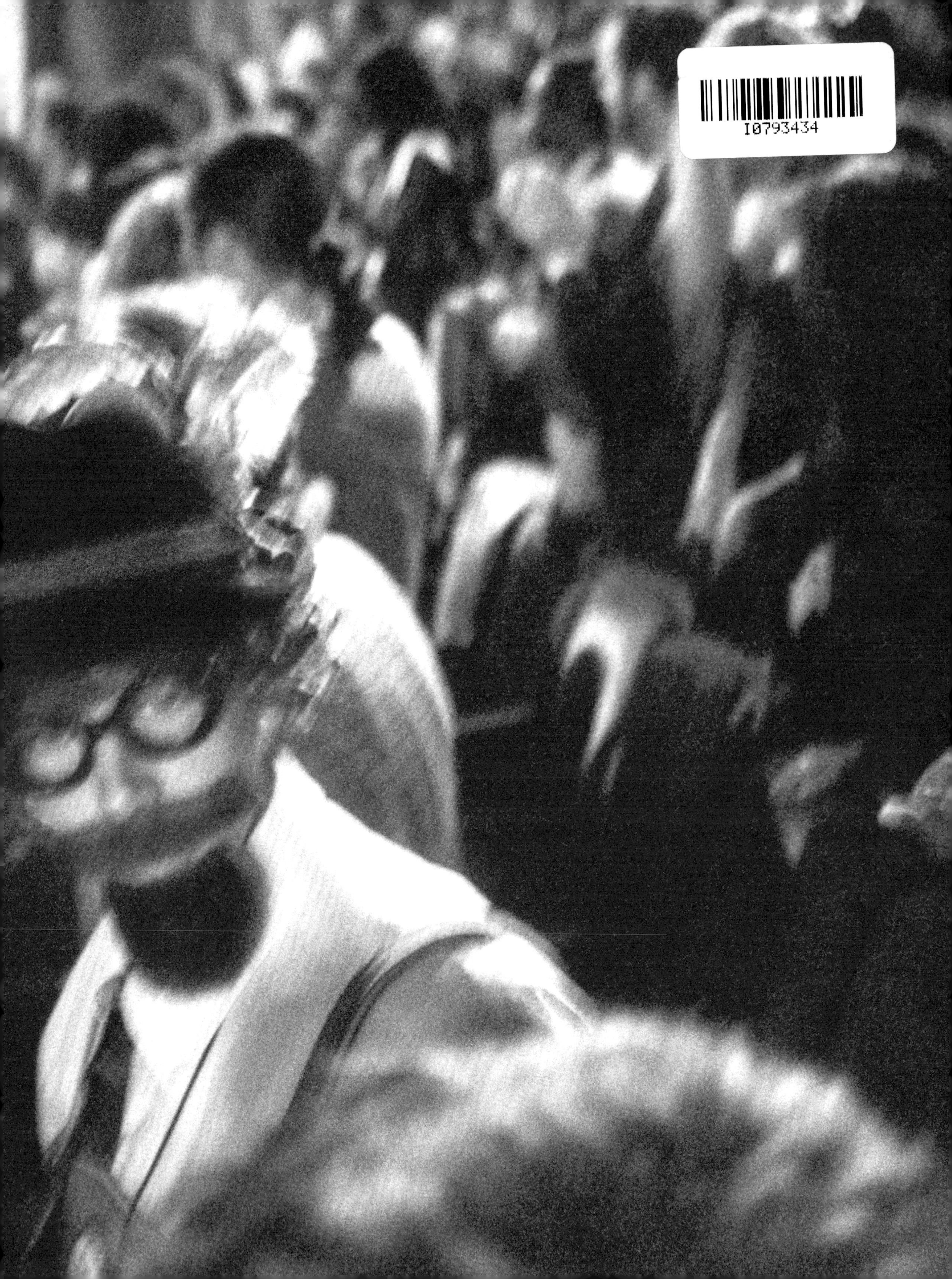

BEASTIE BOYS

BEASTIE BOYS • SPIKE JONZE

RIZZOLI
NEW YORK
New York Paris London Milan

Beastie Boys • Spike Jonze • SJ4

First published in the United States of America in 2020
by Rizzoli International Publications, Inc.
300 Park Avenue South
New York, NY 10010
www.rizzoliusa.com

For Rizzoli—
Publisher: Charles Miers
Editor: Jacob Lehman
Design: Jaime Perlman
Design Coordinator: Olivia Russin
Production Manager: Maria Pia Gramaglia
Managing Editor: Lynn Scrabis

For Spike Jonze—
Editorial Direction: Humberto Leon,
Amanda Adelson, Laura Klein
Archivist: Suzanne Zumbrunnen
Senior Vice President in Charge of
Photographic Reproduction: Stef Mitchell

Images hand-printed, scanned, and retouched by
Richard Foulser, Liz Klebieko, Jimmy Serkoch, Lacy
Weathersbee, Jessica Stocker, and all at
Picturehouse + TheSmallDarkroom

All rights also reserved to ask you why you are reading
all of this. Not that there's anything wrong with it,
just curious. If you want to let us know, just email us at:
whyireadthesmalltype@gmail.com.

Printed in Italy

2020 2021 2022 2023 / 10 9 8 7 6 5 4 3 2

ISBN: 978-0-8478-6838-4
Library of Congress Control Number: 2020930742

Facebook.com/RizzoliNewYork
Twitter: @Rizzoli_Books
Instagram.com/RizzoliBooks
Pinterest.com/RizzoliBooks
Youtube.com/user/RizzoliNY
Issuu.com/Rizzoli

For Yauch

When we first met Spike he was a little kid. No, seriously. Like a child. And we were like, "Who the fuck is this little kid trying to take our photo?"

That's how it is when you're 22 years old and you think you're a rock star and your new album is about to come out and you think it's going to take over the world and you meet this kid with the high-pitched voice of an 8-year-old who says: "Hi, I'm Spike. I'm here to shoot you guys for *Dirt* magazine."

"Wait, what? *Dirt* magazine? What the f is that?"

Spike: "Oh, me and my friends started it. You're gonna be the cover of our first issue."

Our thought bubble was like: "*Dirt* magazine? This kid looks 12 years old and sounds like he is 8. Is this thing even legit?"

But here we were, rock stars, meeting this poor, unsuspecting child straight outta Maryland at Hamburger Hamlet[1] in West Hollywood, and we're kind of putting him through the ringer, like: "What do you like to order, kid?"

"Umm... I dunno, is fries and Coke not good?"

We're looking at each other and shaking our heads, thinking, "Wait, we're big time, we should have some fancy German/Swiss/French photographer with leather pants and 10 assistants, and they send this little kid to photograph us? What the fuck?" We start to walk to our first location with him. Us seasoned veterans in the game are like, "Ok kid, what's the first setup? Where is your studio?"

We realize there is no studio, and he has no assistants. He's gonna just shoot us out on the street, and he's carrying all his equipment in a camera bag. When he opens it up, it's filled with different lenses and gear and Yauch instantly becomes interested, and he and Spike start talking in secret technical camera talk. "So, is this lens a 220 or 221?"

Suddenly we stop walking, and we're standing in the middle of La Cienega Boulevard, awkwardly, waiting to see what this kid wants us to do. A van pulls up, and a couple of Spike's friends pull a couch out of it and drop it on a little island in the middle of this super-busy intersection.

Spike somehow gets us to sit down on this thing, and before we know it, he's already snapping photos. We start posing a bit. Honestly, we're not so comfortable being on La Cienega Boulevard in the middle of L.A. with a lot of cars and people cruising by as we're trying to somehow look cool or b-boy or whatever the fuck we were trying to do. Spike's just saying stuff to us, or maybe not. I don't remember. Maybe he was just smiling, laughing and taking photos.

Then it hits us. "Shit, what the fuck are we doing sitting on a couch in the middle of La Cienega? People are driving by, staring at us like we're stoned idiots,[2] fuck this." We stood up, and that was the end of that. My memory is that we only sat there for like 8 seconds and we were over it, but looking at the photos now, he seemed to have gotten a lot of photos out of us in those 8 seconds.

He had a way of lulling everyone in a direction. Explaining absurdist things very earnestly and sweetly, so it sounded not only funny, but like the natural way it should be. He gets you to pop out of your comfort zone, and that's one of the consistently magical things about Spike. That's right, y'all. I said magical. Through all the shoots and hanging out together, Spike would just manifest things out of nowhere.

A couch on a busy boulevard in the middle of L.A.? Sure. Filming with a 16mm camera in a casino where it's illegal to film, just by holding the camera by his hip and covering the red lights with tape? Yup. Jumping a 1980s Ford LTD

[1] Yes, the now defunct Hamburger Hamlet used to be on Sunset Boulevard on the border of West Hollywood and Beverly Hills. To this day, Adam Horovitz mourns the closing of this institution from another era.

[2] Well, yes, in fact we kind of were stoned fools.

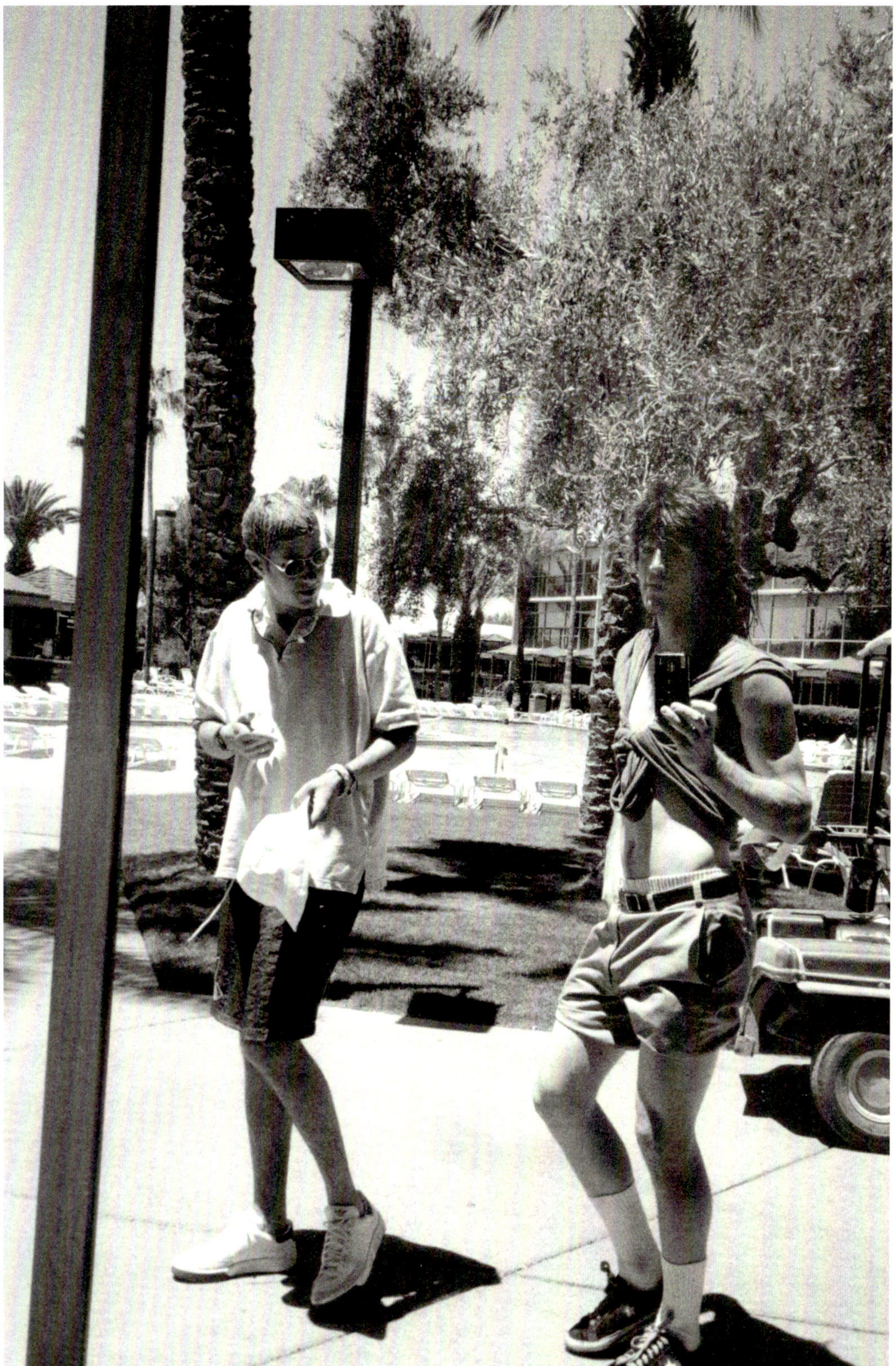

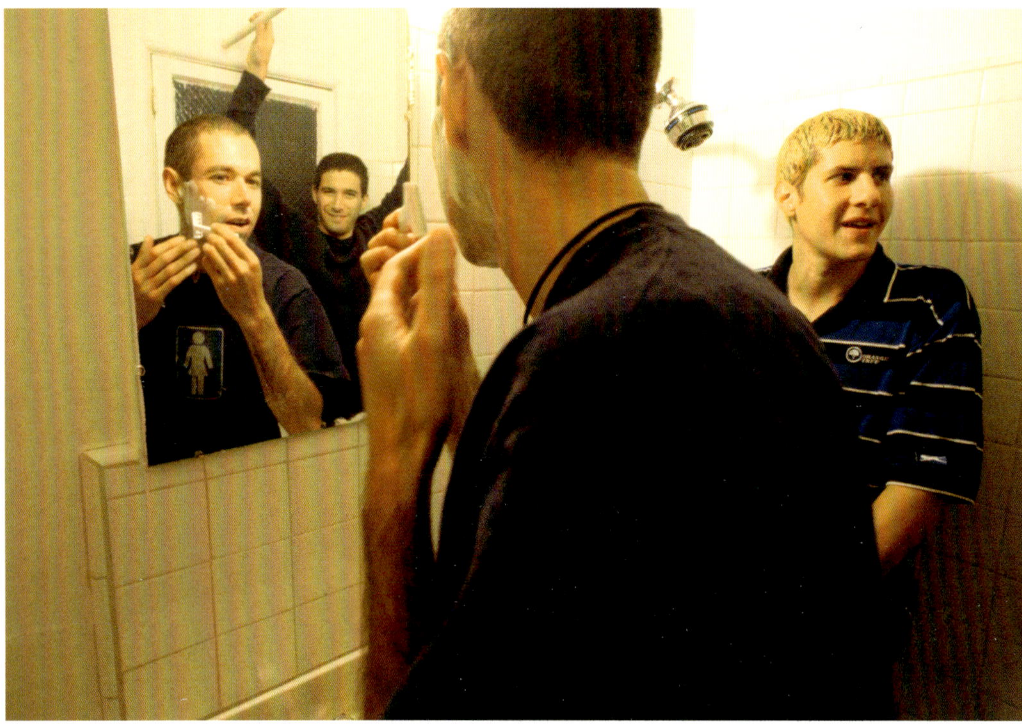

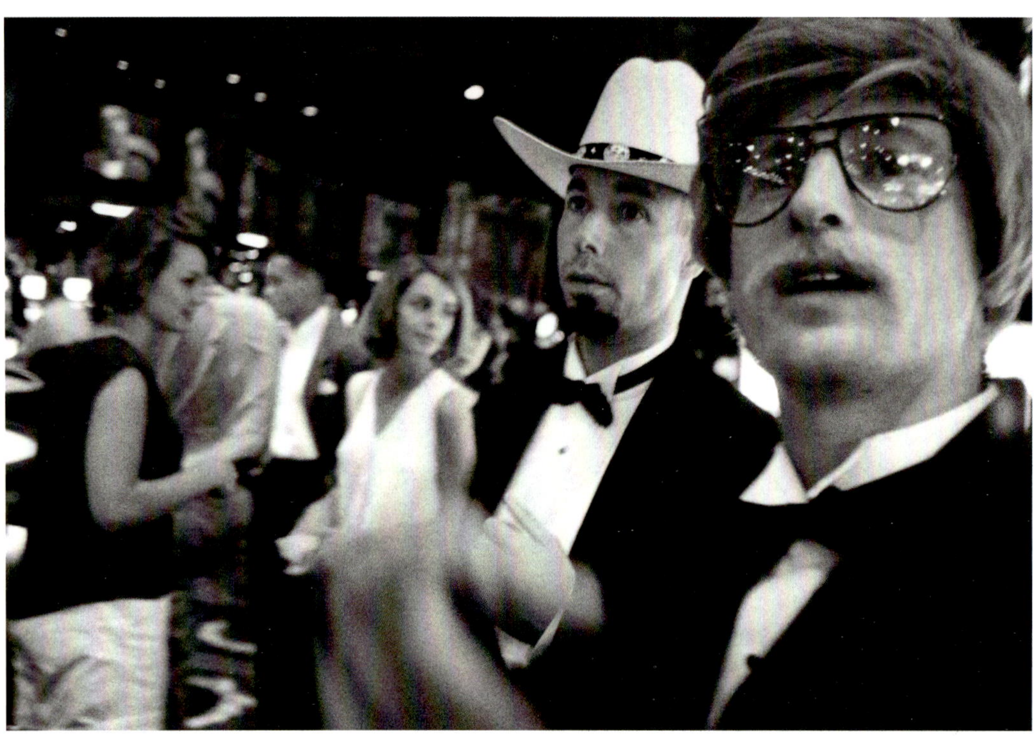

over a San Francisco–steep hill in residential Echo Park with no police or permission or anyone holding traffic? Check. And wait, Yauch's gonna be the stunt driver? "Do the brakes in this thing even work?"

Yauch was the same way, and with both of them, never was there asking permission or were ideas off limits because someone was saying no. So, if some big-time L.A. producer is saying, "Spike, that can't happen. This is illegal, we don't have a permit for this," Spike would say, with a smile that was both mischievous and committed, "Yeah, but it'll be good, we're just gonna put the camera right here, and we'll just do it a couple times. And Yauch, make sure to go fast enough. Yeah, it'll be great." Spike just made things happen because he said, "That's what we're doing." And then he didn't blink.

Going back to our timeline. That album we knew was going to take over the world? Well, it was *Paul's Boutique*, and that takeover... it never happened. That gave us countless days, hours, months to just fuck around, trying to make stuff. Not just songs or records, but record covers, videos, magazines. Spike was there, not only capturing it, but being a full member and facilitator of our creative chaos. And, at the same time, he was also always interested in asking, "What are you feeling?"

These photos are beyond outtakes. These are the moments that happened while we were all making stuff together. They're the whole process, the moments in between, every minute leading up to that recording or that shoot or that show or whatever.

Not us on the mic as much as us thinking about what we were going to do on the mic. Us eating a snack or getting dressed or talking on the phone or putting on a mustache. Or the look we would give each other when we were just even thinking about putting on a mustache or eating a snack.

Being in a band, the photos you end up seeing repeatedly are those ones from formal photo shoots, or these big moments. I feel kinda silly saying this, but looking back at all these photos, most of which I've never seen before, there's a palpable intimacy that only he could have gotten because we knew him so well.

And a lot of these in-between moments I don't even remember happening, and actually, there's one set of photos of a whole in-between apartment I had that I'd forgotten about, too. It was on 12th Street, and for some reason I just never got around to buying furniture for it, except a mattress for me, a few folding chairs, and a blow-up raft for Spike, who was staying with me then.

The four of us were writing a script for a movie together at the time, and we were just having so much fun hanging out and doing it that I guess it never crossed our minds to get furniture.

And we were very busy, because when we weren't doing that, we were just fucking around in the city or going to see our friends' bands or dressing up as Carl Sagan to shoot some photos... and actually, just getting dressed up for no reason at all.

I remember this one time in N.Y.C. at this kinda fancy fashion-type party—I'm talking big names in the fashion game: Kate Moss, Anna Sui, Coco Chanel, people of that nature—Spike and Yauch show up in the middle of it wearing mustaches and wigs and weird shiny polyester suits bought at some sleazy men's store on 8th Avenue near the Port Authority. They didn't look like they were dressed up in costumes, but more like they were just some weird guys who spilled drinks on themselves that you wouldn't want to be stuck talking to. Why were they dressed up? Not for a shoot (although Spike would always dress up for those, too), but just to meet Adam and me there and to crack us up. And the fashion people there were trying to act entertained and in on the joke, but they were really actually uncomfortable and maybe even a little grossed out. As the crowd tried to slowly stay away from them, they just stood there with big dumb smiles on their faces. Without blinking.

Good times.

Mike Diamond
2019

Meet on La Cienega

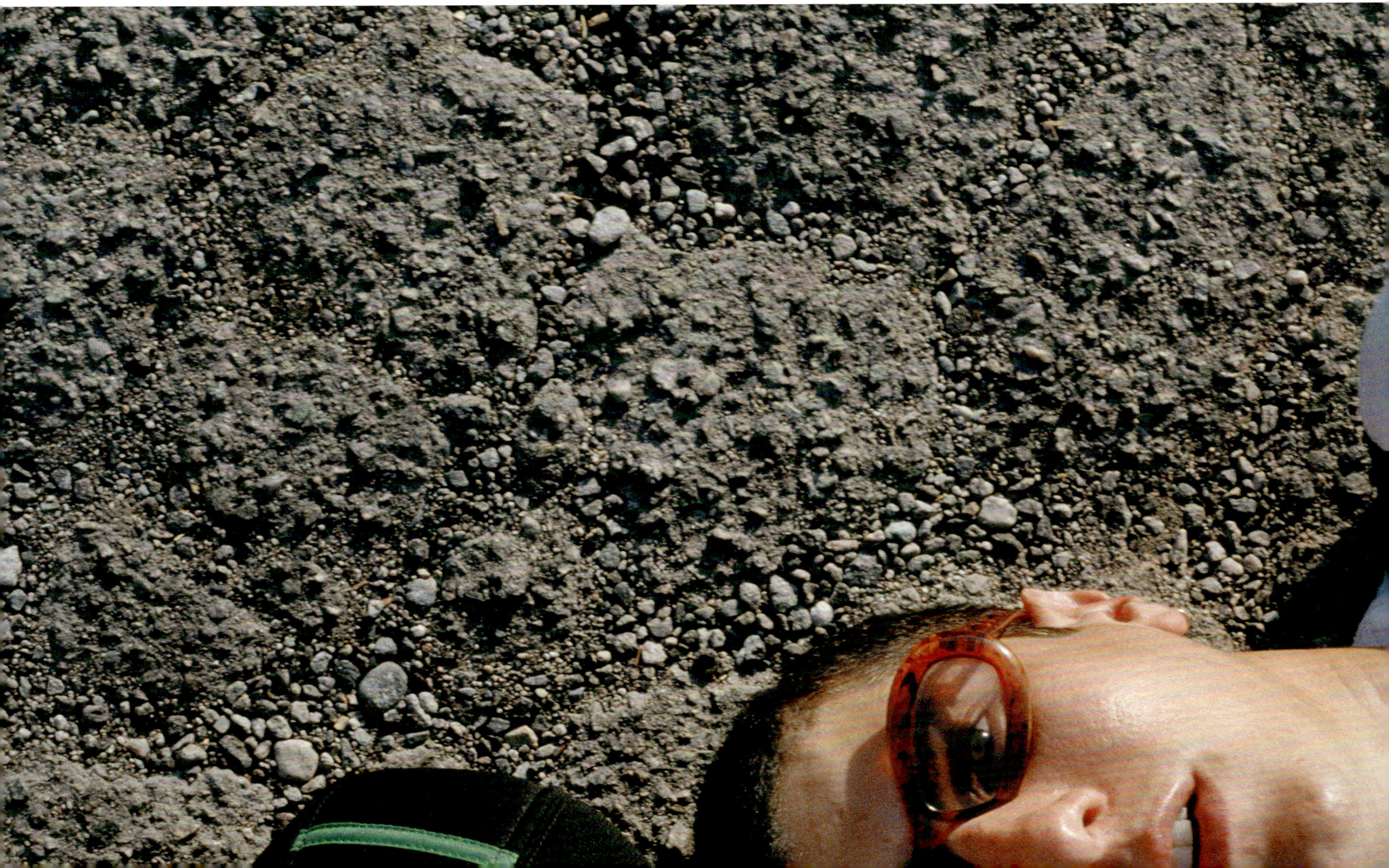

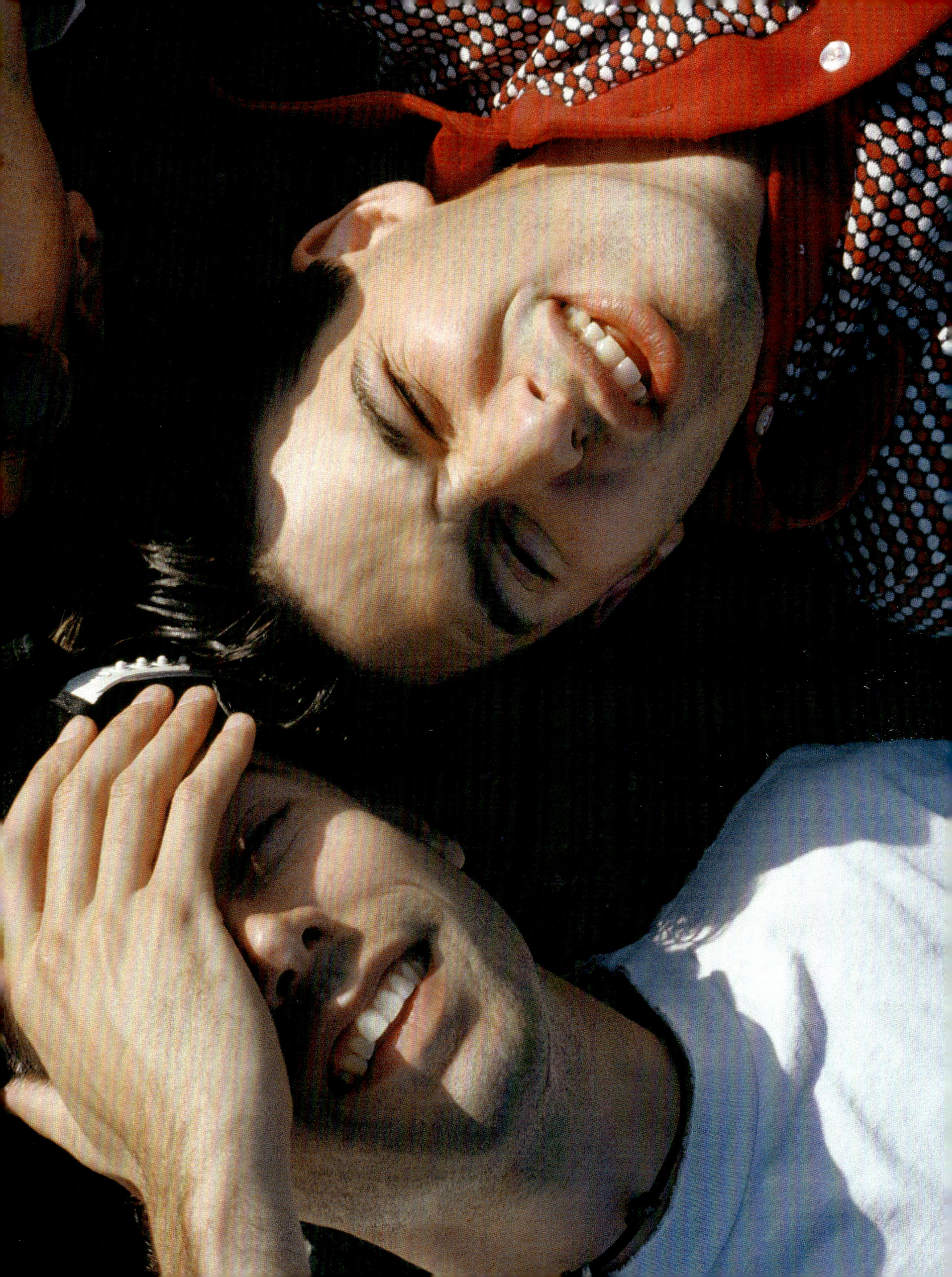

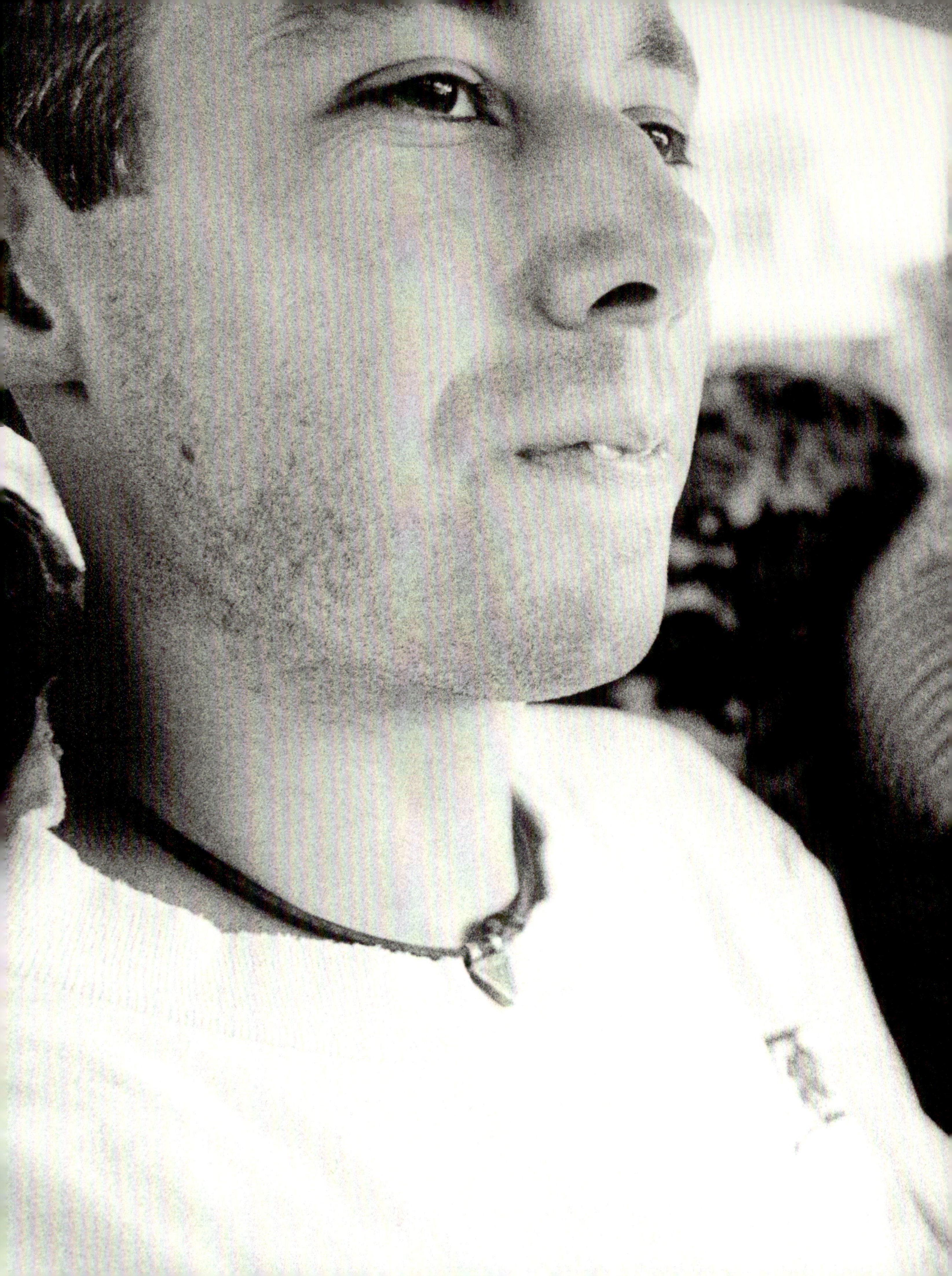

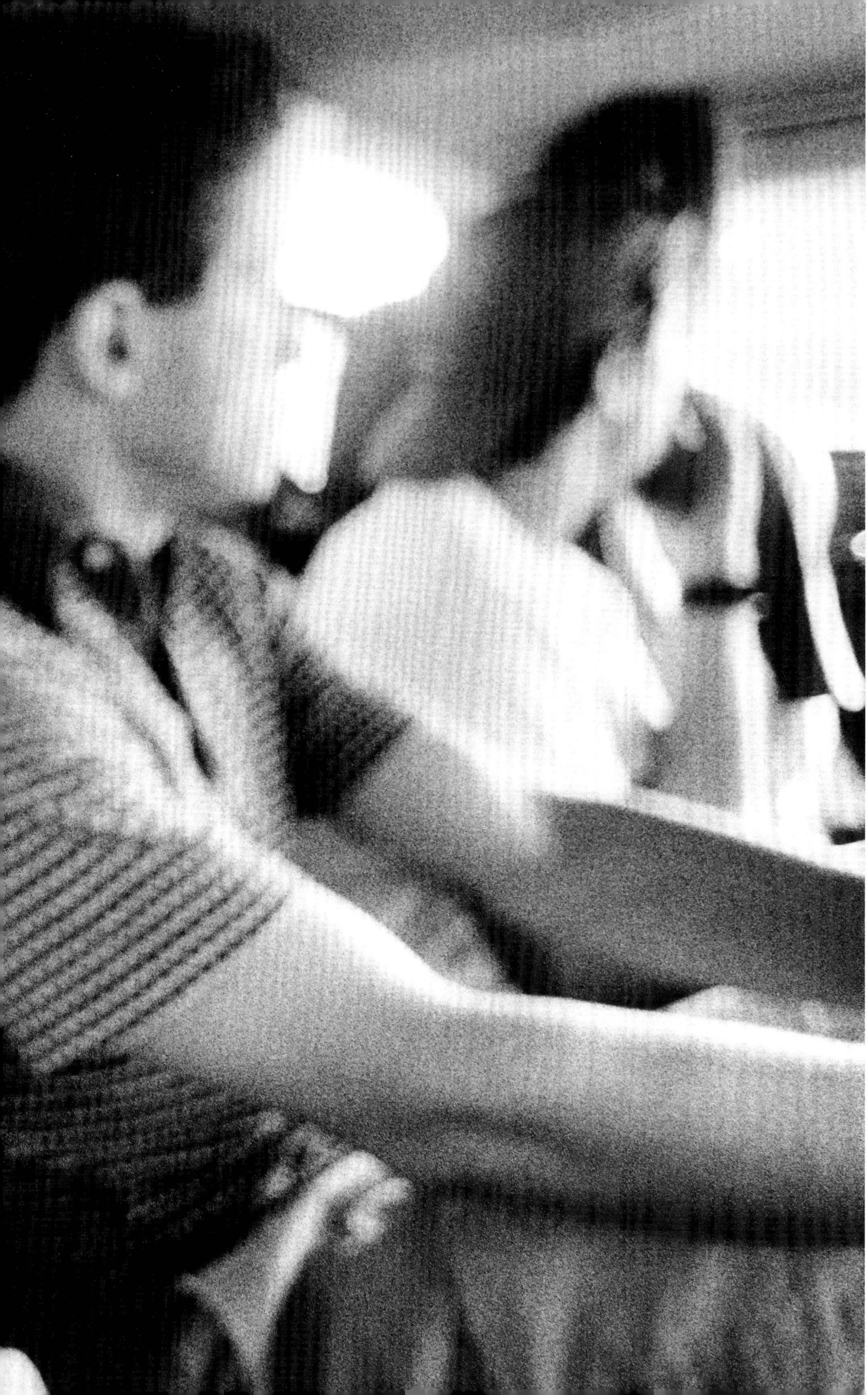

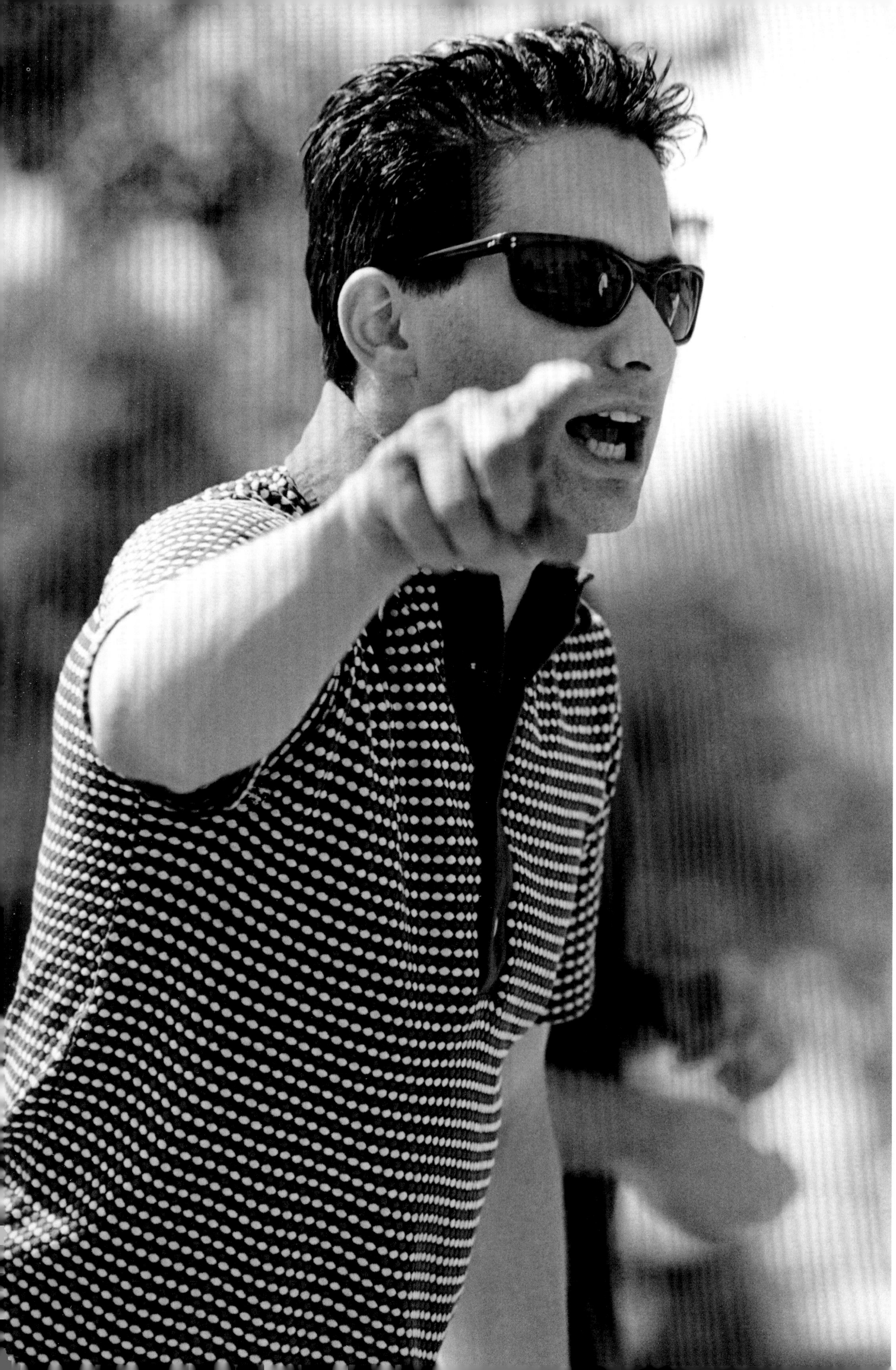

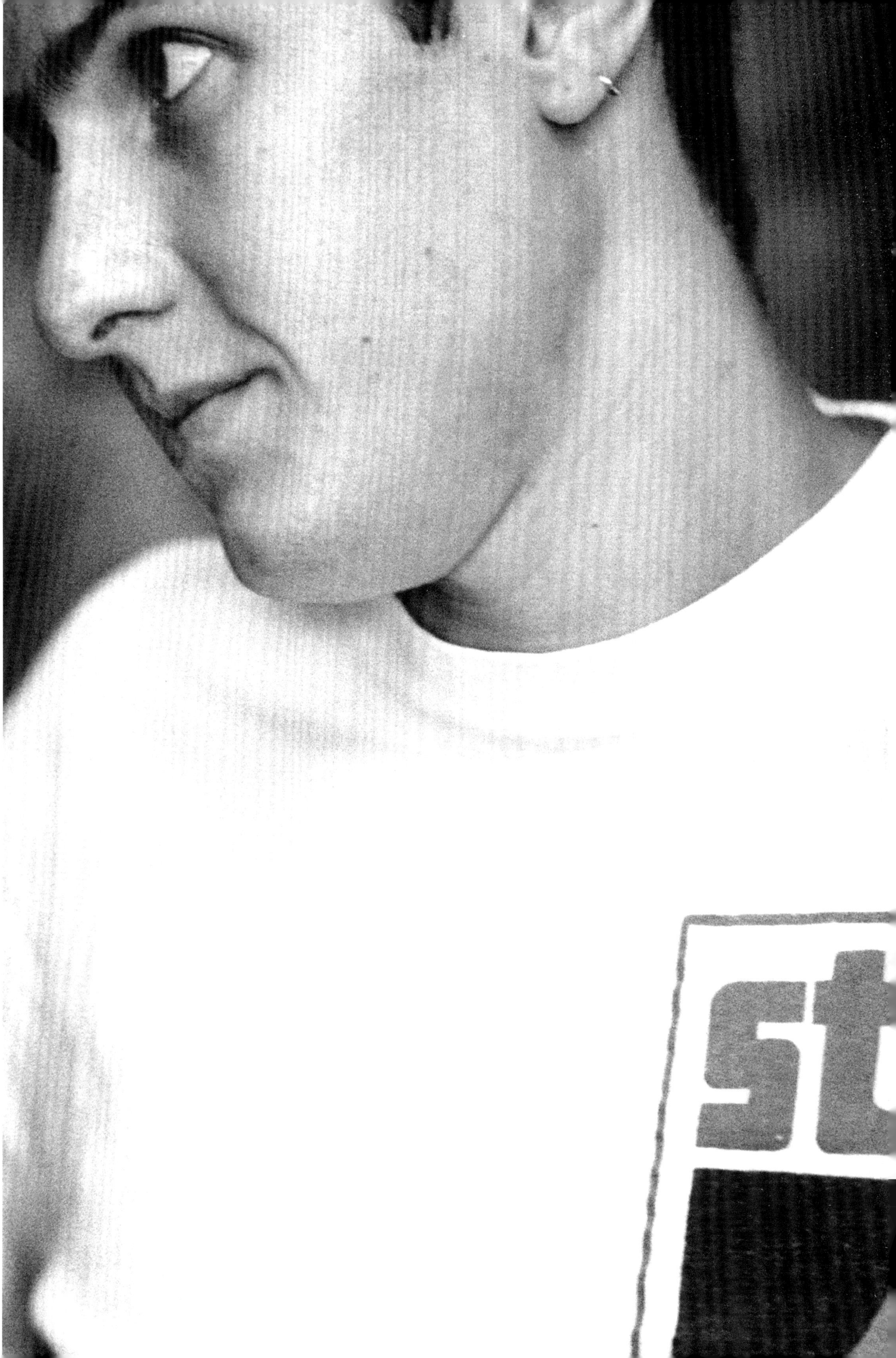

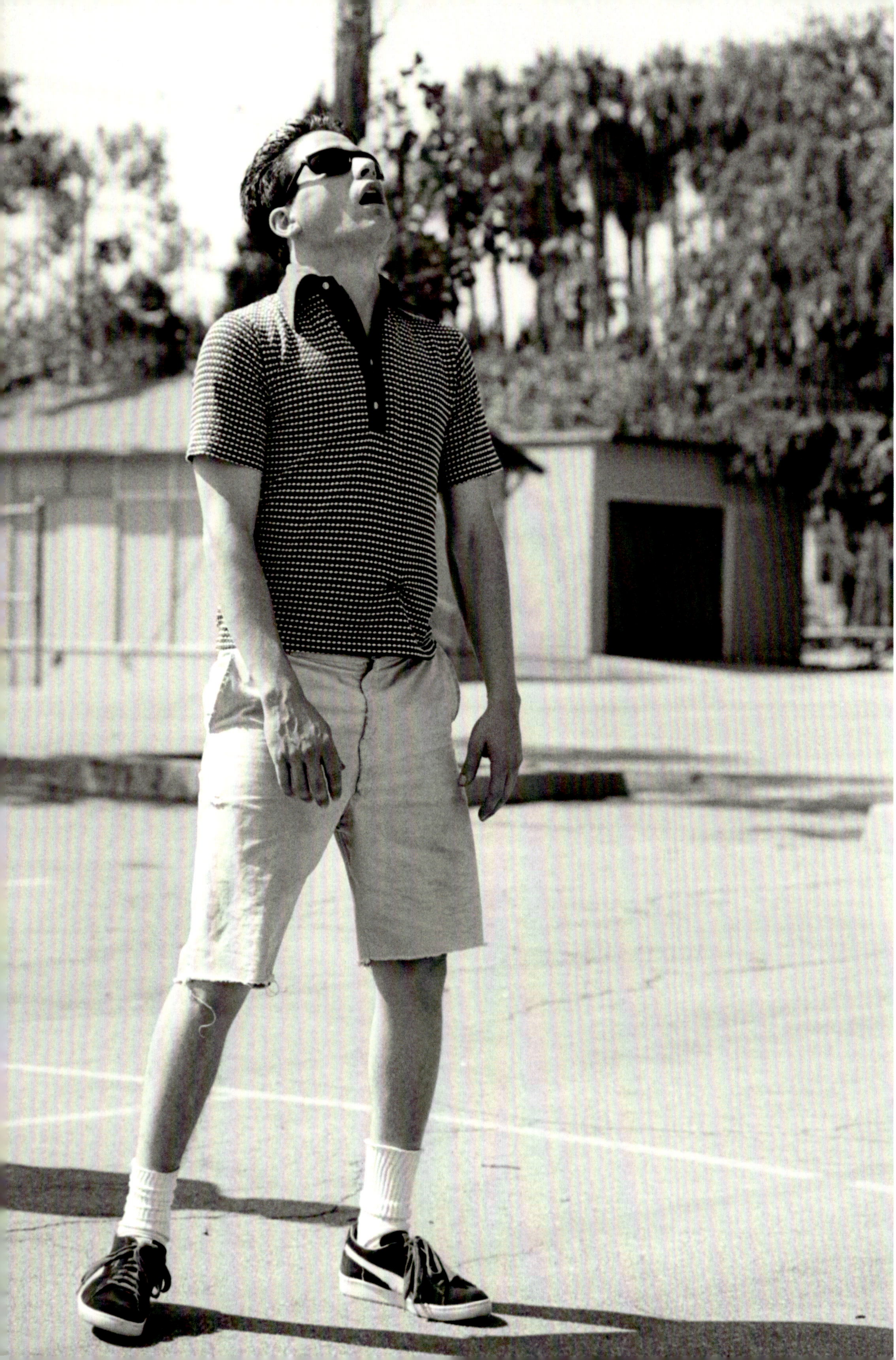

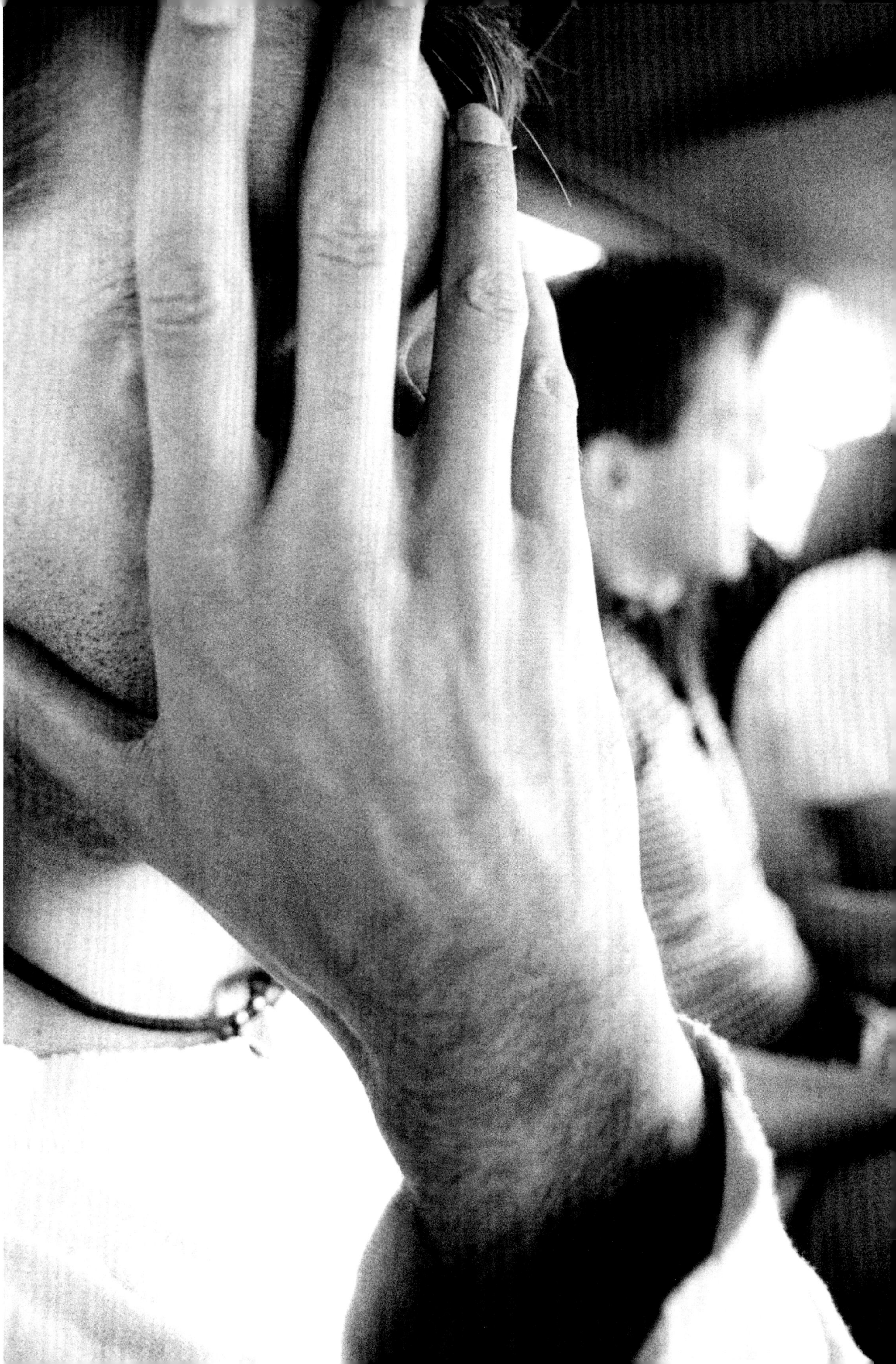

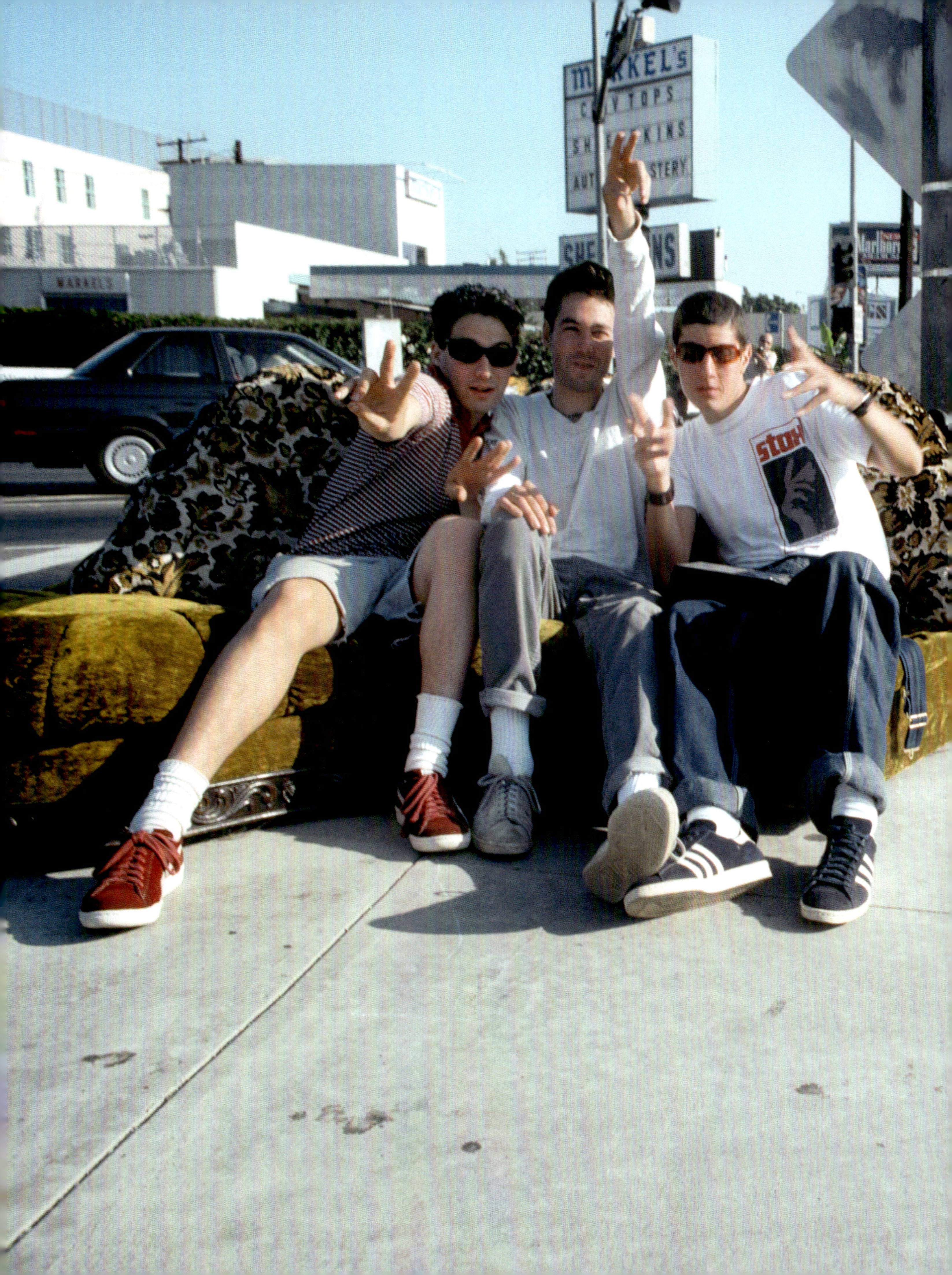

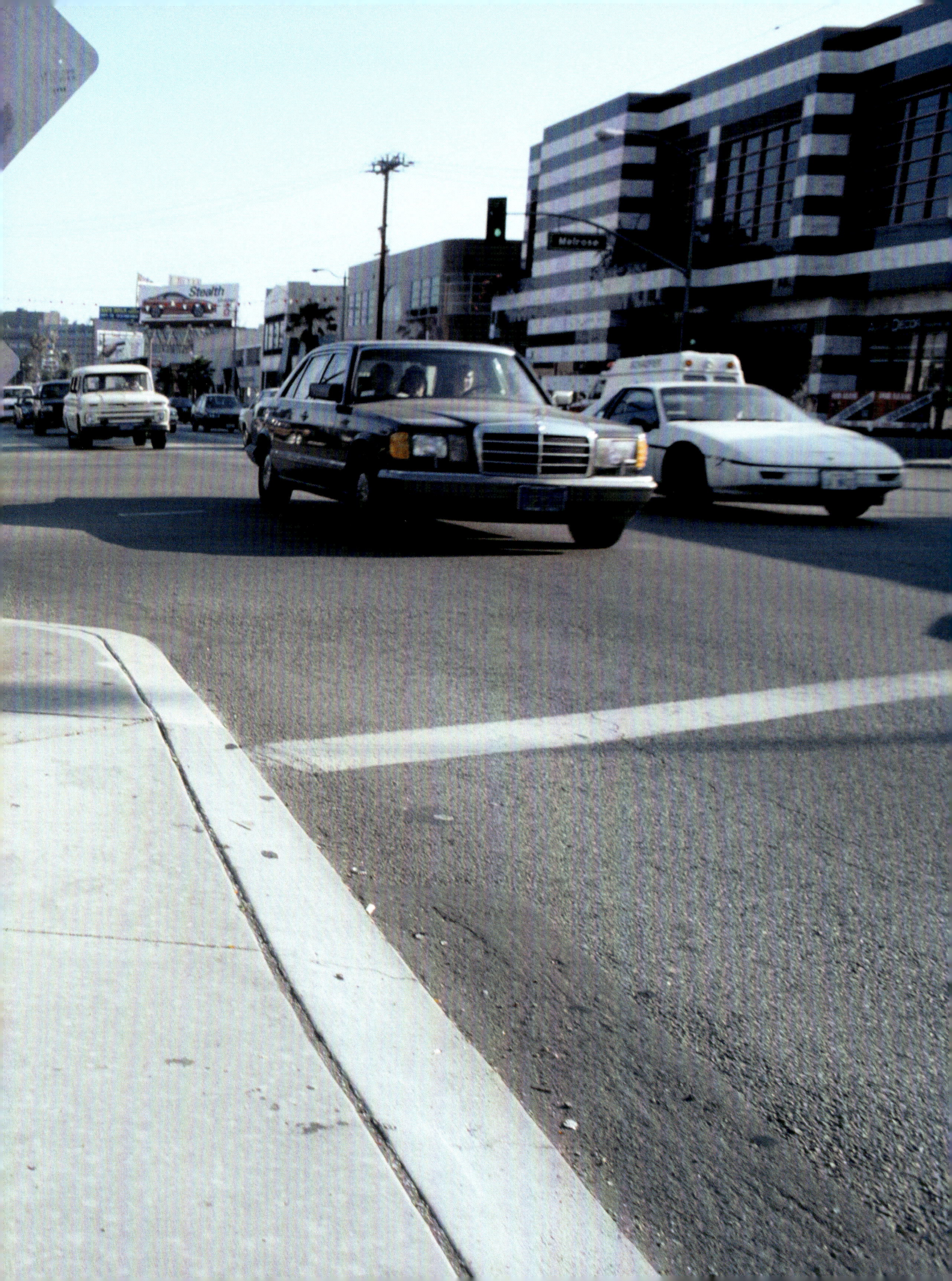
Melrose
Stealth

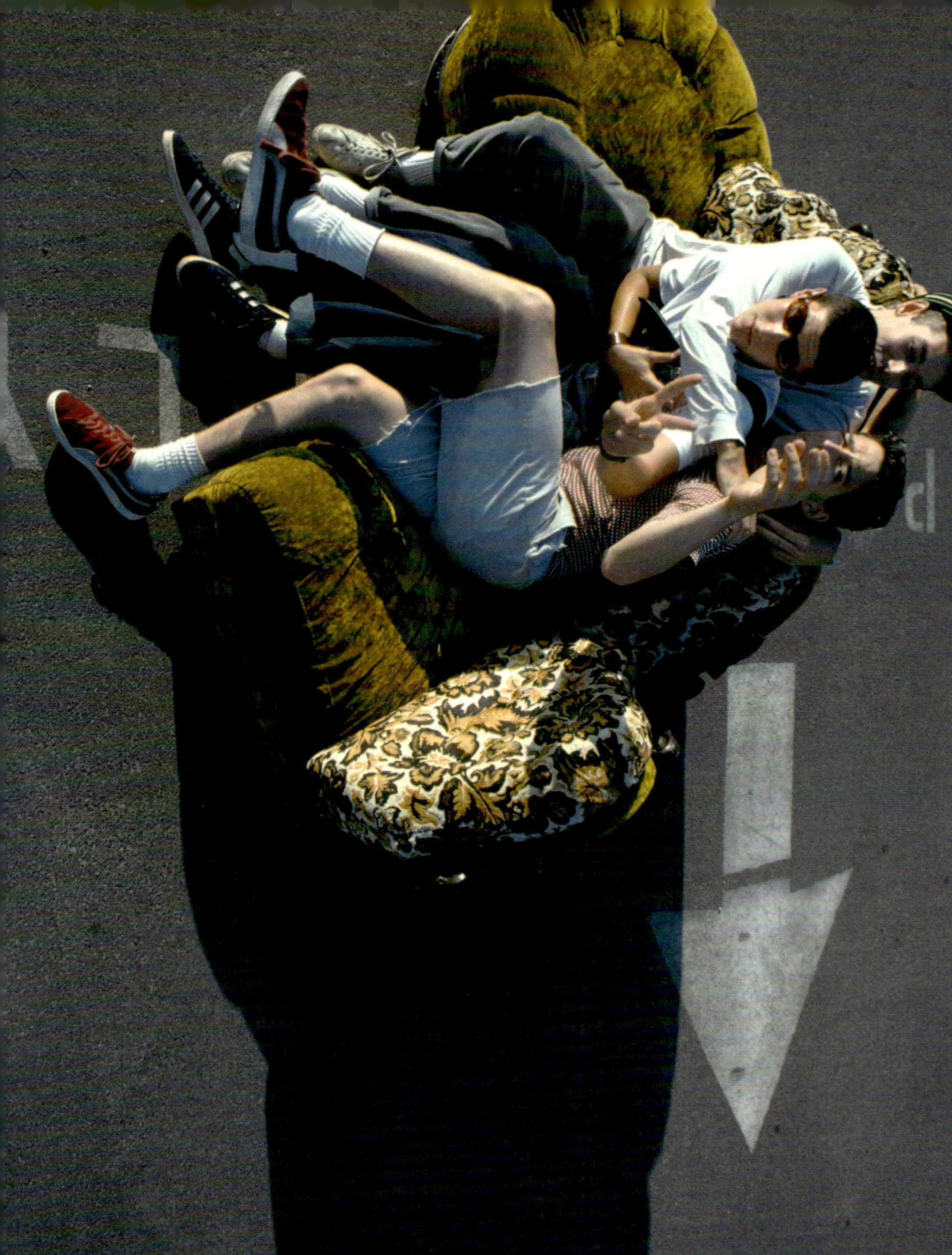

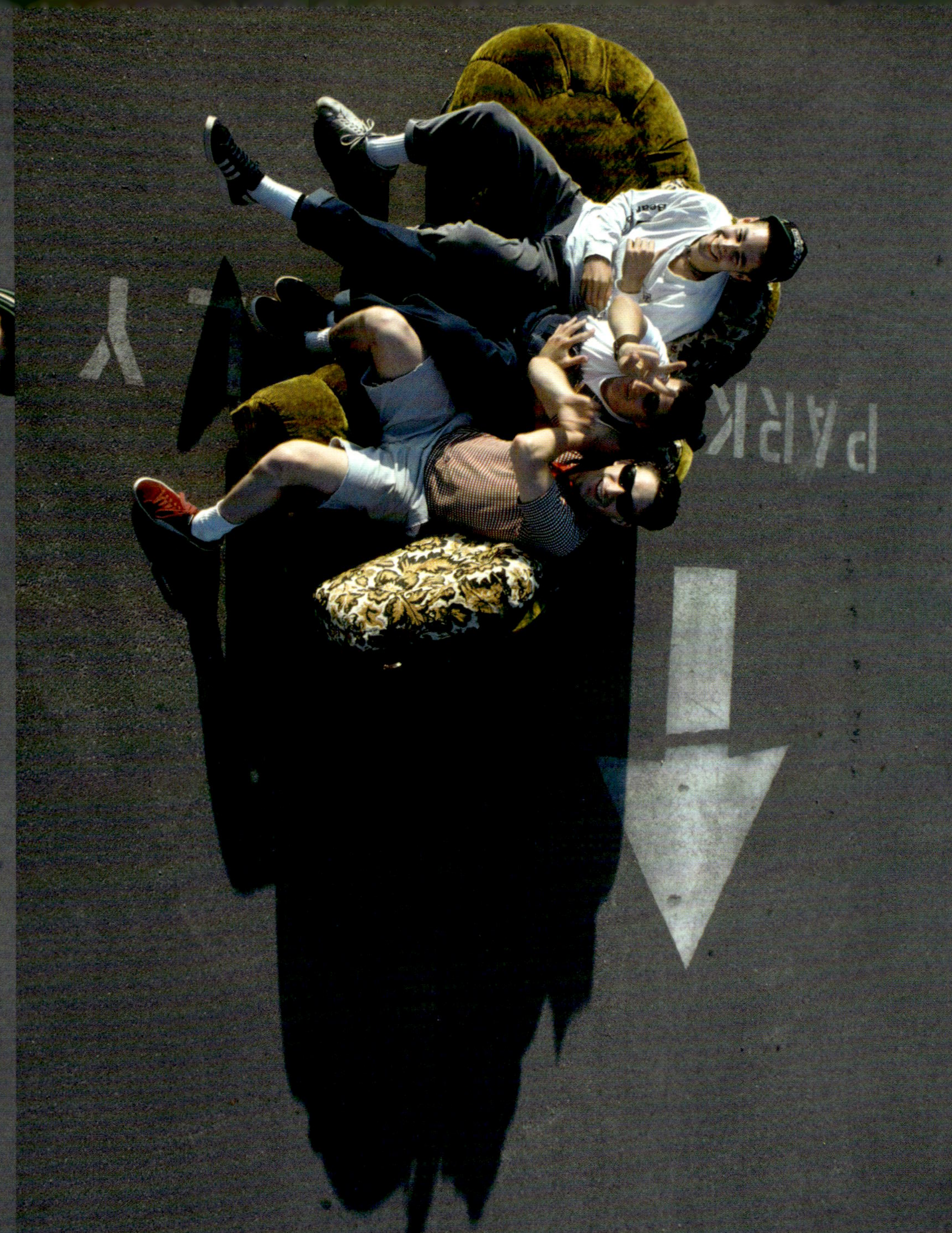

Lewman's Couch.

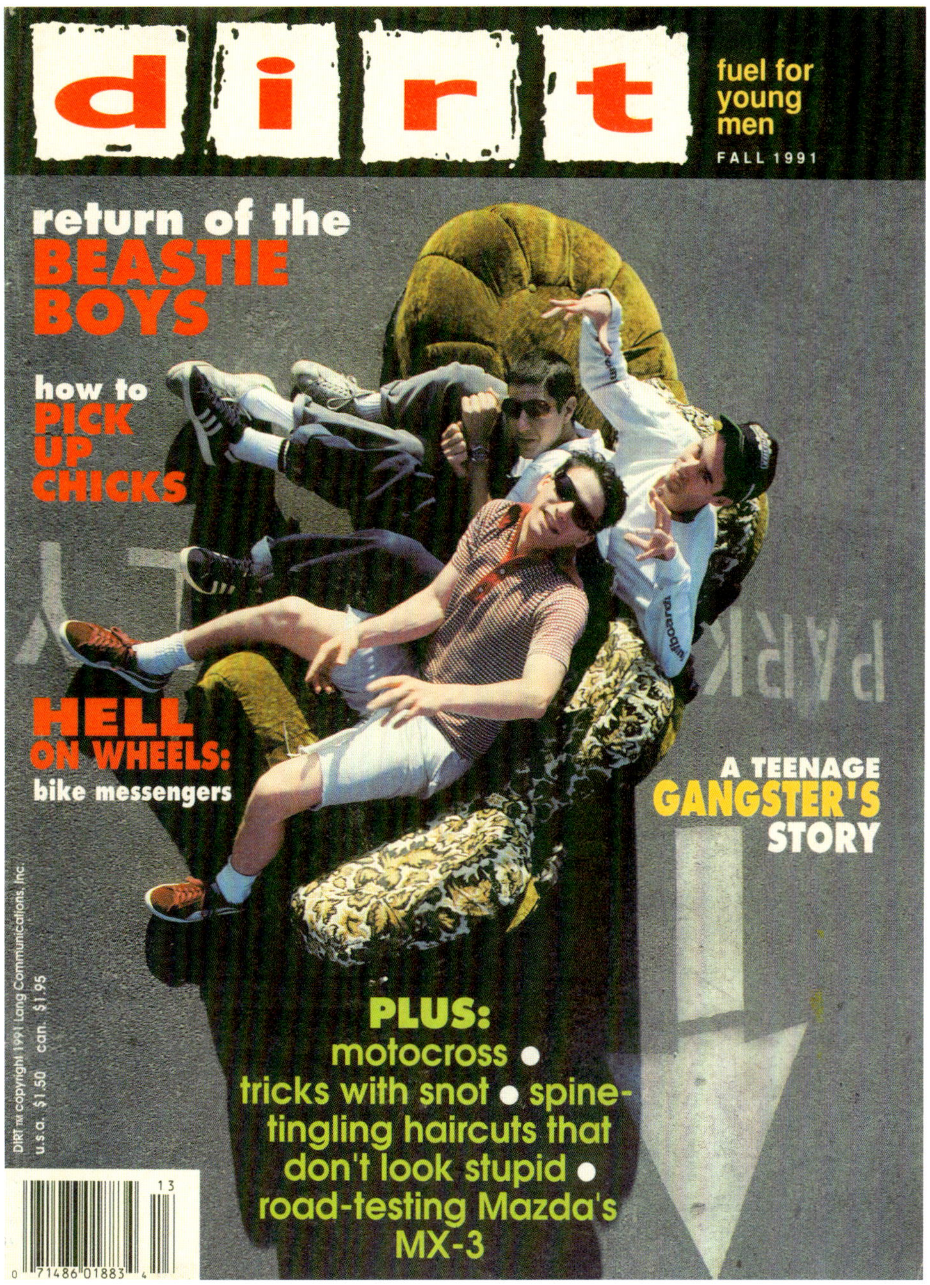
dirt
fuel for young men
FALL 1991
return of the BEASTIE BOYS
how to PICK UP CHICKS
HELL ON WHEELS: bike messengers
A TEENAGE GANGSTER'S STORY
PLUS:
motocross • tricks with snot • spine-tingling haircuts that don't look stupid • road-testing Mazda's MX-3
DIRT ™ copyright 1991 Lang Communications, Inc.
u.s.a. $1.50 can. $1.95
PARK

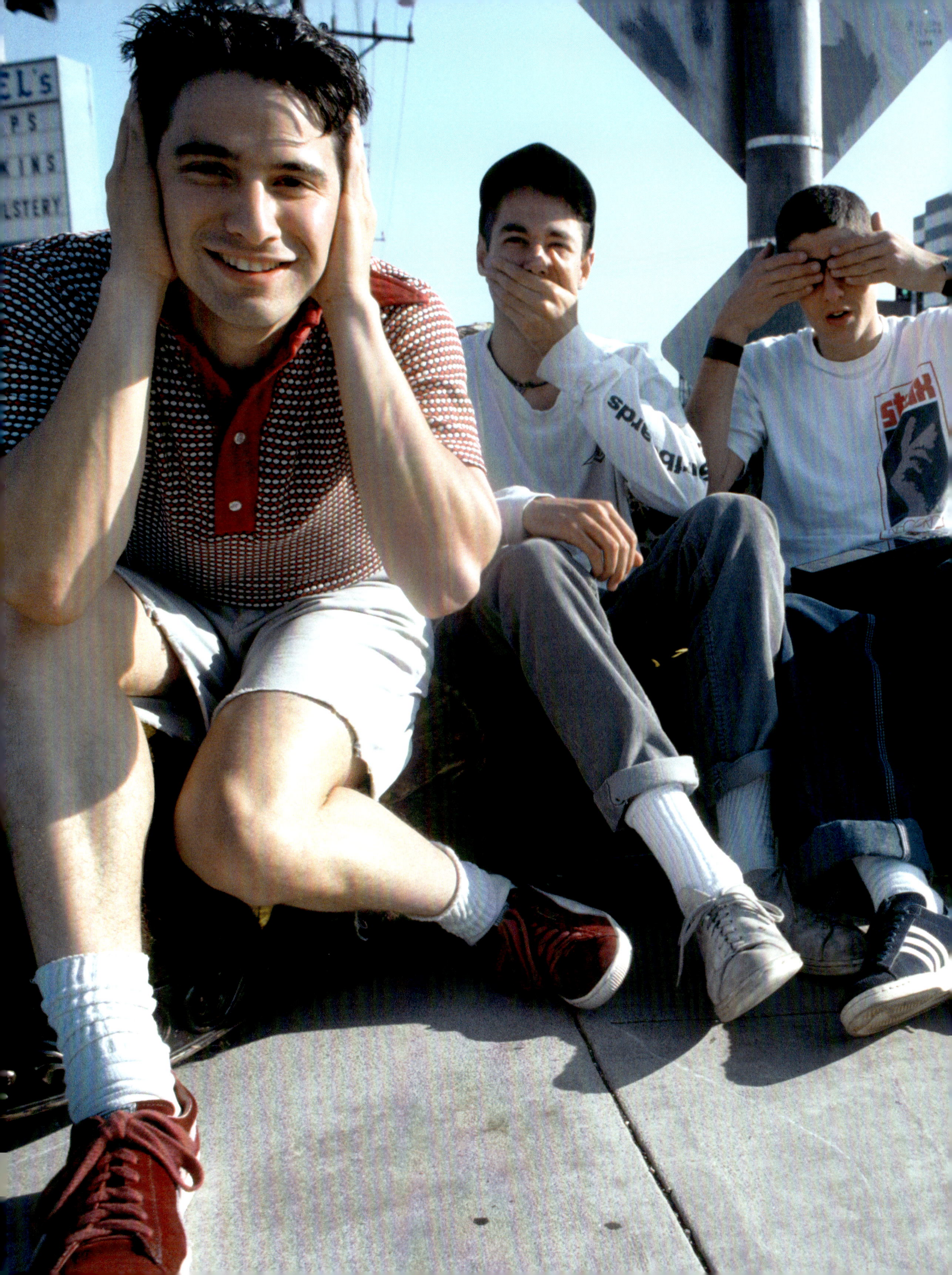
EL's
PS
KINS
LSTERY
stax

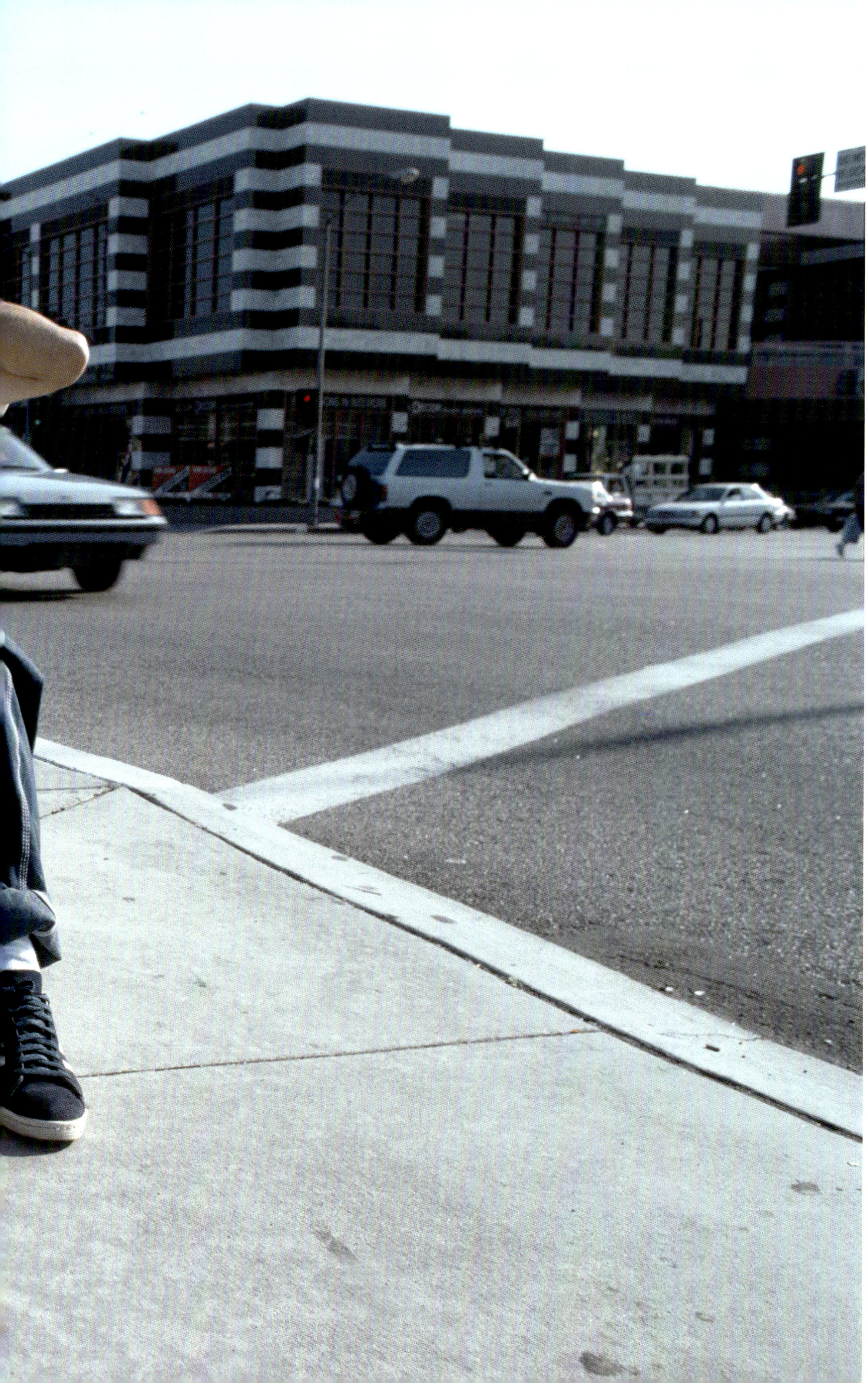

Mike D

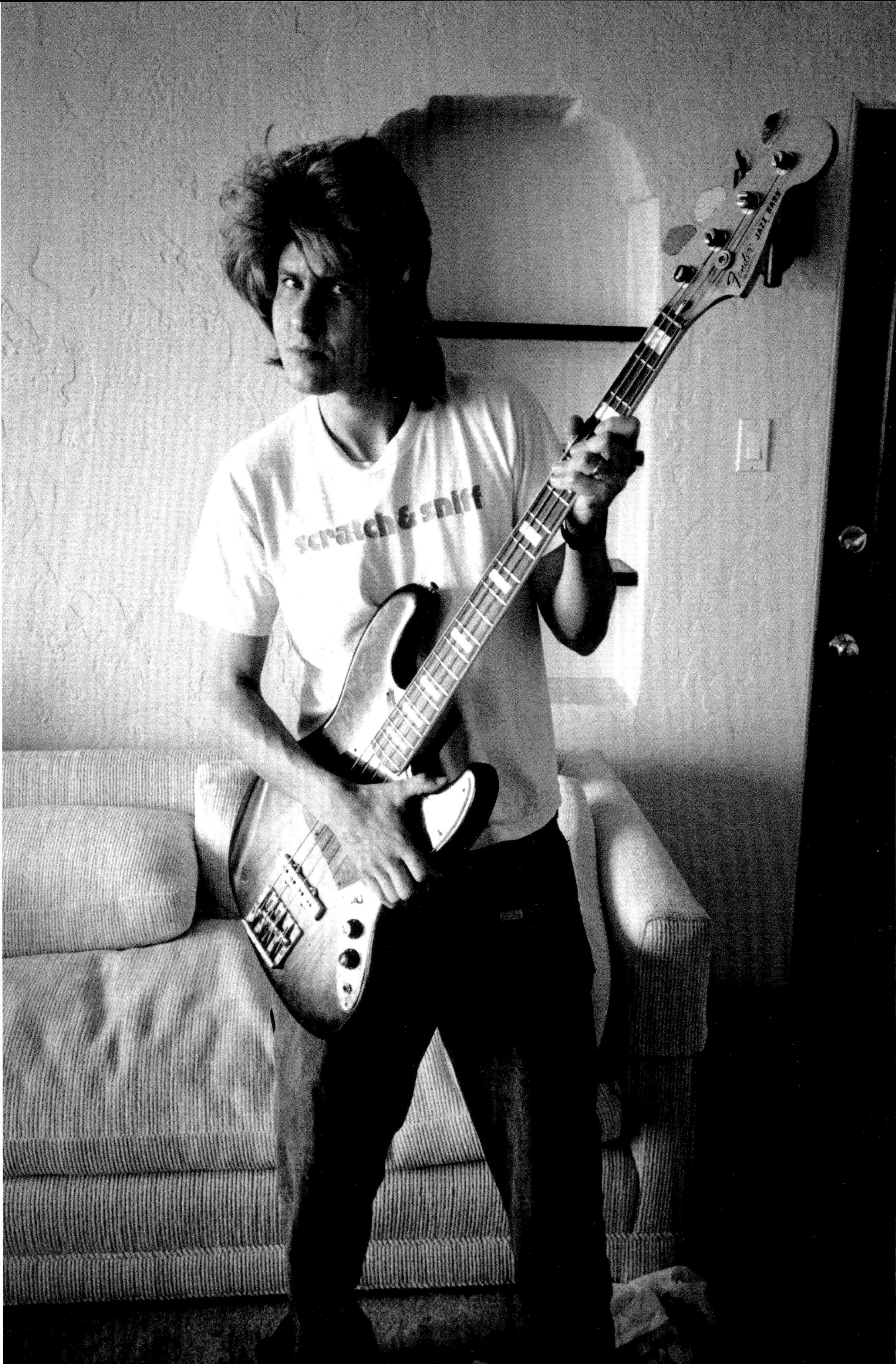
scratch&sniff

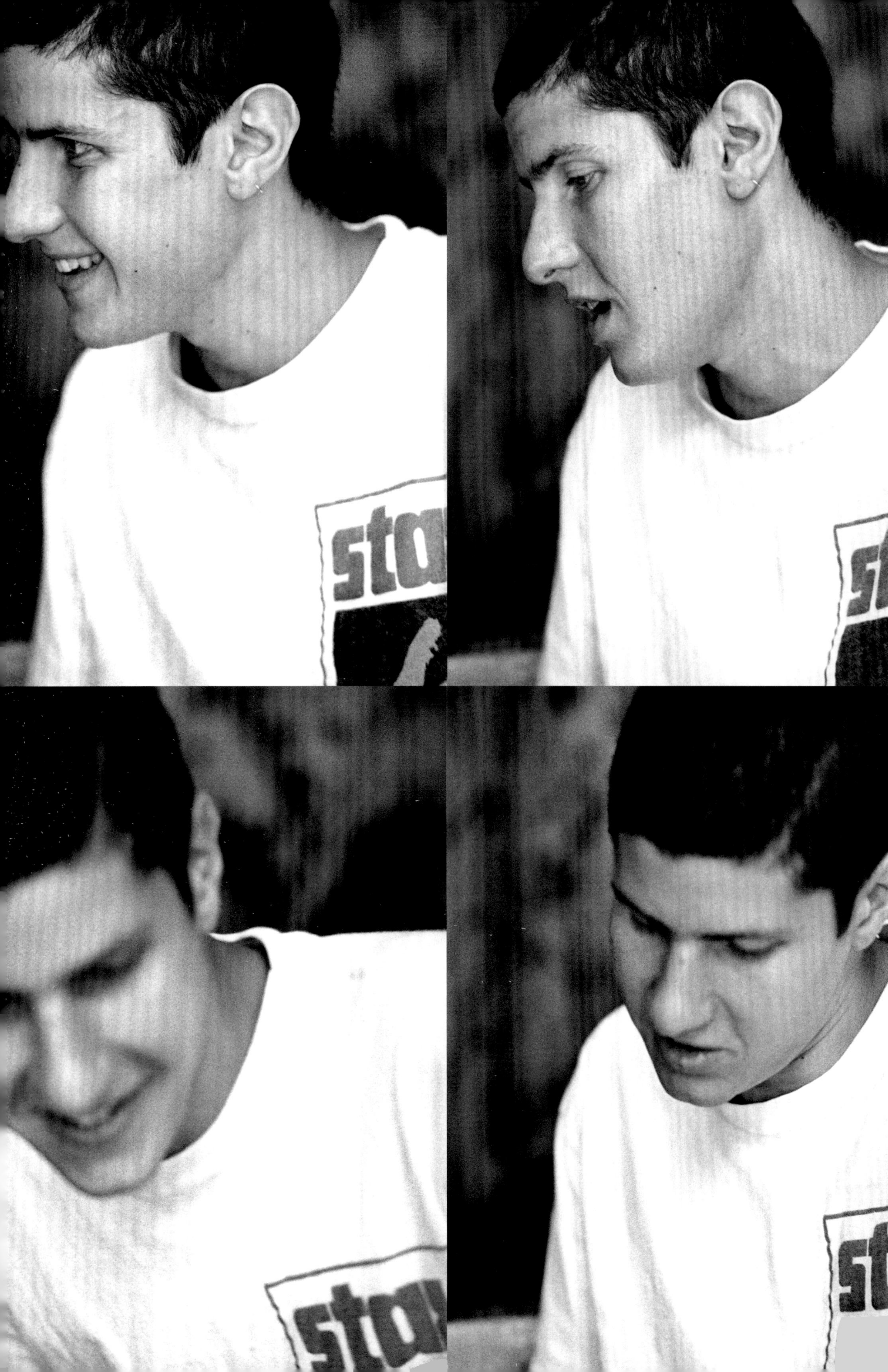

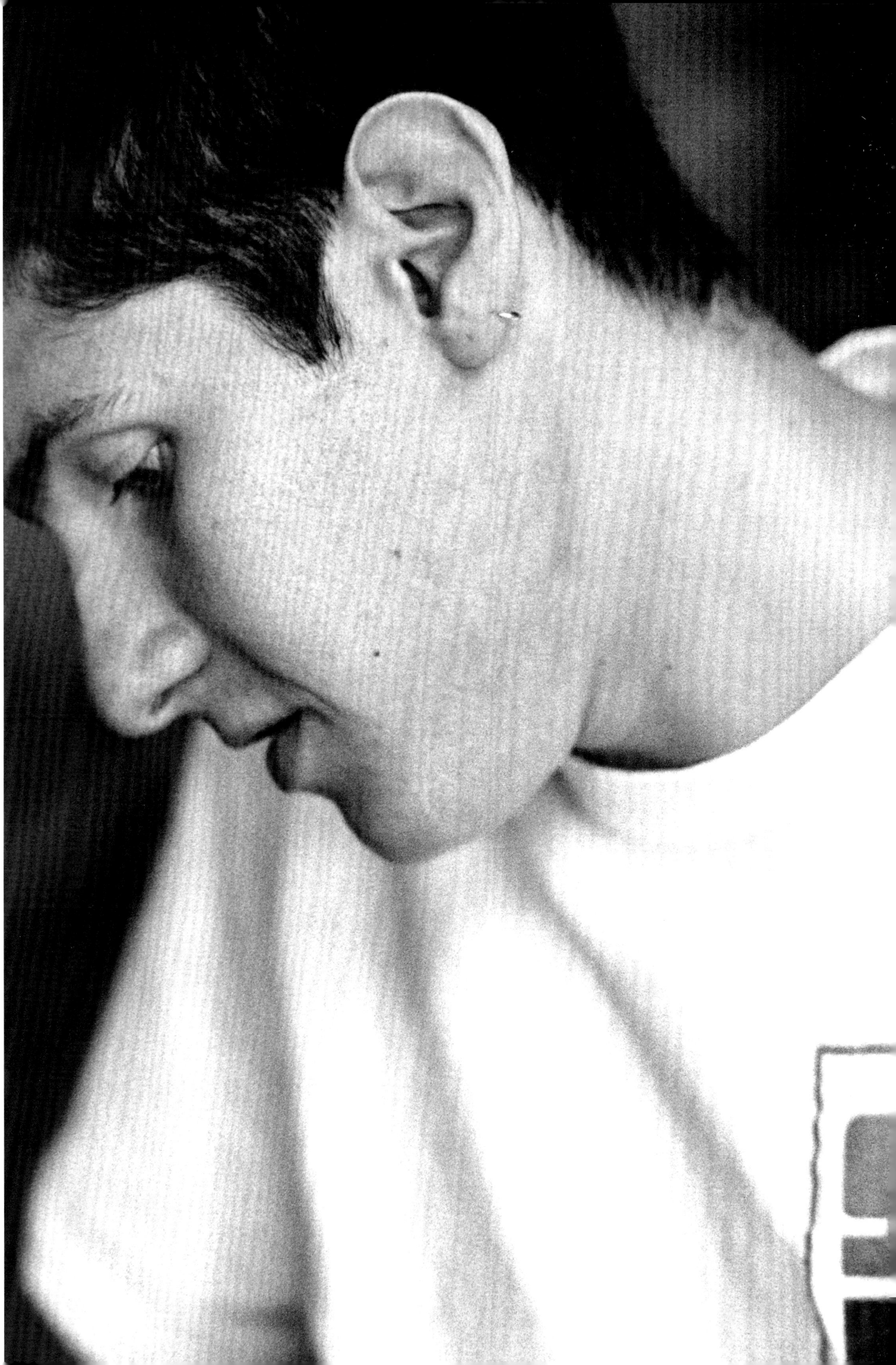

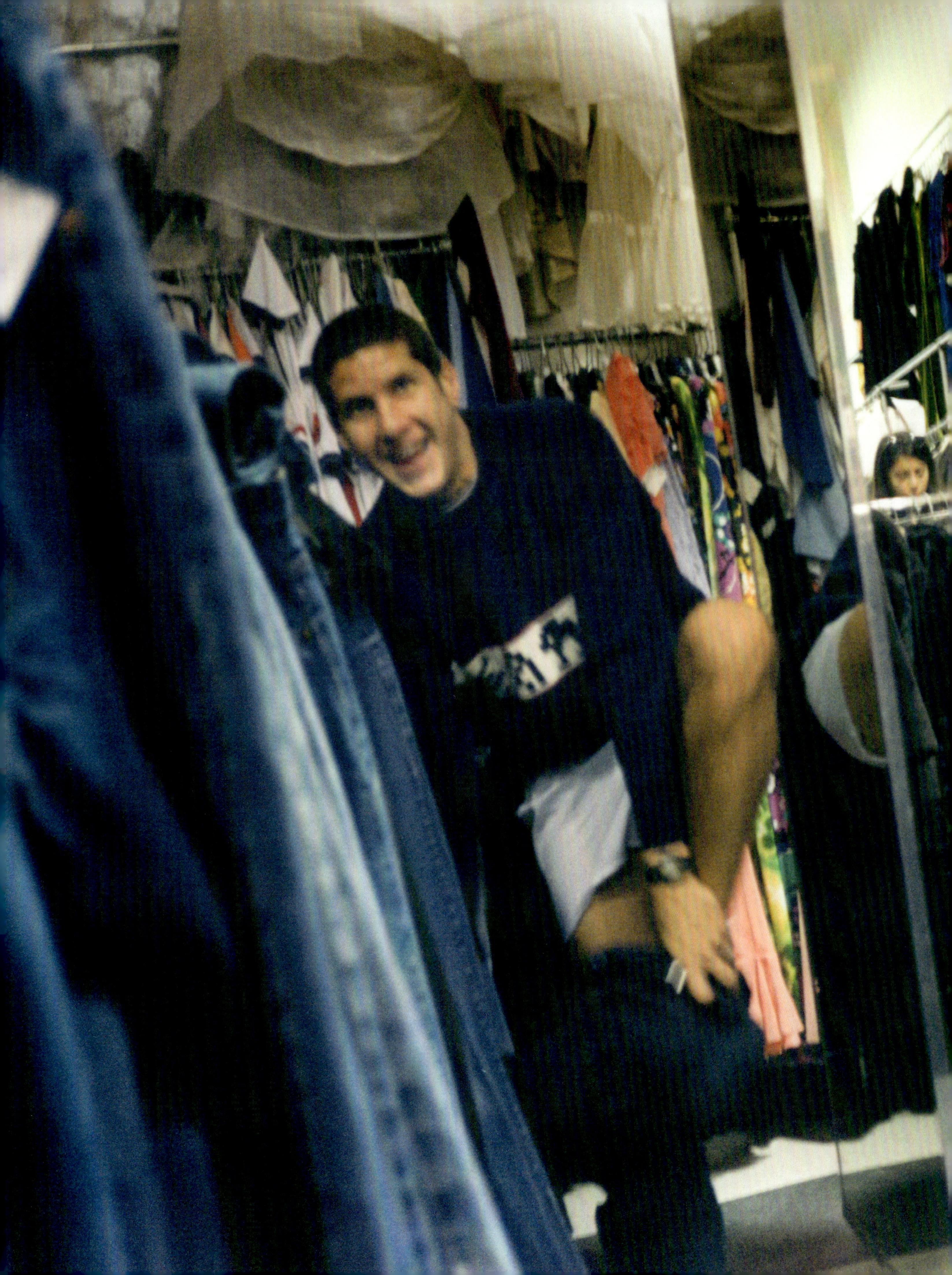

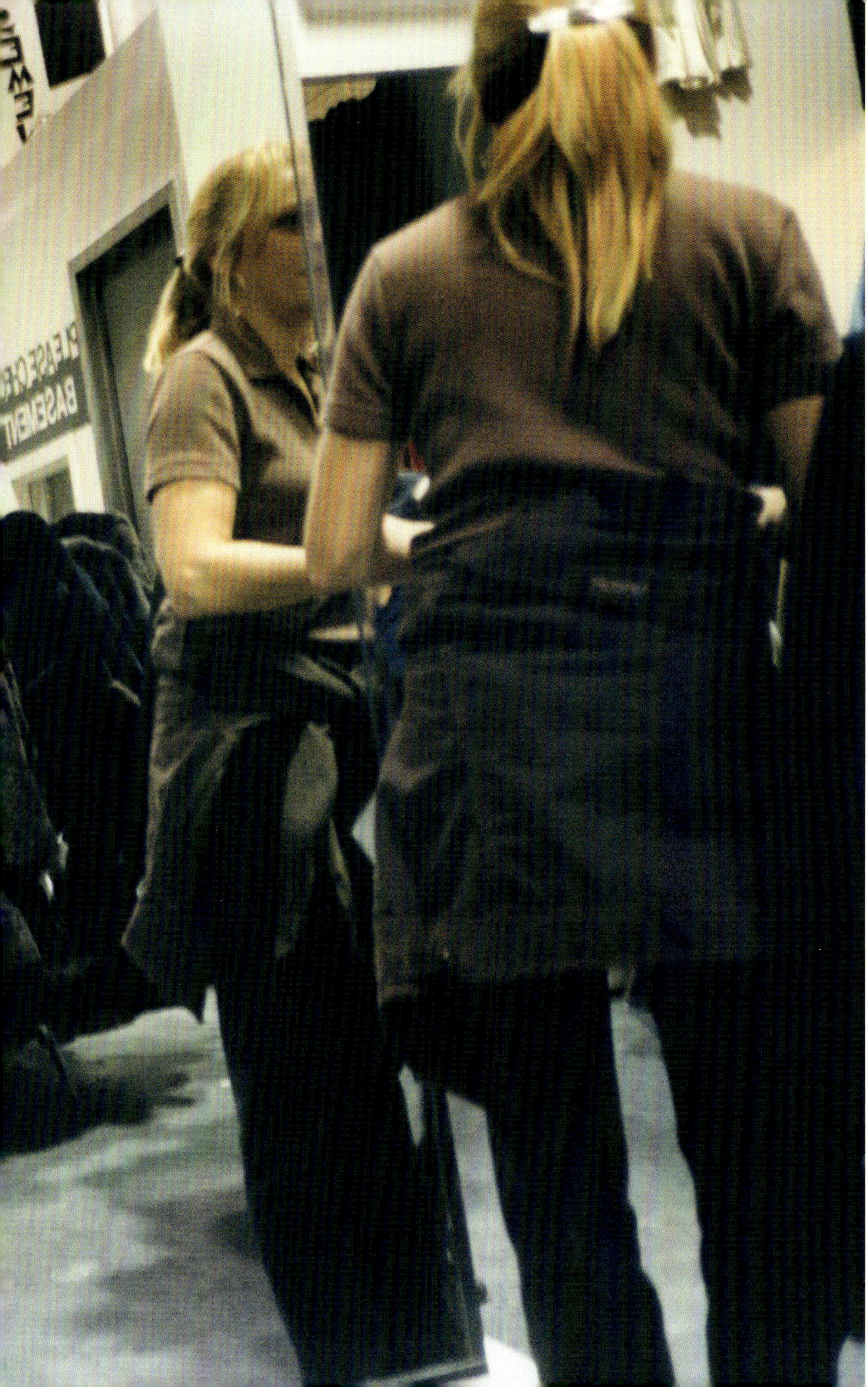

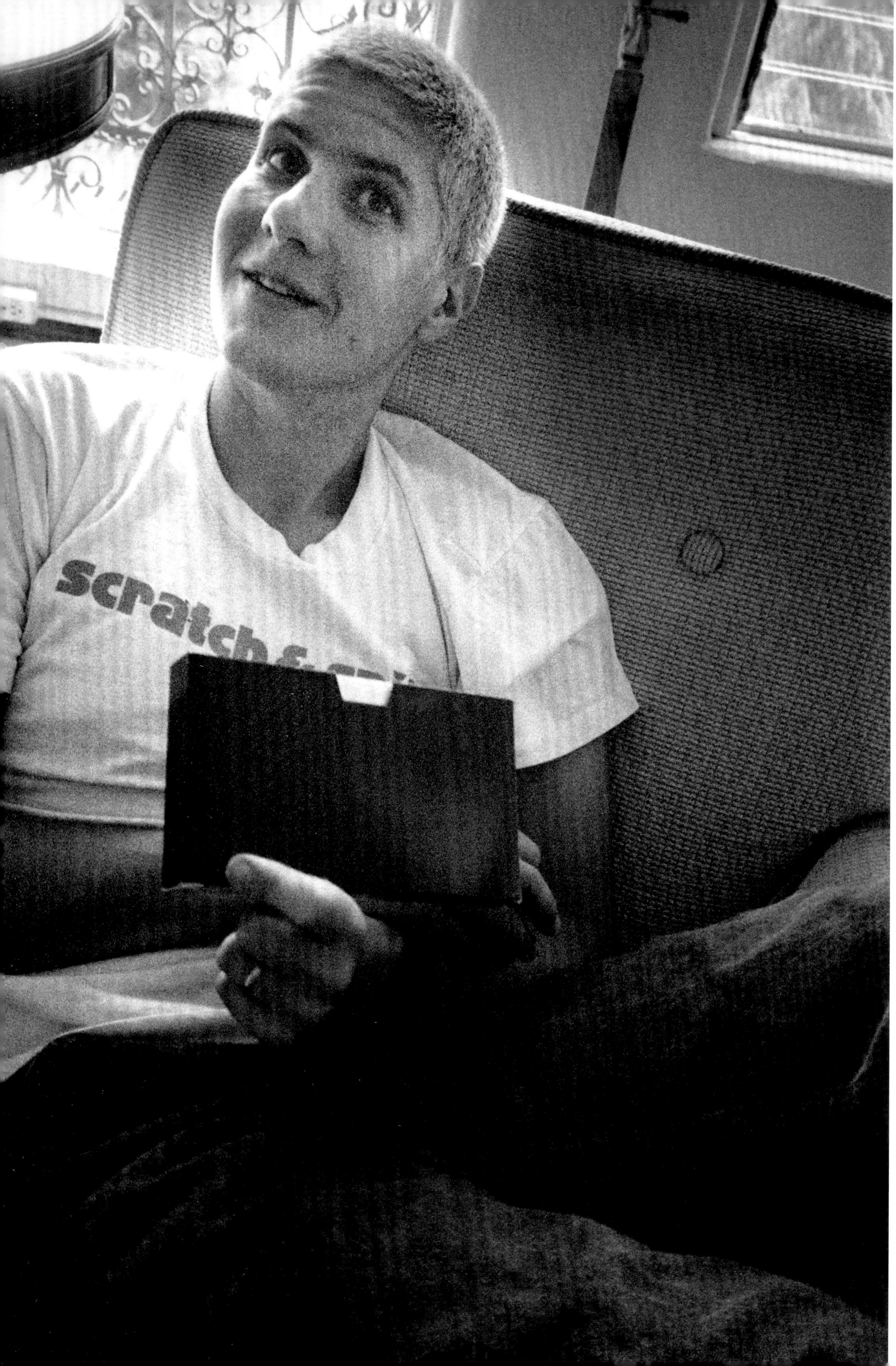
scratch

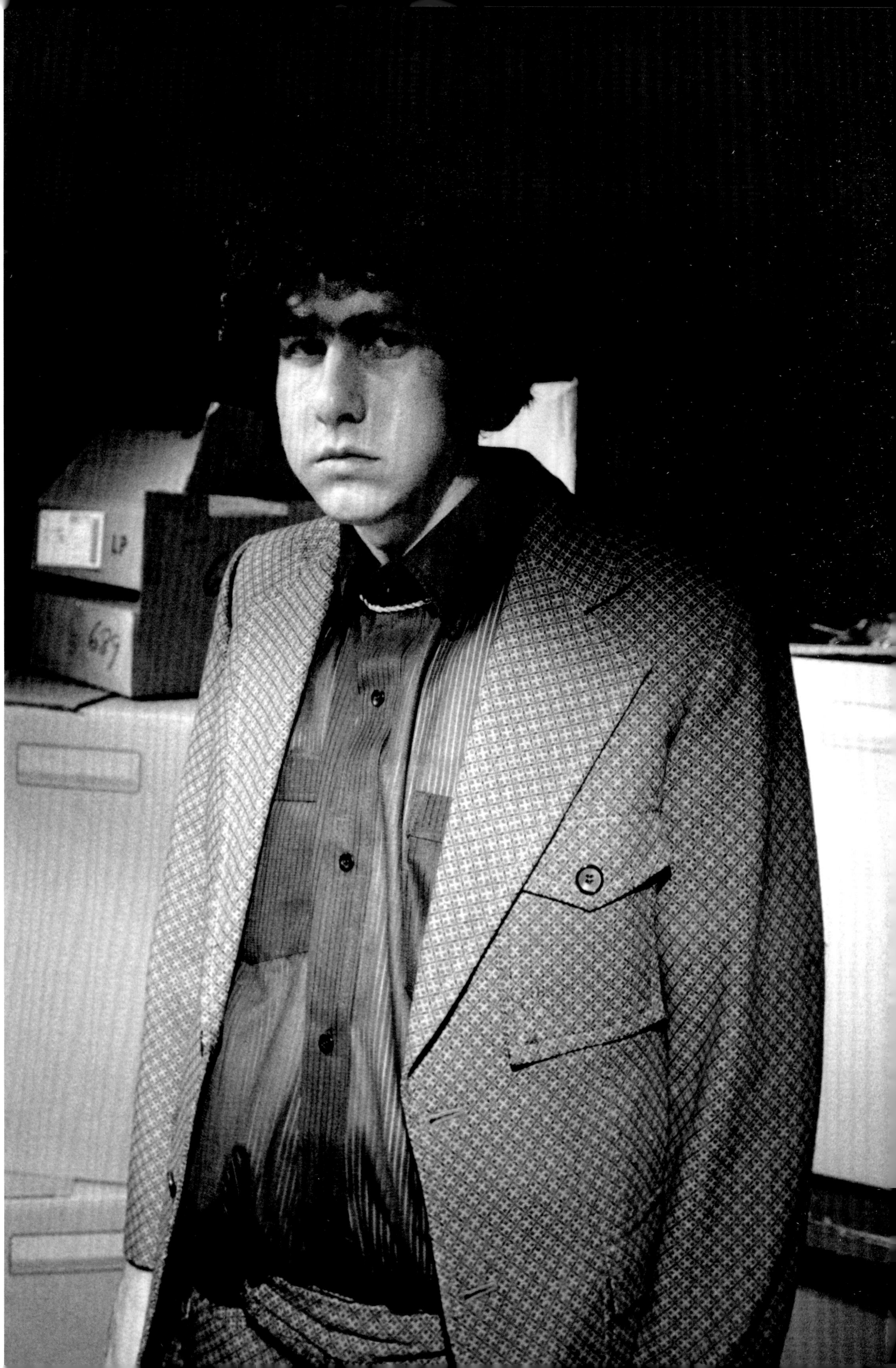
LP

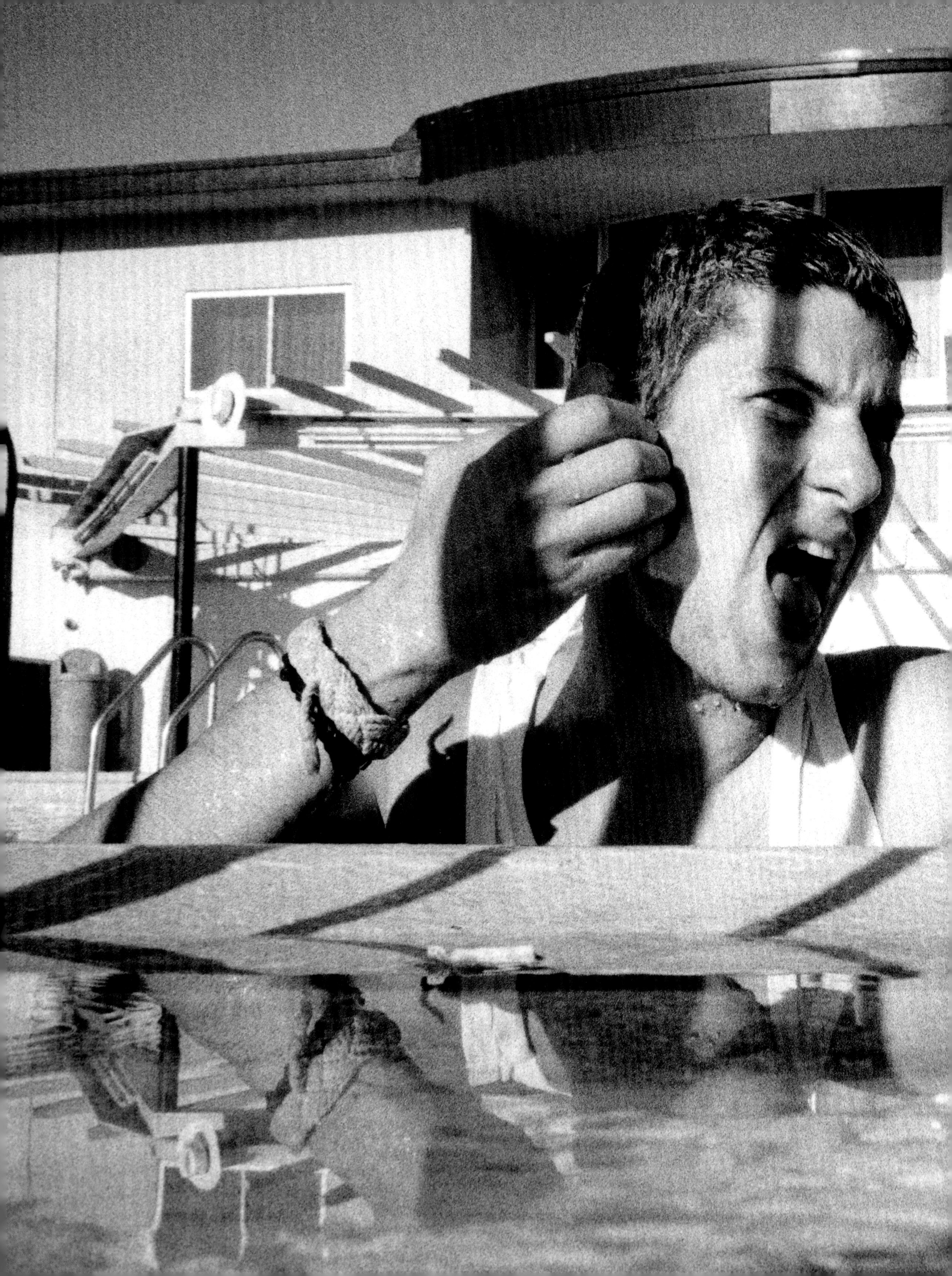

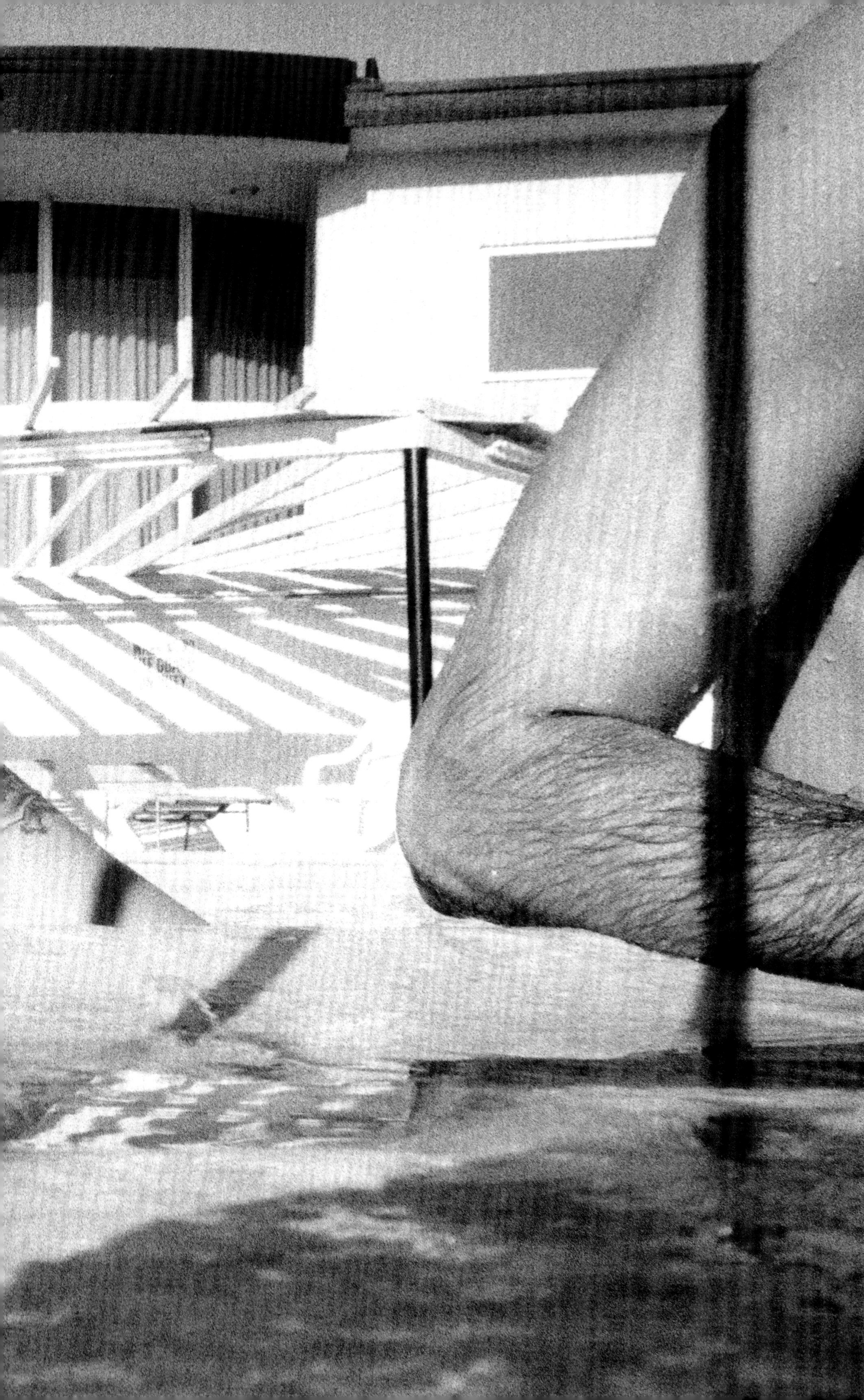

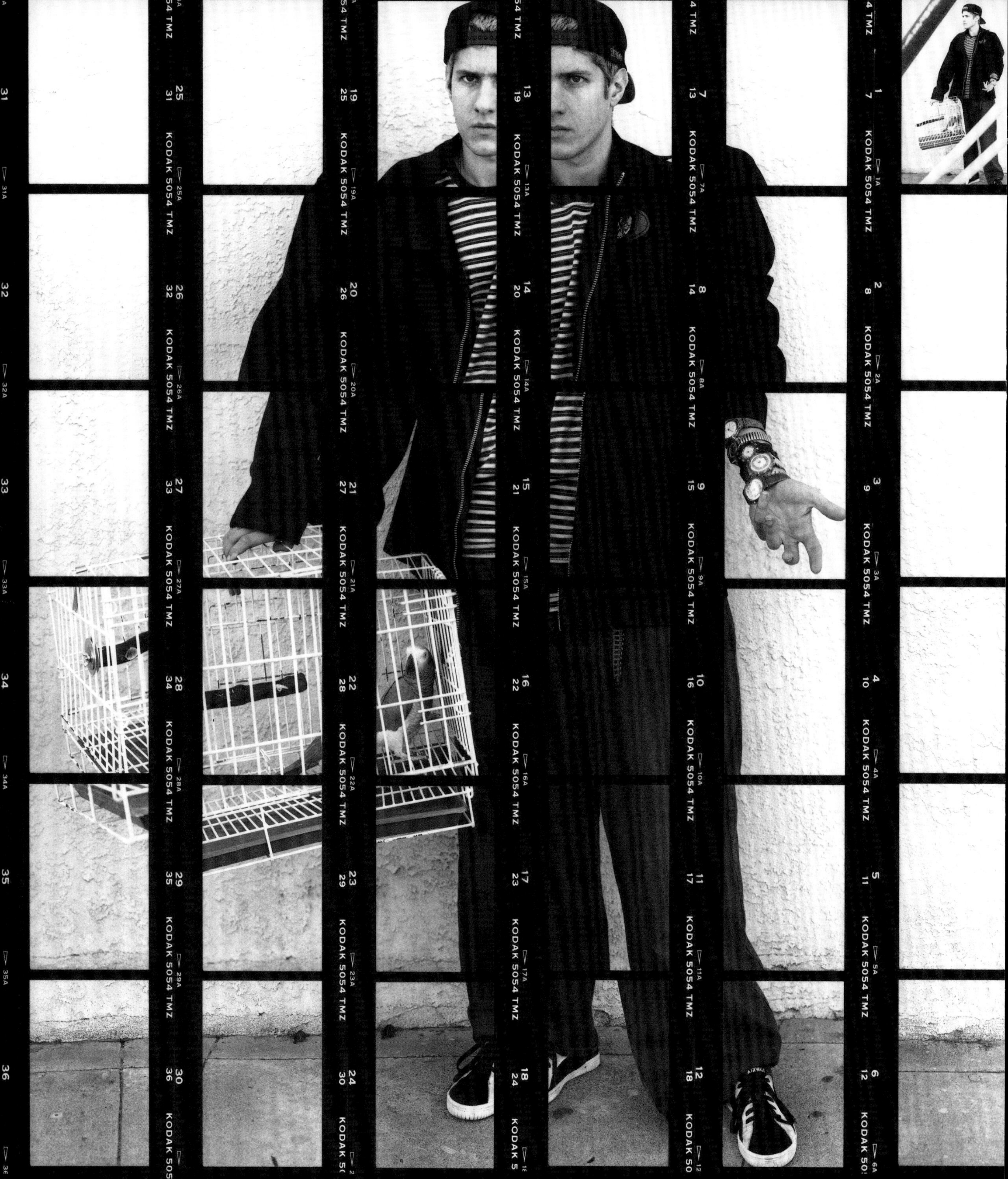

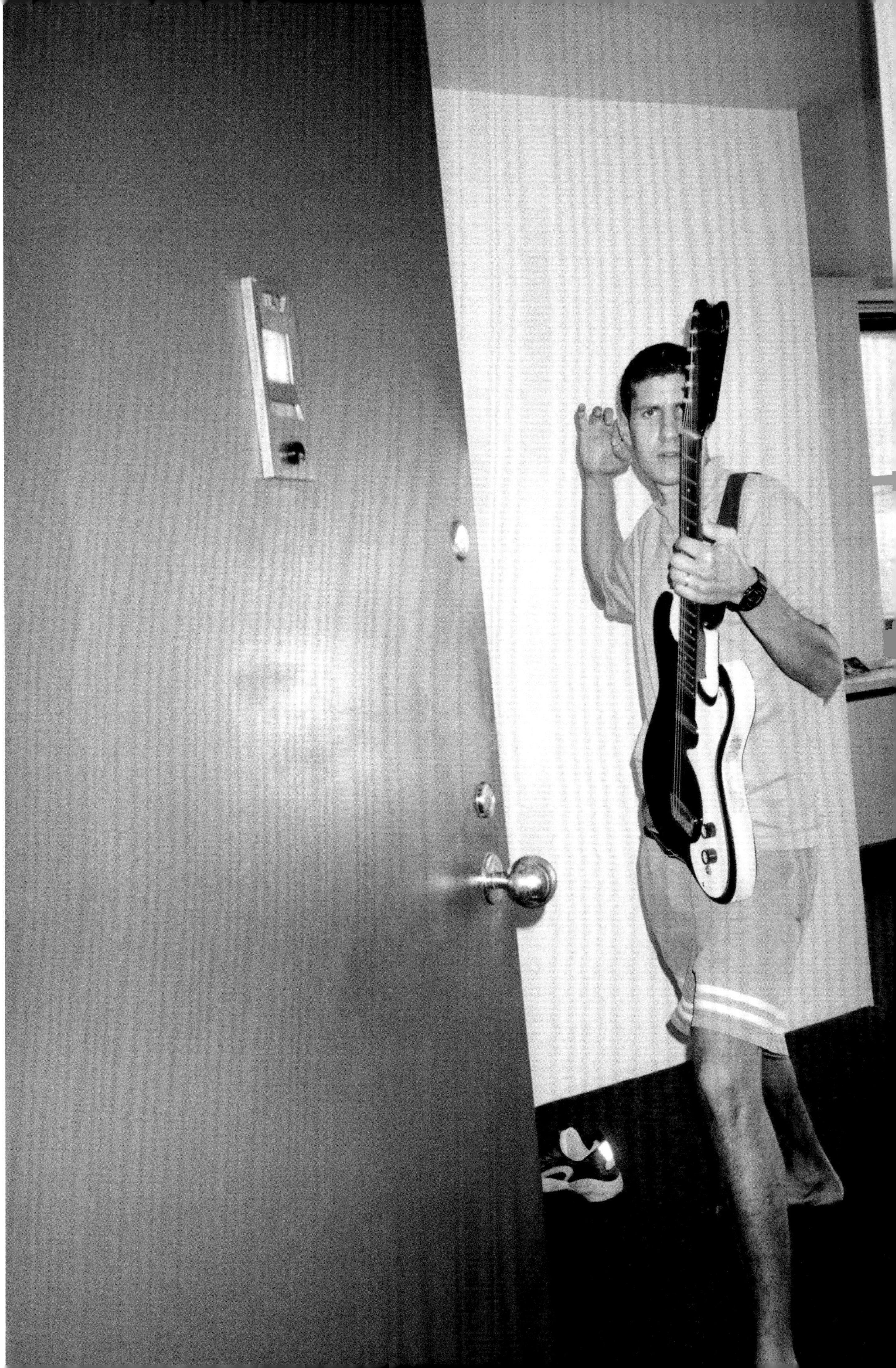

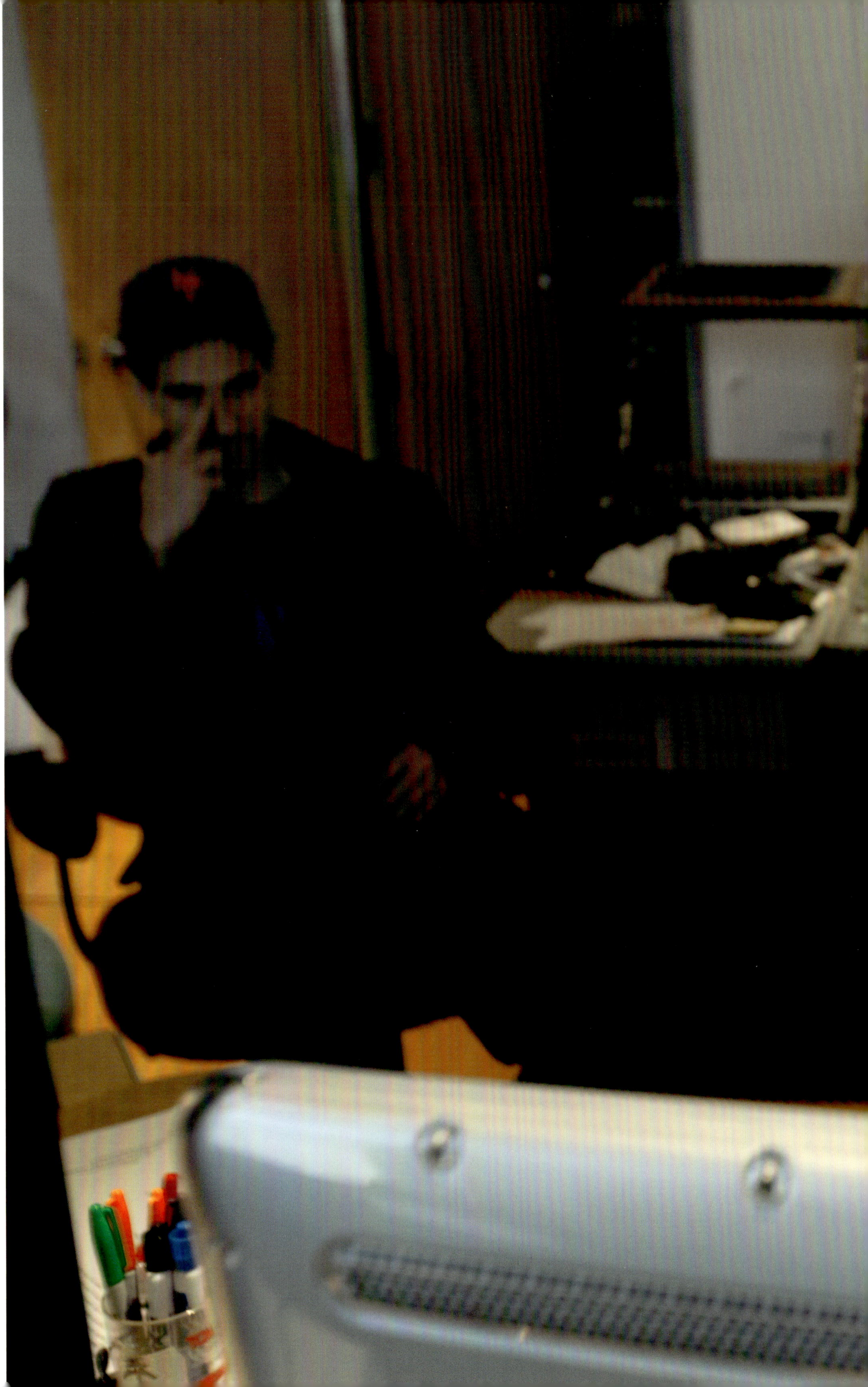

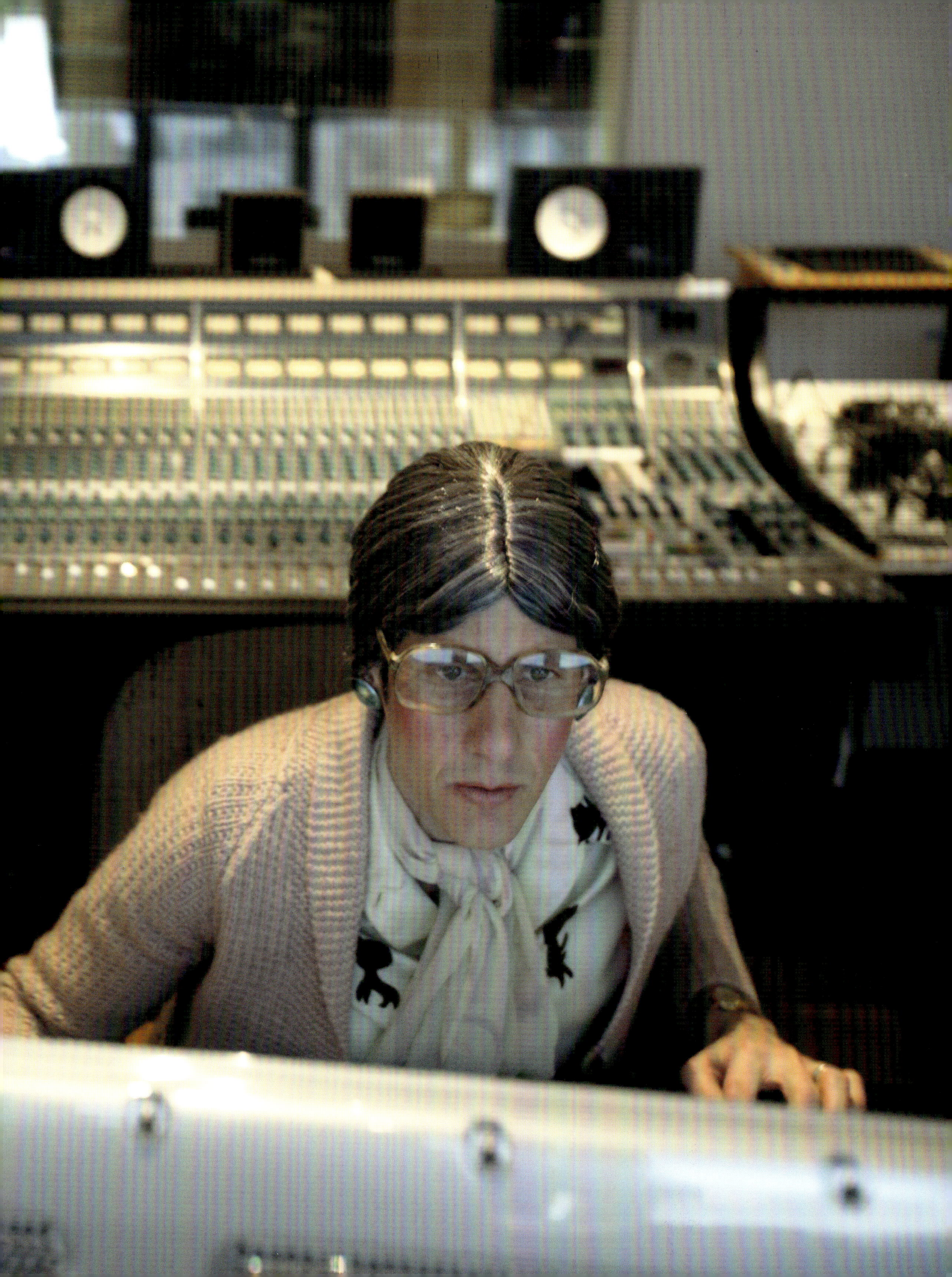

Adam

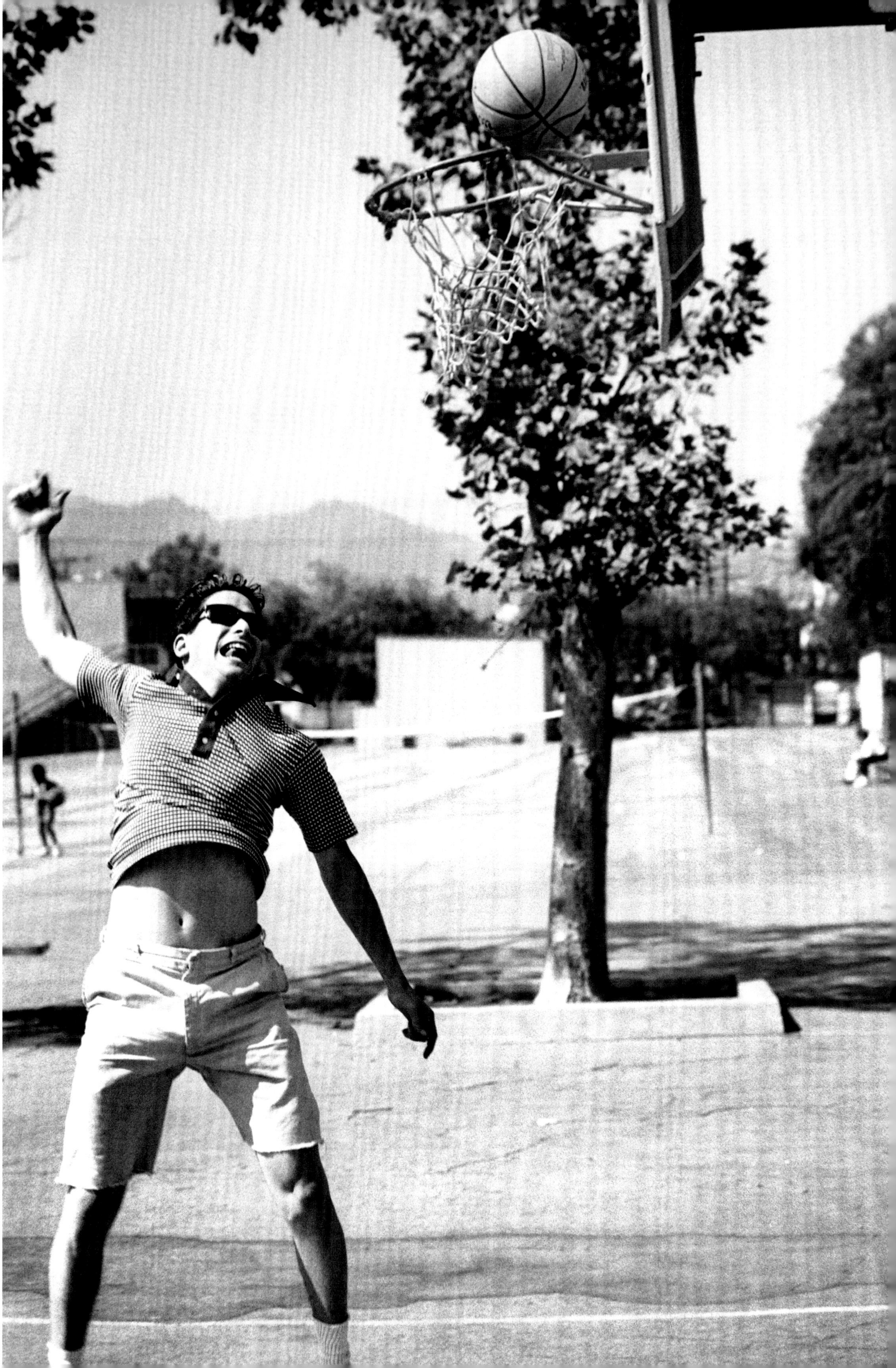

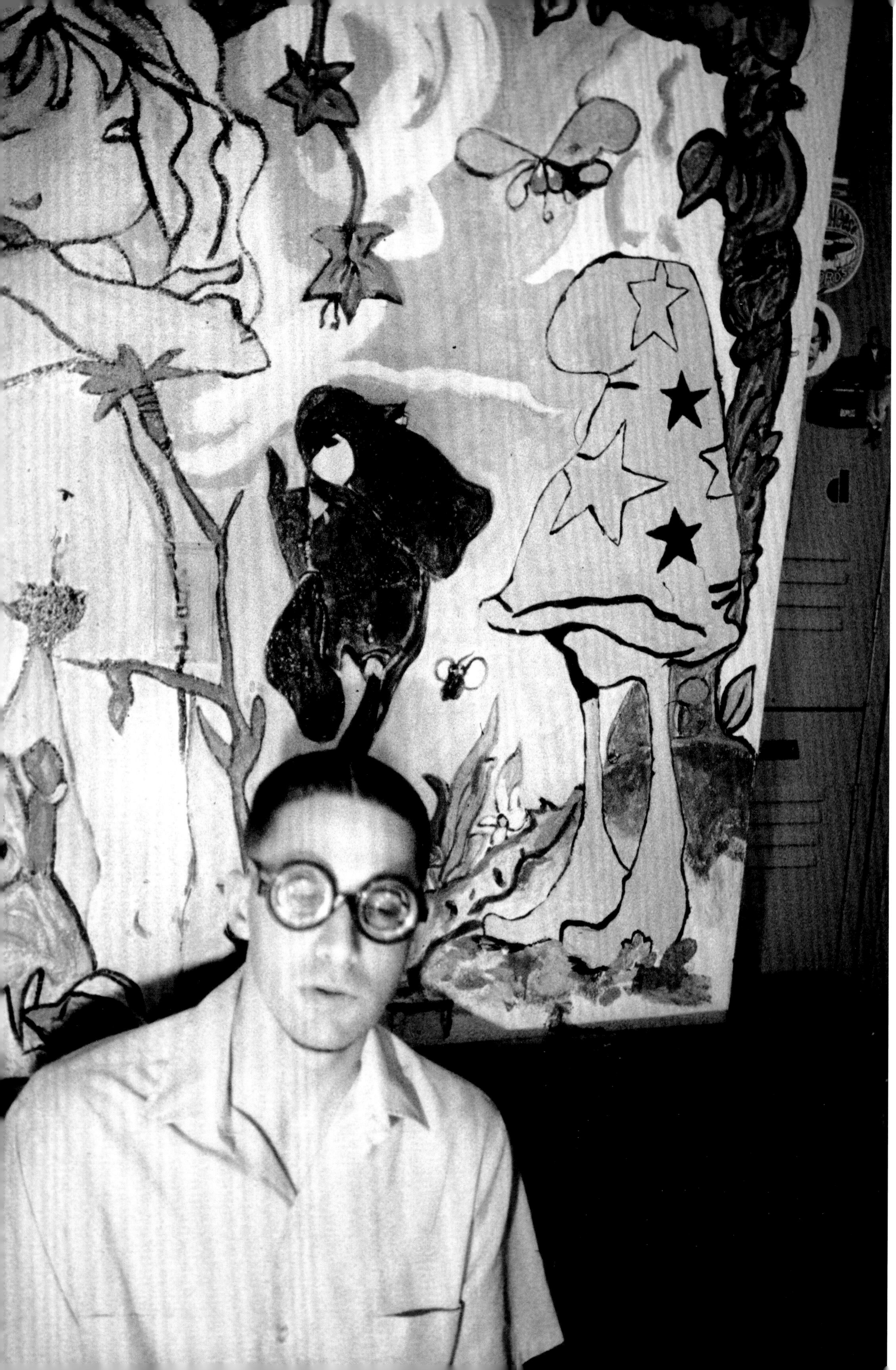

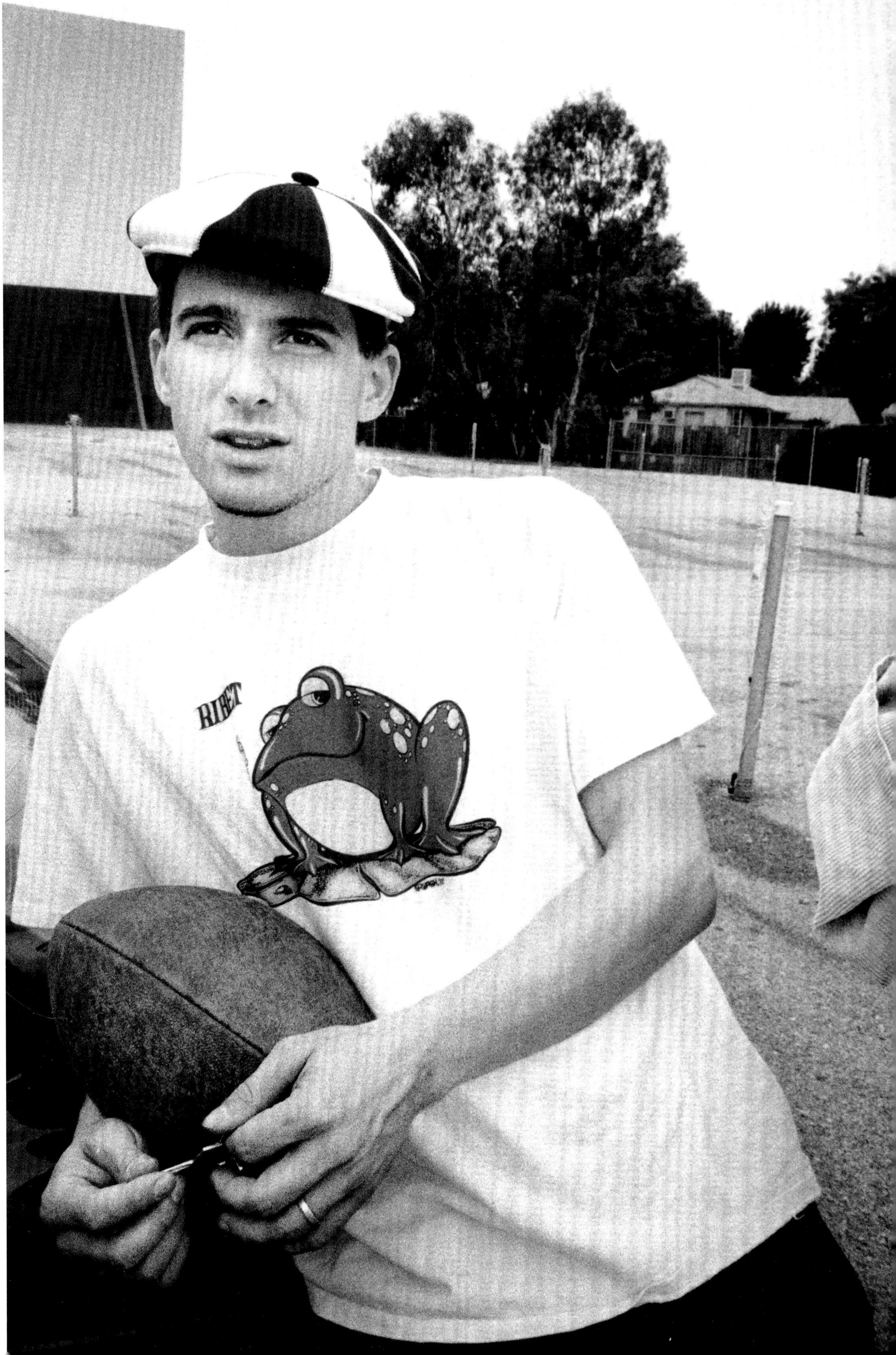

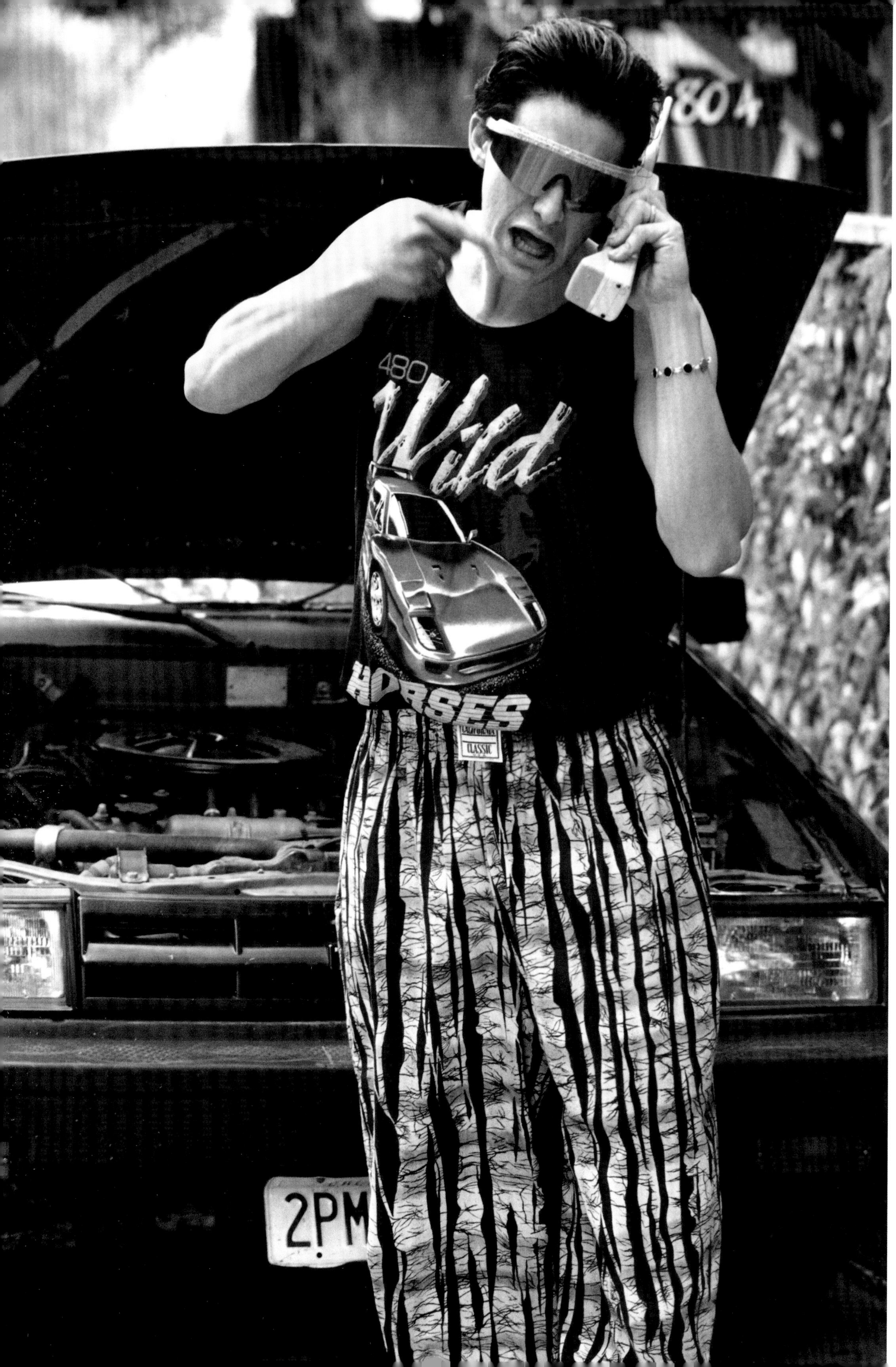
804
480
Wild
HORSES
CLASSIC
2PM

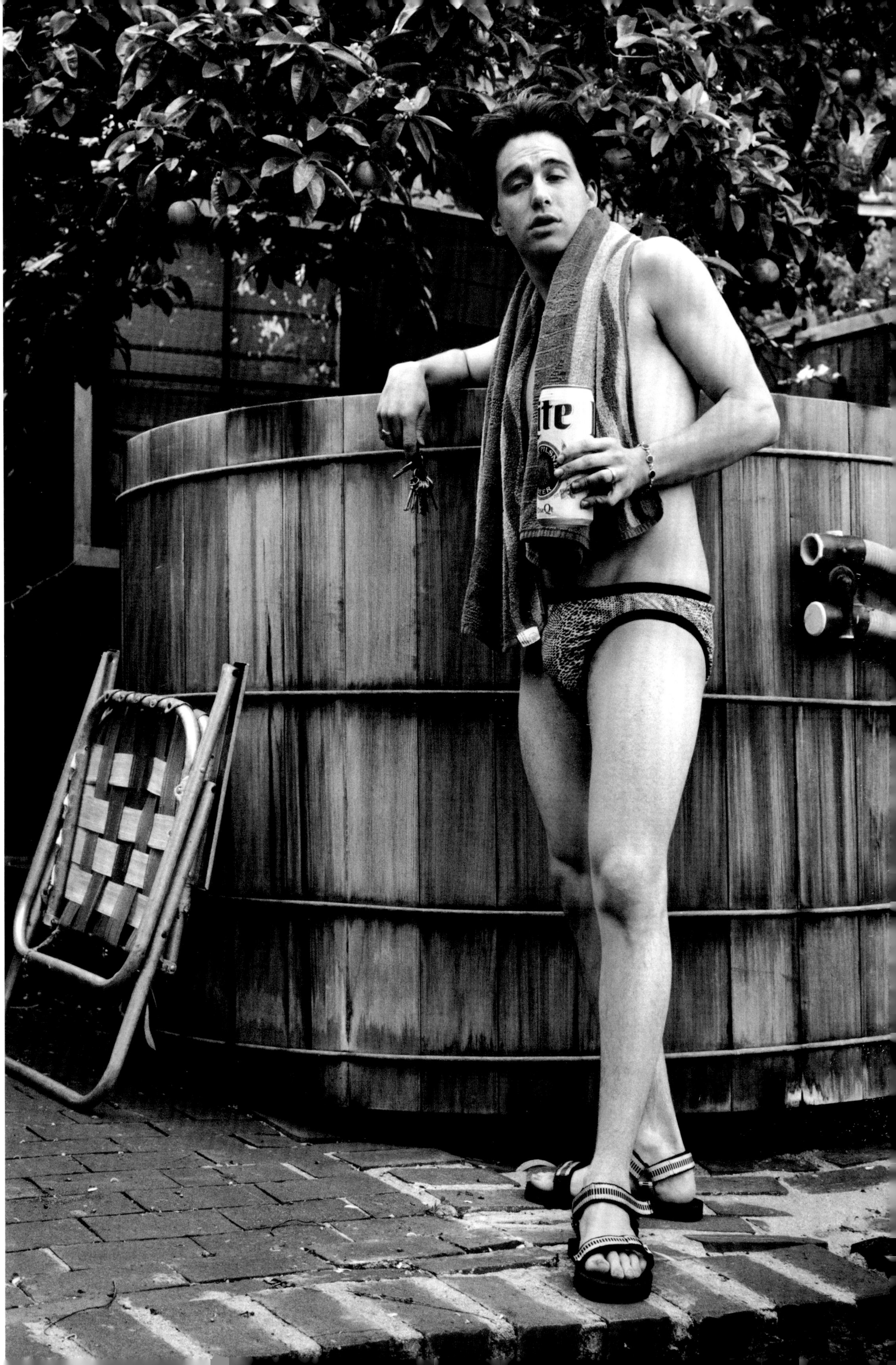

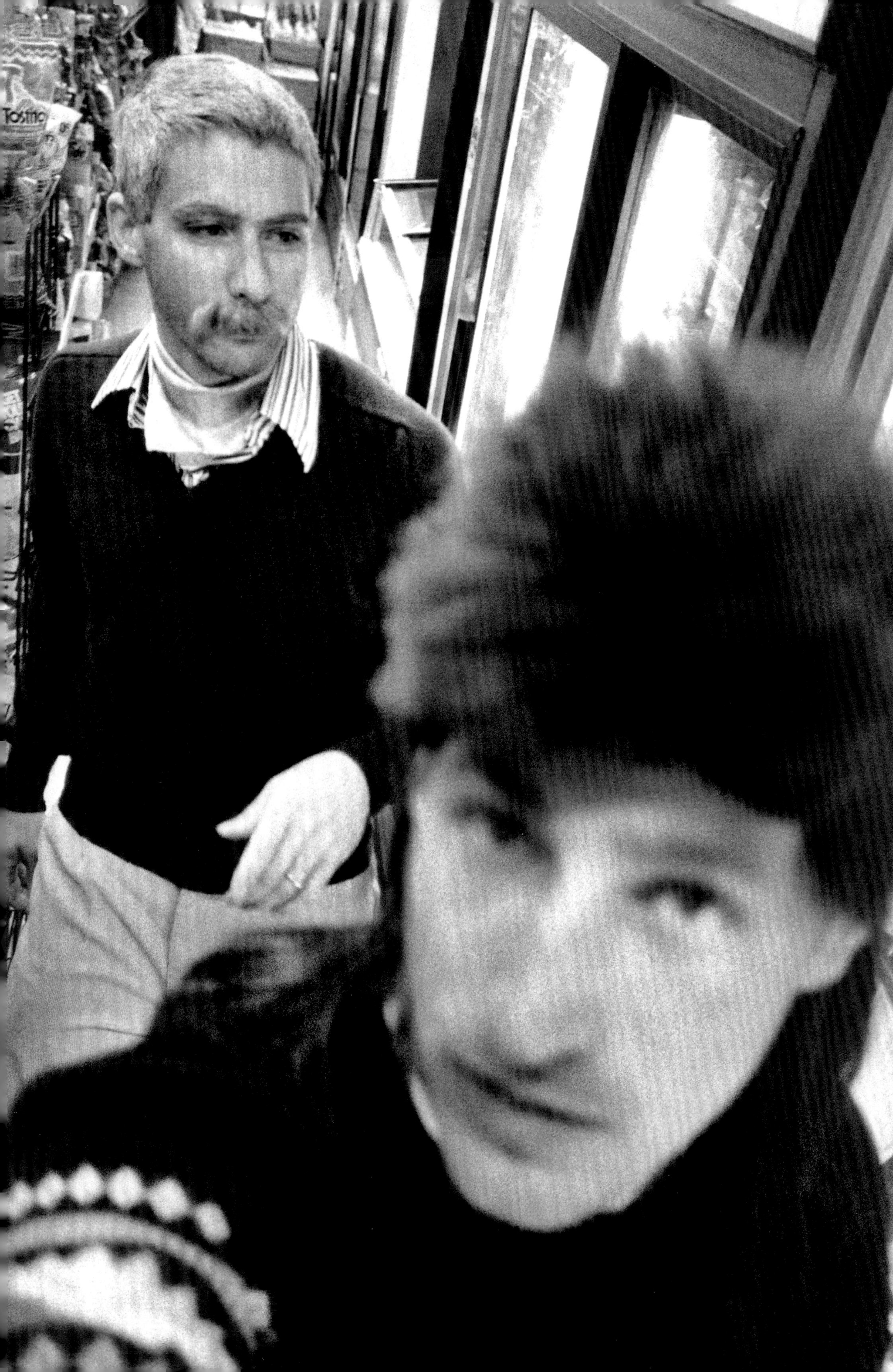

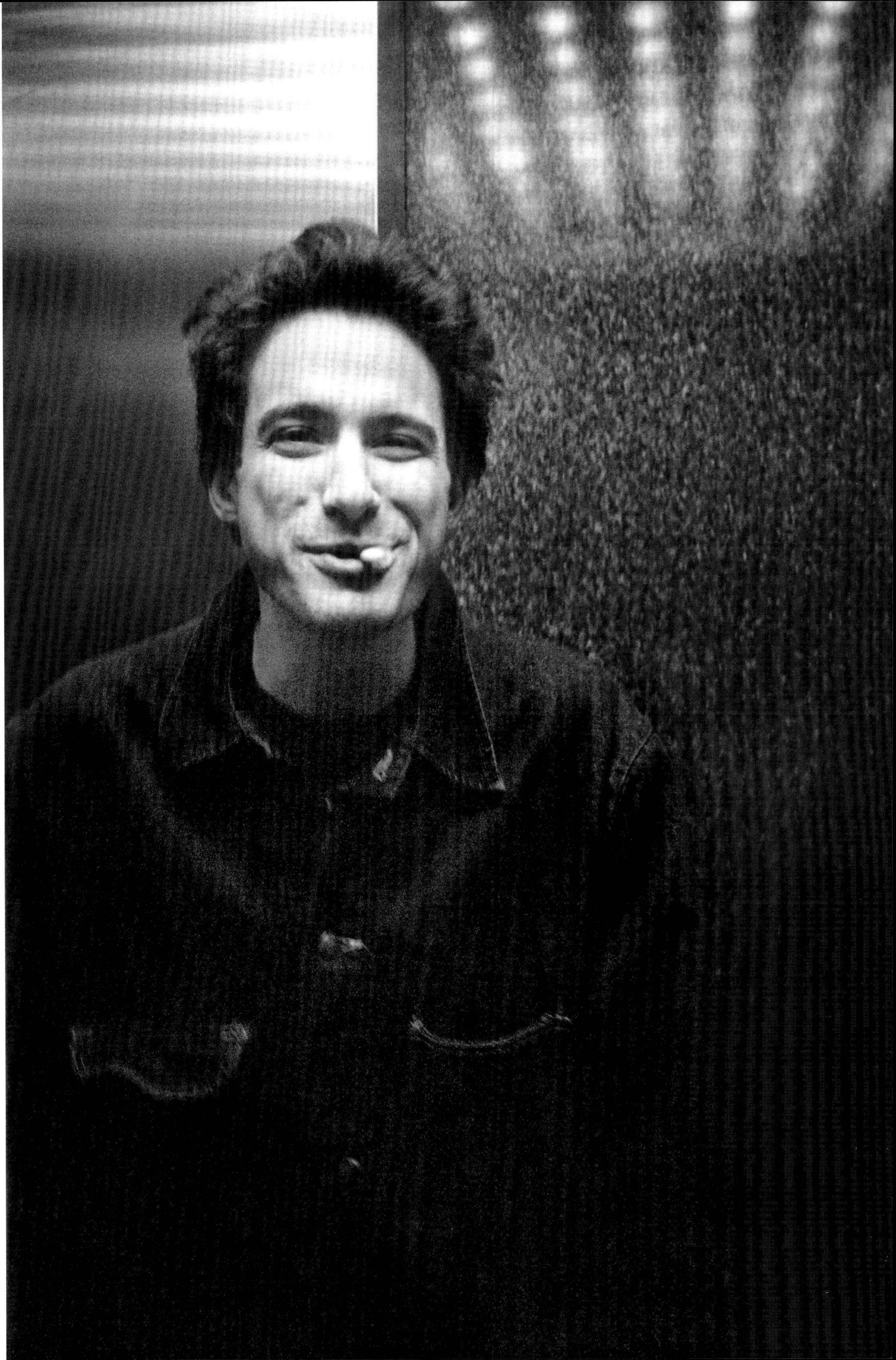

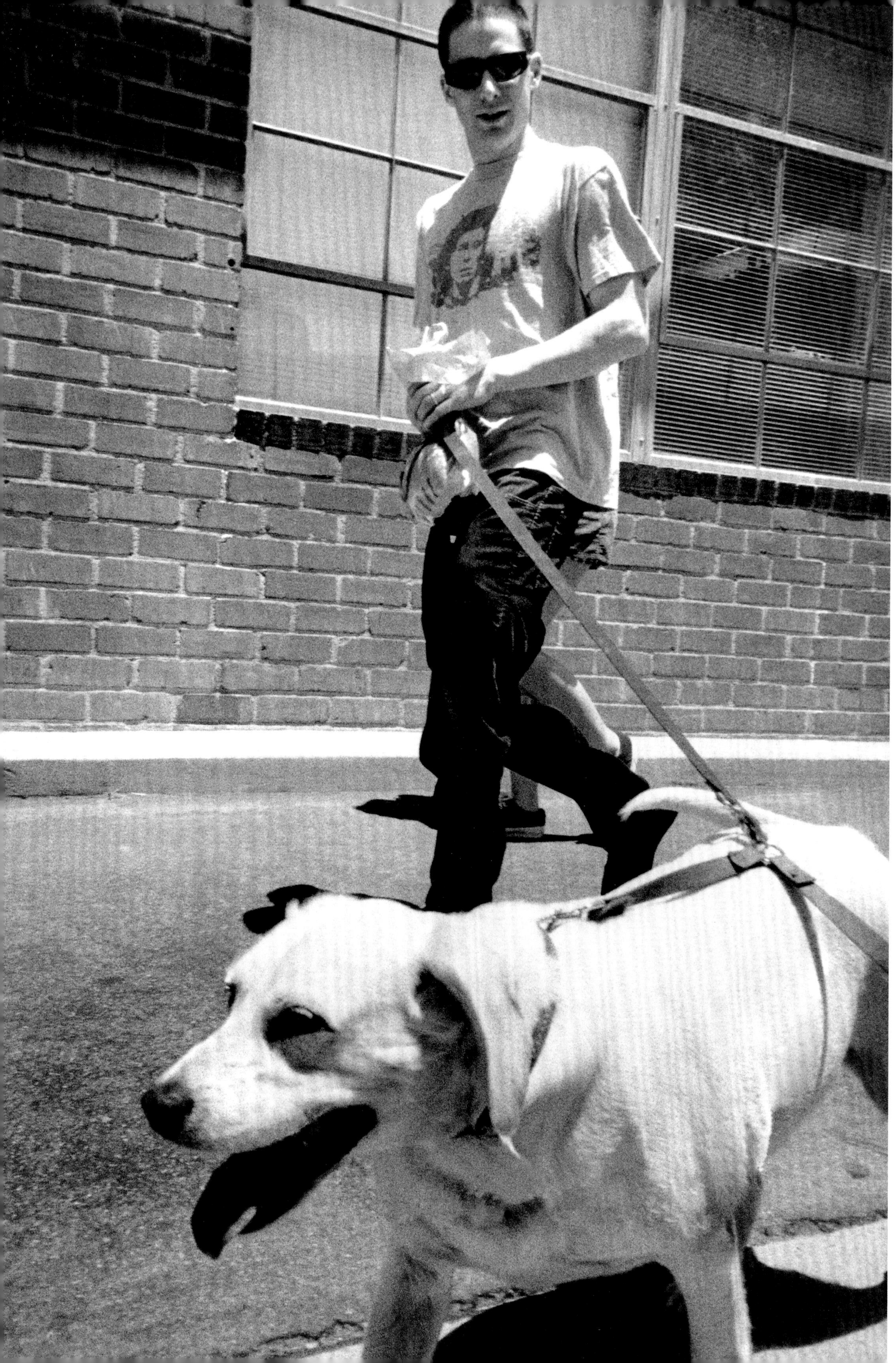

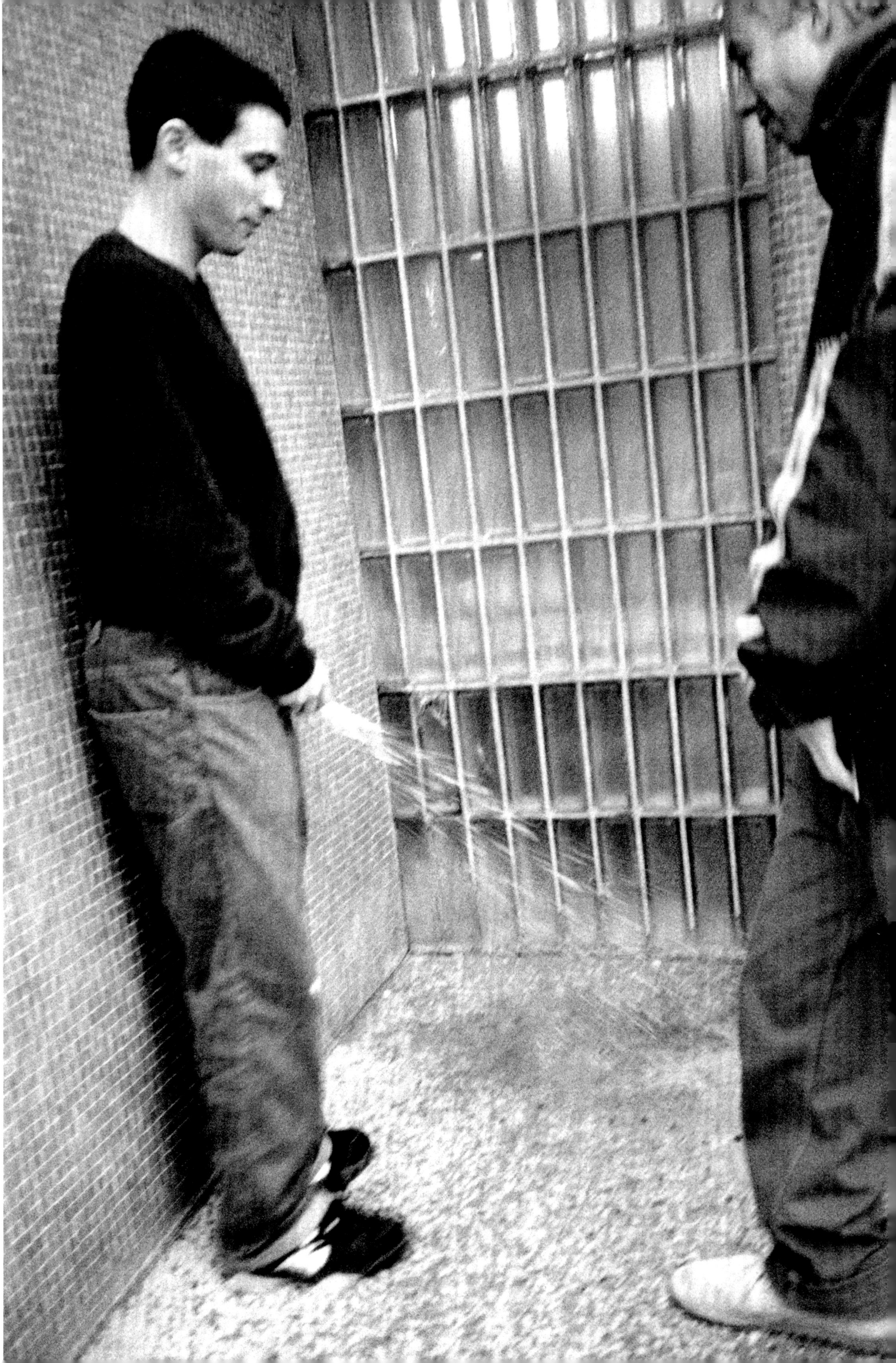

Yauch

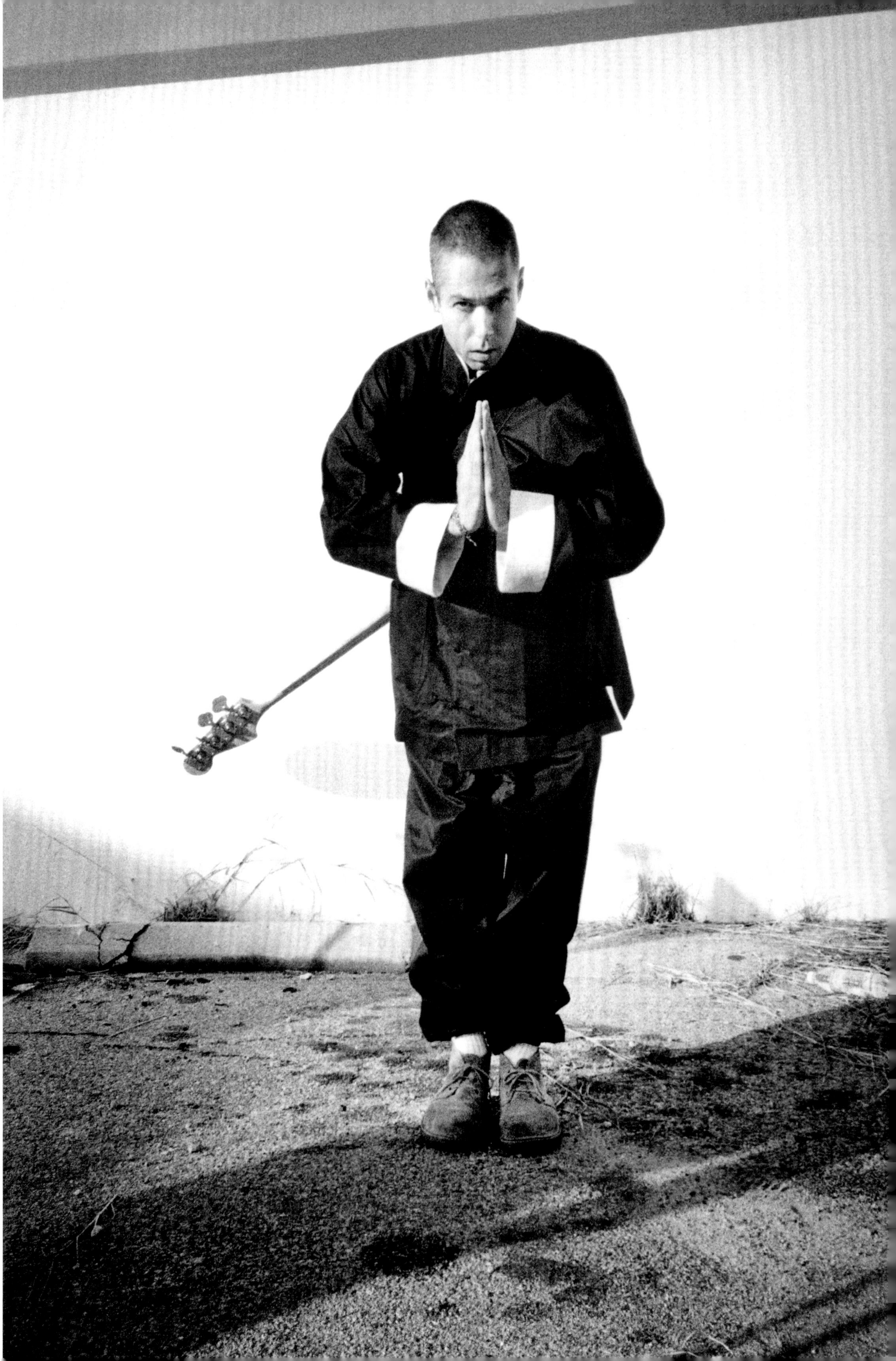

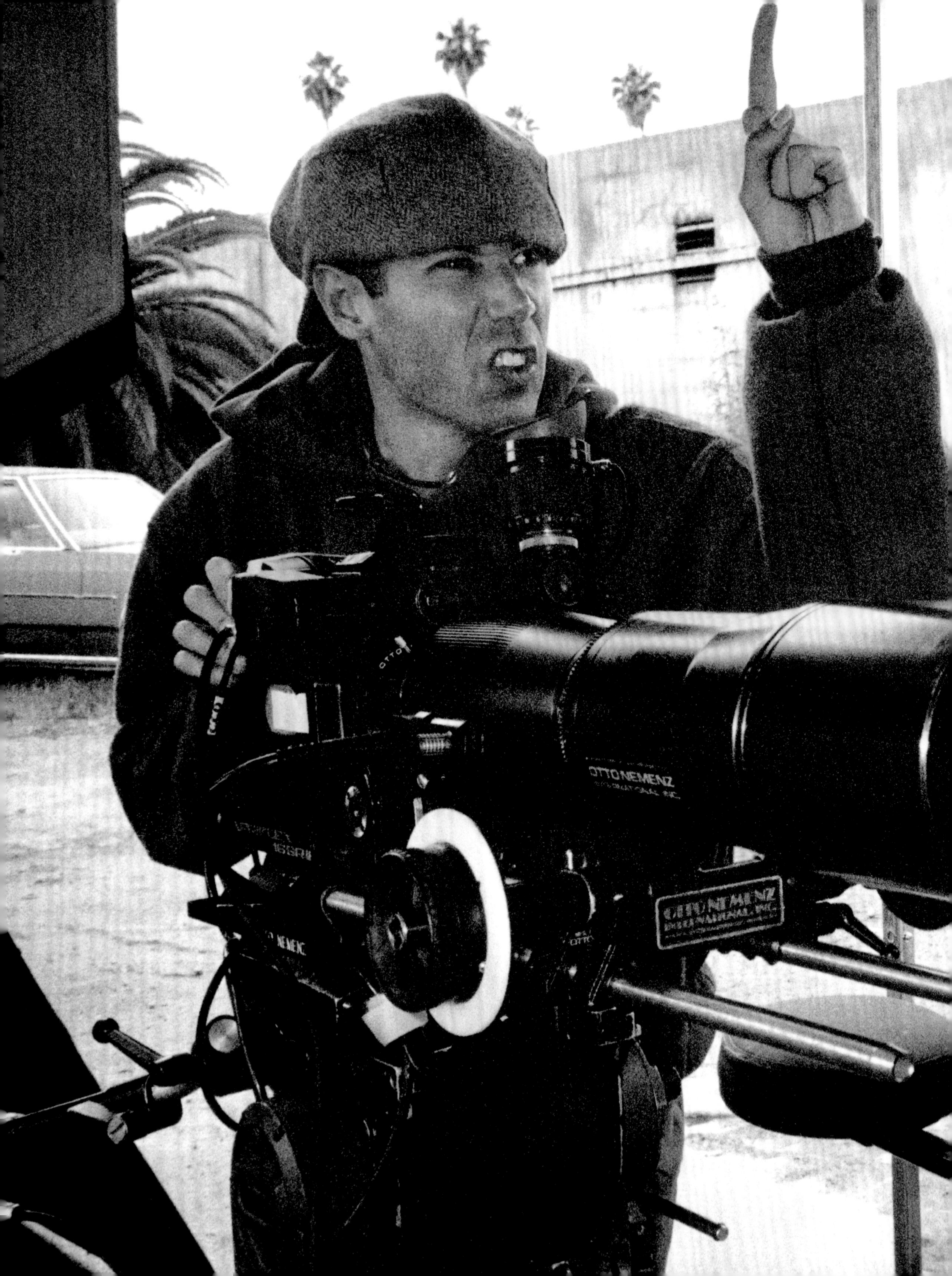
OTTO NEMENZ

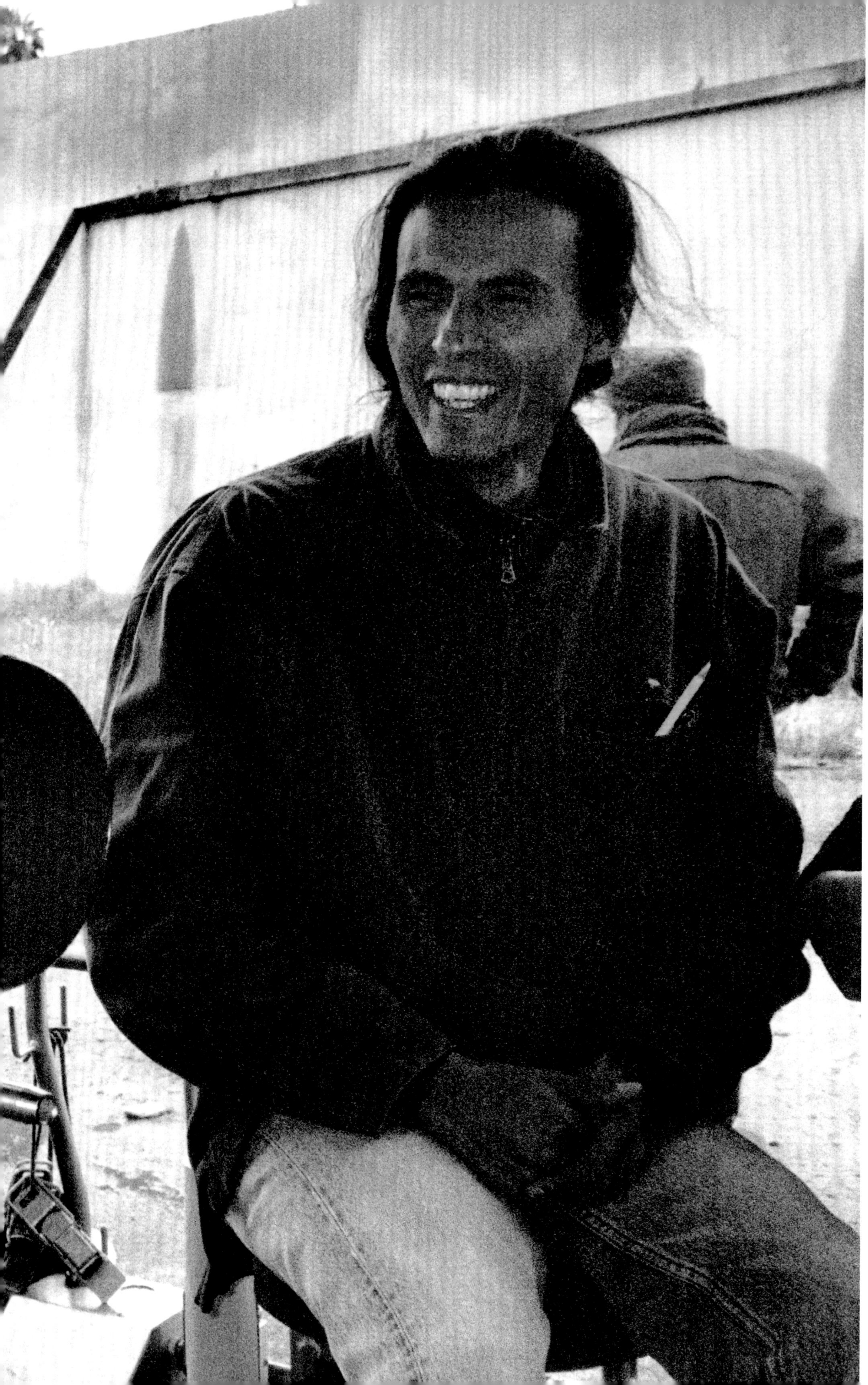

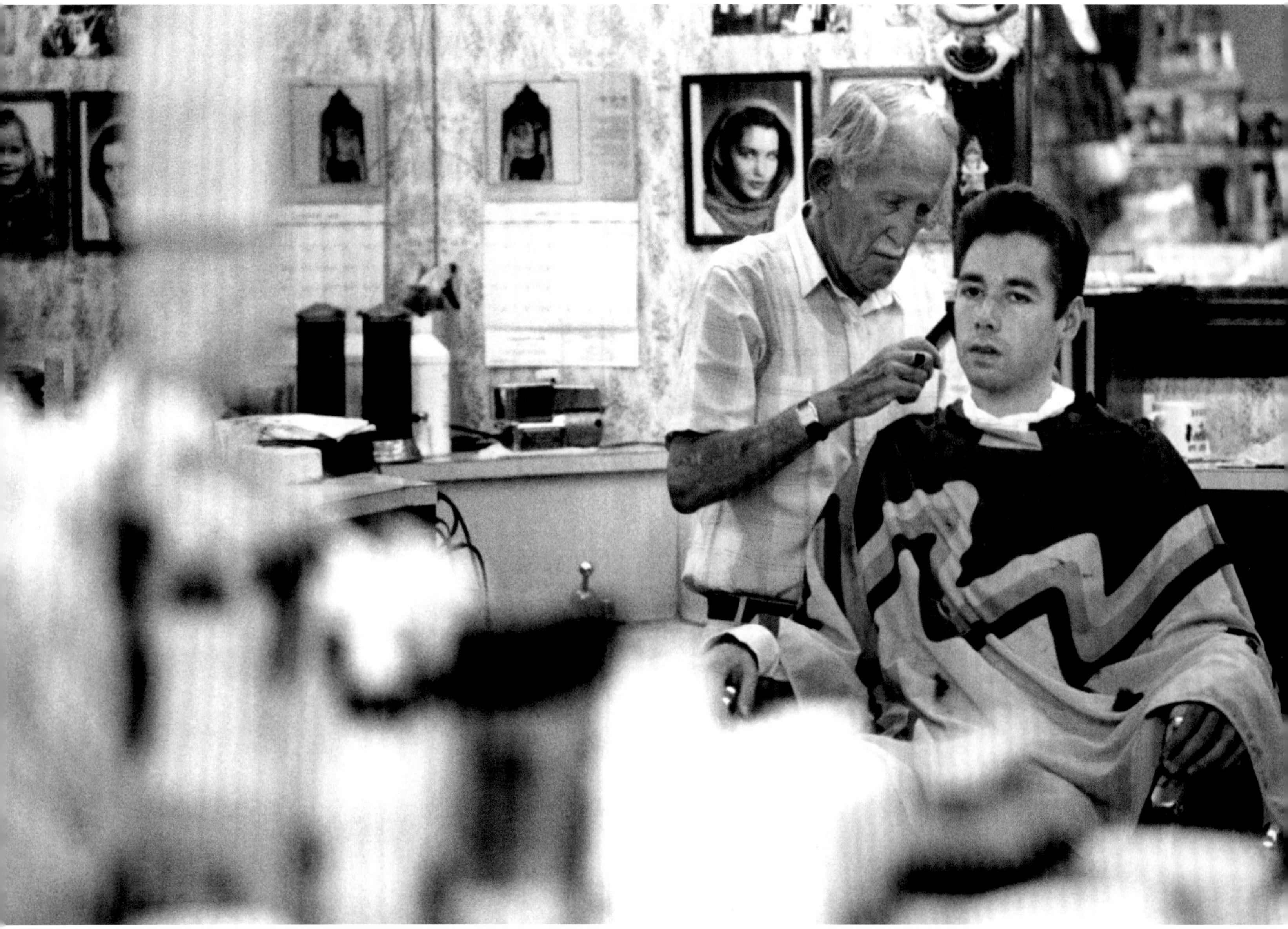

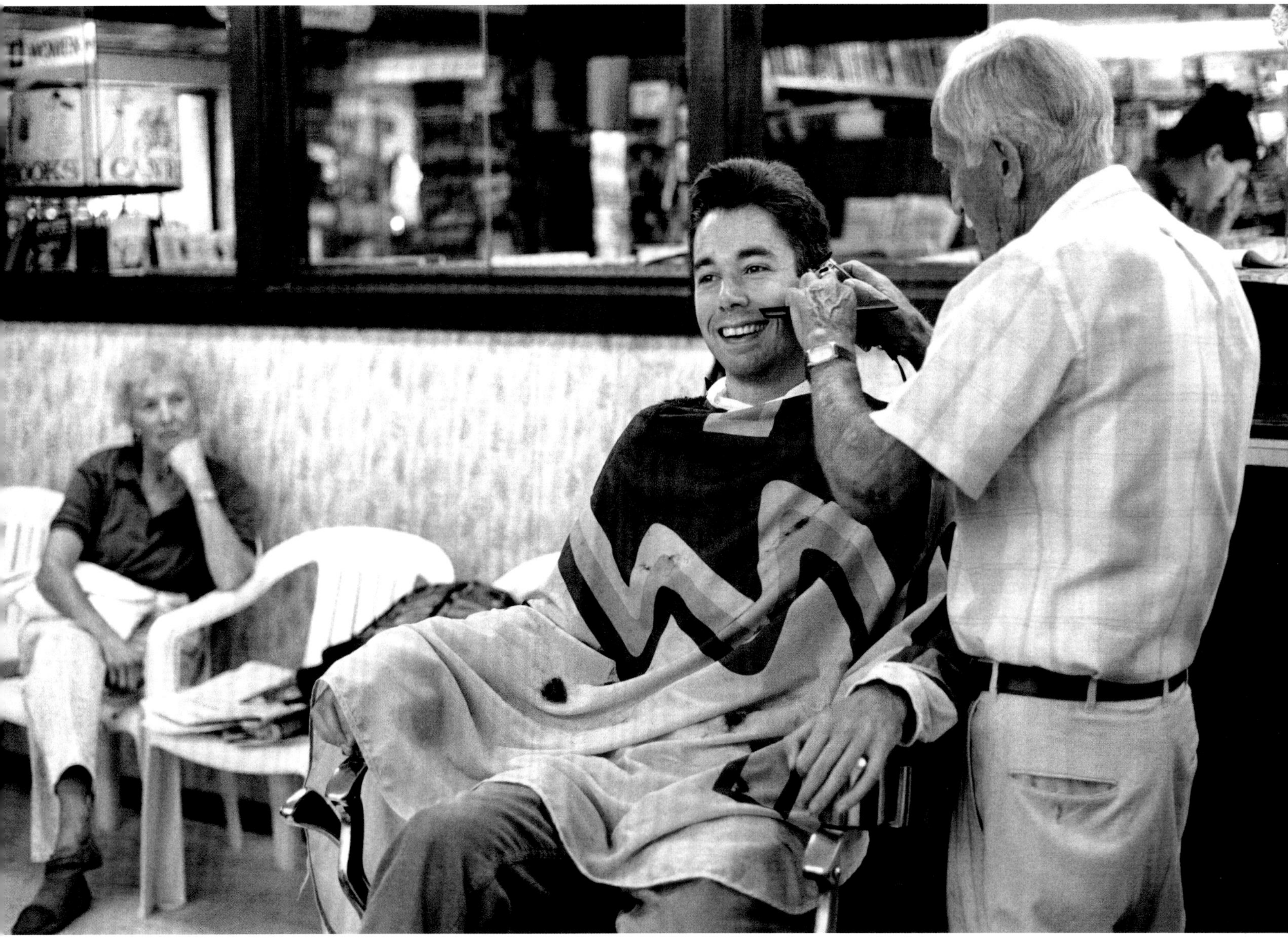

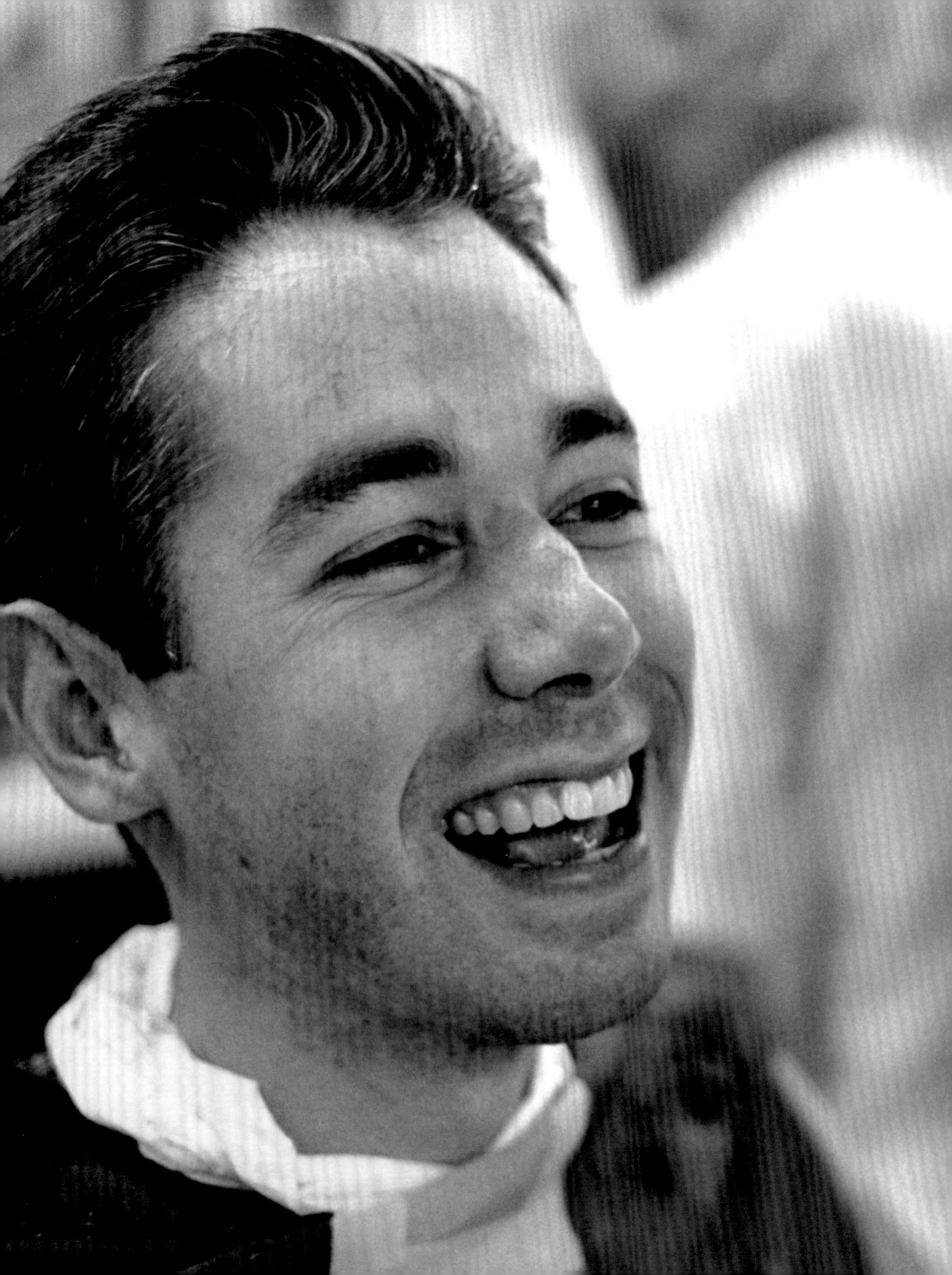

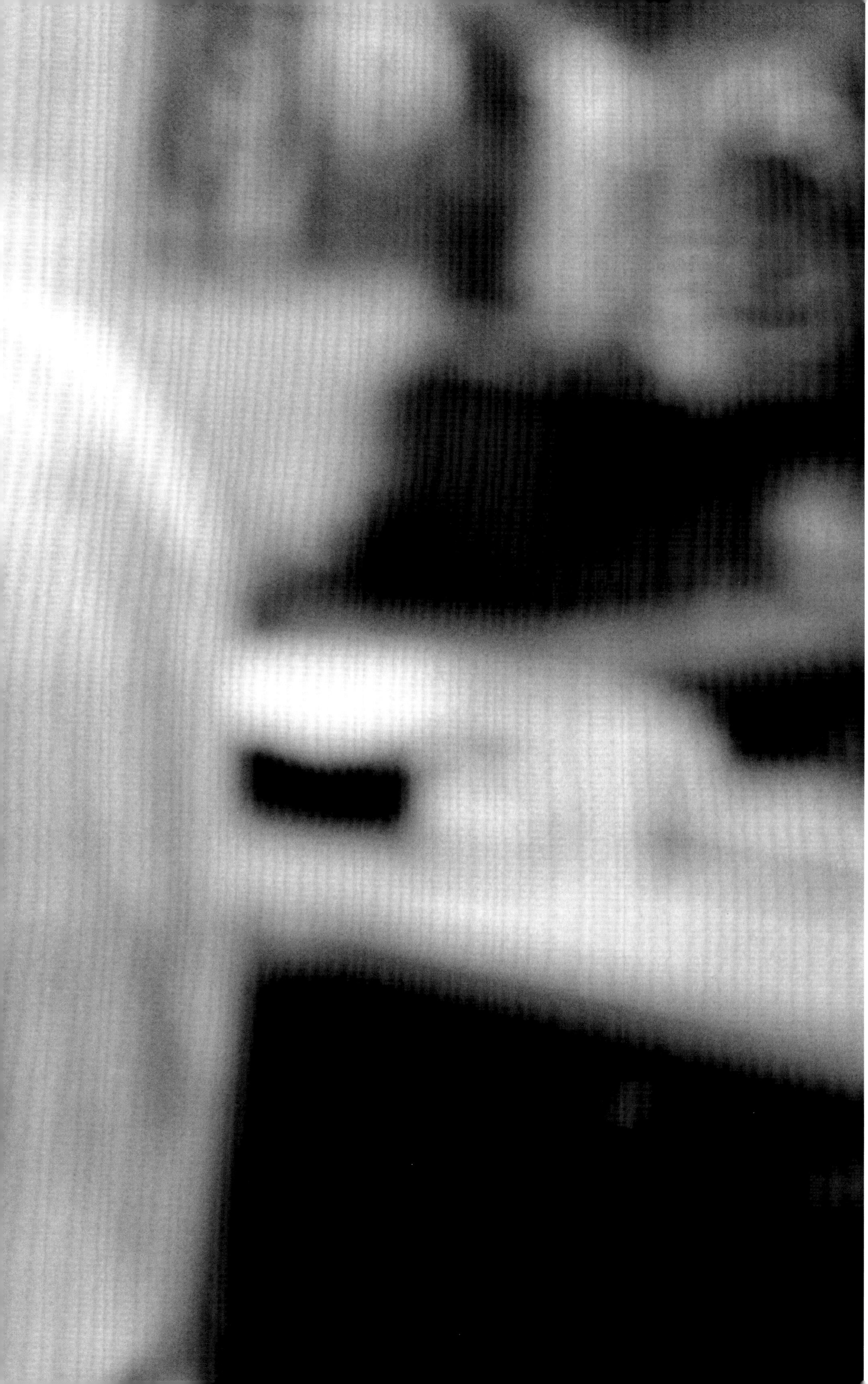

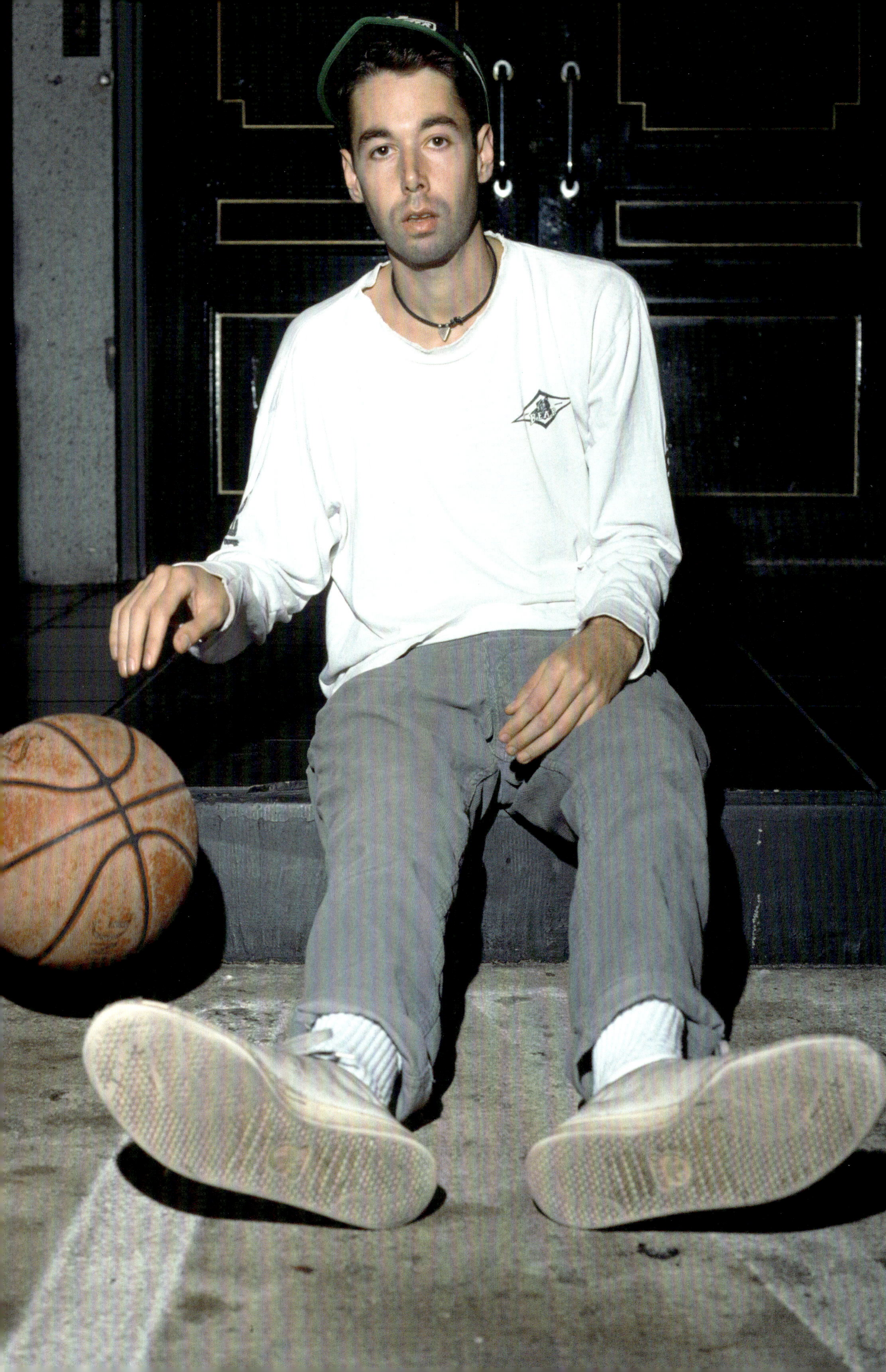

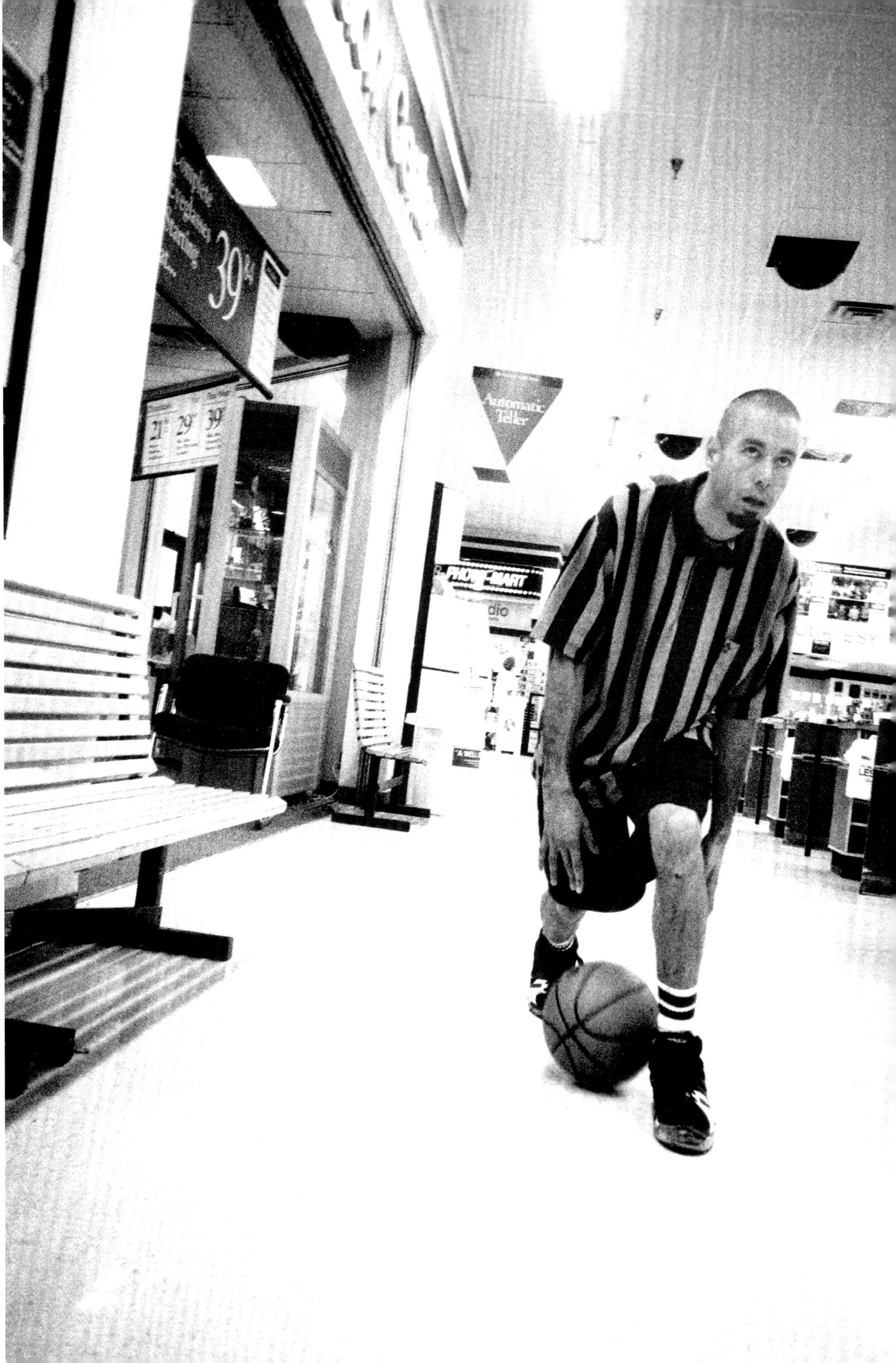
Automatic Teller
PHONE-MART

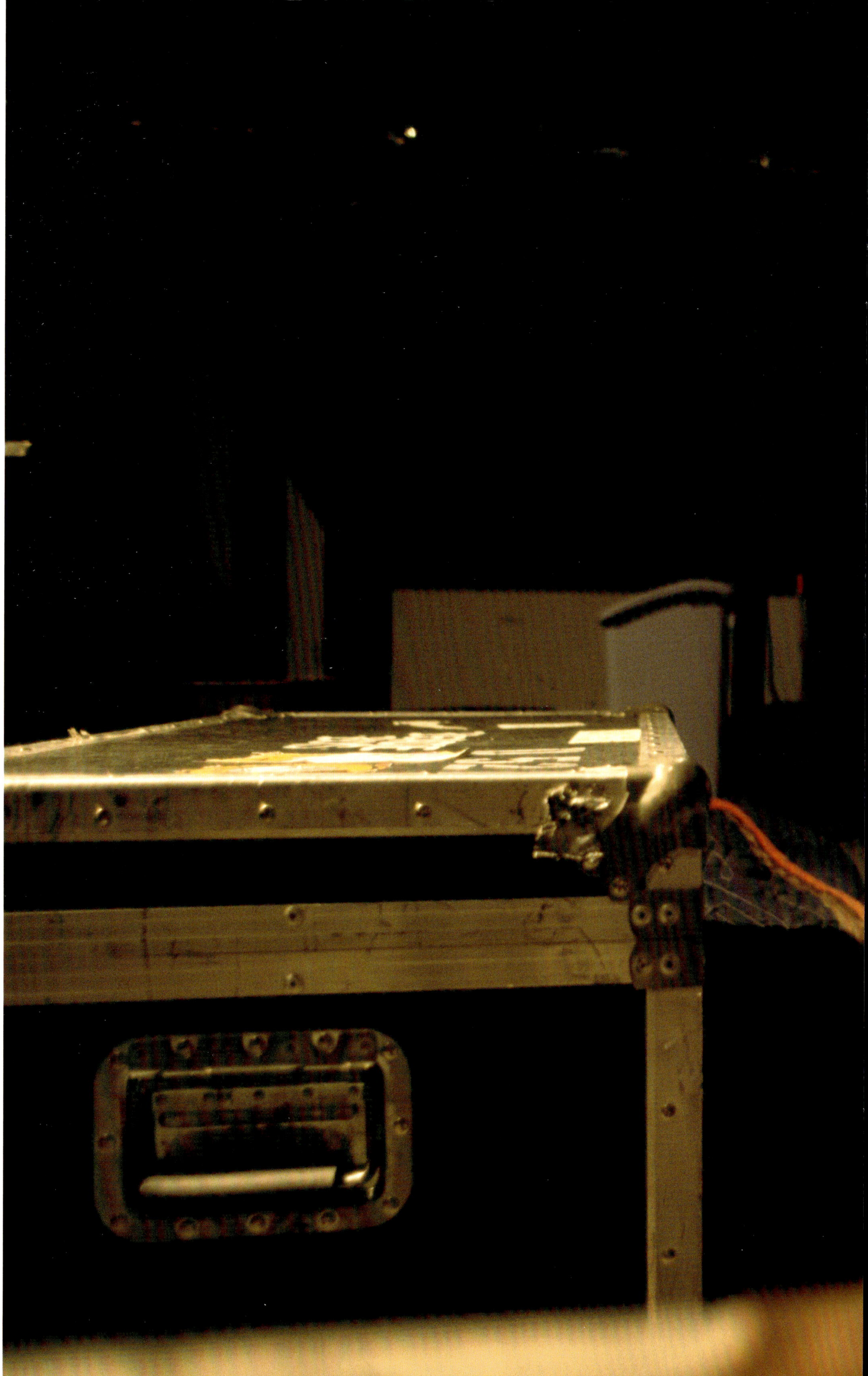

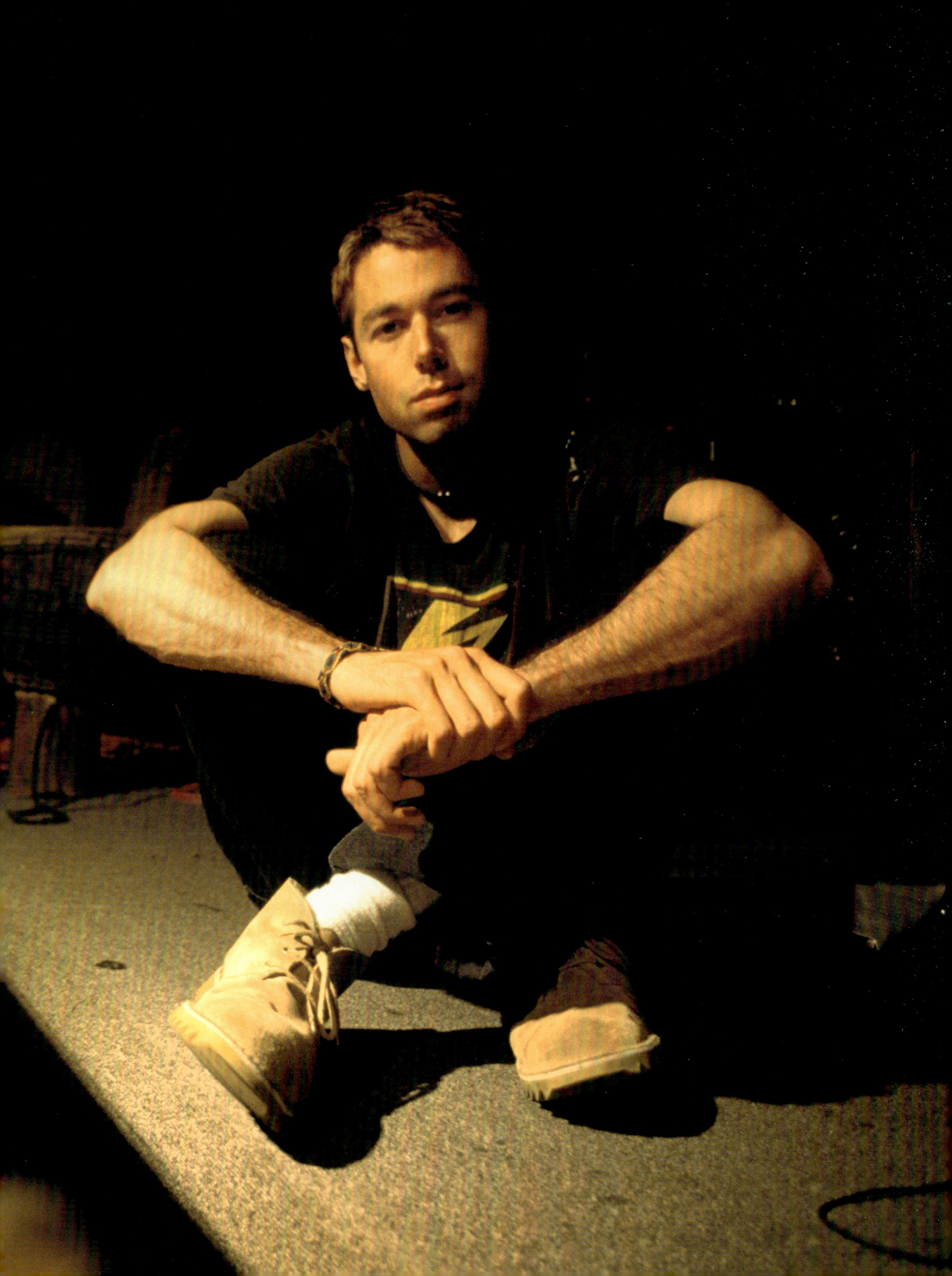

Wake up call

Desert Sands Hotel Room 809

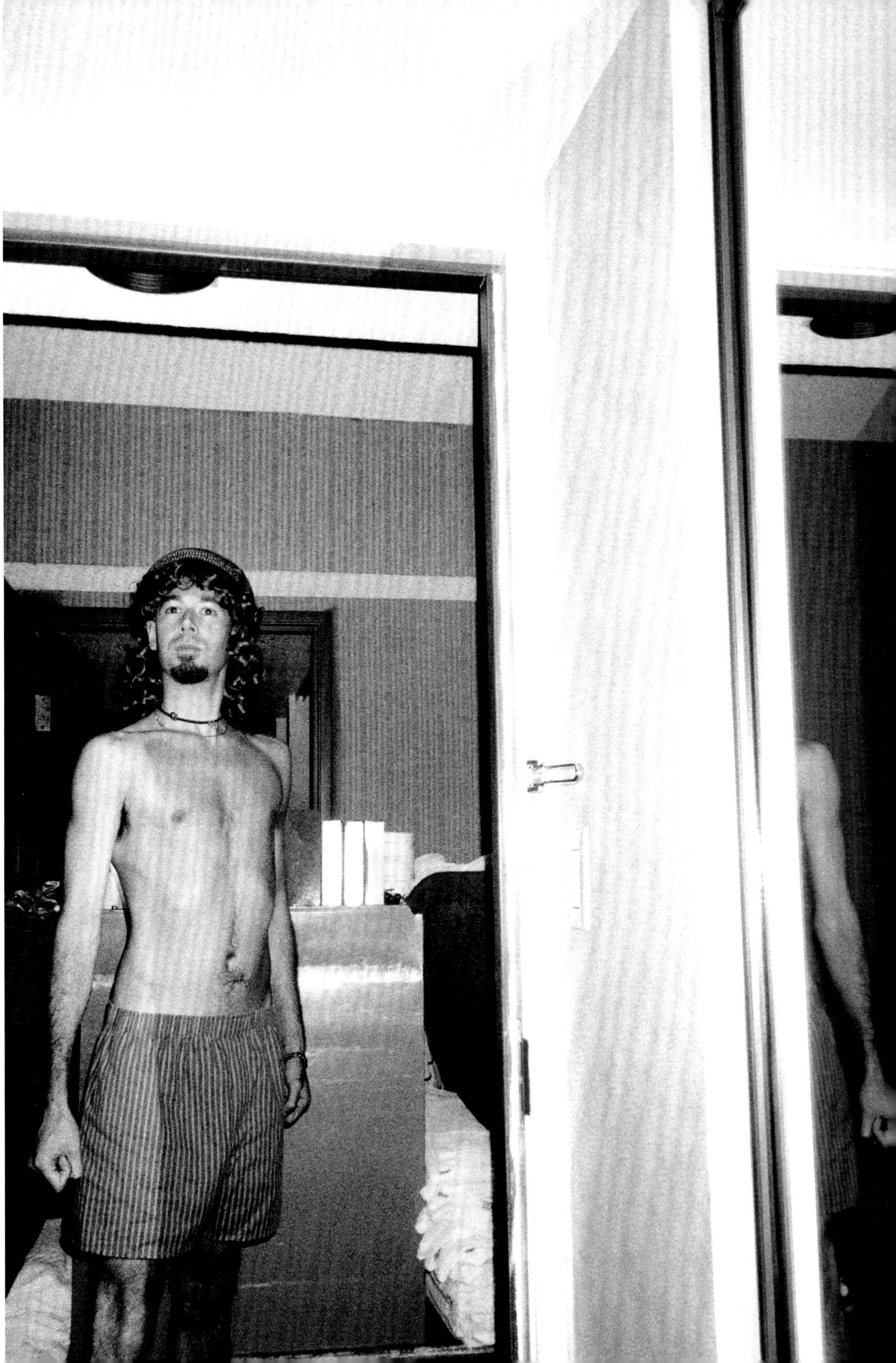

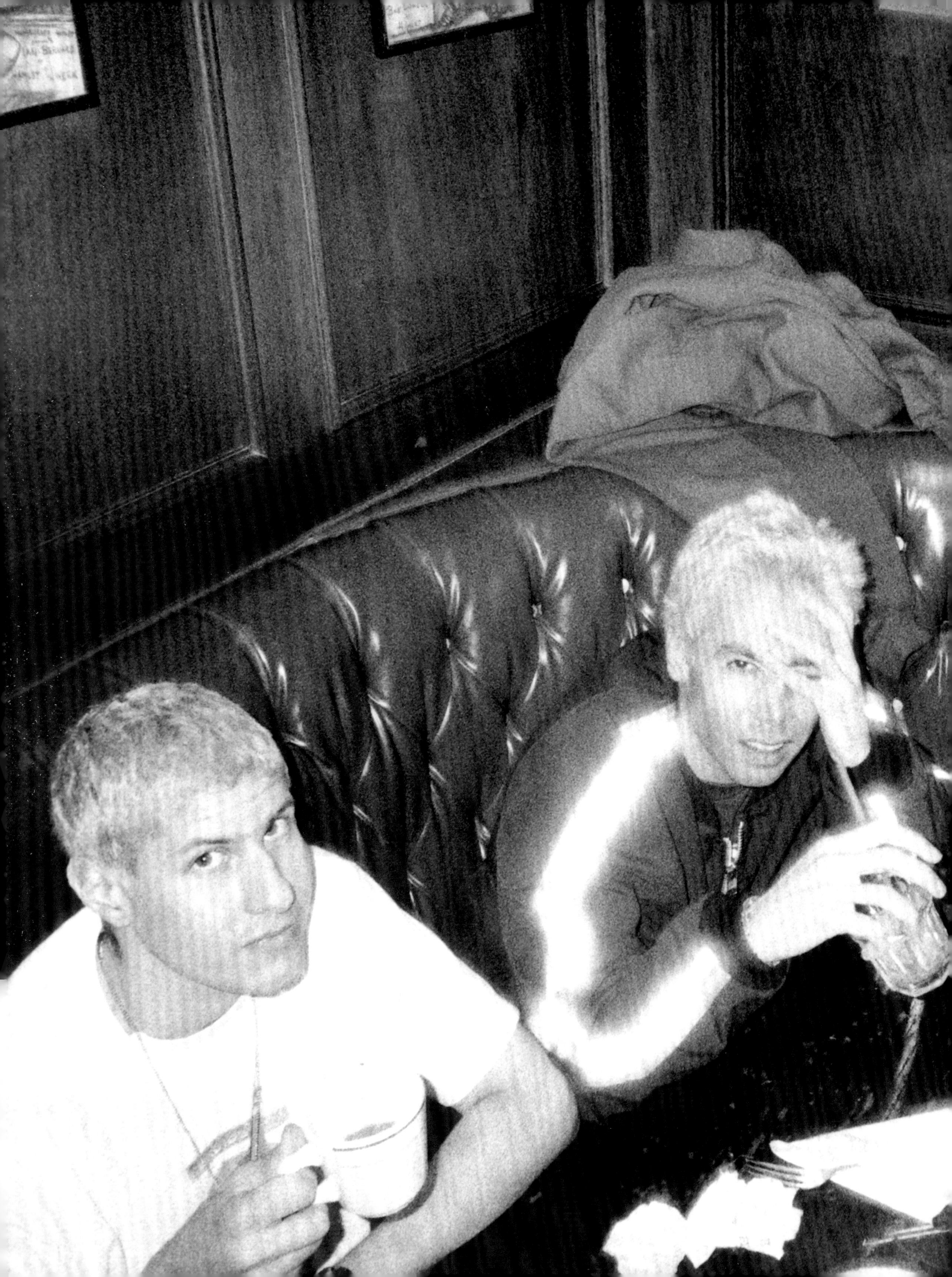

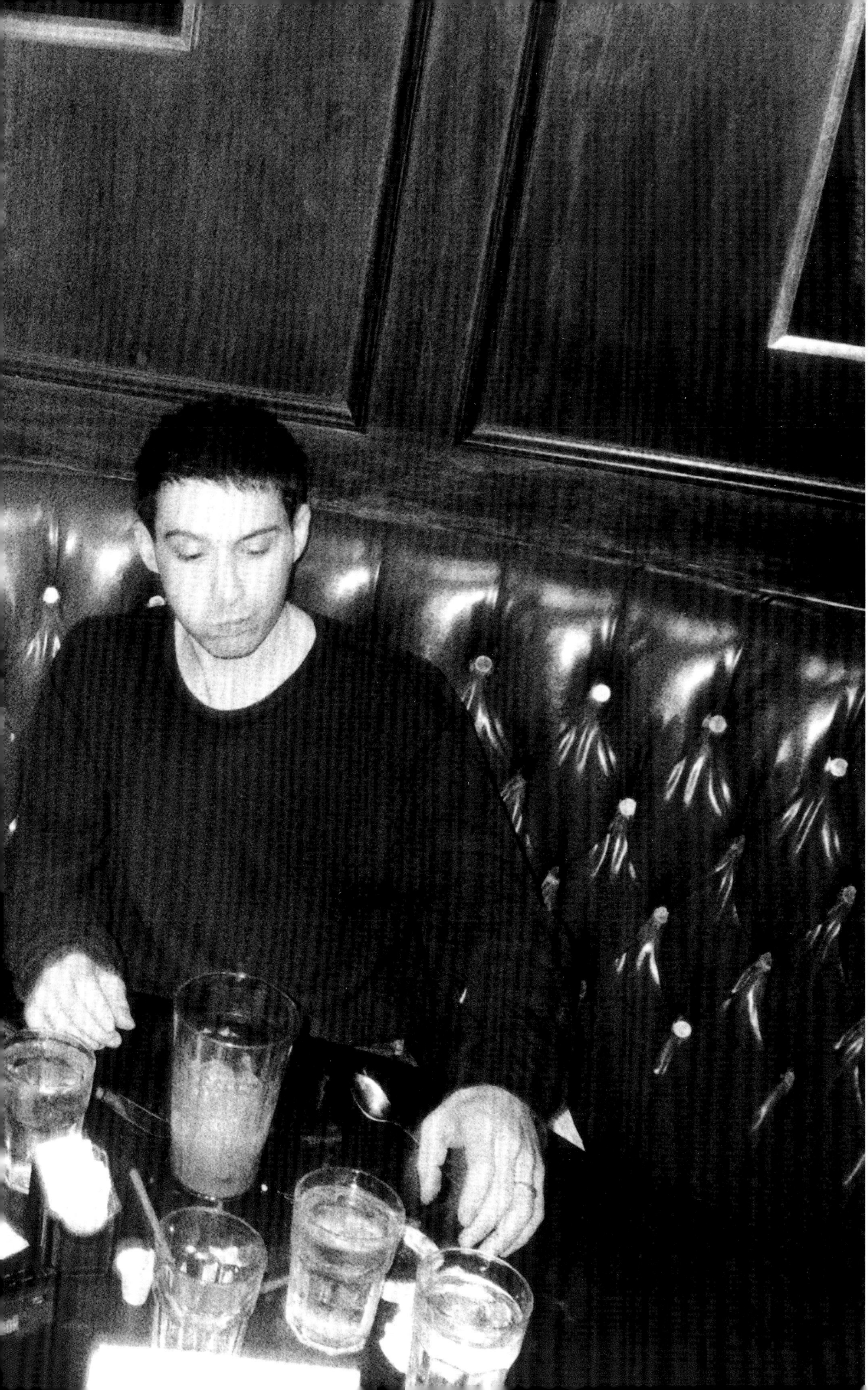

Hamburger Hamlet

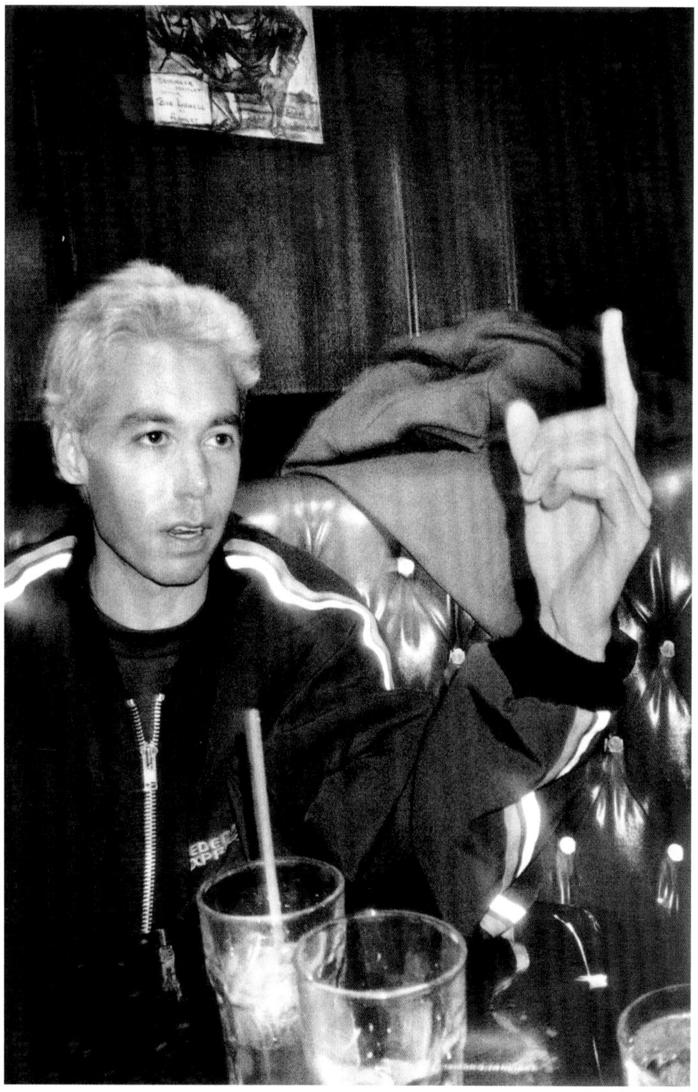

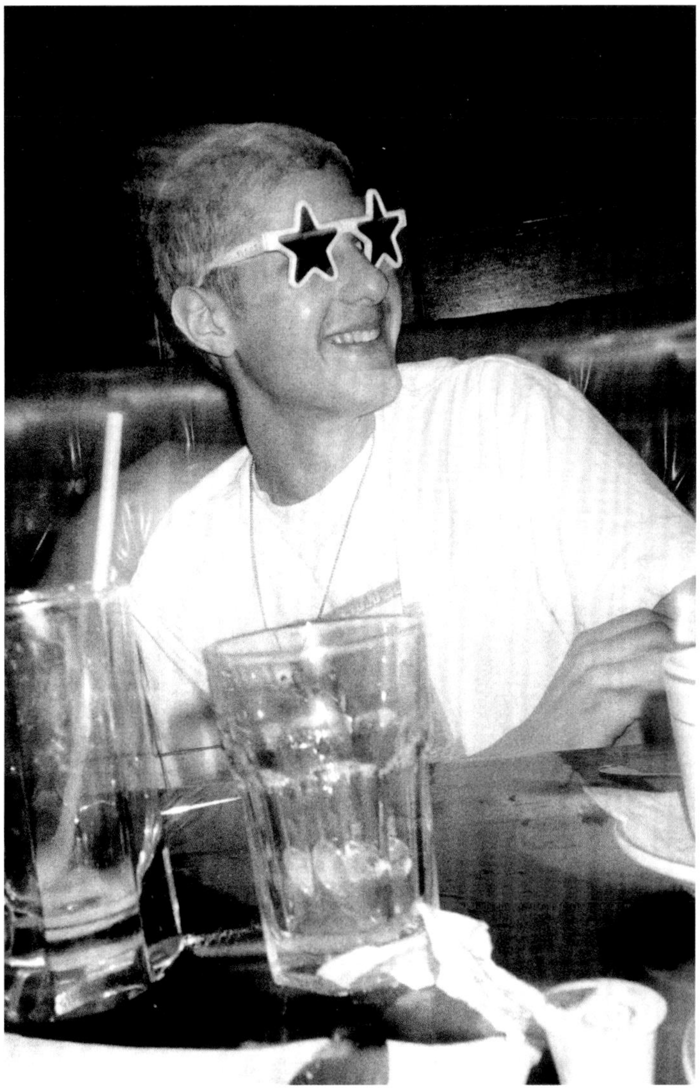

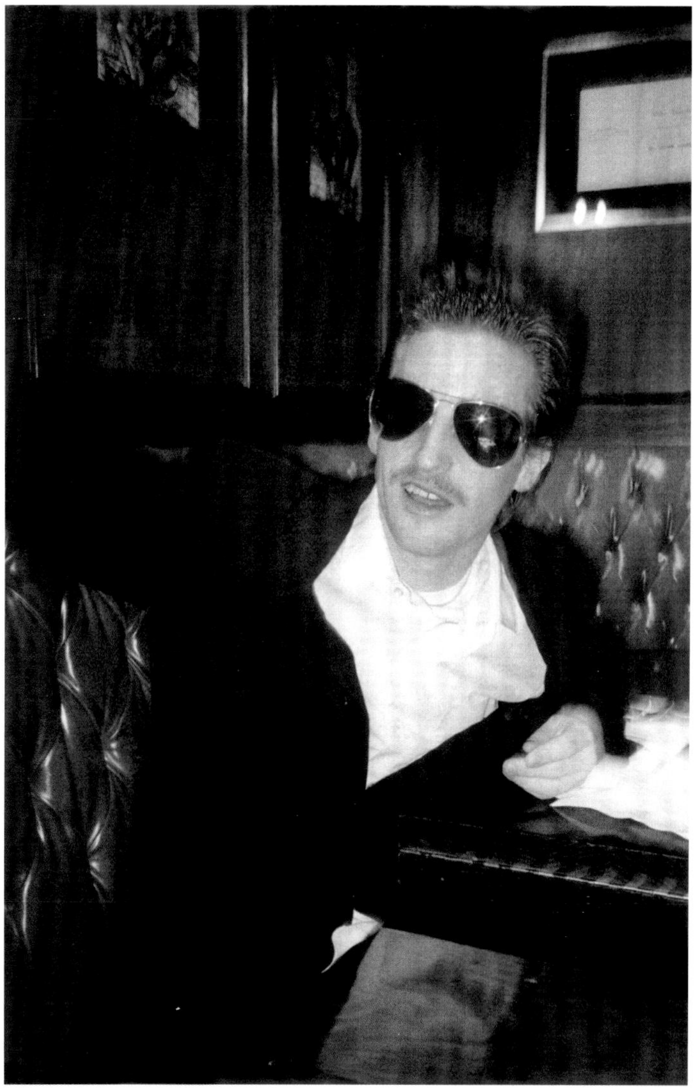

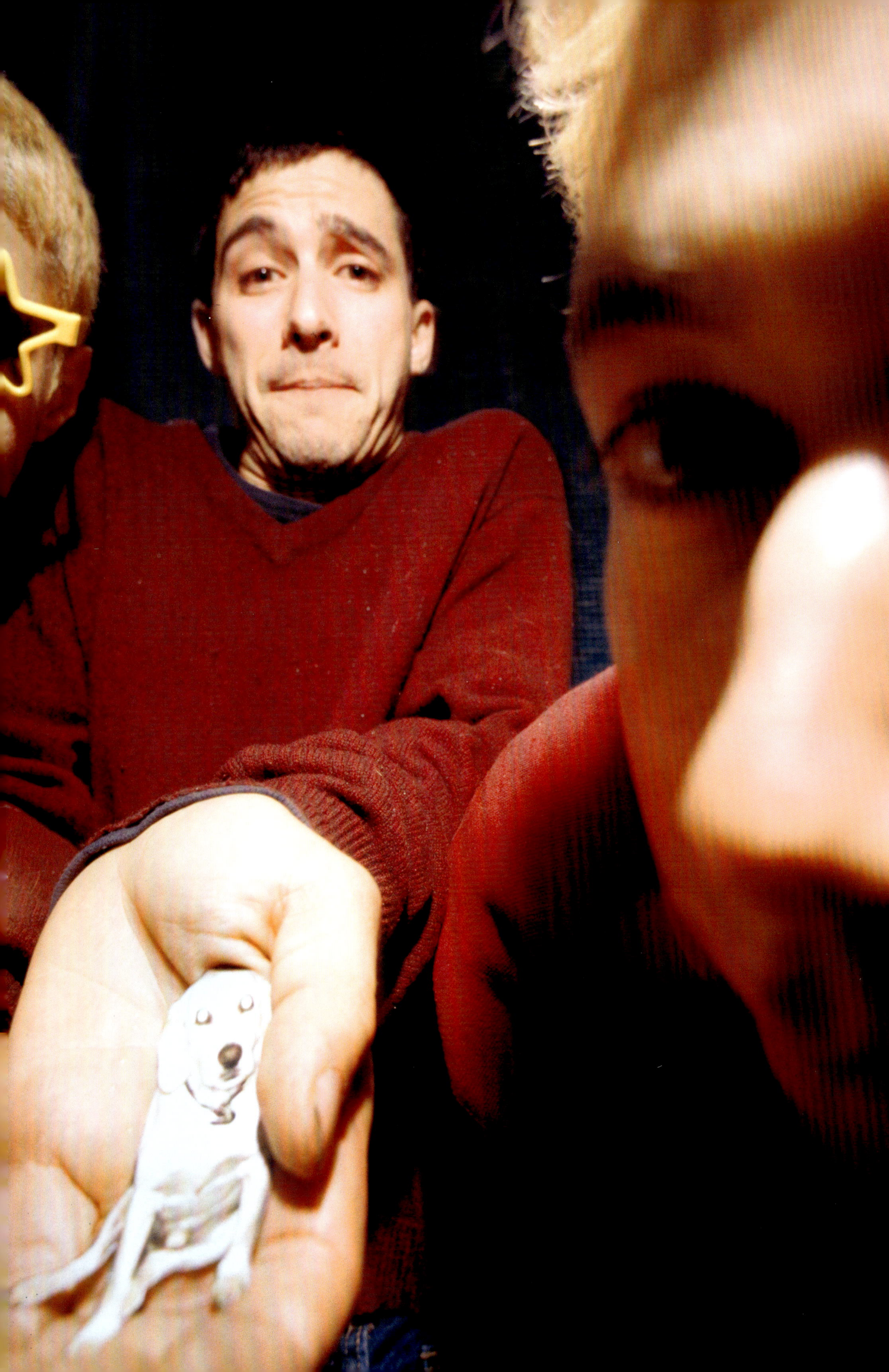

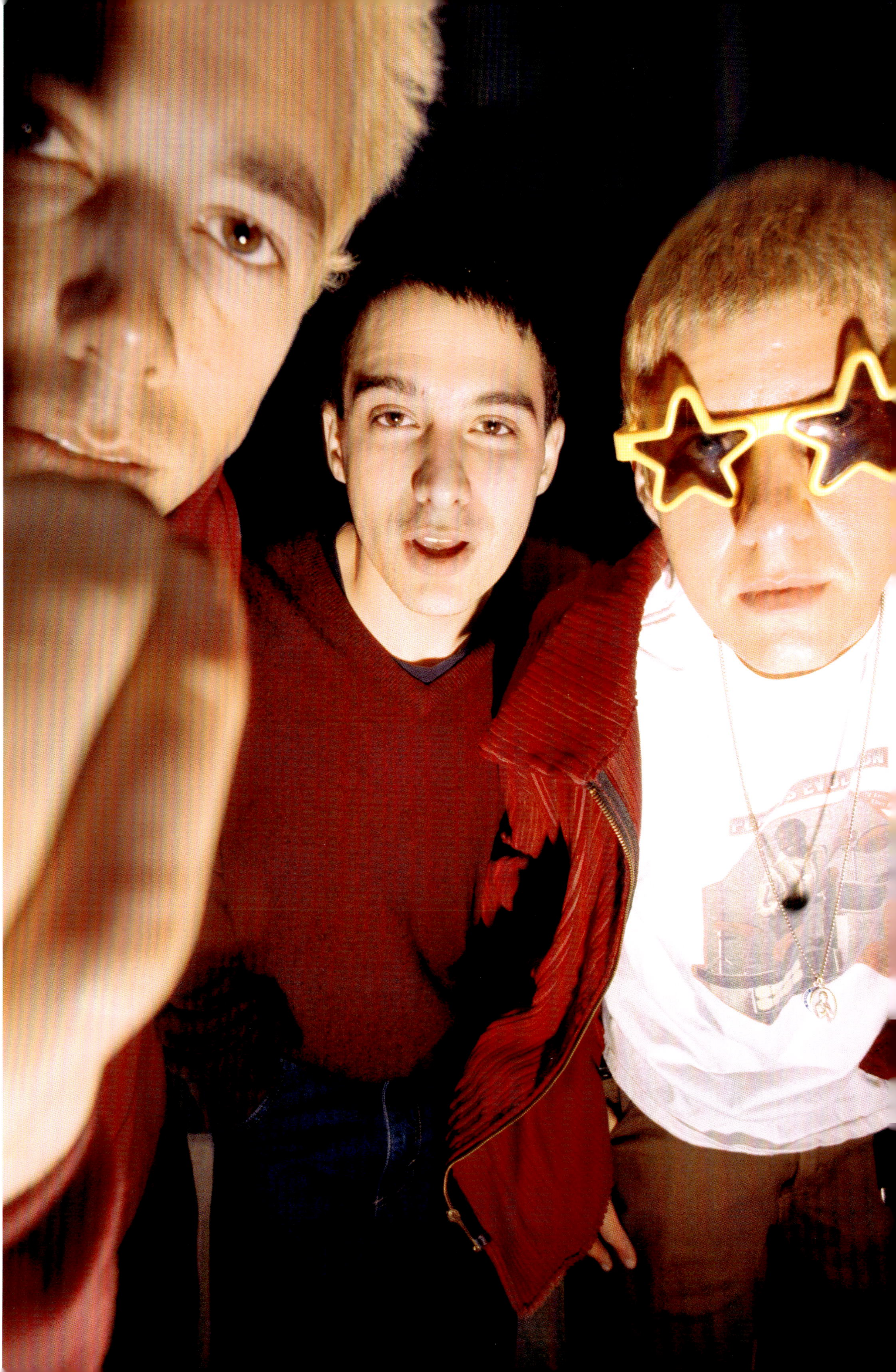

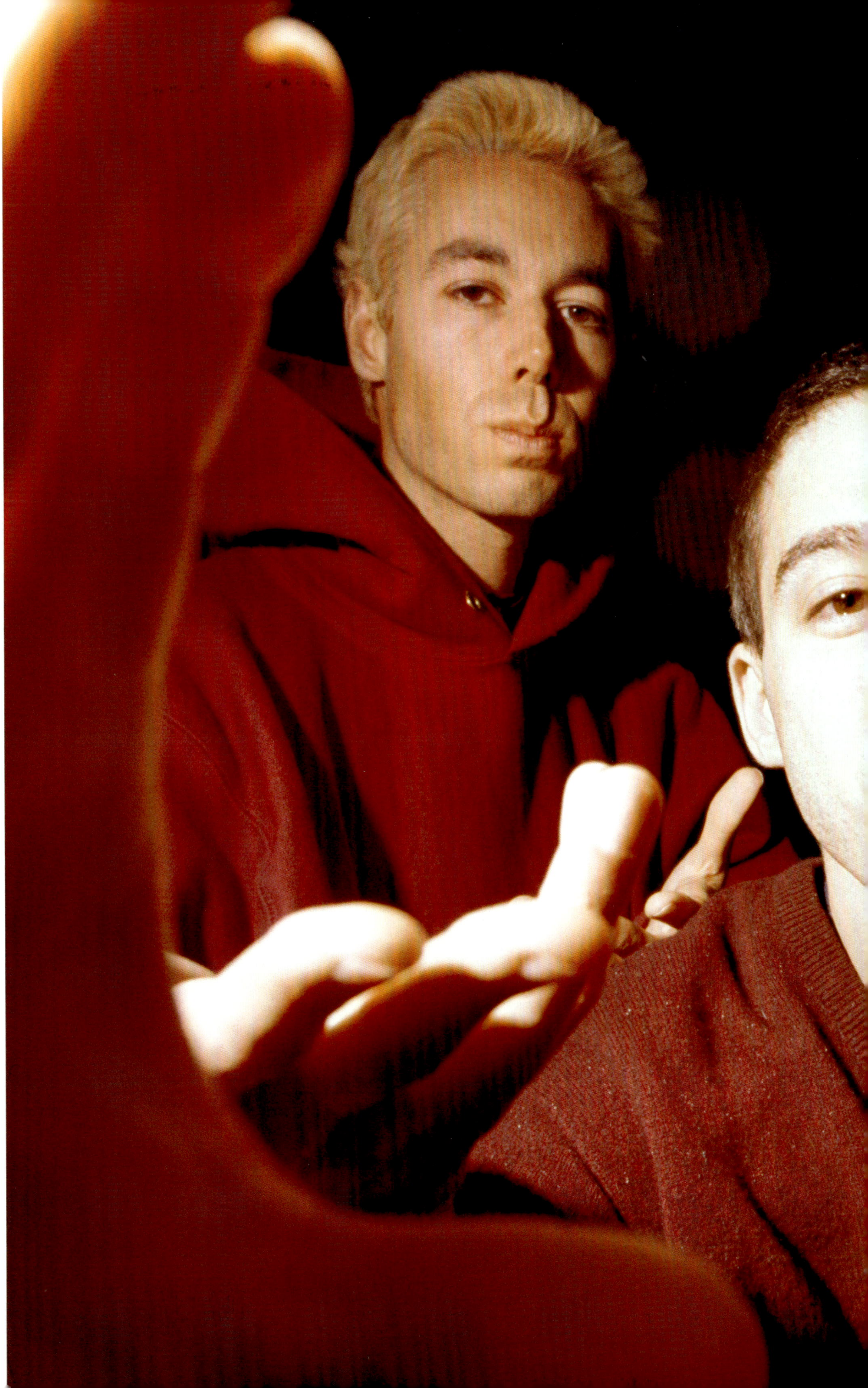

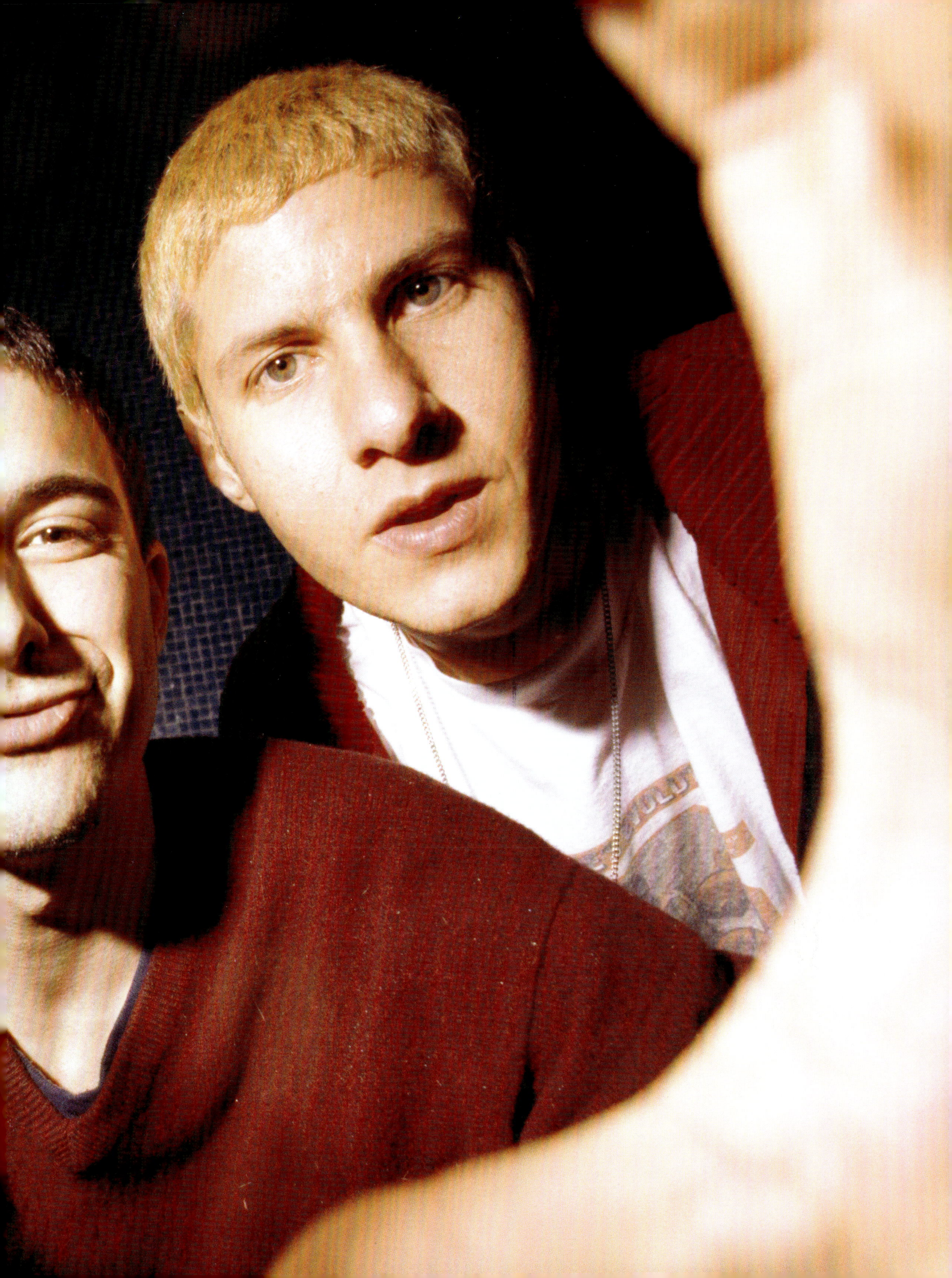

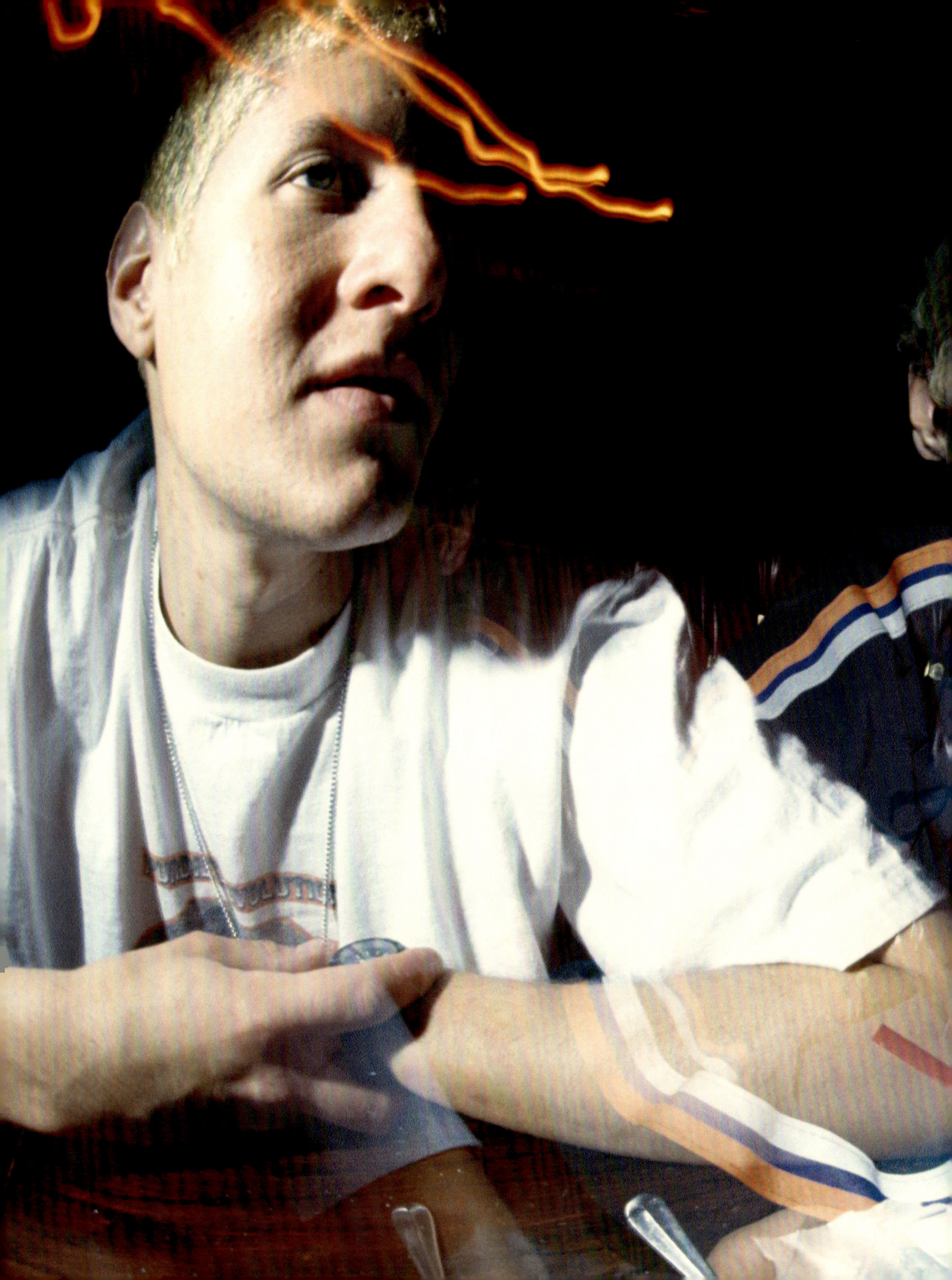

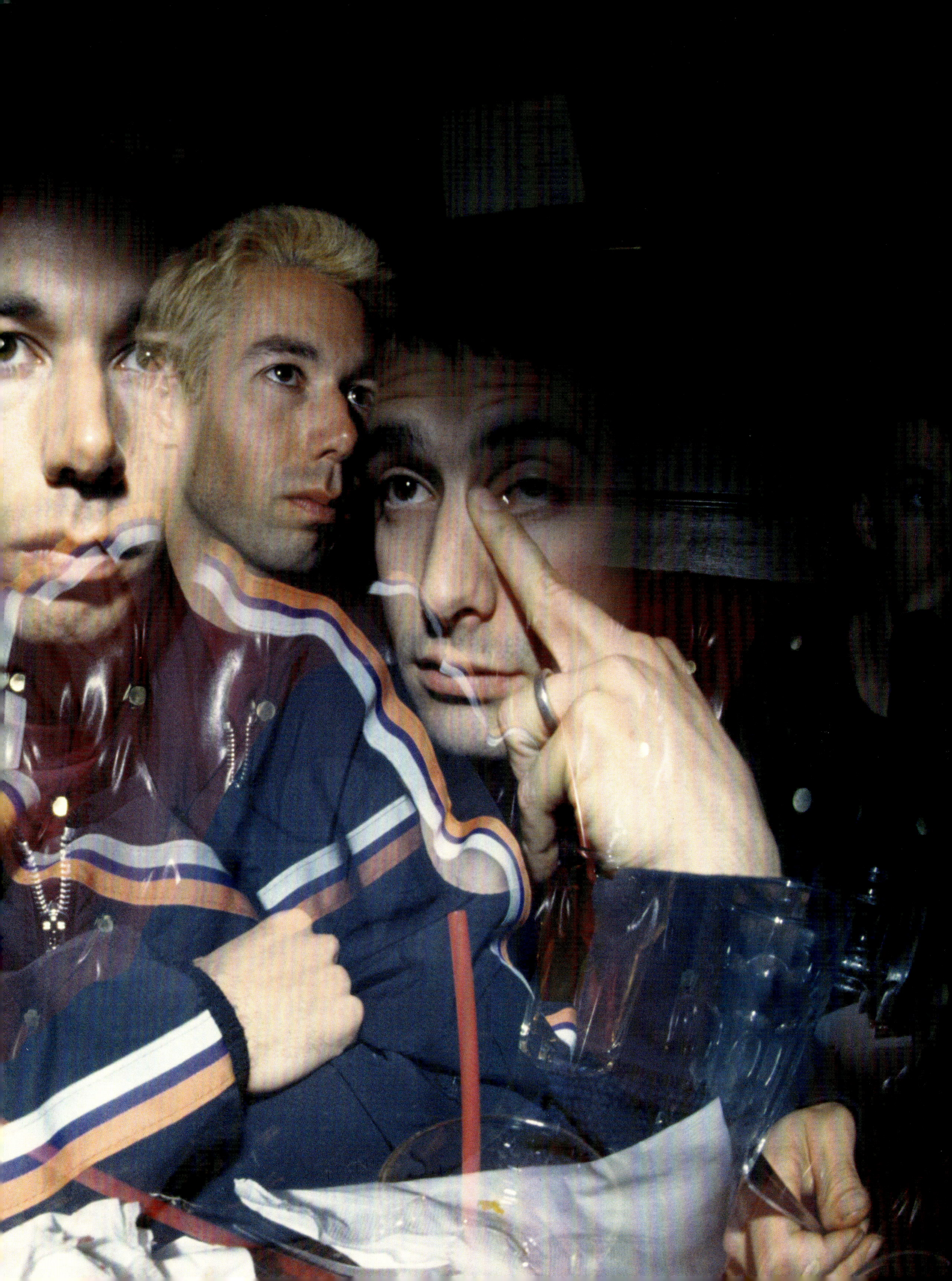

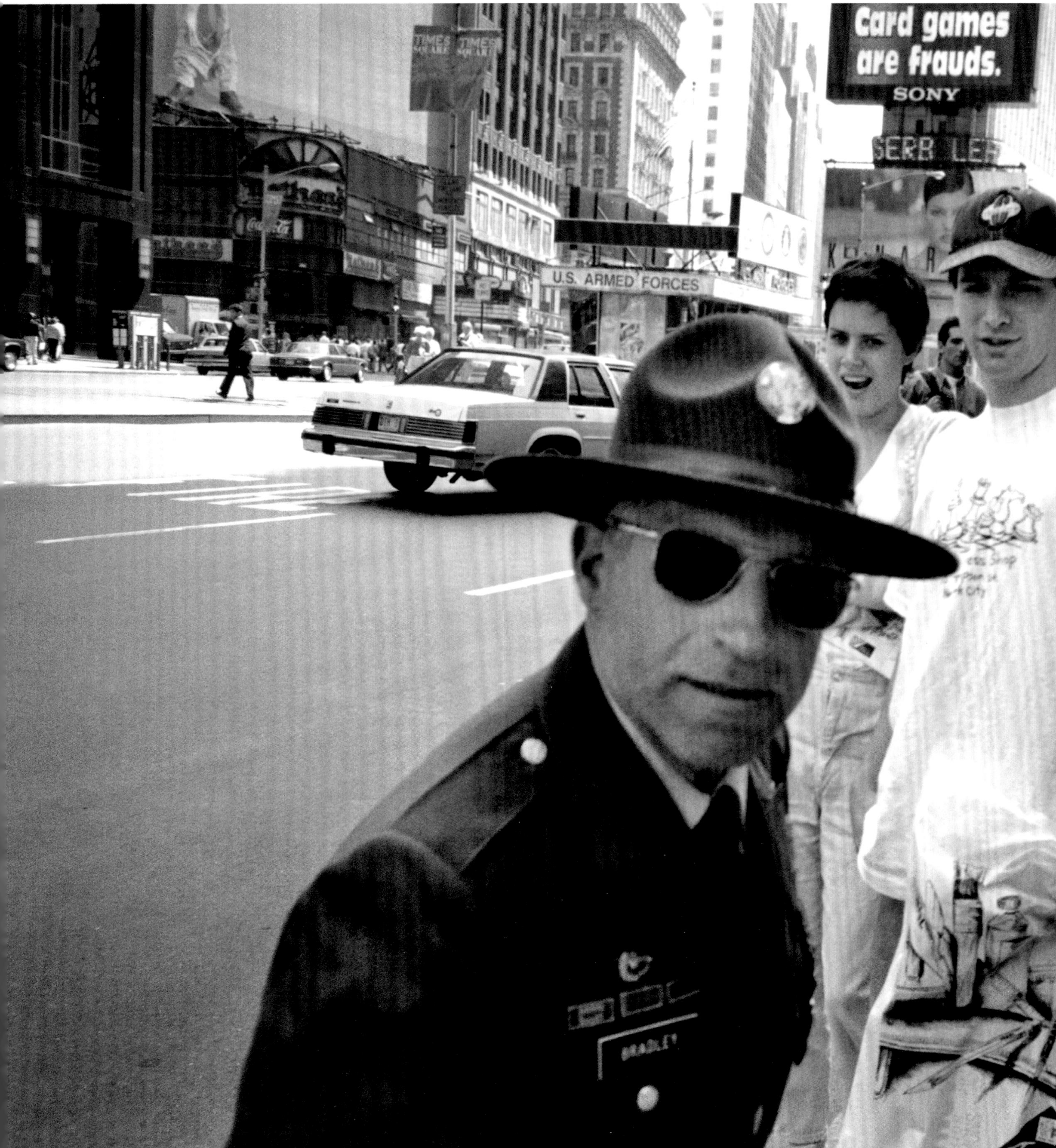
Card games
are frauds.
SONY
U.S. ARMED FORCES

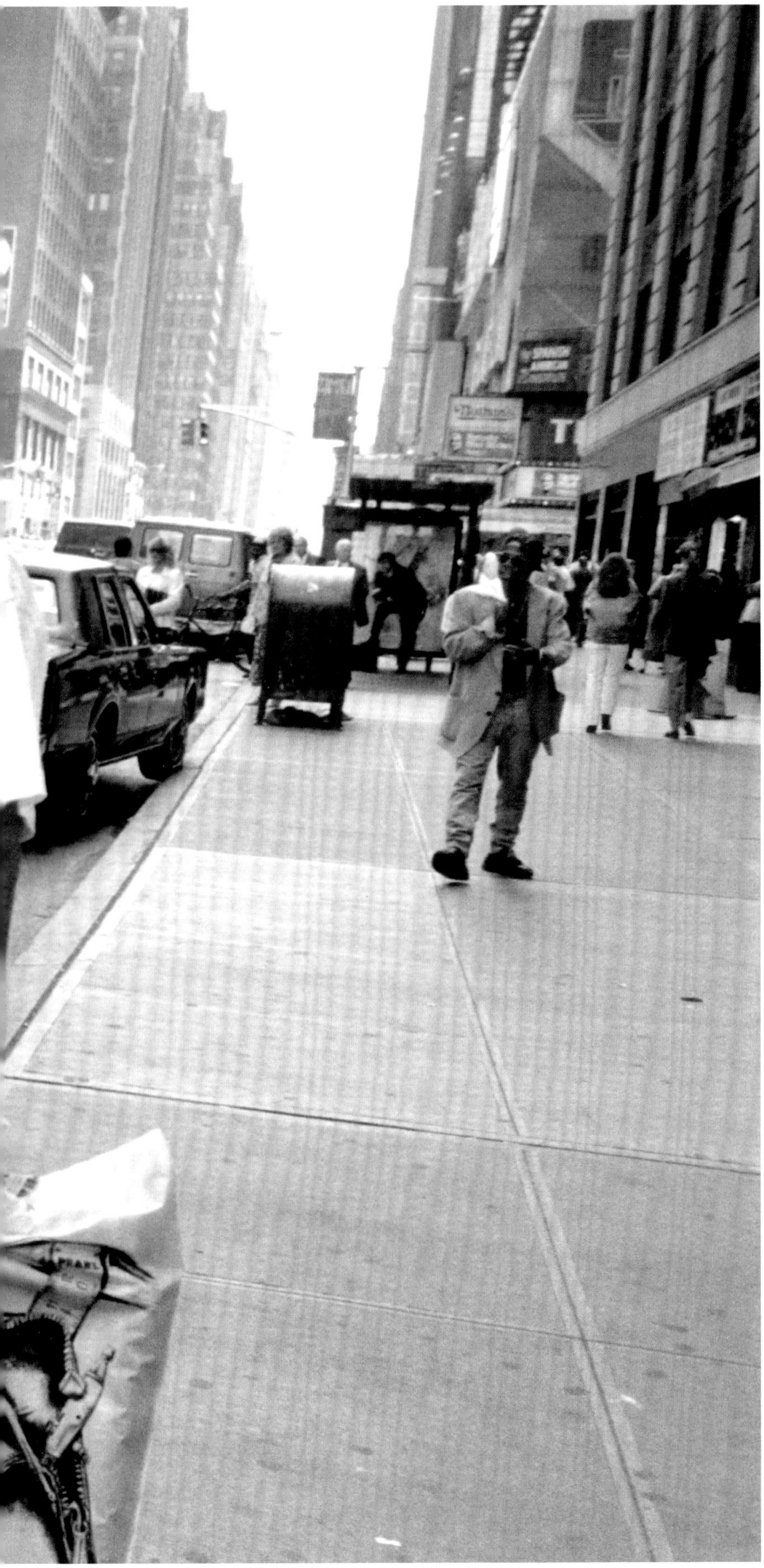

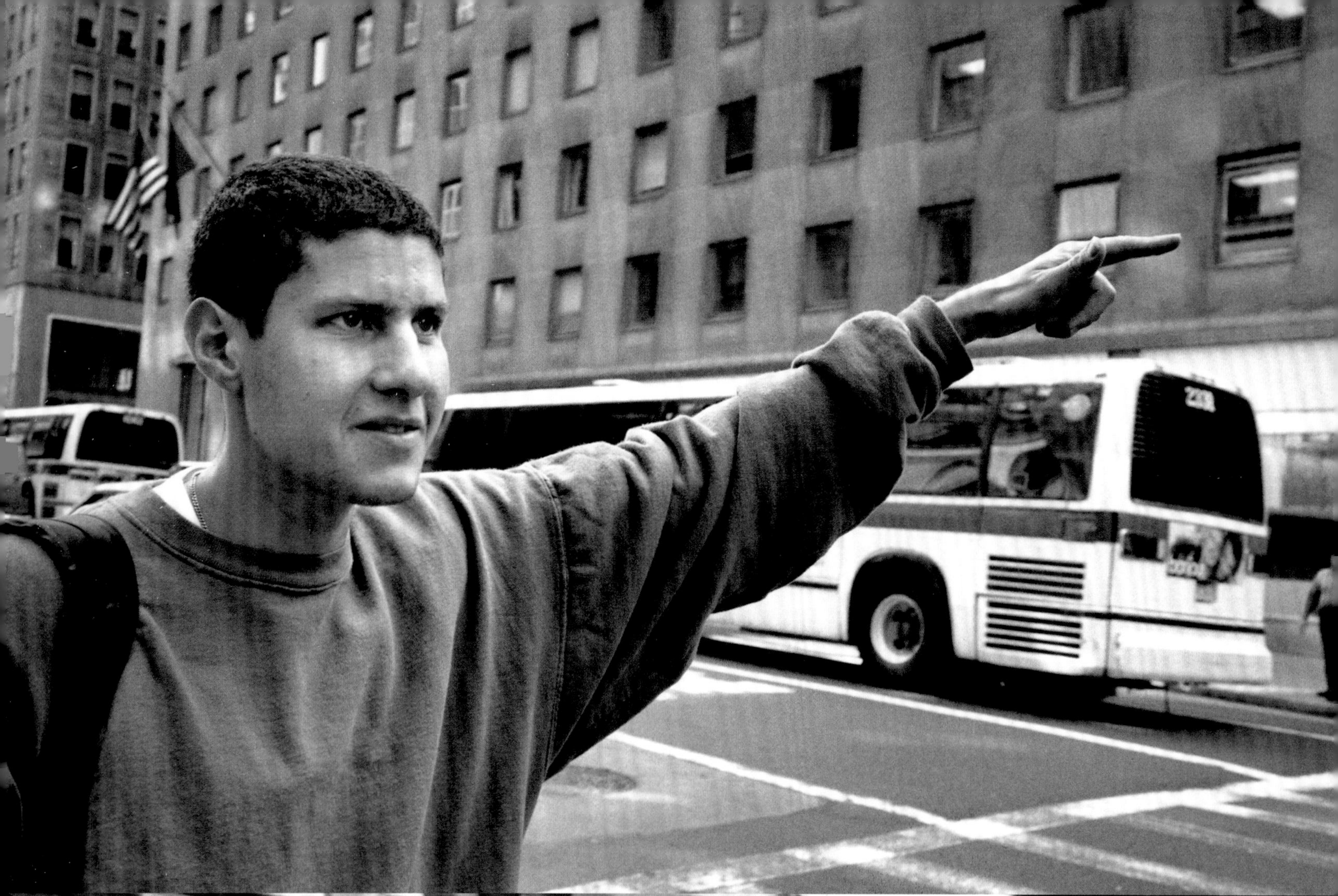

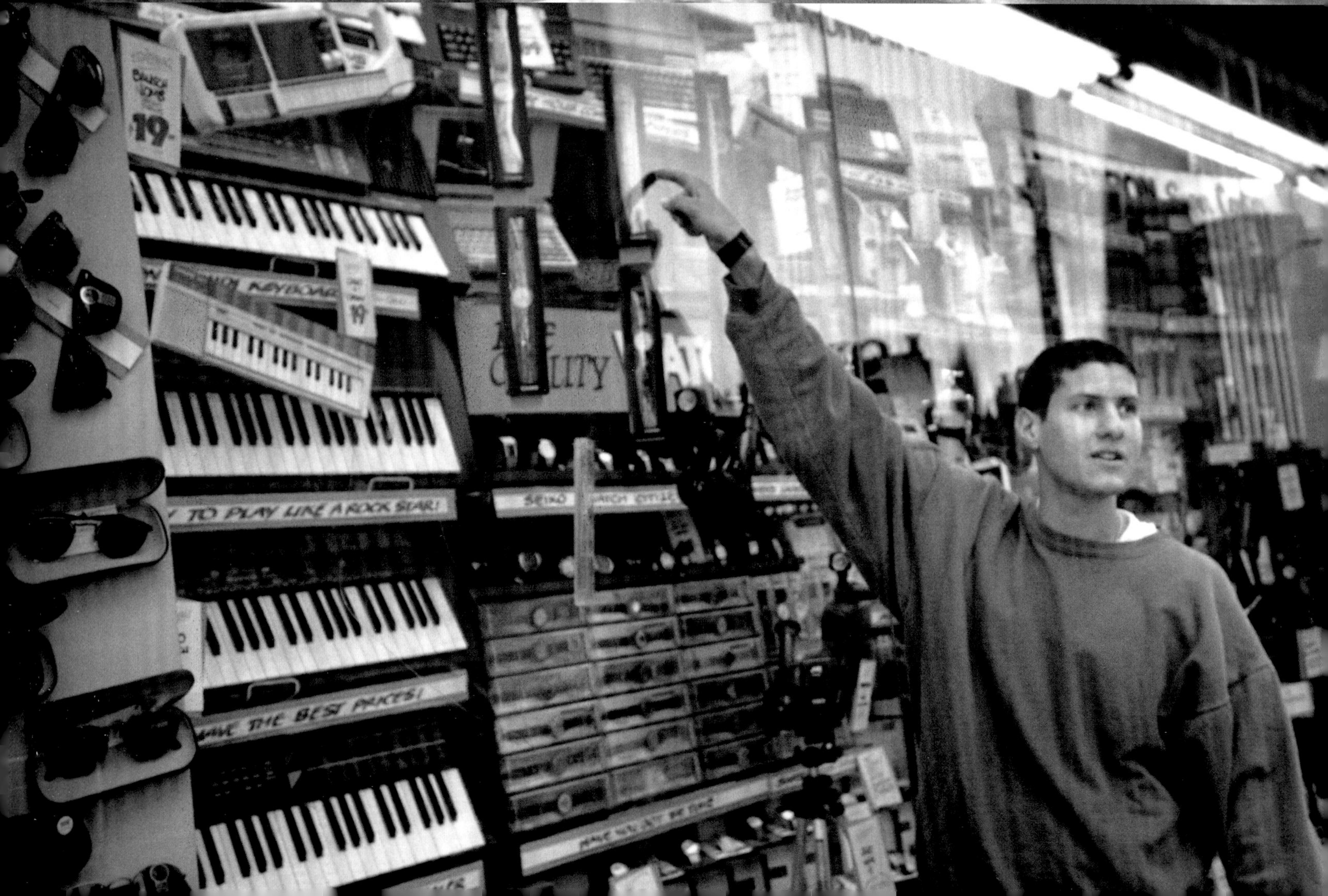
KEYBOARD
QUALITY
TO PLAY LIKE A ROCK STAR!
THE BEST PRICES!

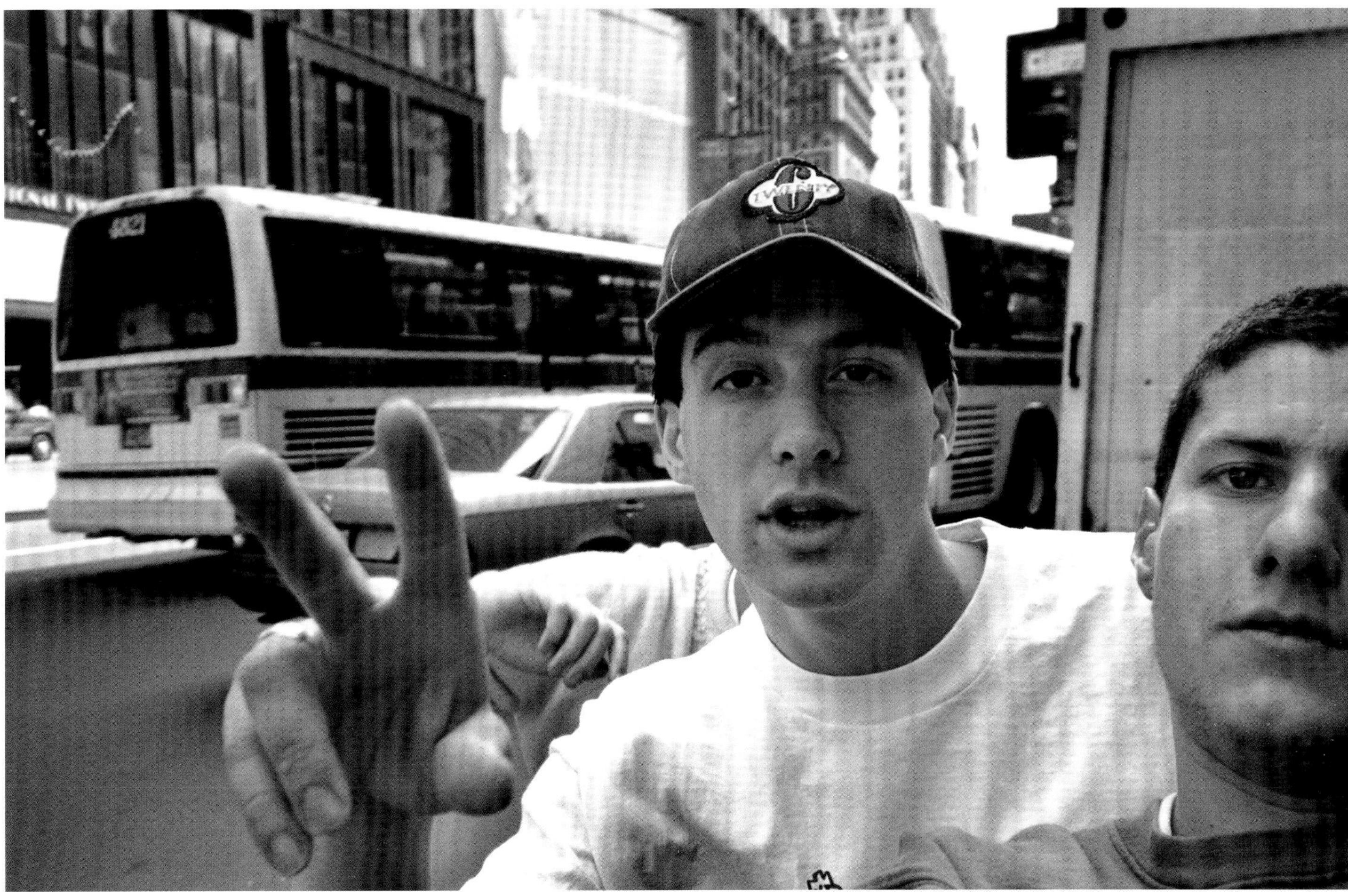

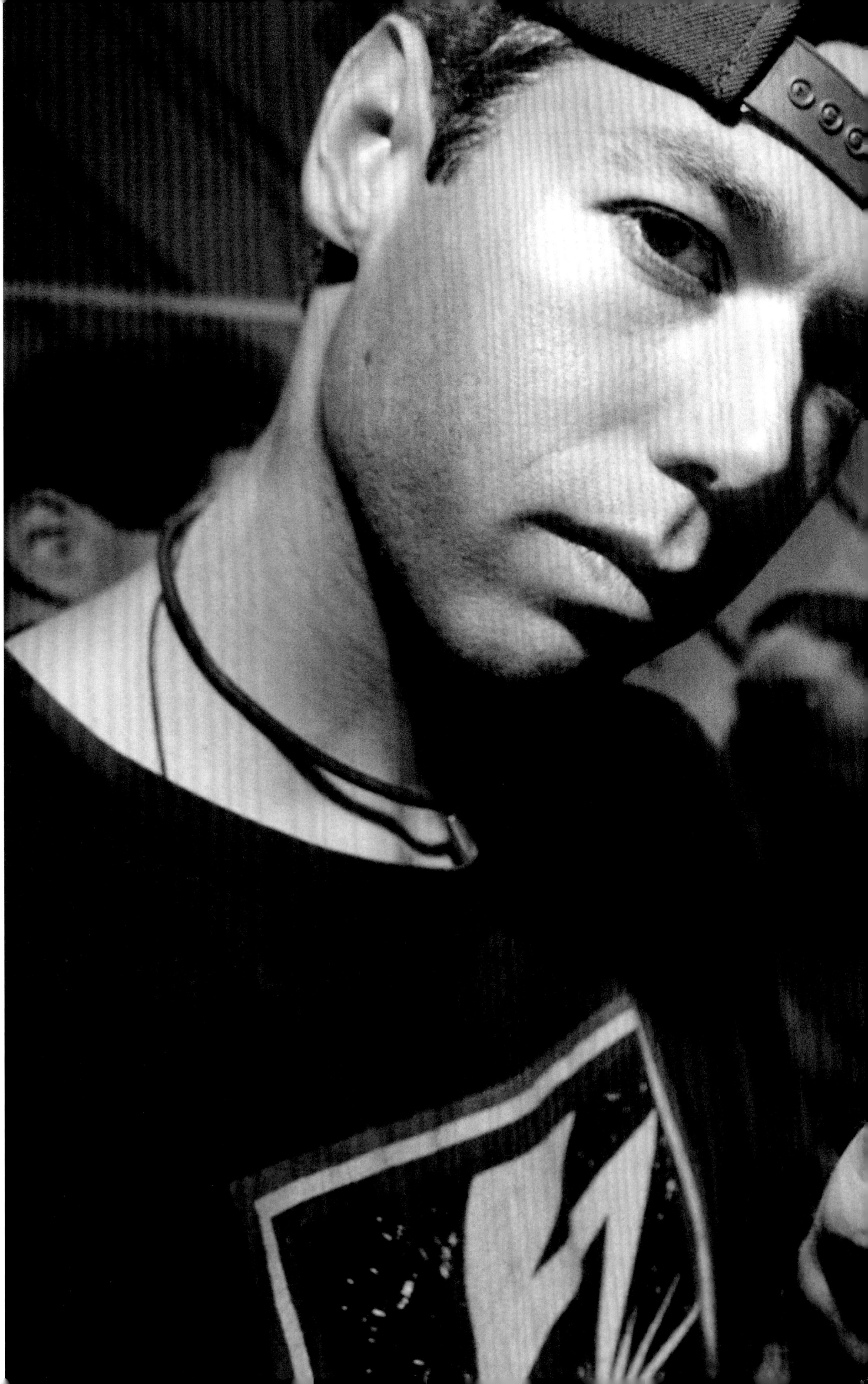

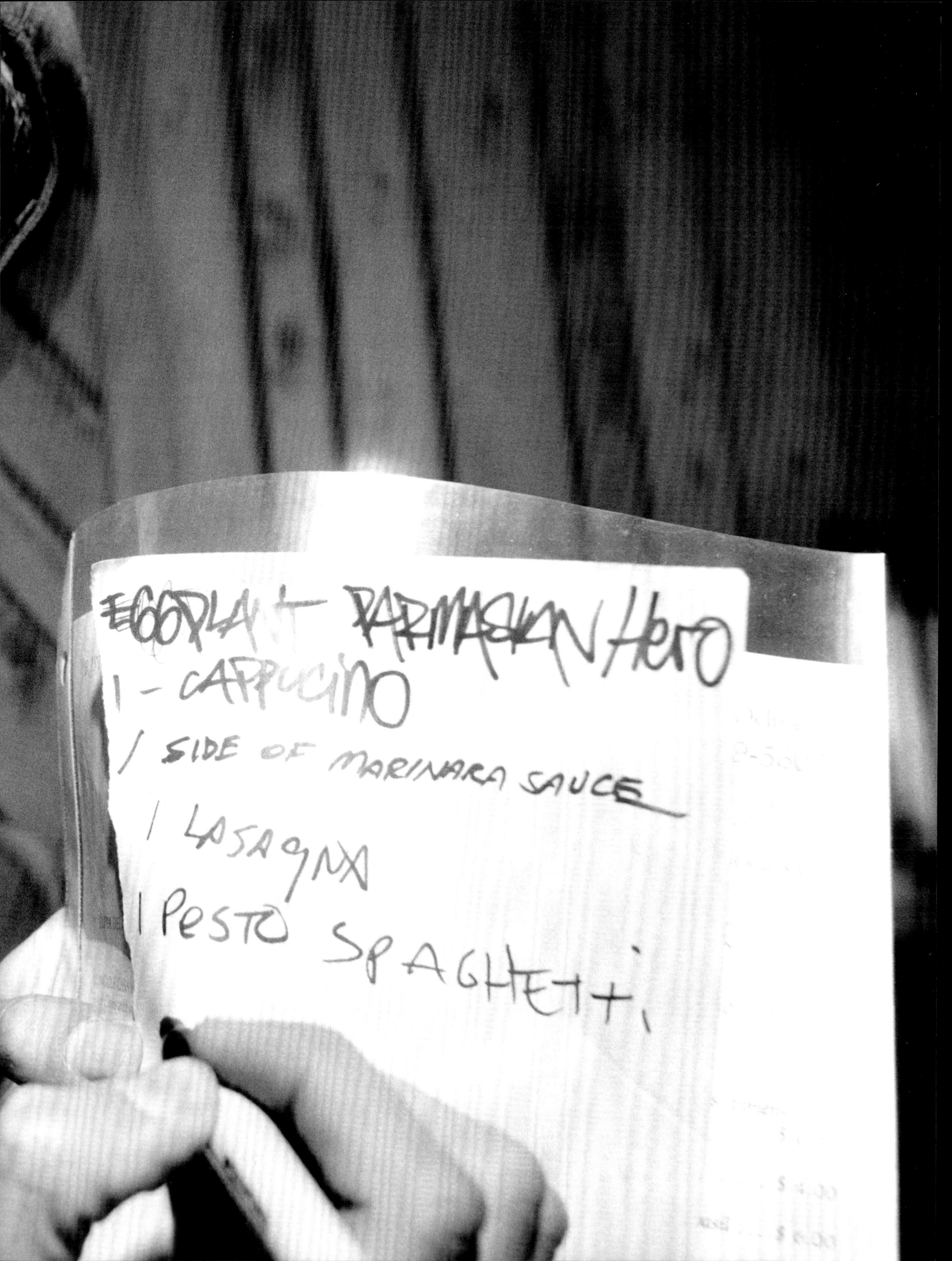
EGGPLANT PARMASAN Hero
1 - CAPPUCINO
1 SIDE OF MARINARA SAUCE
1 LASAGNA
1 PESTO SPAGHETTI

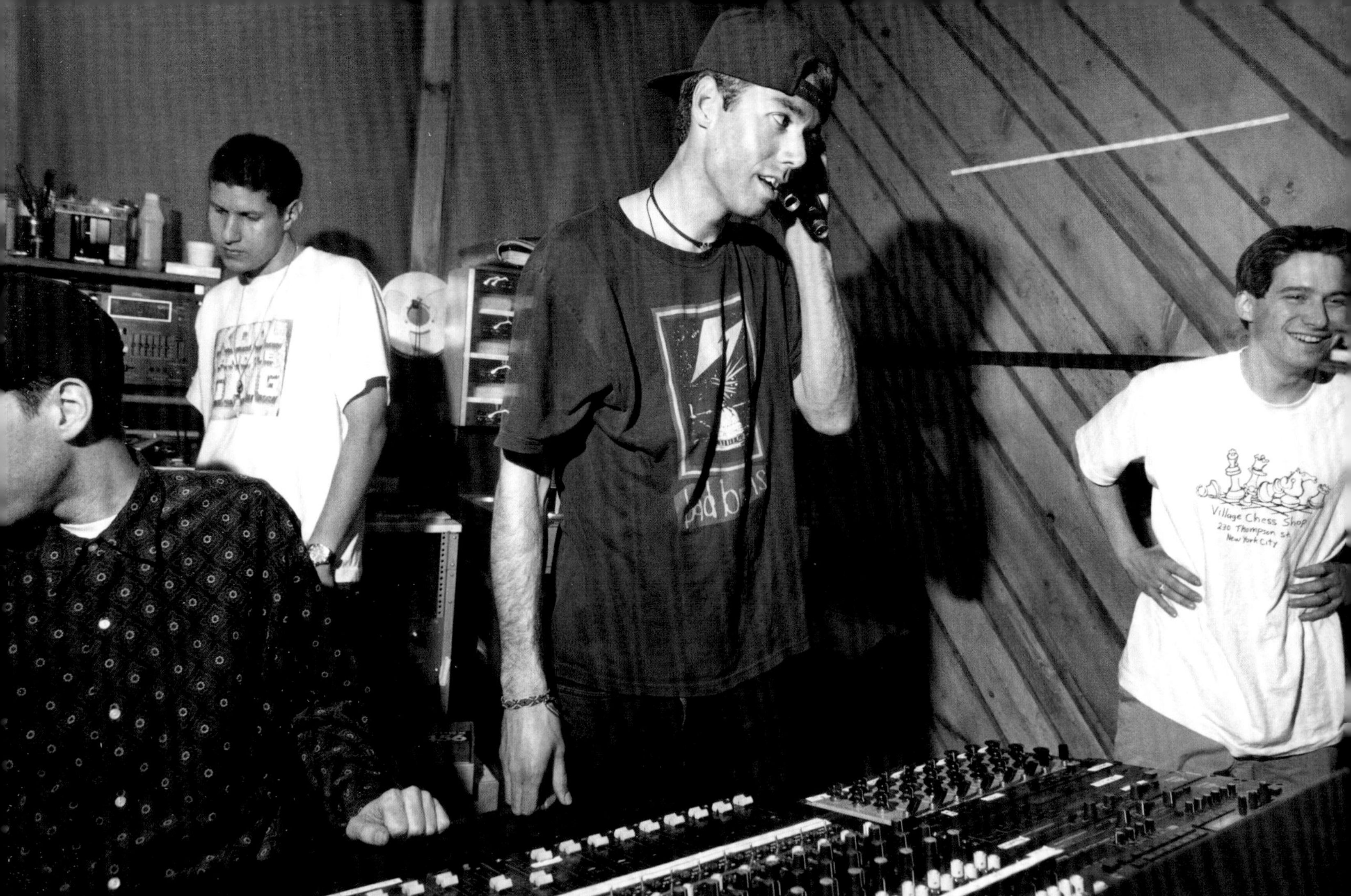
Village Chess Shop
230 Thompson St
New York City

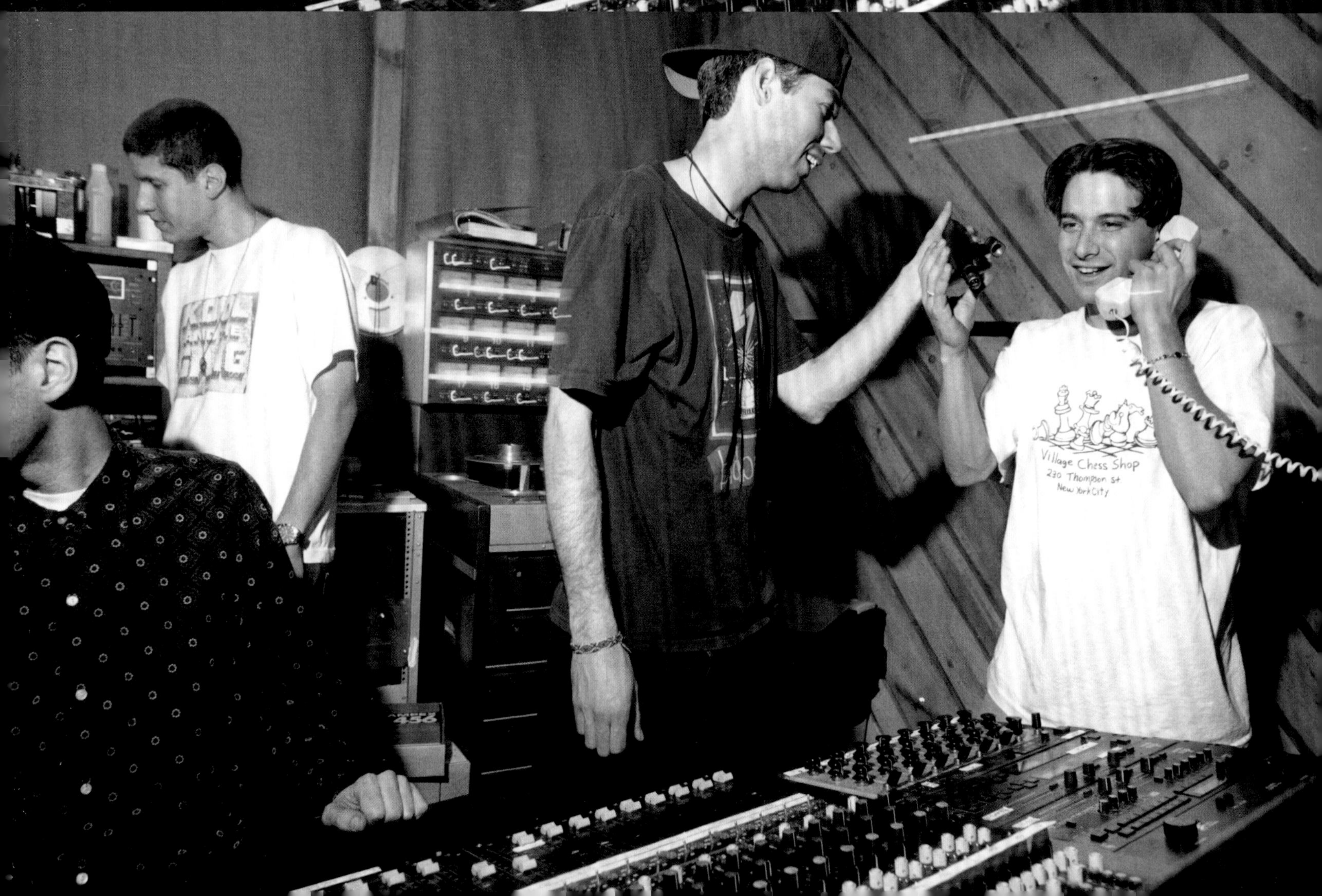
Village Chess Shop
230 Thompson St
New York City

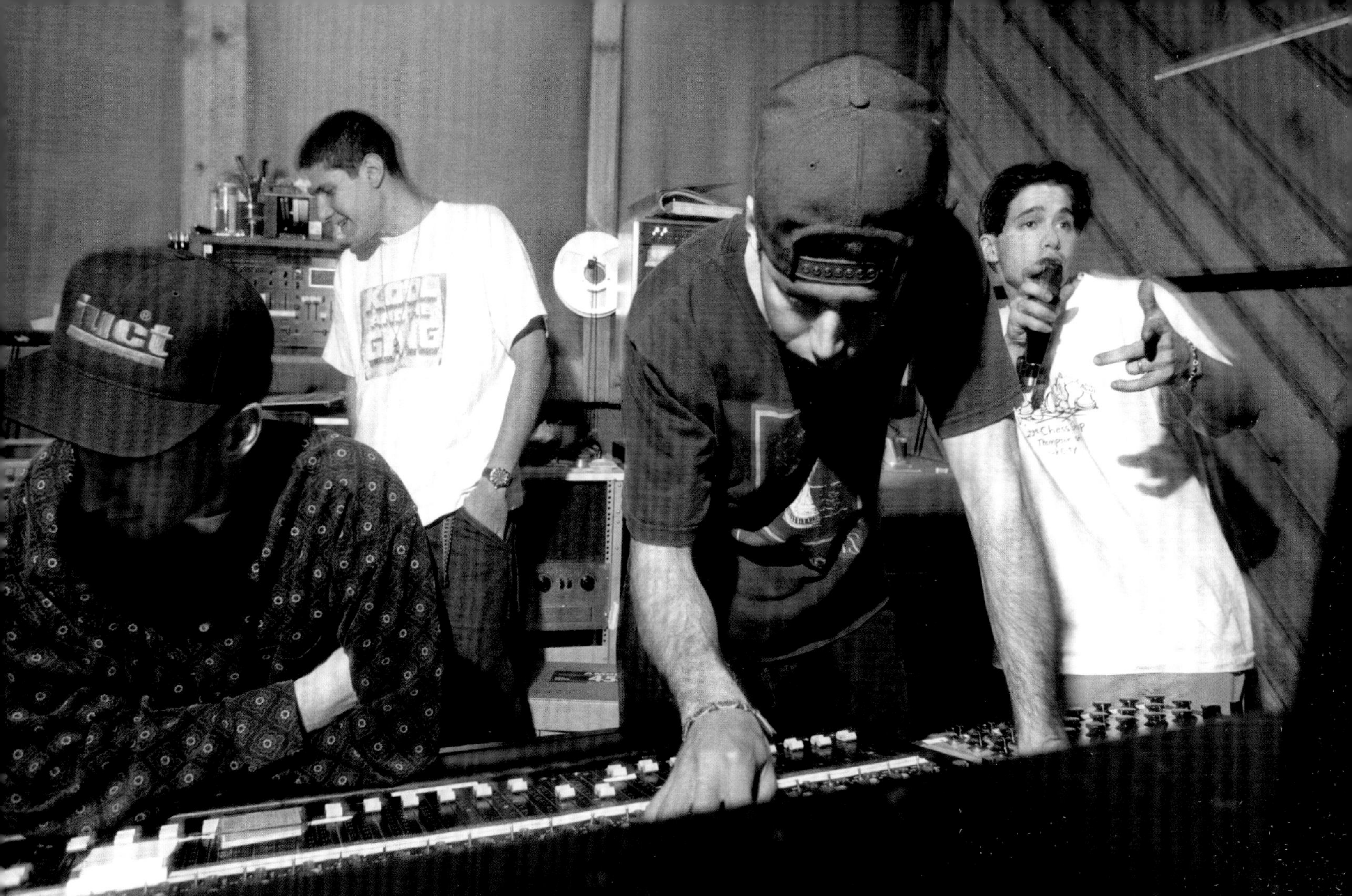

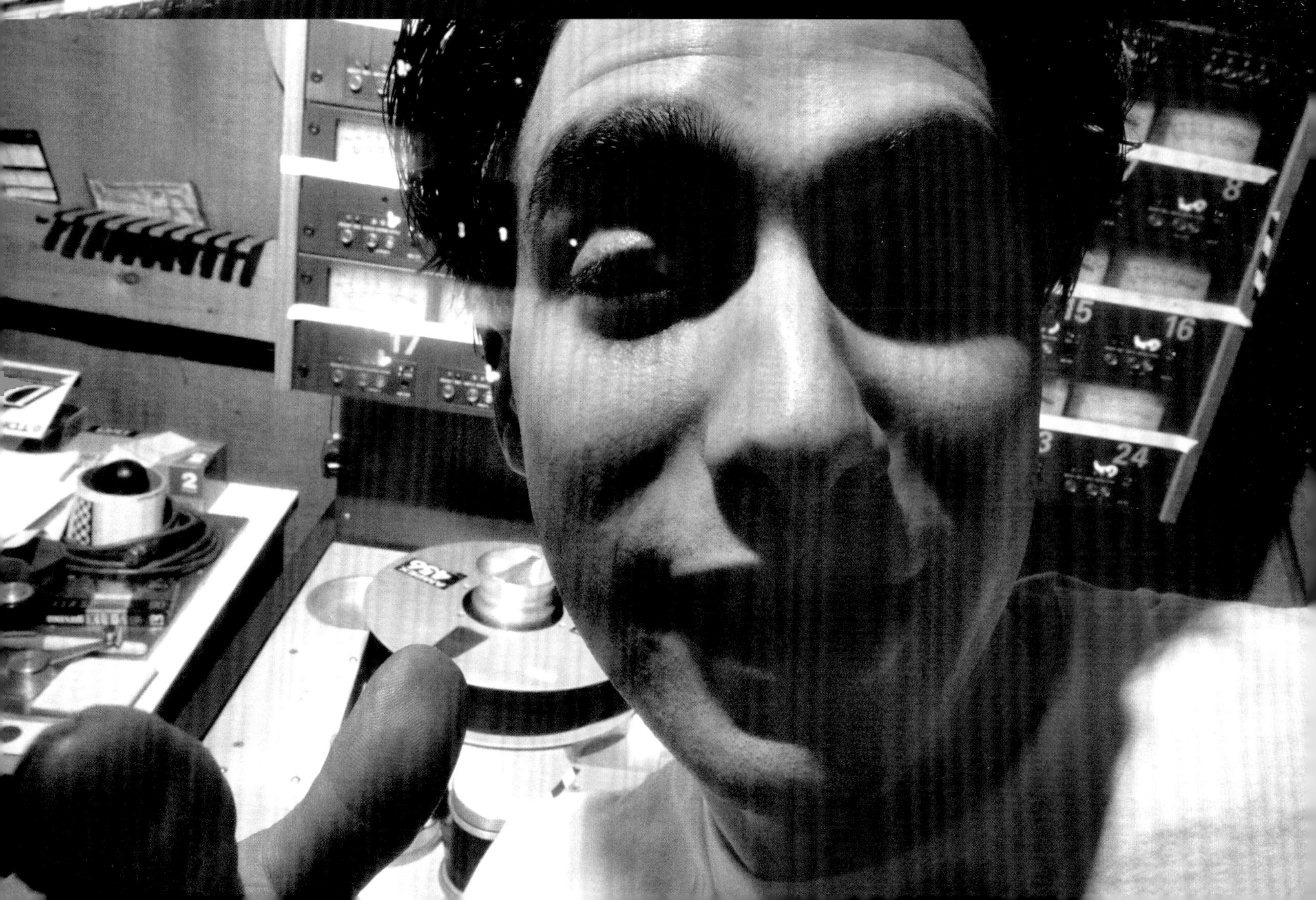

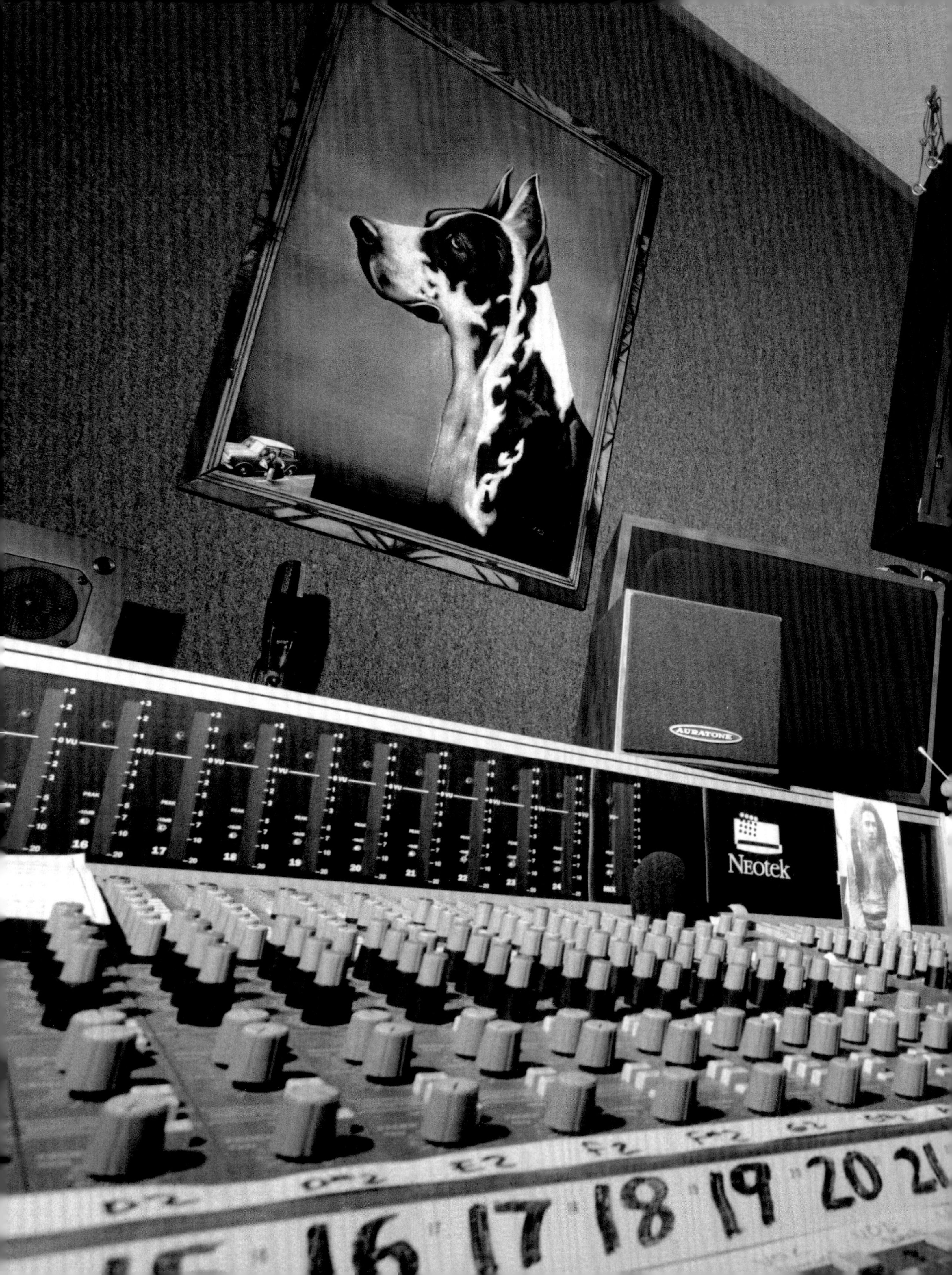
AURATONE
Neotek

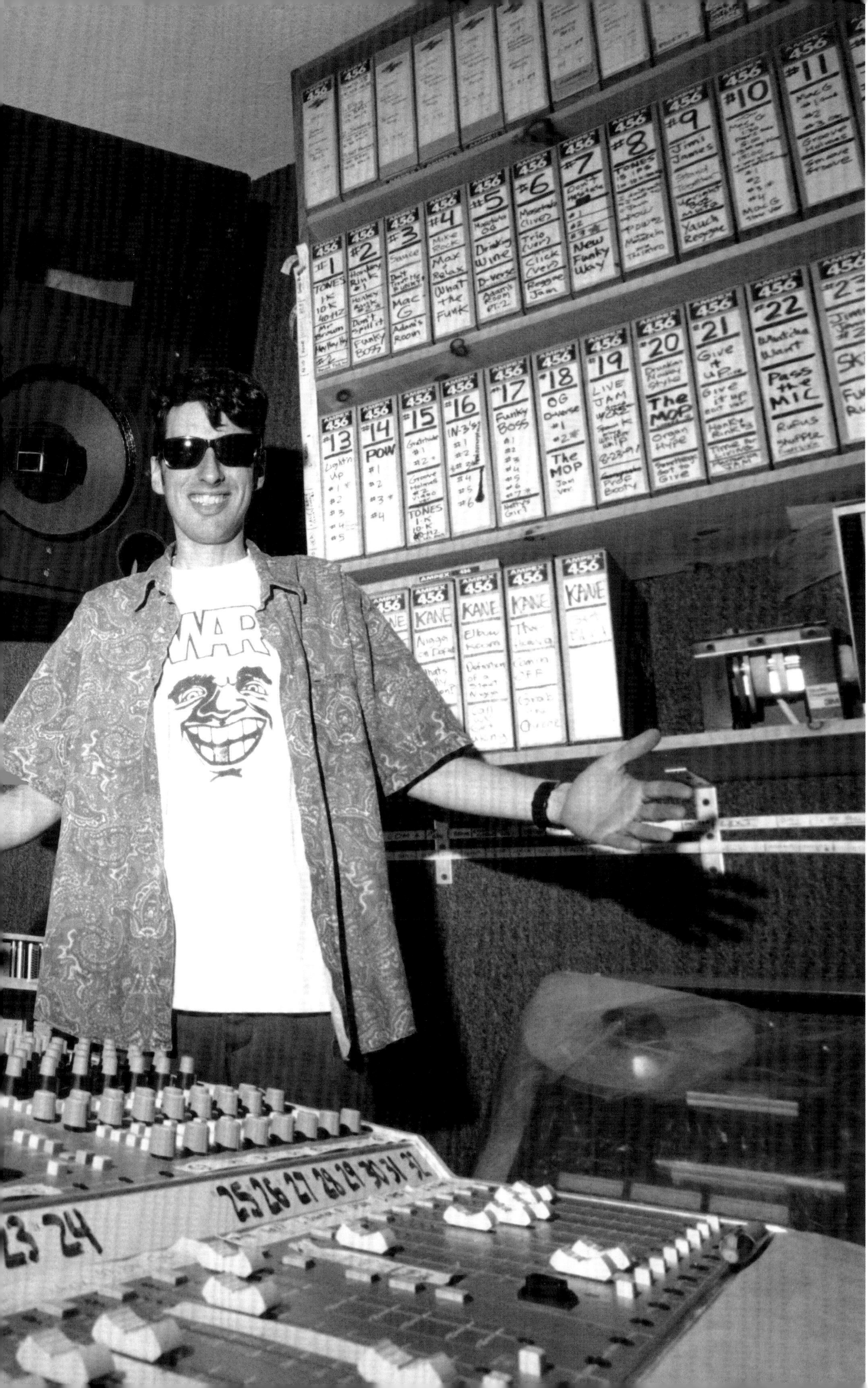
WAR
AMPEX 456
POW
LIVE JAM
The MOP
Pass the MIC
New Funky Way
What the Funk
Mac G
Funky Boss
KANE
25 26 27 28 29 30 31 32
23 24

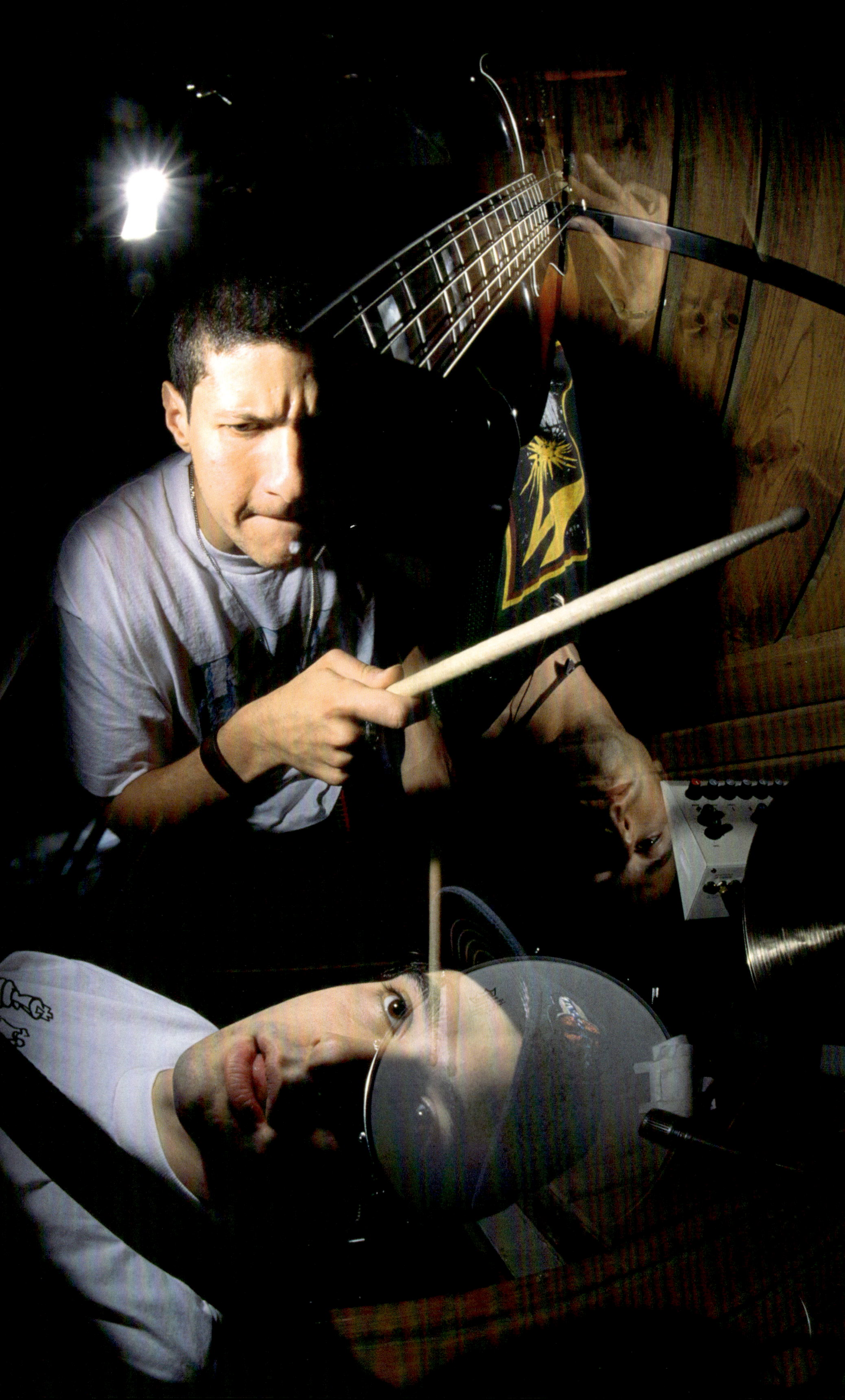

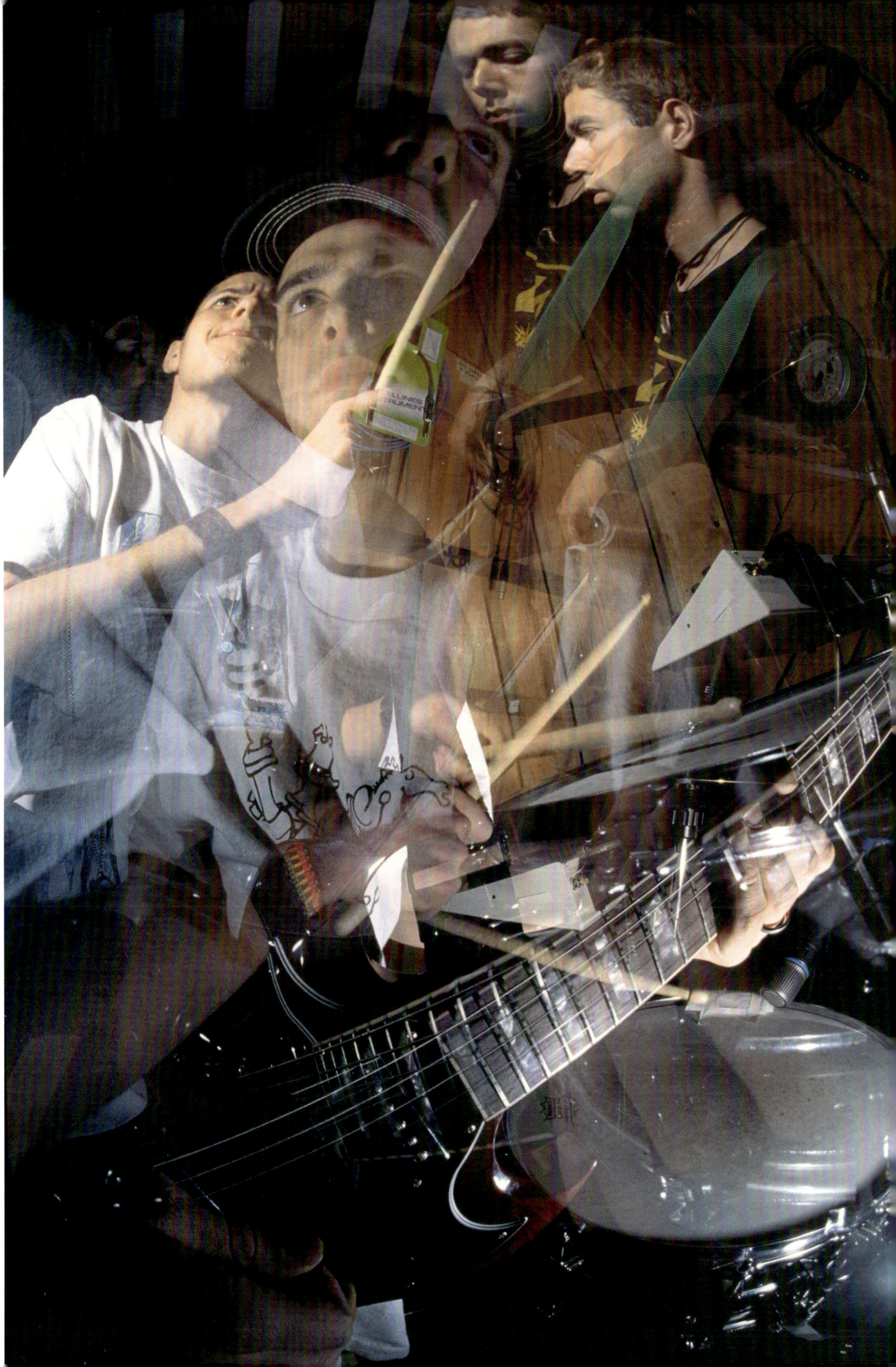

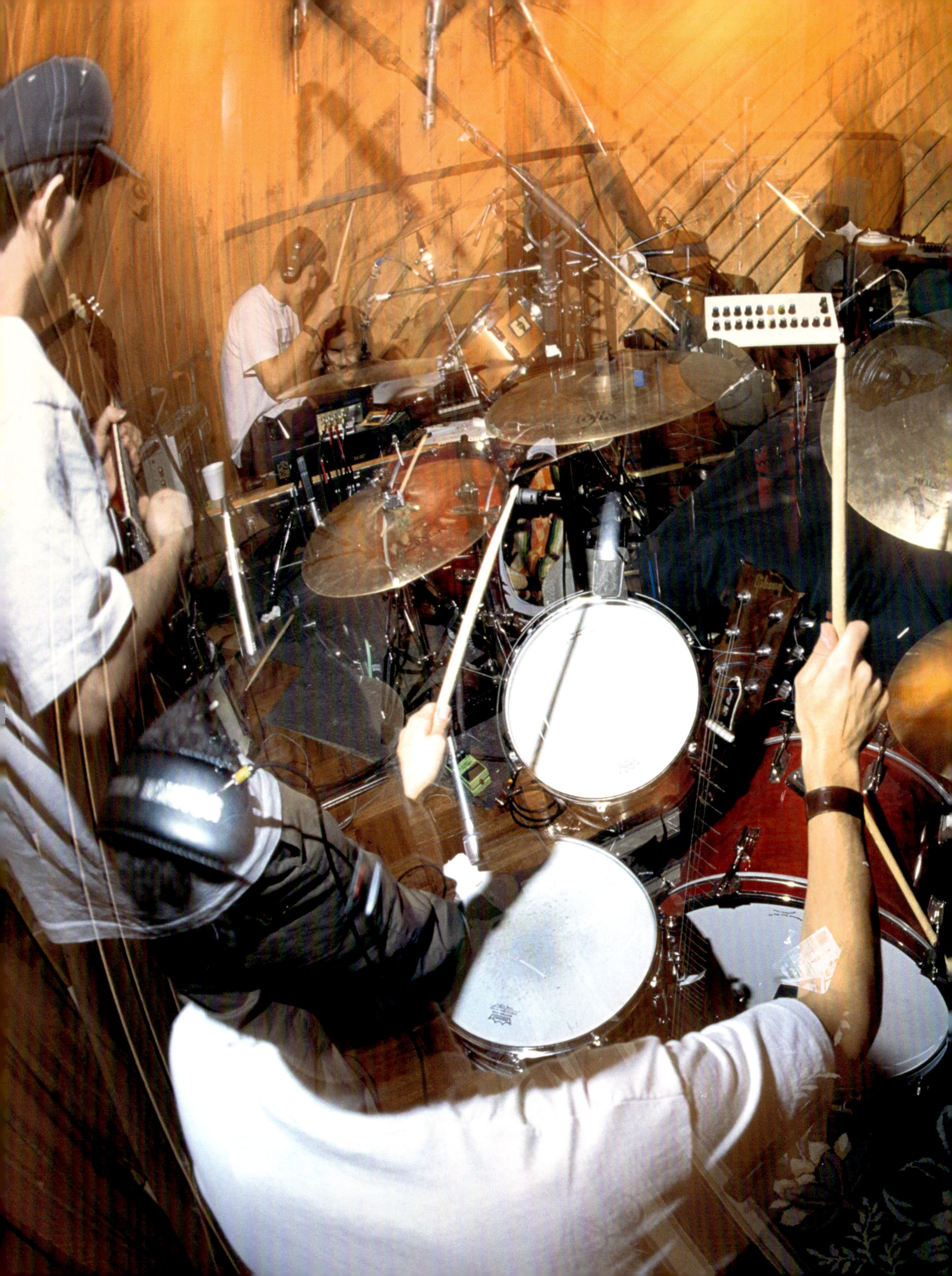

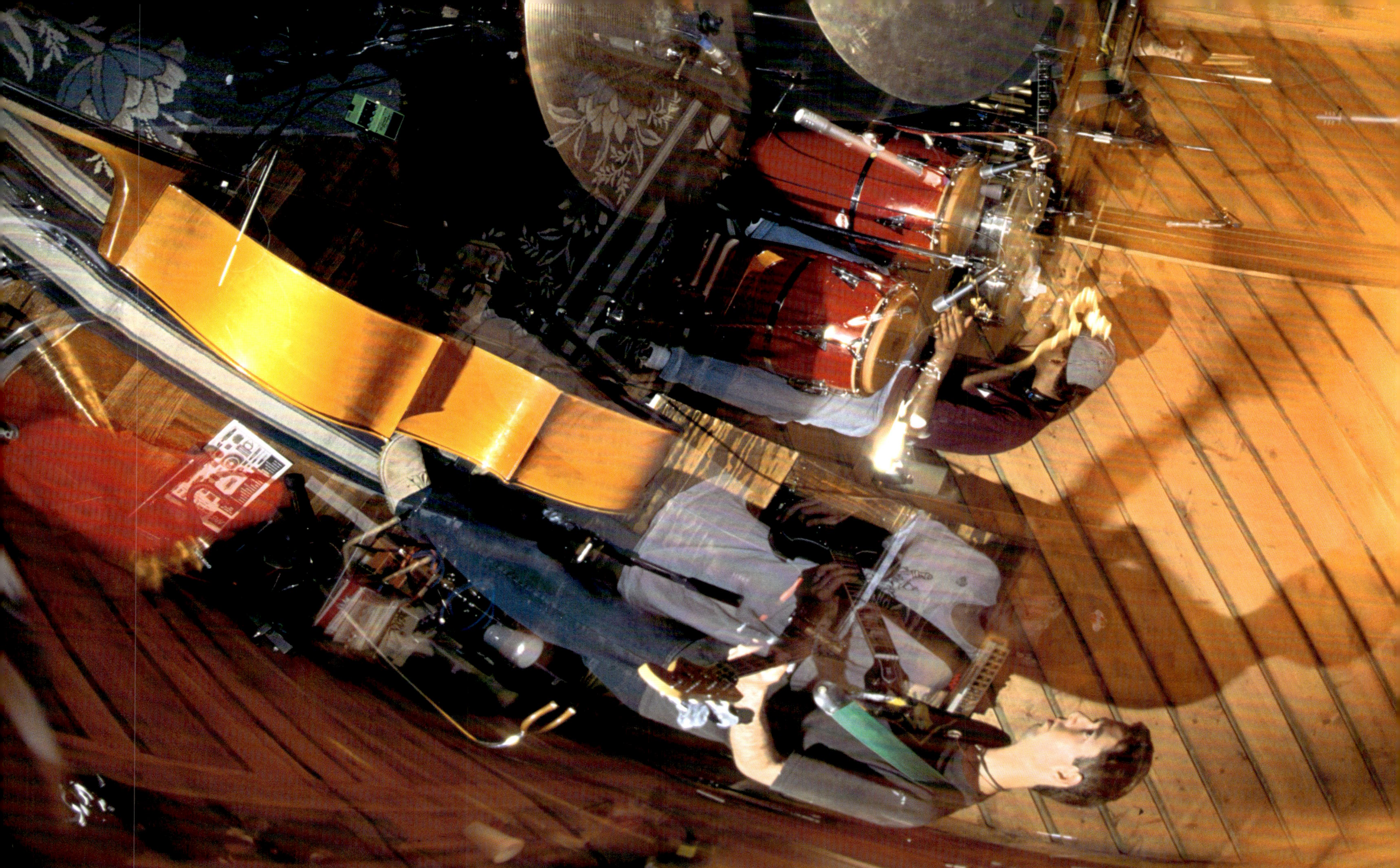

Don't cuss... Call us.

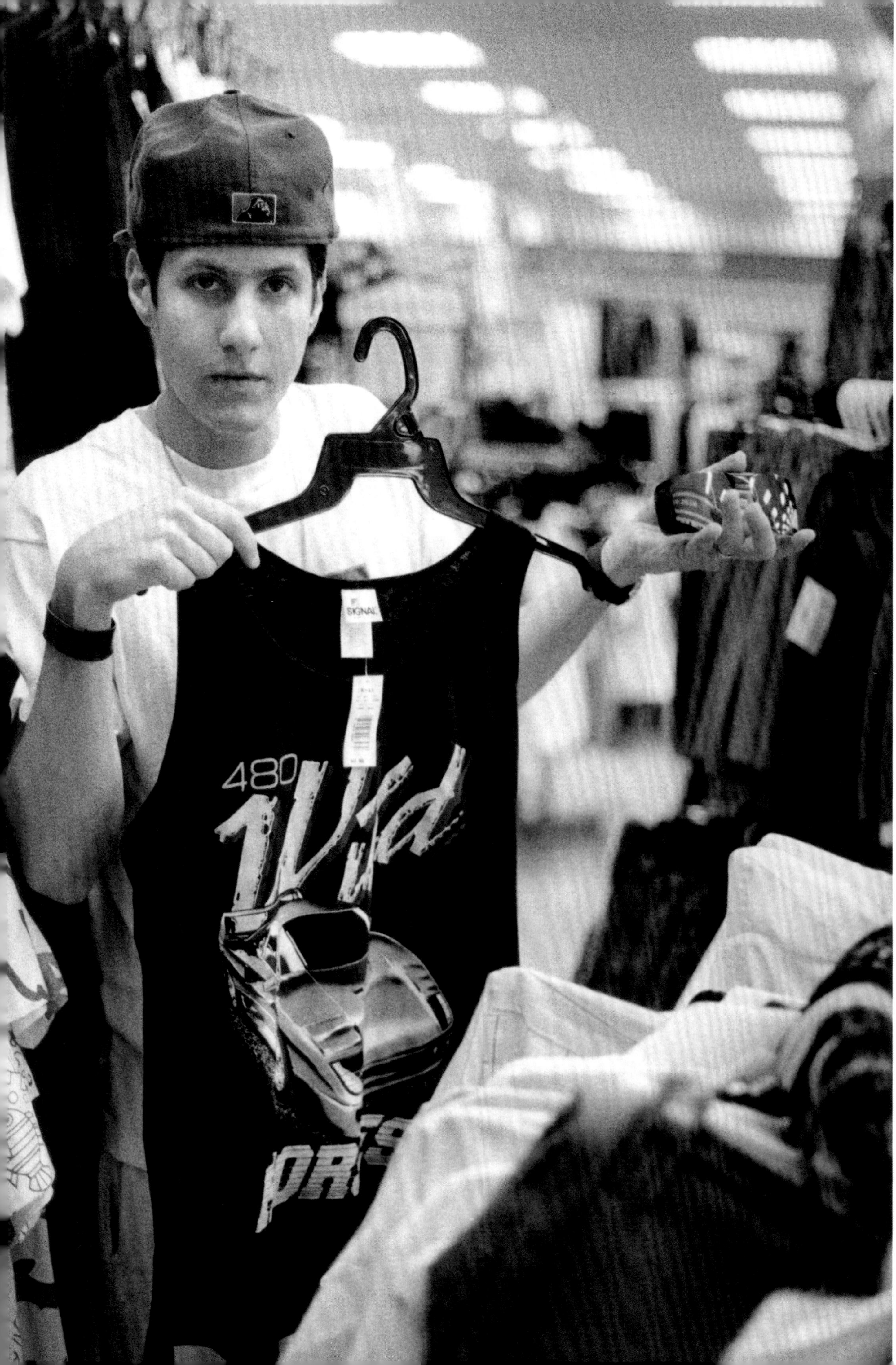
SIGNAL
480

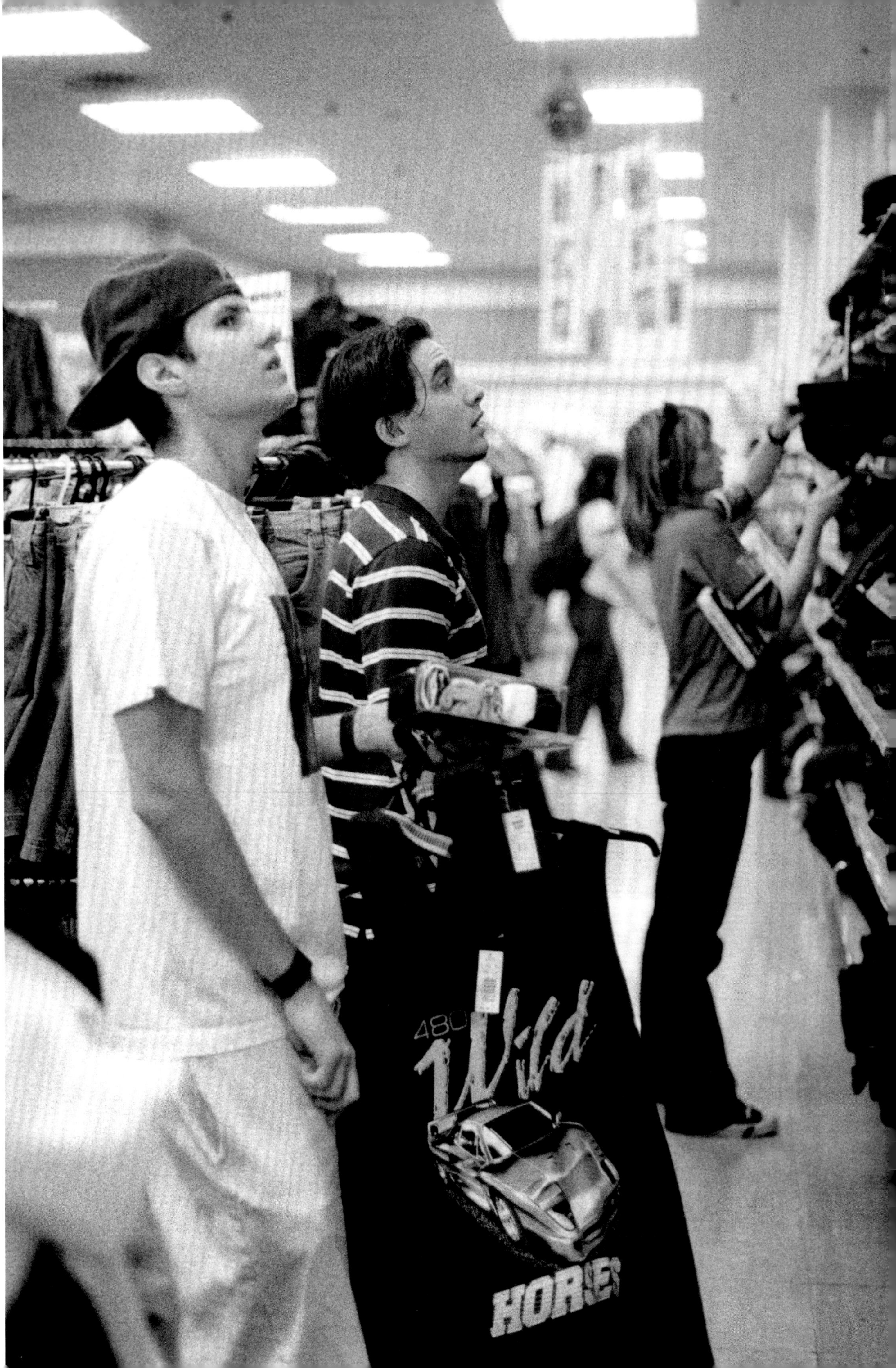
480
Wild
HORSES

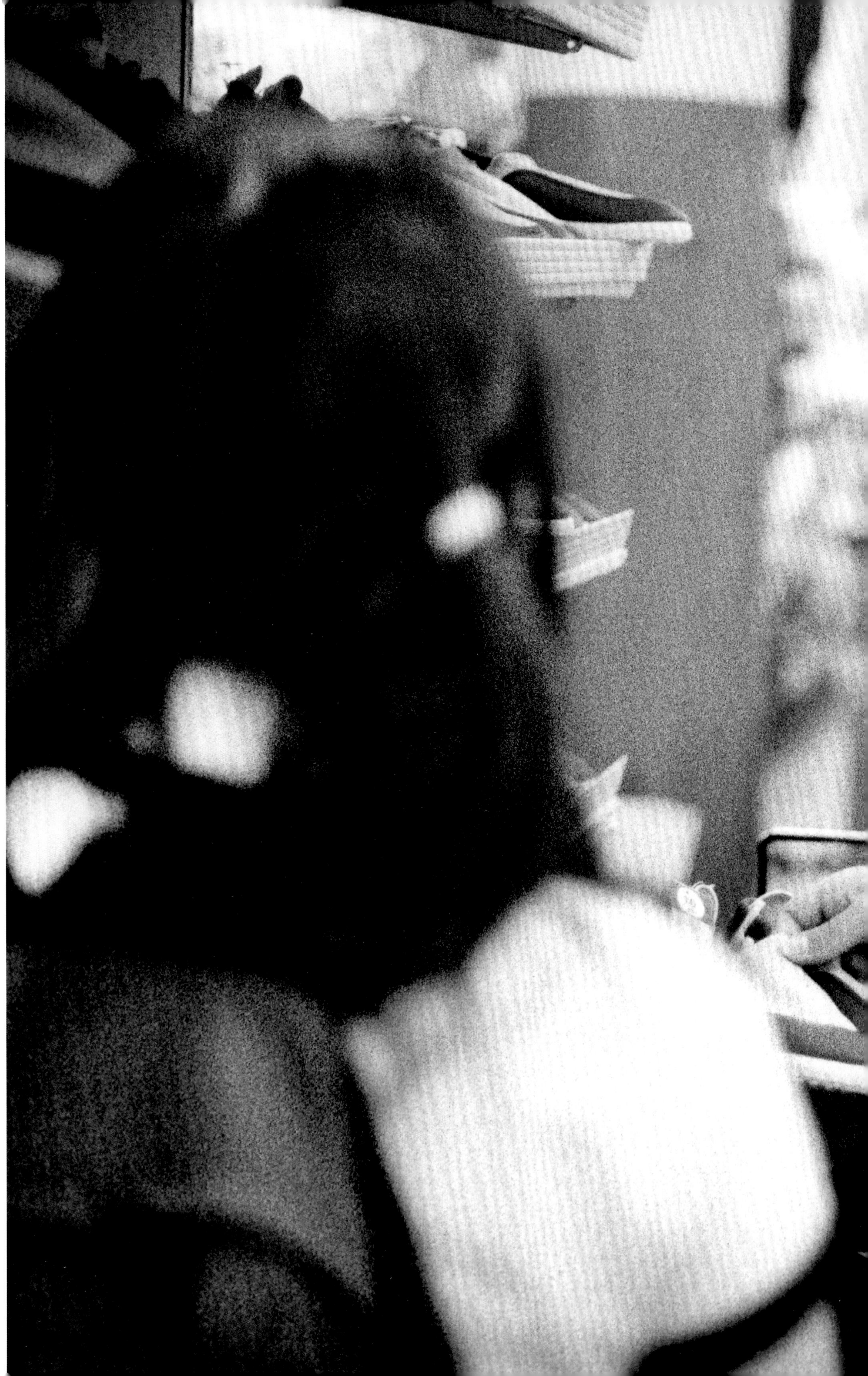

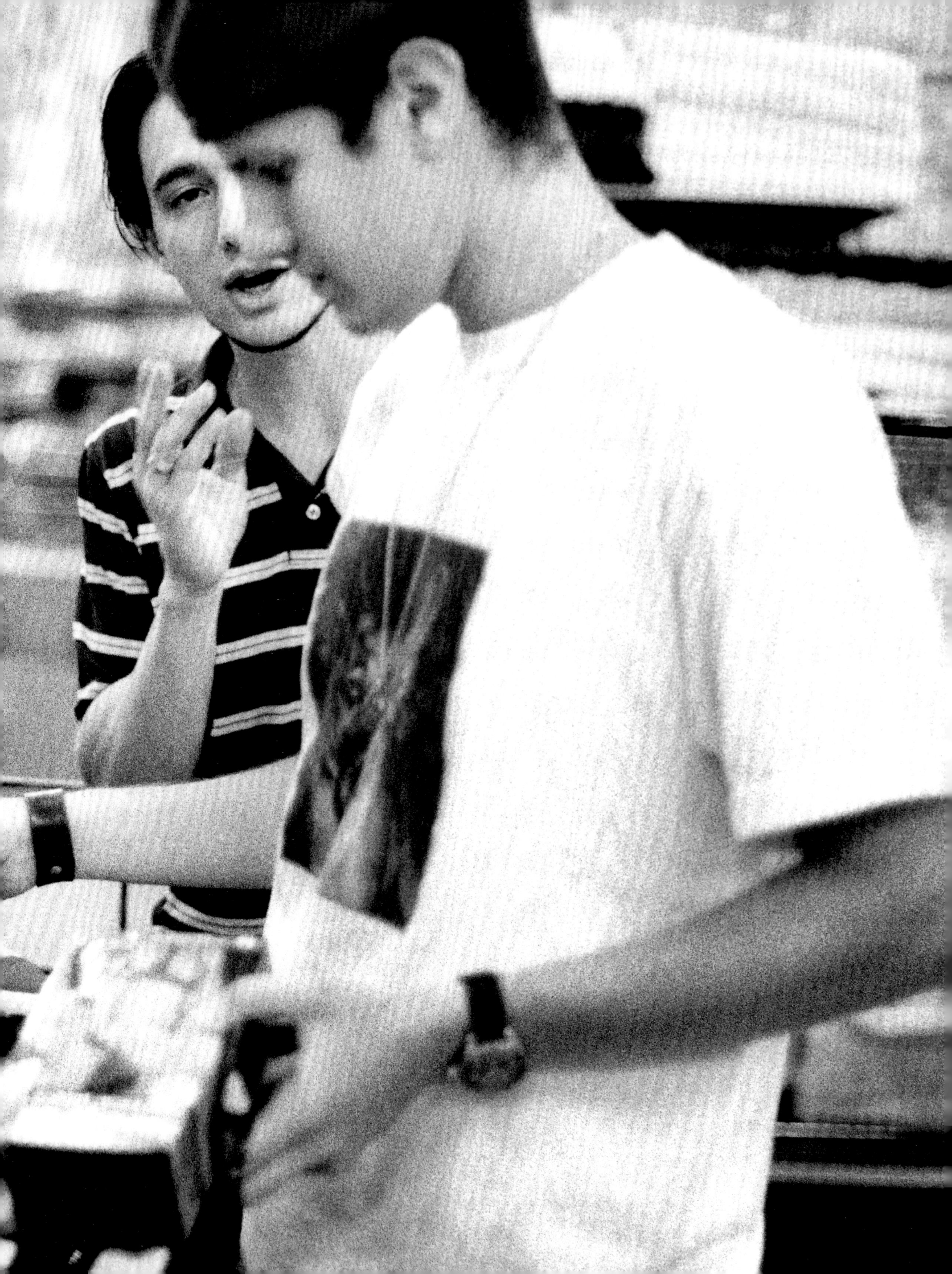

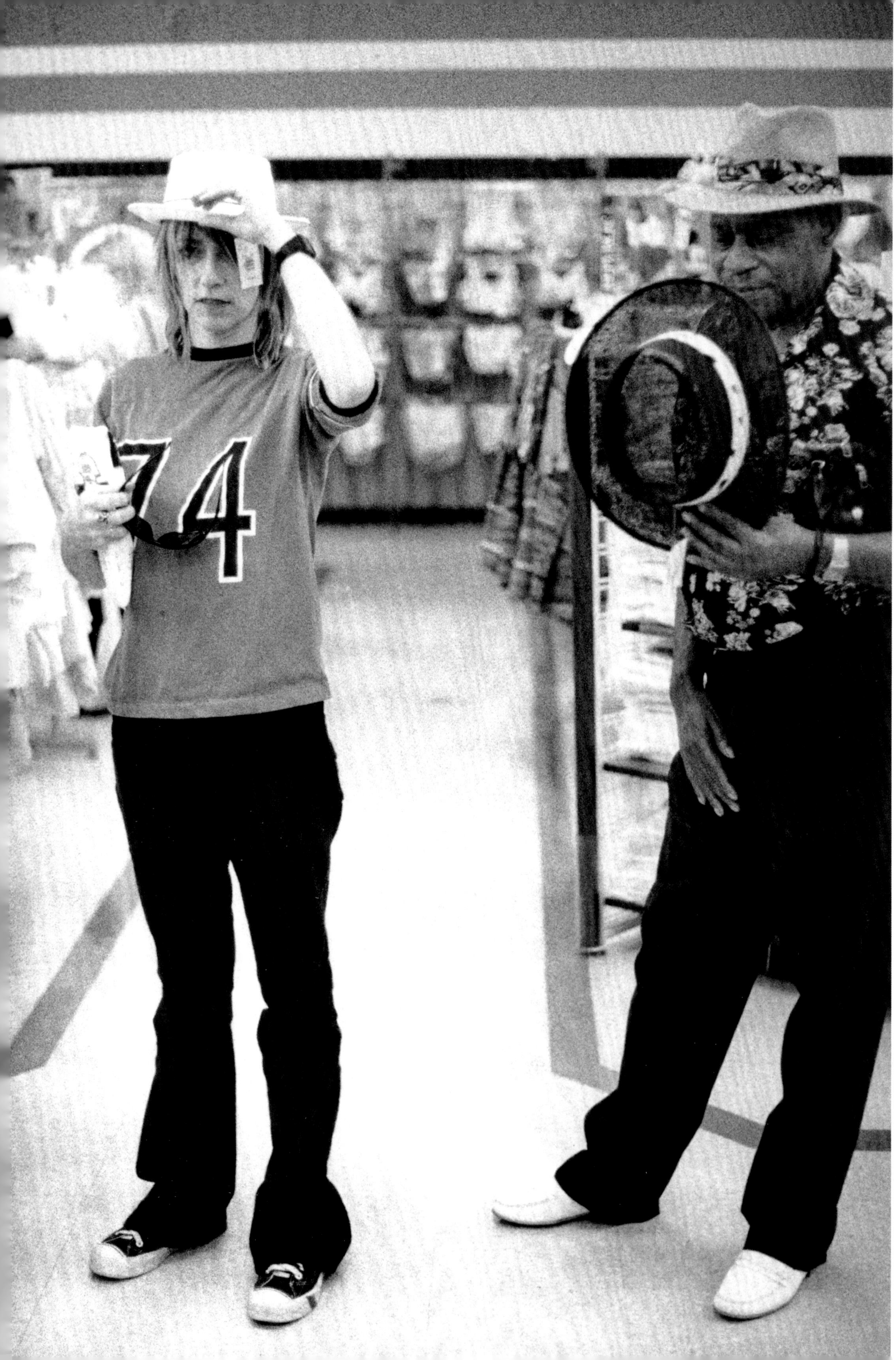
74

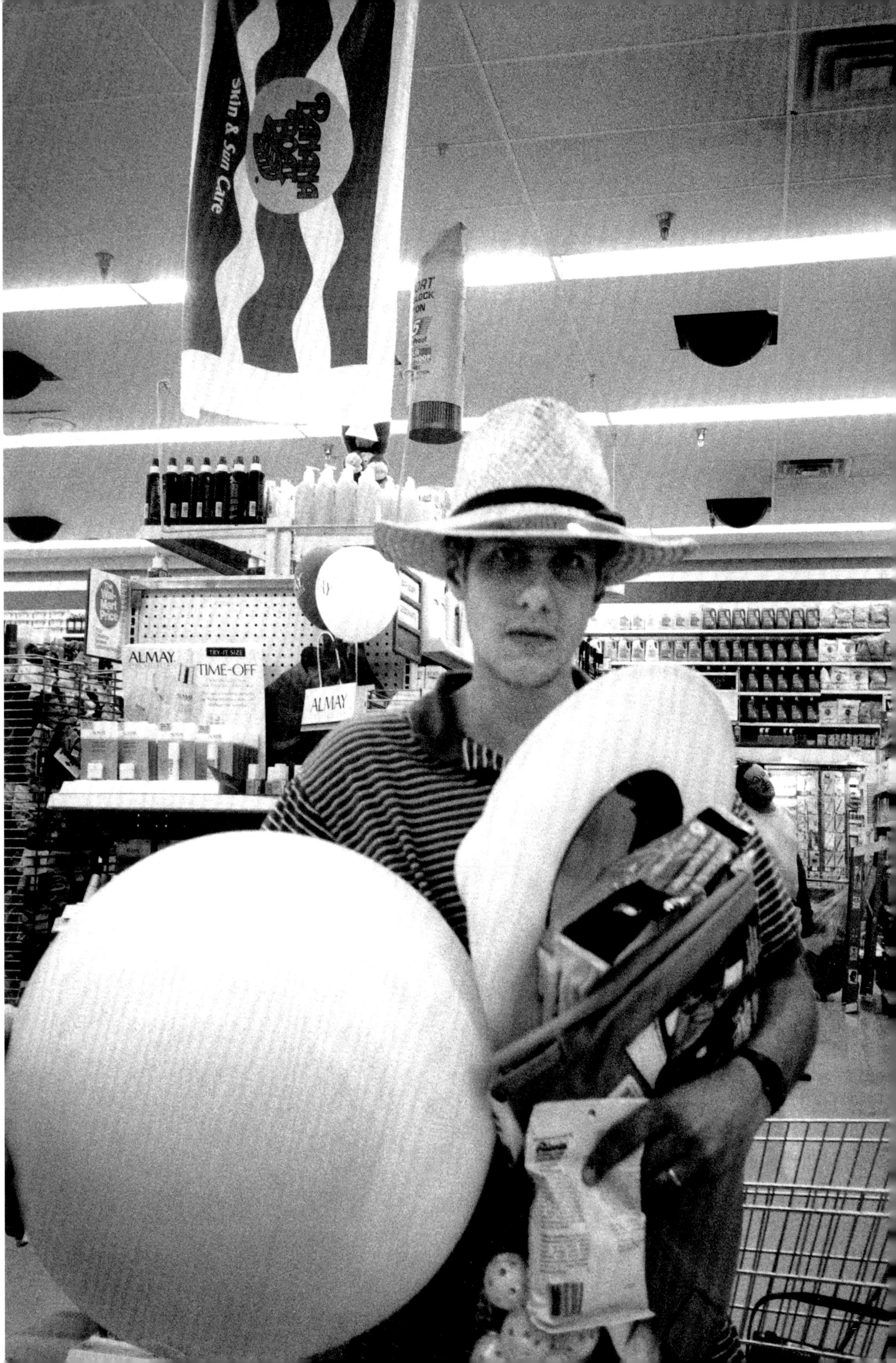

Skin & Sun Care
ALMAY
TRY-IT SIZE
TIME-OFF
ALMAY

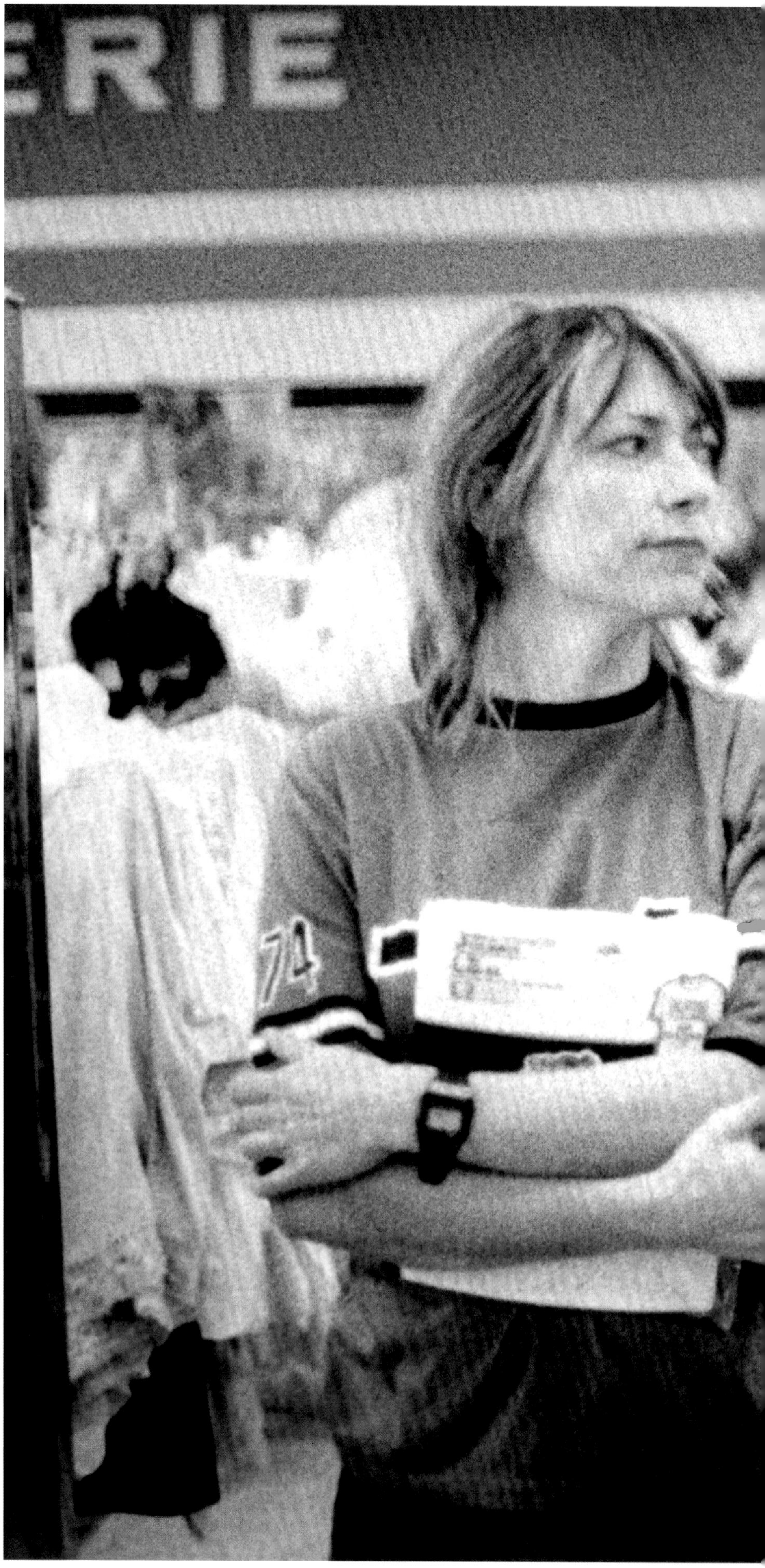
ERIE

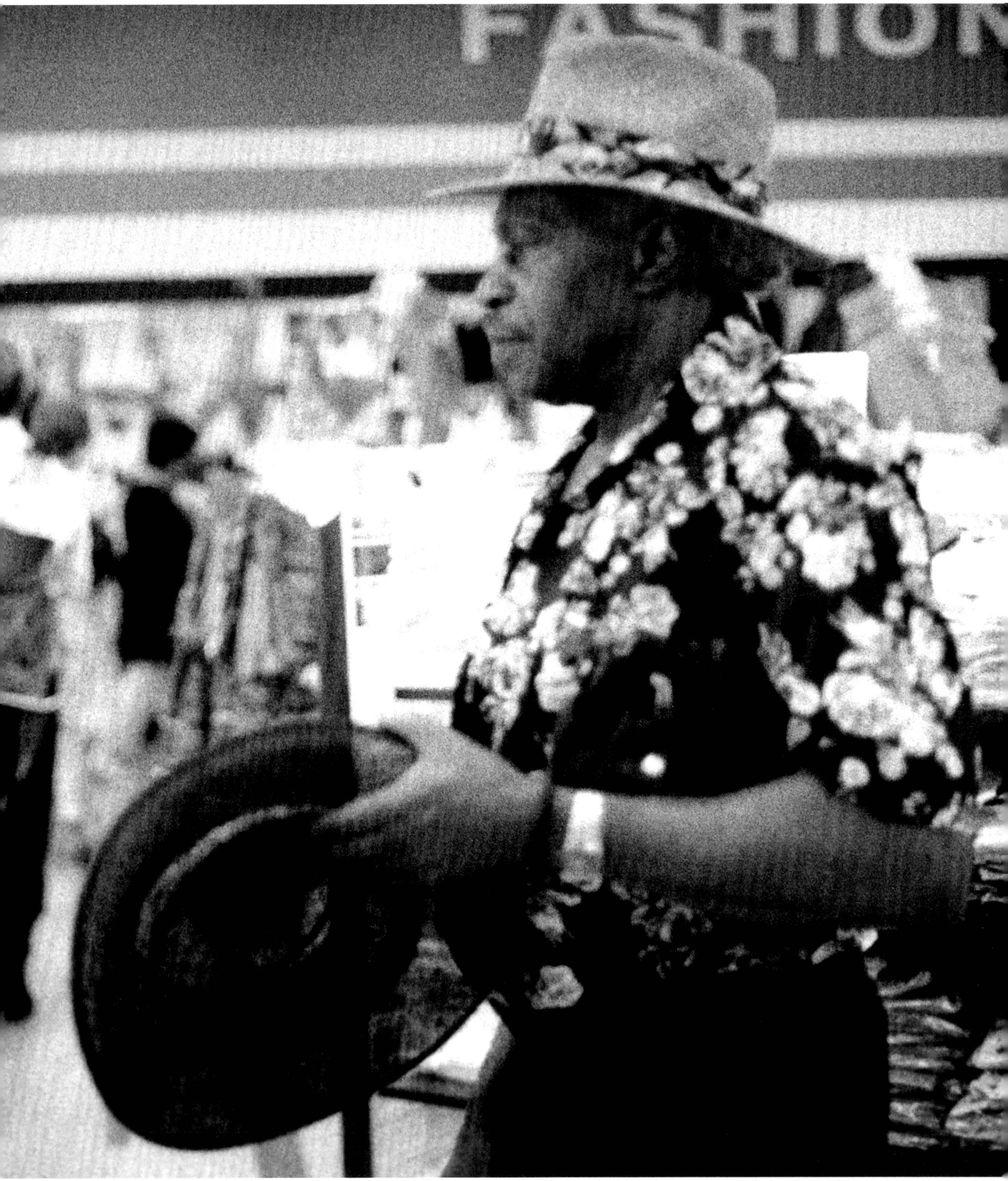

Virgil + Temple

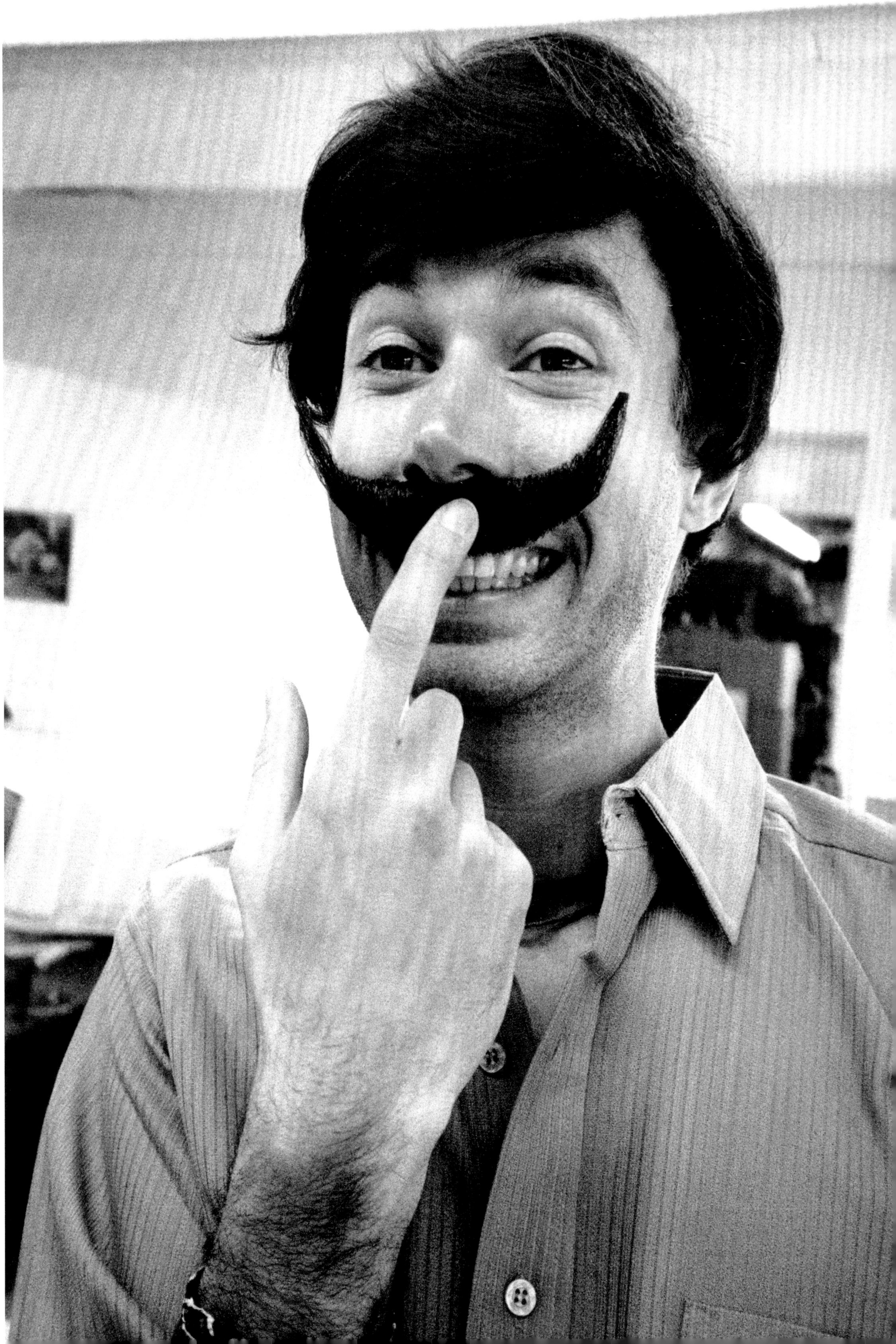

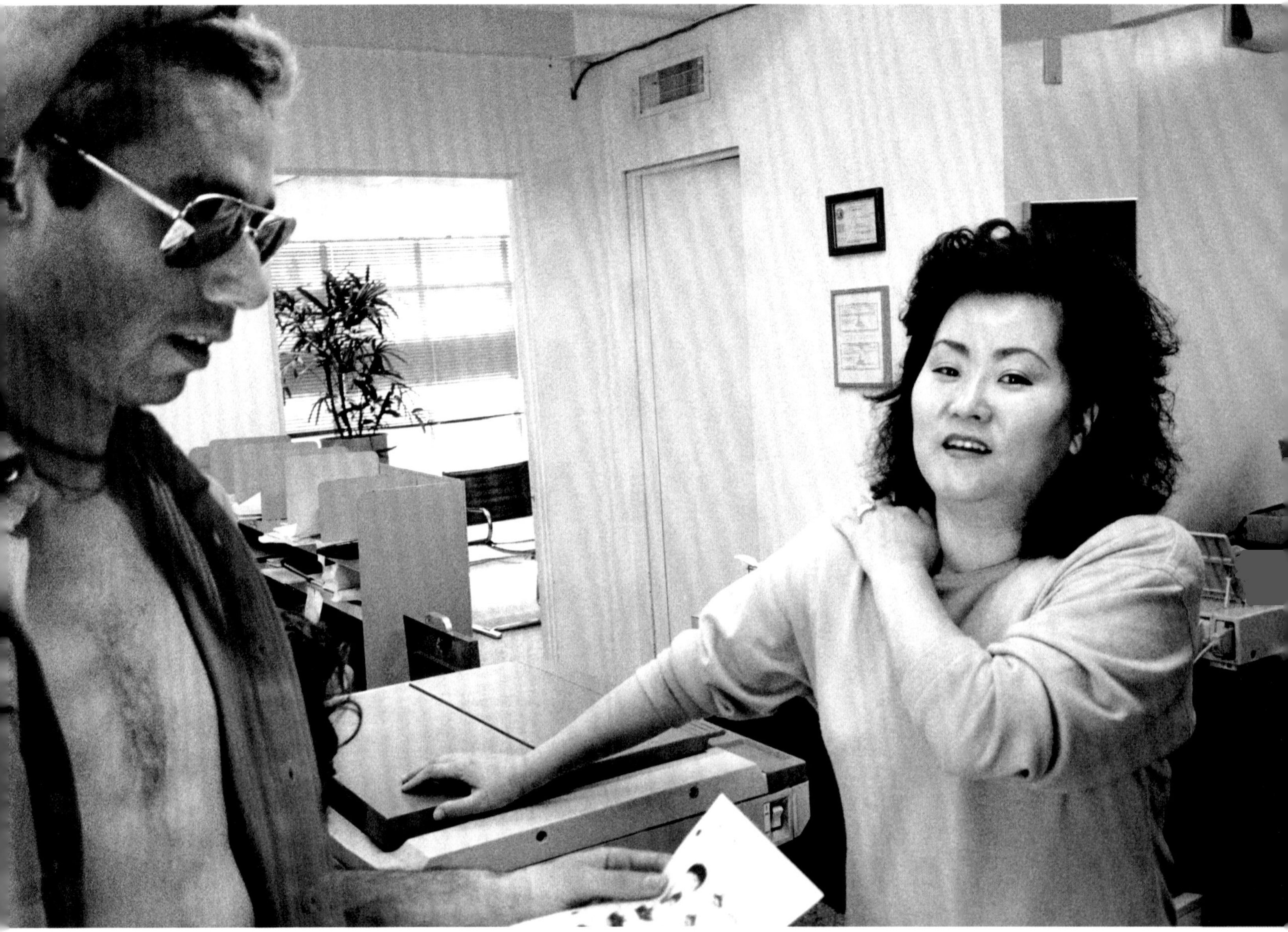

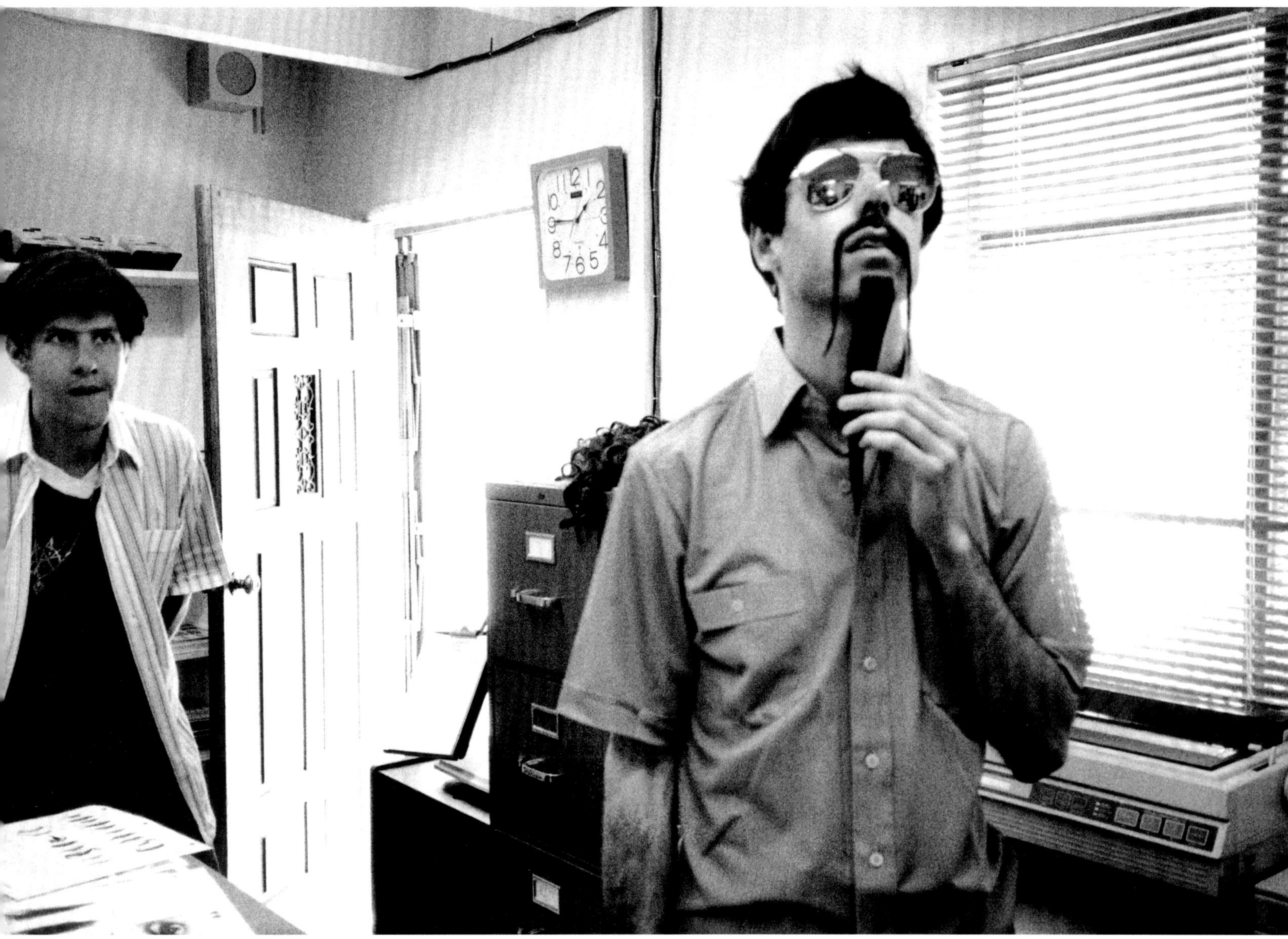

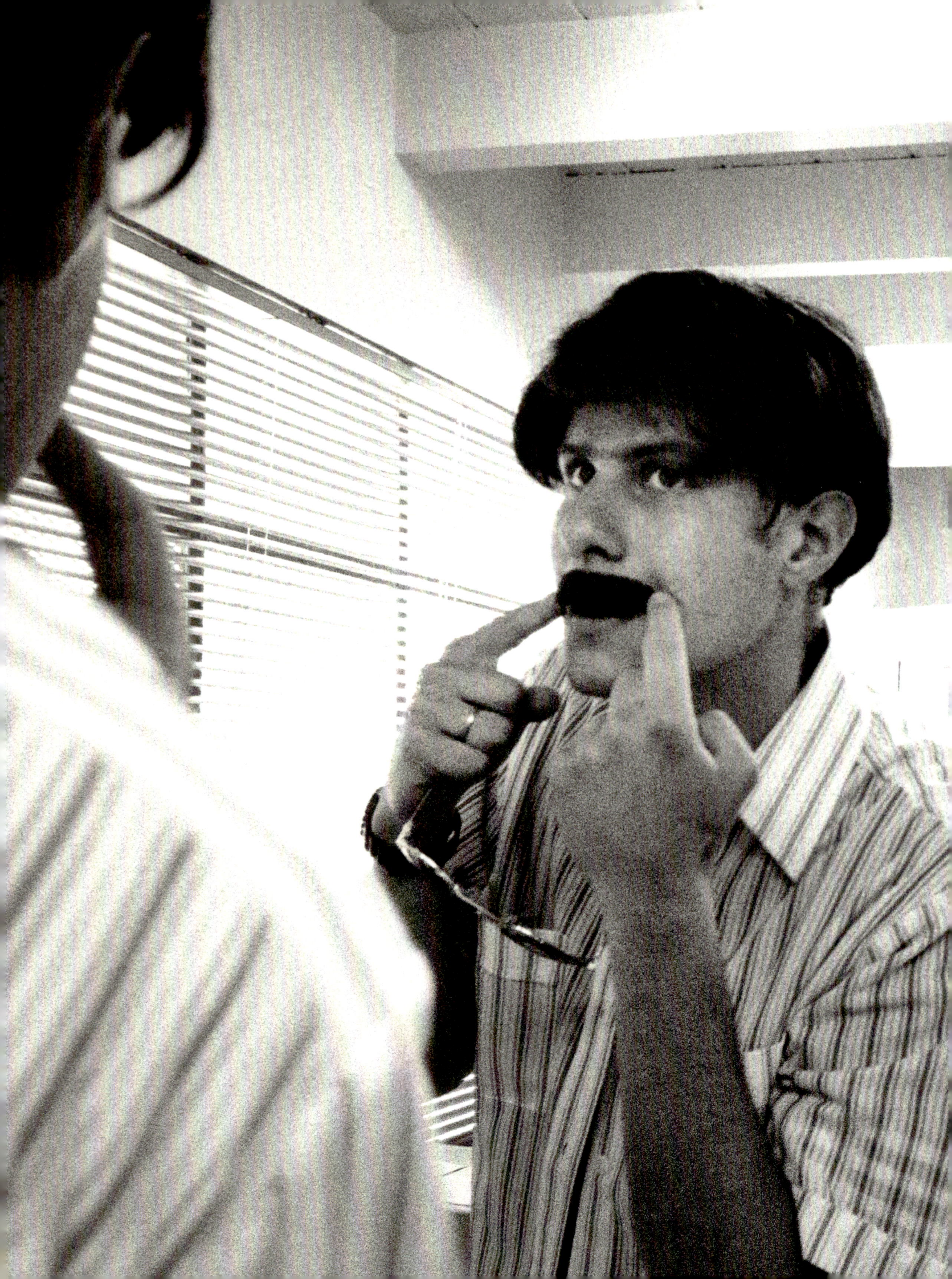

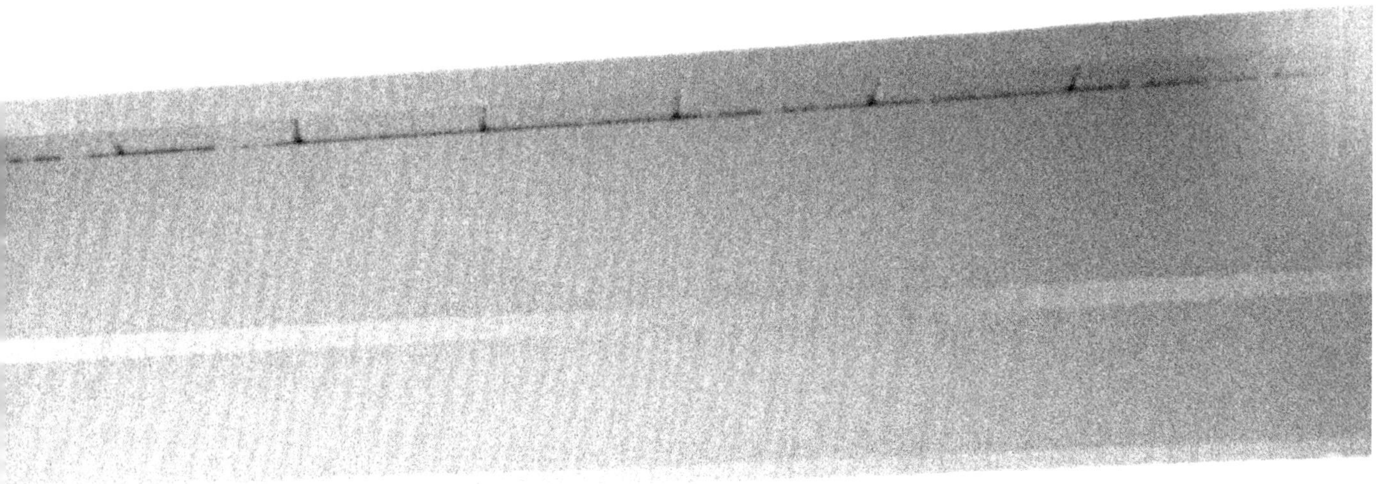

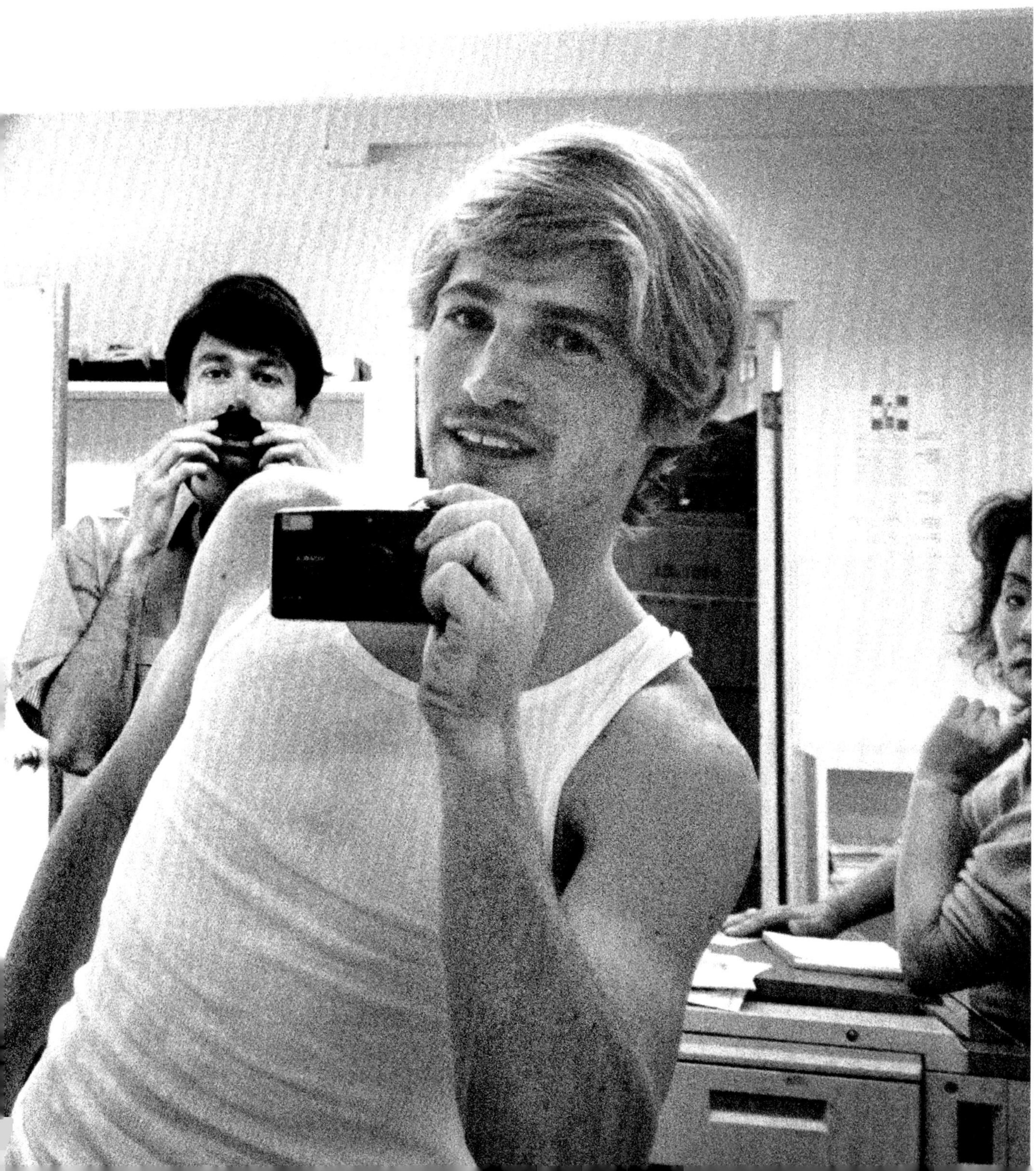

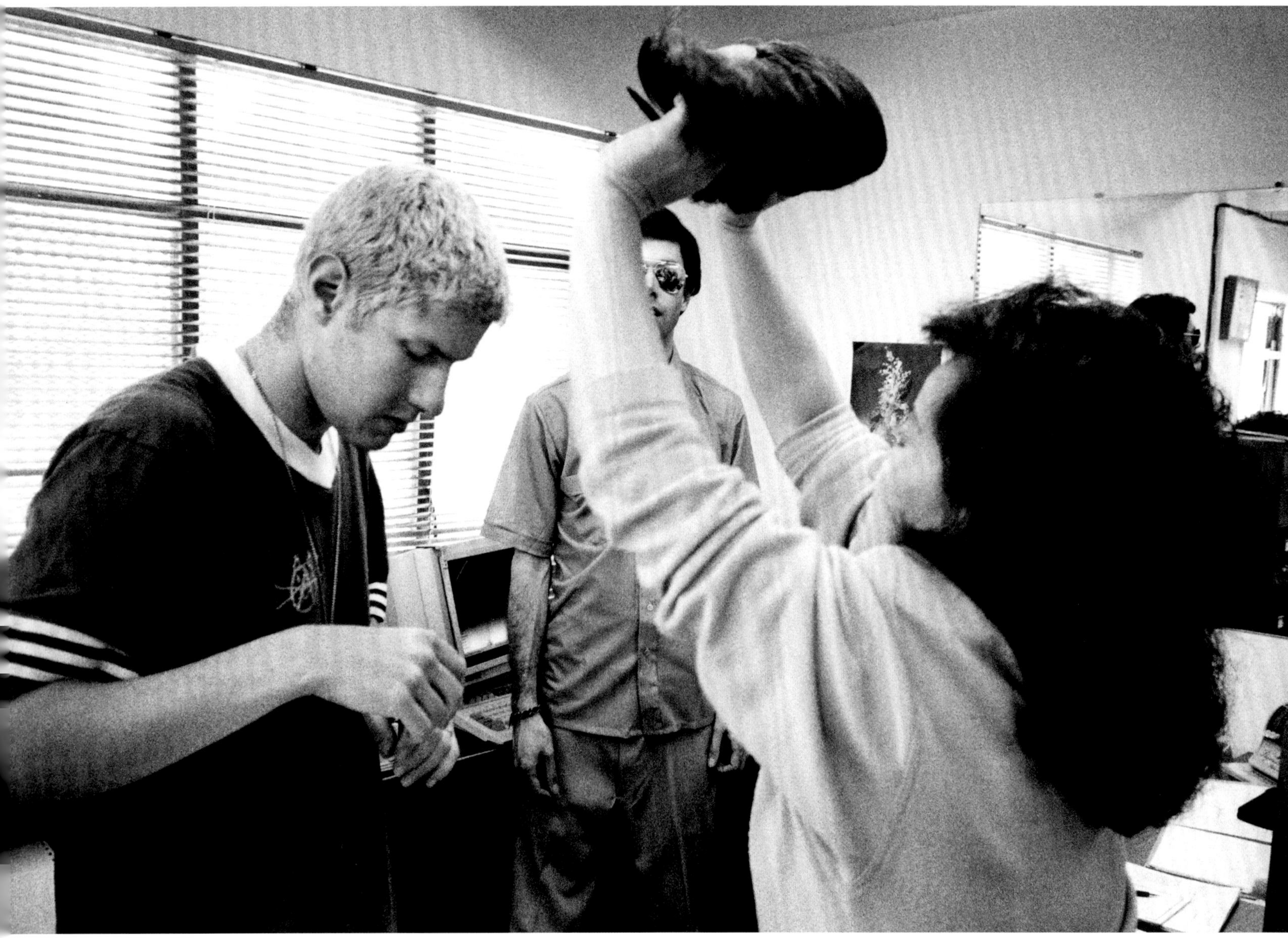

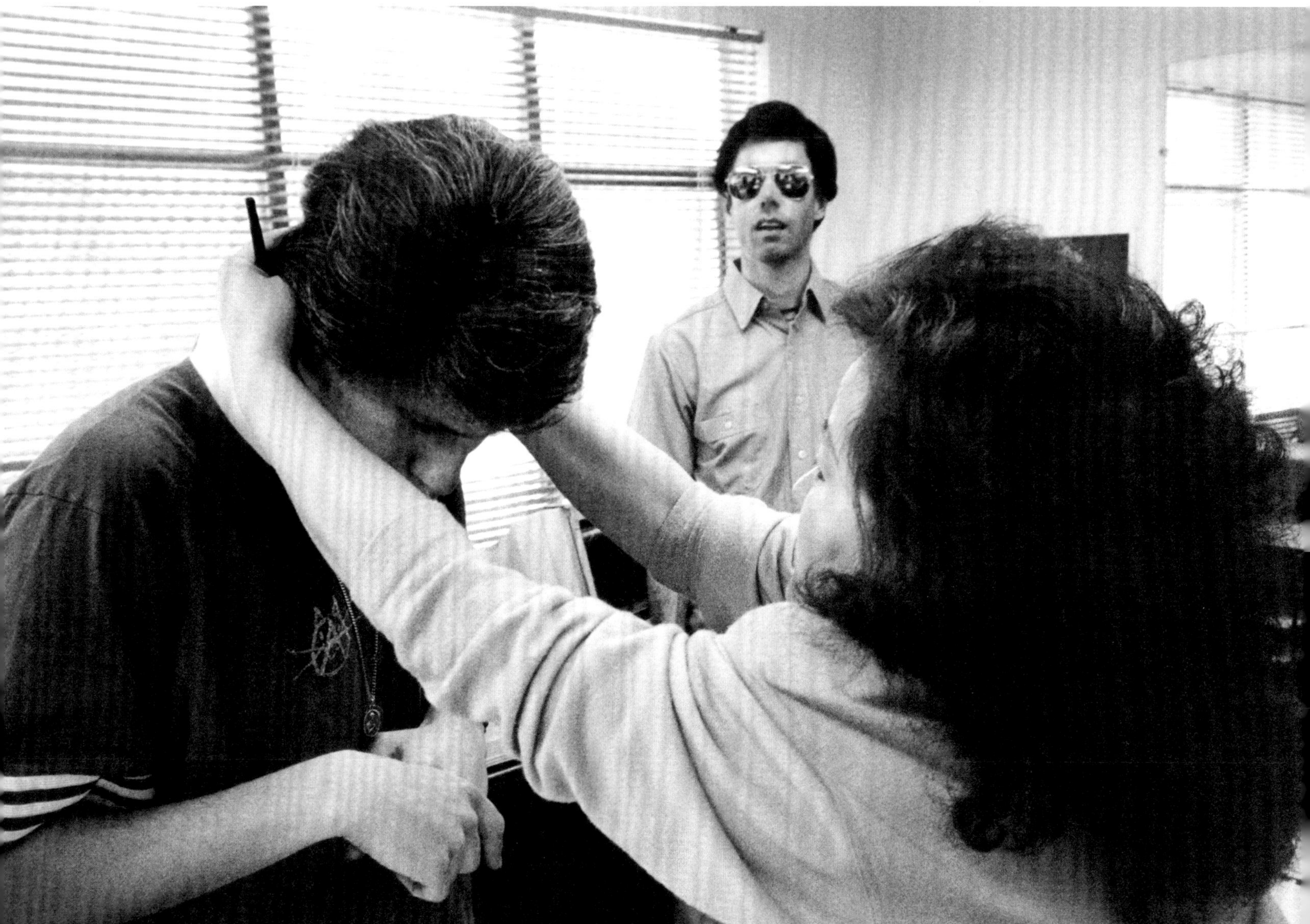

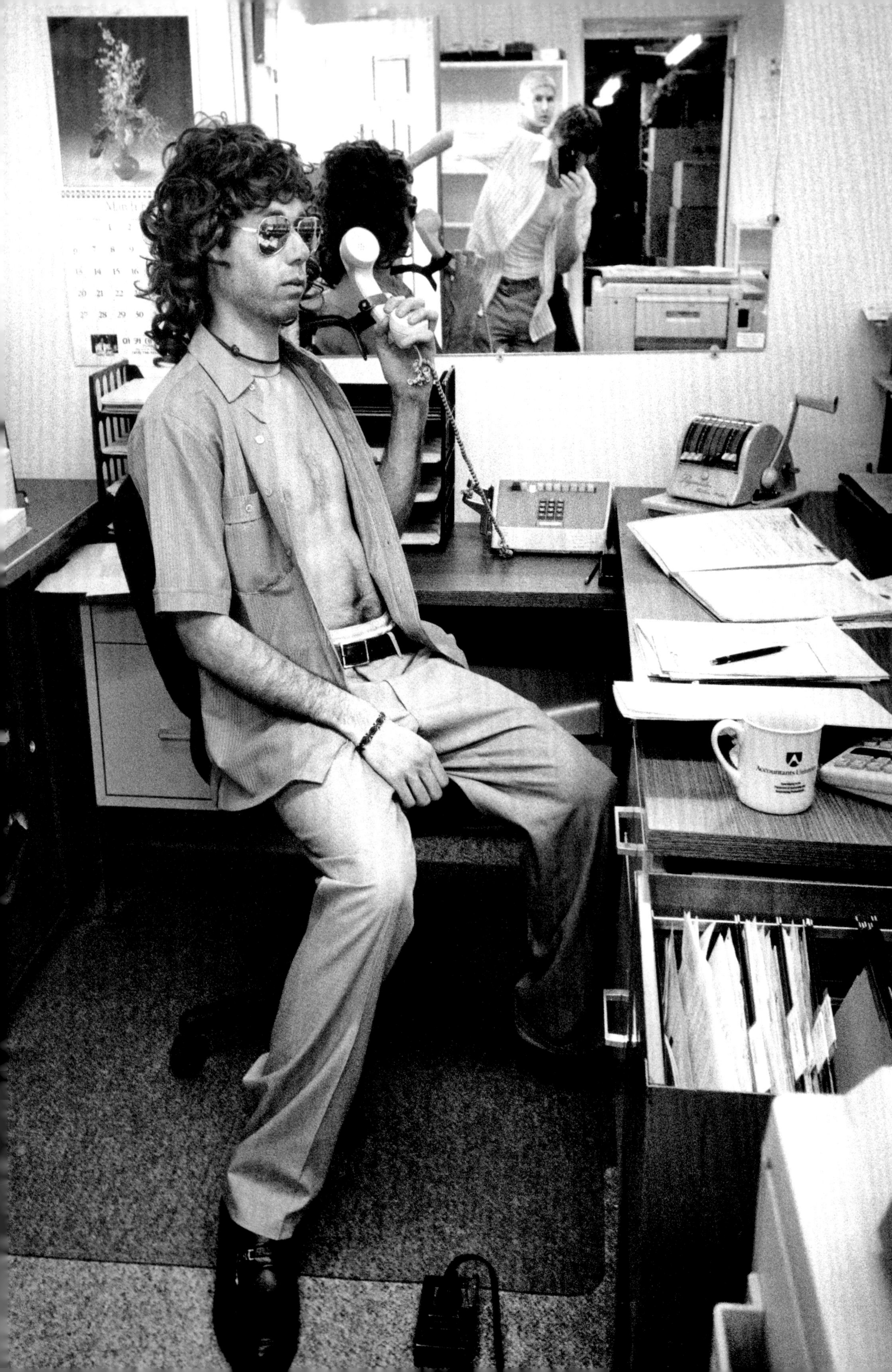

czar of HR

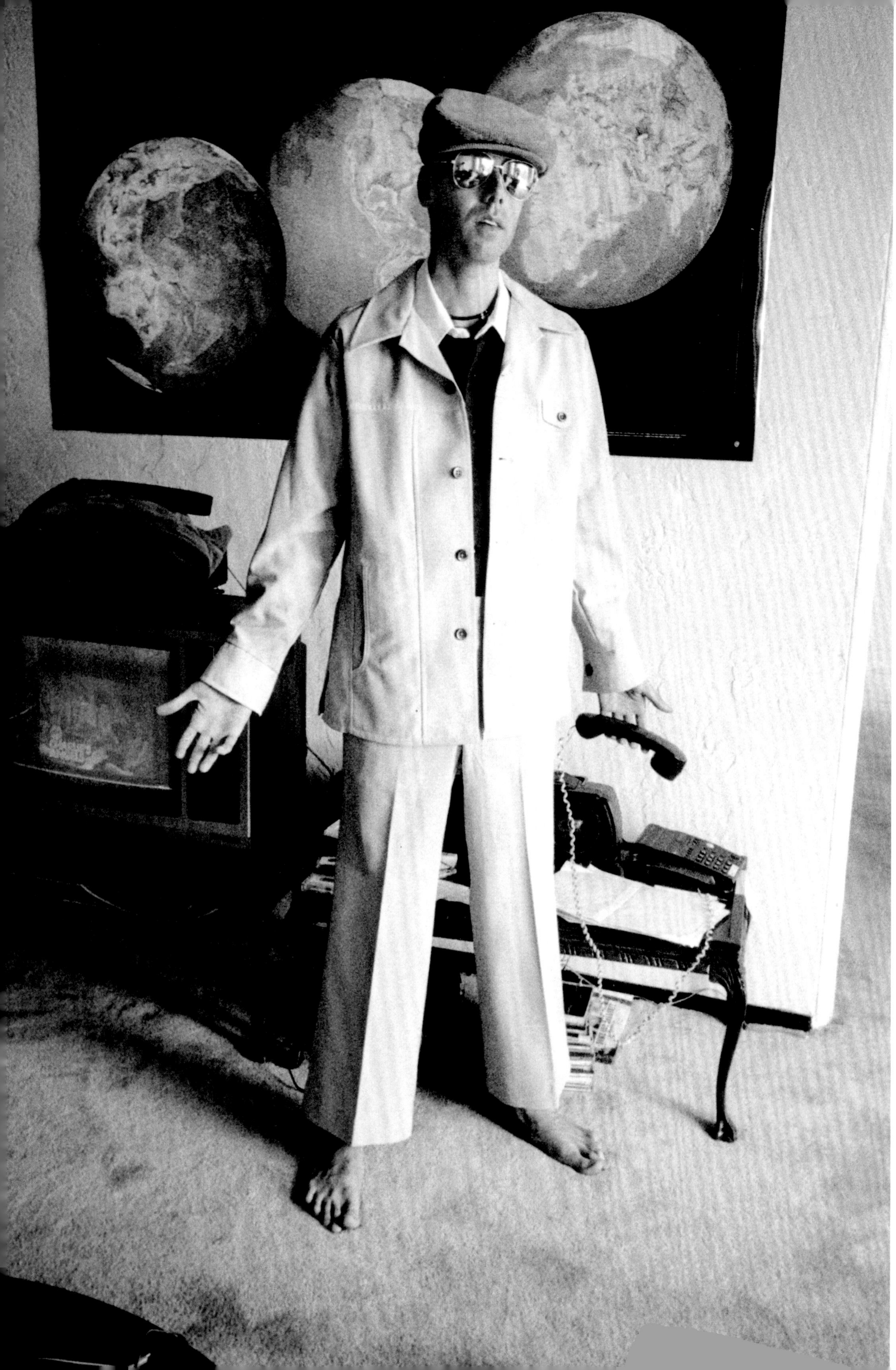

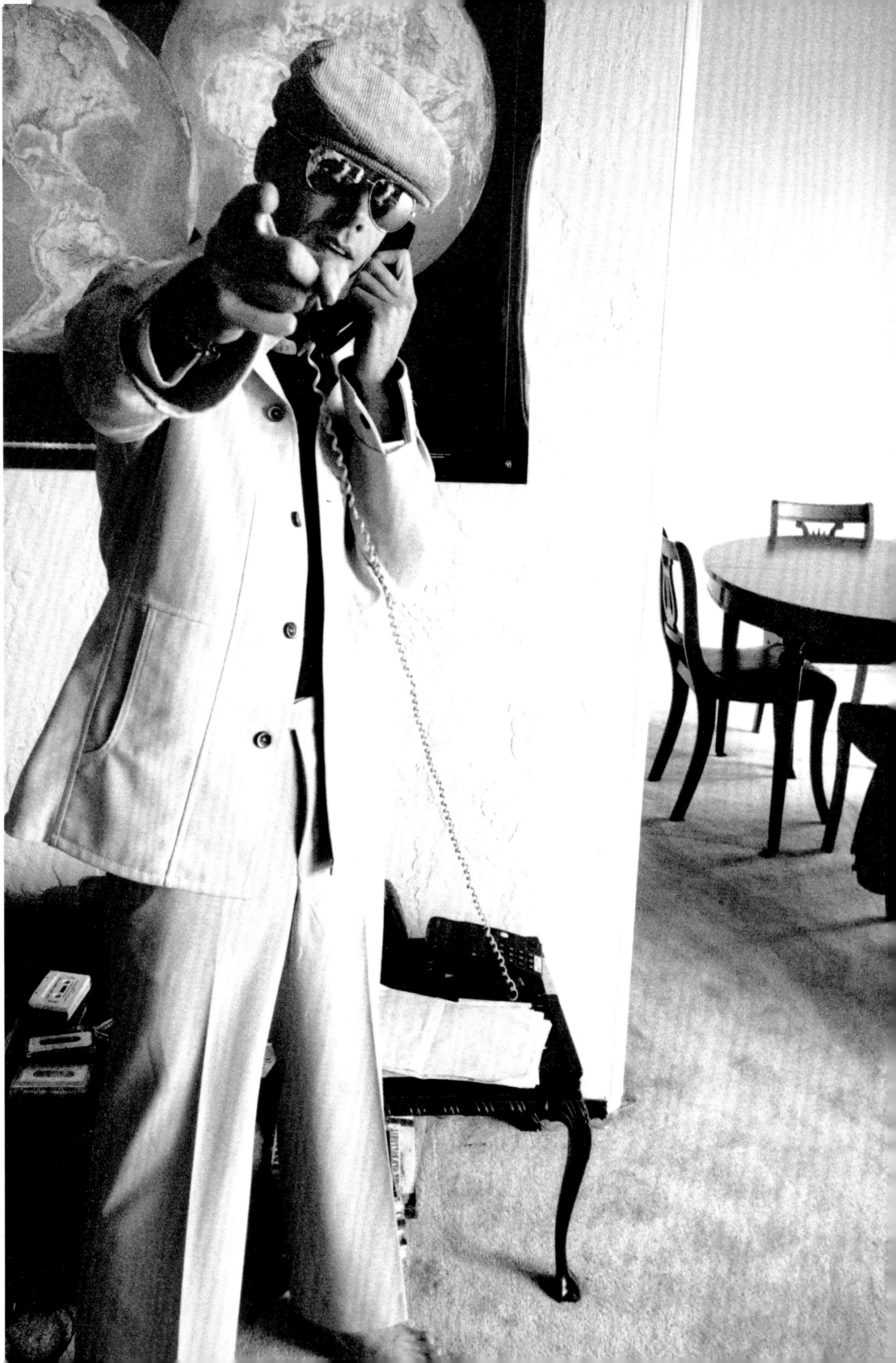

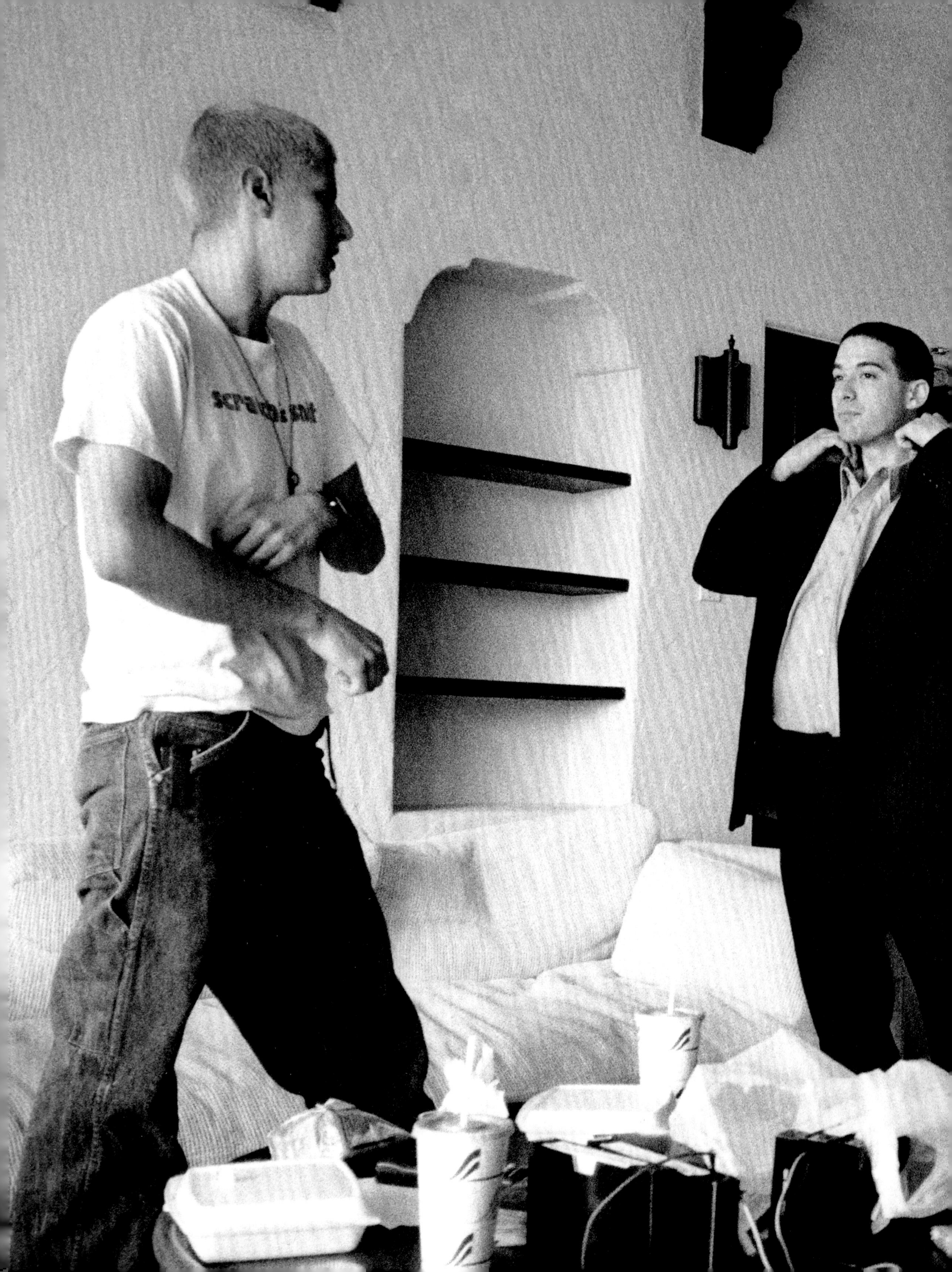

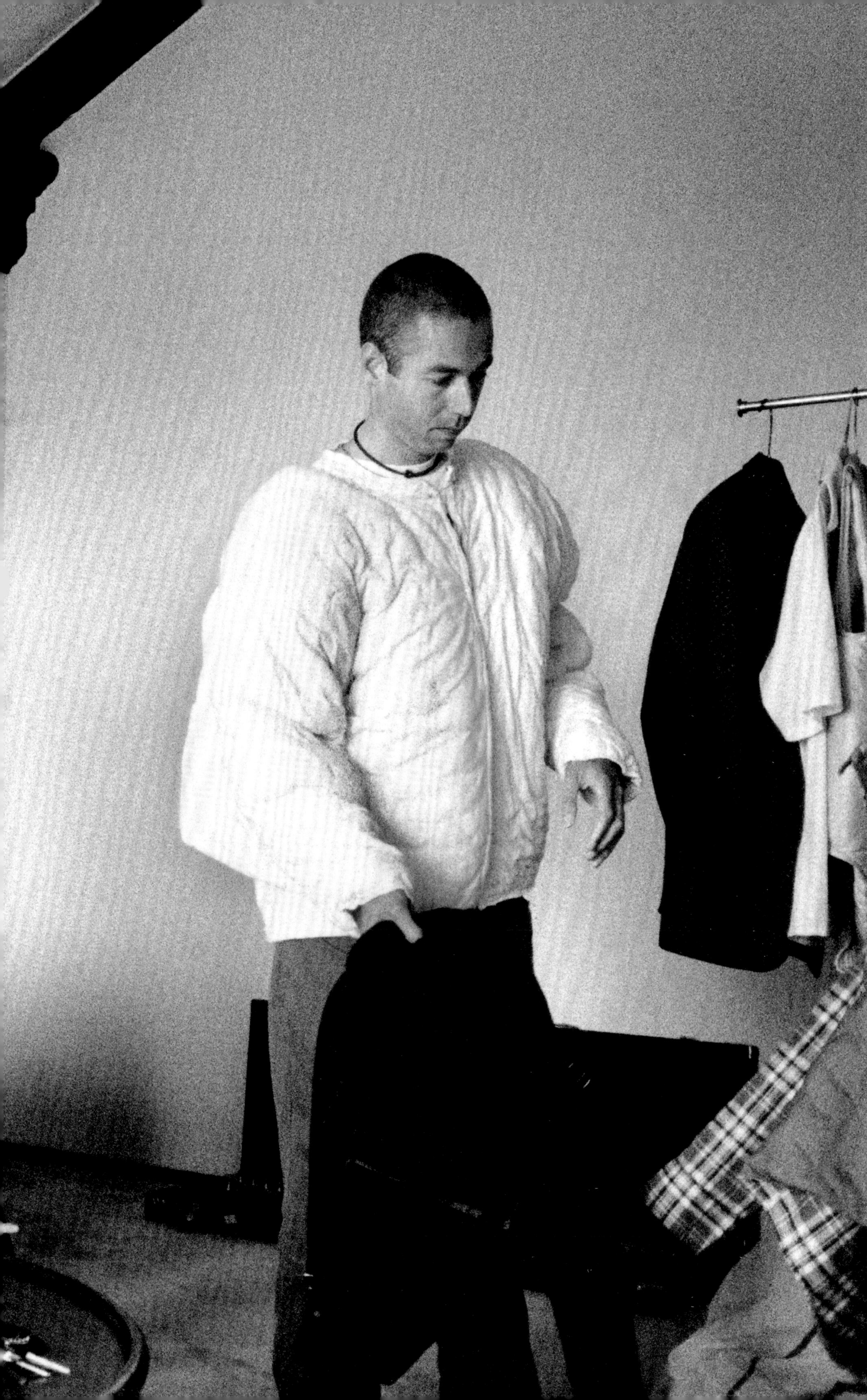

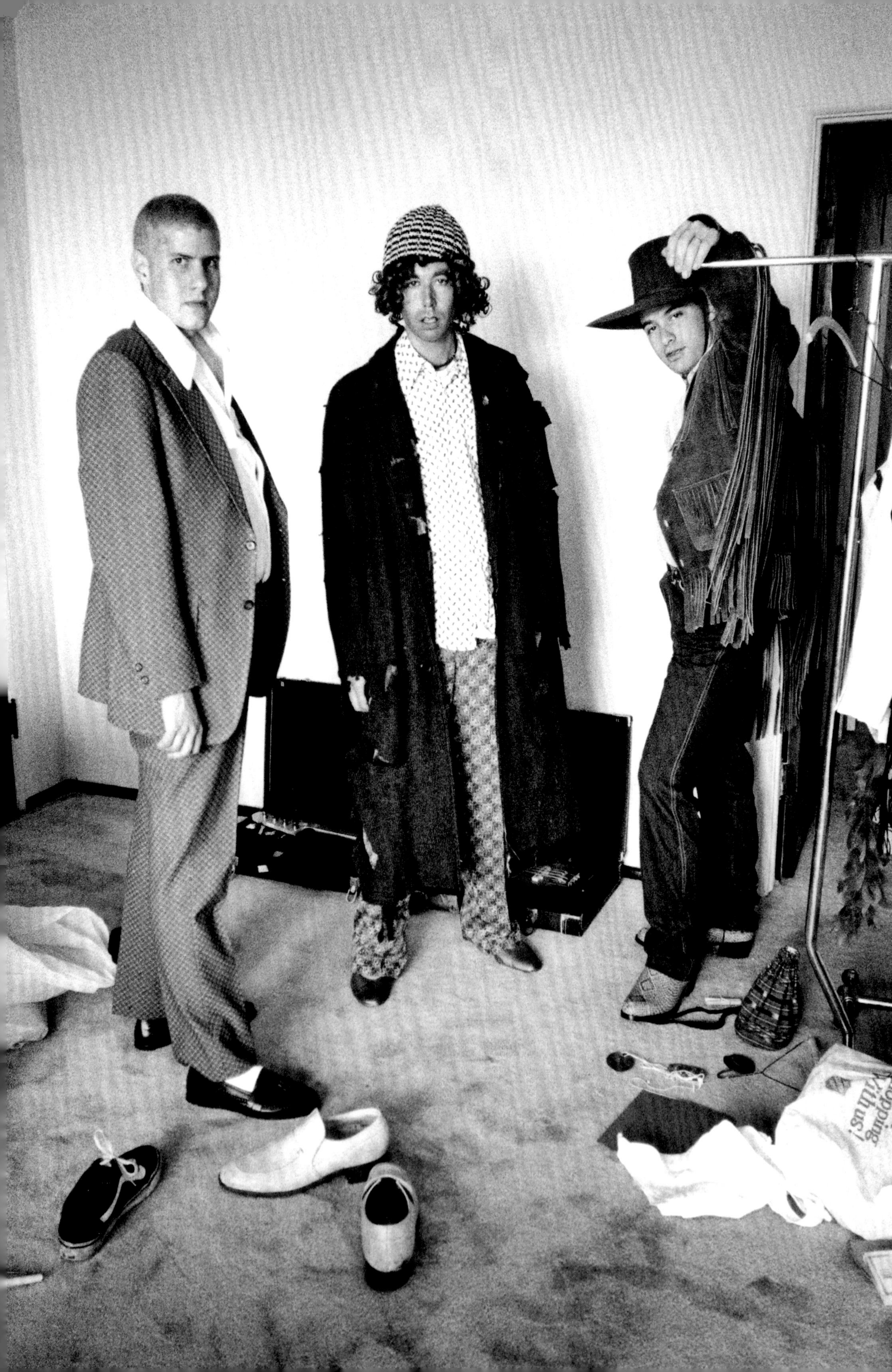

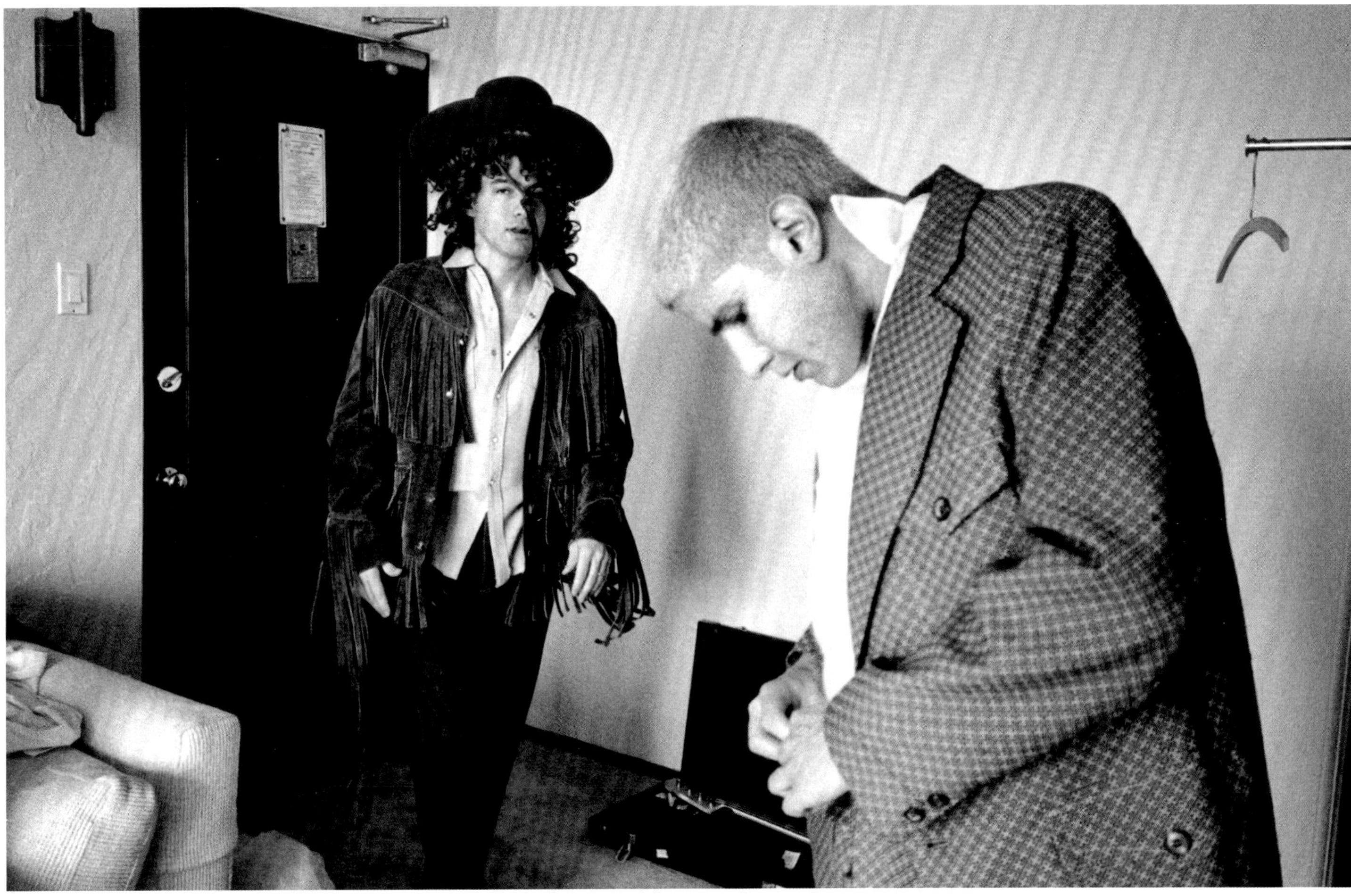

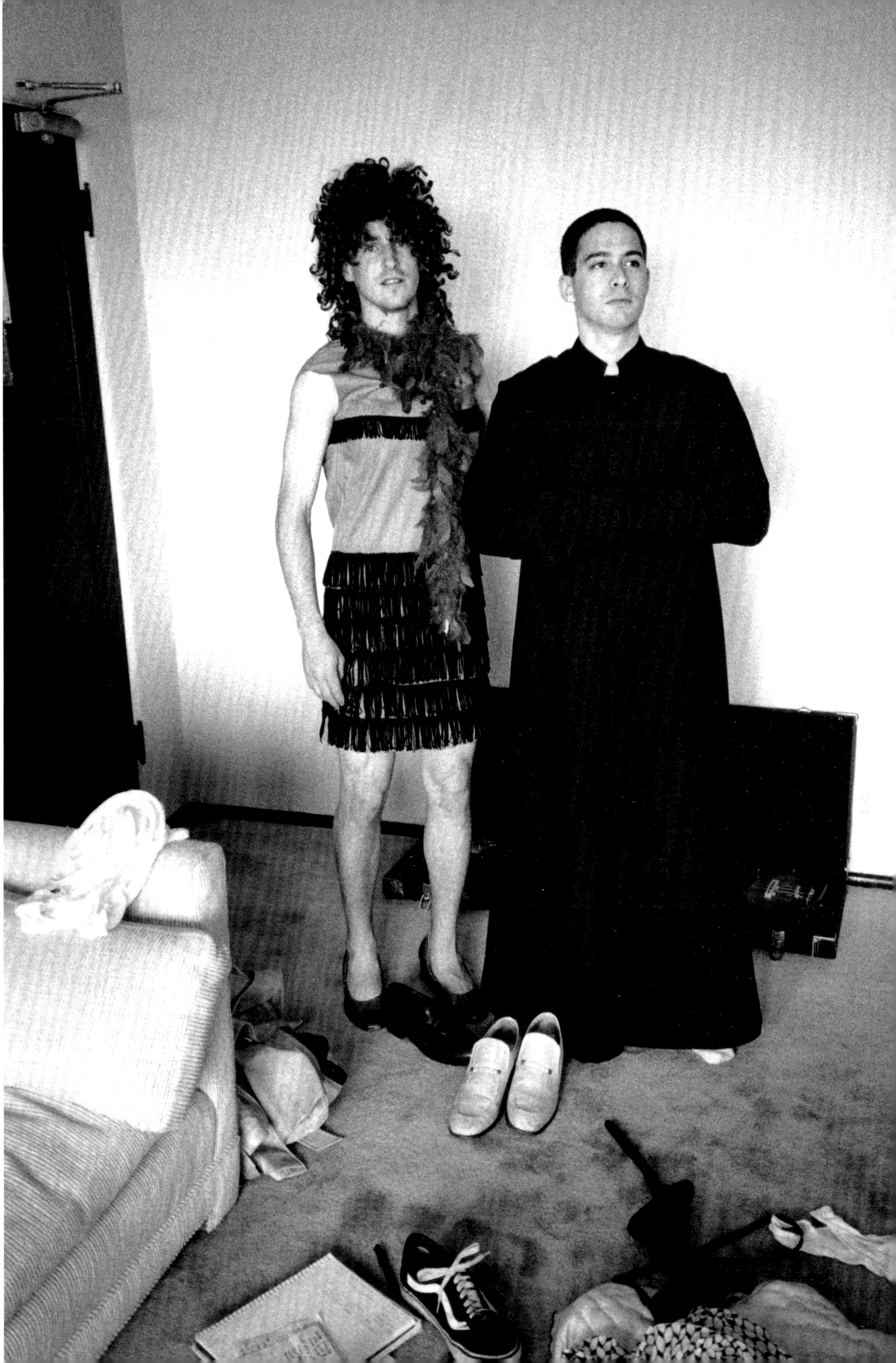

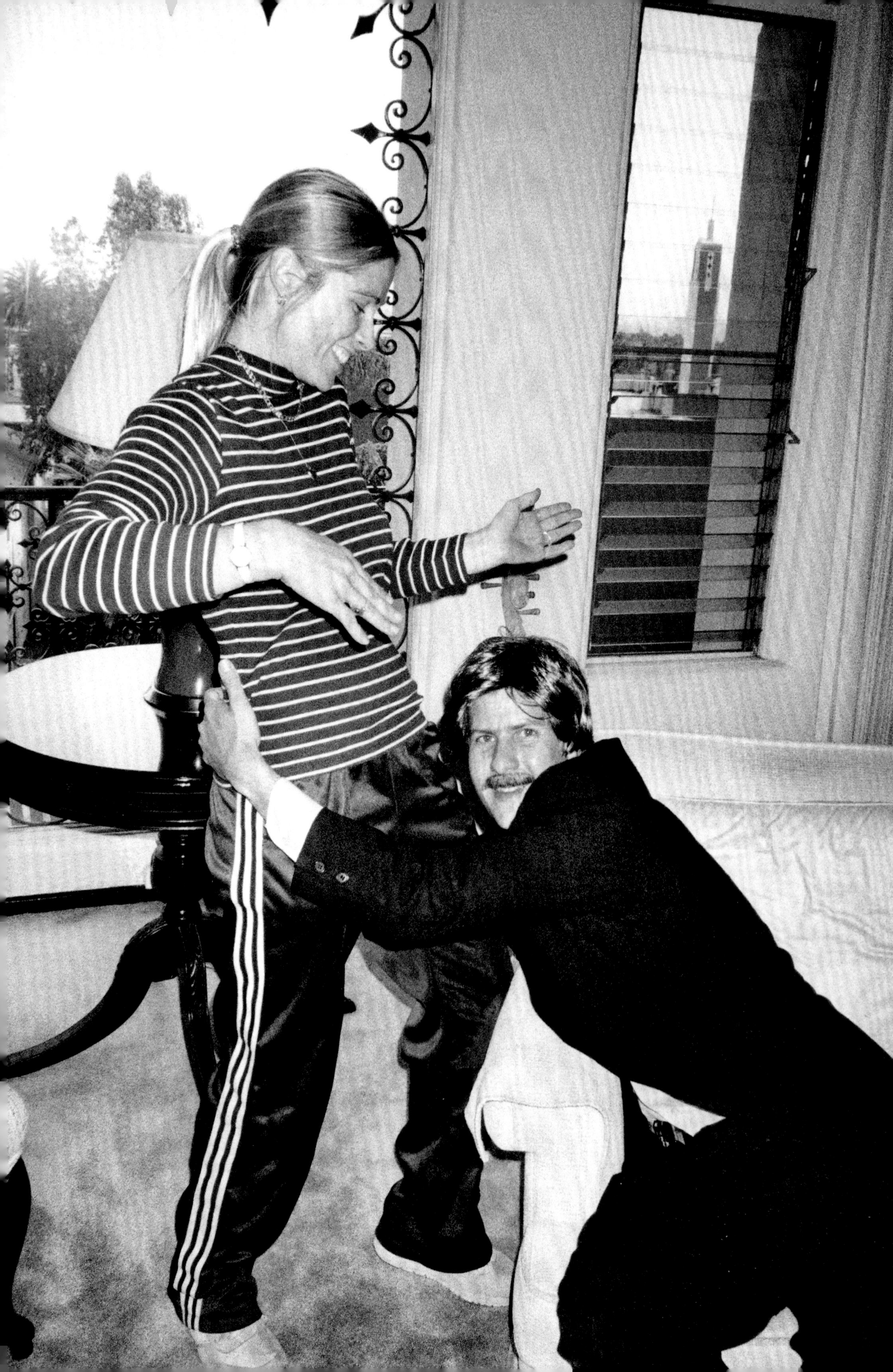

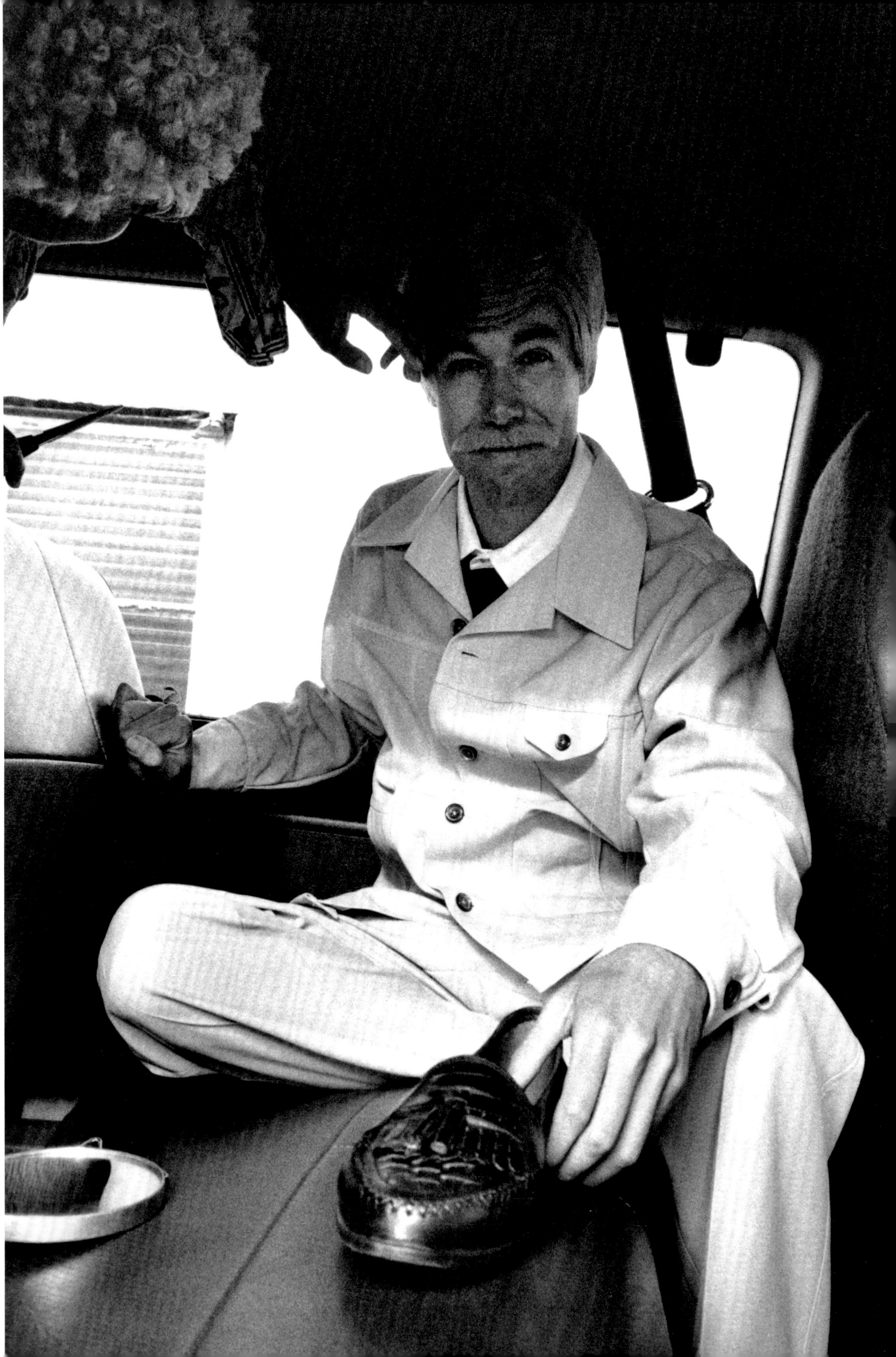

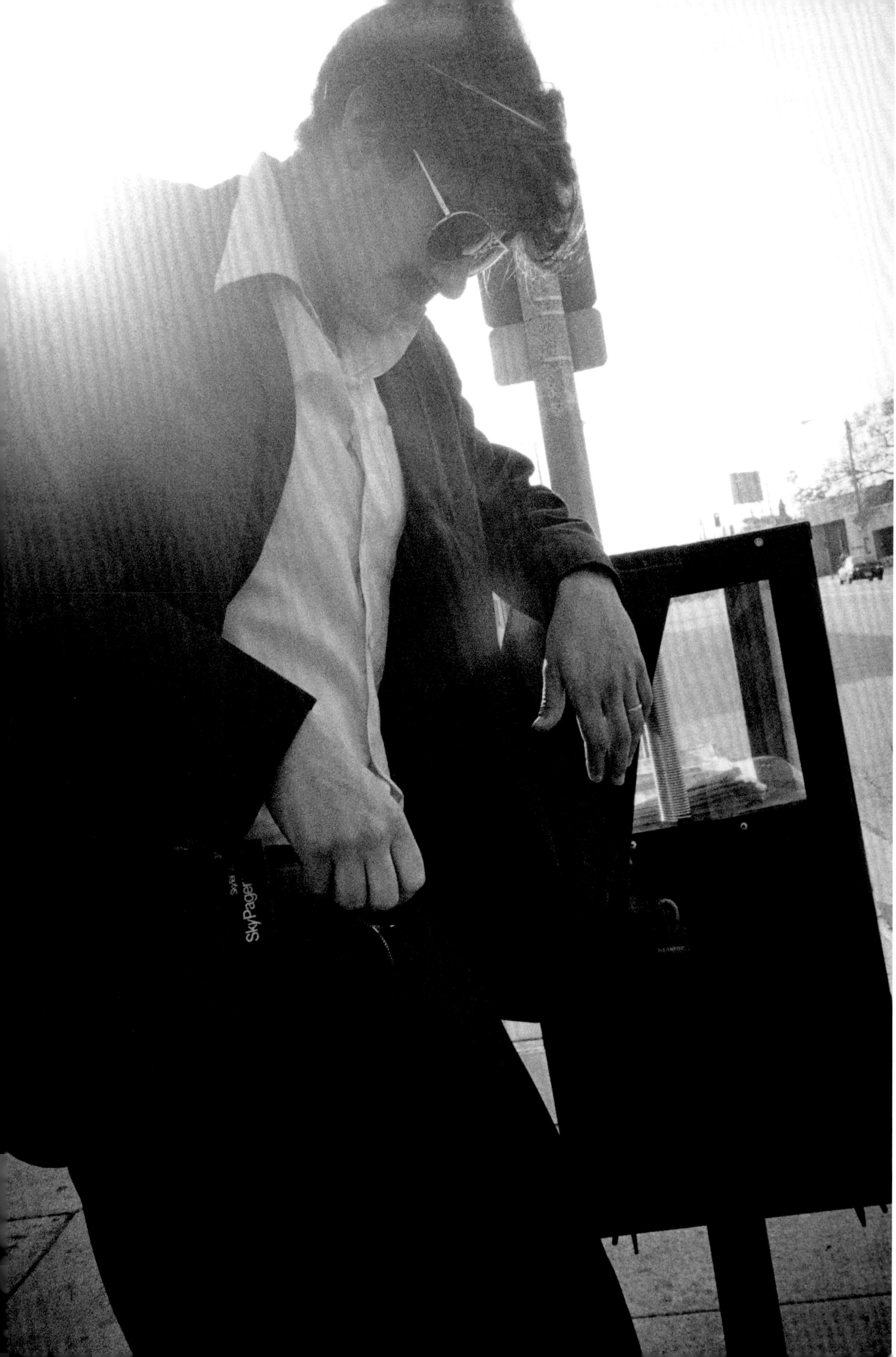
SkyPager

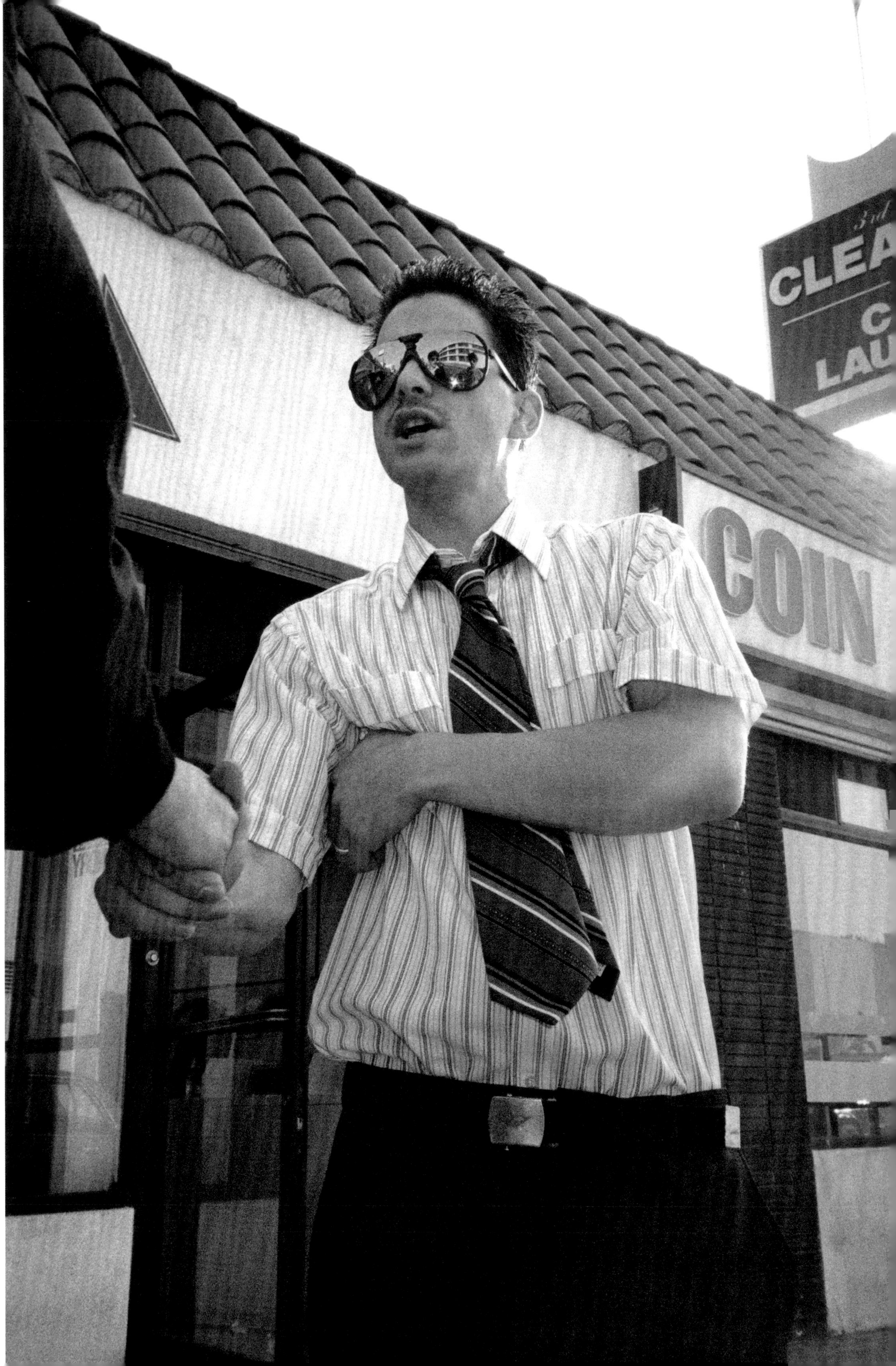
COIN

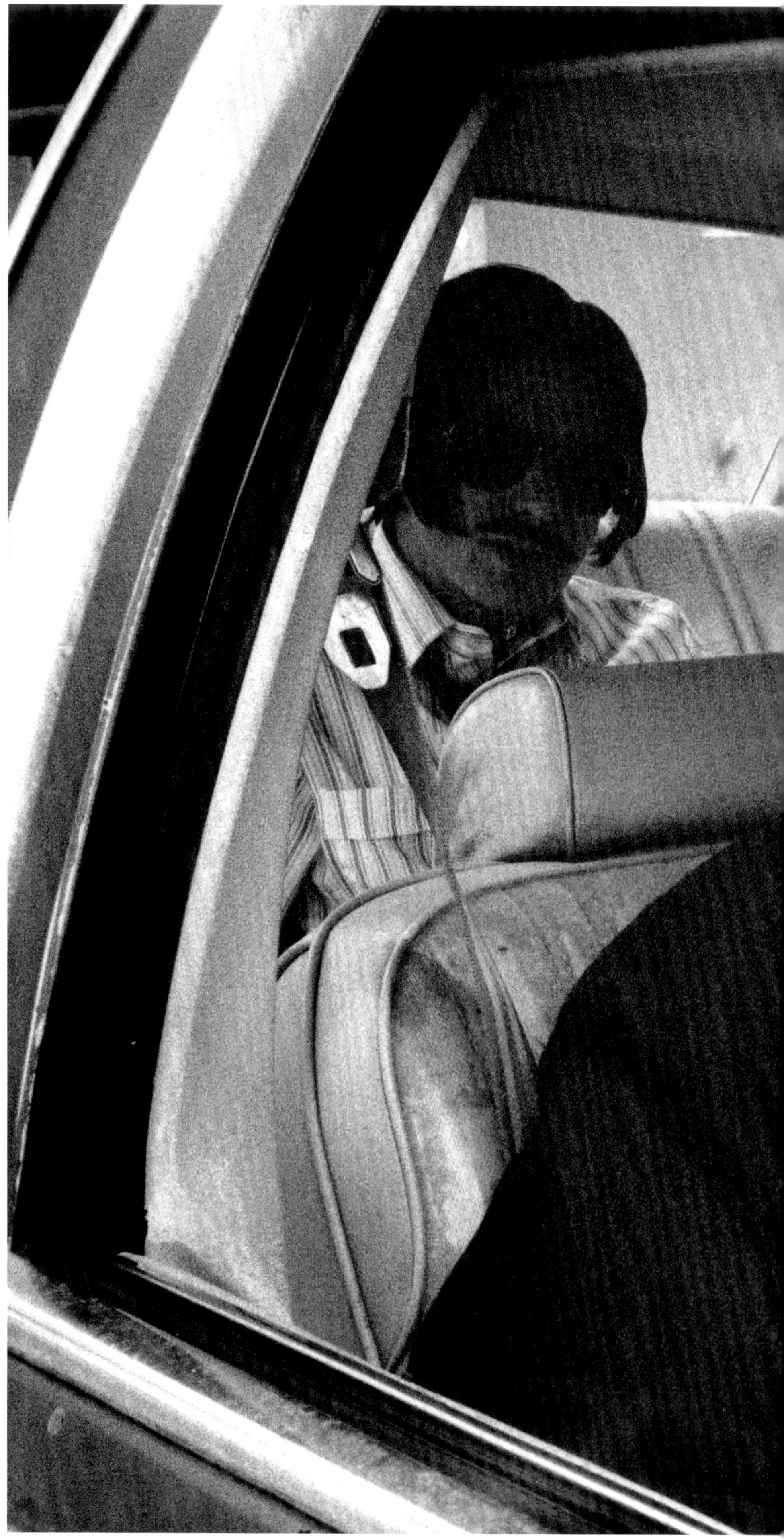

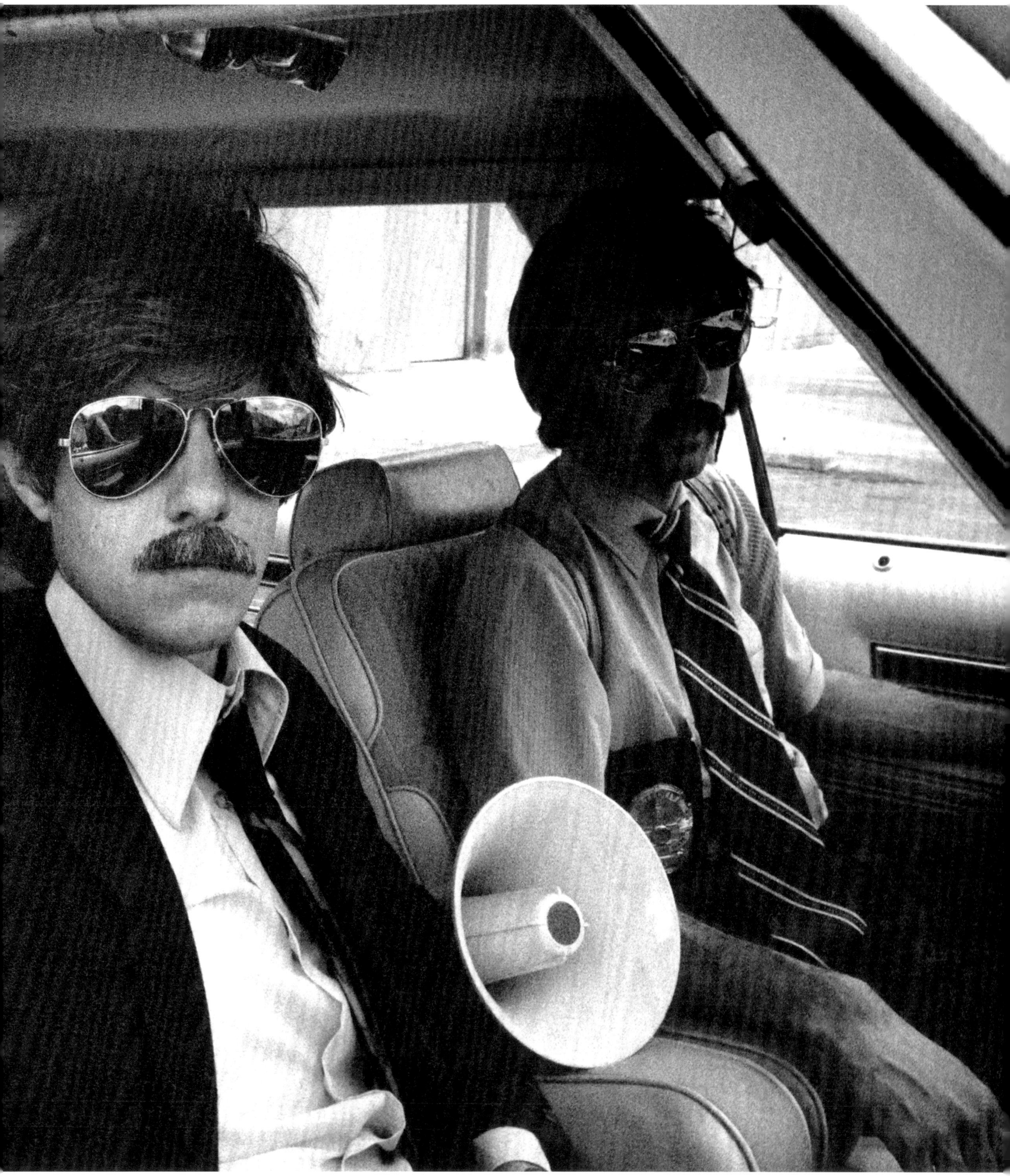

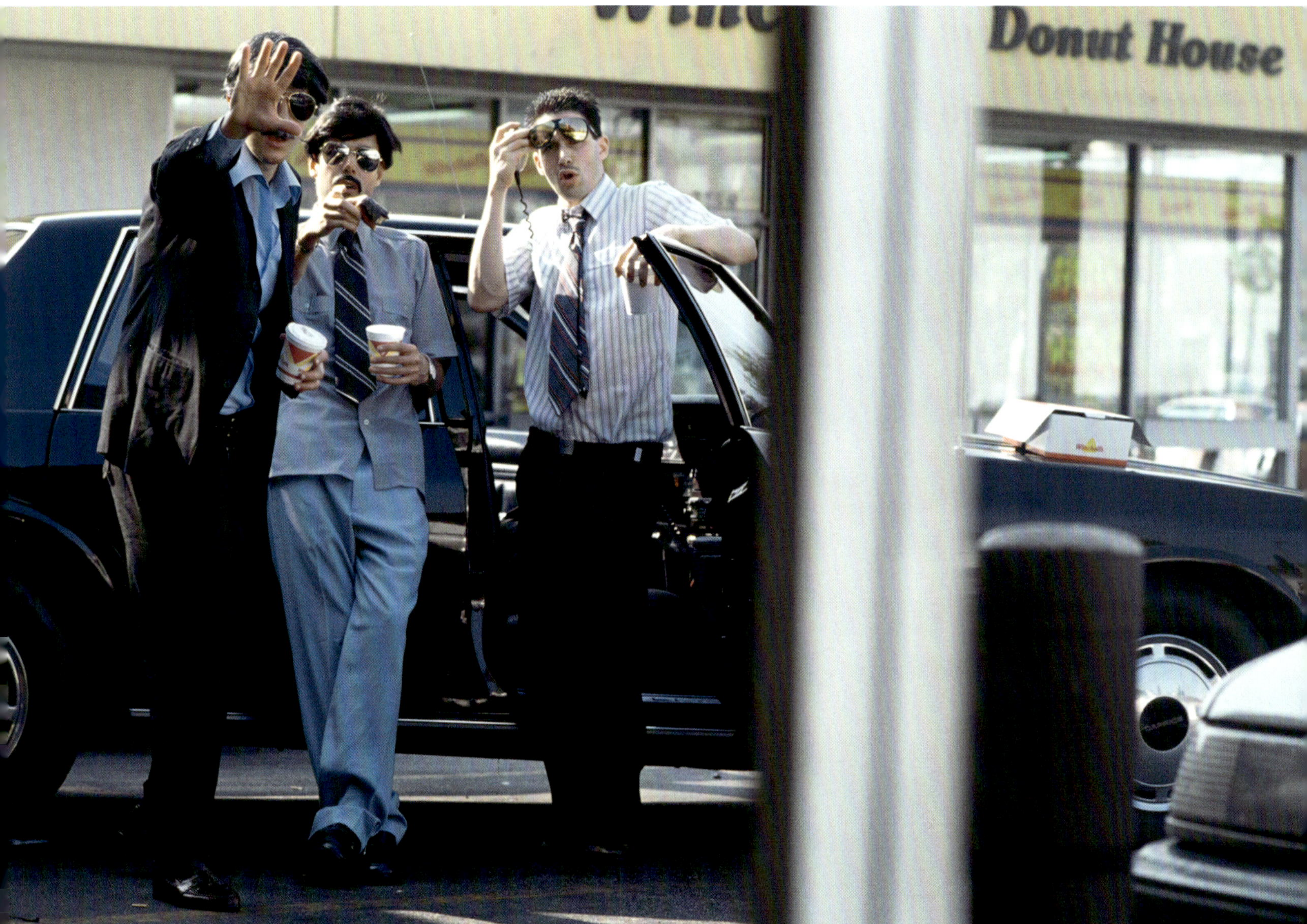
Donut House

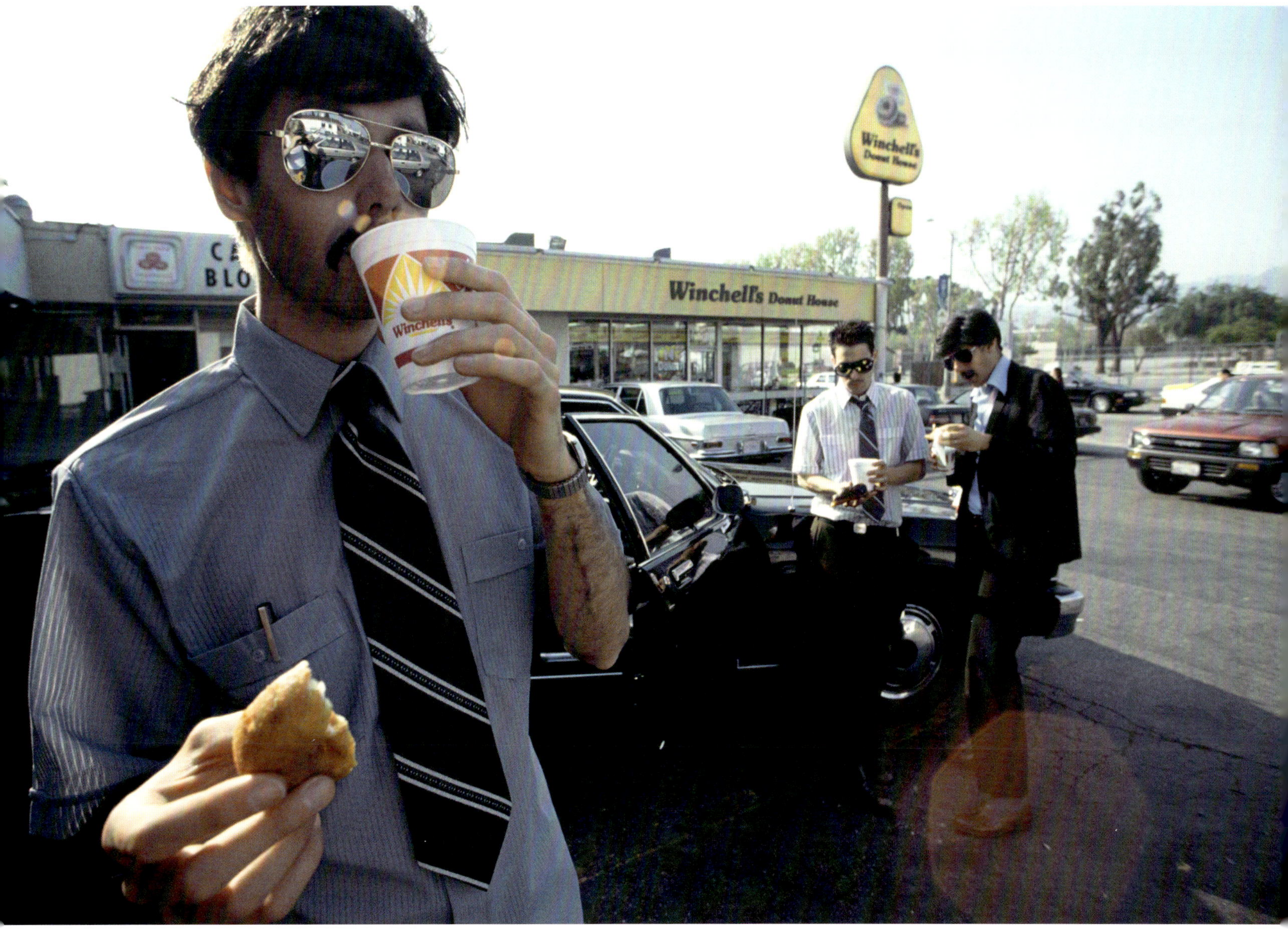
Winchell's
Donut House
Winchell's Donut House
Winchell's

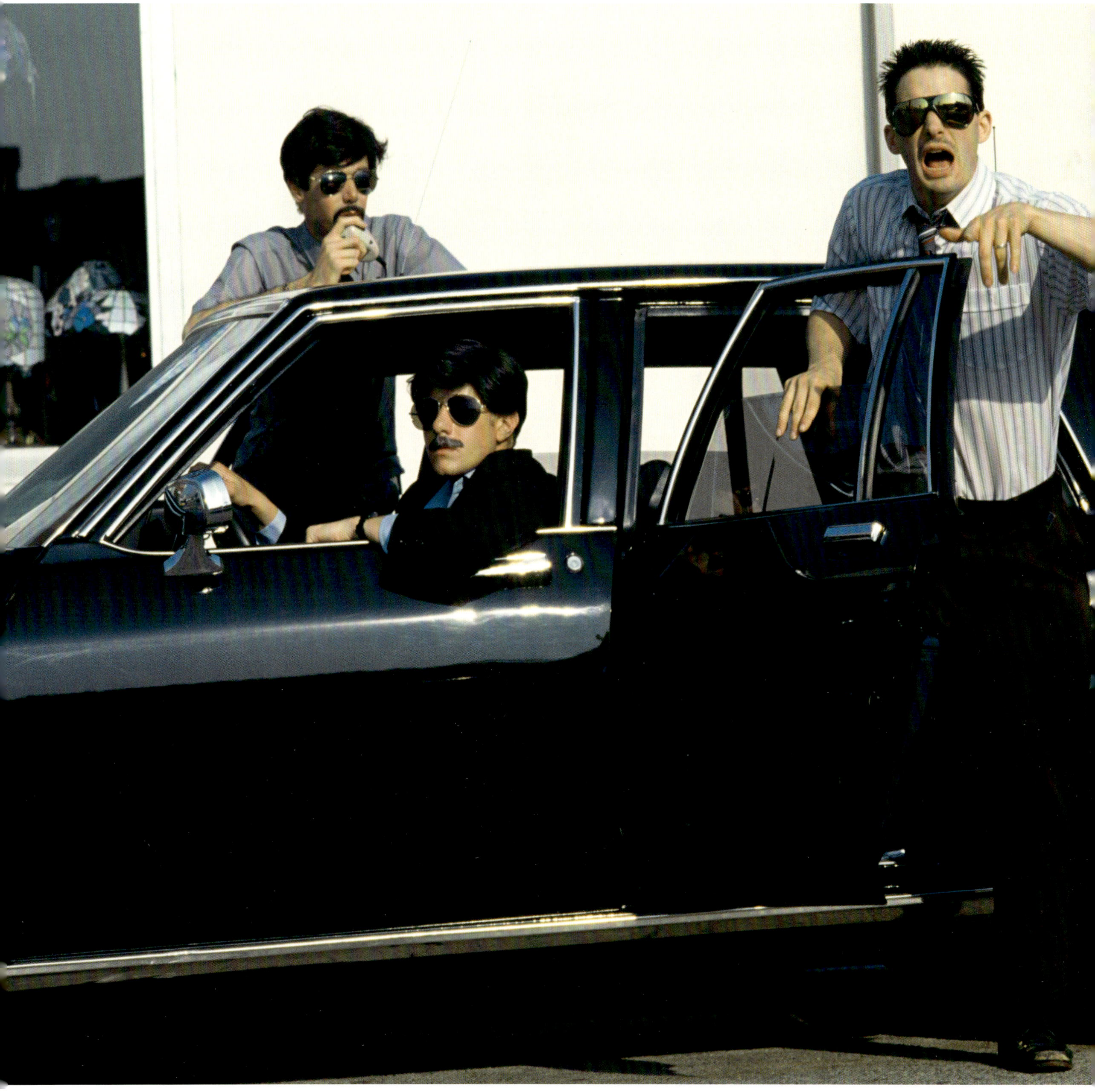

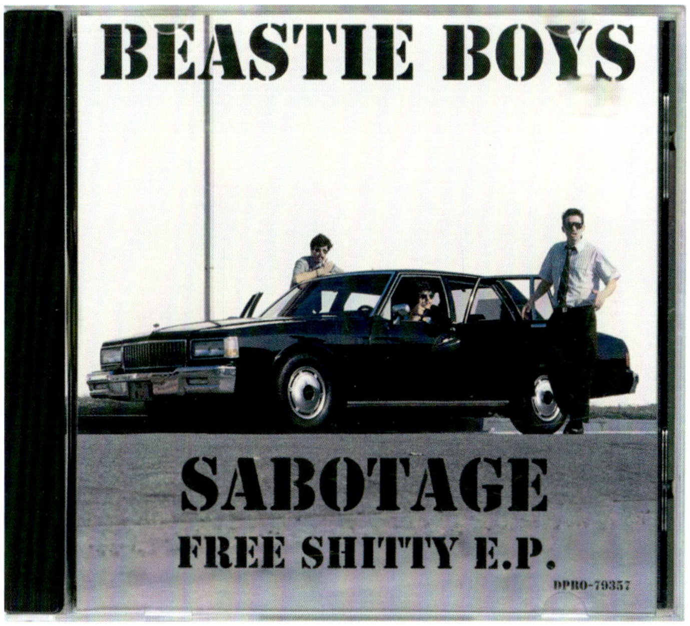
BEASTIE BOYS
SABOTAGE
FREE SHITTY E.P.
DPRO-79357

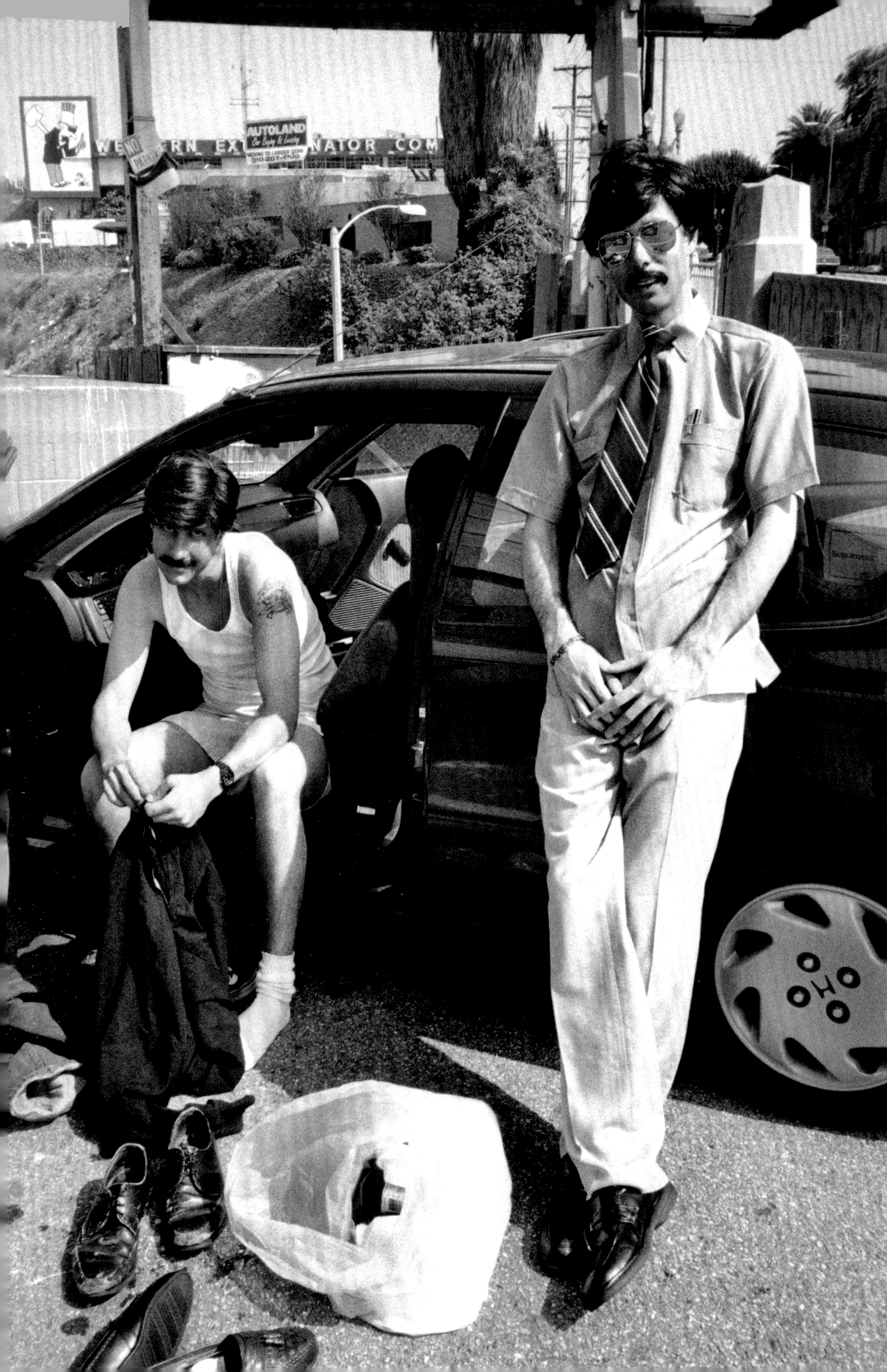
AUTOLAND

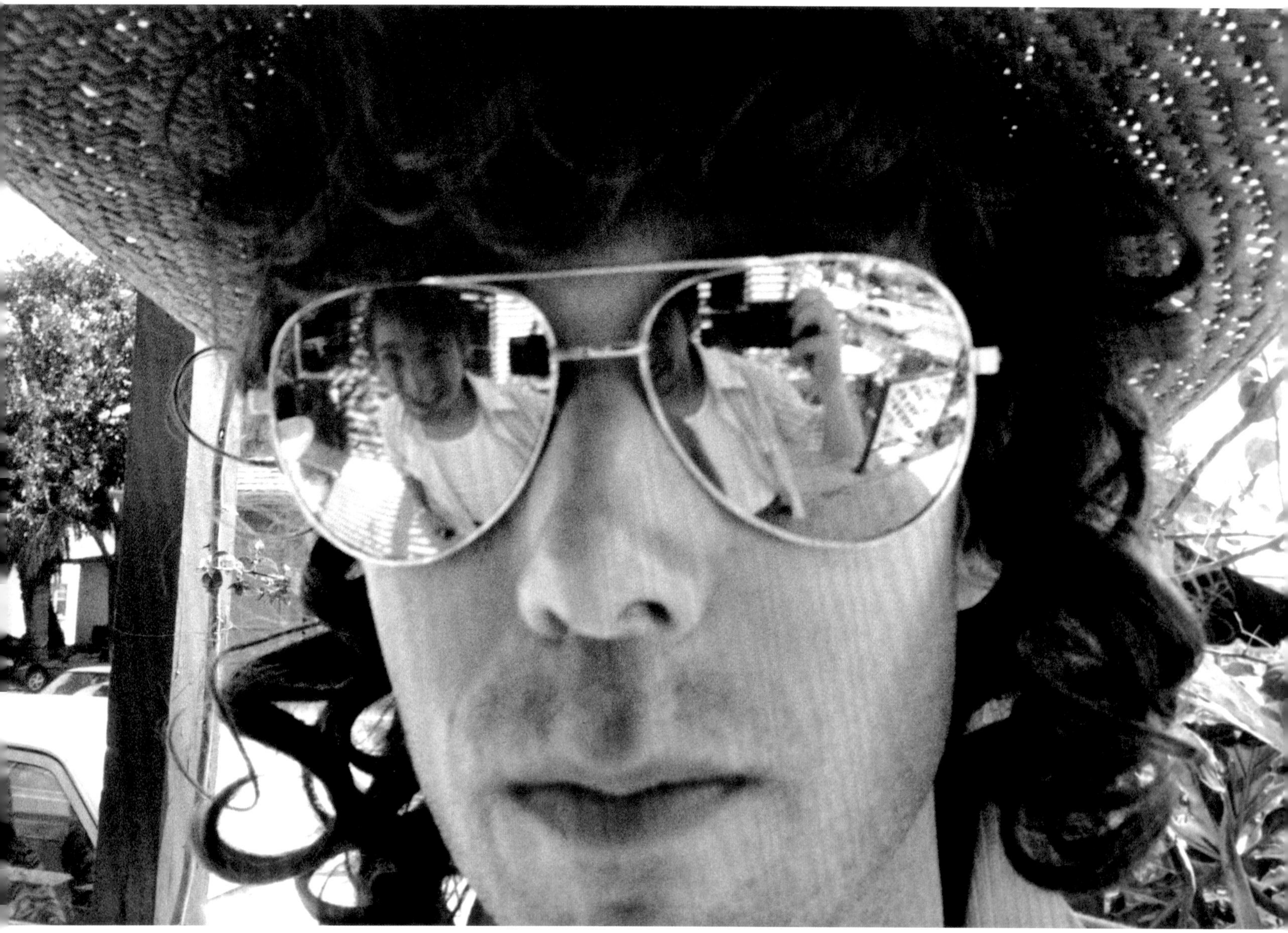

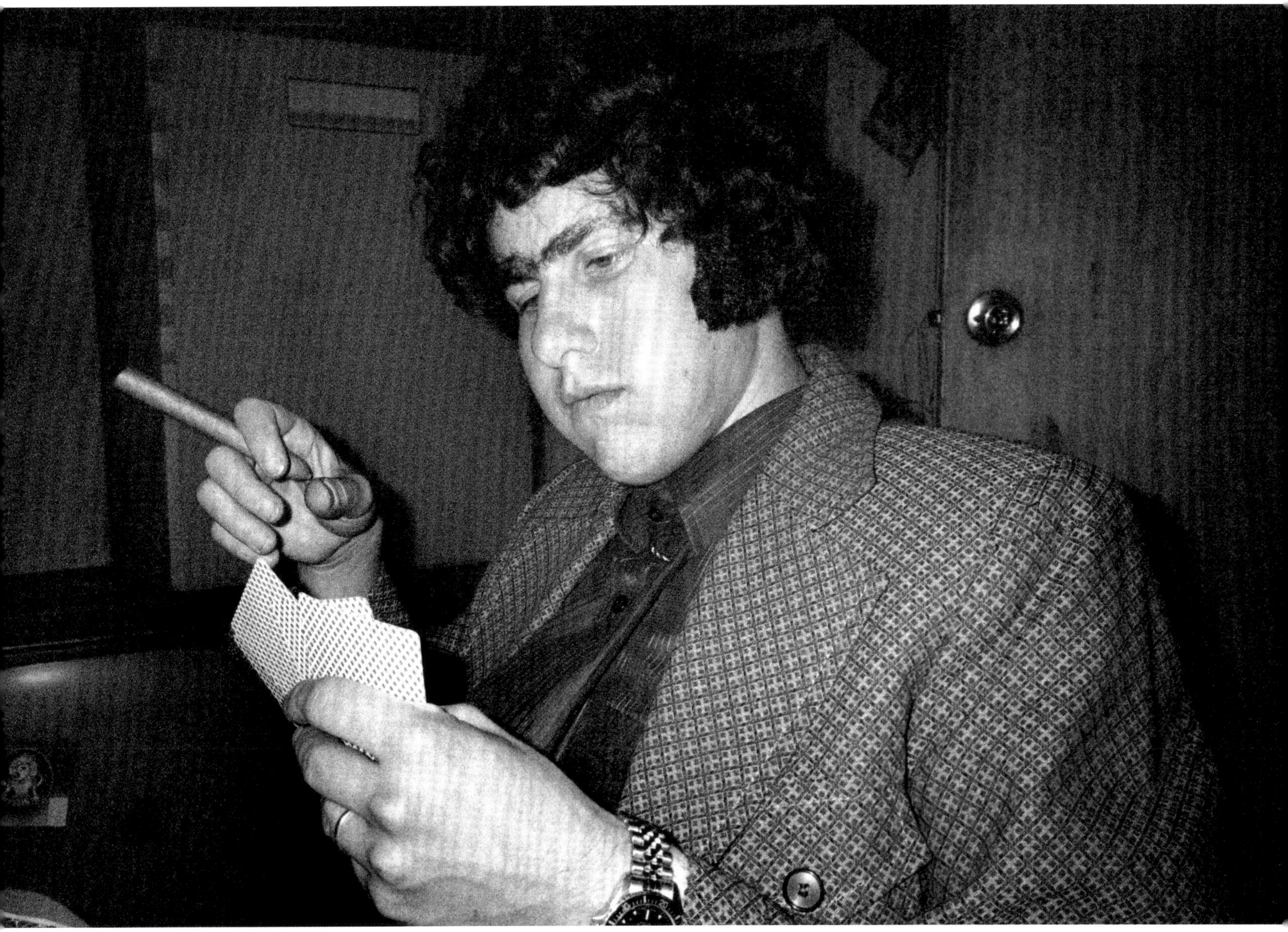

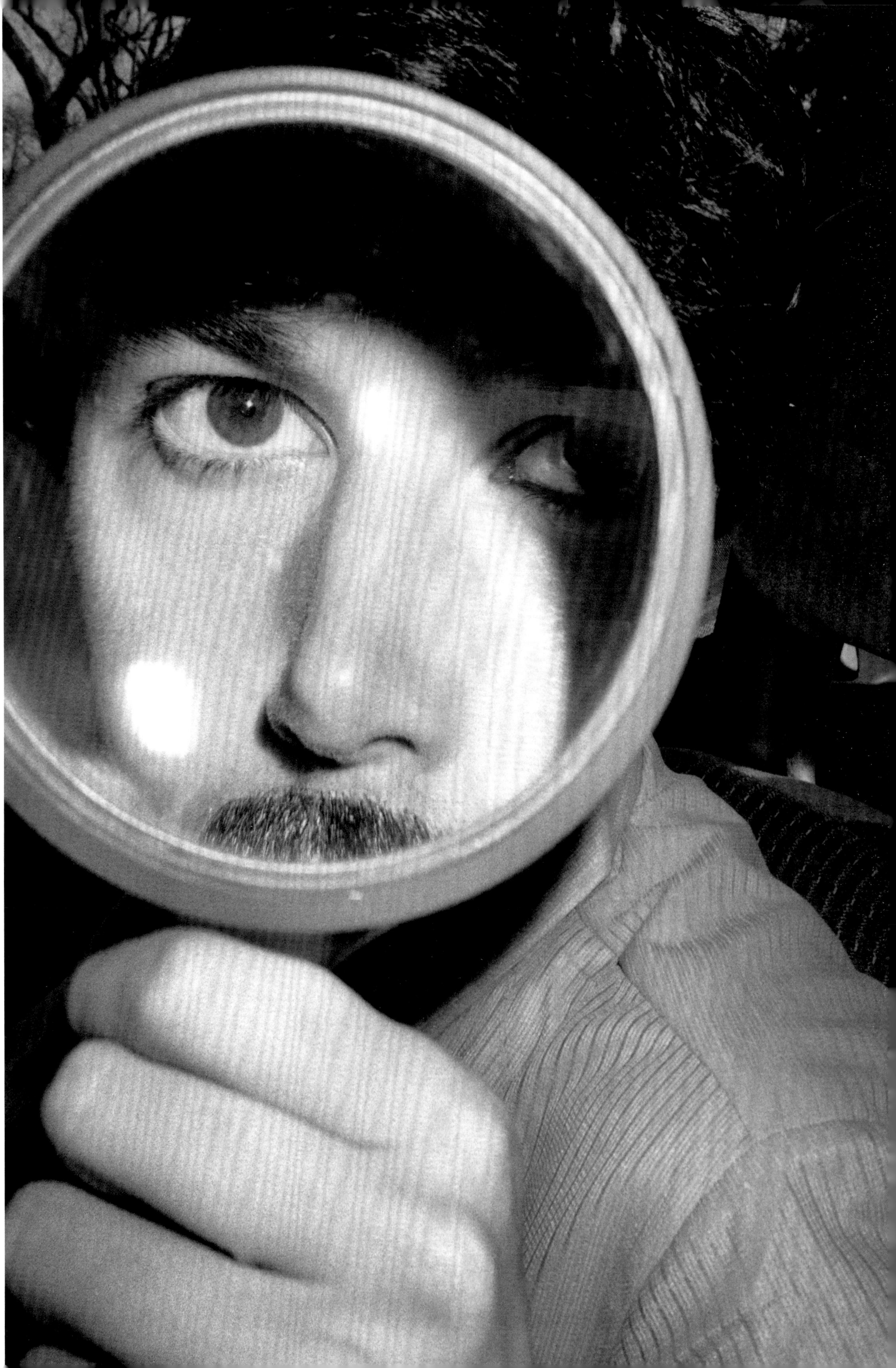

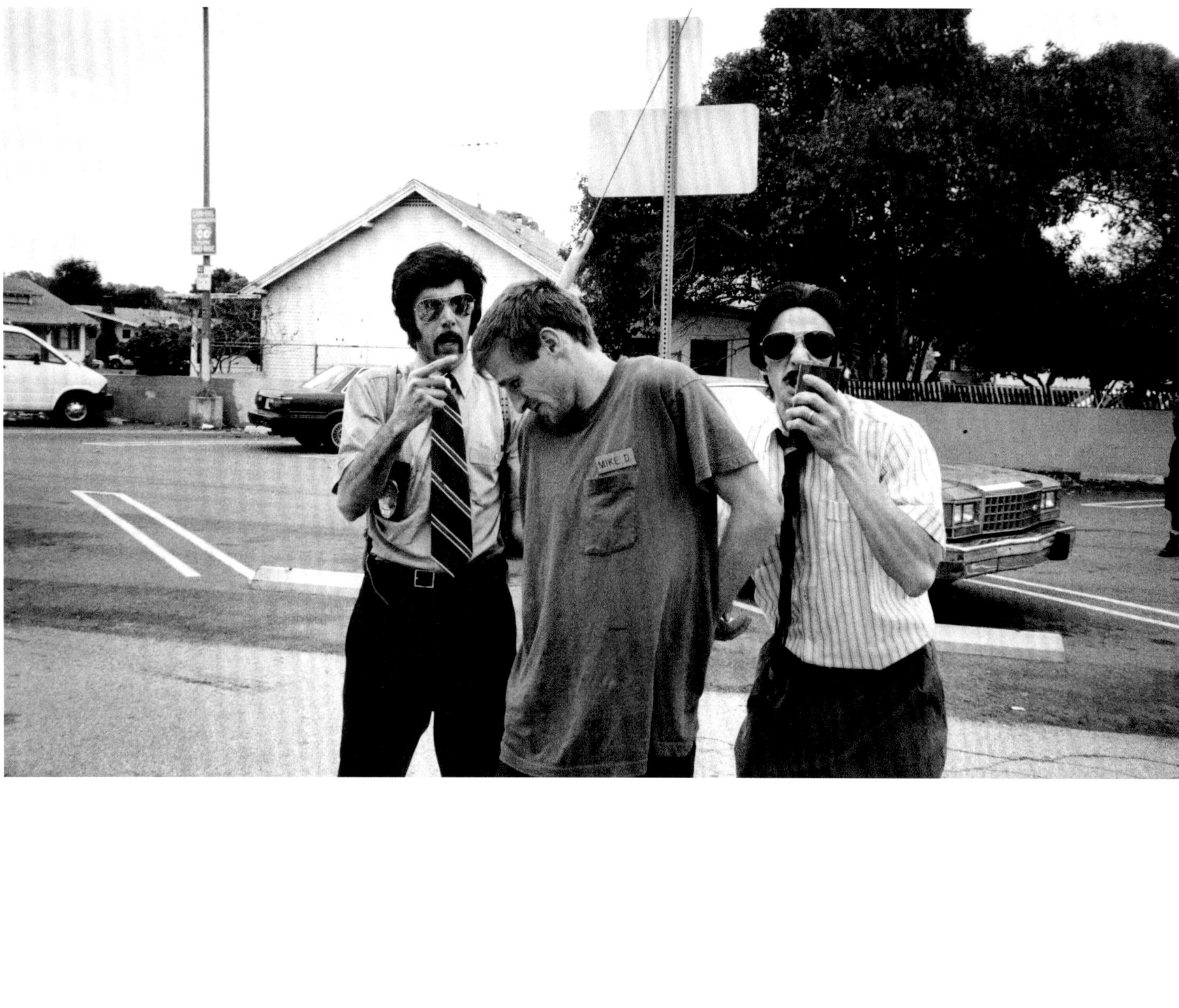
MIKE D.

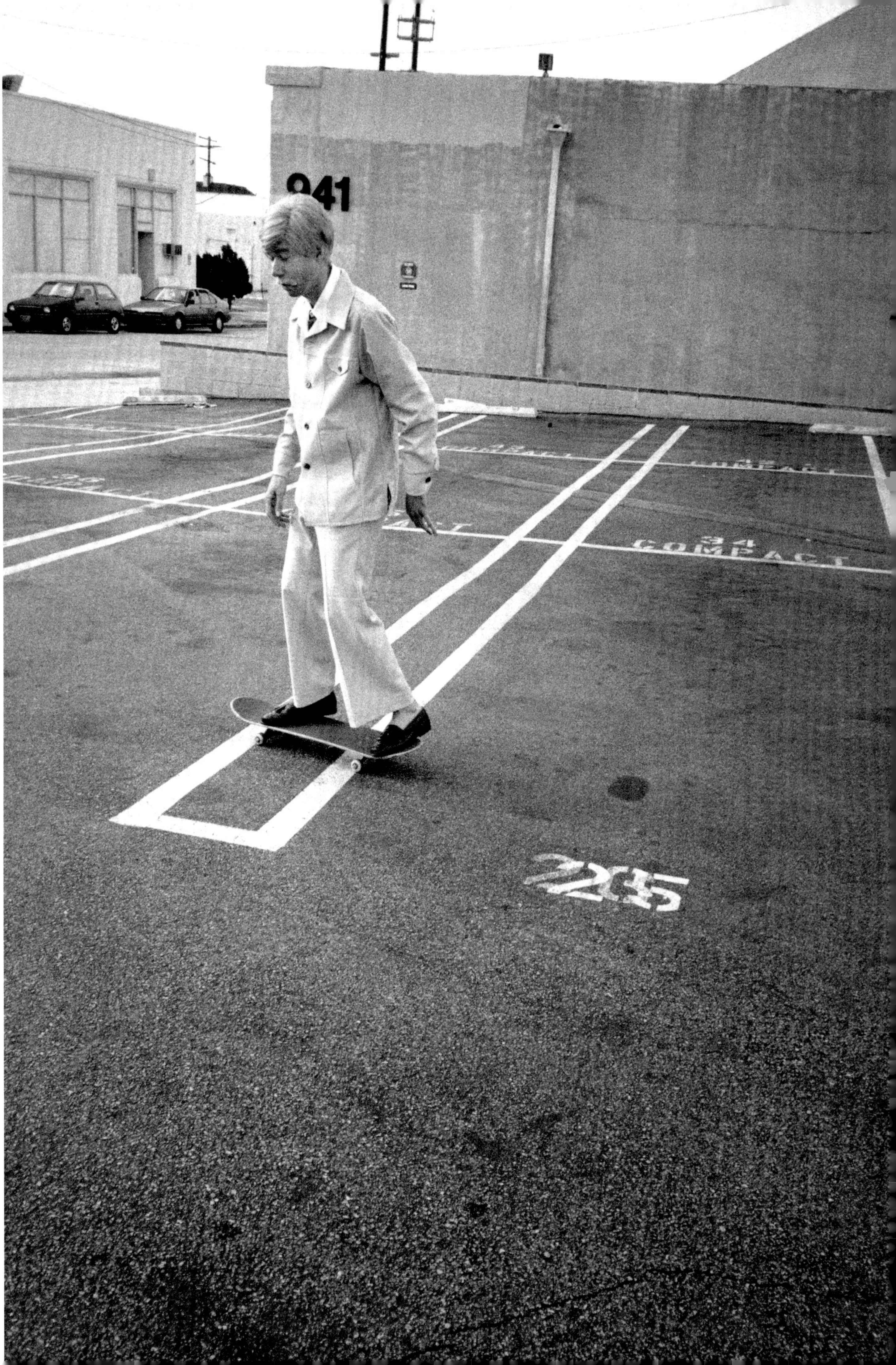
941
34
COMPACT

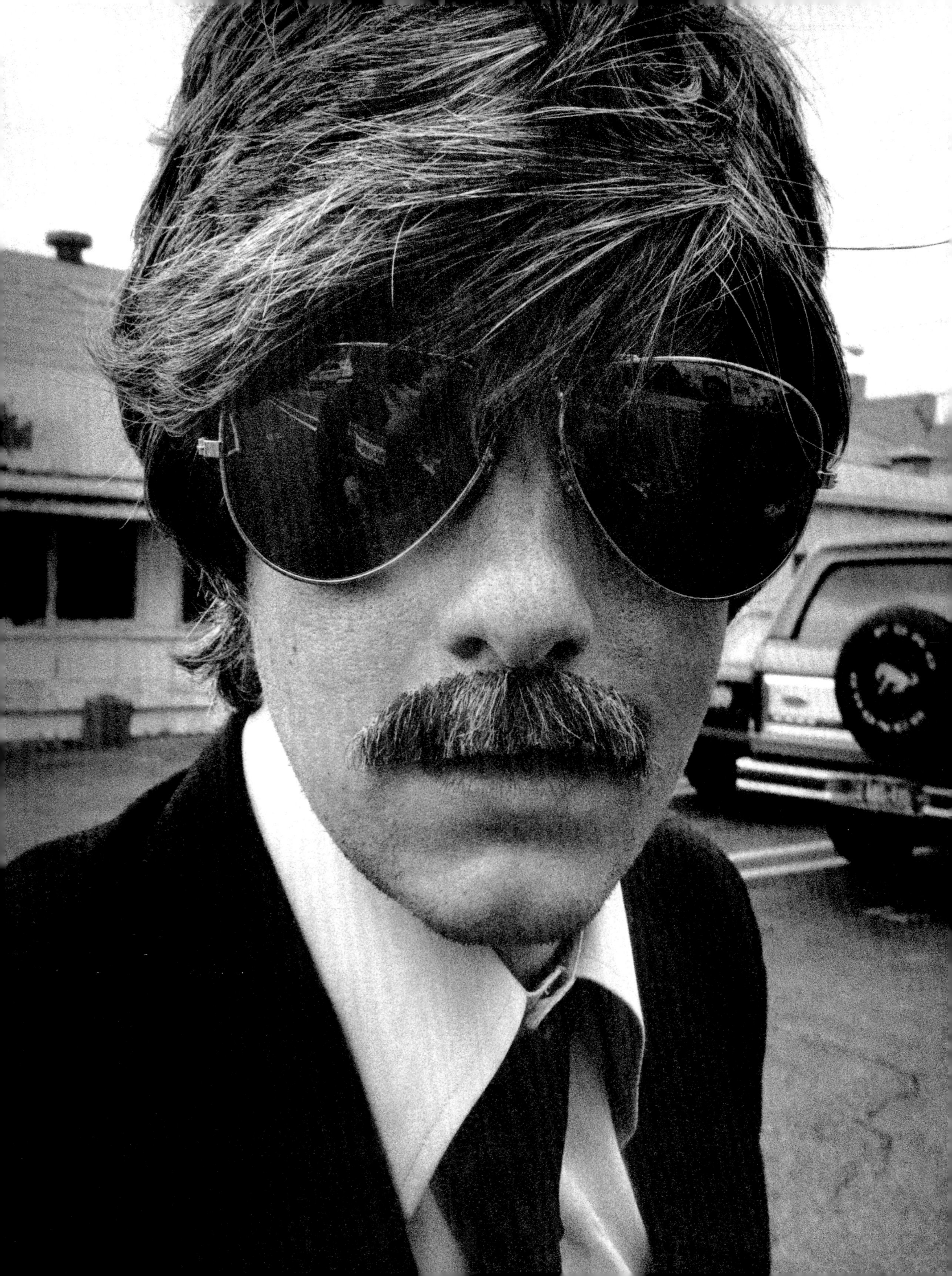

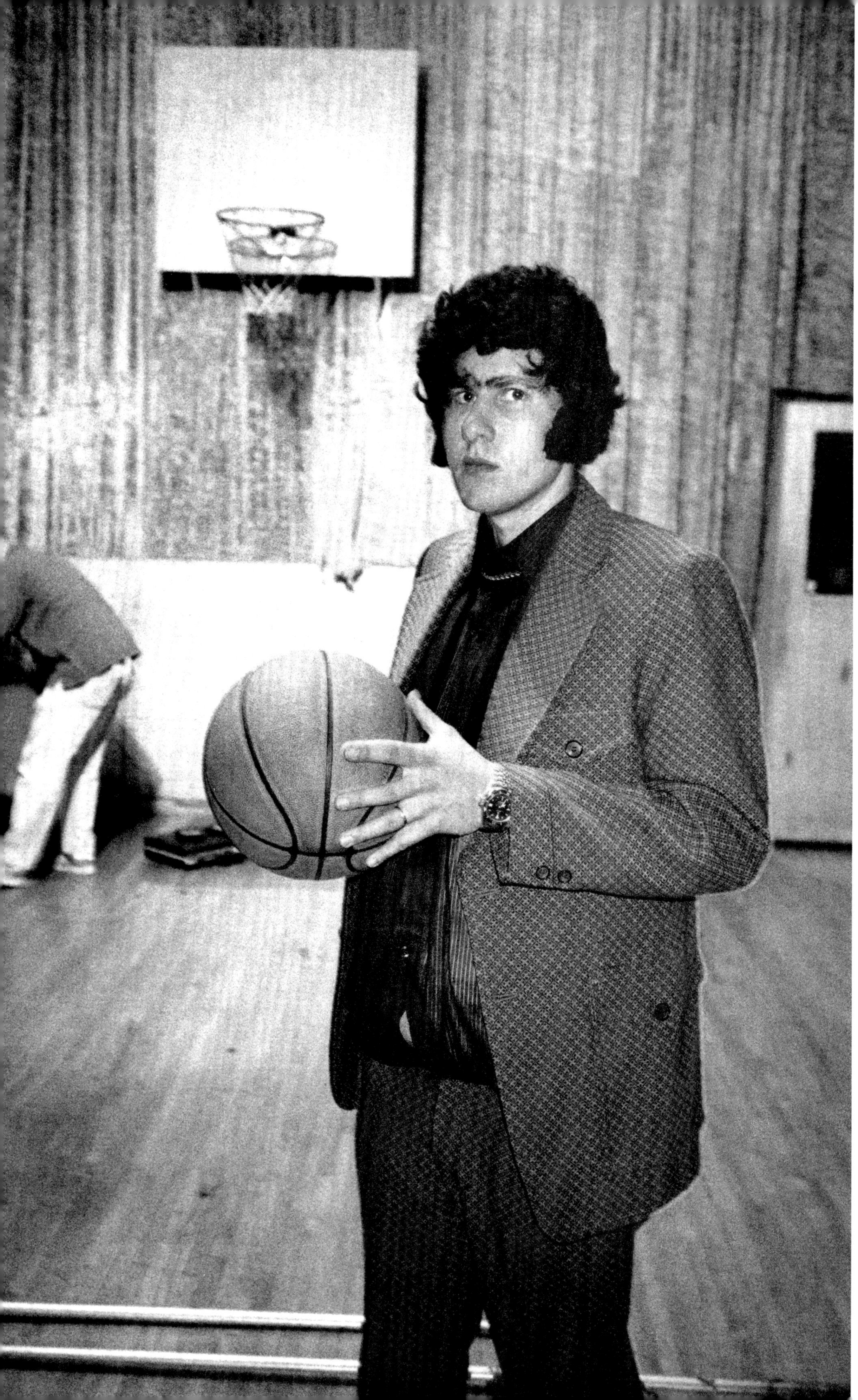

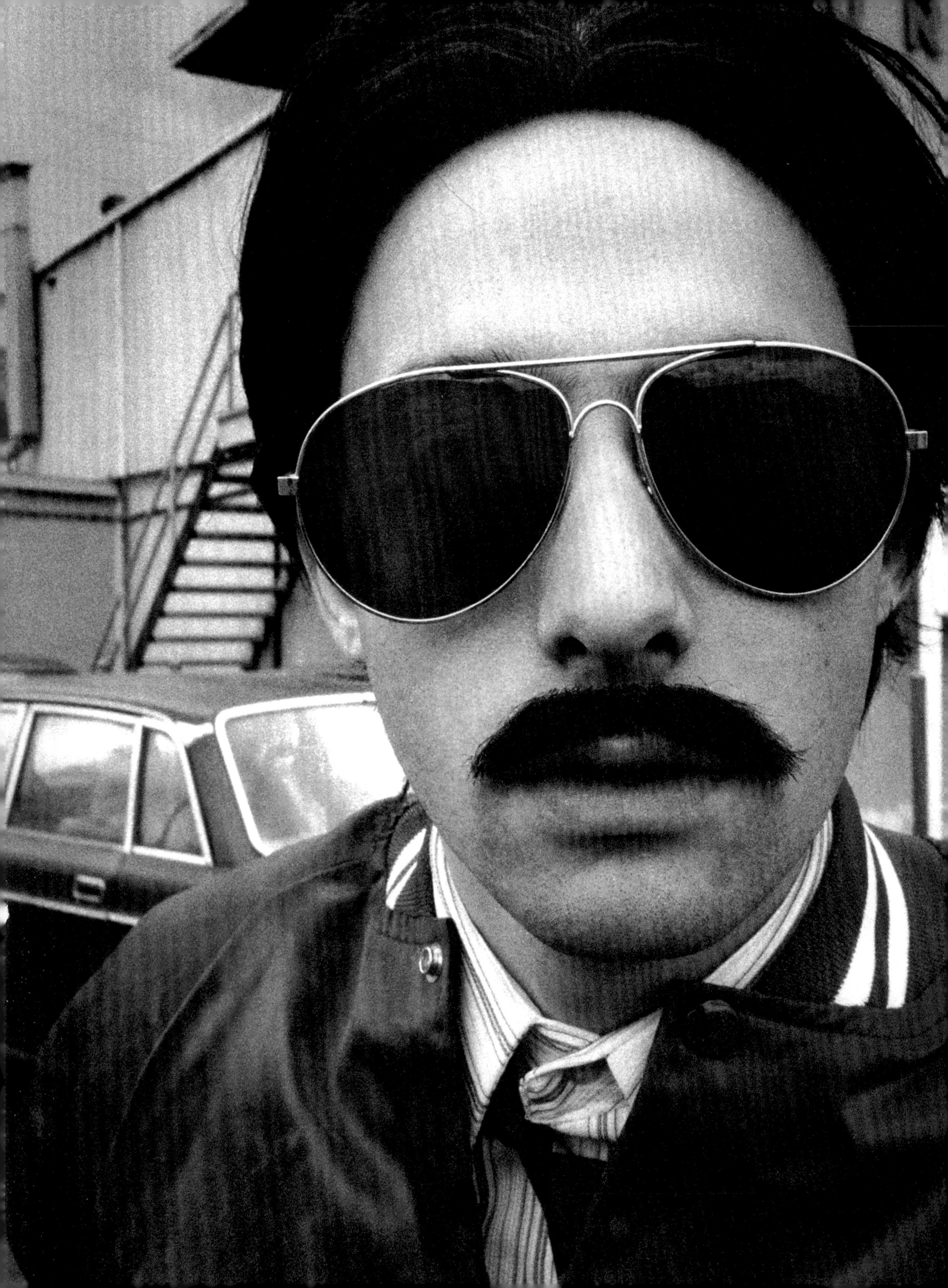

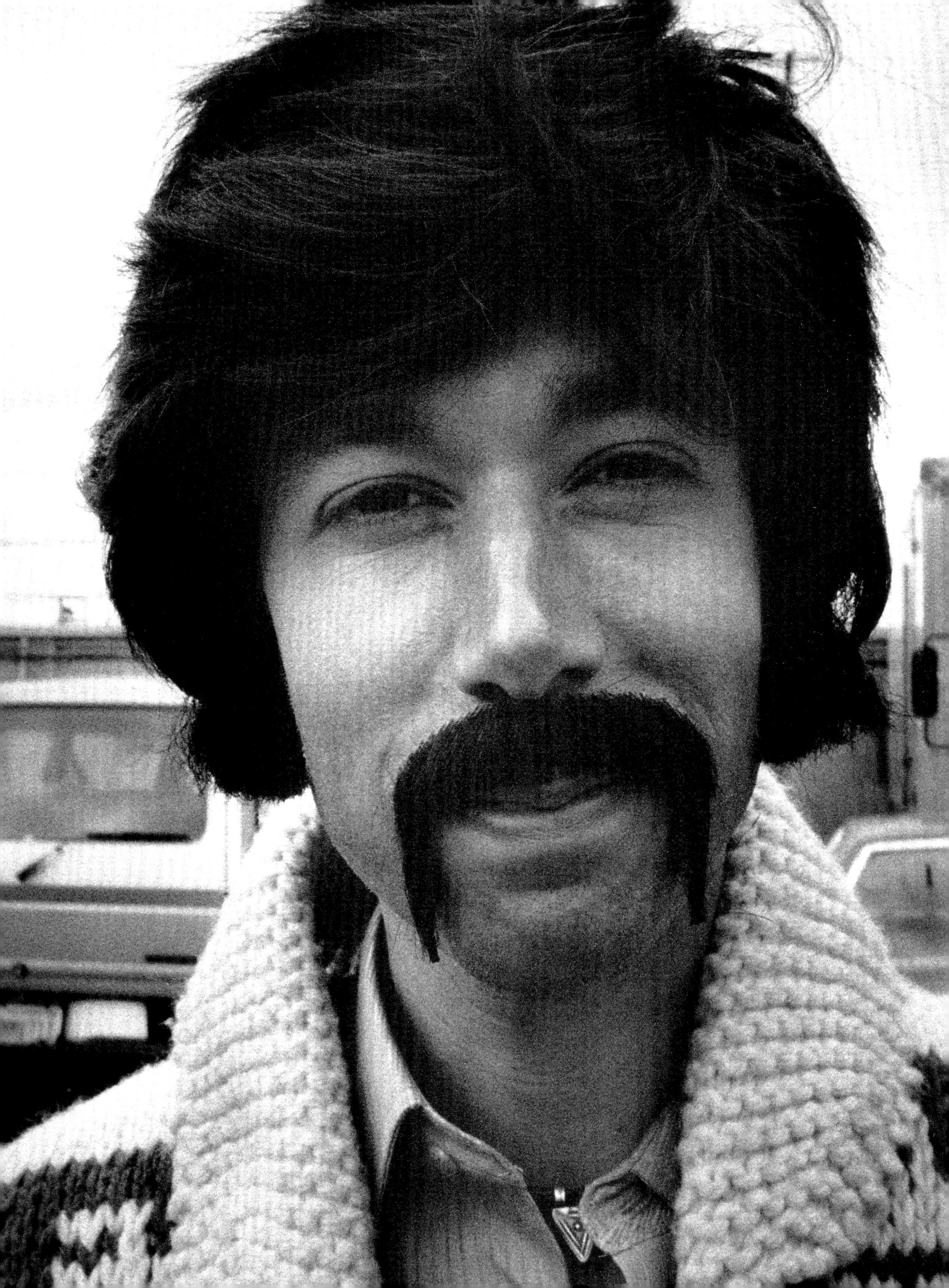

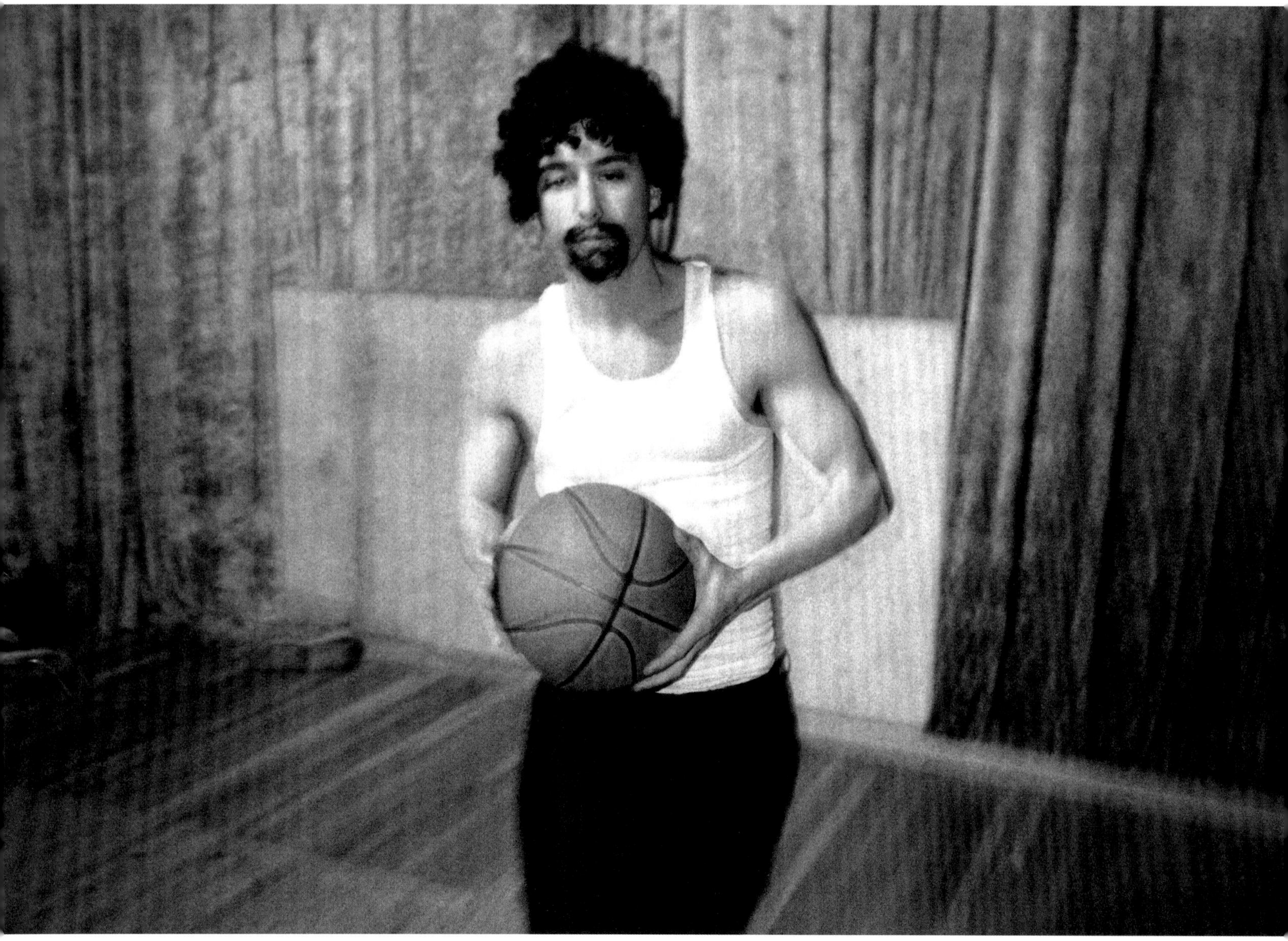

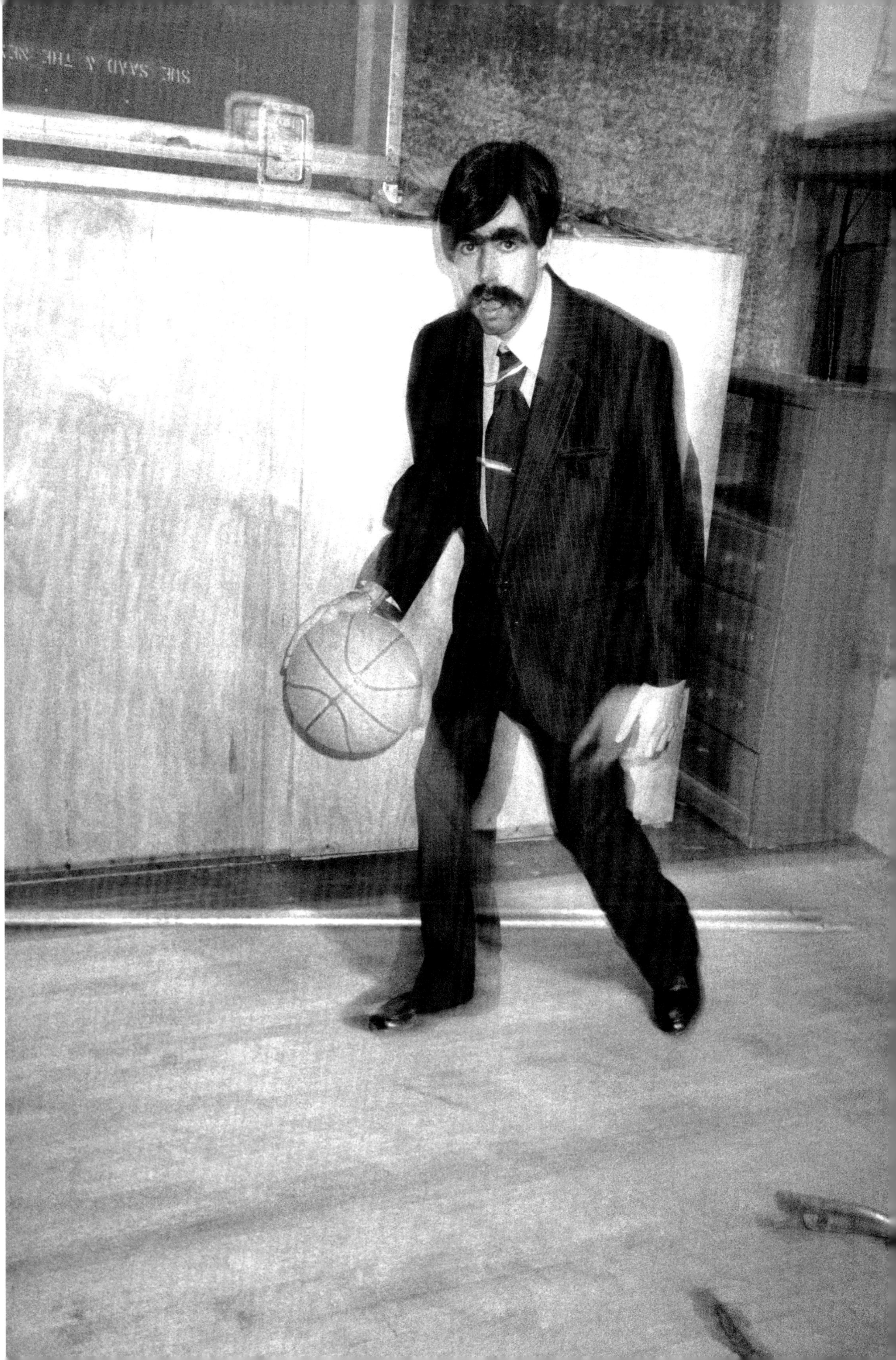

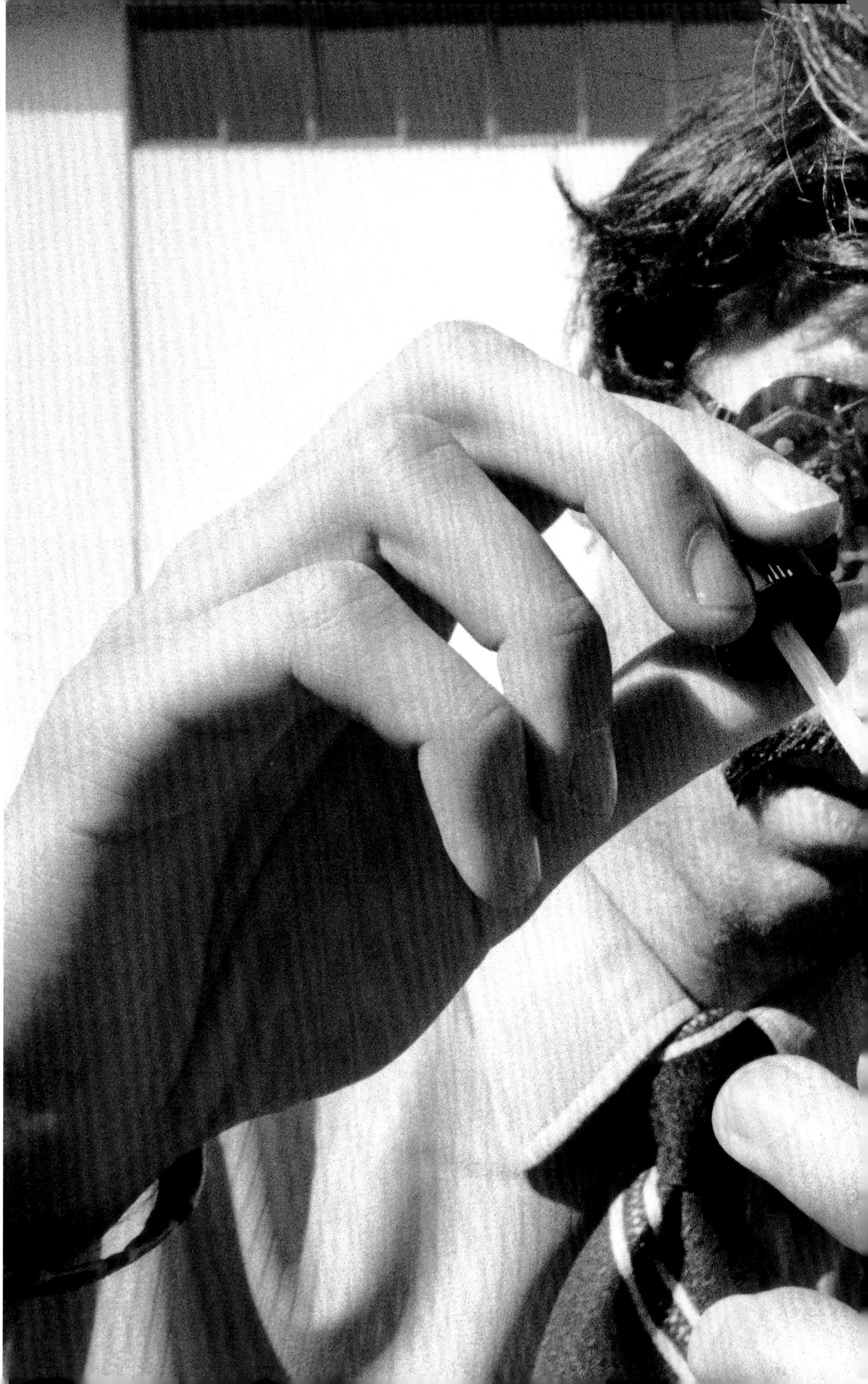

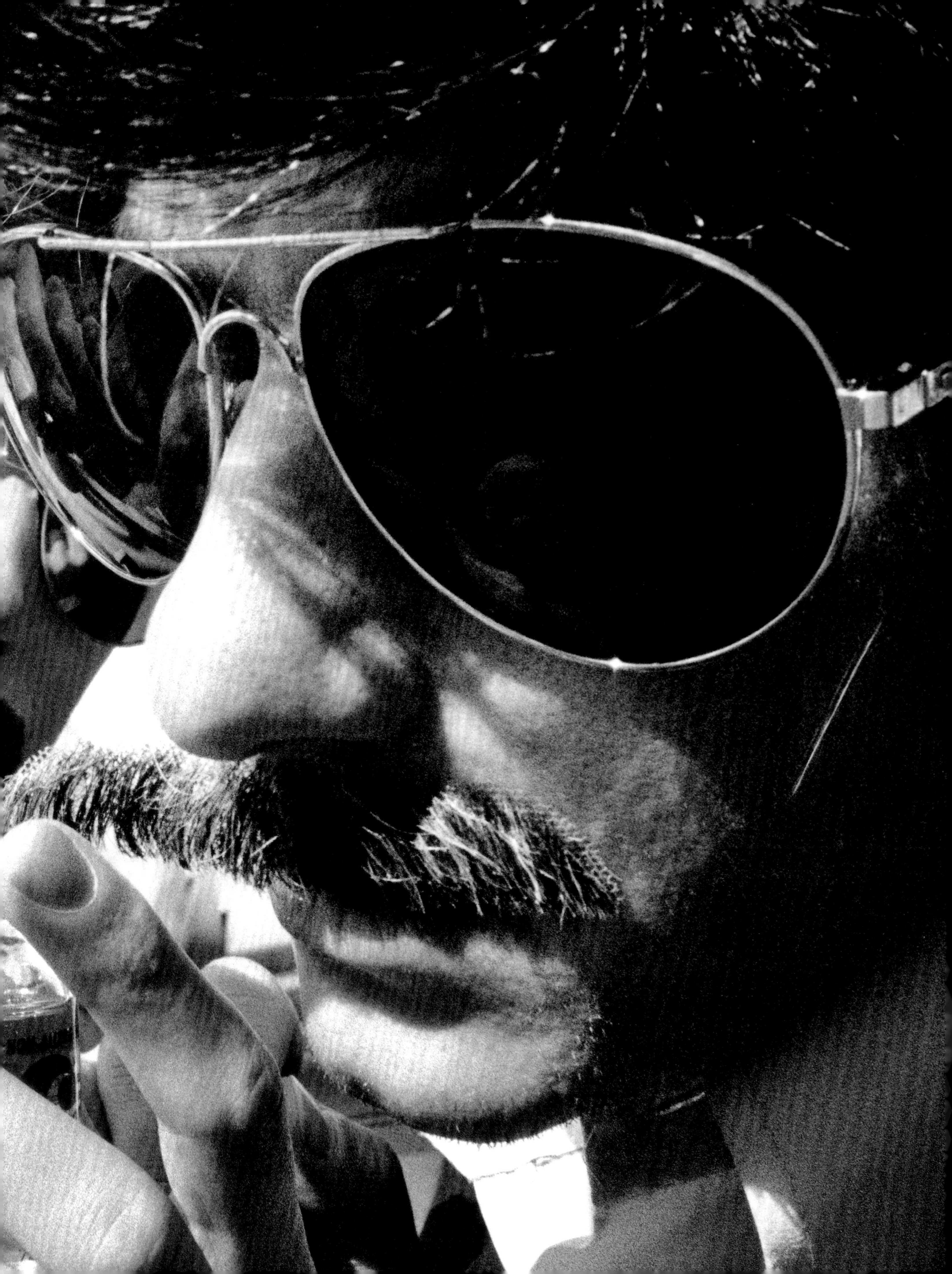

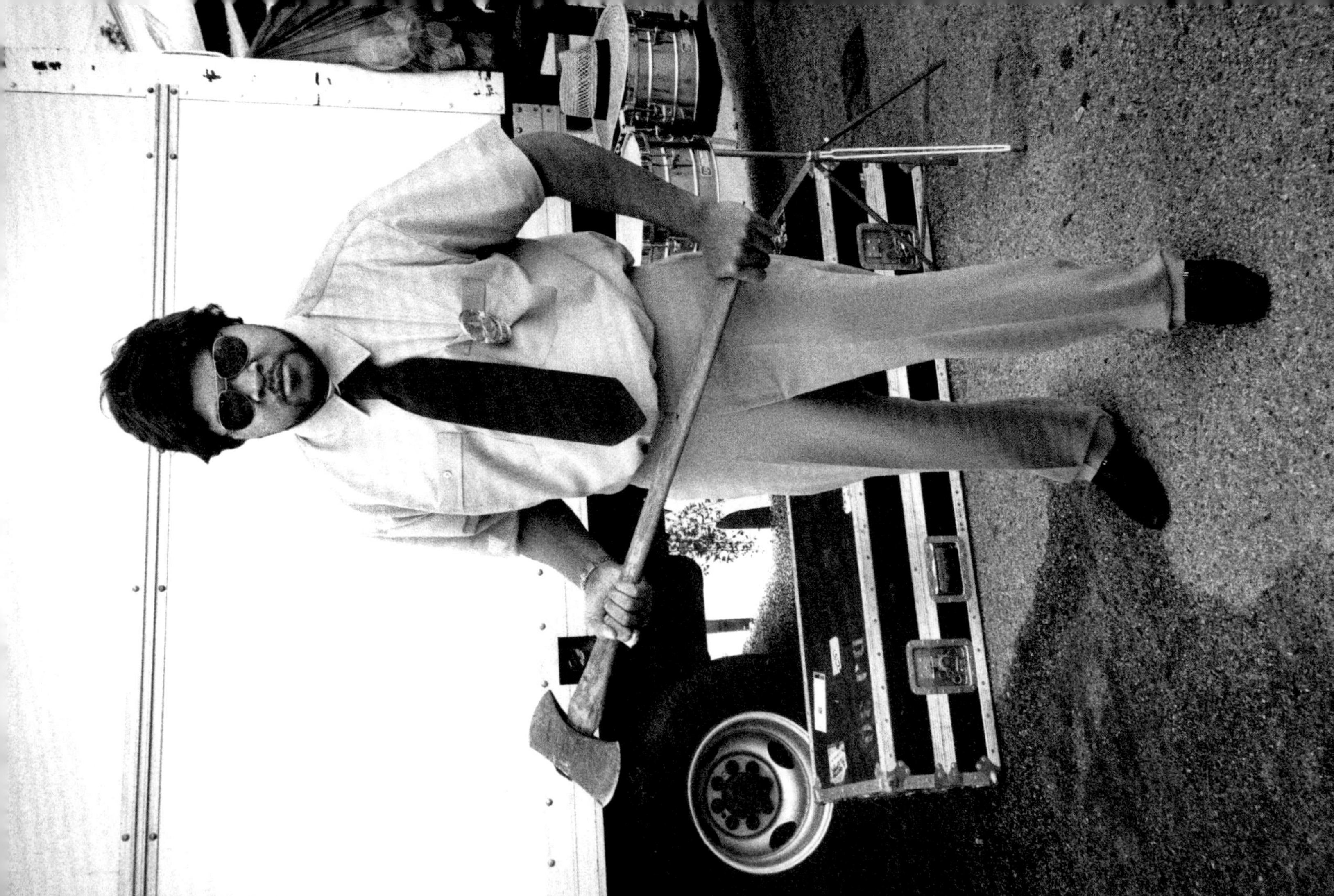

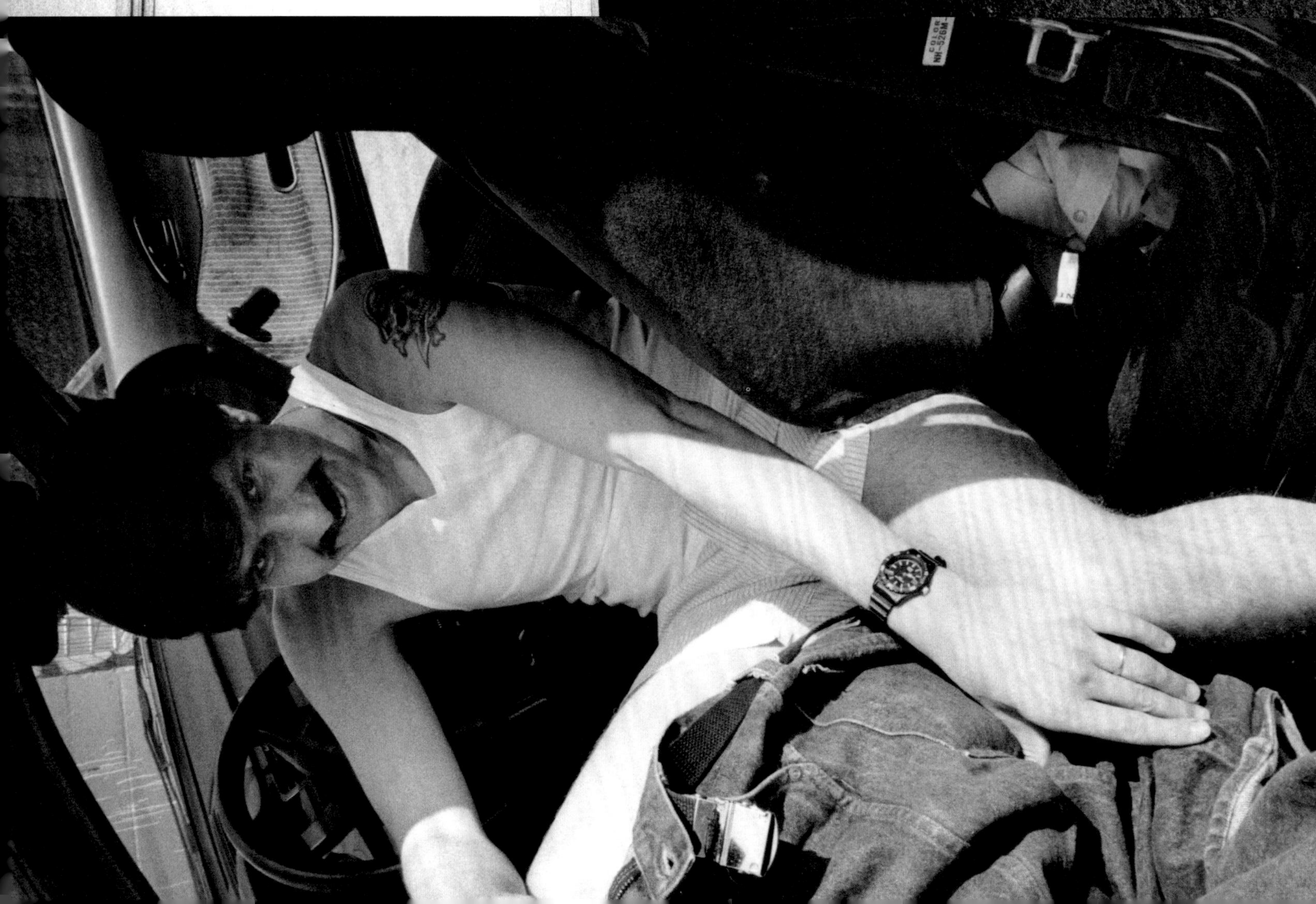

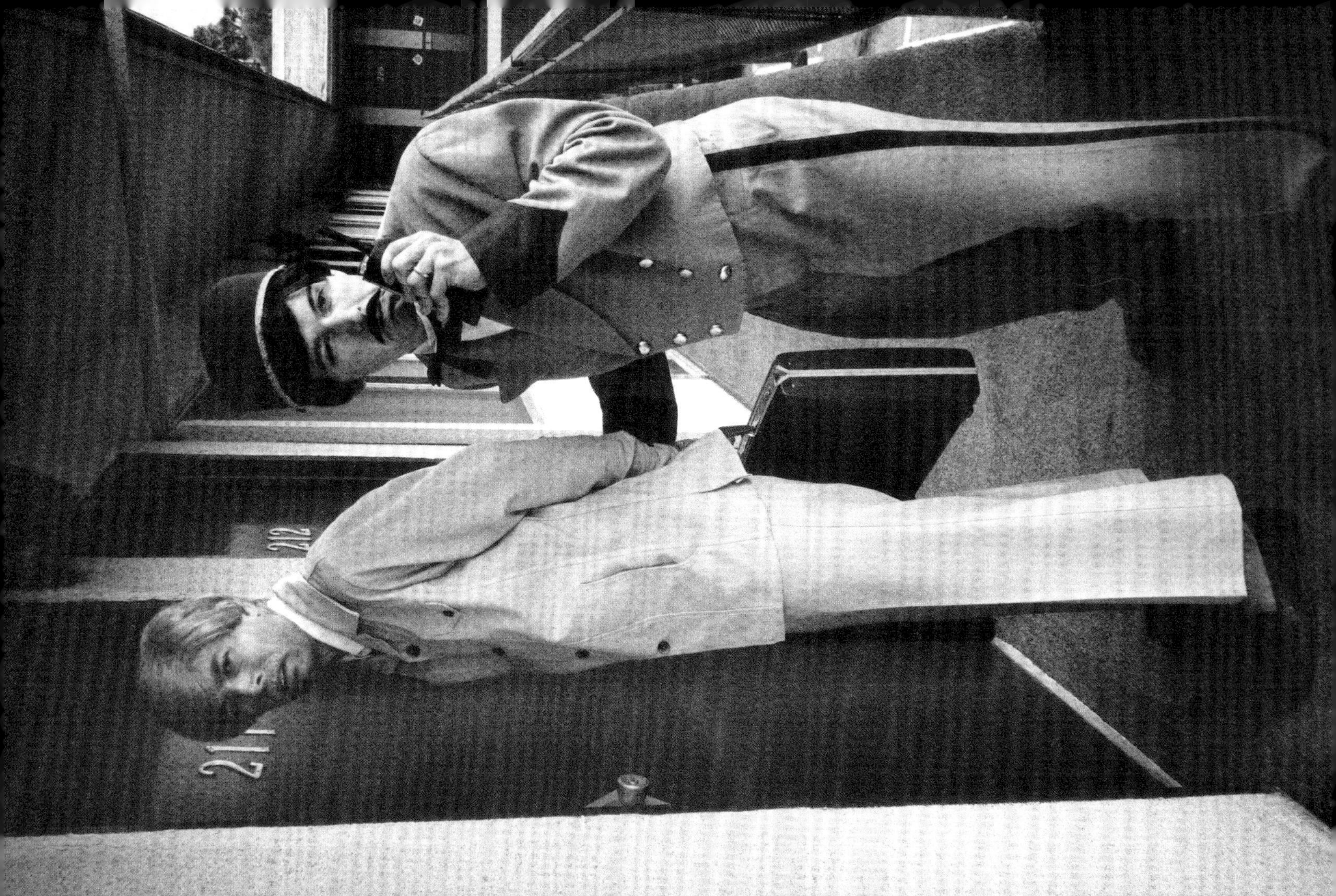
211
212

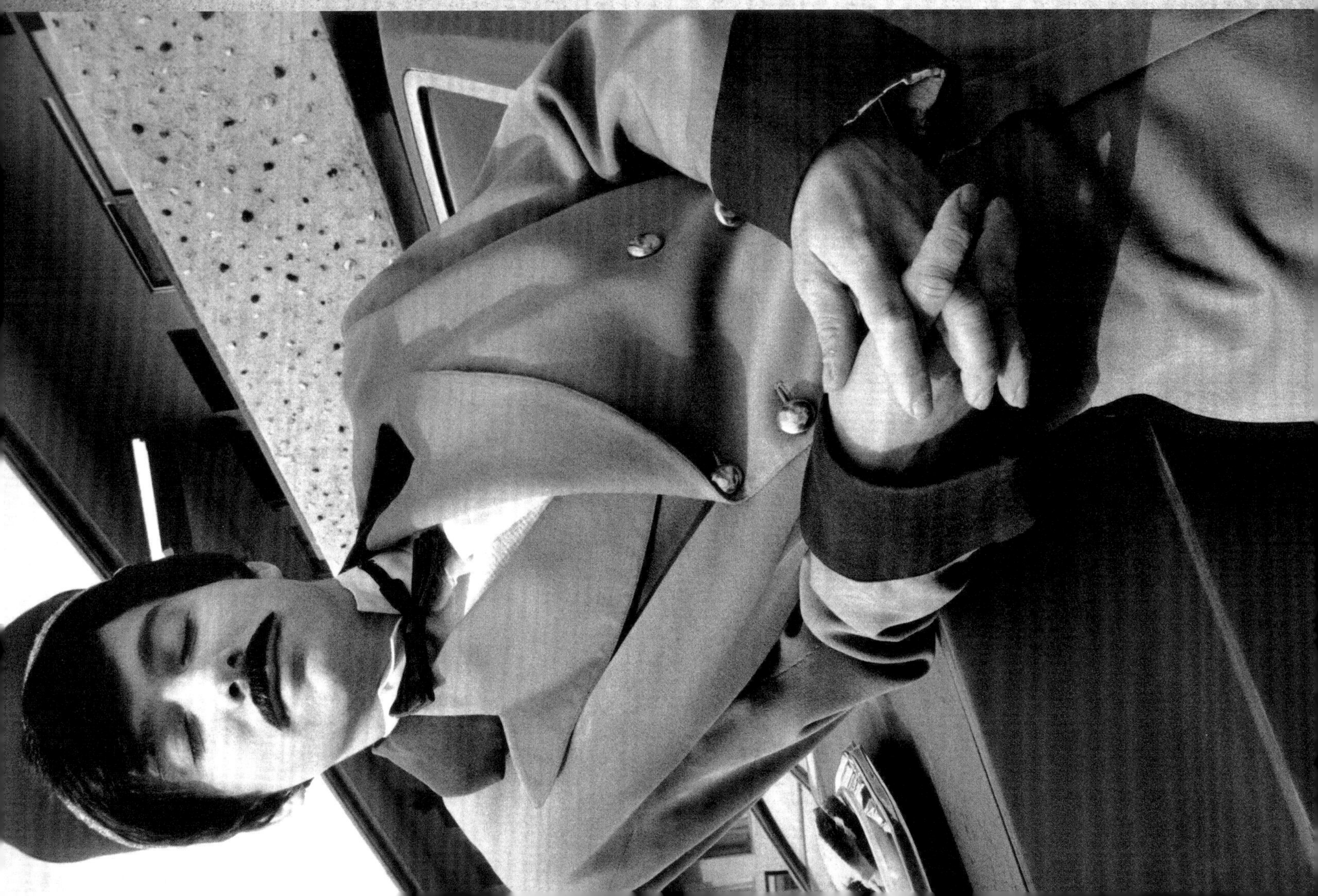

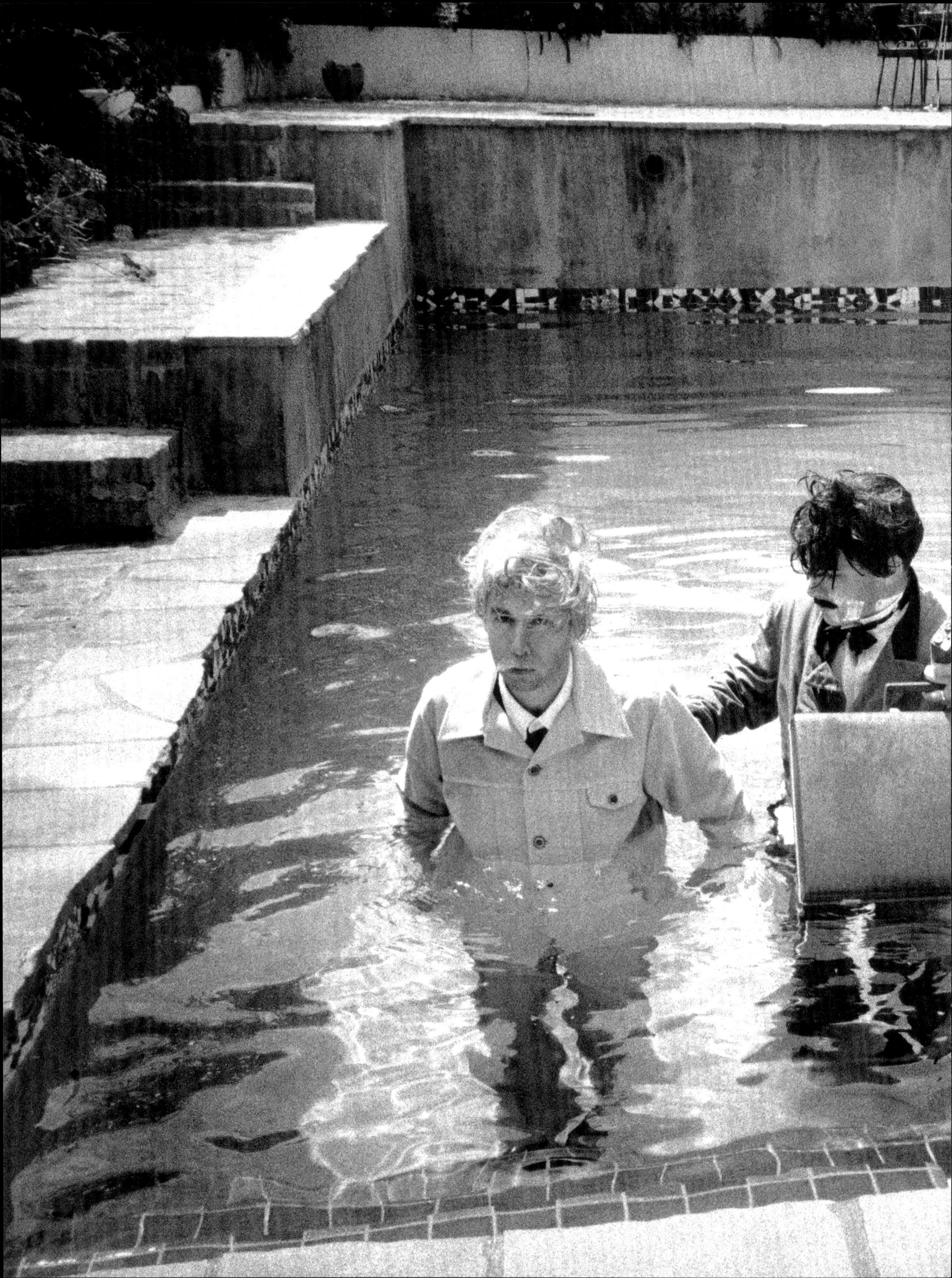

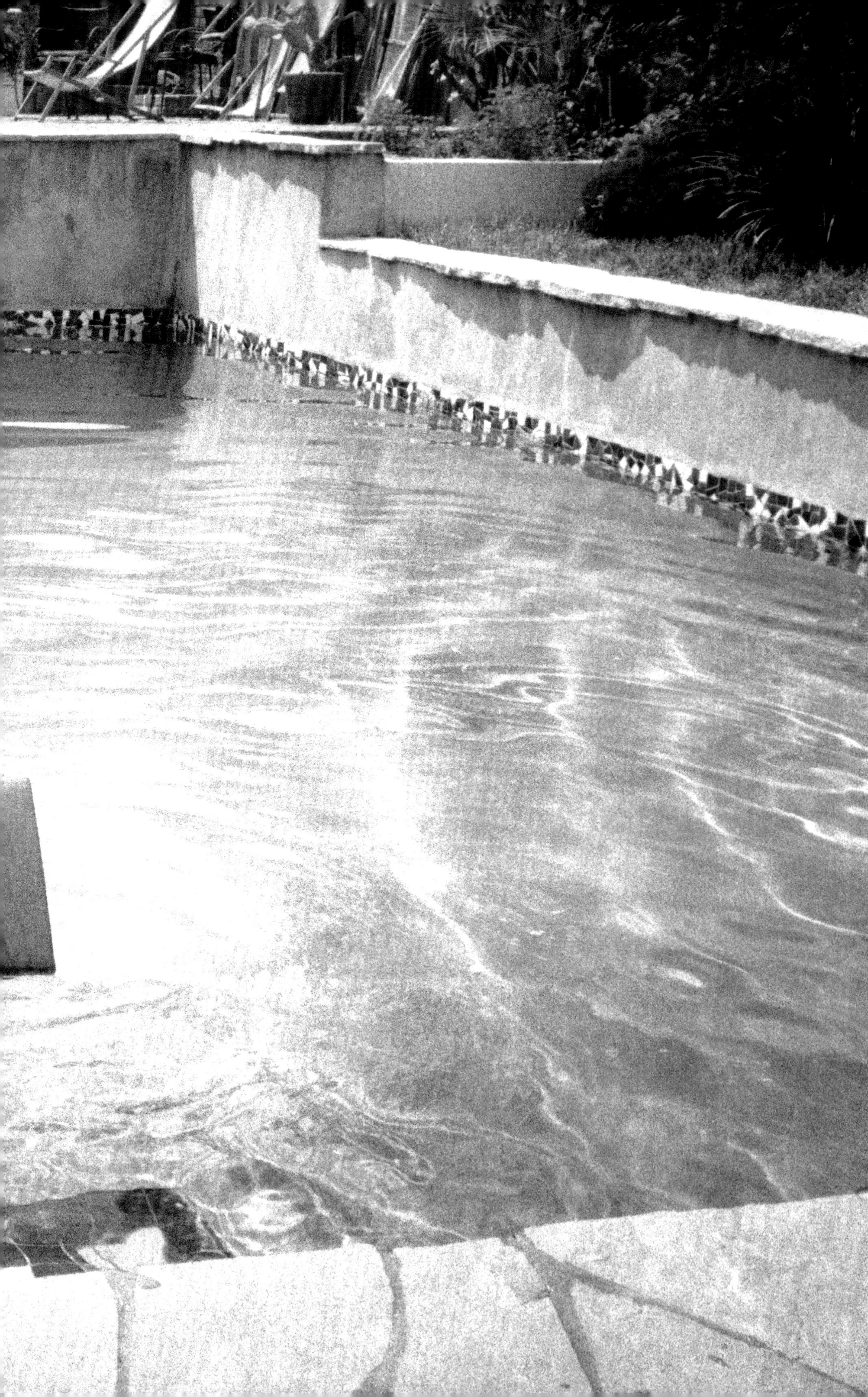

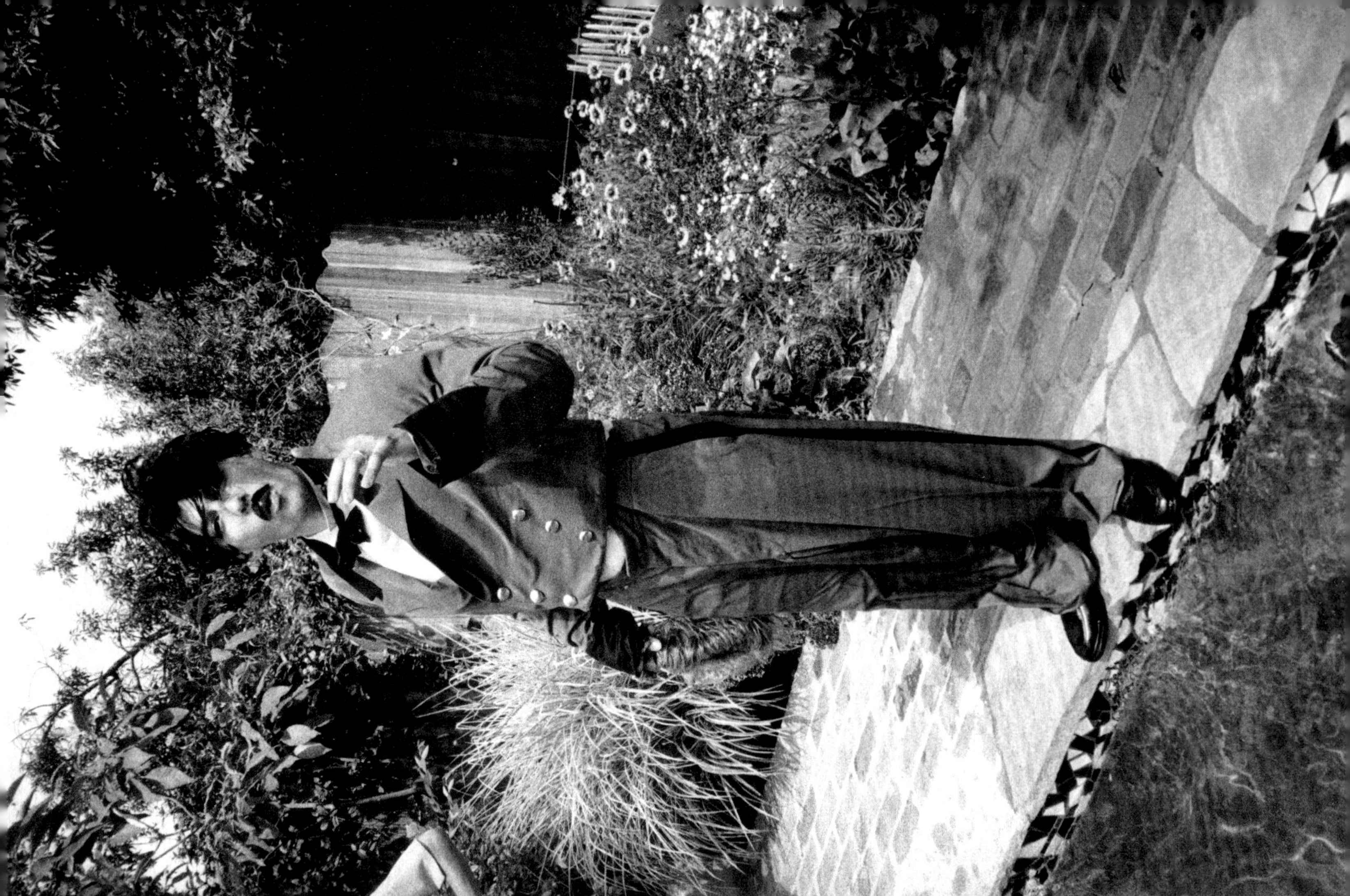

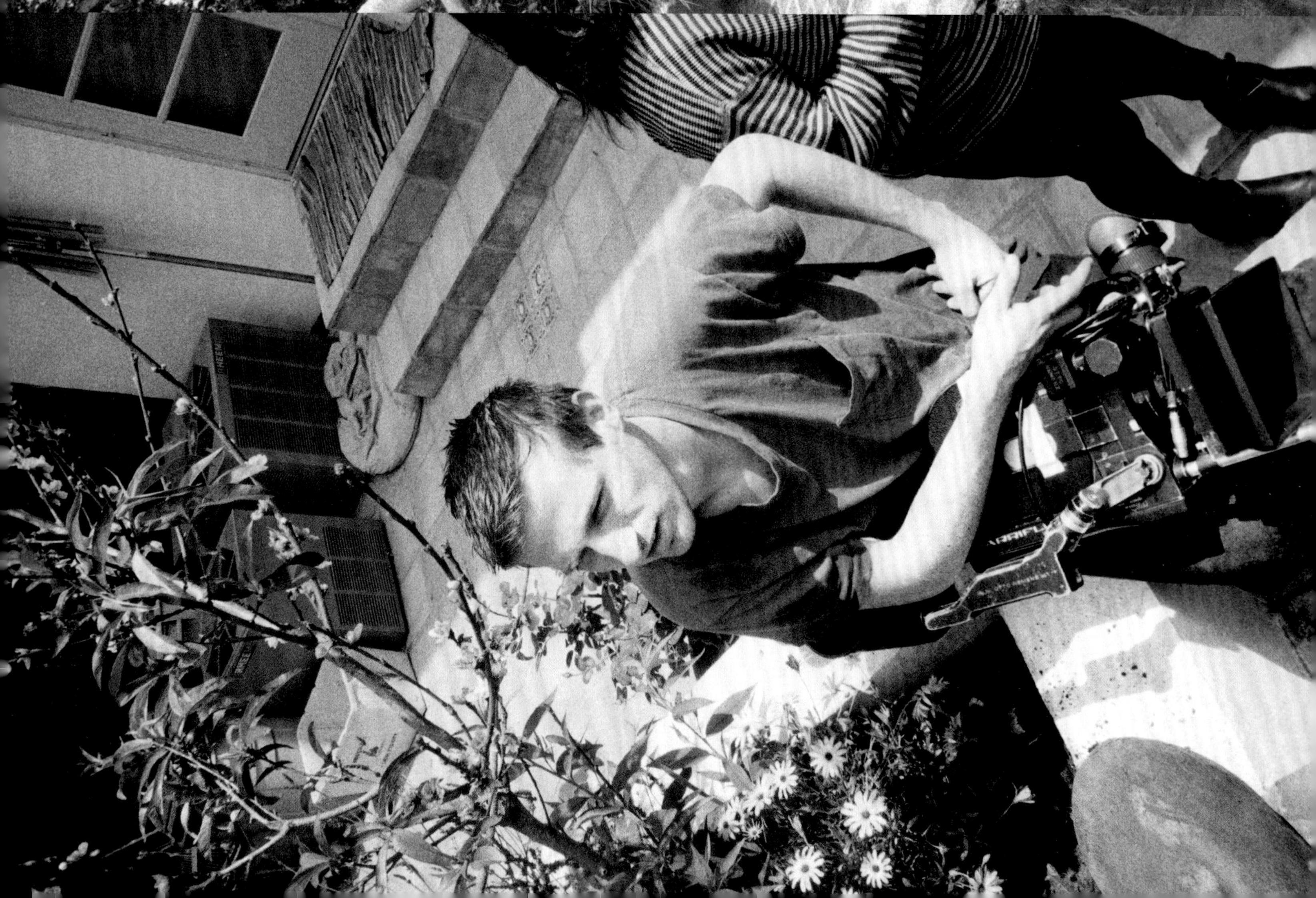

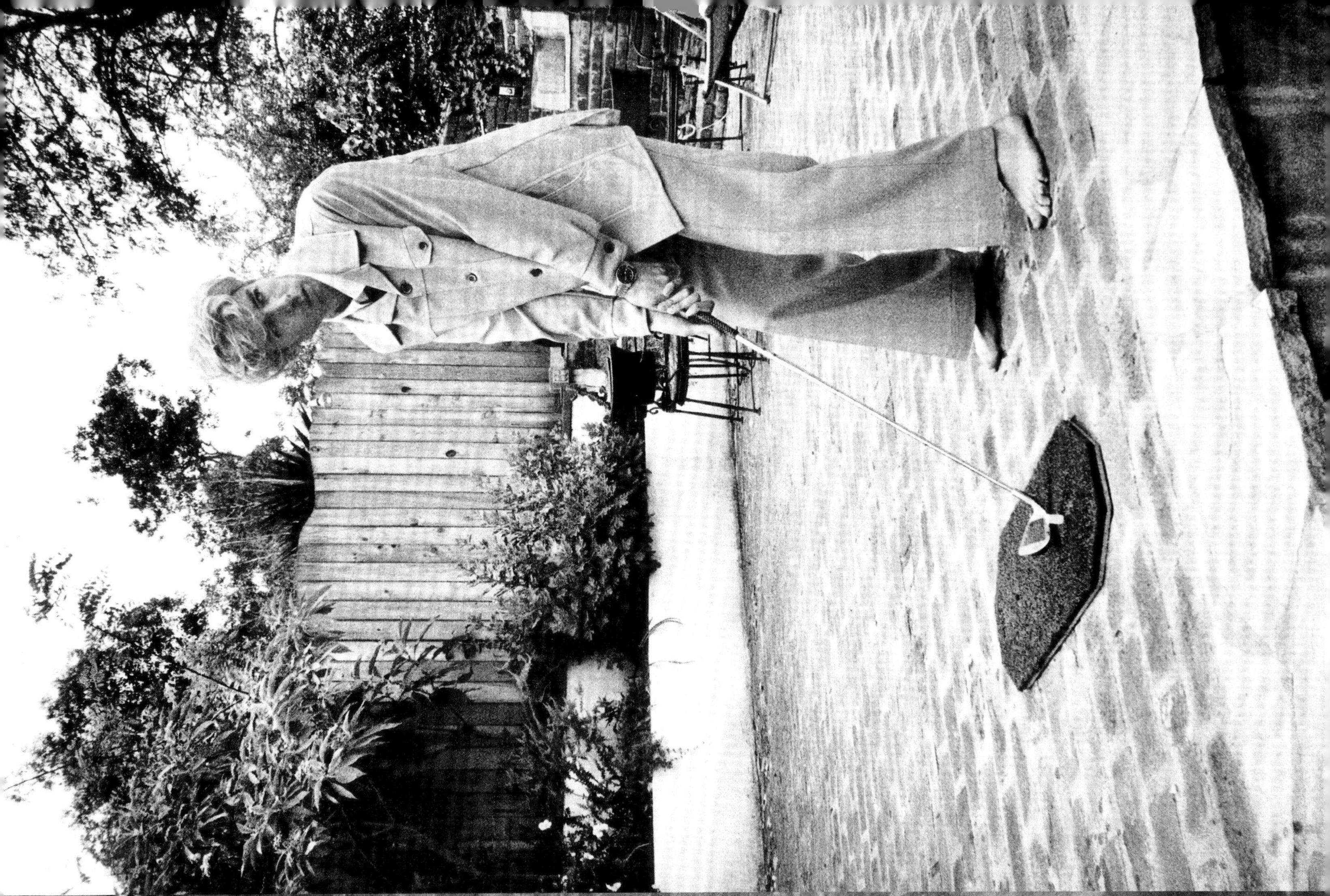

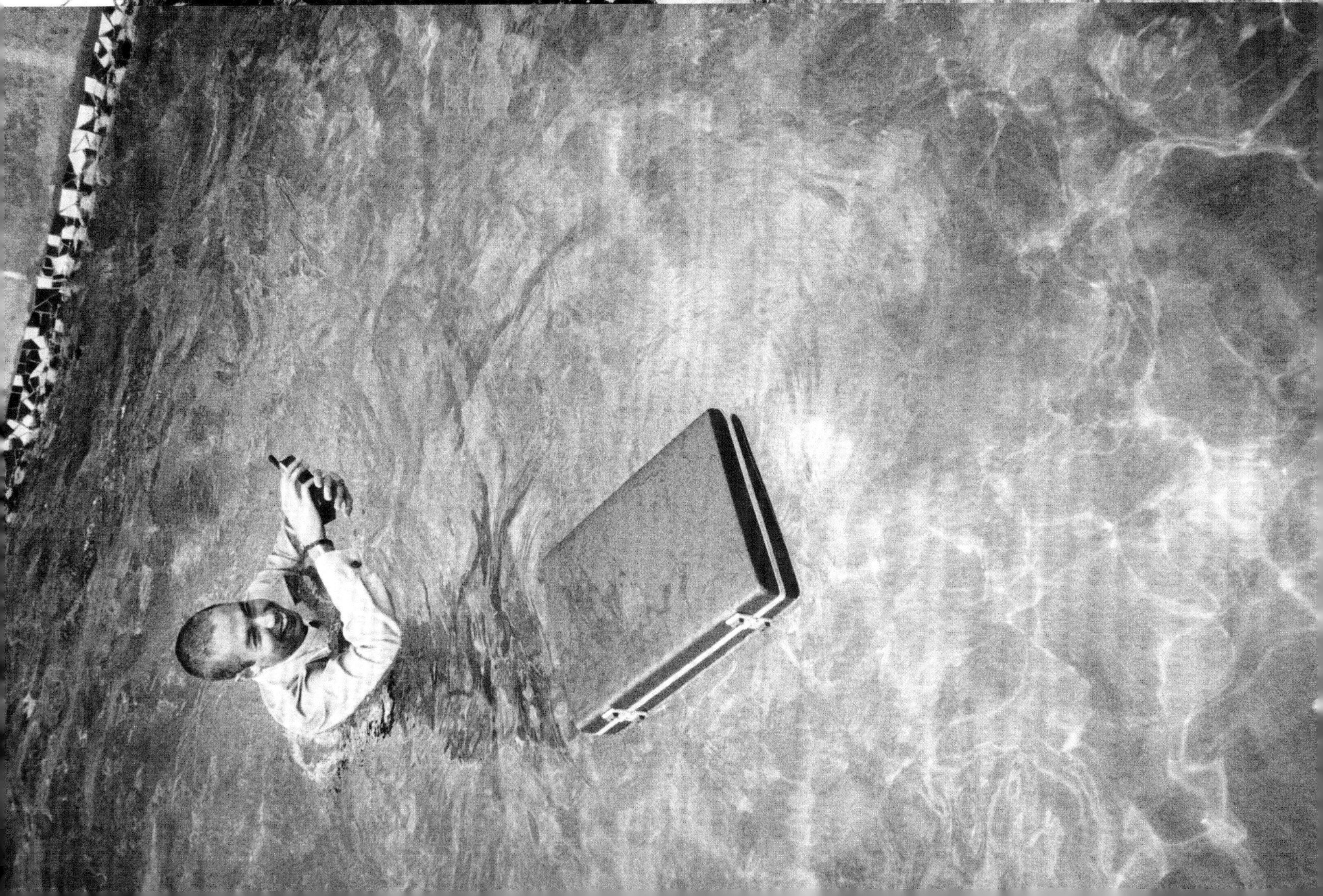

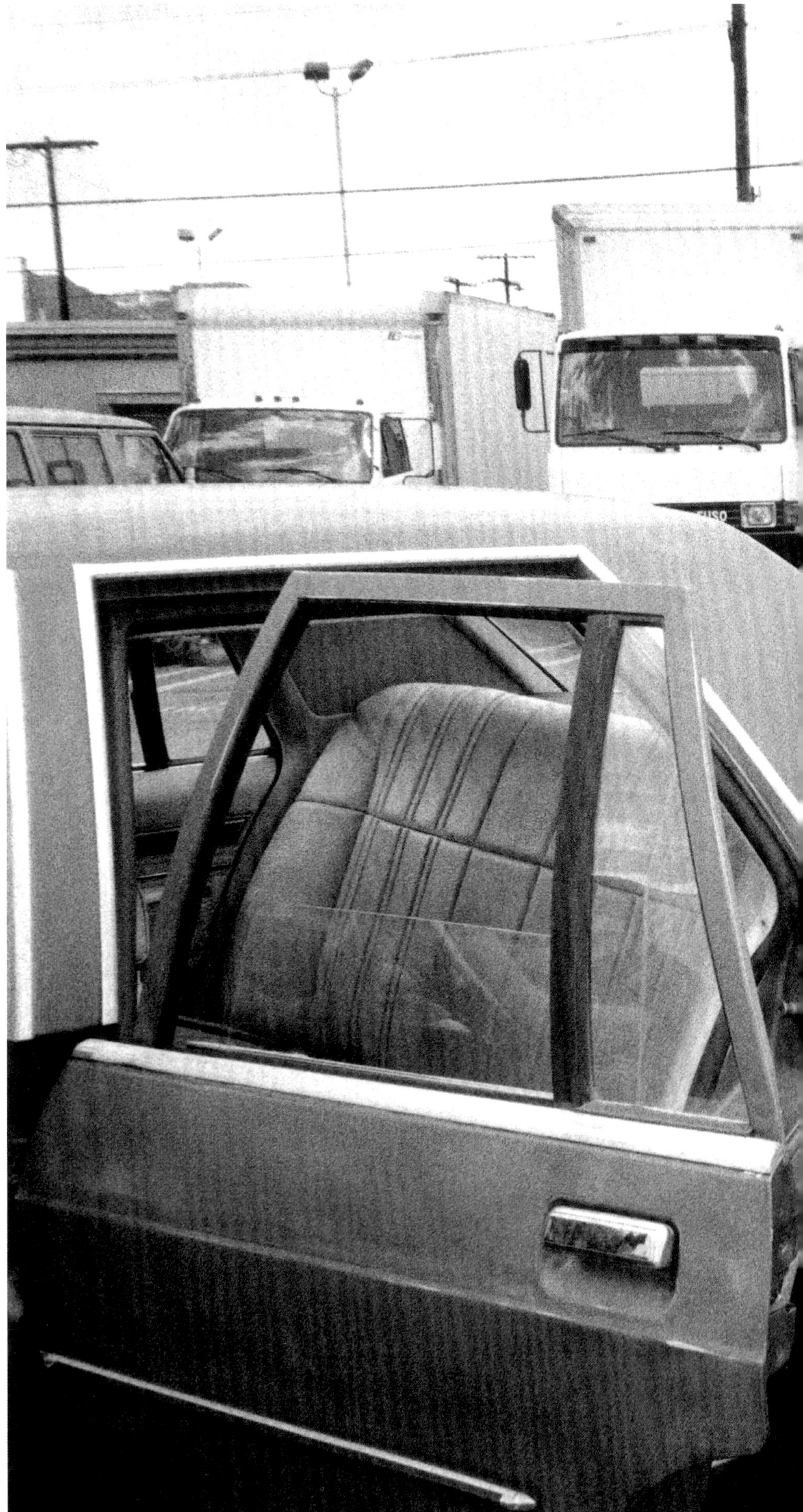

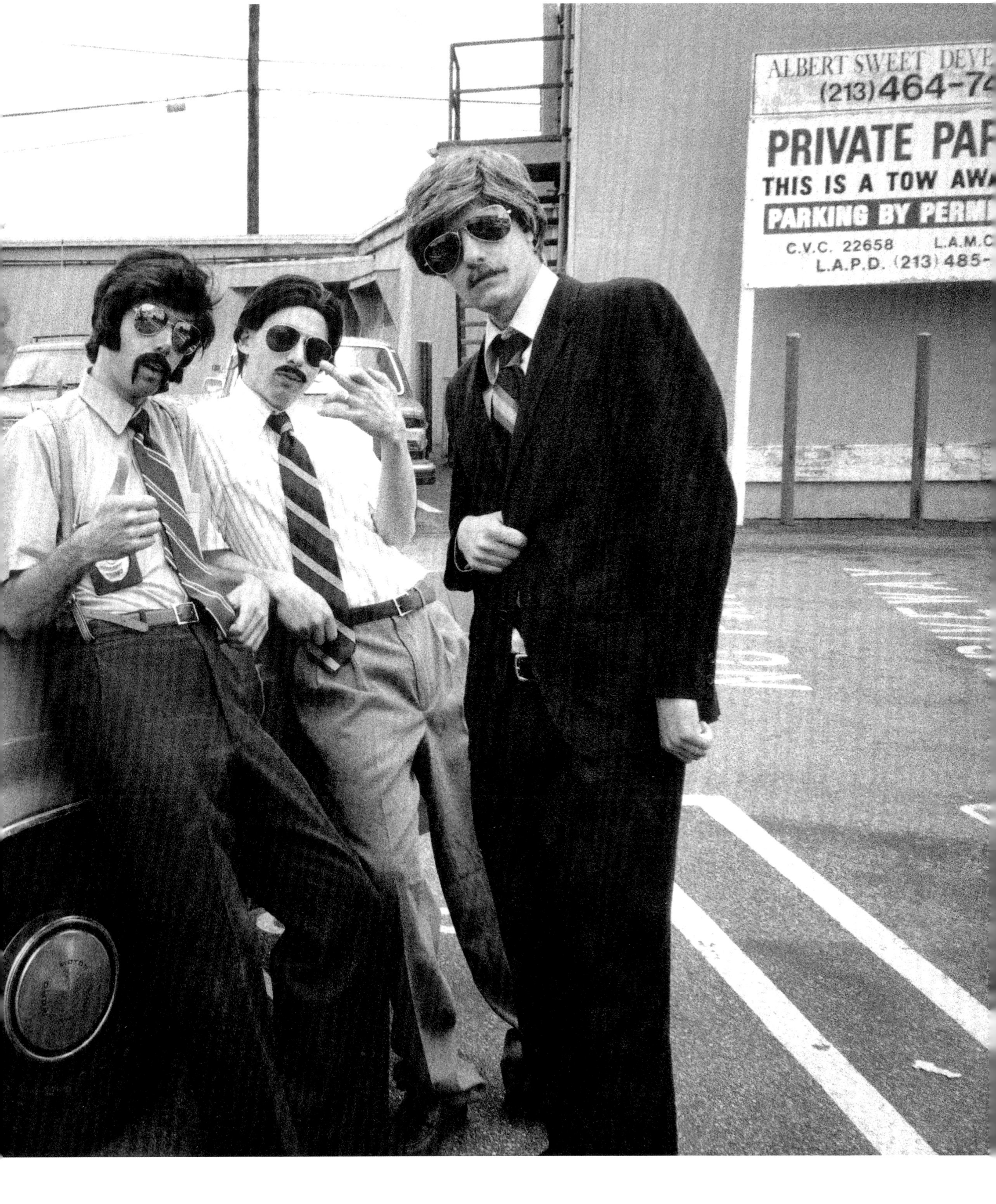
ALBERT SWEET DEVE
(213)464-74
PRIVATE PAR
THIS IS A TOW AWA
PARKING BY PERM
C.V.C. 22658
L.A.M.C
L.A.P.D. (213) 485-

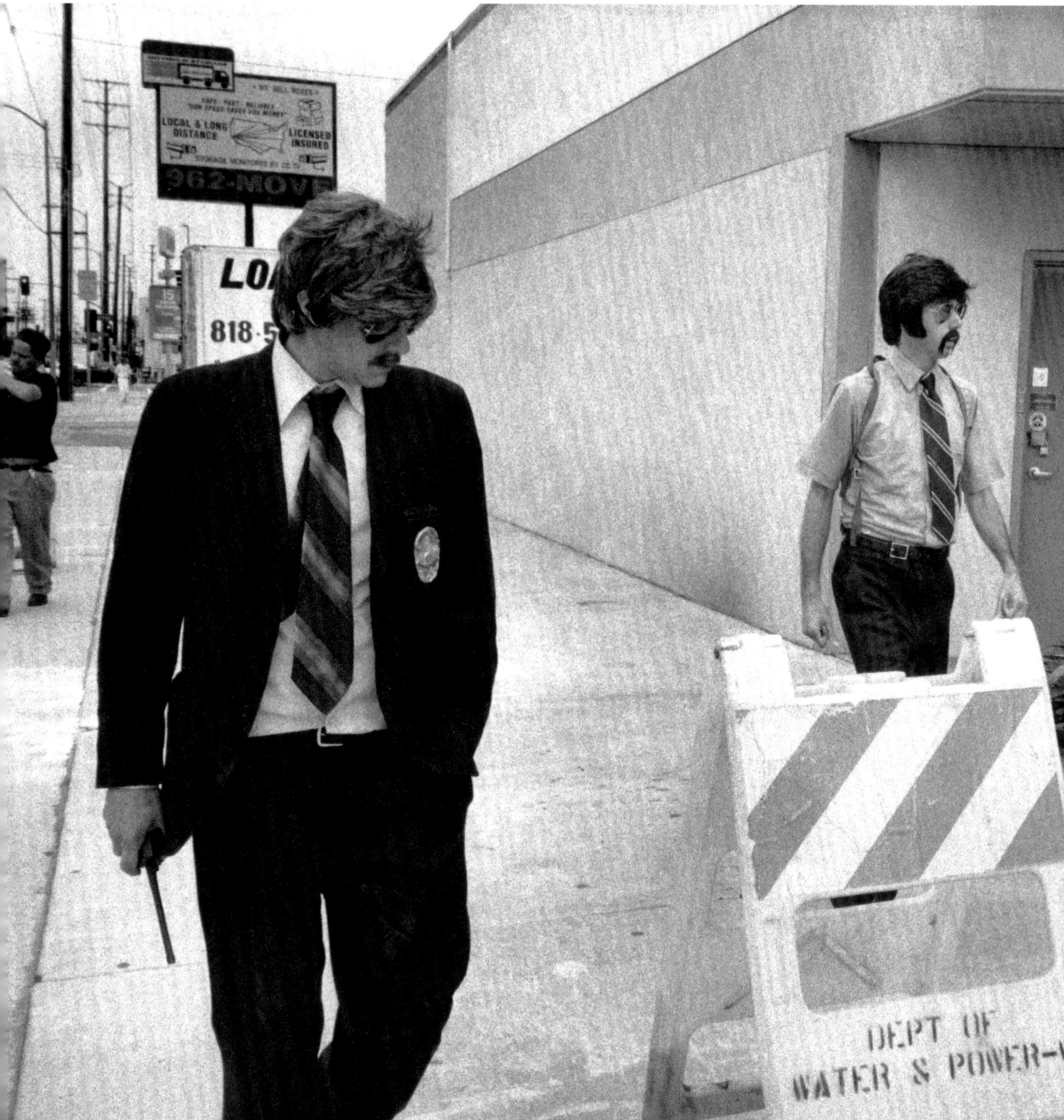
LOCAL & LONG DISTANCE
LICENSED INSURED
962-MOVE
DEPT OF
WATER & POWER

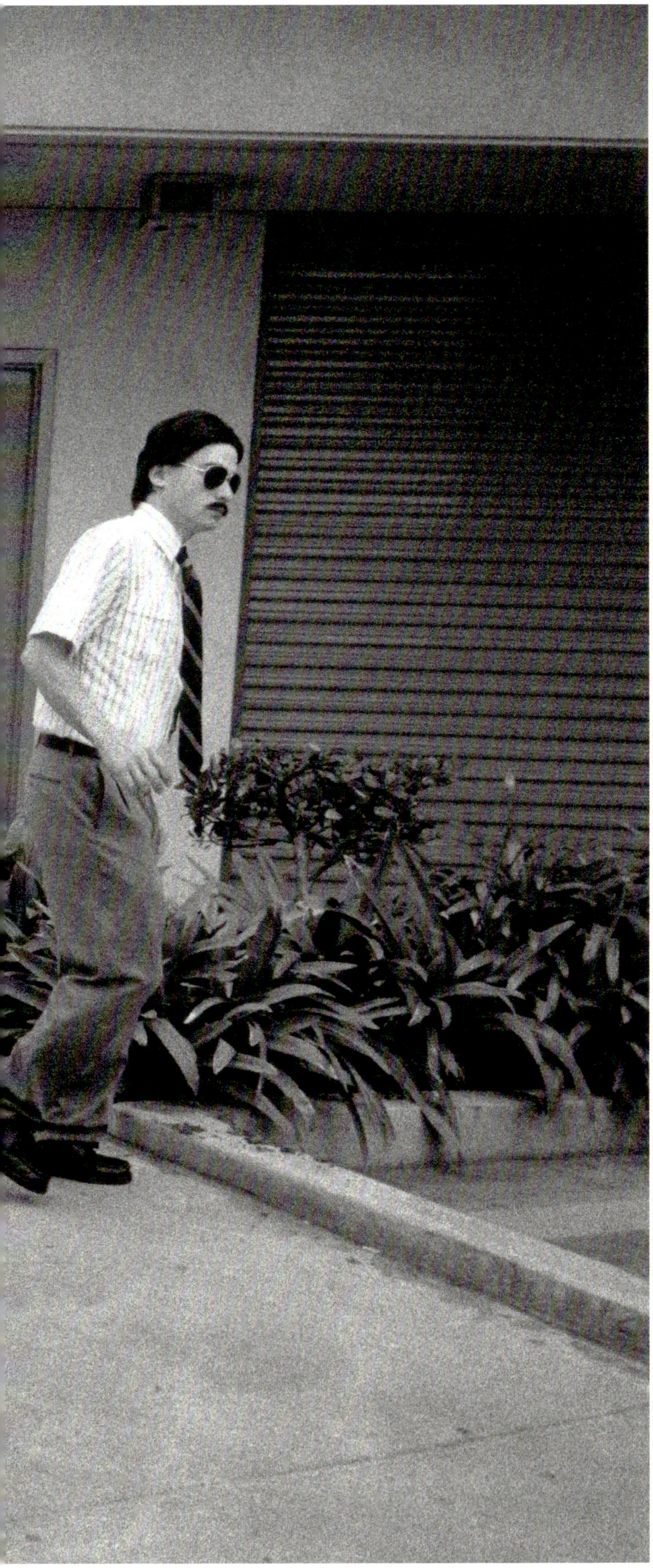

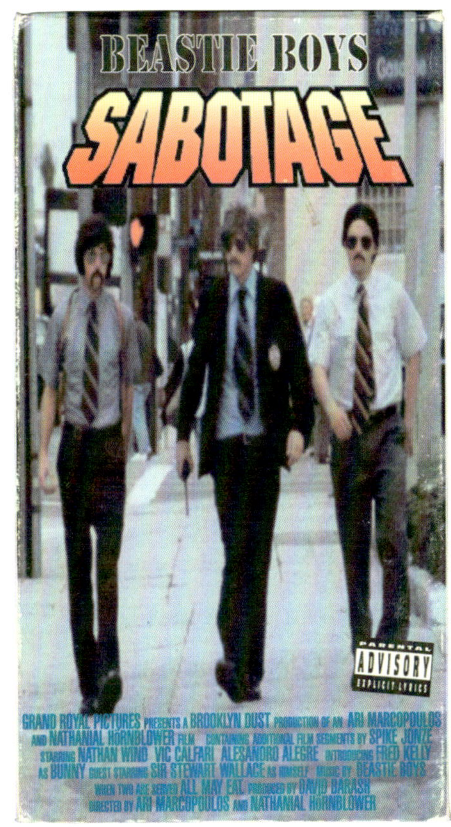
BEASTIE BOYS
SABOTAGE
PARENTAL ADVISORY EXPLICIT LYRICS
GRAND ROYAL PICTURES PRESENTS A BROOKLYN DUST PRODUCTION OF AN ARI MARCOPOULOS AND NATHANIAL HORNBLOWER FILM CONTAINING ADDITIONAL FILM SEGMENTS BY SPIKE JONZE
STARRING NATHAN WIND VIC CALFARI ALESANDRO ALEGRE INTRODUCING FRED KELLY AS BUNNY GUEST STARRING SIR STEWART WALLACE AS HIMSELF MUSIC BY BEASTIE BOYS
WHEN TWO ARE SERVED ALL MAY EAT PRODUCED BY DAVID BARASH
DIRECTED BY ARI MARCOPOULOS AND NATHANIAL HORNBLOWER

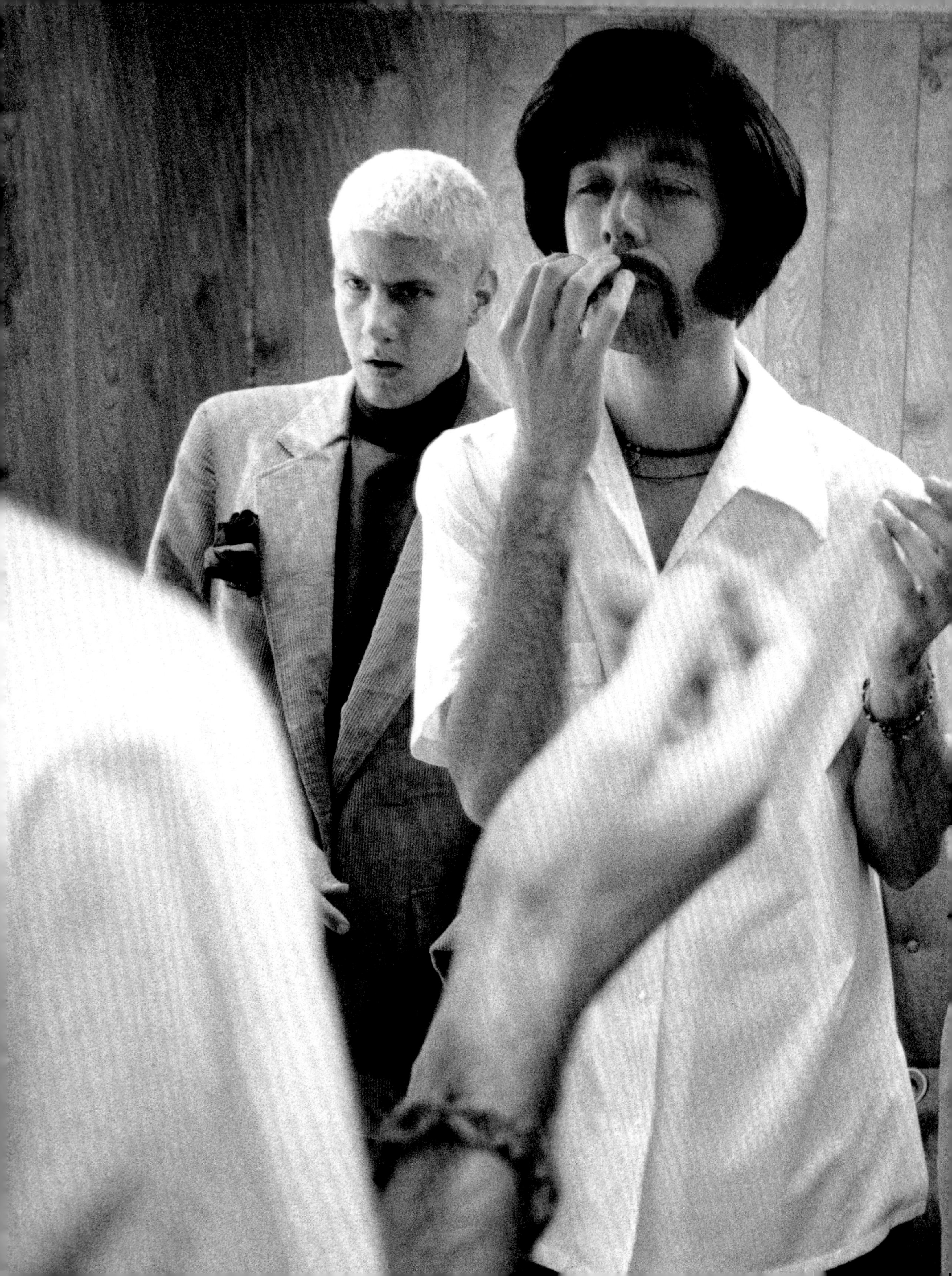

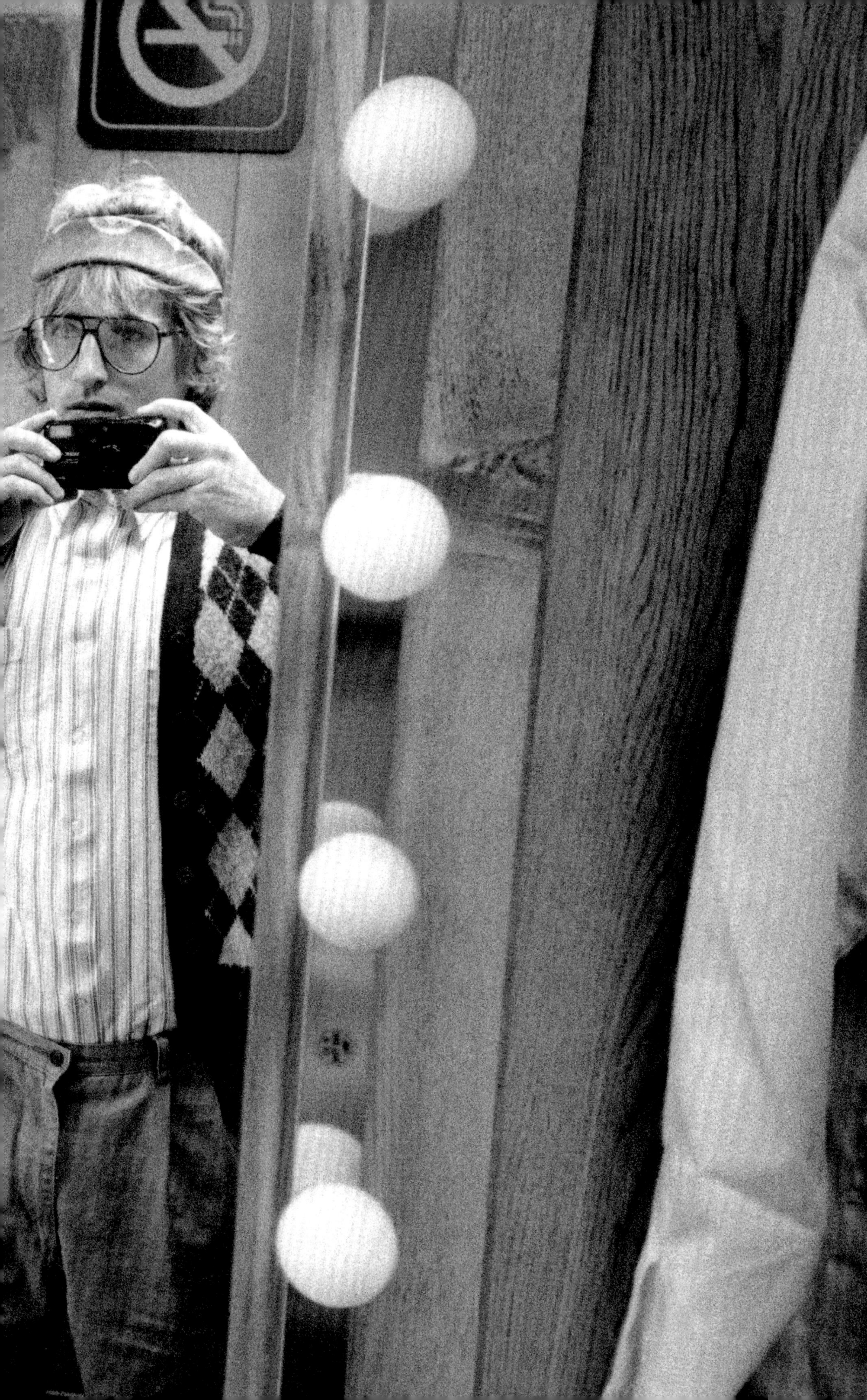

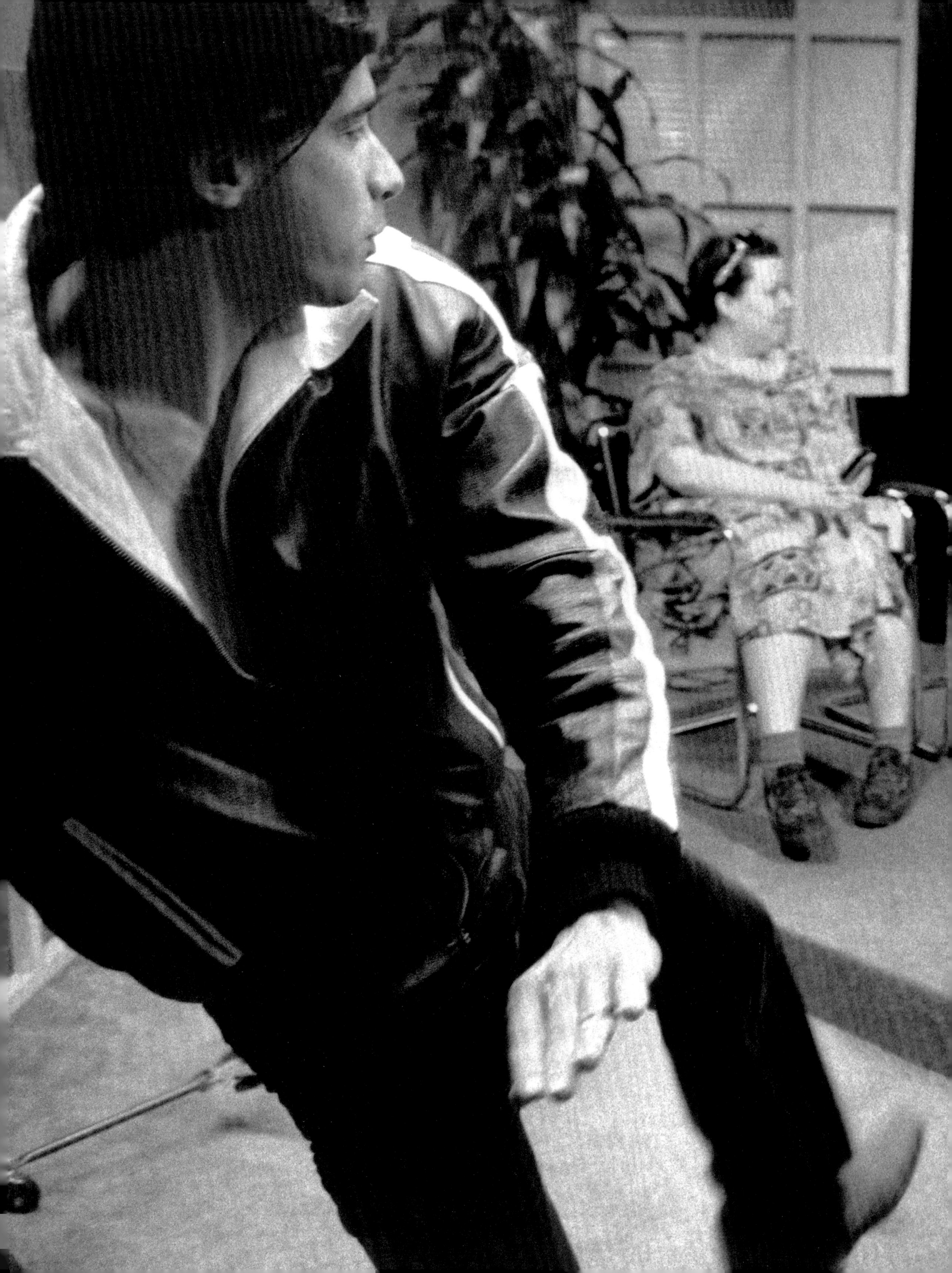

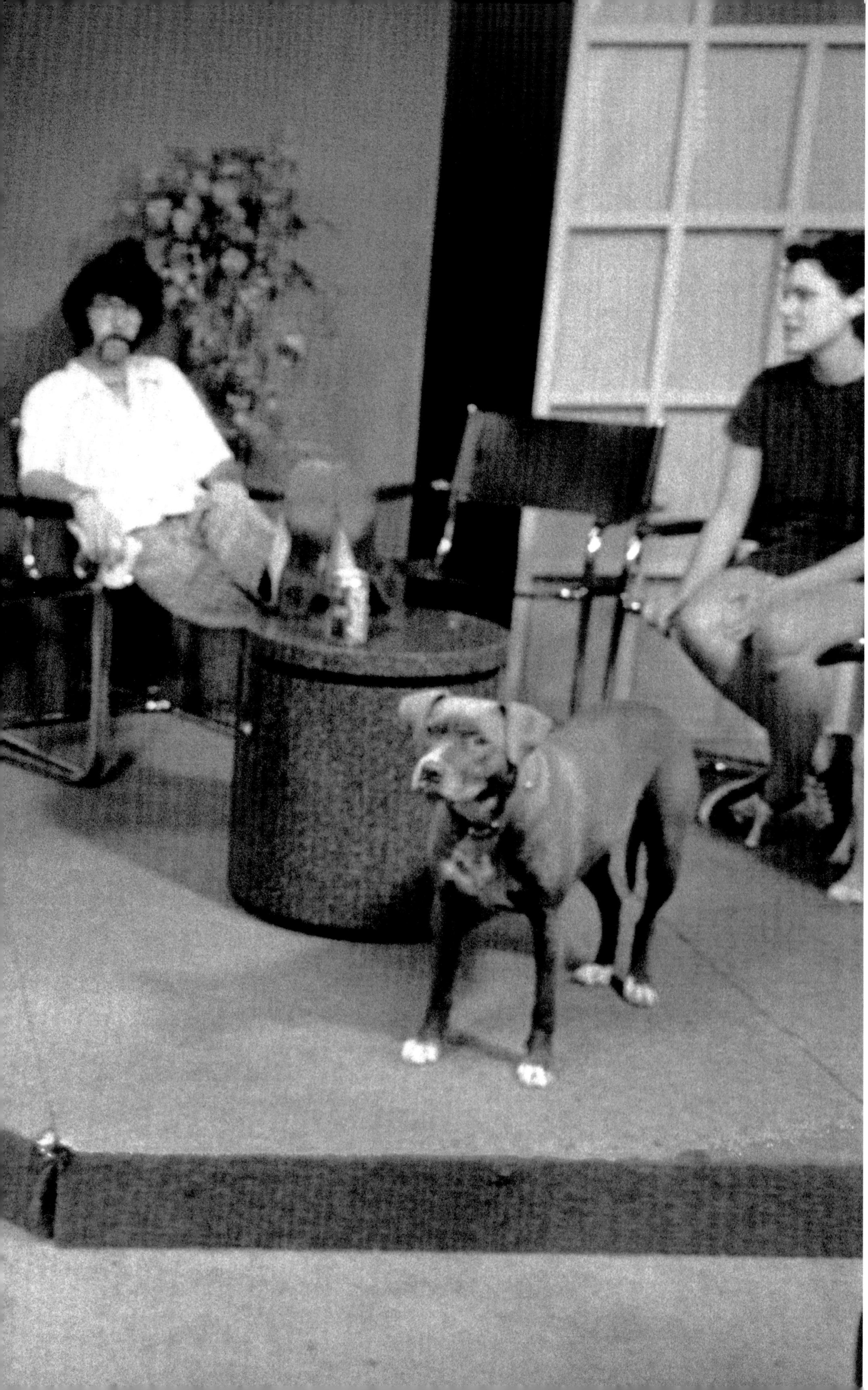

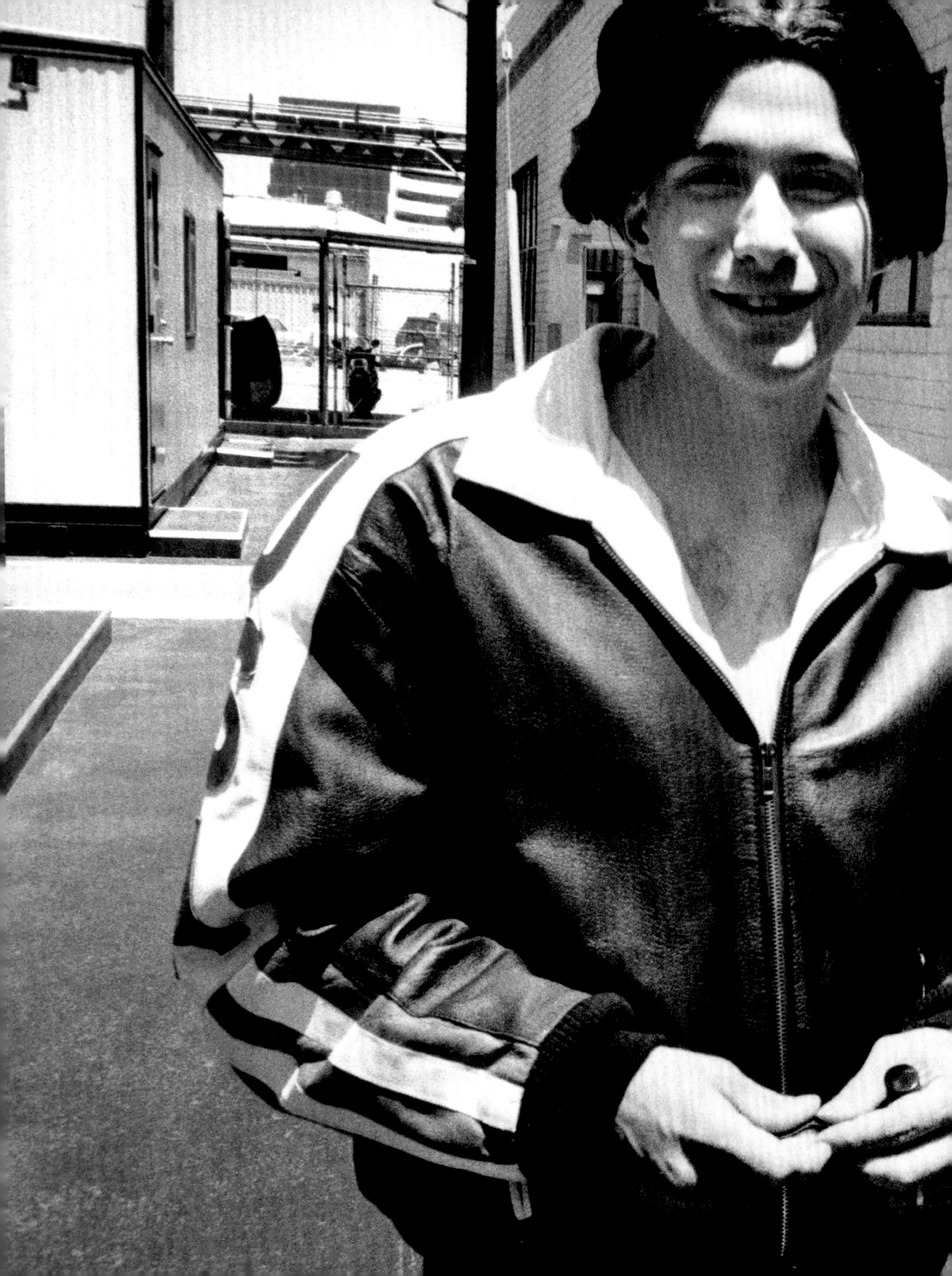

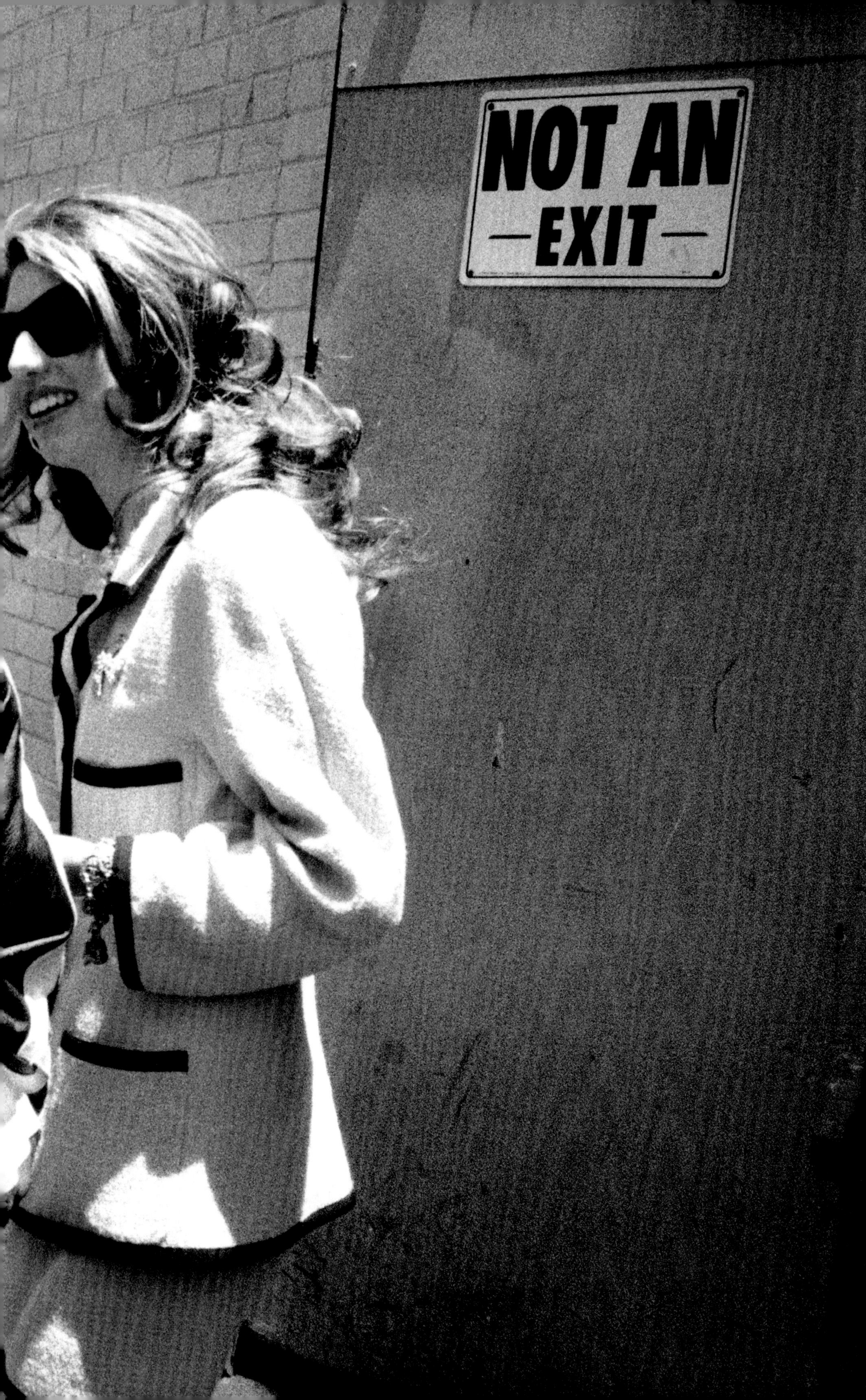
NOT AN
EXIT

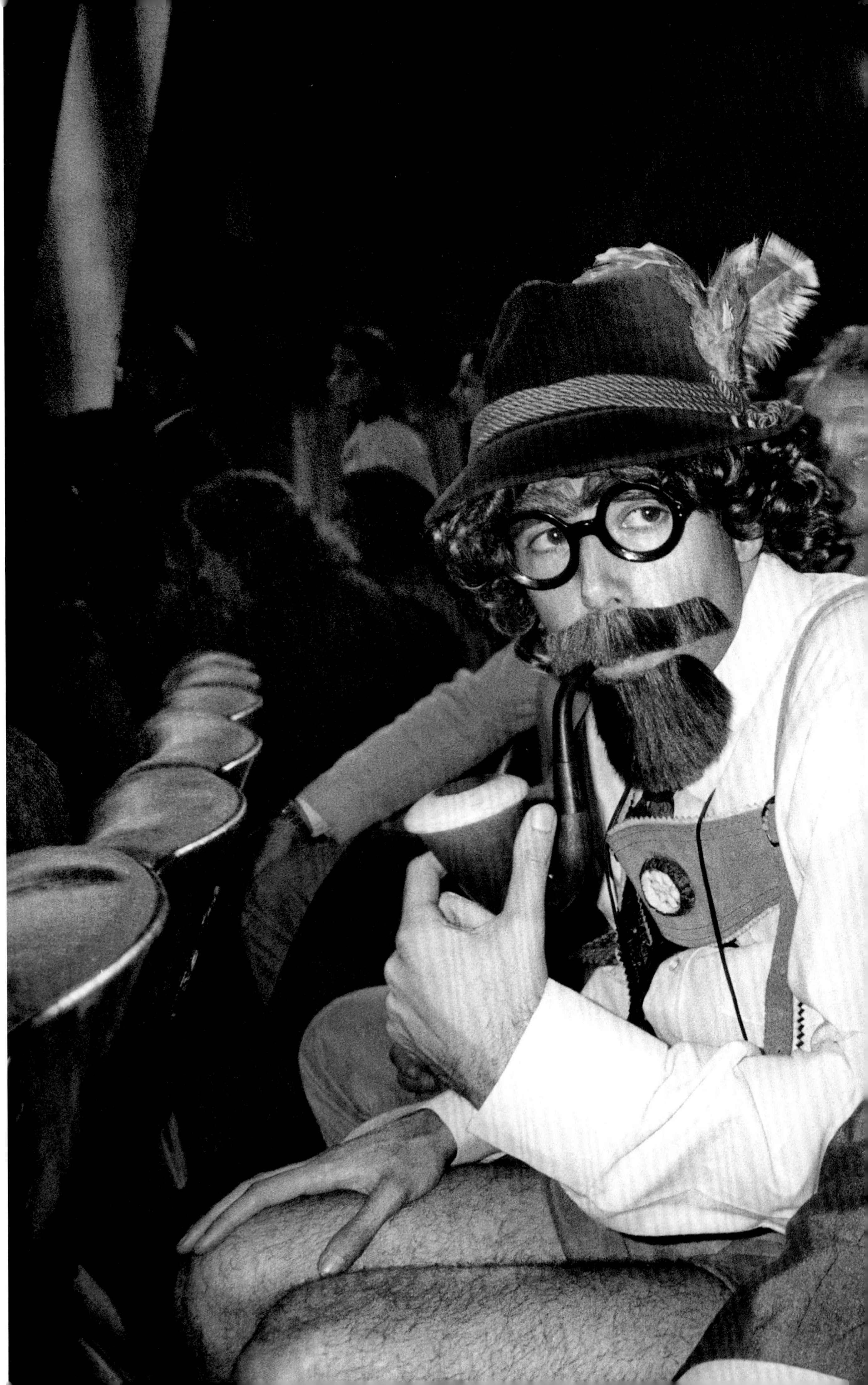

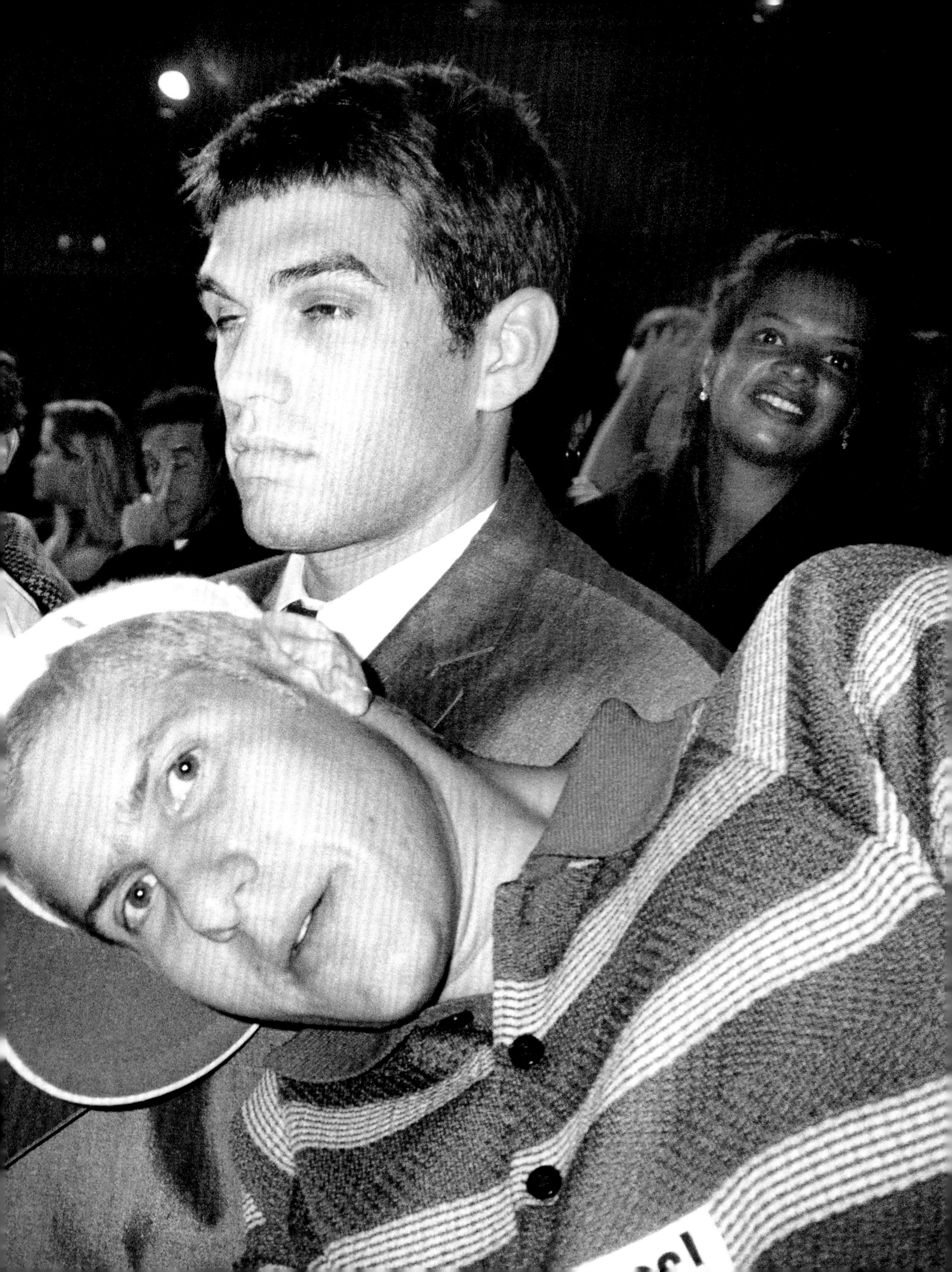

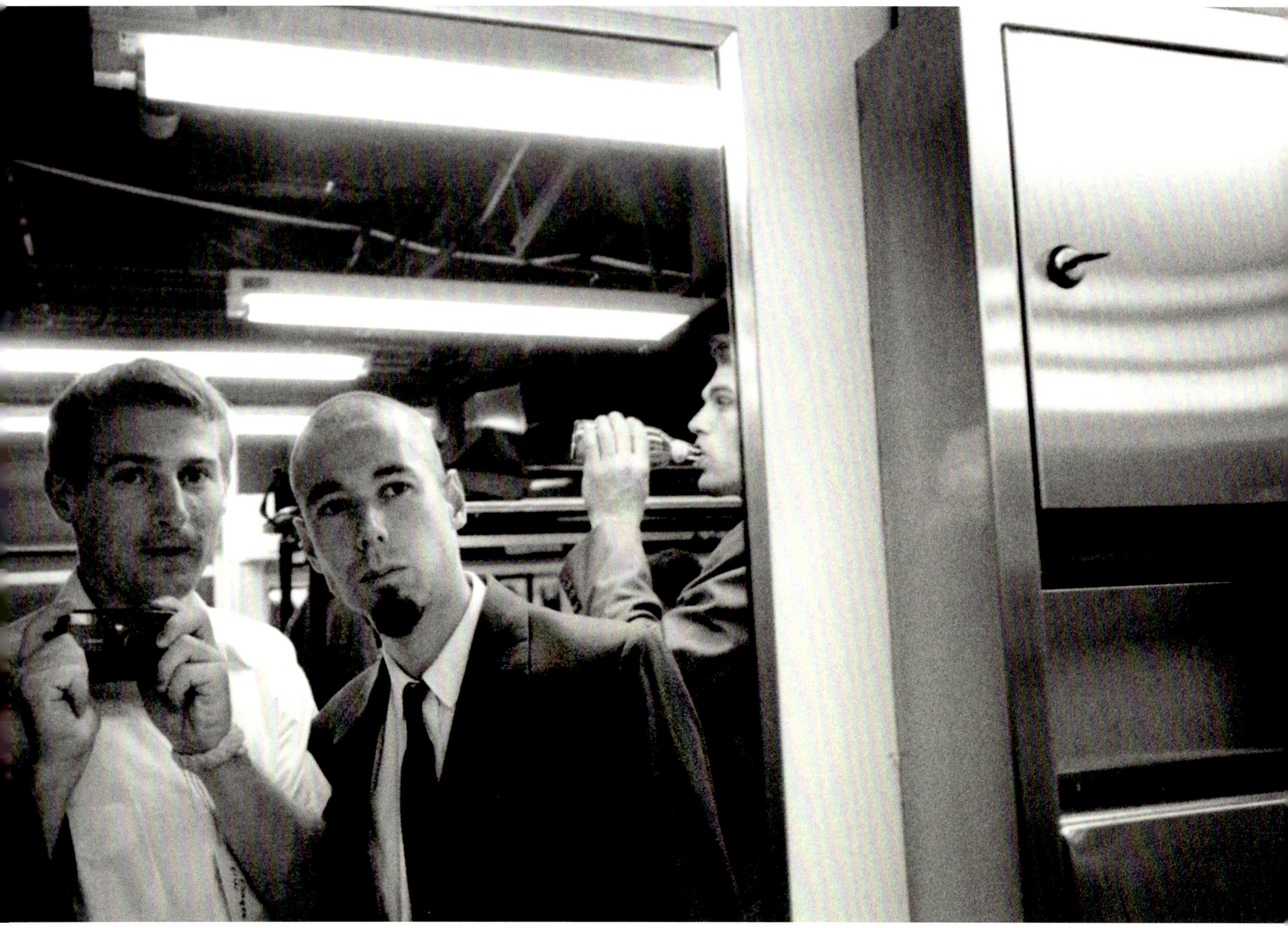

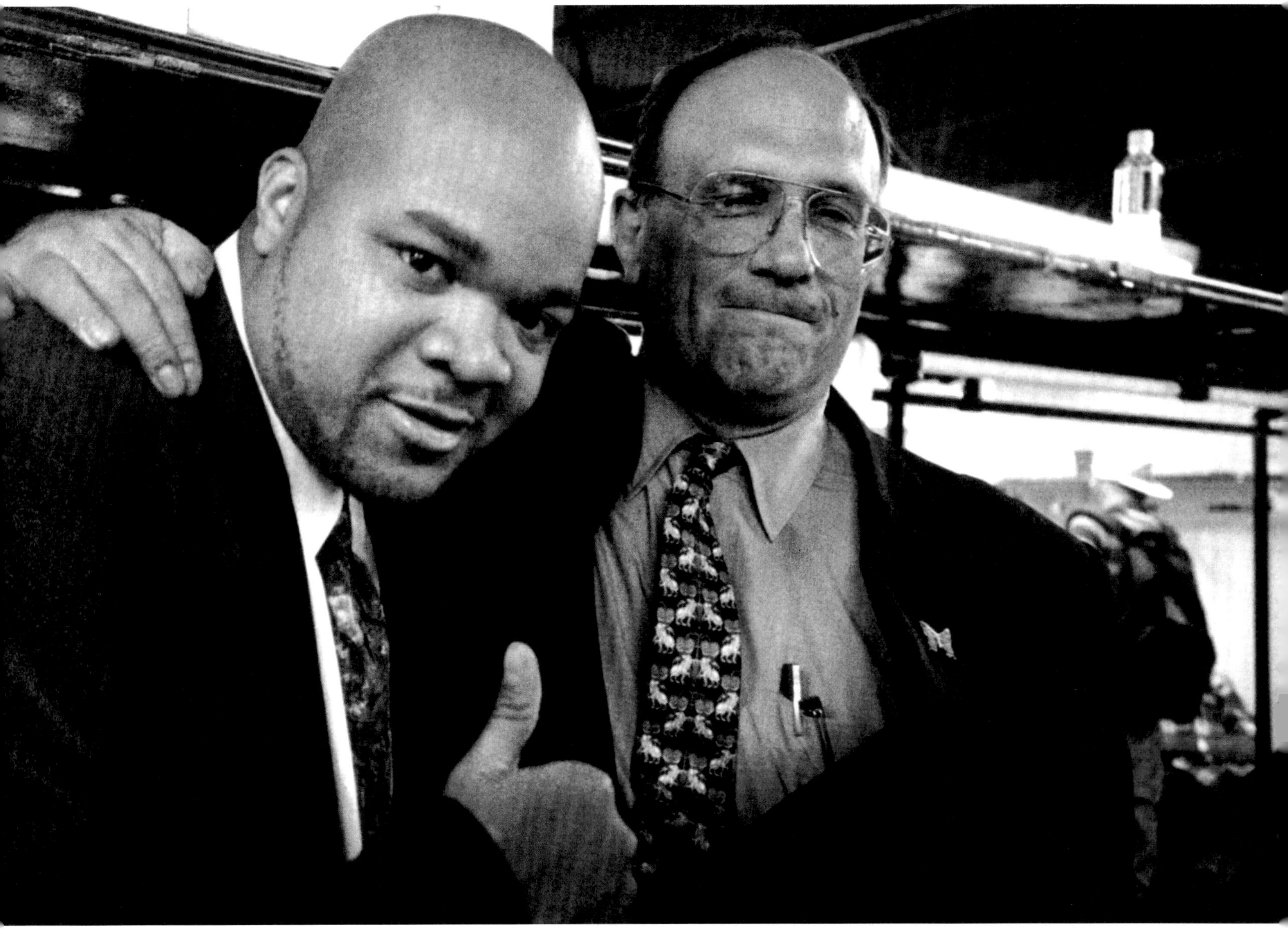

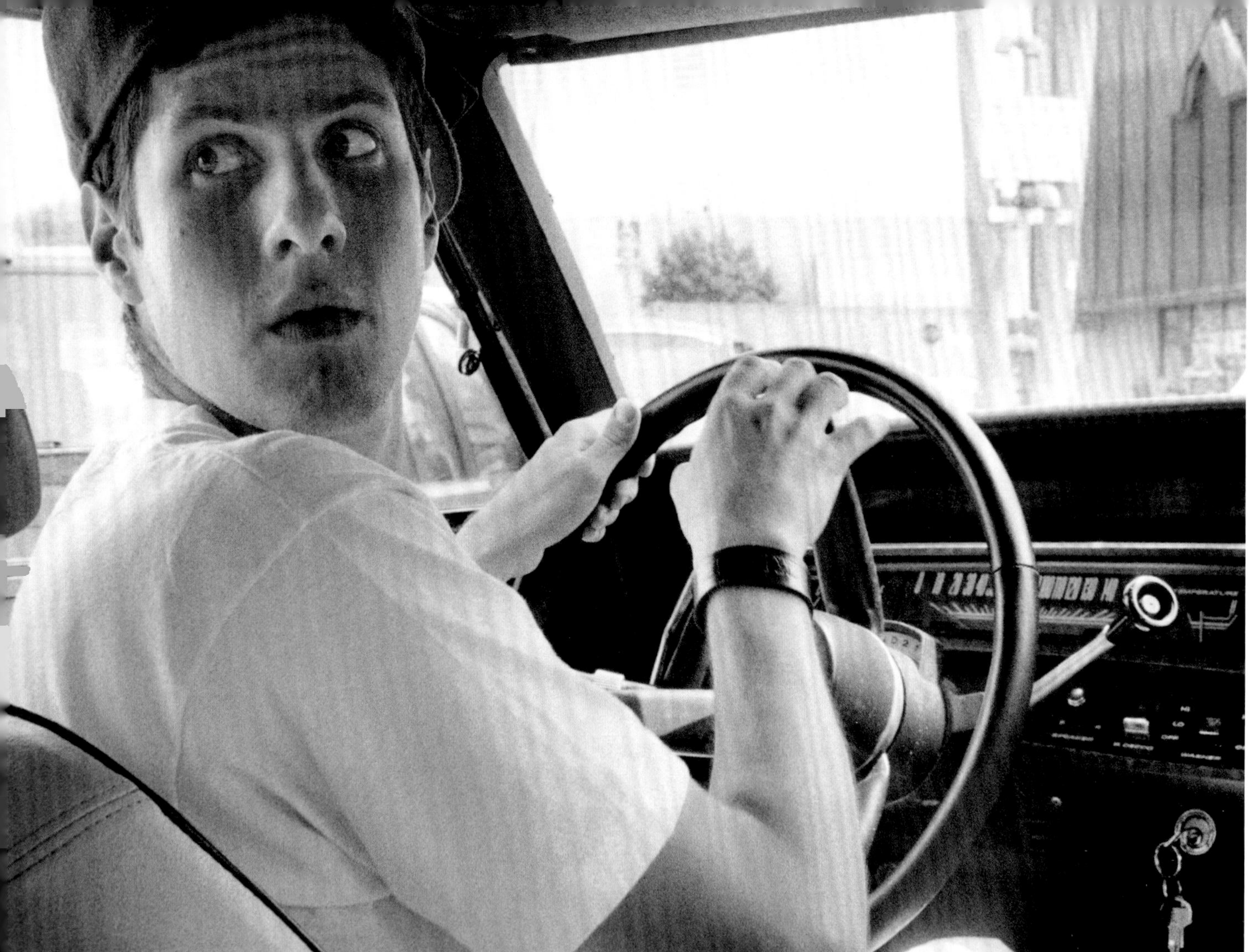

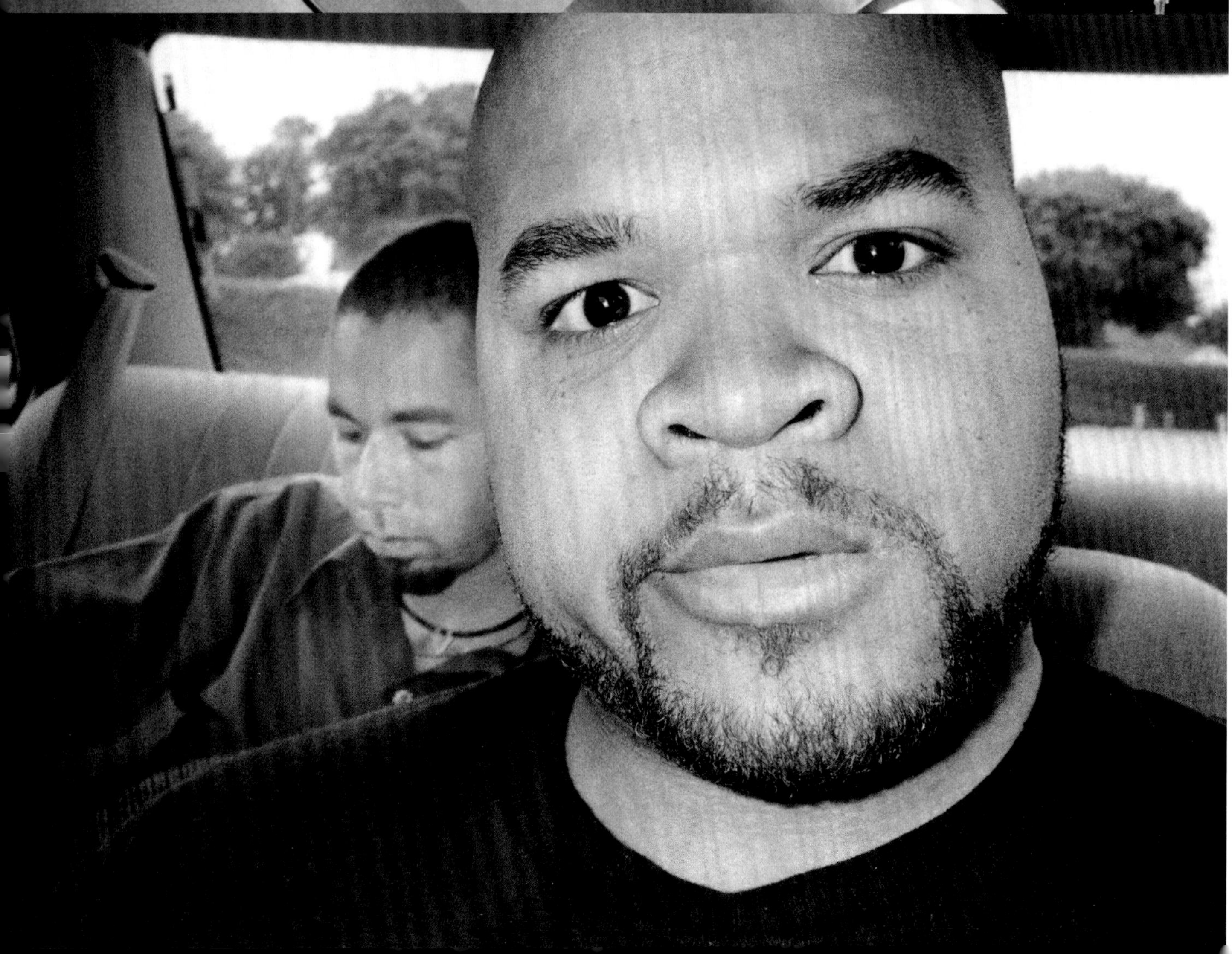

Hurricane's got Clout

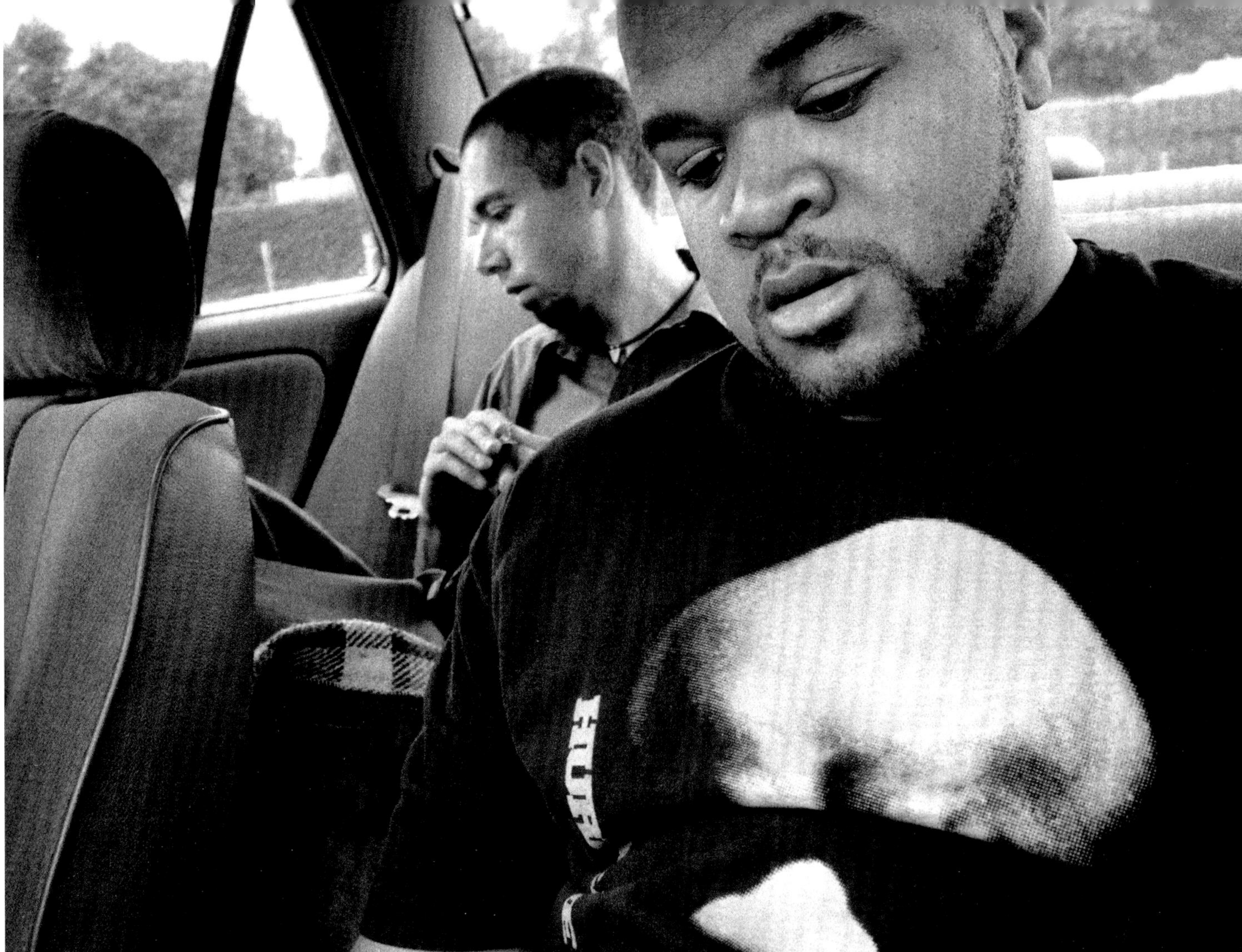

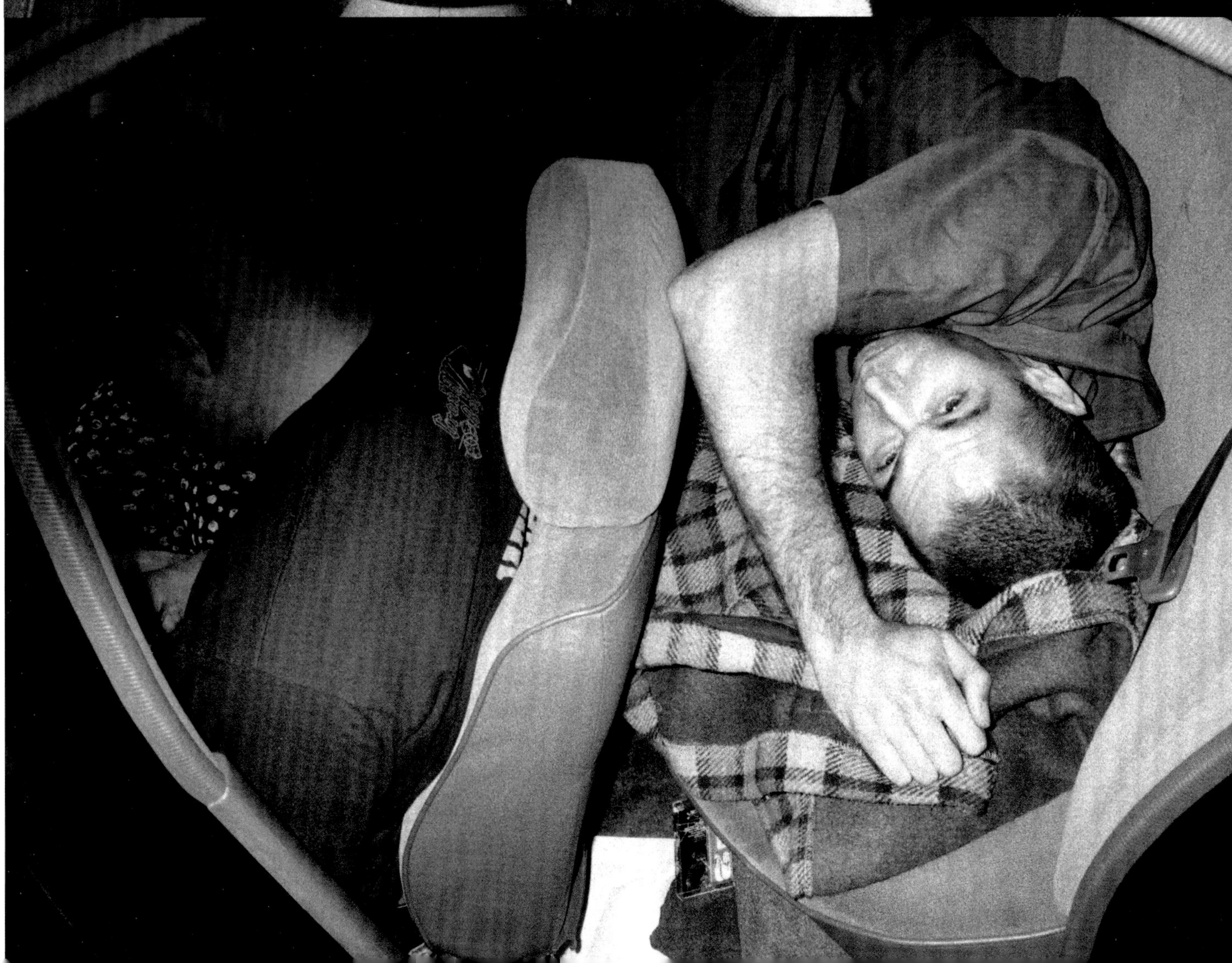

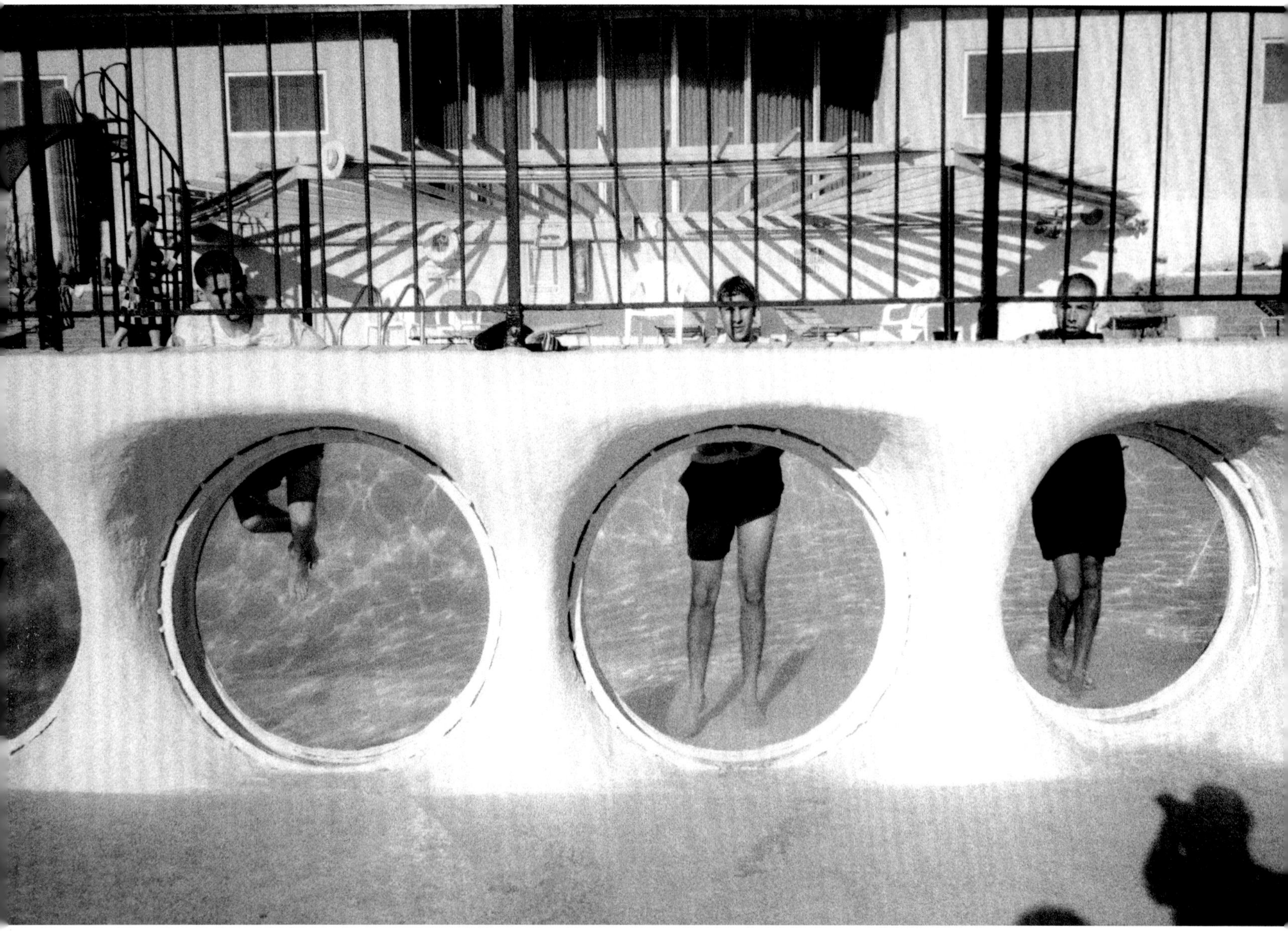

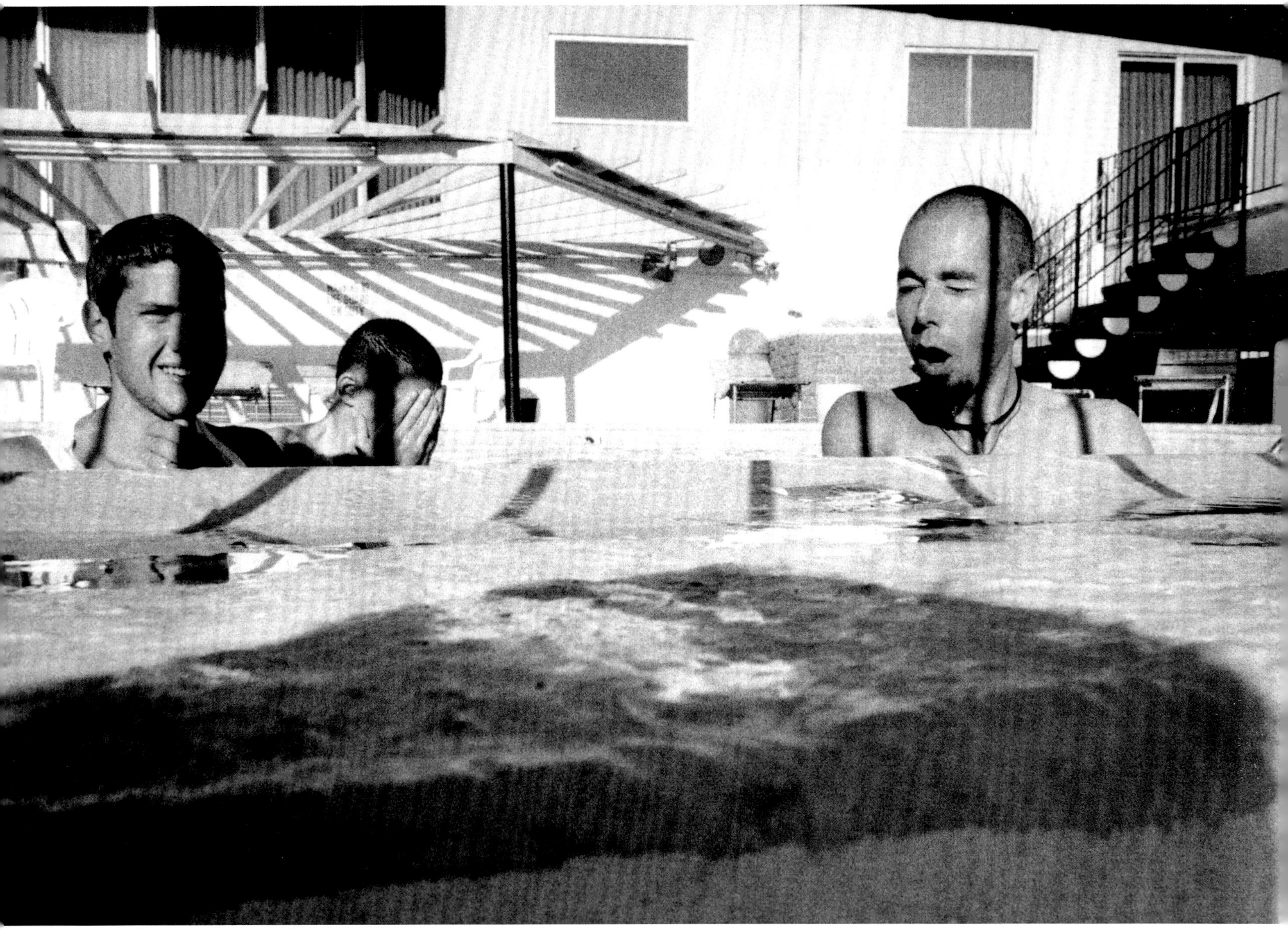

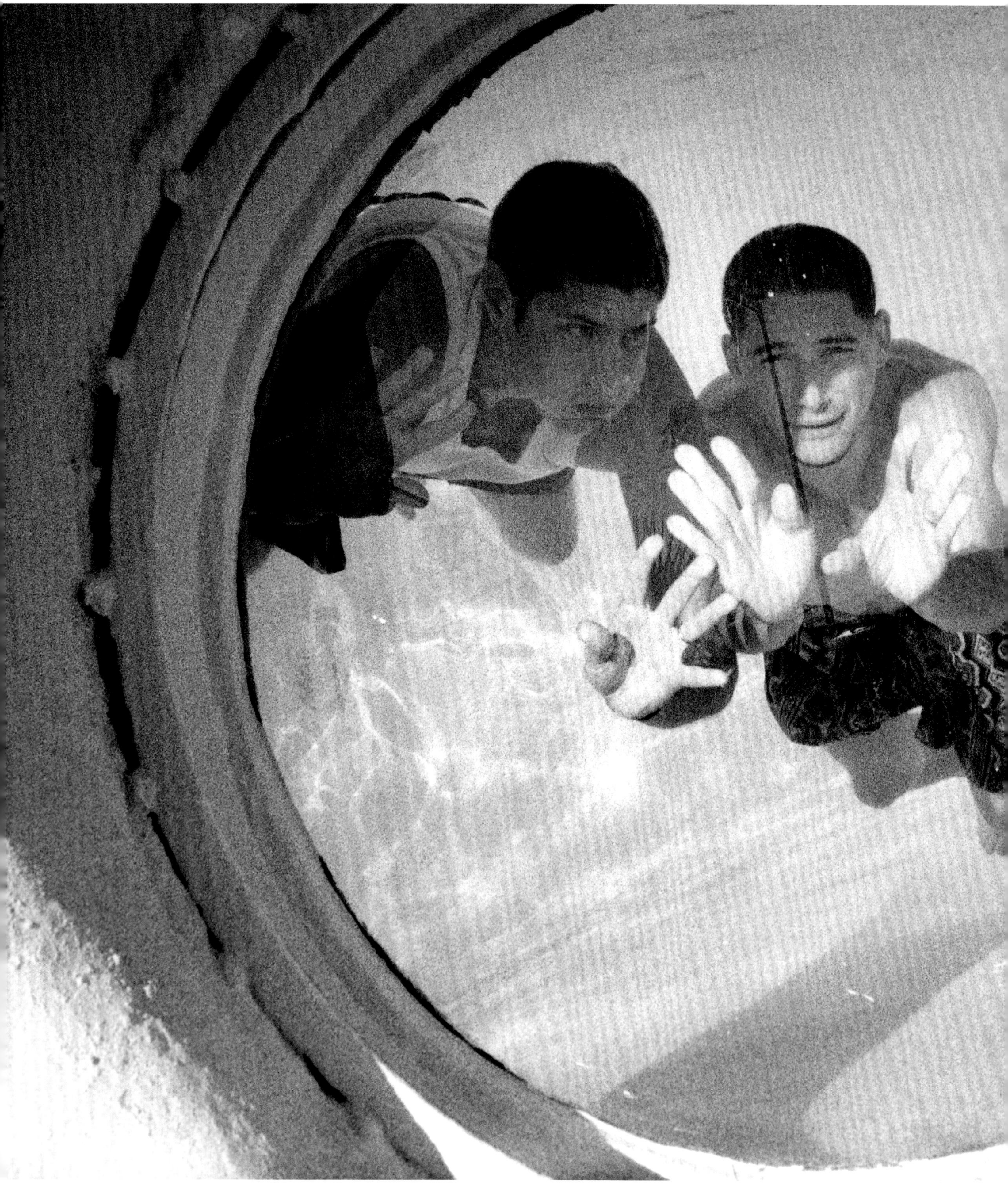

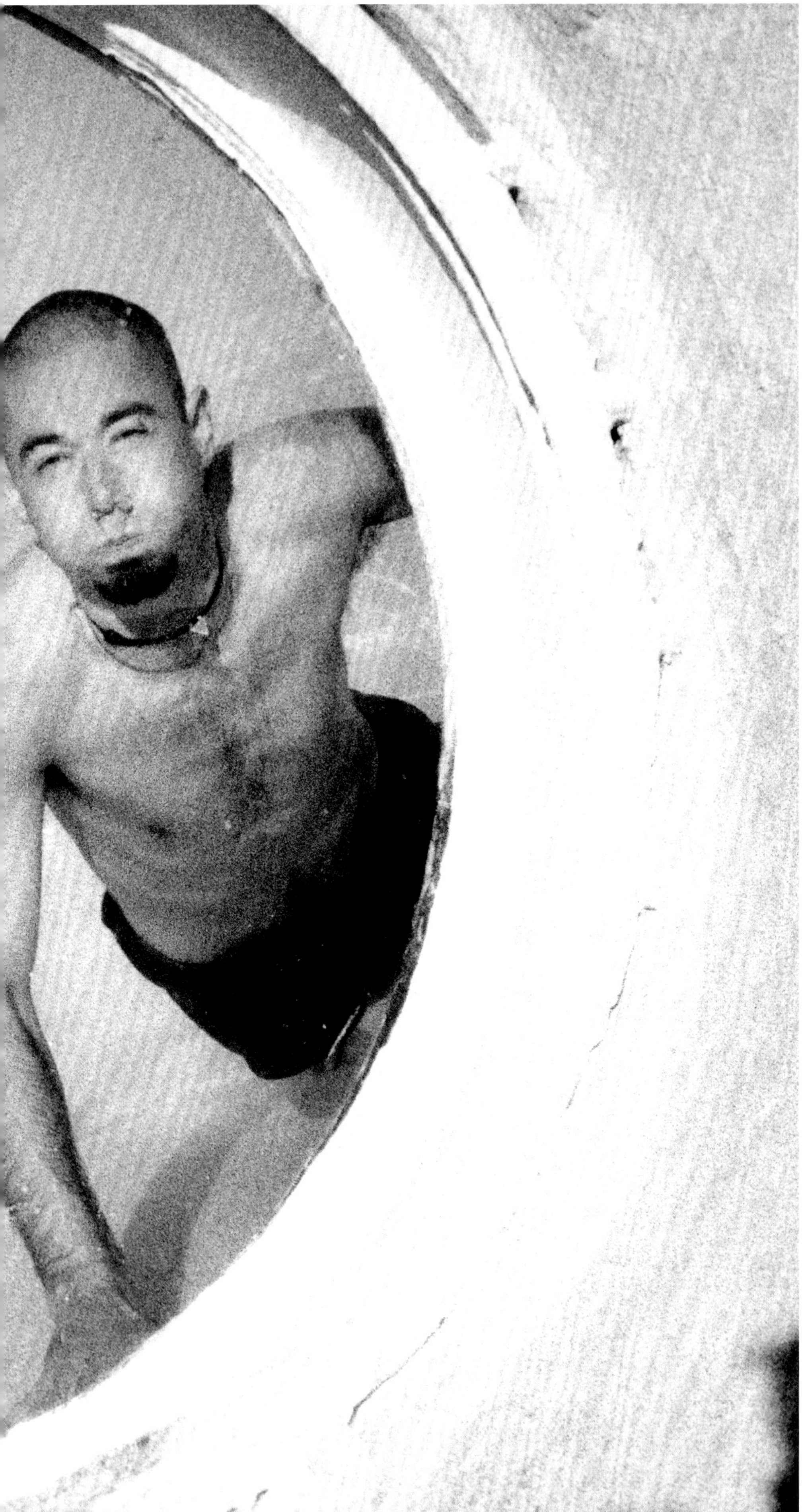

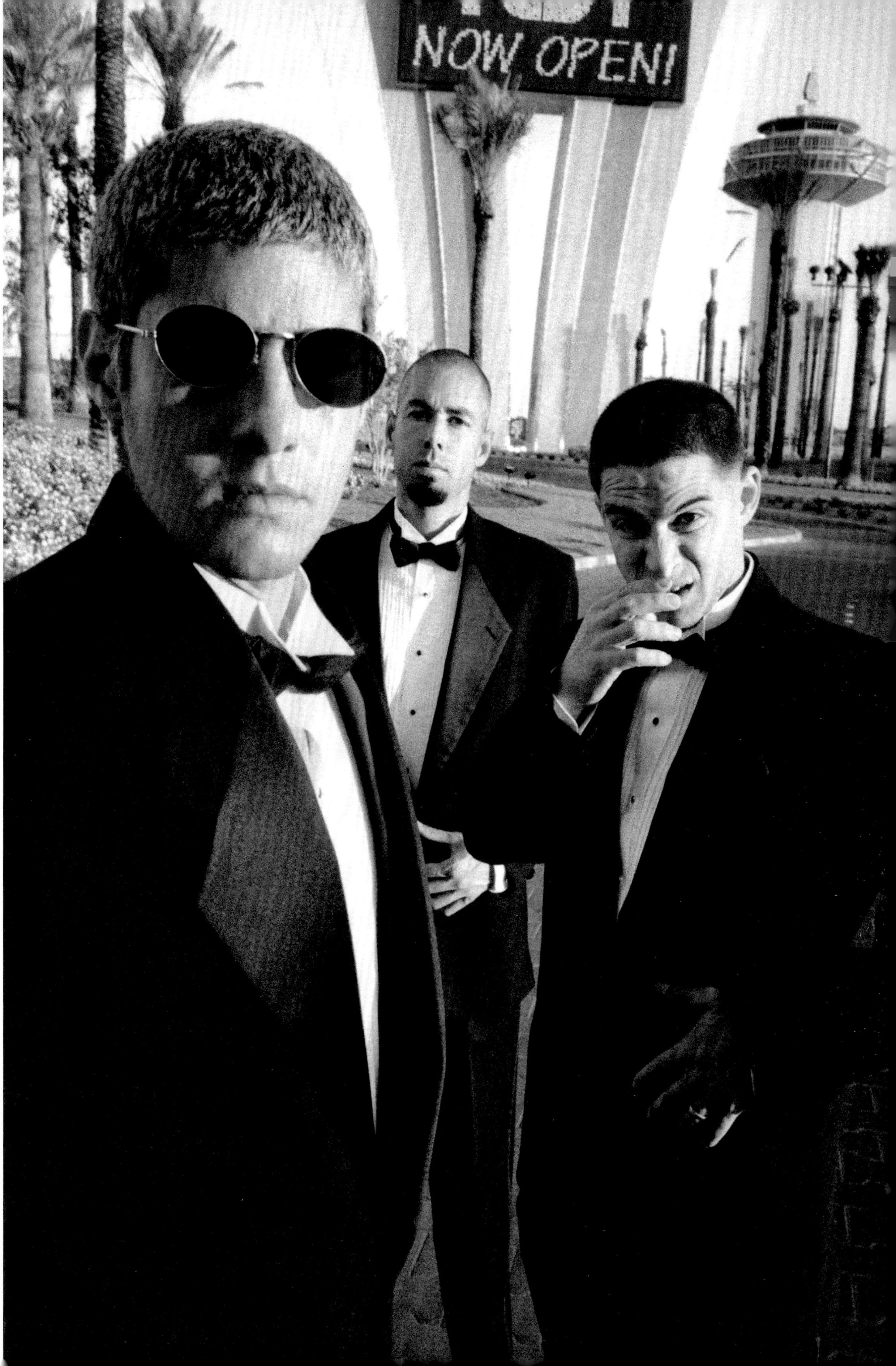
NOW OPEN!

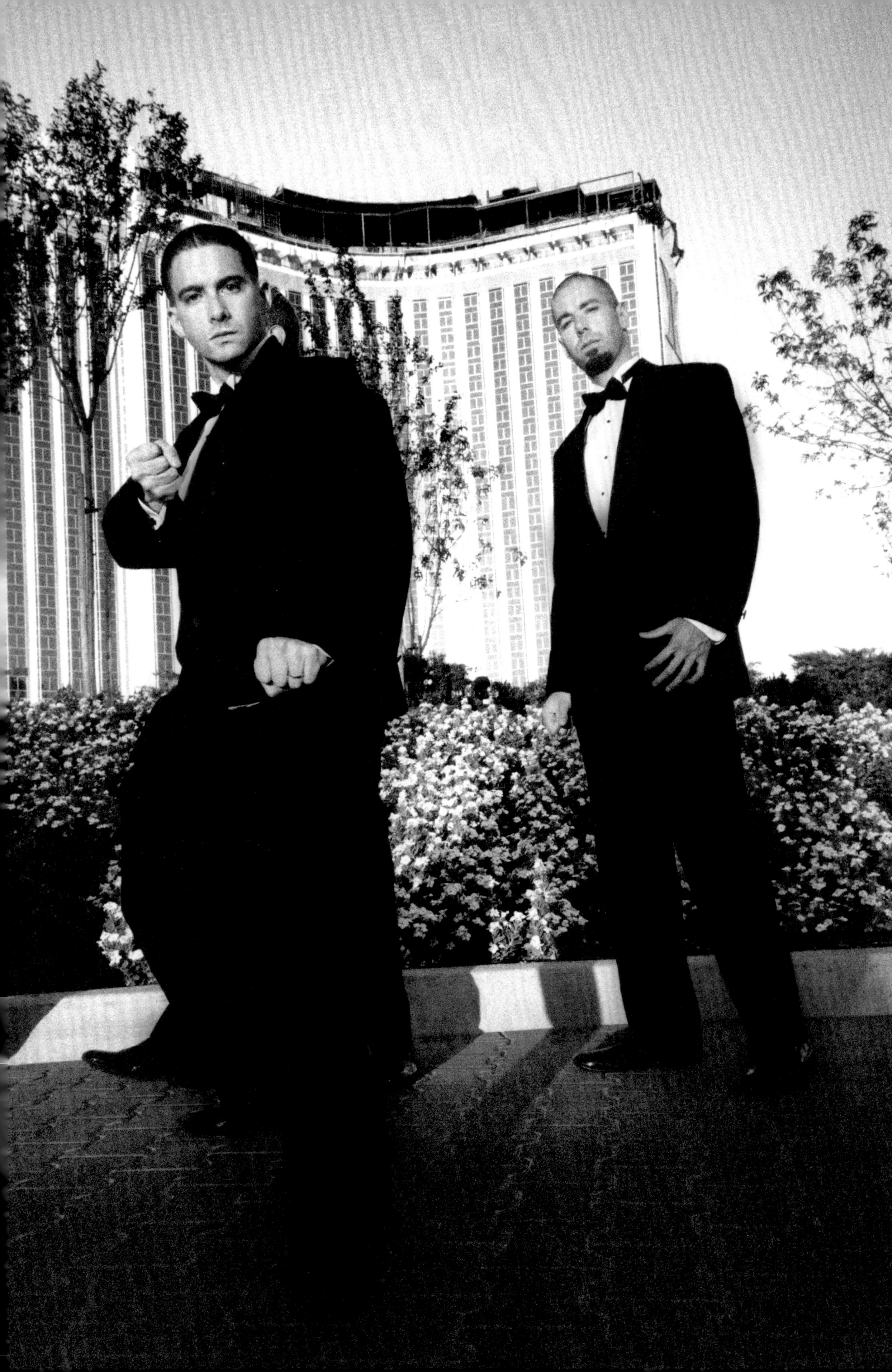

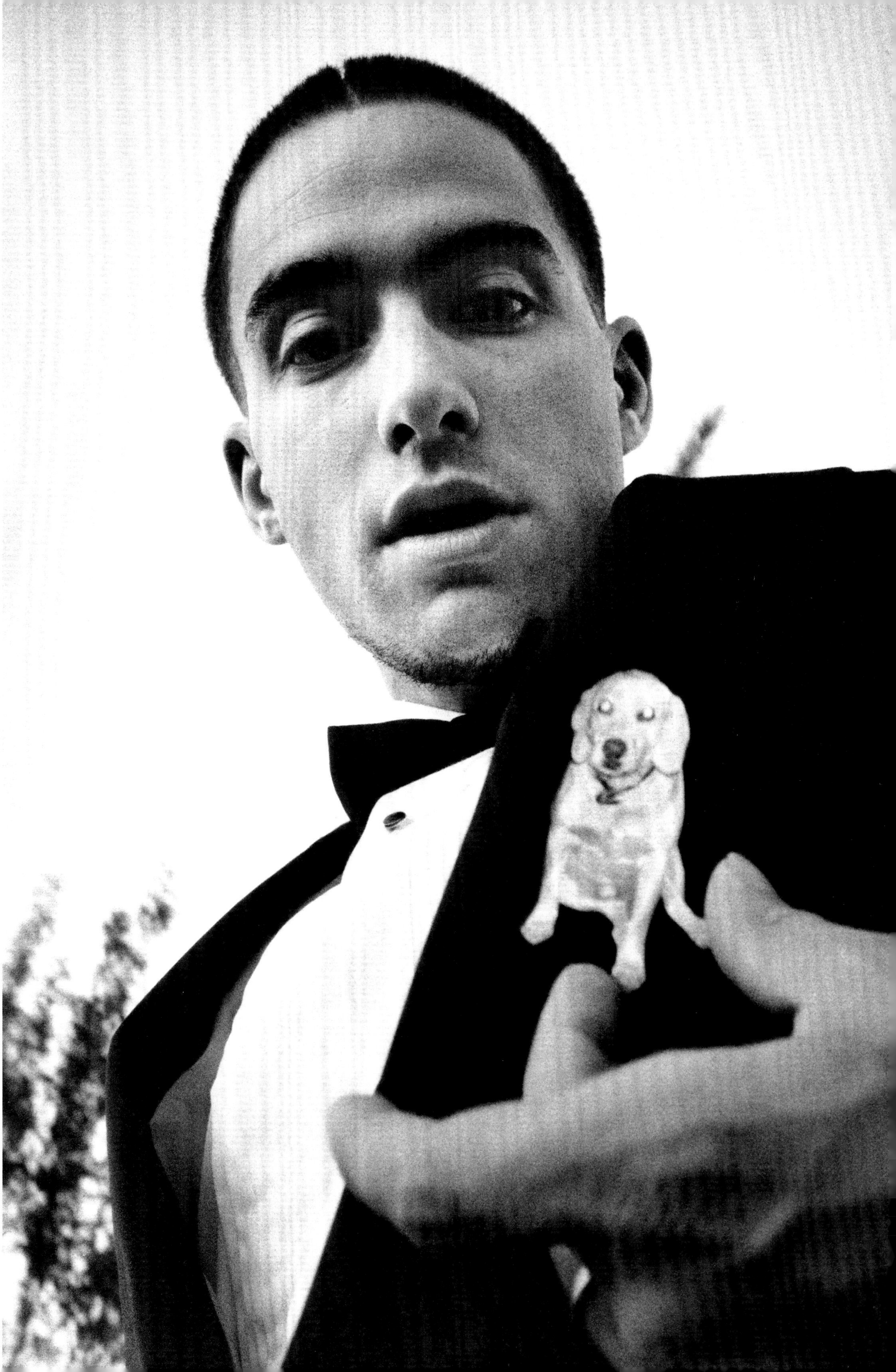

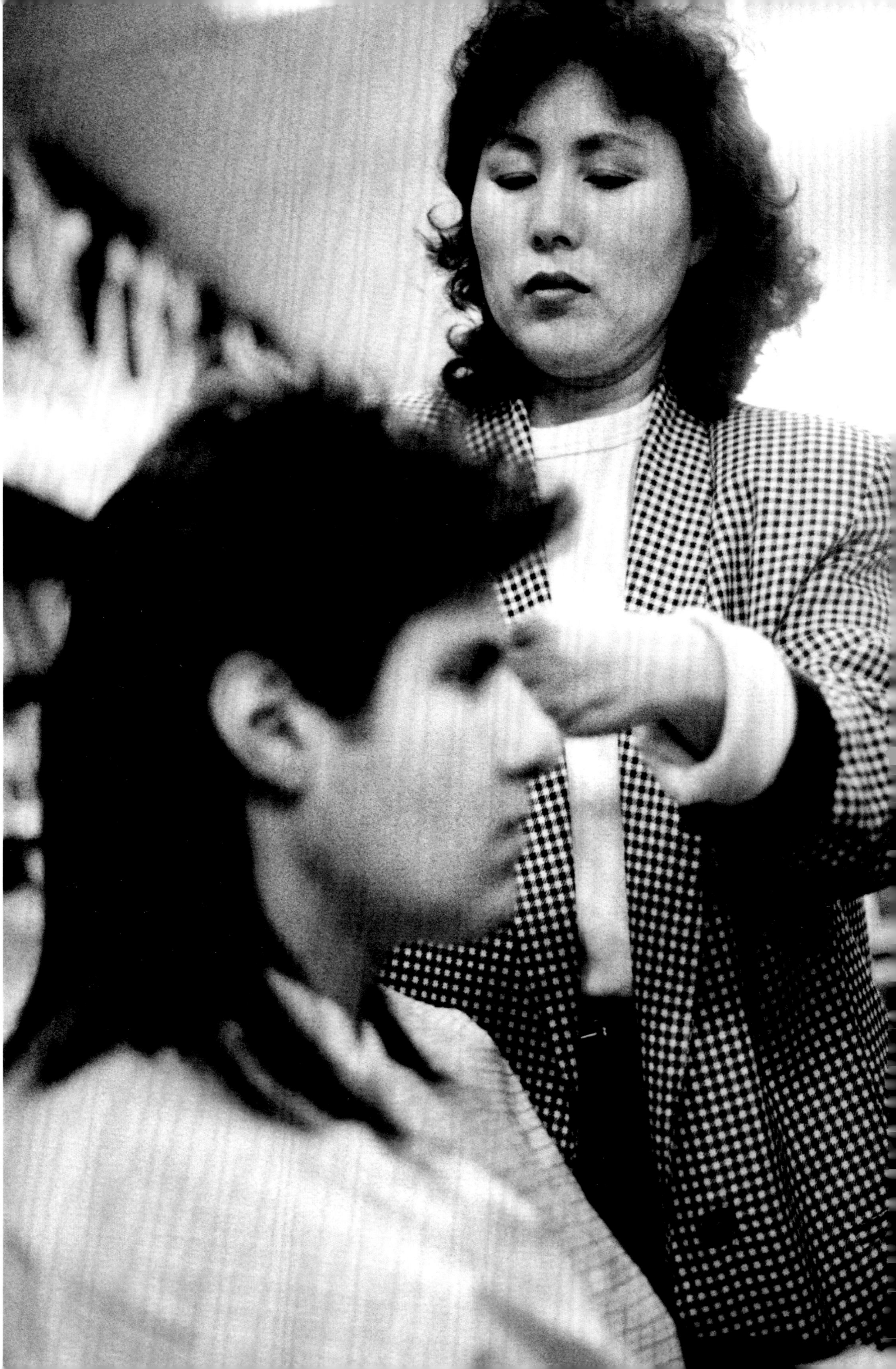

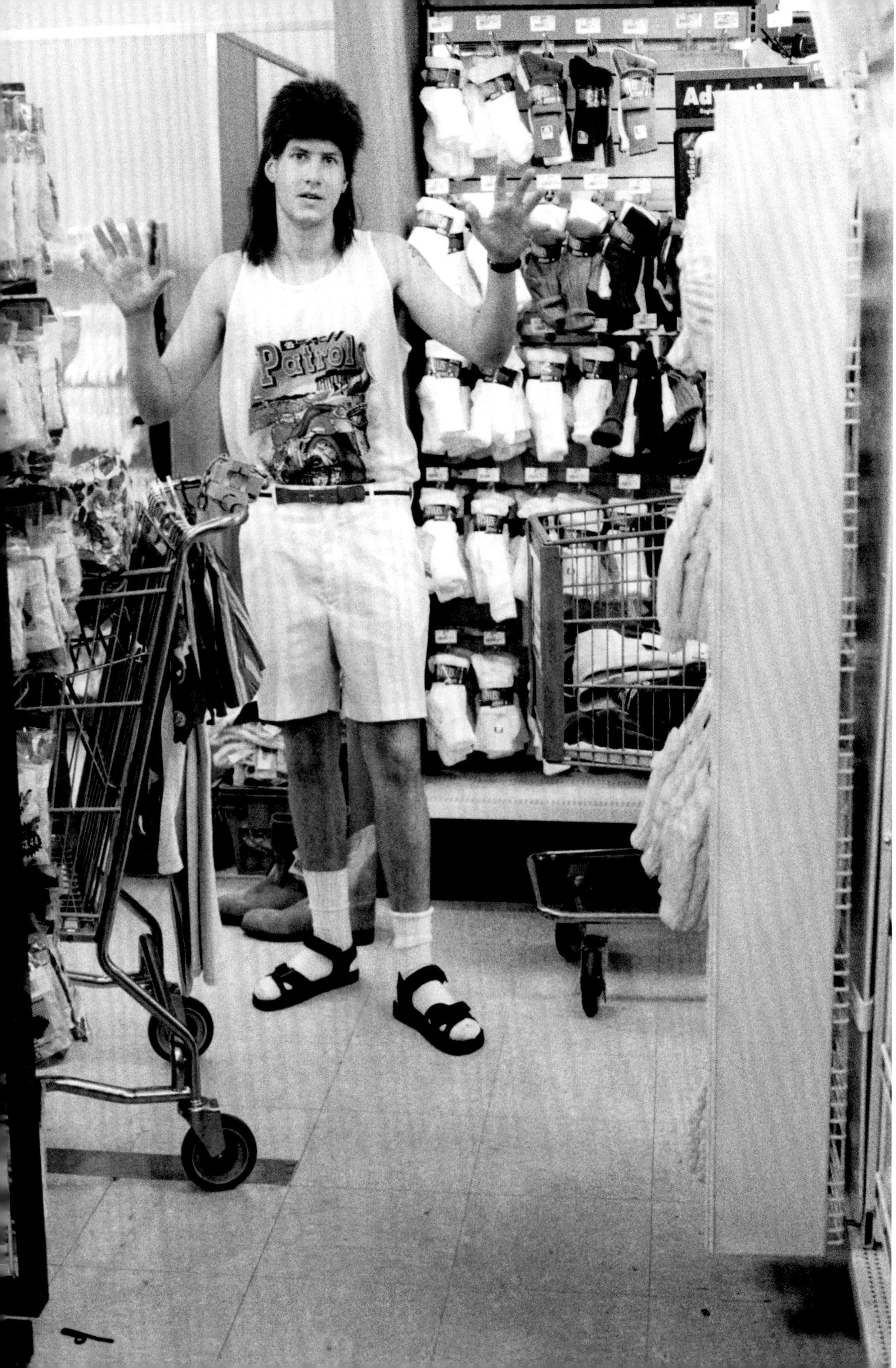
Patrol

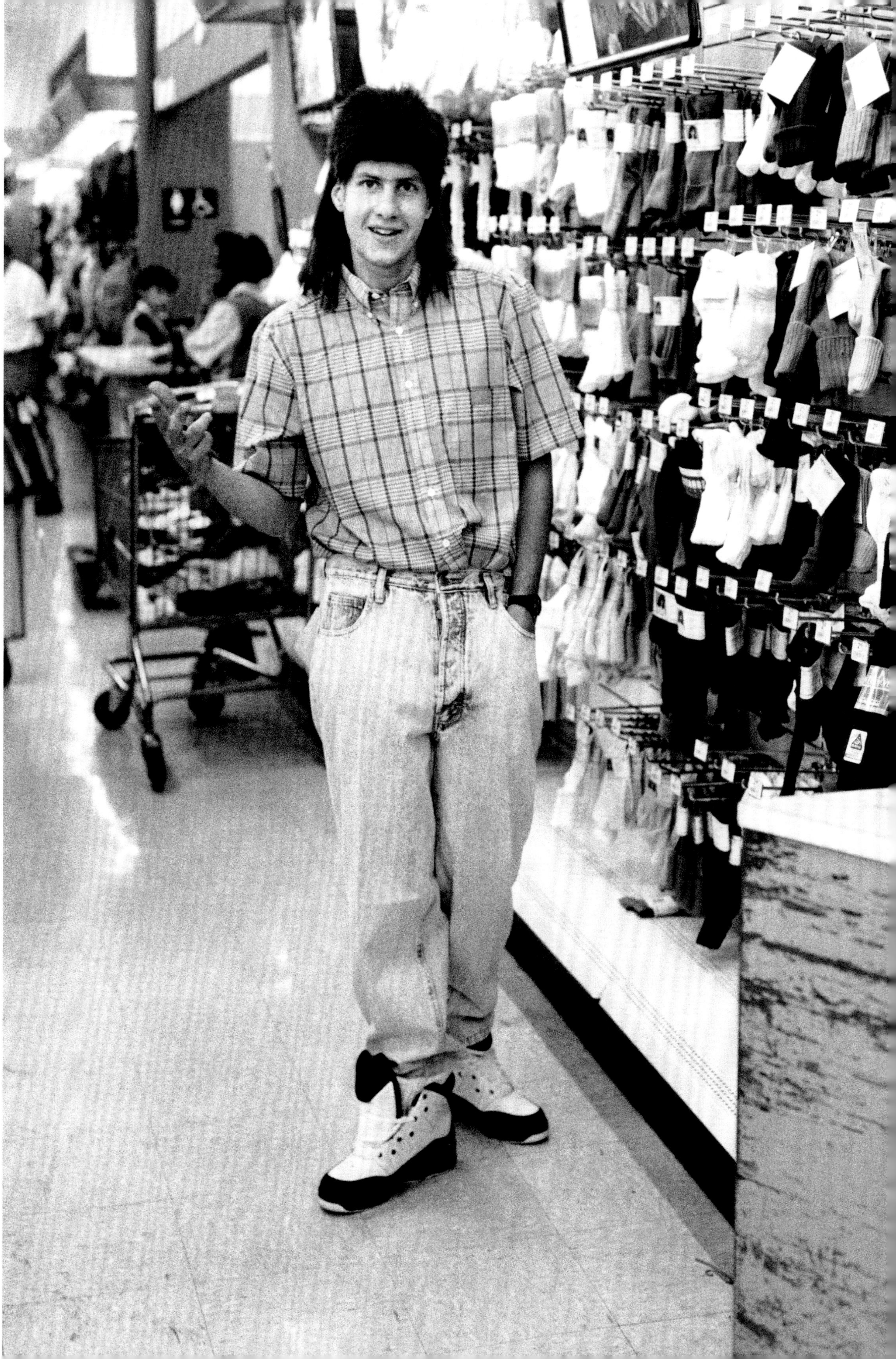

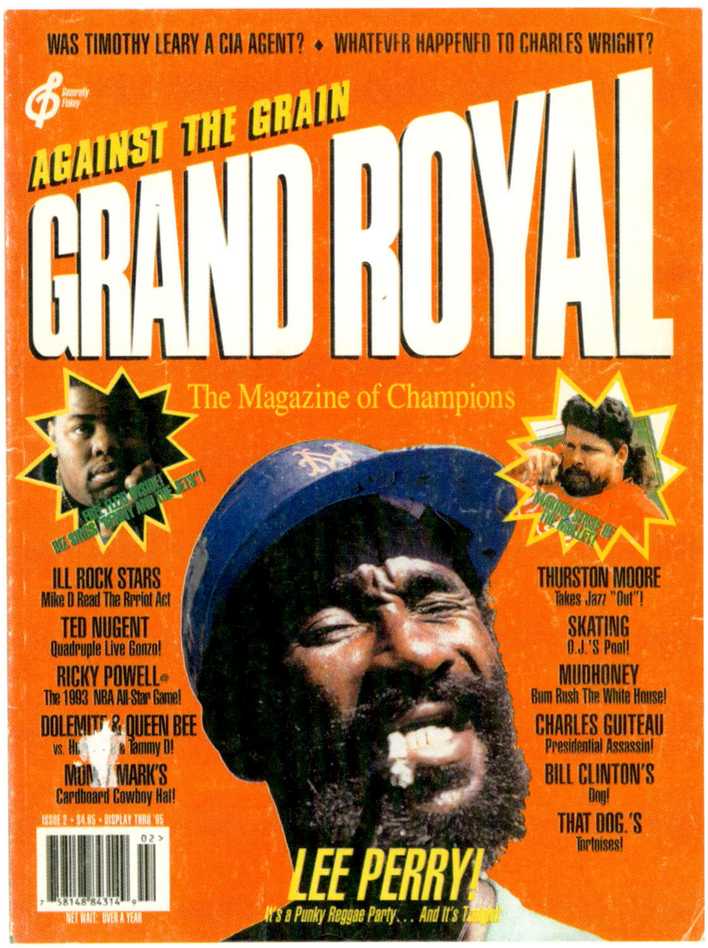

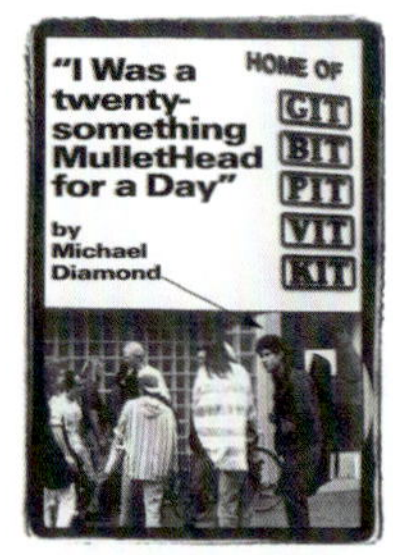

11:00 a.m. Spike and I let our fingers do the walking (that's '70s speak for check the Yellow Pages) and decide on Hollywood Wigs on Hollywood Boulevard in Hollywood, California. We are reassured that the Mullet wig is in stock when the woman on the phone goes, "Ohh, the shag!"

12:00 p.m. Depart for Hollywood dressed in vinyl trousers and listening to KNAC to get into right mood. This leads us to our first and most important Mullet discovery of the day: Smashing Pumpkins are in fact a heavy-metal band, and KNAC is nothing more than a heavy alternative to the already heavily alternative KROQ. We'd bargained for some Priest and Sabbath but got Al Stone Gossard's Pilots instead.

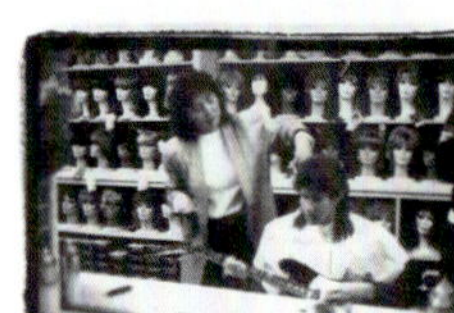

12:30 p.m. Arrive at Hollywood Wigs, purchase light brown shag and obtain custom Mulletization from perplexed Asian proprietor. Only after repeated requests to look like Billy Ray Cyrus does reticent barber cut sides to desired length.

1:00 p.m. Pull up to Musicians Institute of Technology, aka Mullet Institute of Technology, just as classes are letting out. With gig bag in tow, I muster the courage to mingle with students and initiate conversation by asking how the school is. Student Mullet Number One asks me what style of guitar I enjoy playing. I respond, "rock, riffs, licks, you know," while looking at ground. Then I ask if the school is very expensive and he confirms that "it's expensive, but I'm doing it all on loans. I'm paying for it later." Next I ask if it's hard, and he states somewhat cryptically that "anyone can get in, but it's hard to get out. By the time you reach the third level, it's very difficult unless you have theory." He pauses and then asks if I have any theory. I sheepishly but honestly repy no. "Then I strongly suggest you get some before coming here," he advises. Defeated, I try to mill around for a sec but soon head for Hollywood Boulevard in search of more like-minded Mullets.

1:30 p.m. Proceed to generic rock t-shirt shop on Hollywood Boulevard. Amidst row upon row of black Cypress Hill, Pantera and Megadeth merch, we overhear our favorite Mullet quote of the day: "What I like to do is overdub a bunch of tracks of my leads first, and then I do my vocals." We're not exactly sure what that means, but we definitely agree that it's awesome.

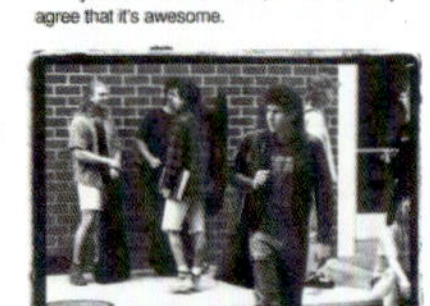

2:30 p.m. Following an uneventful lunch at heavy metal Denny's, where no significant Mullet citings can be reported, we head for Aron's Records in hopes of getting dissed by the high-brow indie-rock cashiers for buying a Joe Satrianni box set. Unfortunately, we soon realize that there are way too many Mullet Heads and assorted Hollywood freaks already frequenting the place for management to be fazed by our appearance. I do, however, earn bonus points for spotting DGC A&R honcho Mark "Kato" Kates and conspicuously brushing up against him with my gig bag while sifting through the bins. At first mildly annoyed and then positively terrified, Kates moves away with increasing alarm before retreating to the far wall of the store, where I finally corner him and brandish a "demo tape" of "my band." Kates begins to bolt, but upon closer inspection recognizes and curses me. I finally go to counter, ask for new Smashing Pumpkins and am mortified to find that the salespeople are more than happy to offer me assistance. (Reached for comment later, Kales revealed that "all I could think was, 'Git!' I know it's been a few years, but this is still L.A. and there are a lot of these guys around. They make me uncomfortable.")

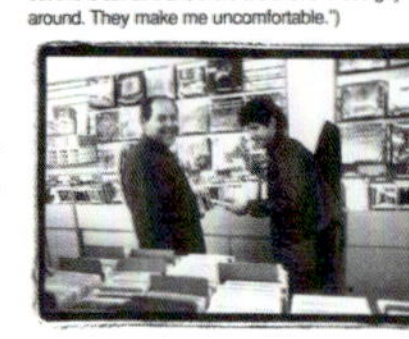

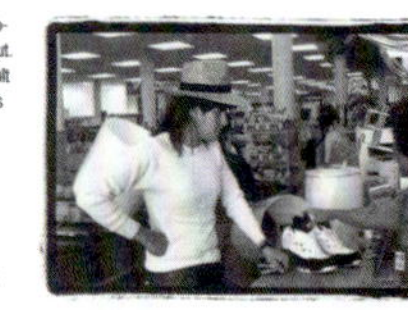

3:30 p.m. After a quick stop at K-Mart to pick up some more Mullet haberdashery, we arrive at Mullet Mecca: The Guitar Center on Sunset. We bow in front of Eddie Van Halen's autographed guitar in the front window and enter the same shrine where

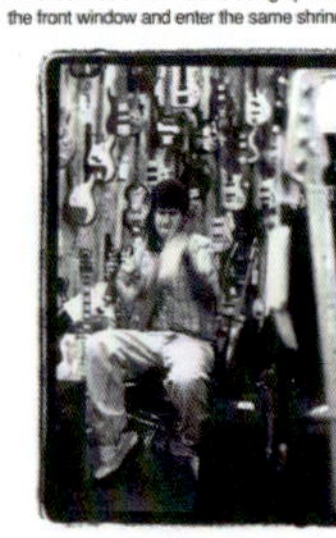

some of the most important Mullets in history have shopped. I test-drive several different Flying Vs, but when Spike's wig becomes entangled in his camera's motor drive, suspicion is aroused. The store manager walks over and asks us if he can help us with something. We try to keep a straight face and say that we're just looking for a "gnarly tool." He then asks us what we really want, and we use the tried and true "we're not from around here" excuse, claiming to be students from out of town in search of only a few snapshots at the world-famous G Center. So why were we putting on wigs and changing our outfits in the parking lot, he asks. We realize that our time as Mullet Heads is almost up.

4:00 p.m. till? Return to studio for rehearsal in my Fletch disguise, which fools Heart Attack Man for a good five minutes. Following rehearsal (during which Chris Rock compliments my phony Air Jordans), I'm dragged to a chi chi Hollywood Hills shindig with my wife, Tamra, who soon becomes buttonholed in conversation with James Woods. "Who is the long-haired gentleman that came with you tonight?" the notorious thespian asks with a hint of smirk, but is visibly dismayed (and Tamra even more visibly embarrassed) when she is forced to admit, "It's my husband." I continue partying on till the wee hours while facing the wrathful snarls of the assembled glitterati.

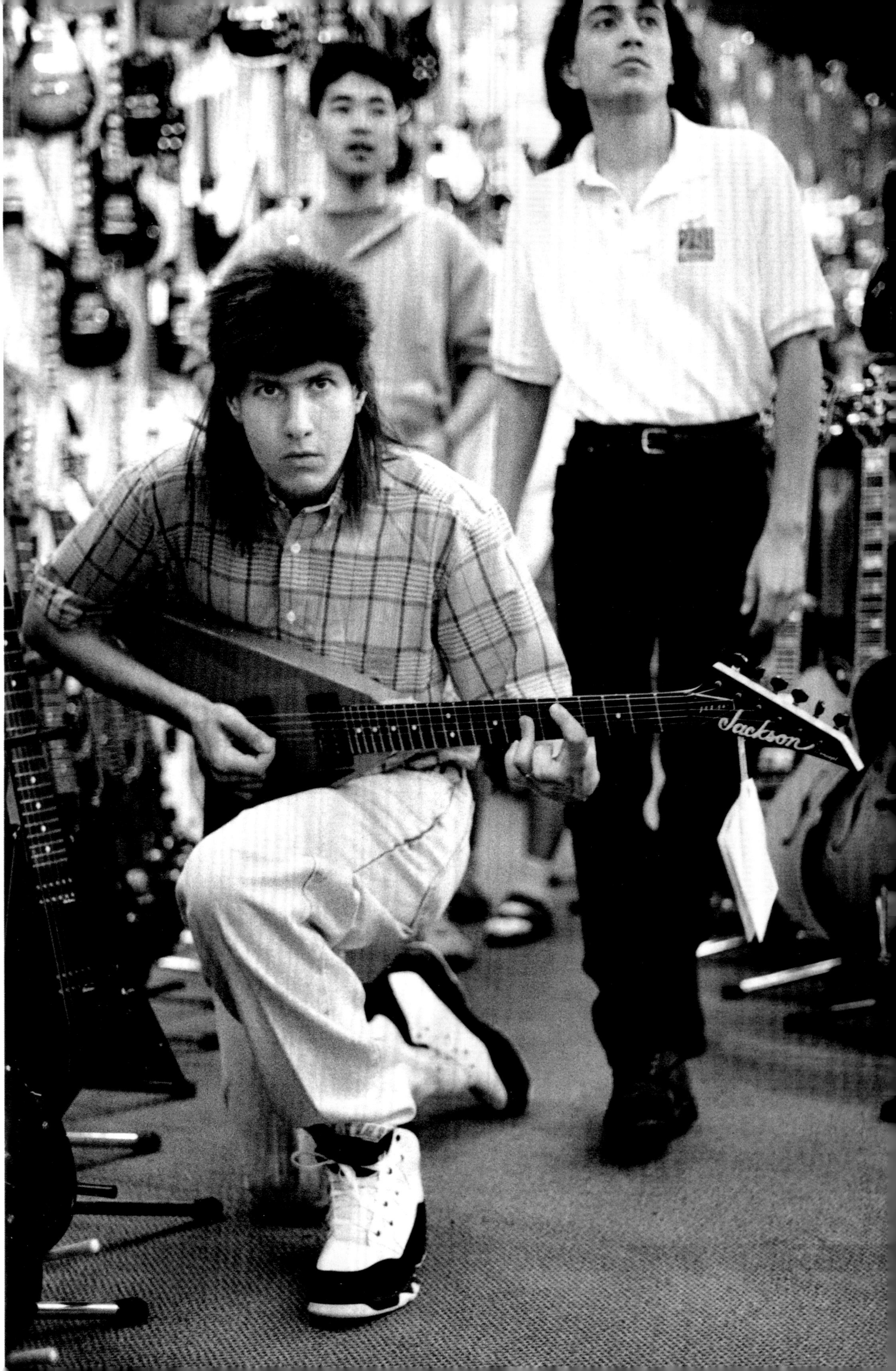
Jackson

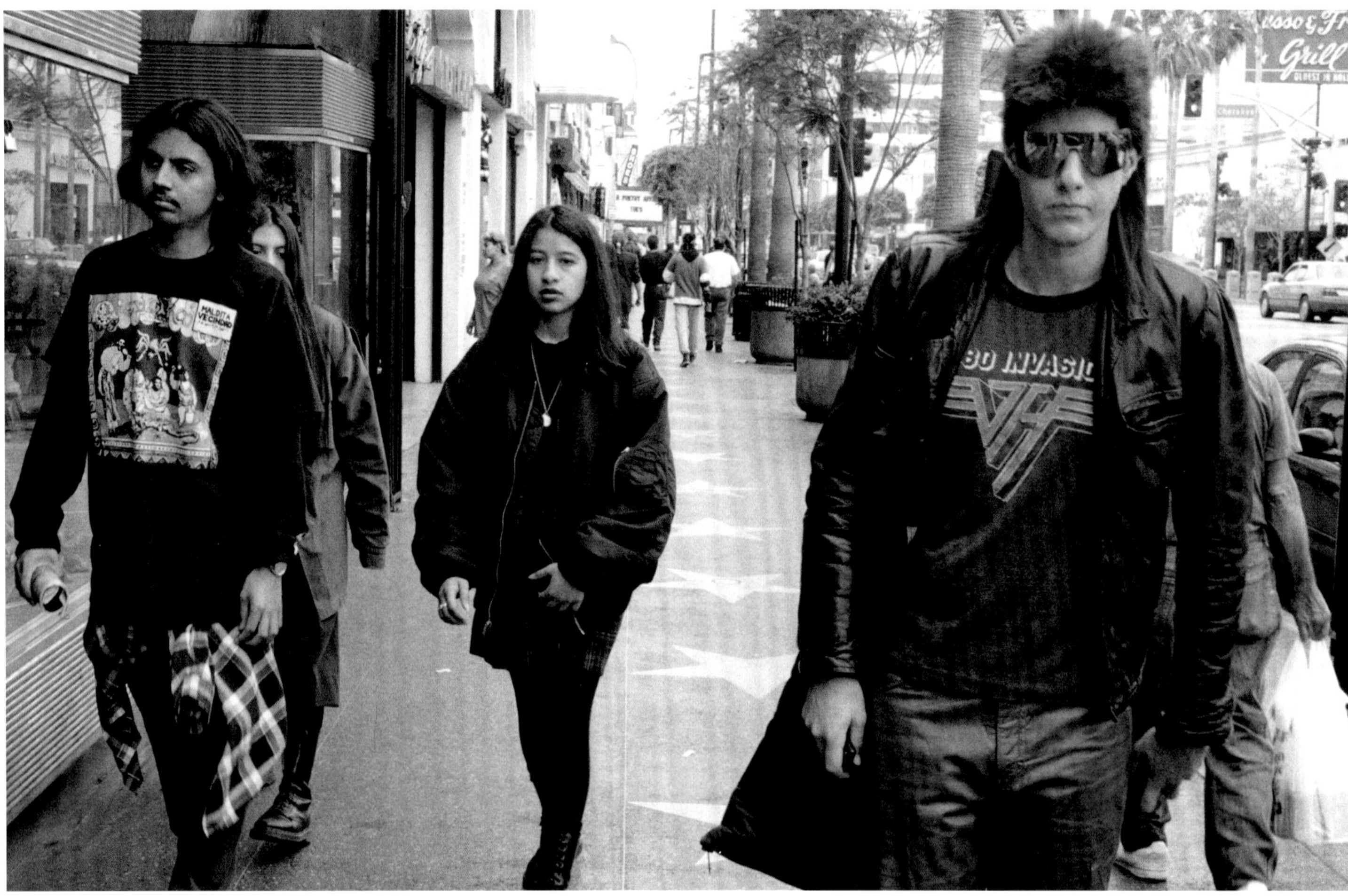
Grill

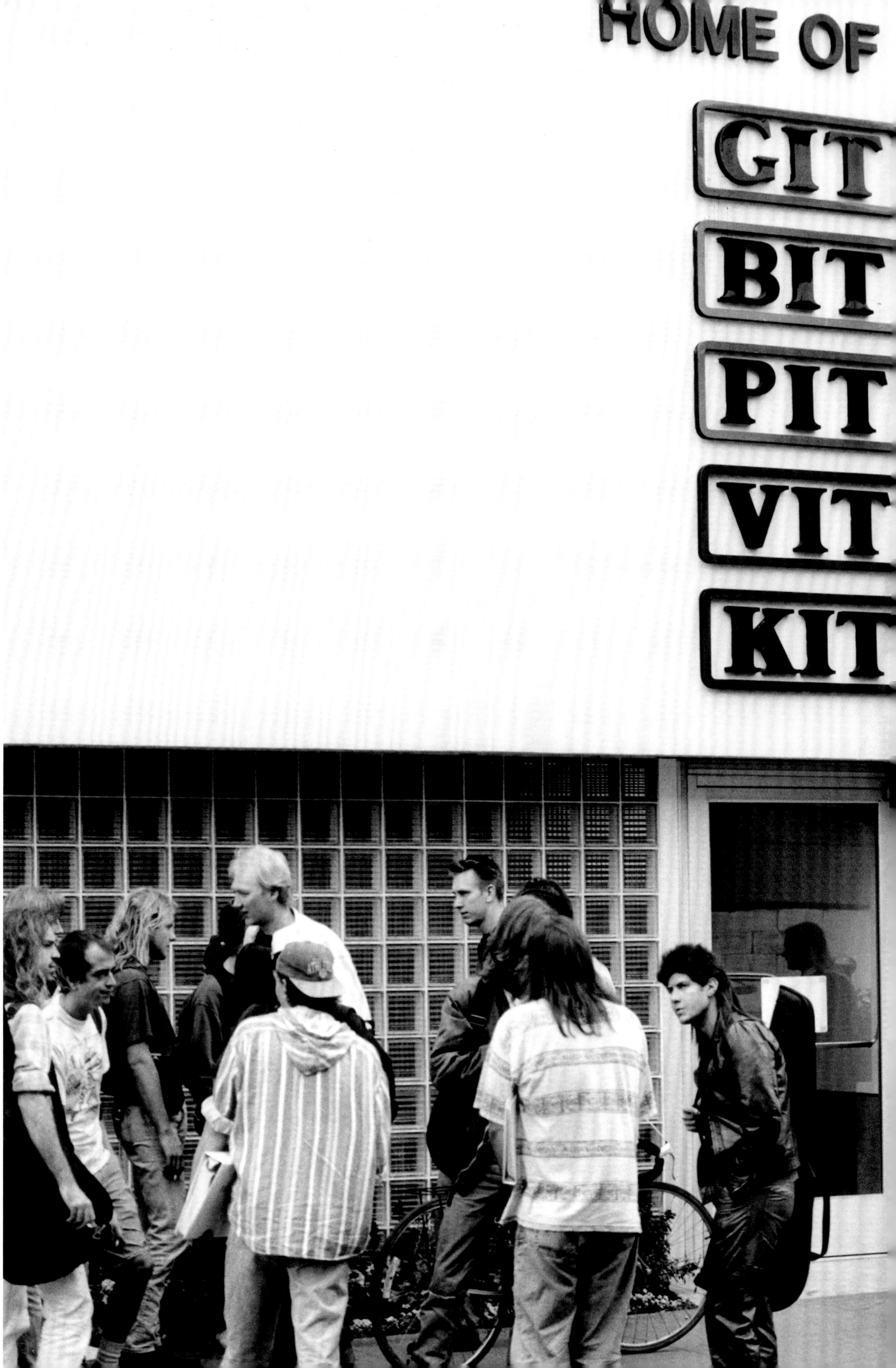
HOME OF
GIT
BIT
PIT
VIT
KIT

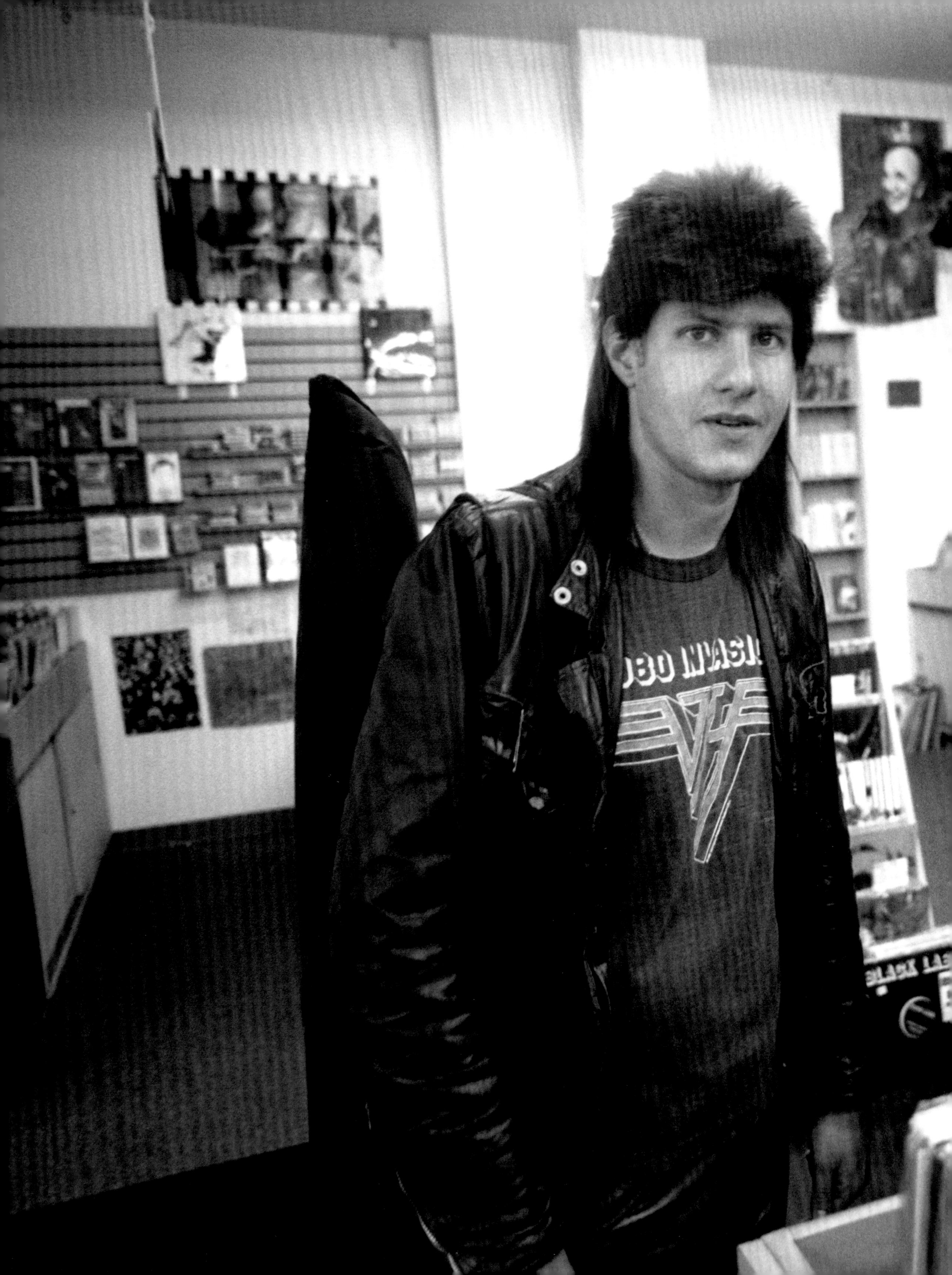

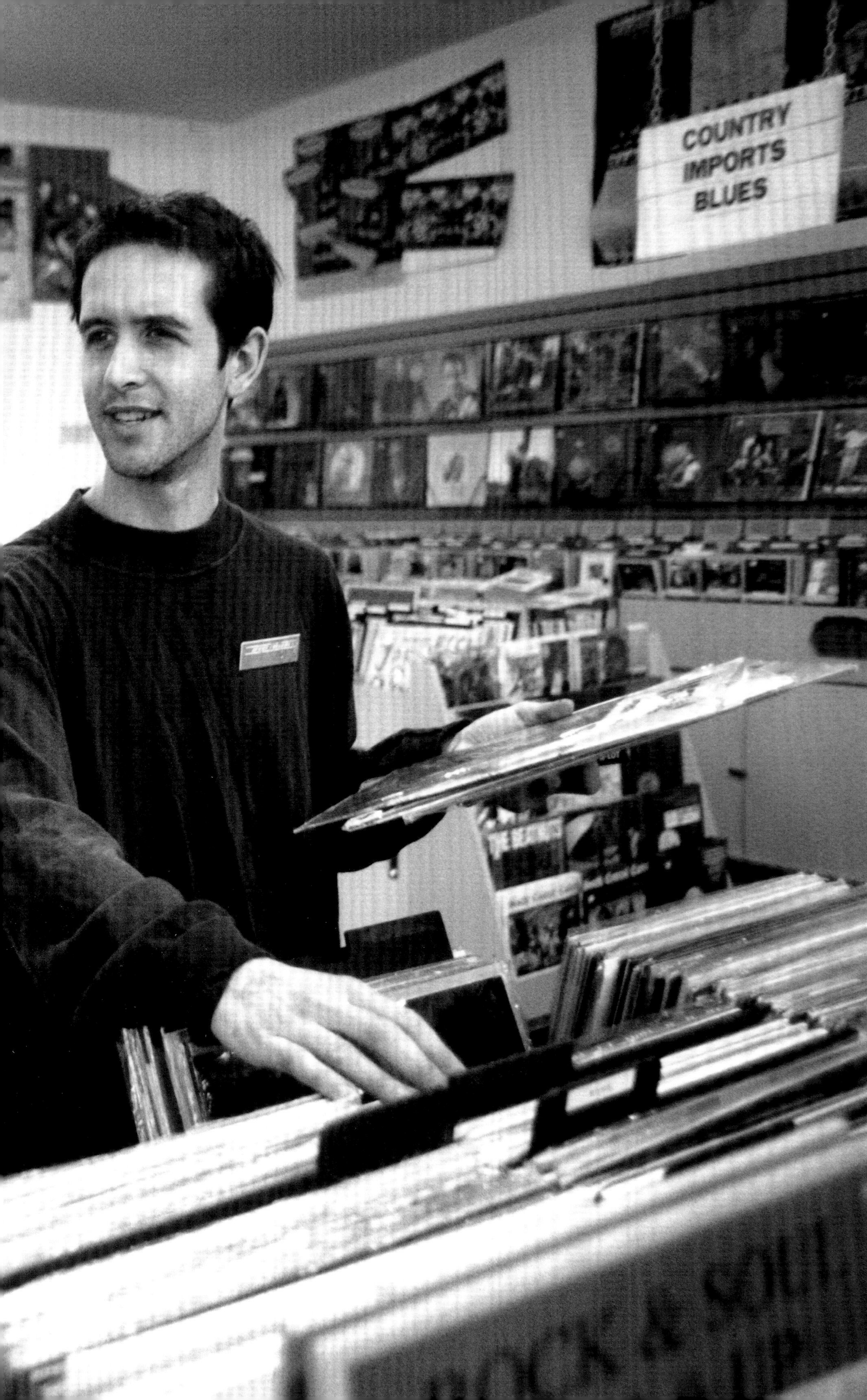
COUNTRY
IMPORTS
BLUES

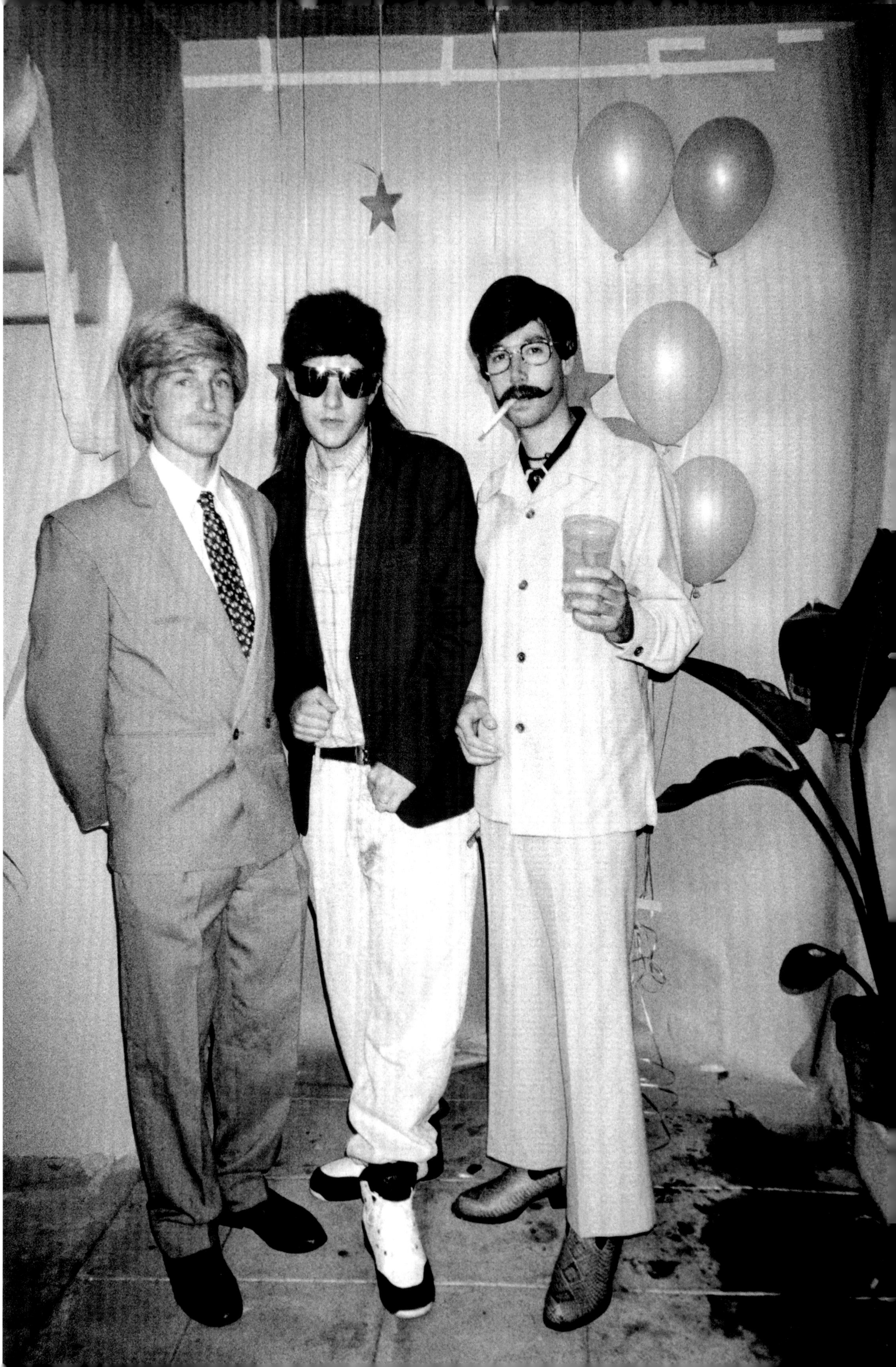

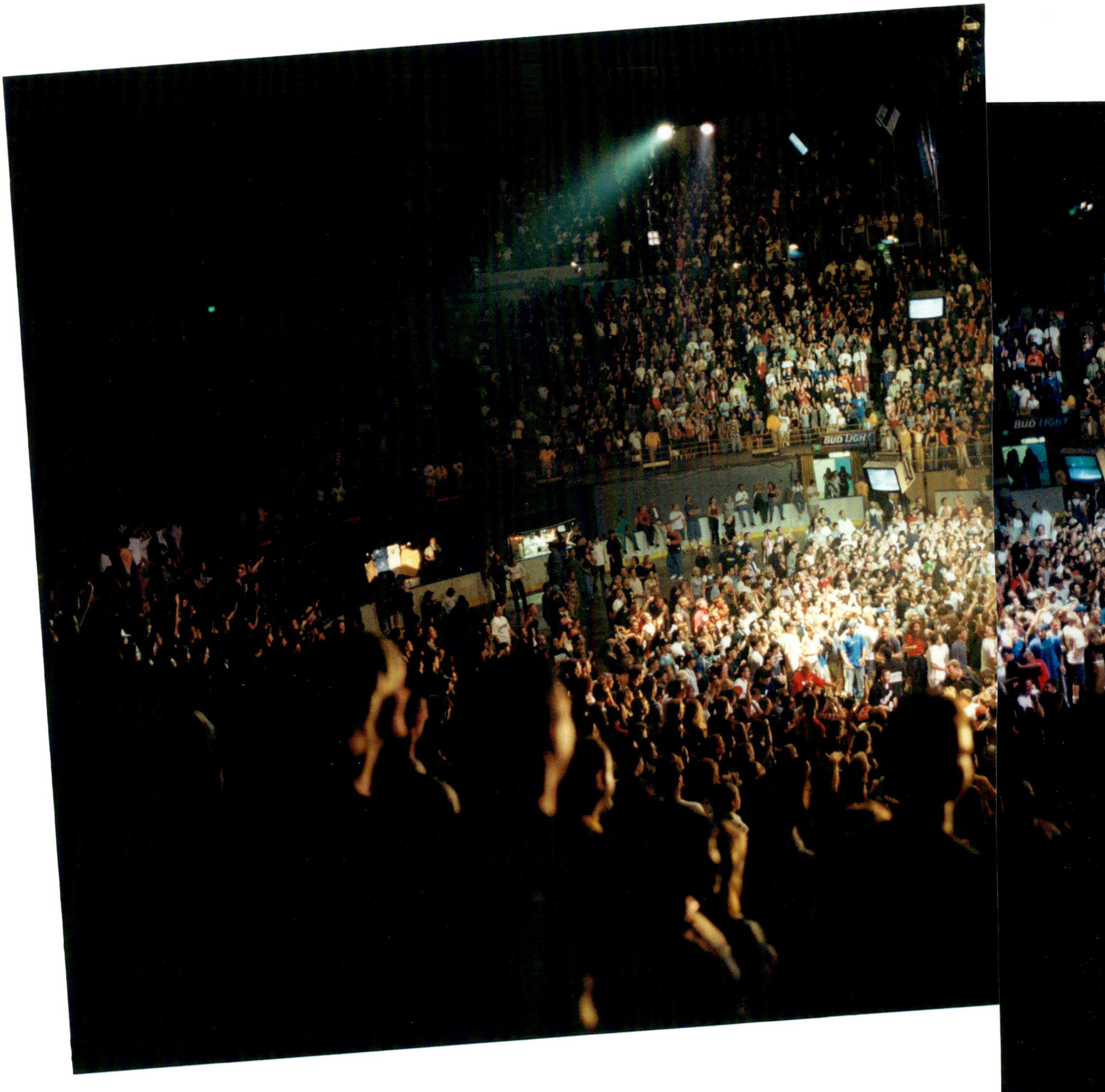
BUD LIGHT

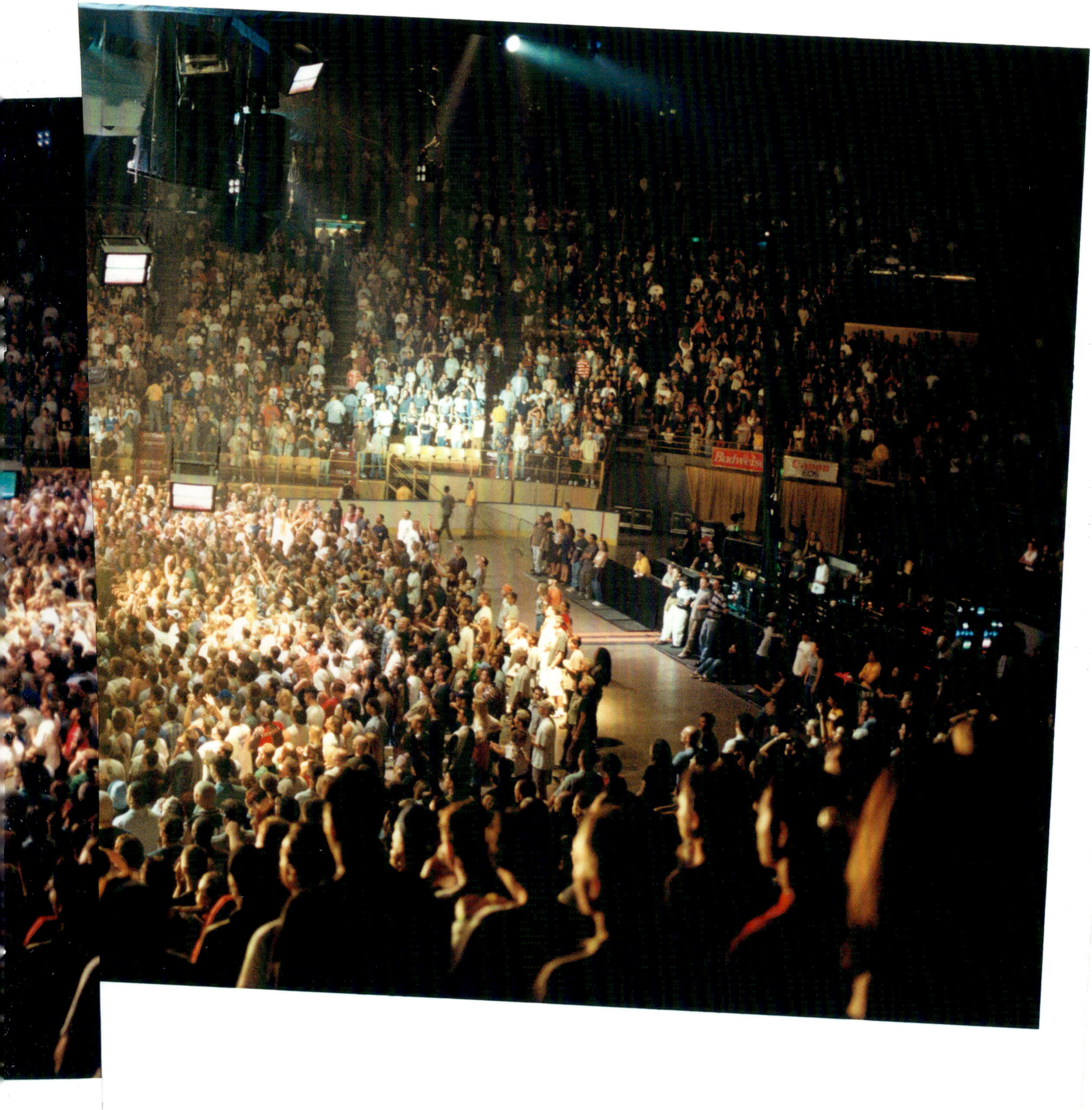

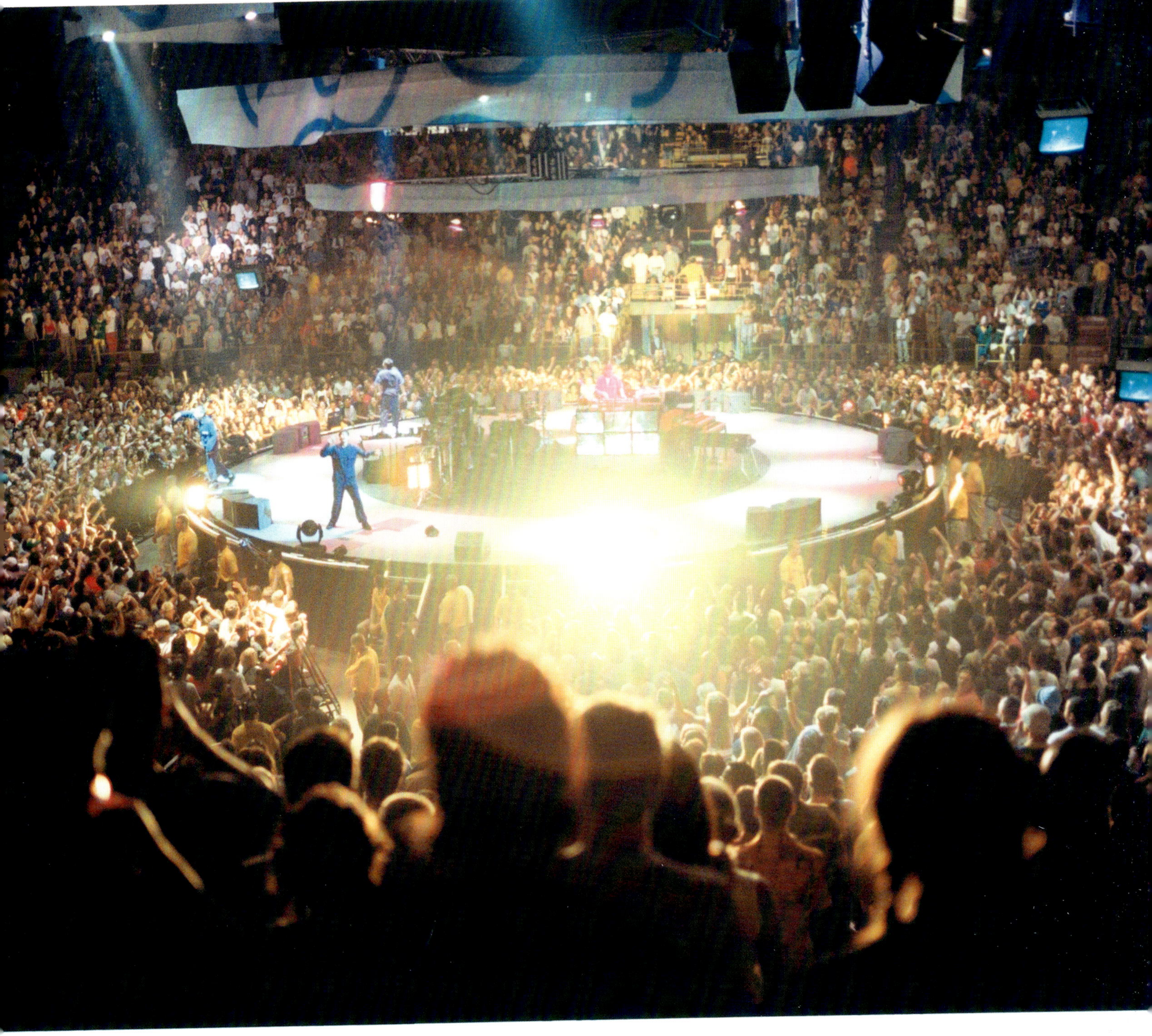

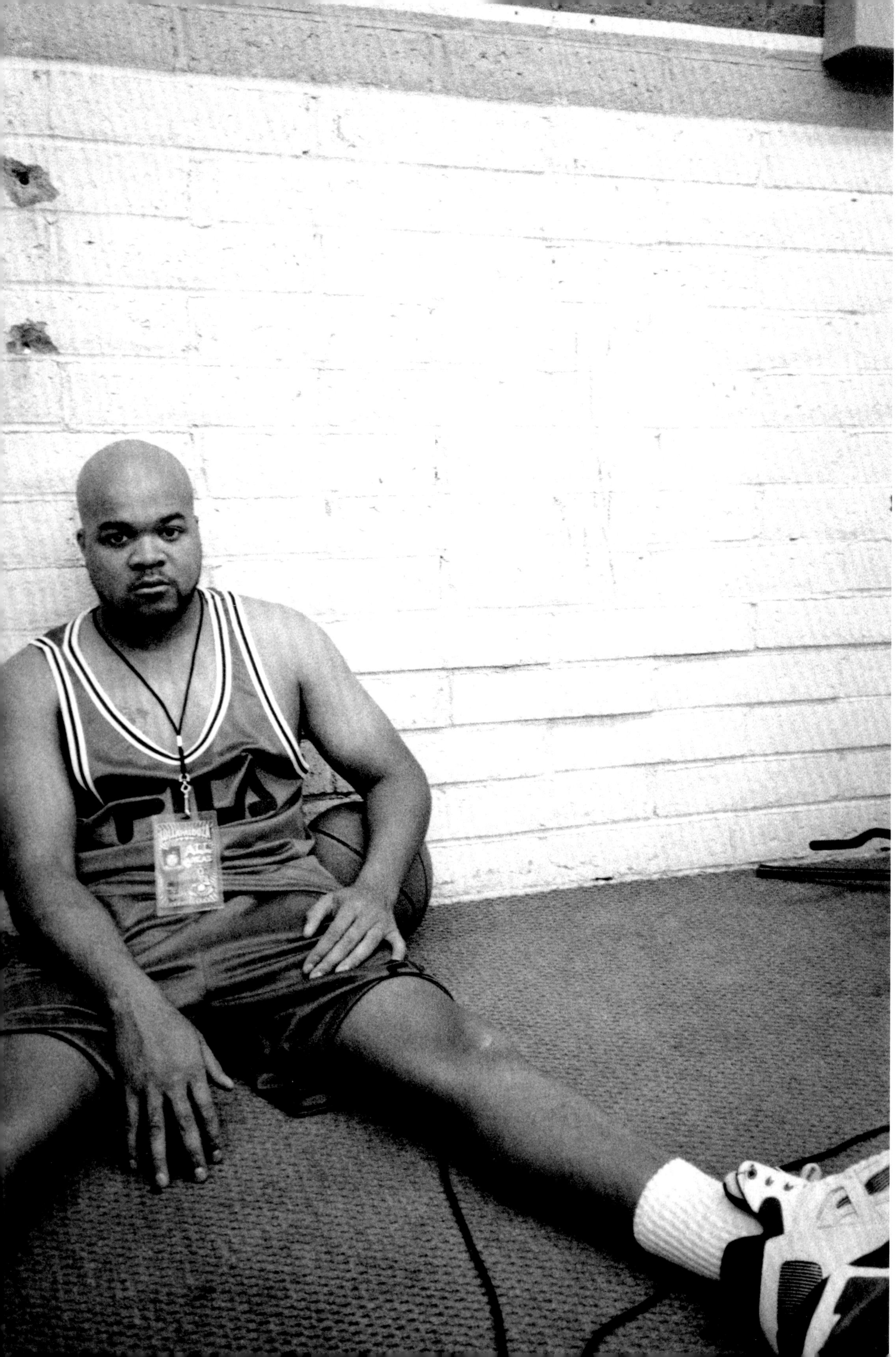

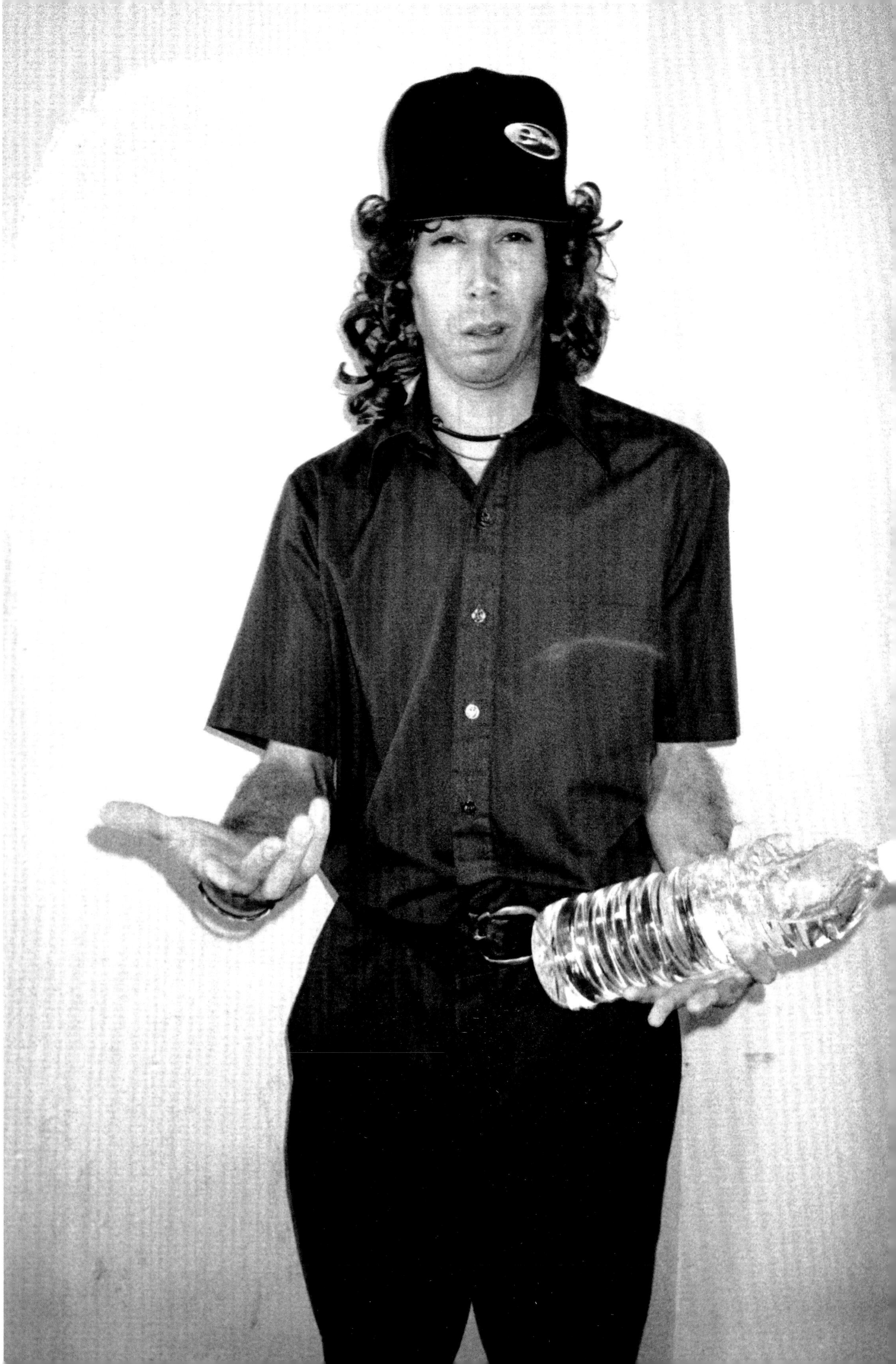

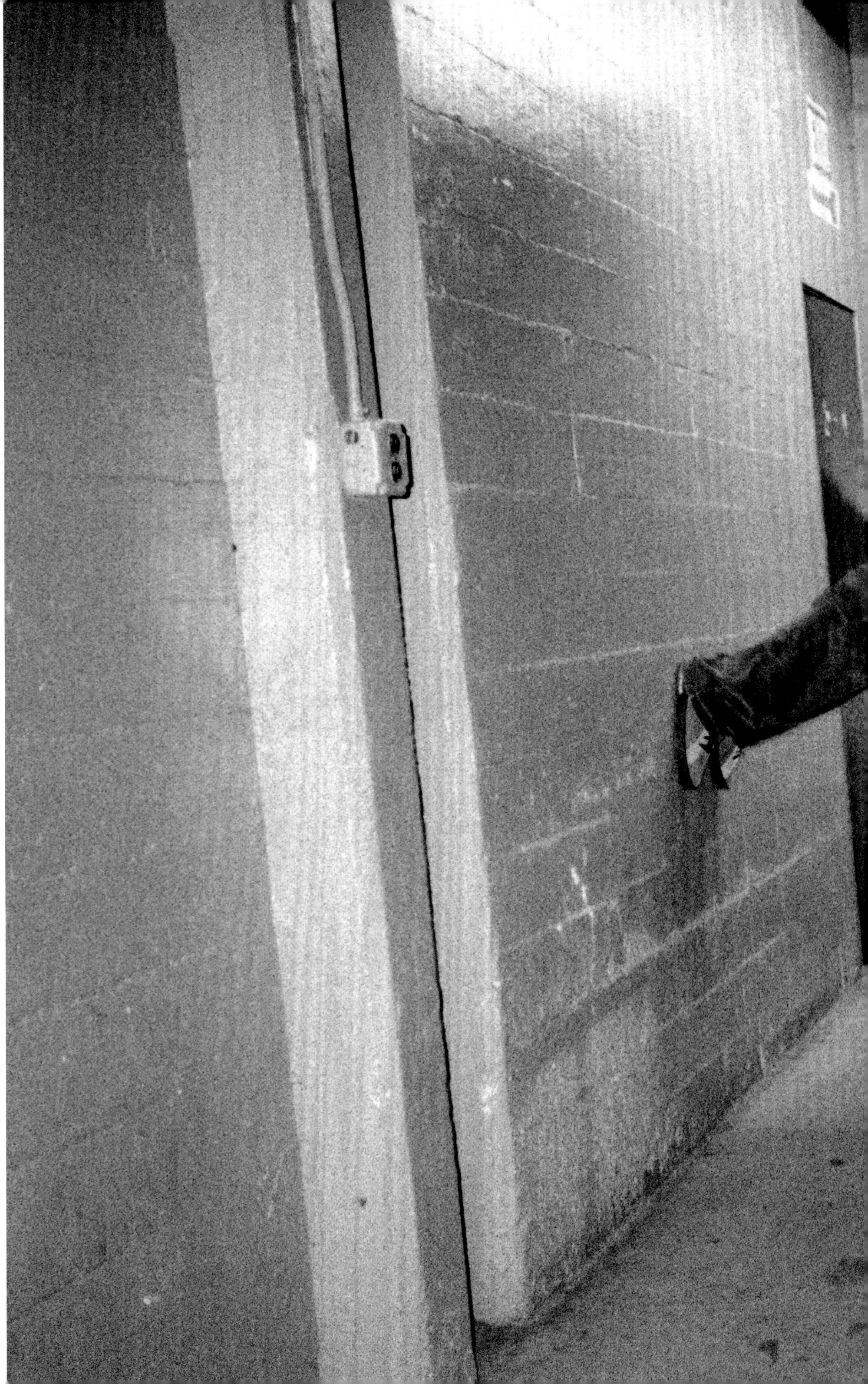

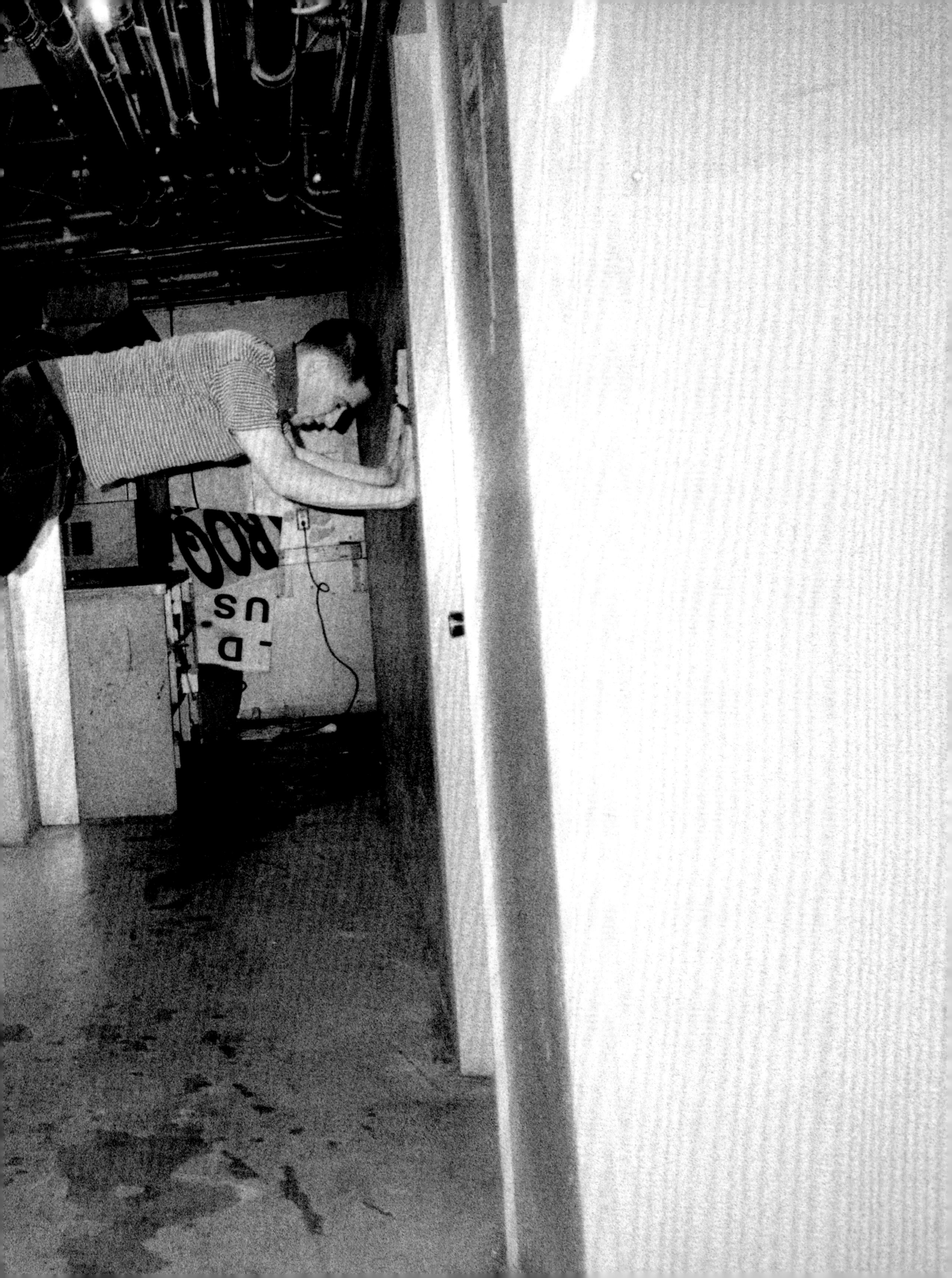

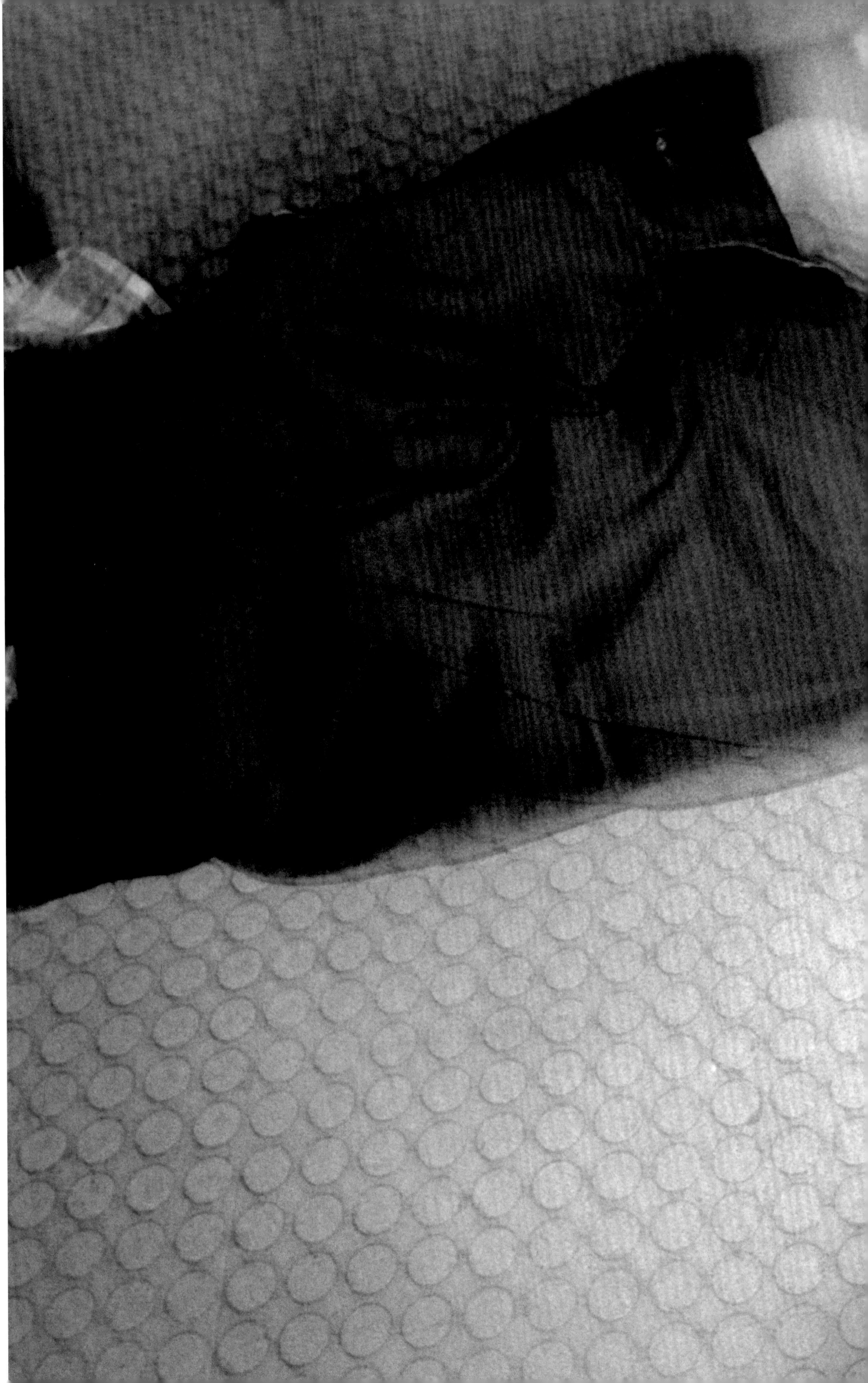

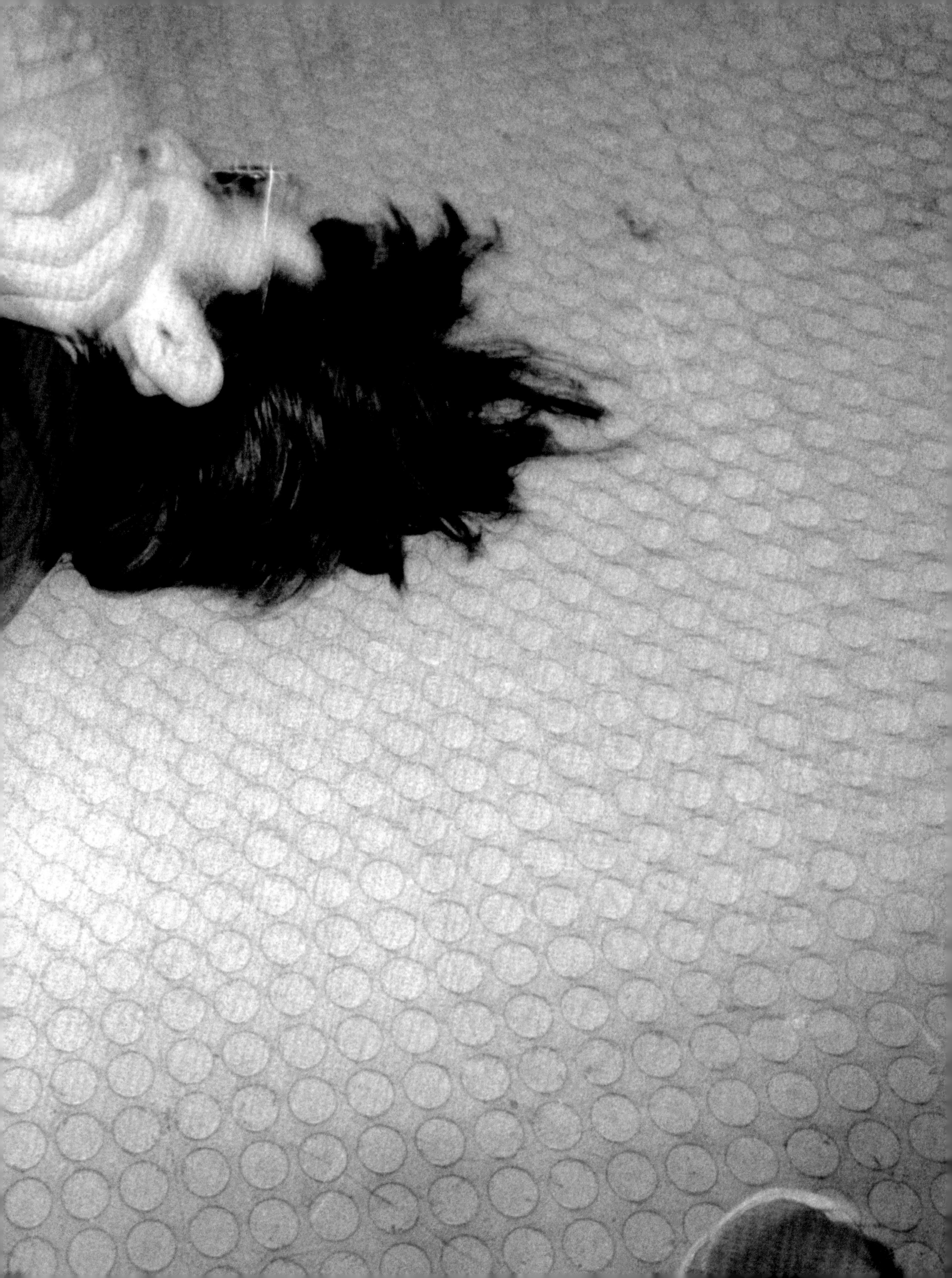

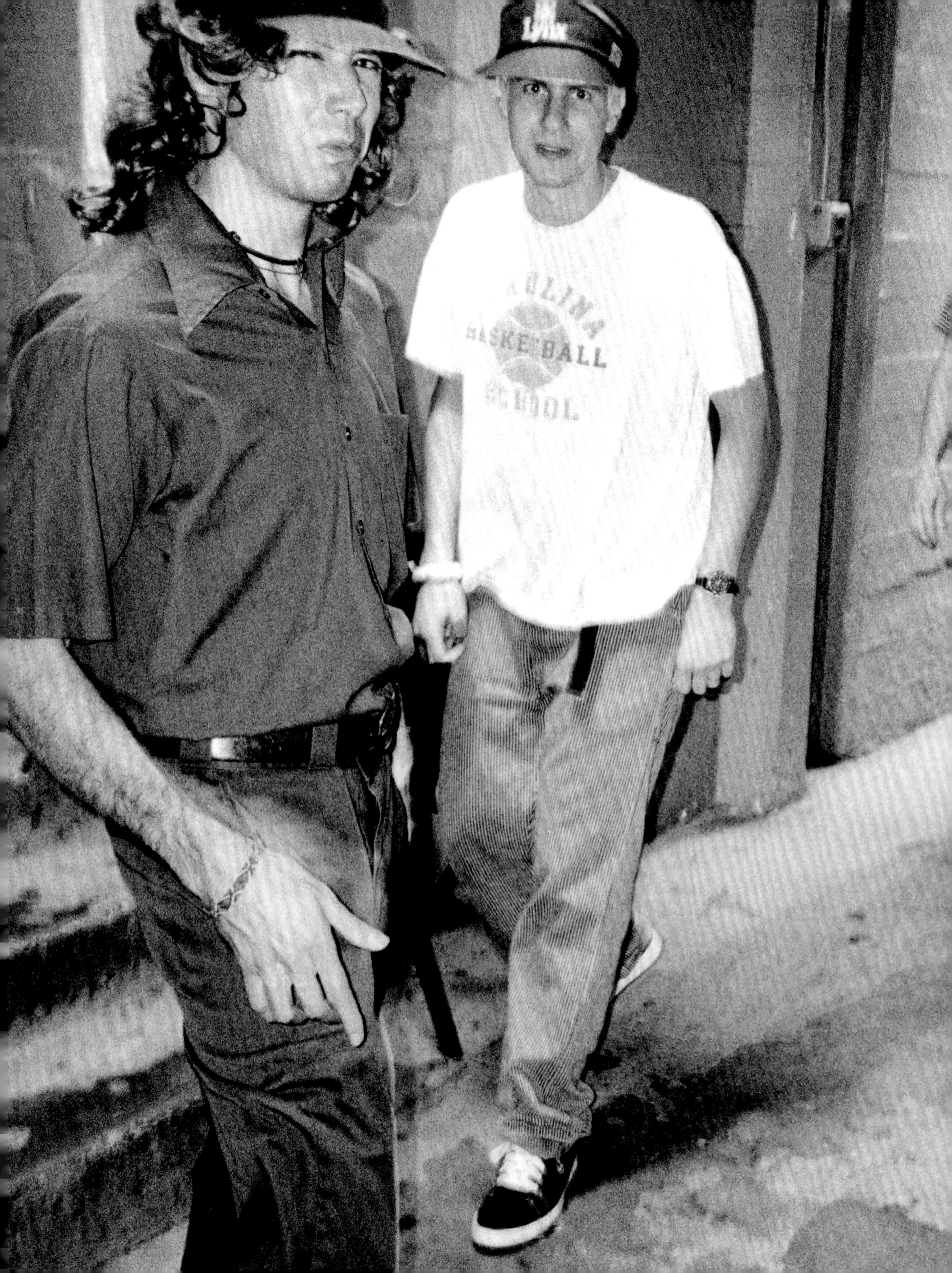

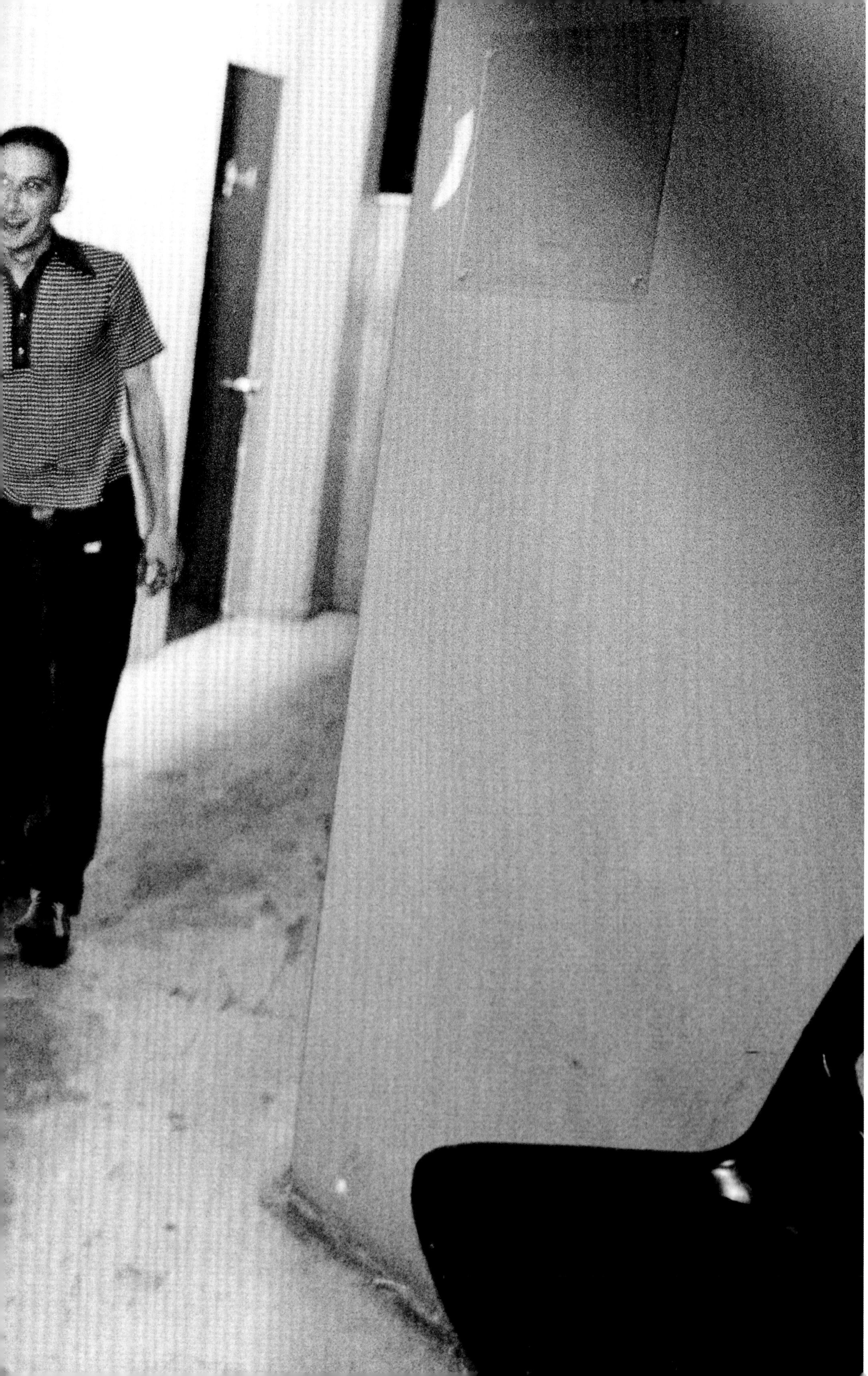

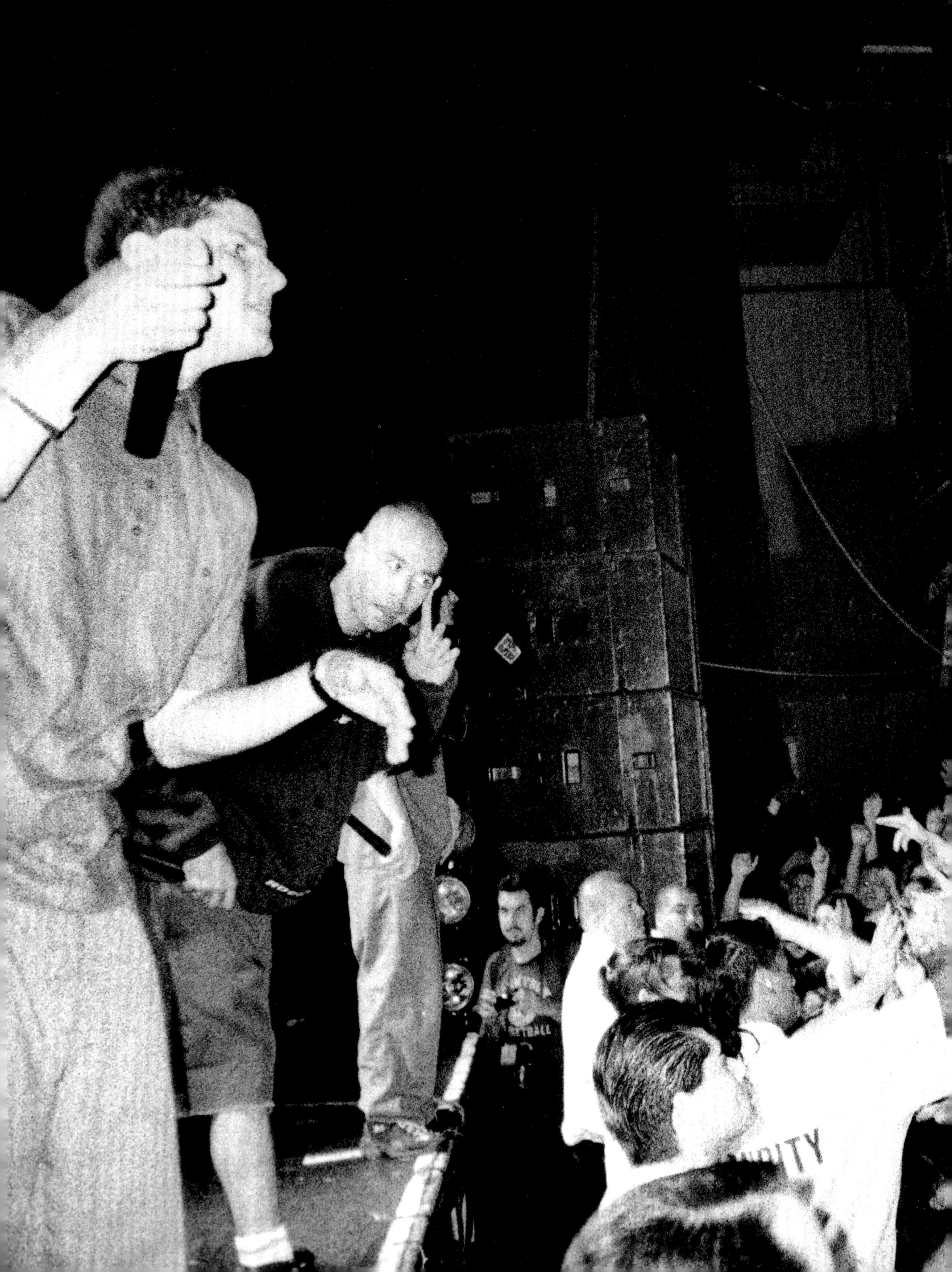

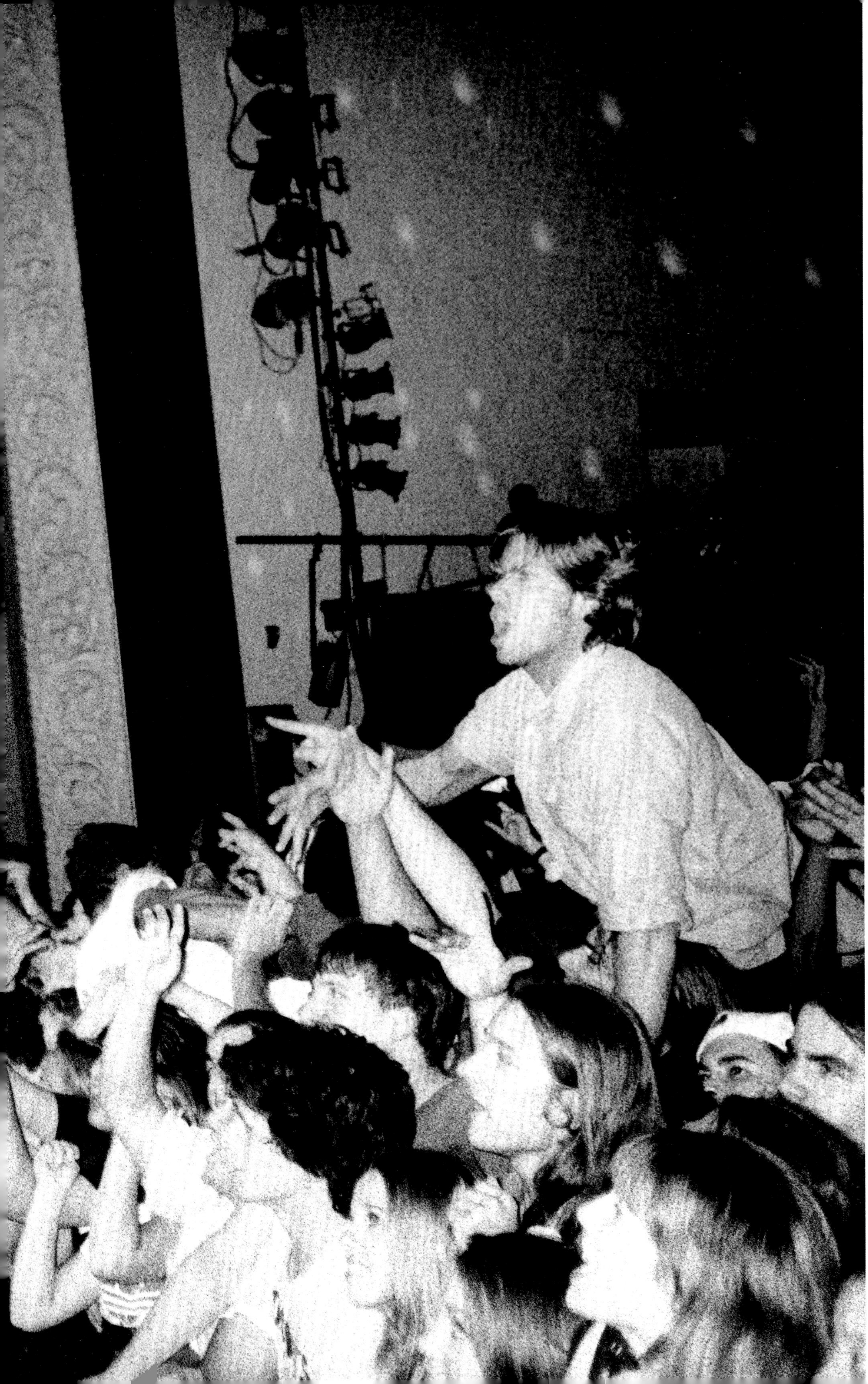

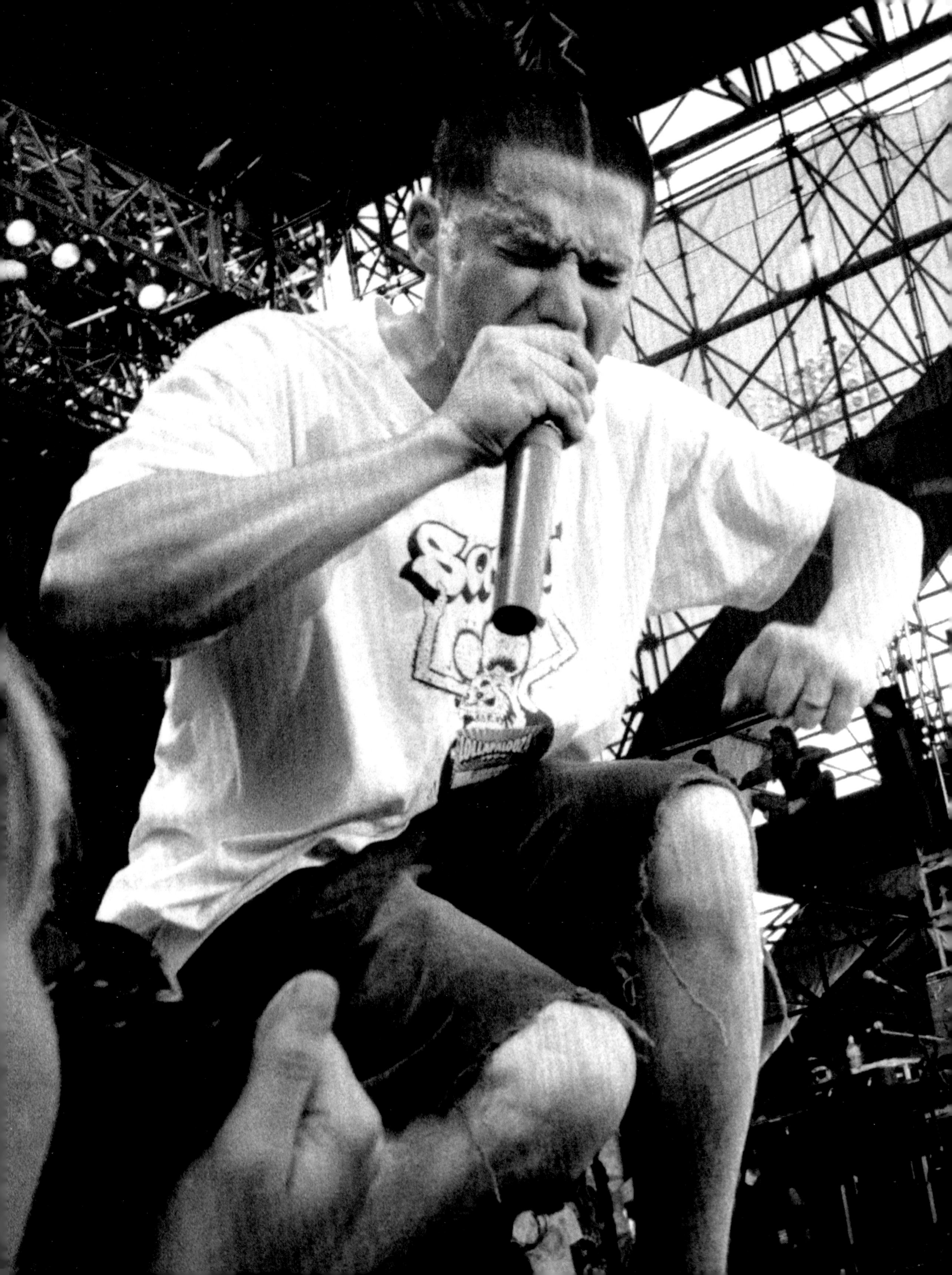

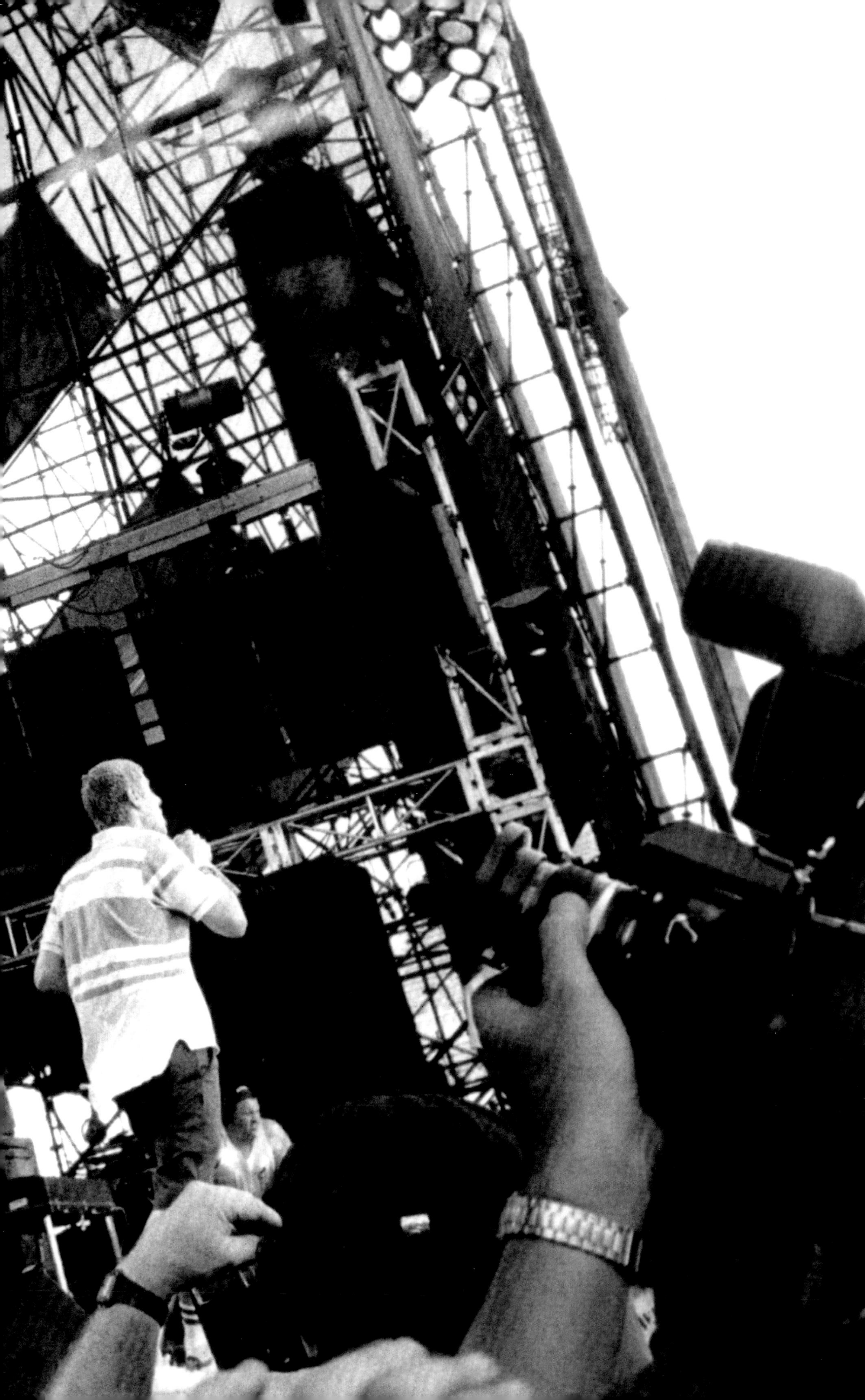

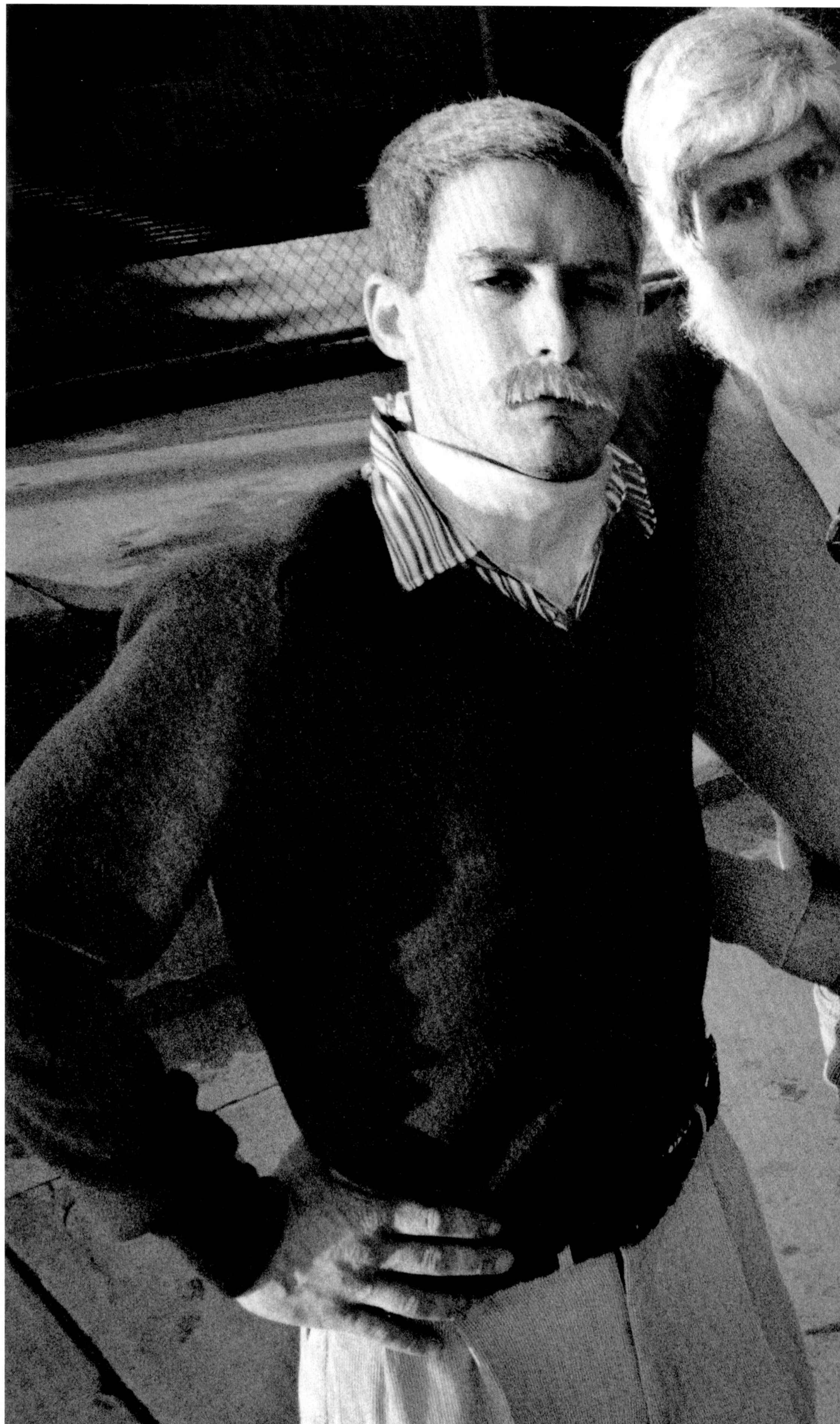

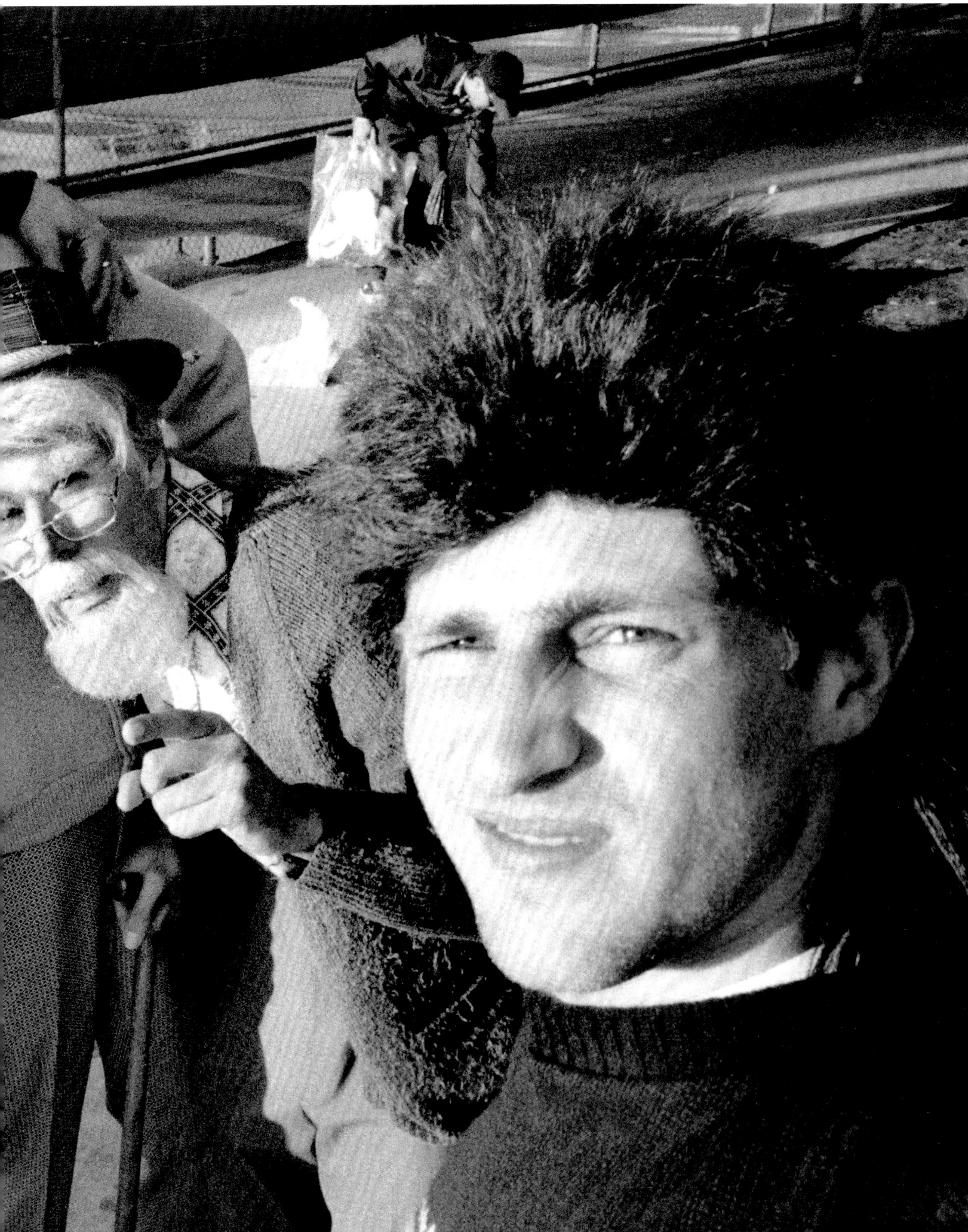

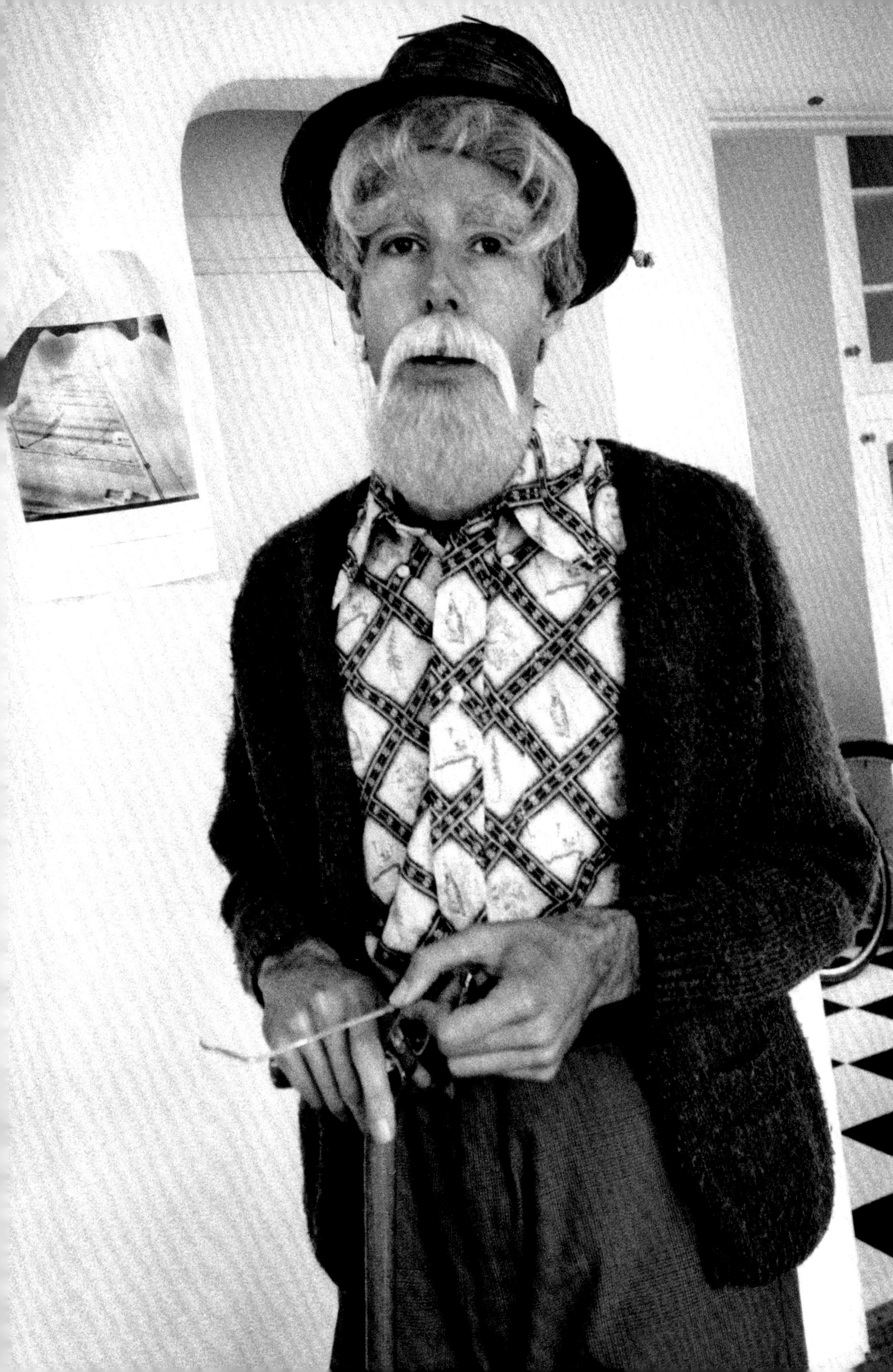

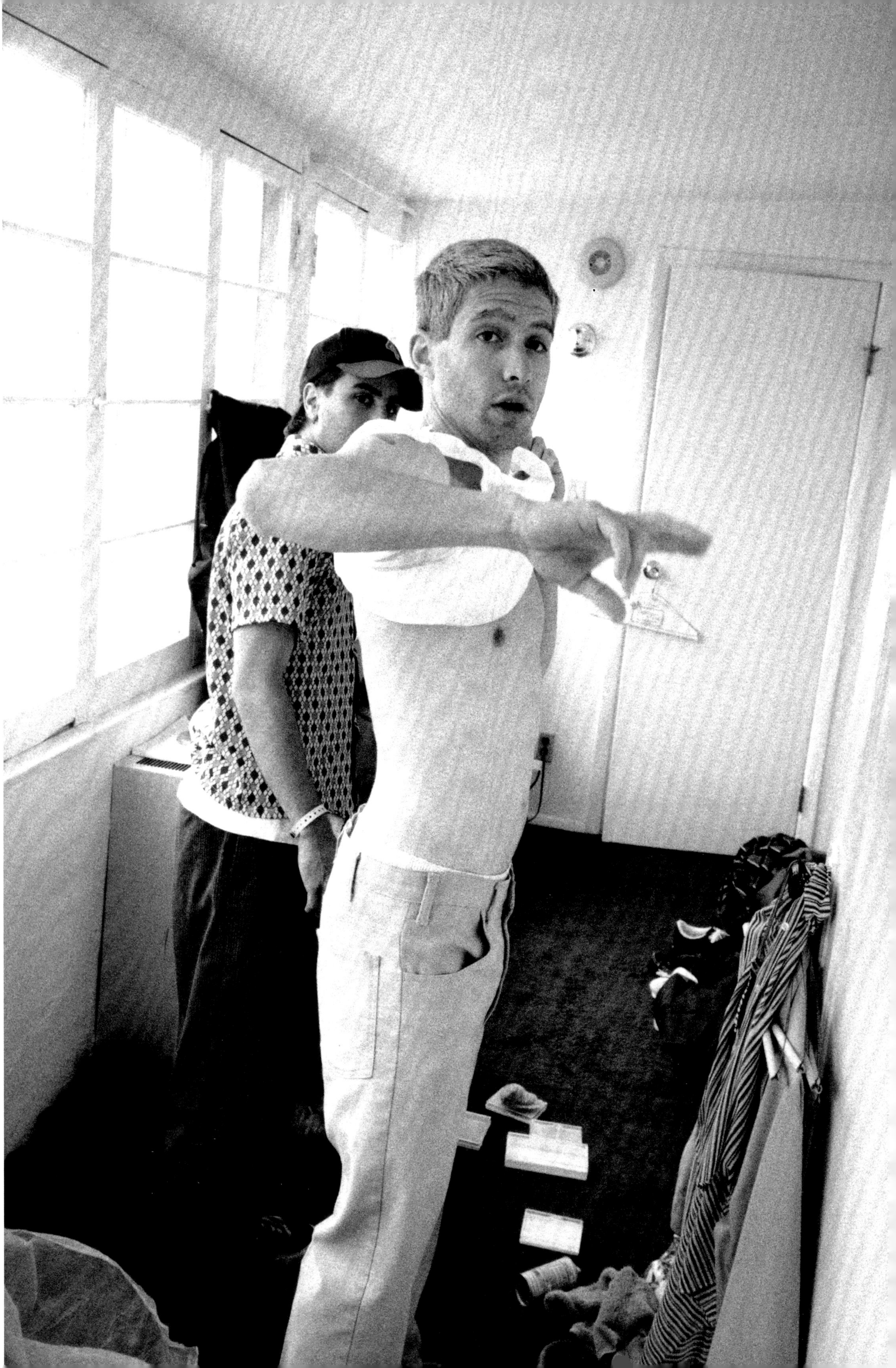

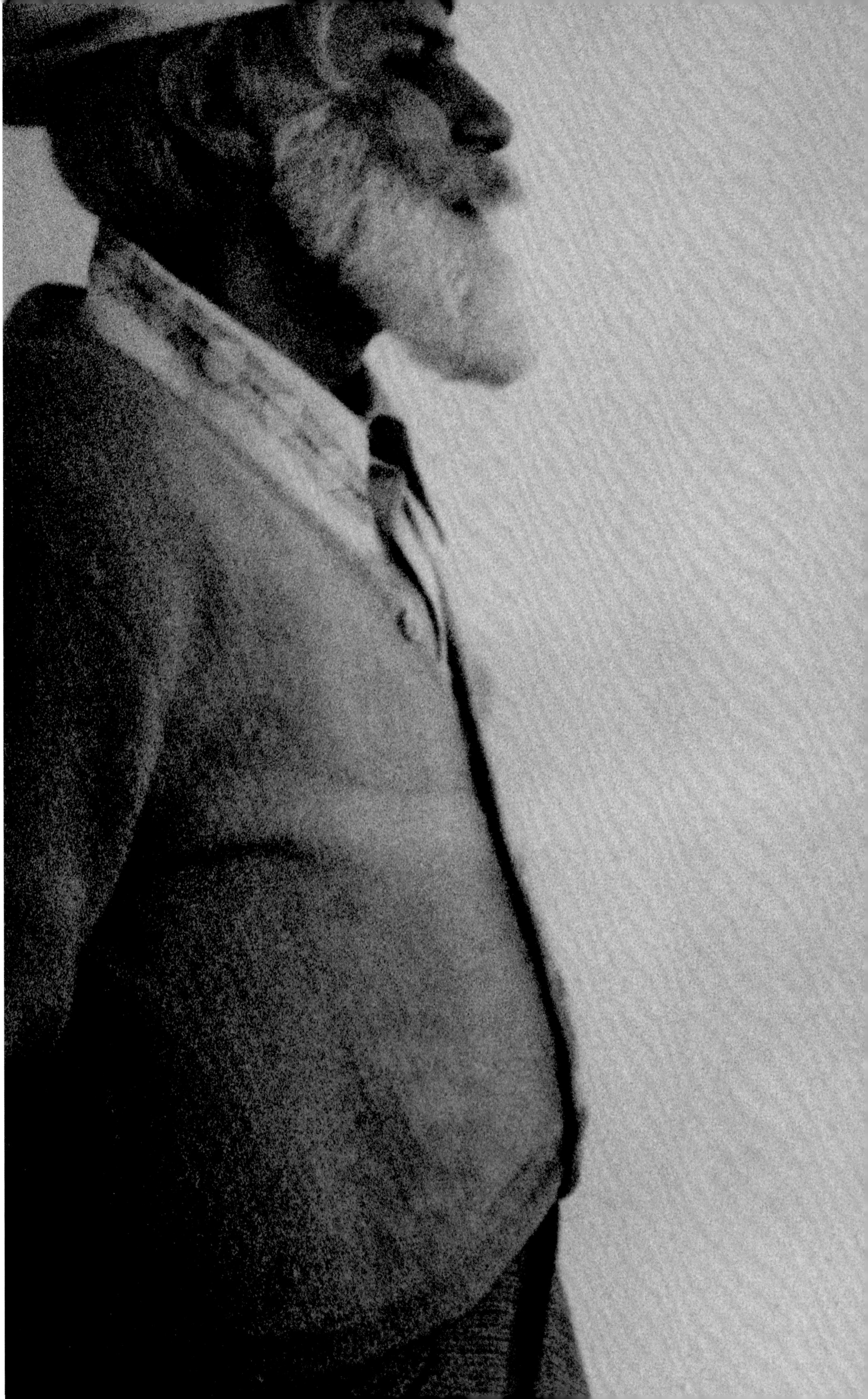

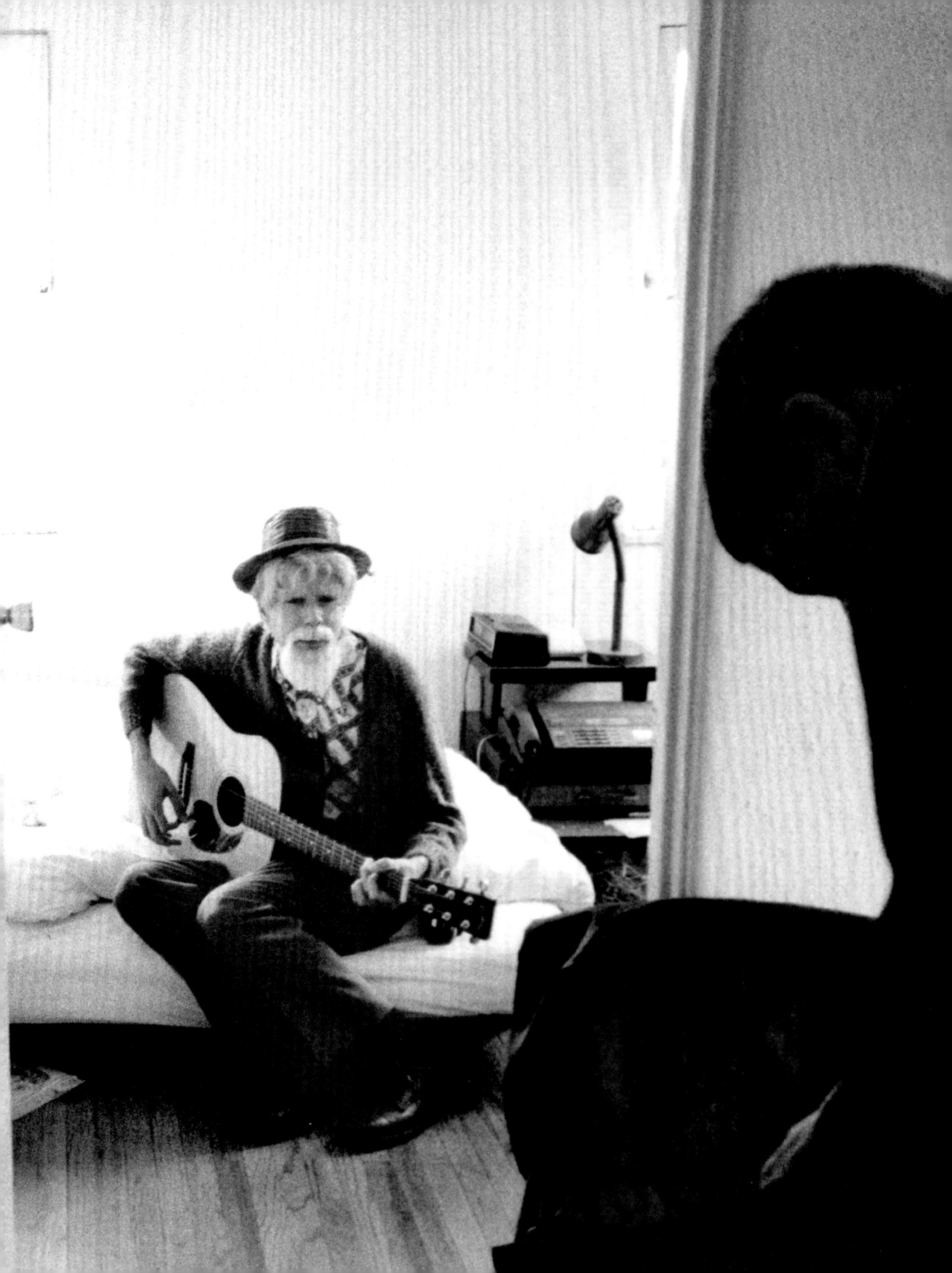

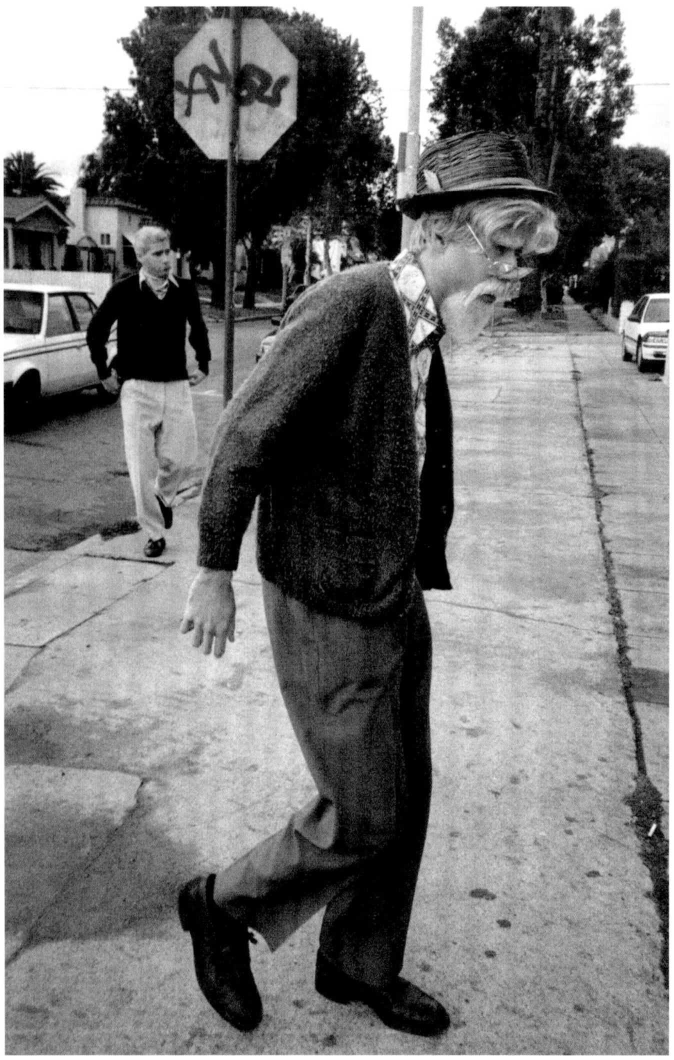

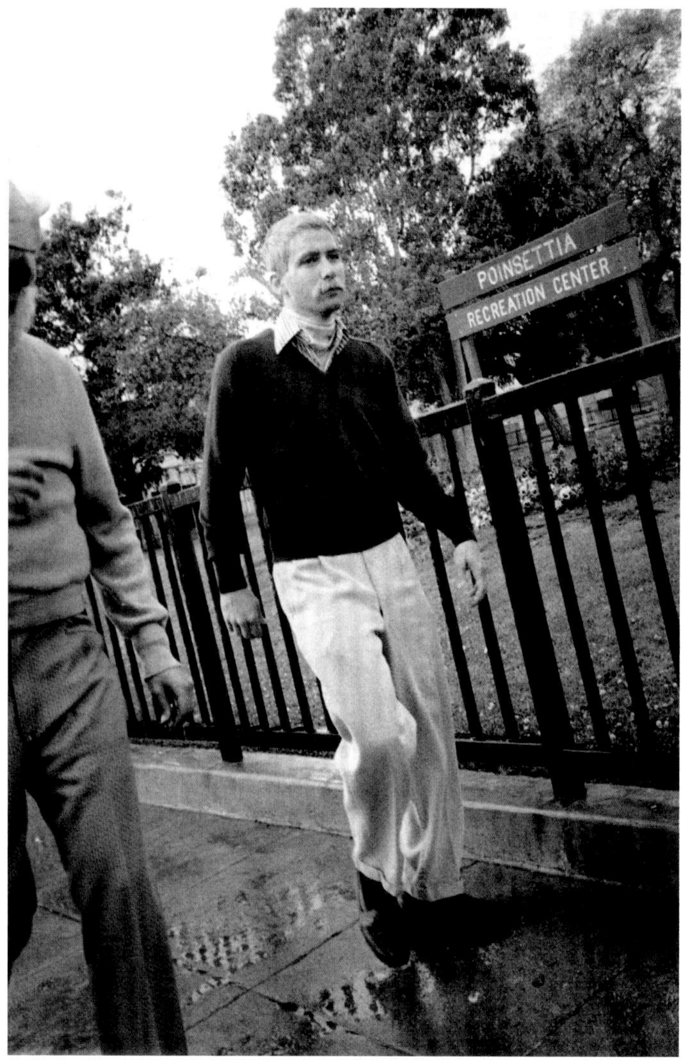
POINSETTIA
RECREATION CENTER

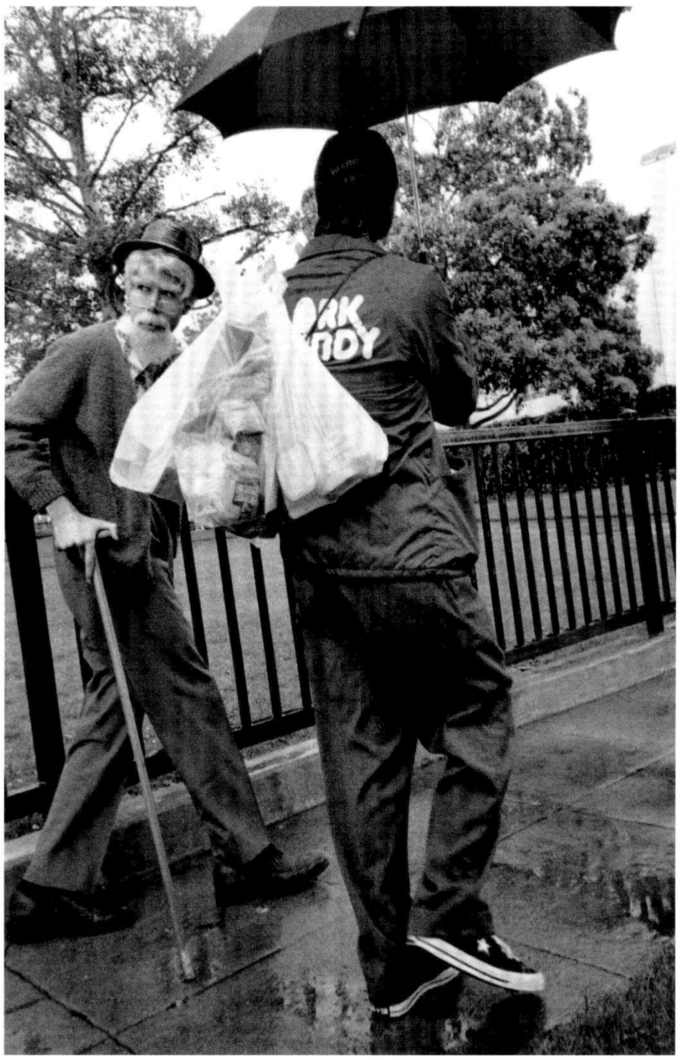

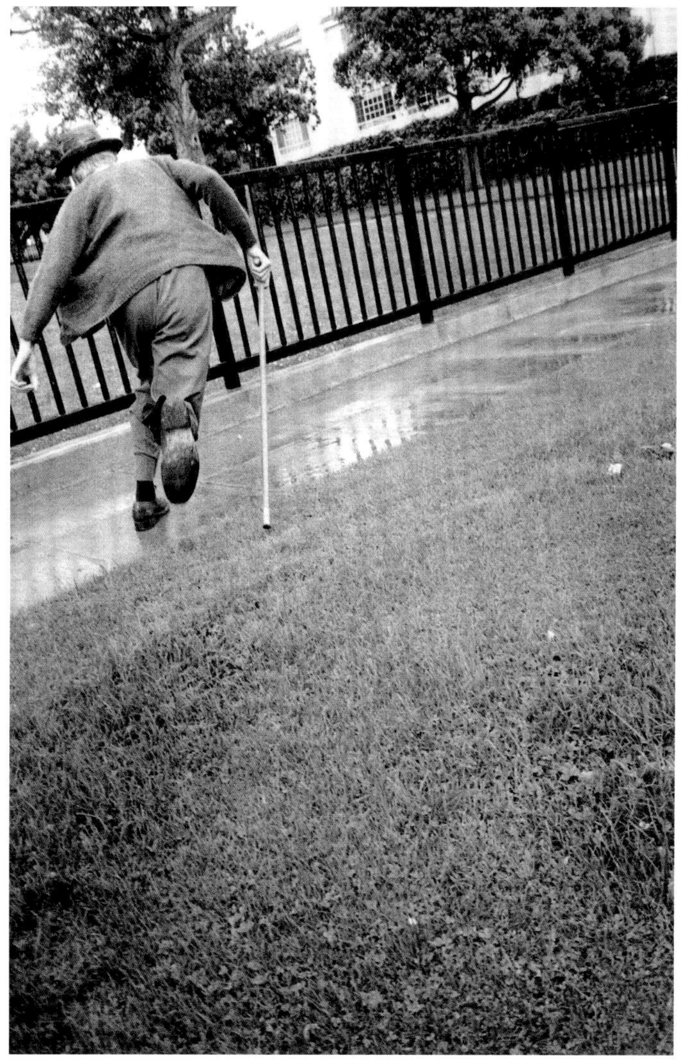

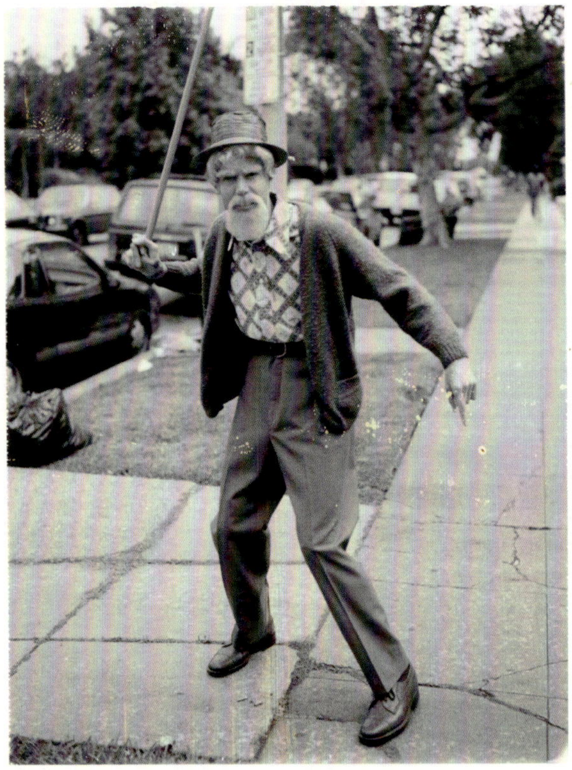

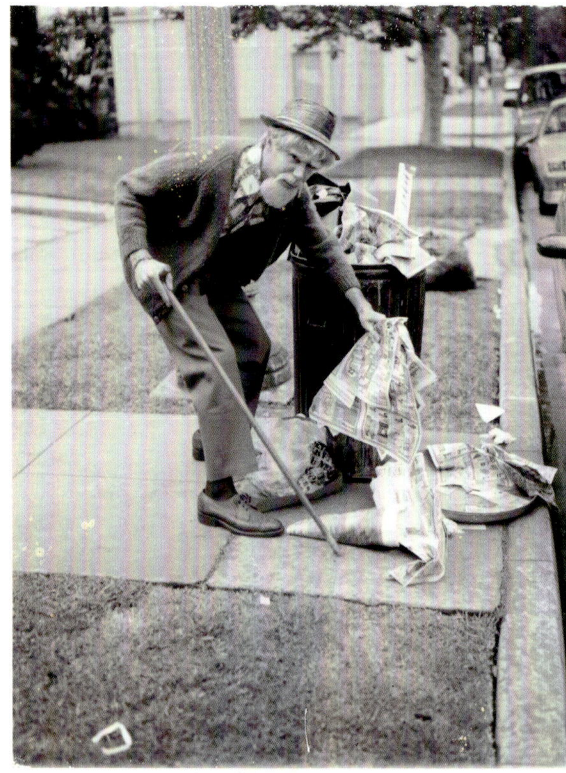

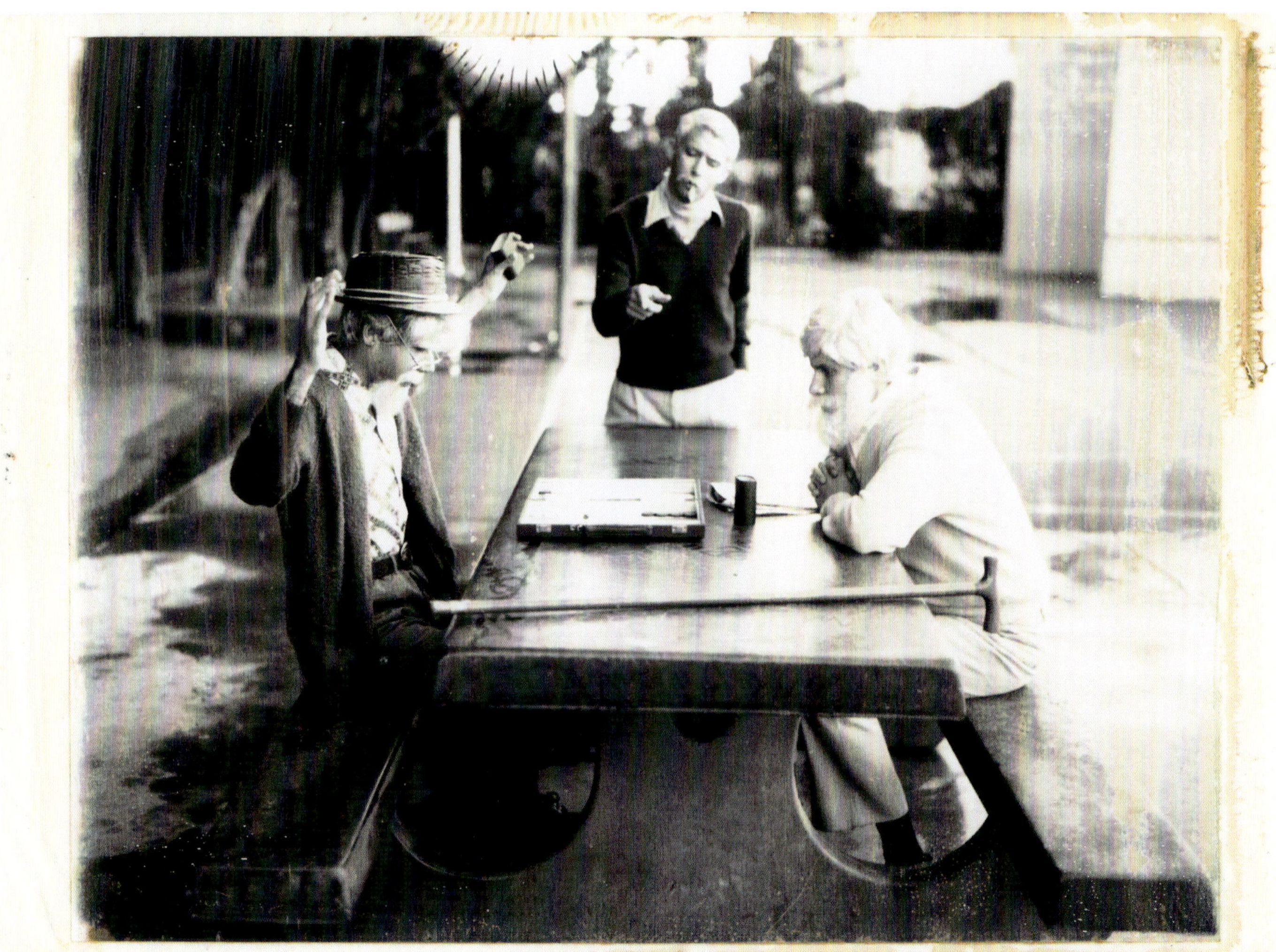

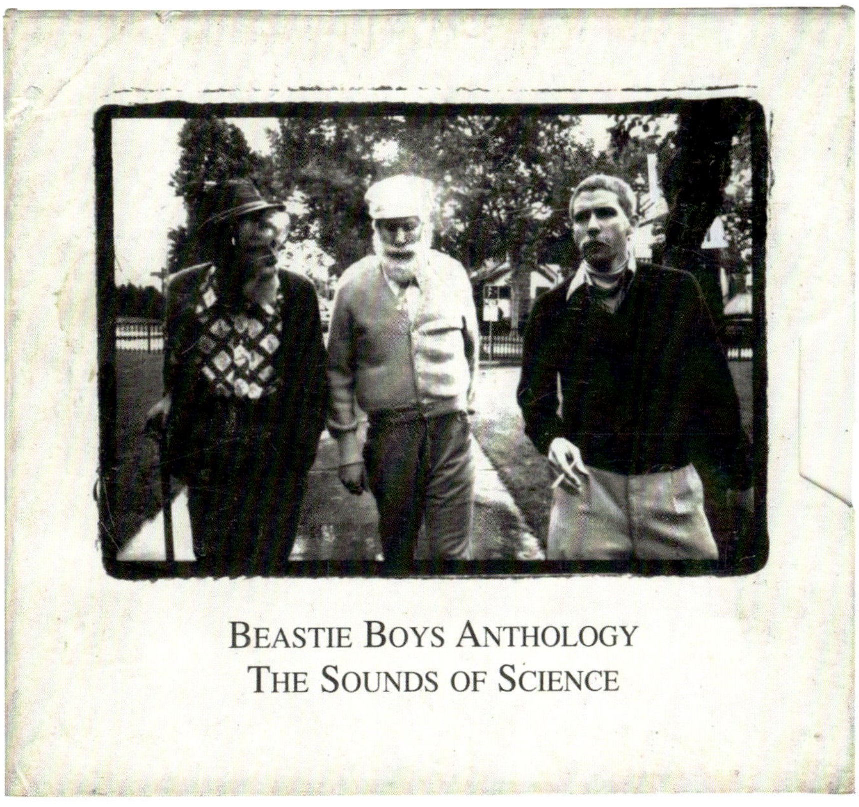
BEASTIE BOYS ANTHOLOGY
THE SOUNDS OF SCIENCE

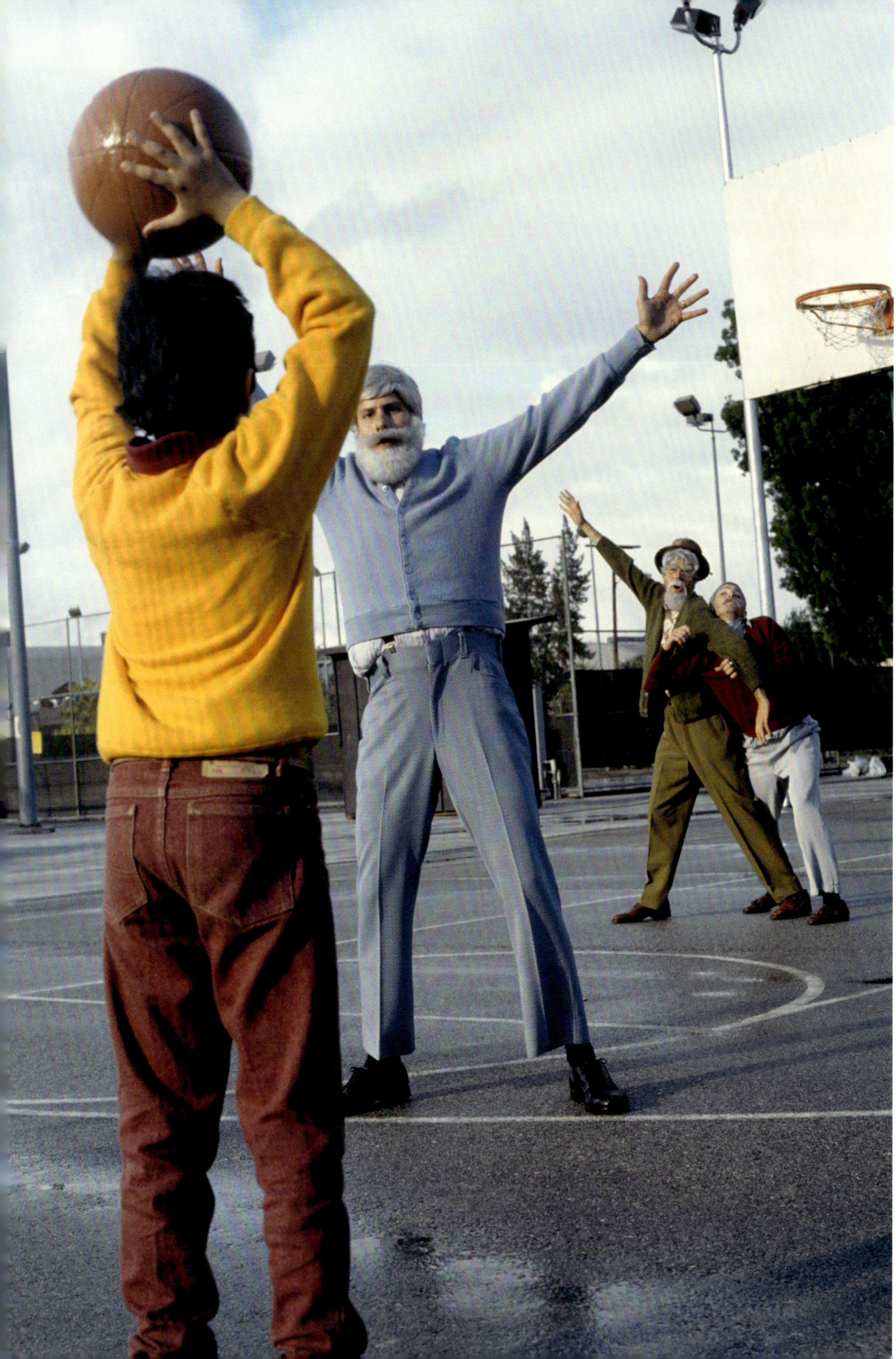

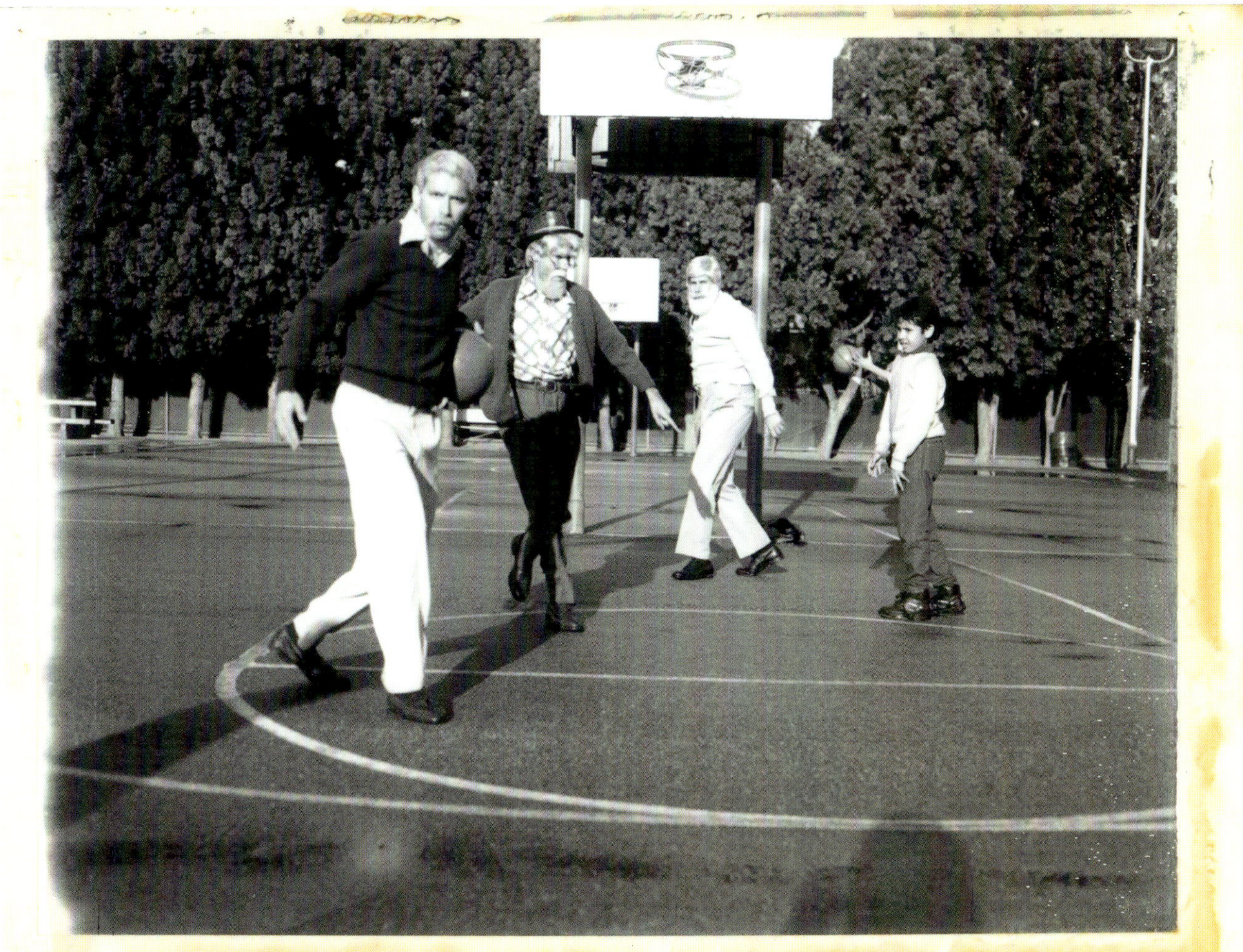

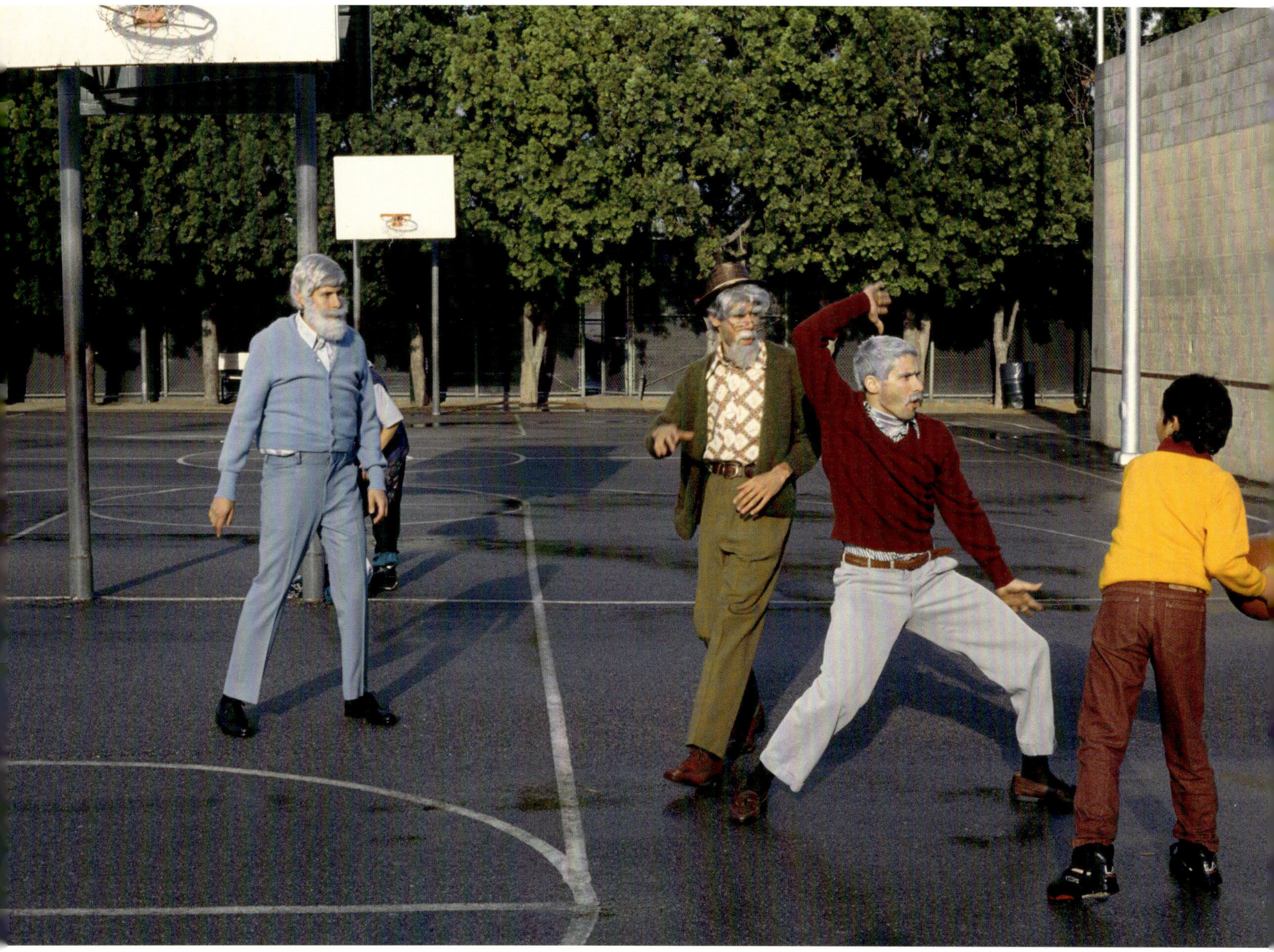

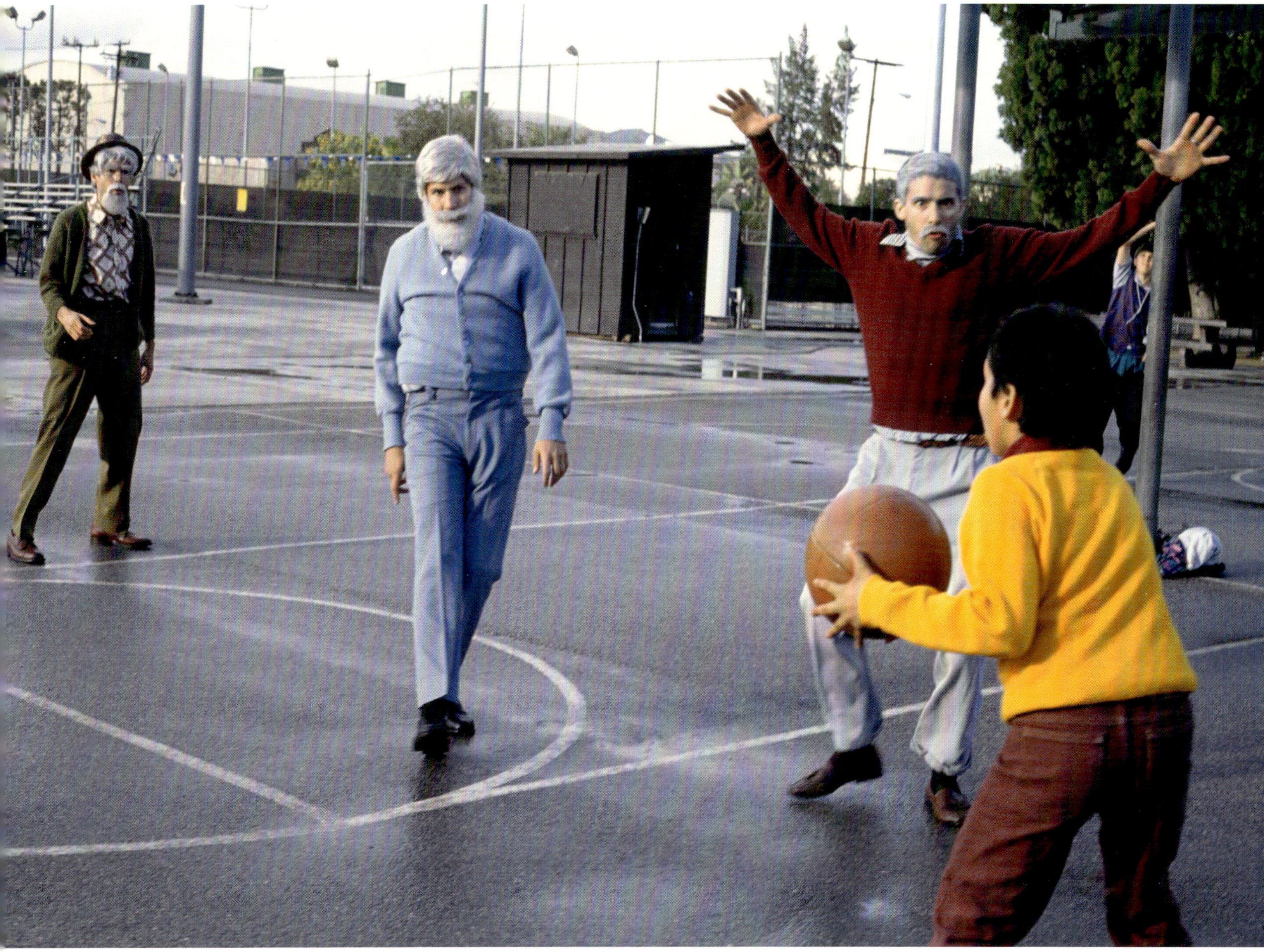

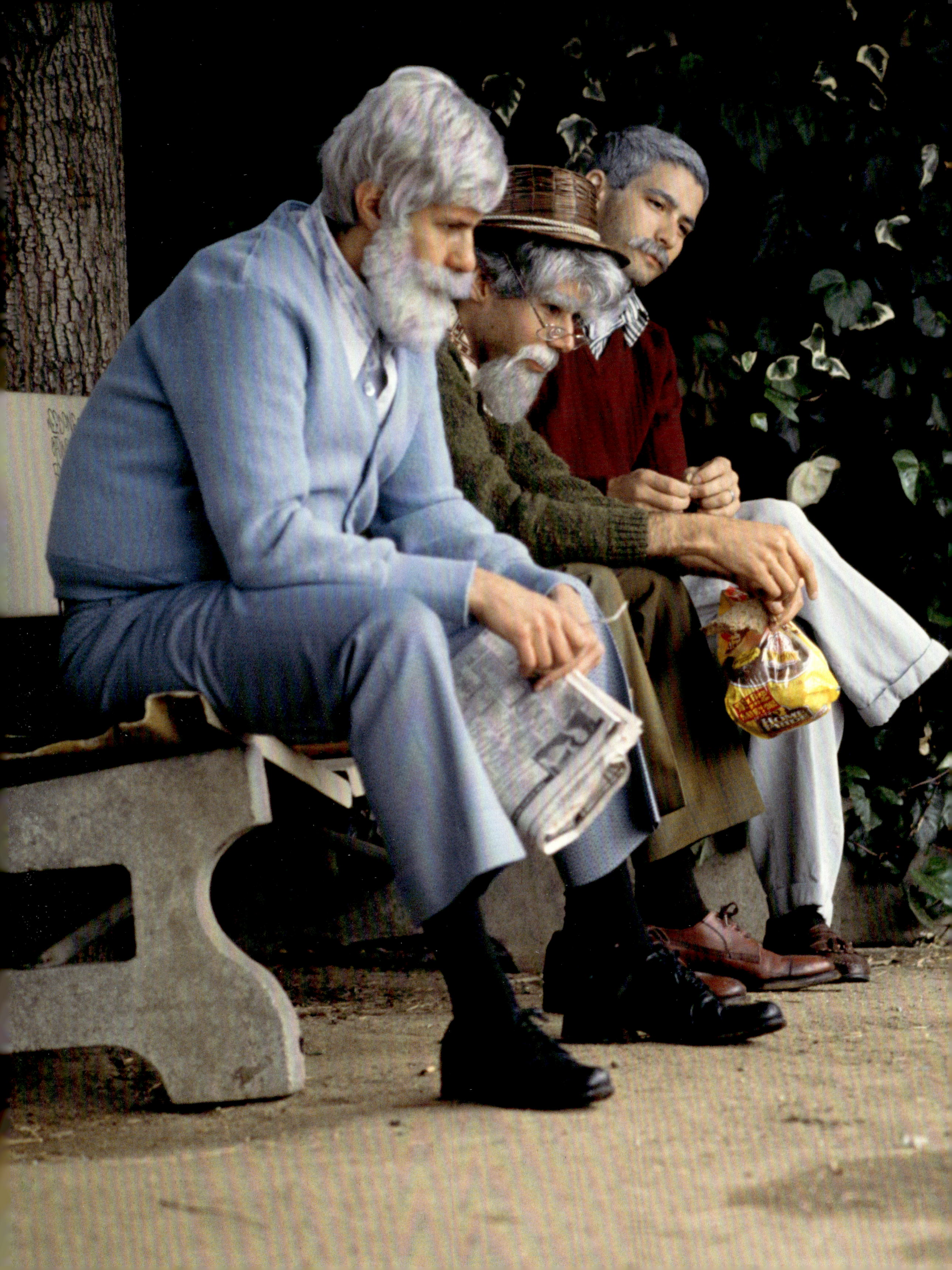

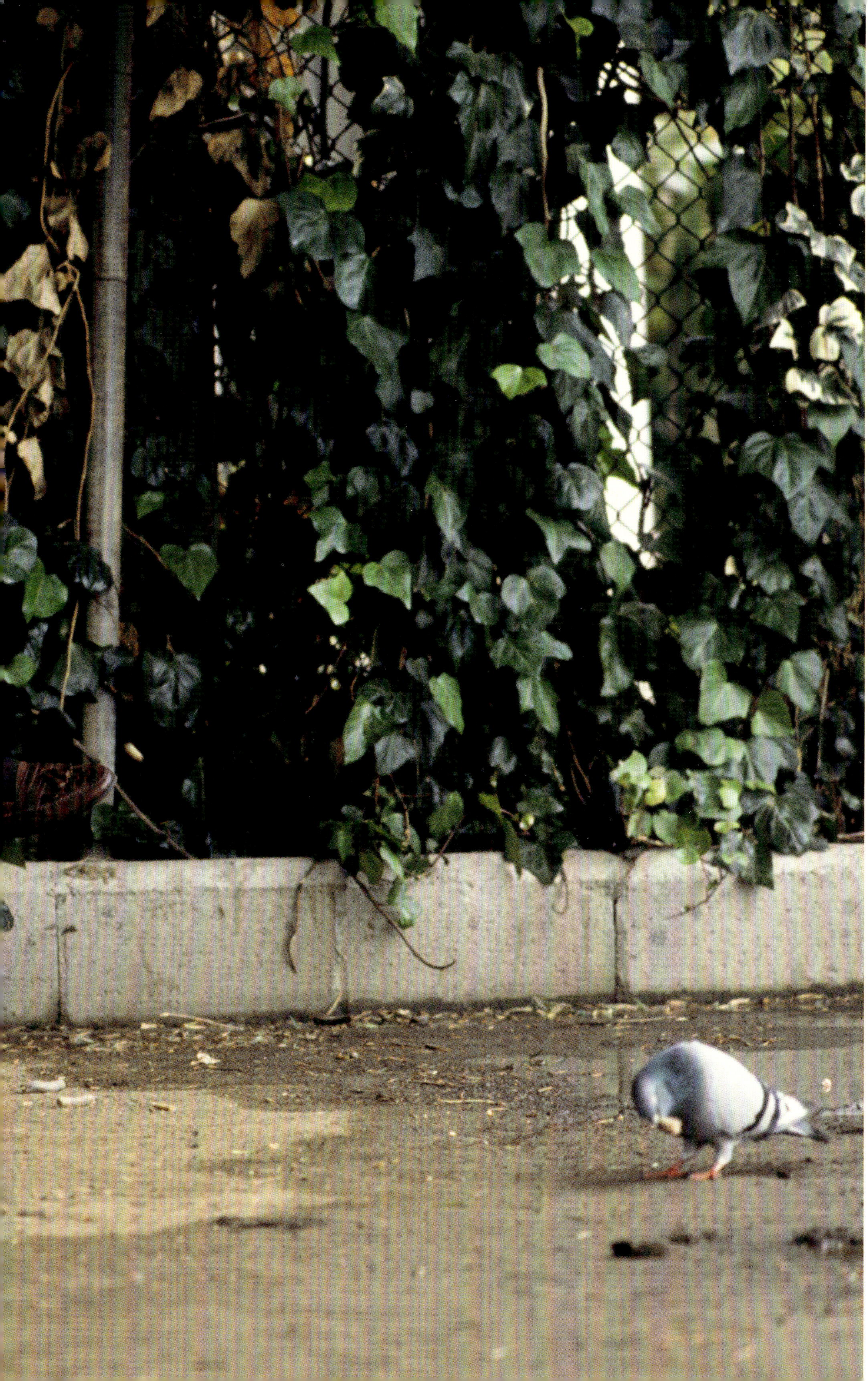

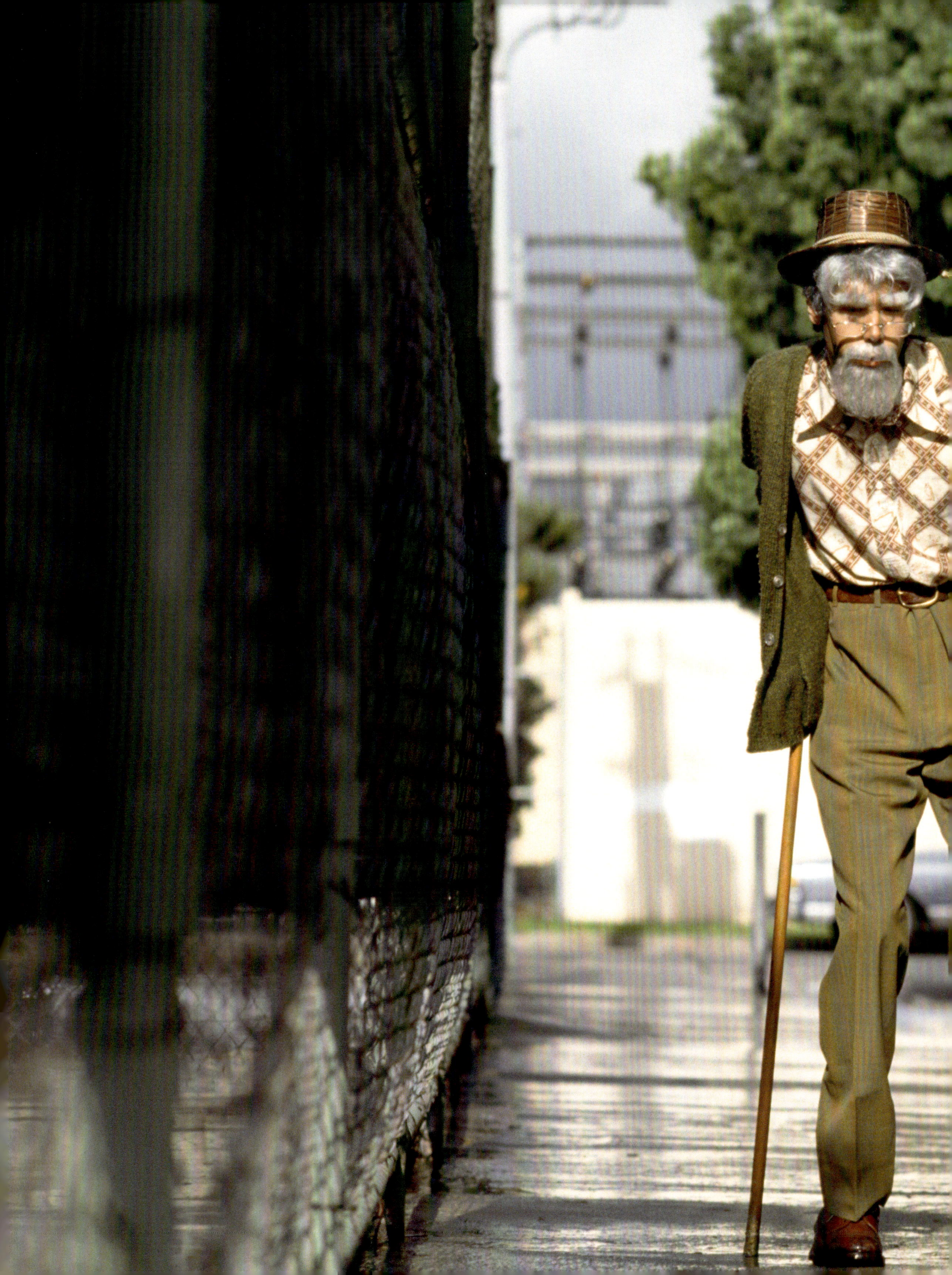

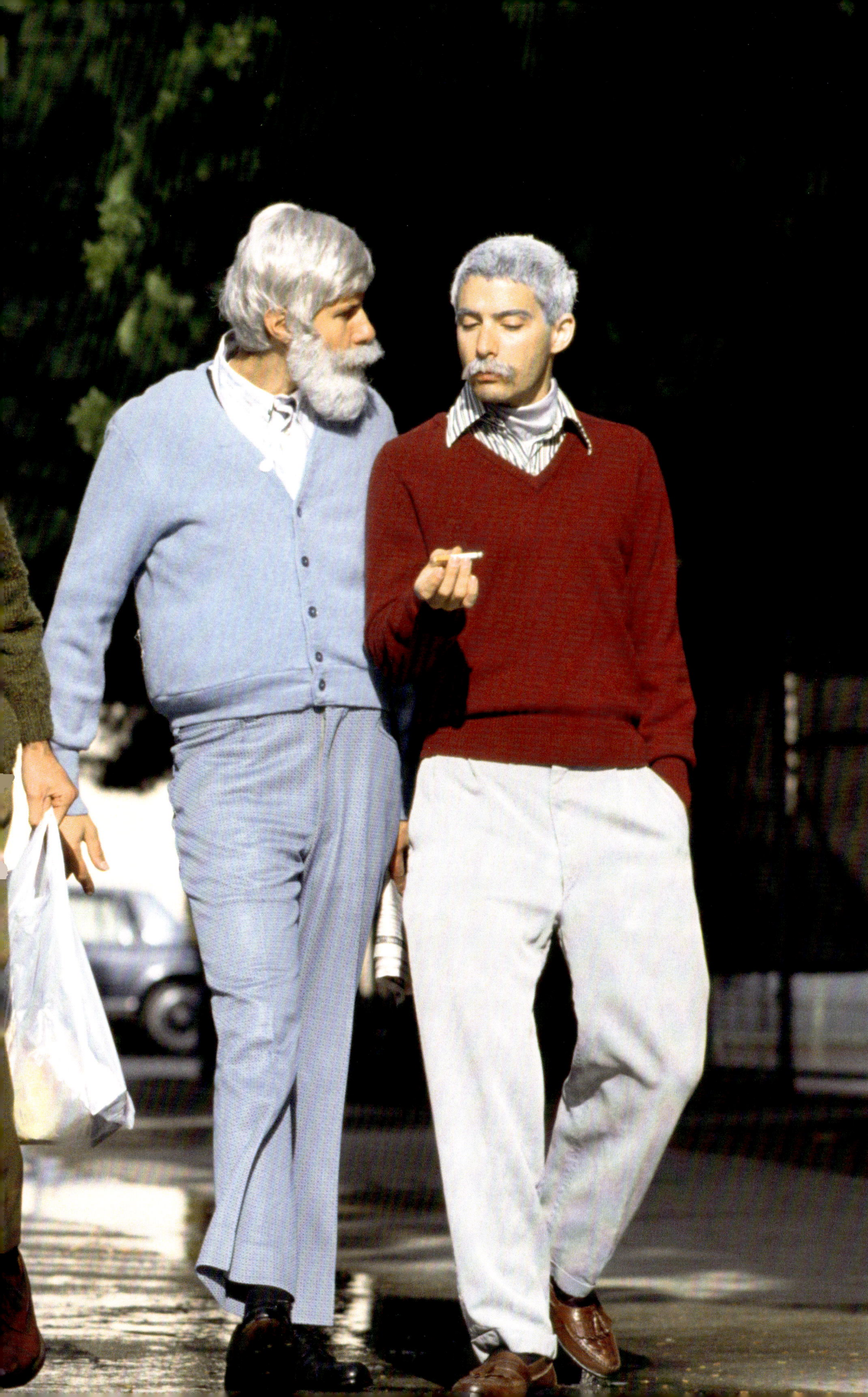

Mike
Call Carl Sagan Back

Mike
Call Carl Sagan Back

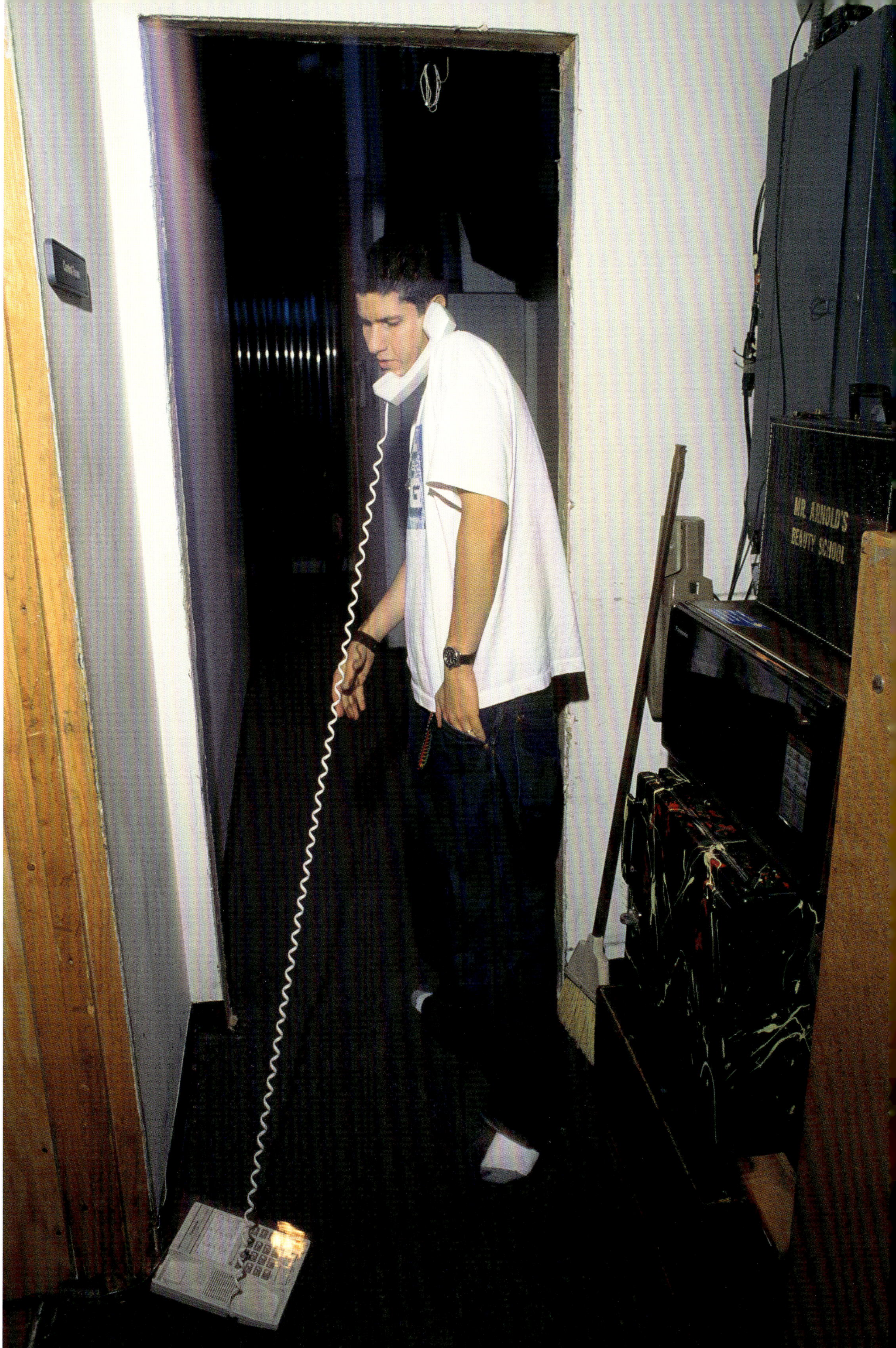
MR. ARNOLD'S
BEAUTY SCHOOL

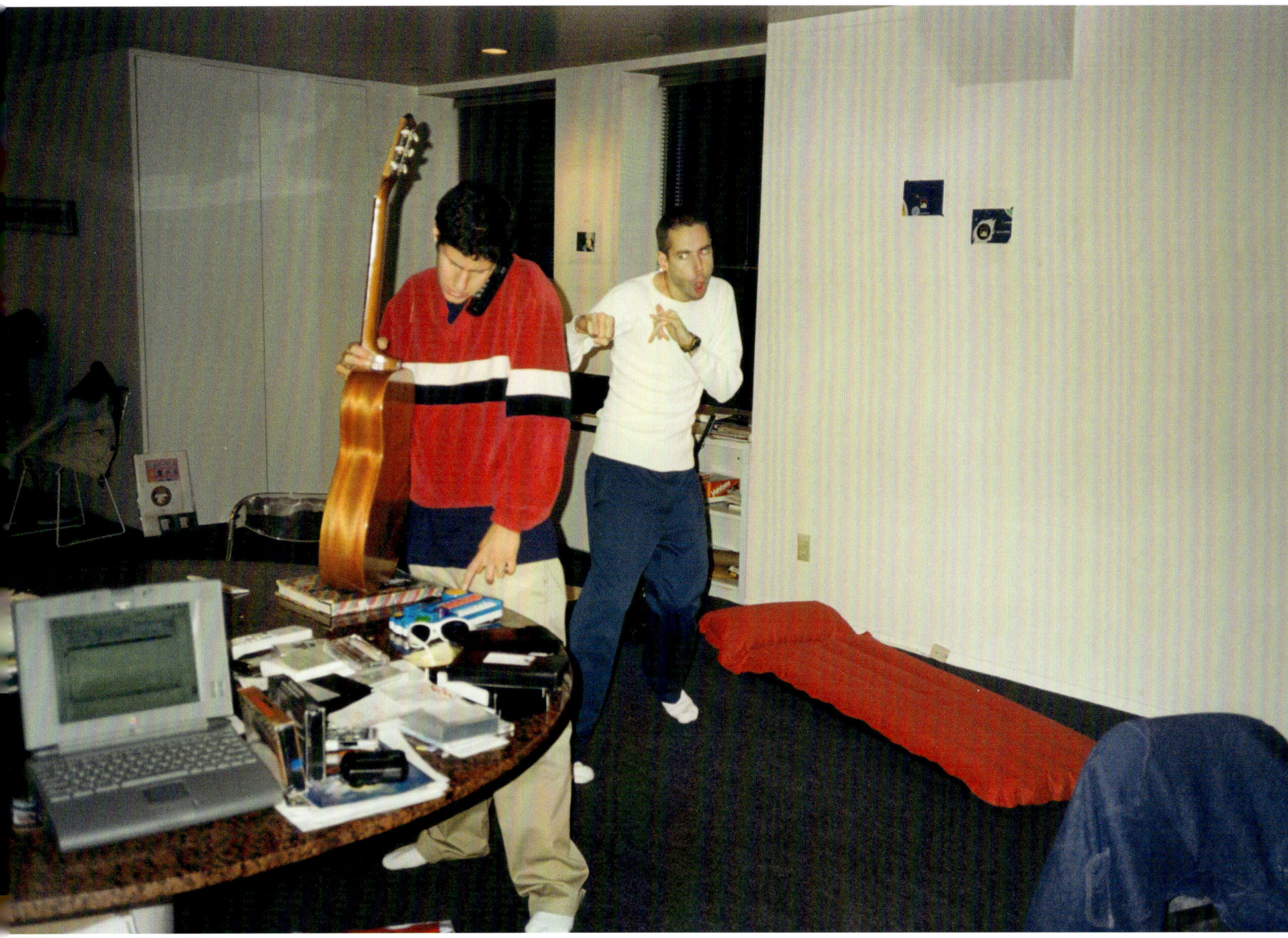

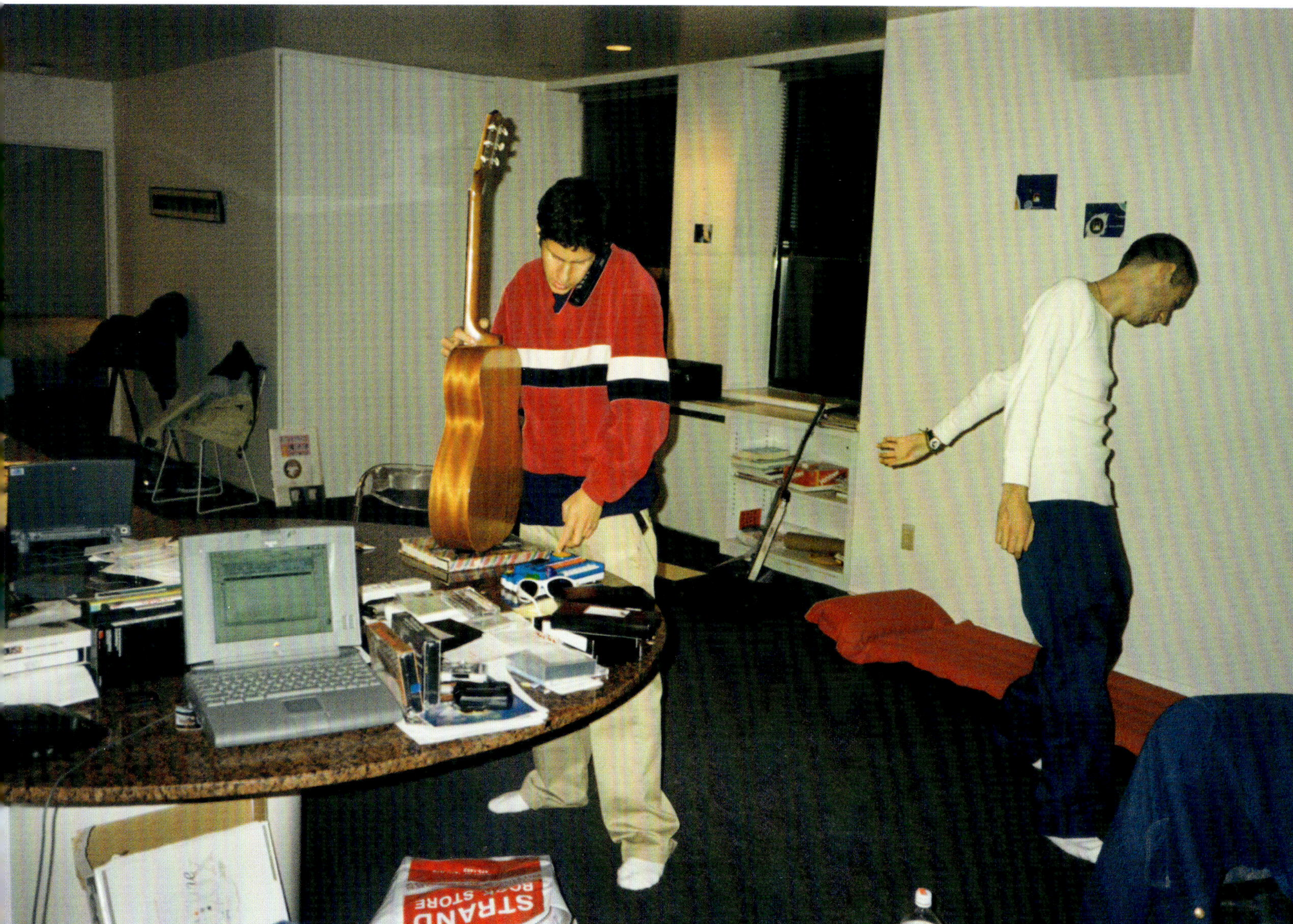
STRAND

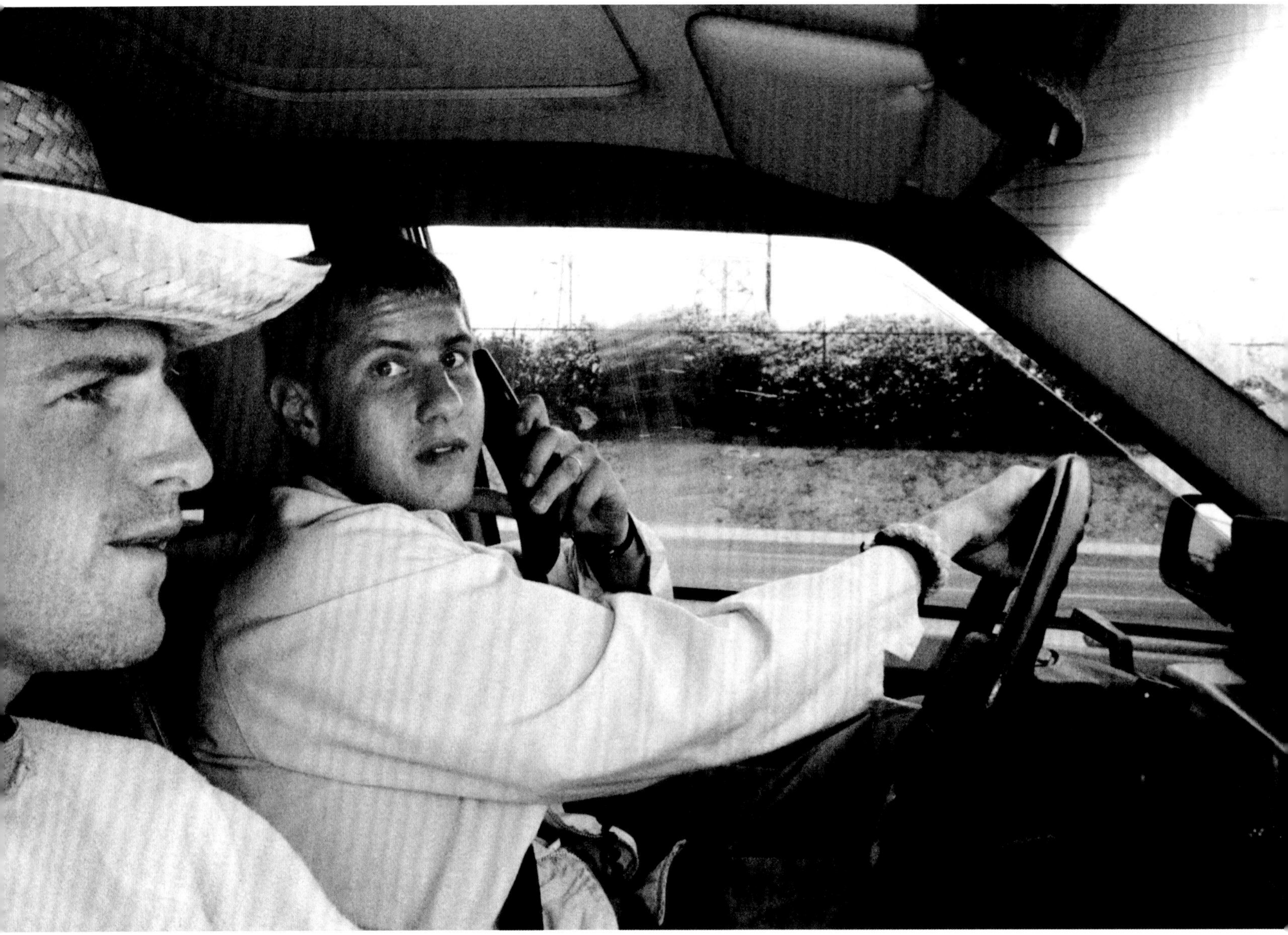

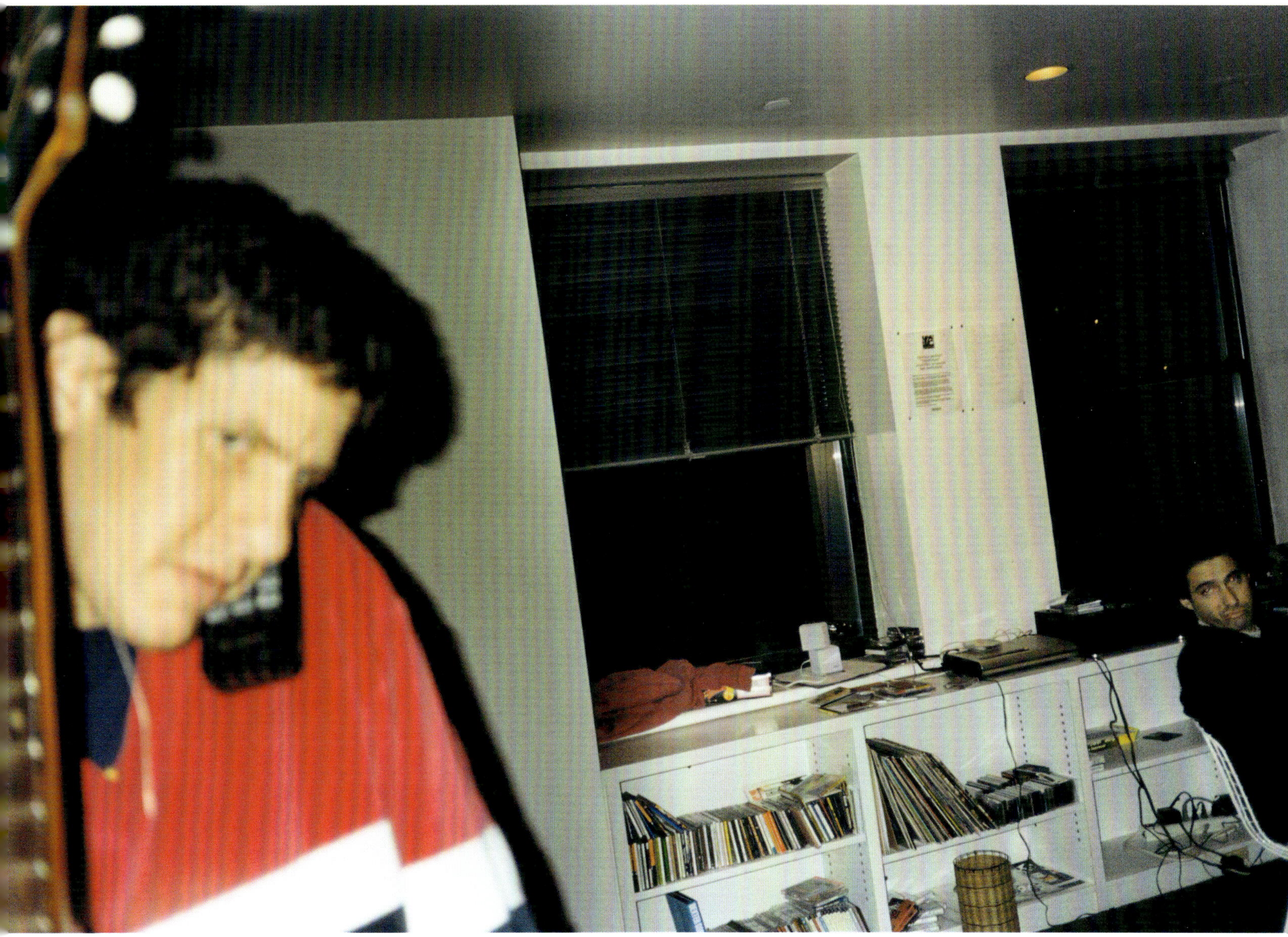

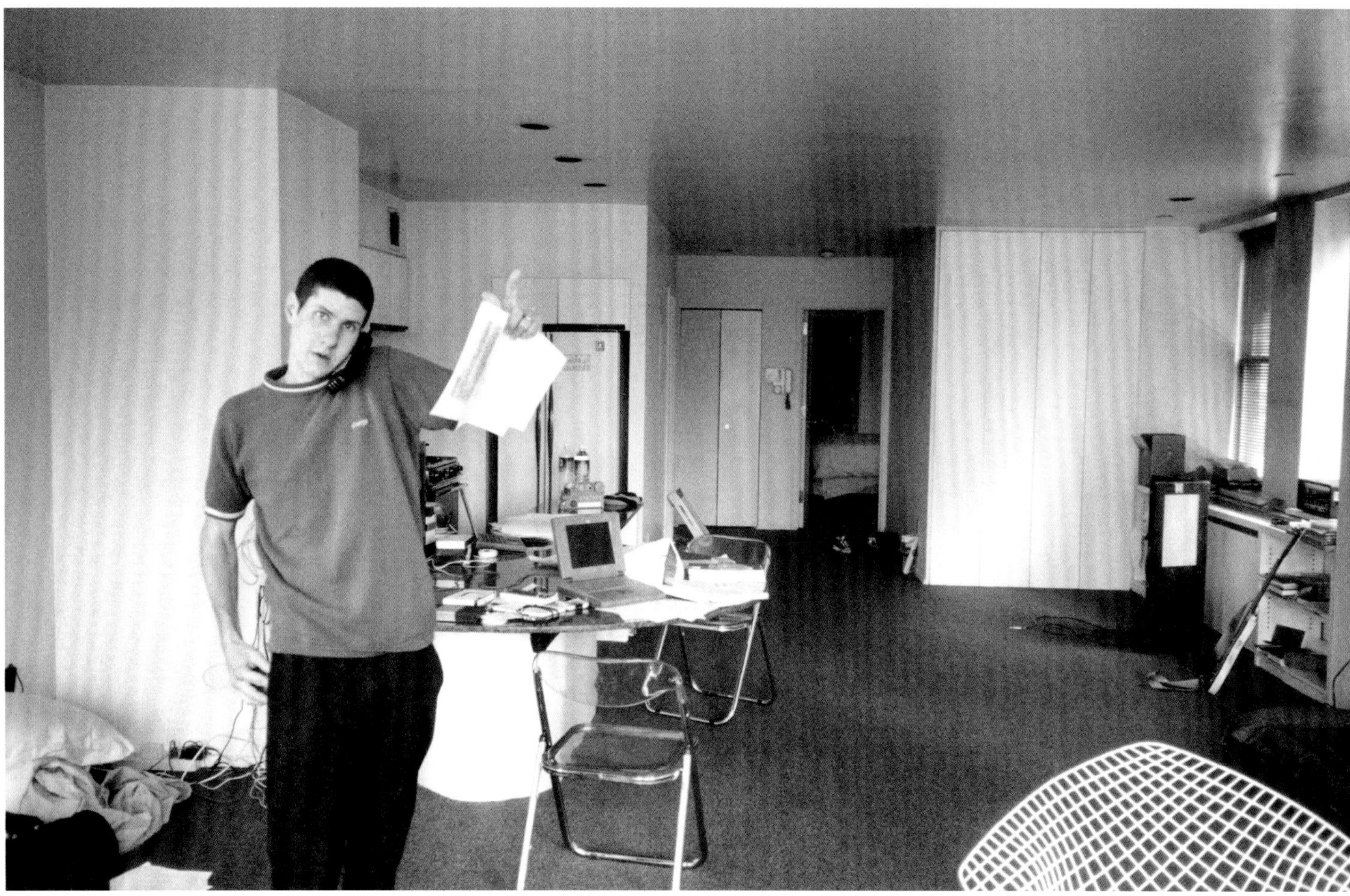

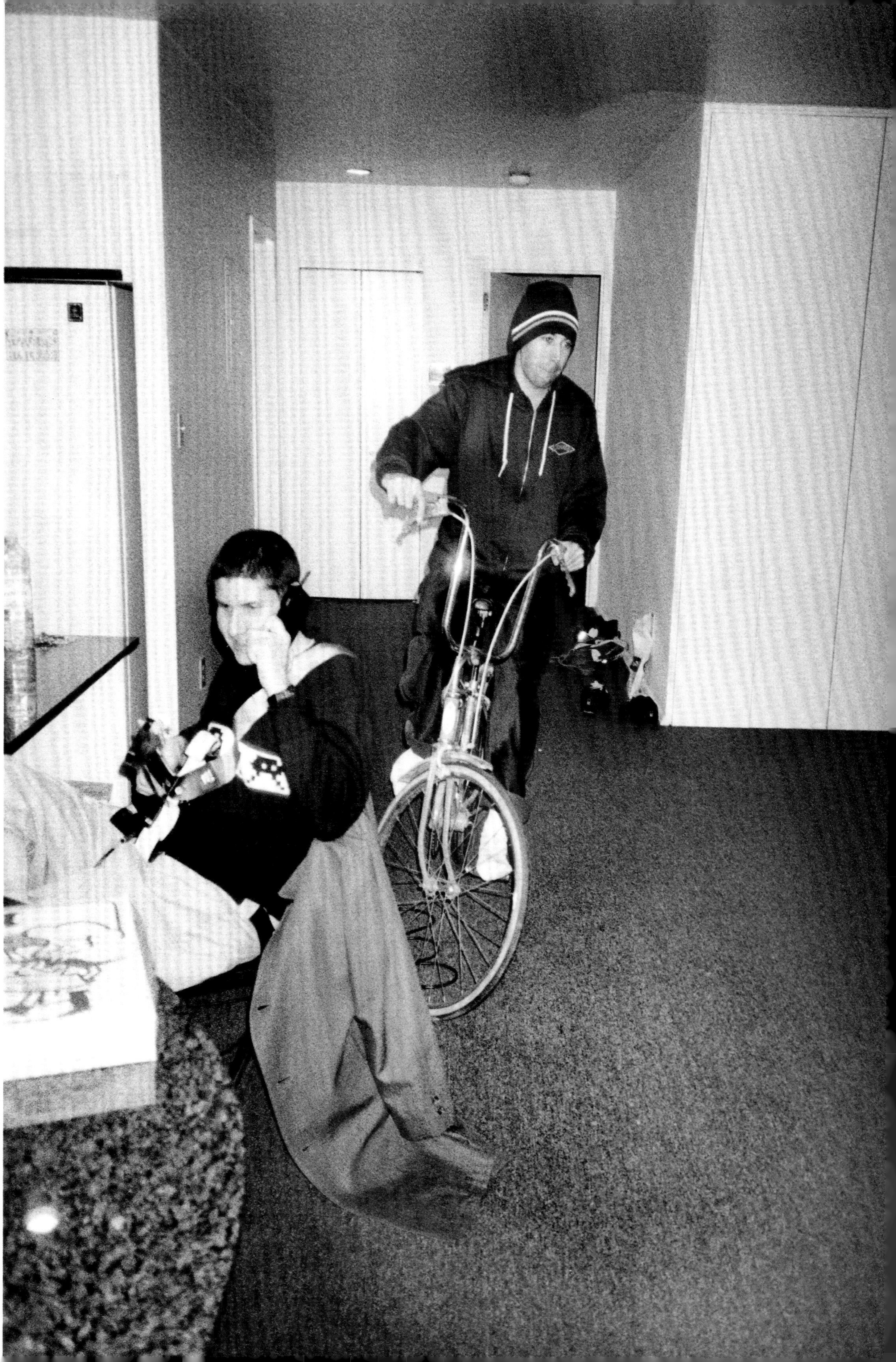

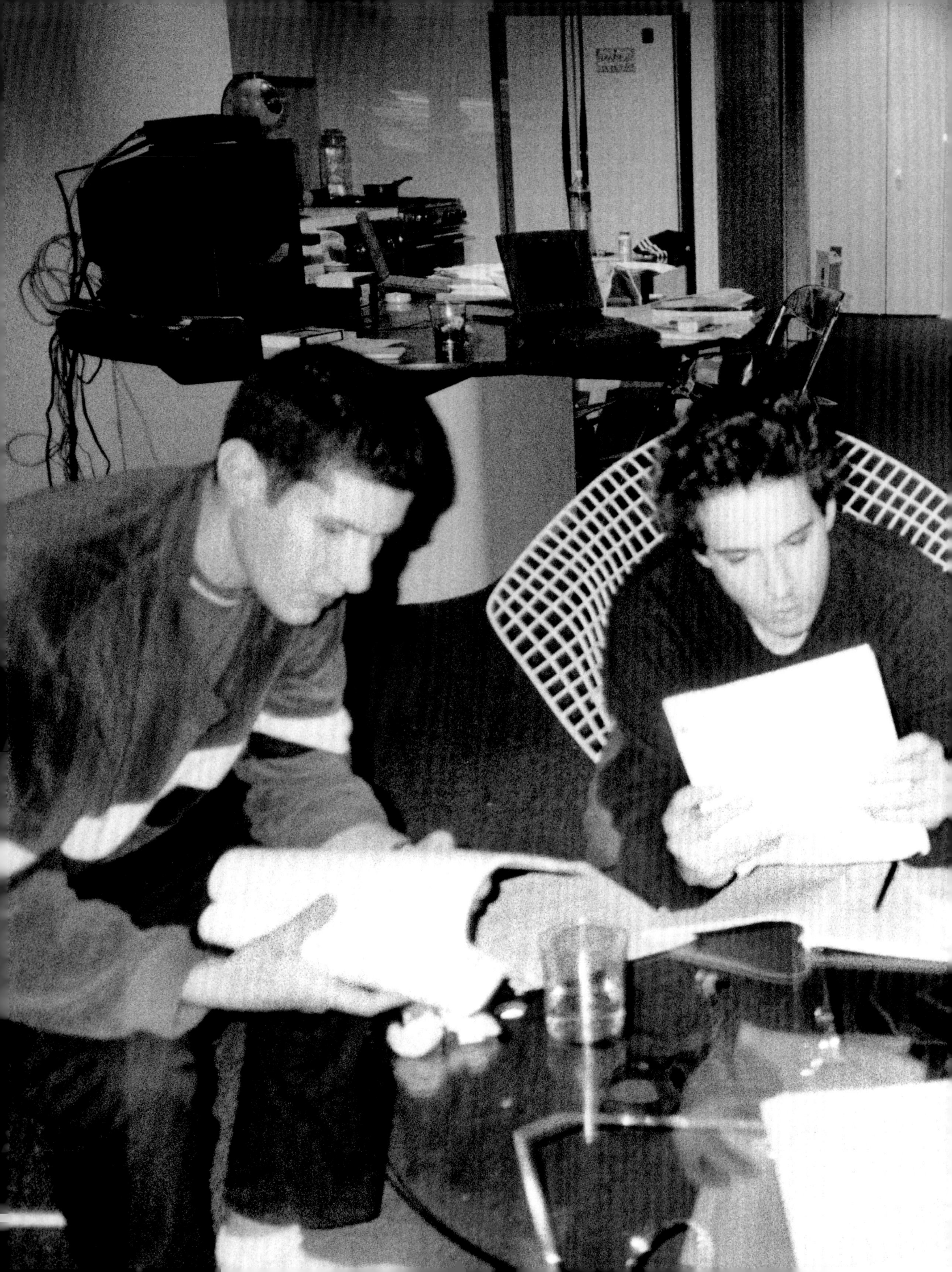

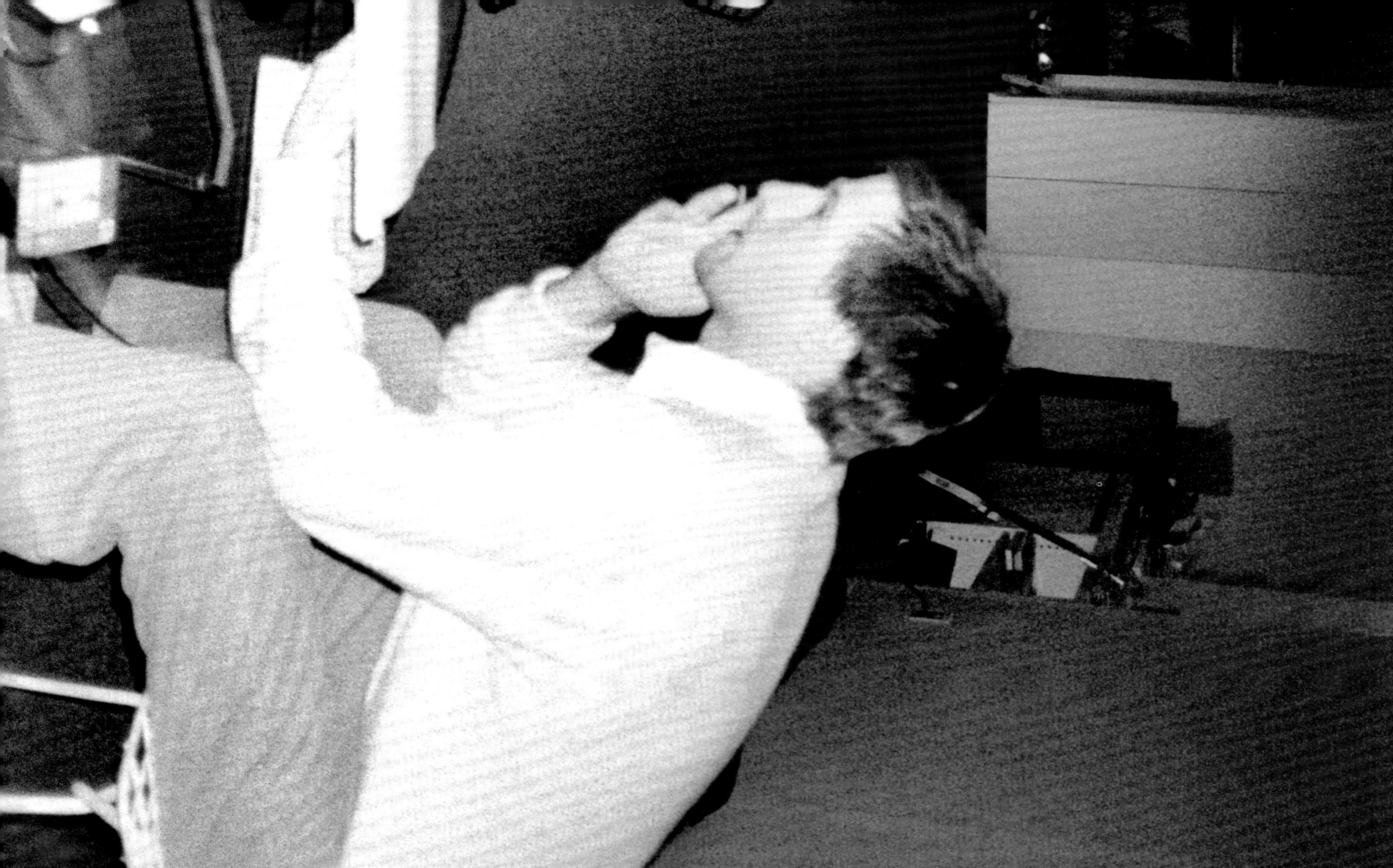

Yauch and i called the script
we all wrote, "Our Weird Brick."

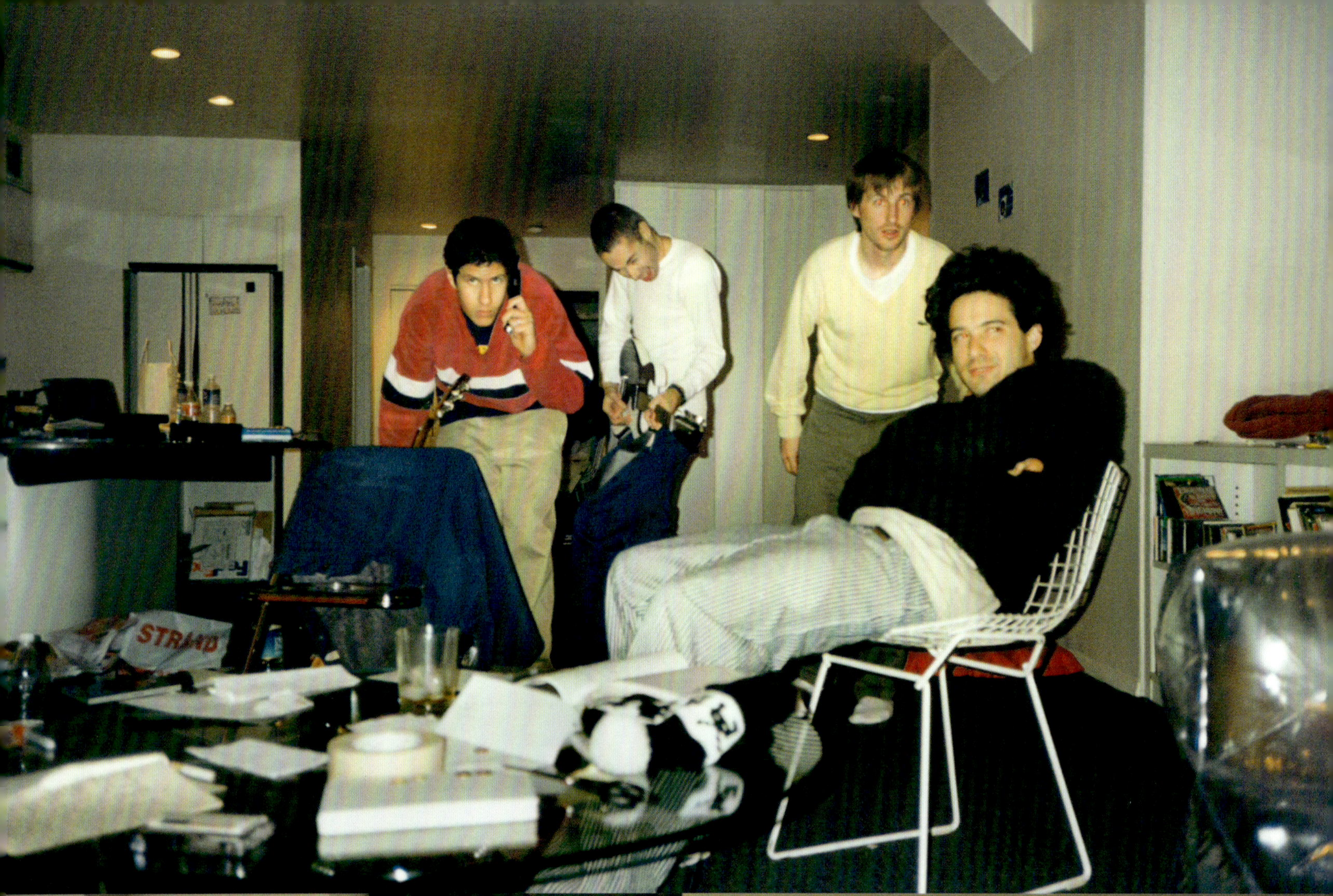
STRAND

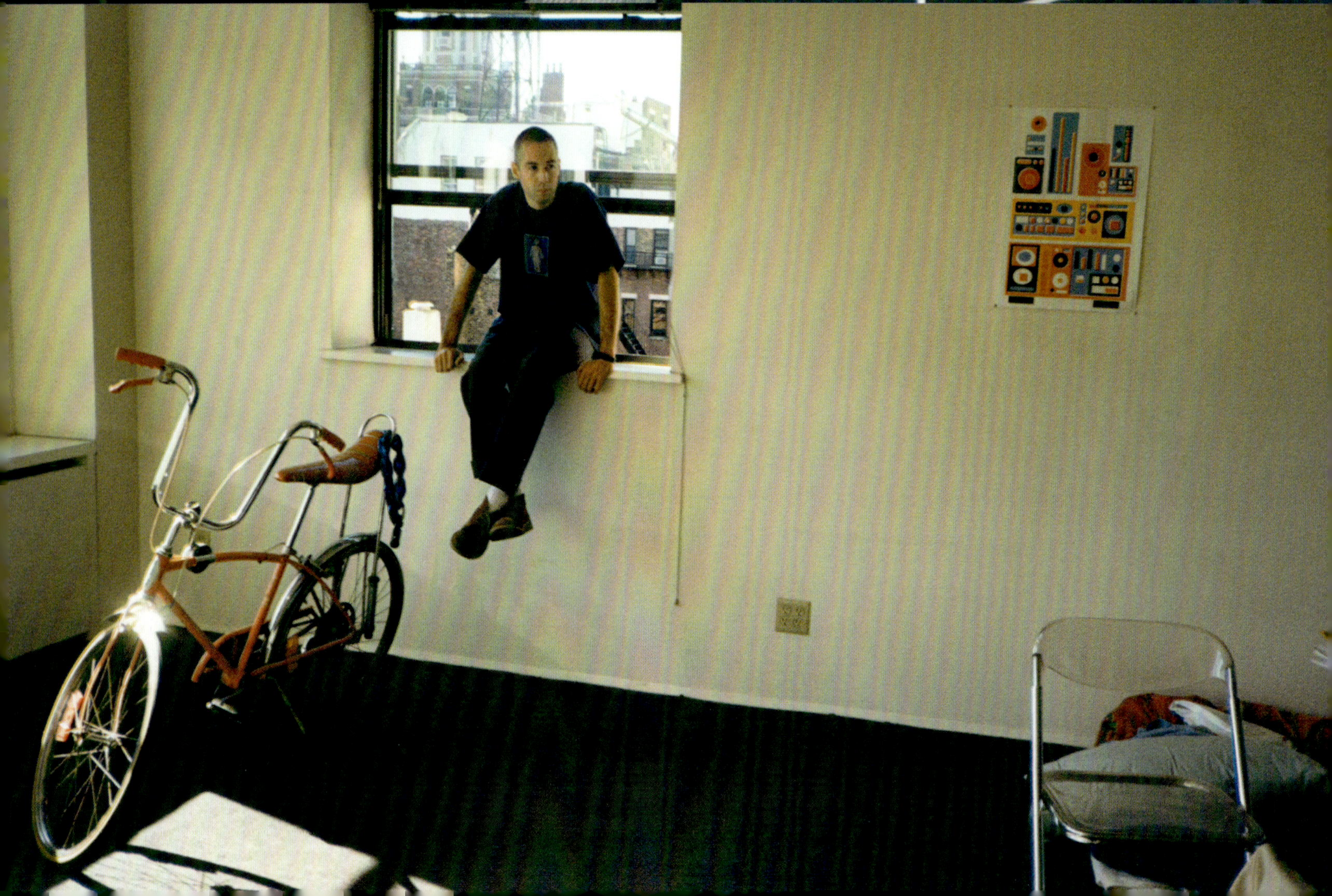

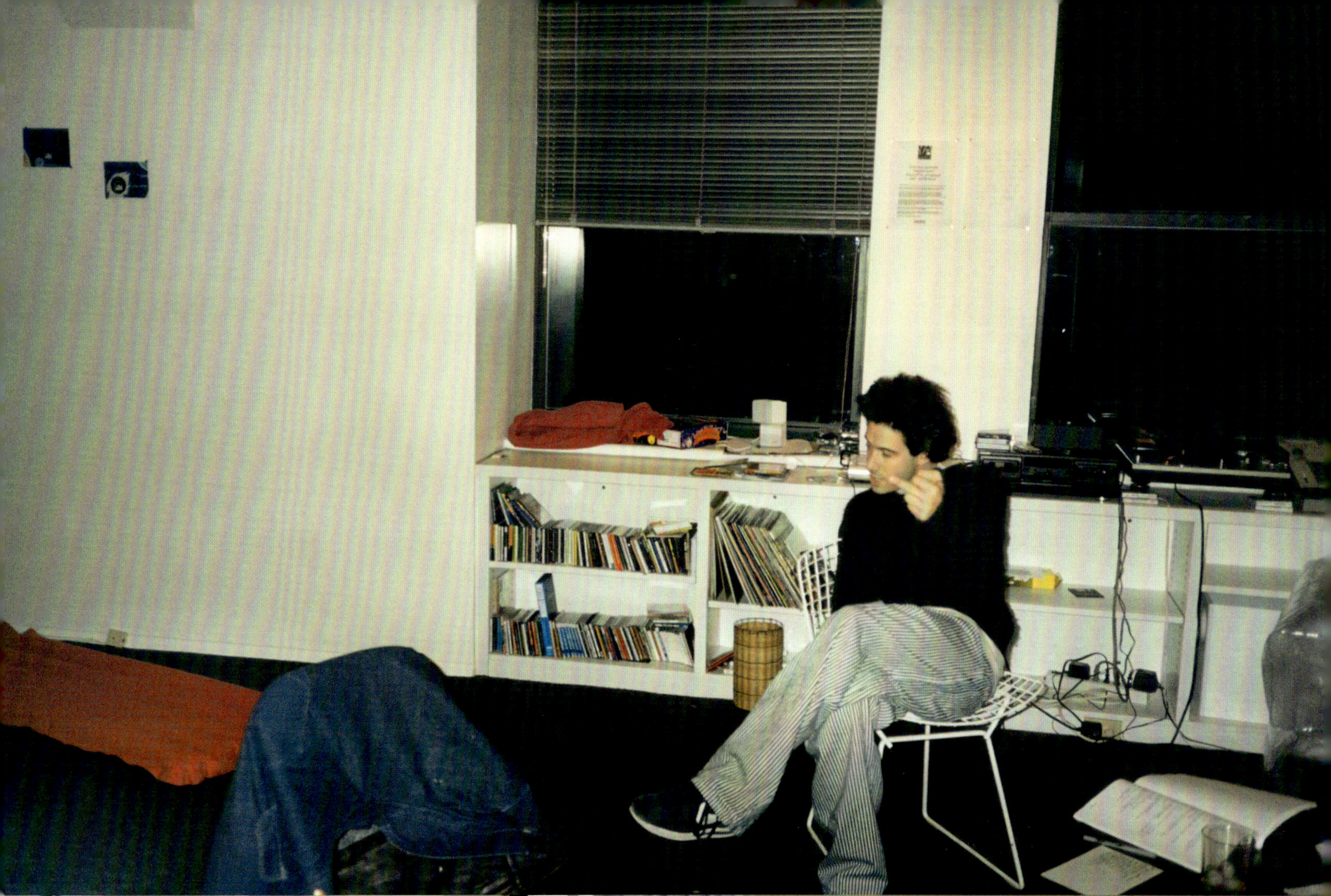

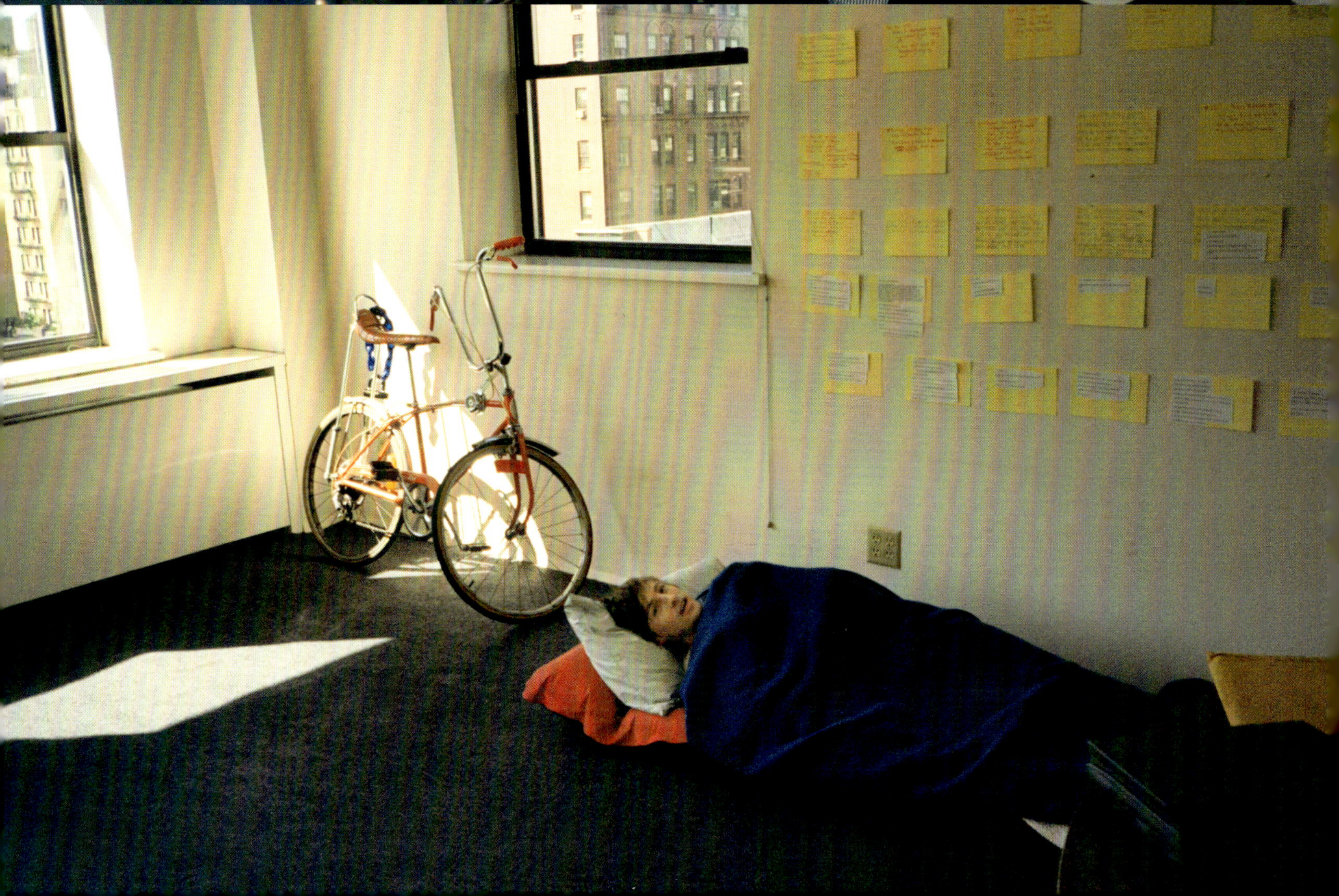

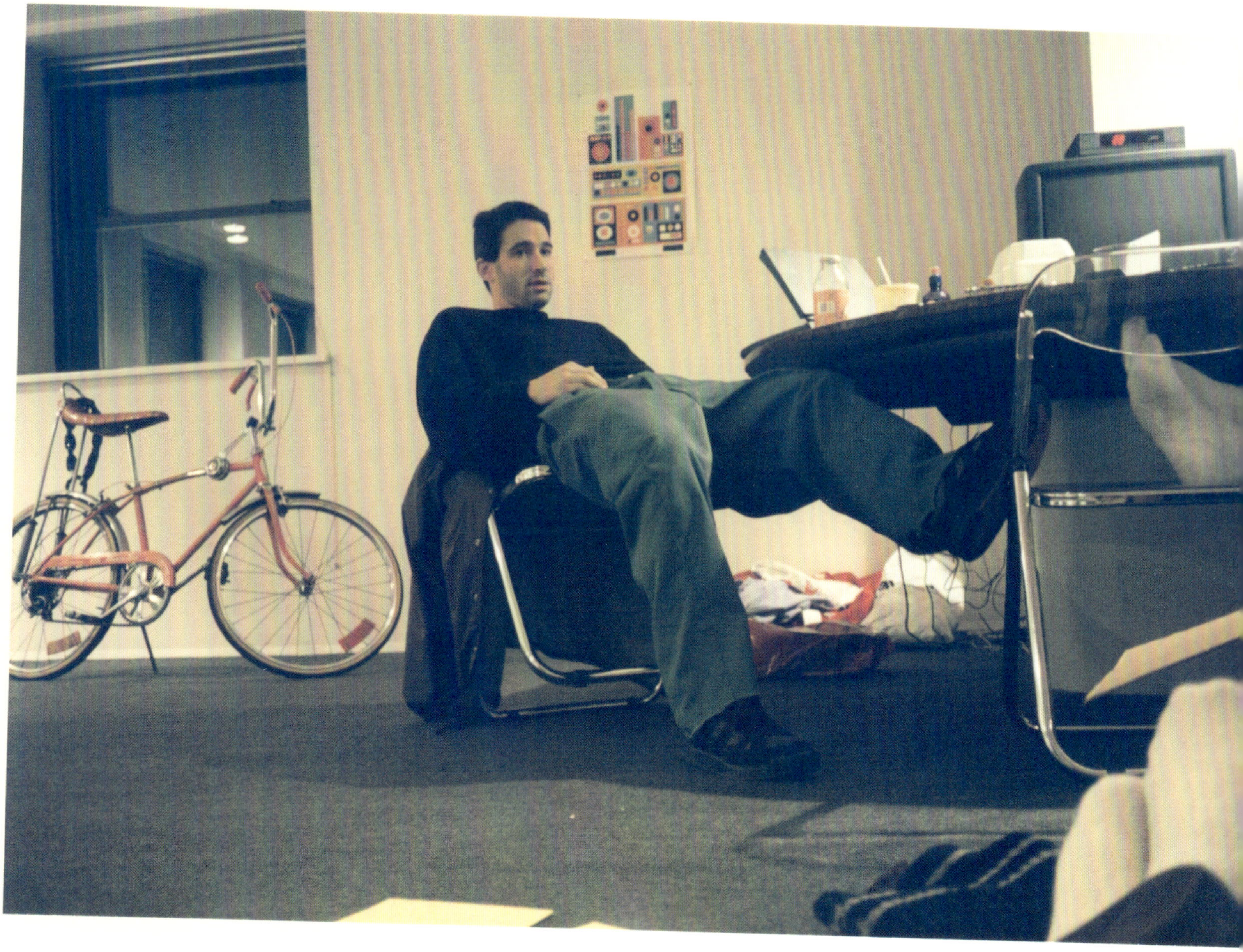

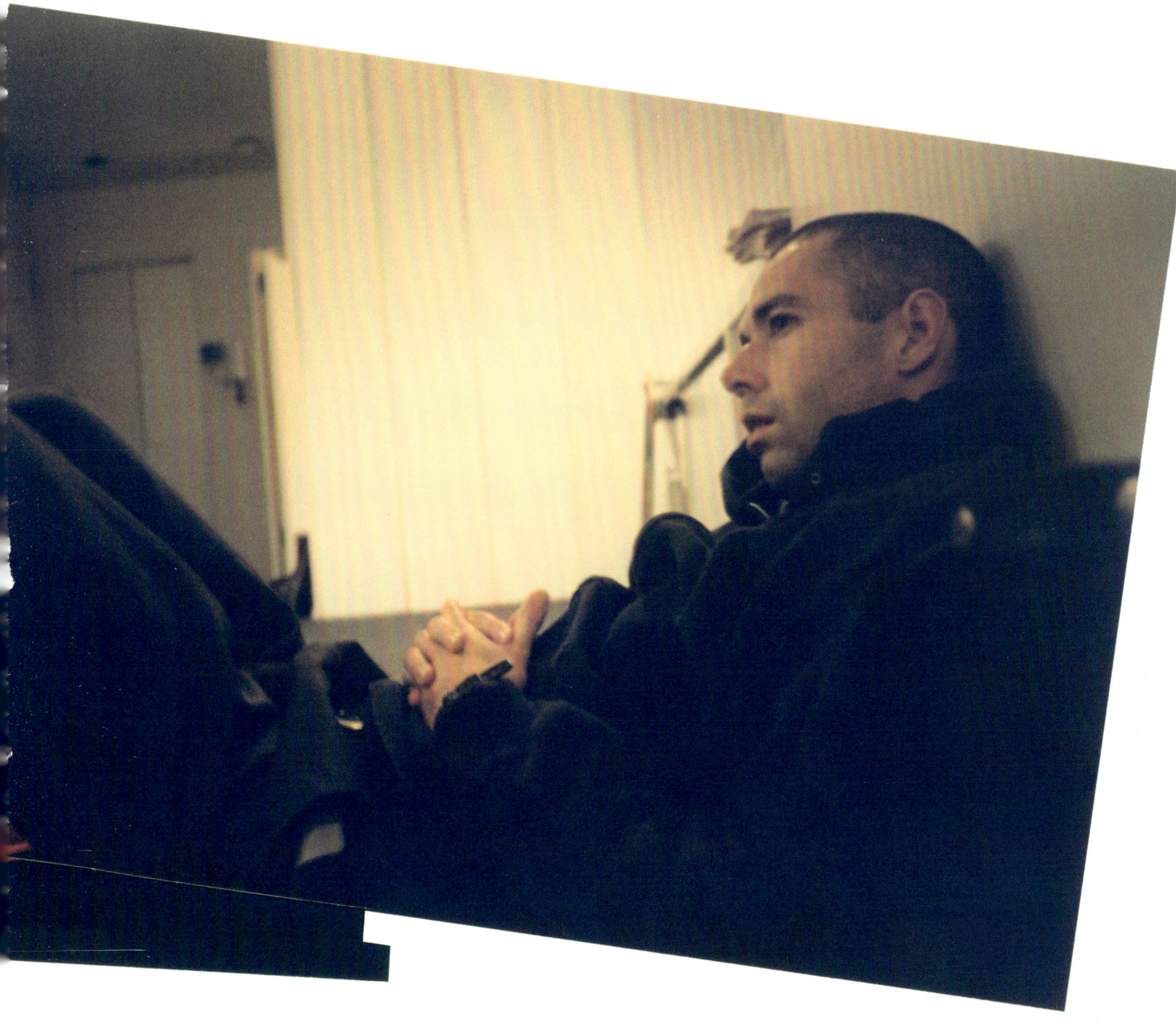

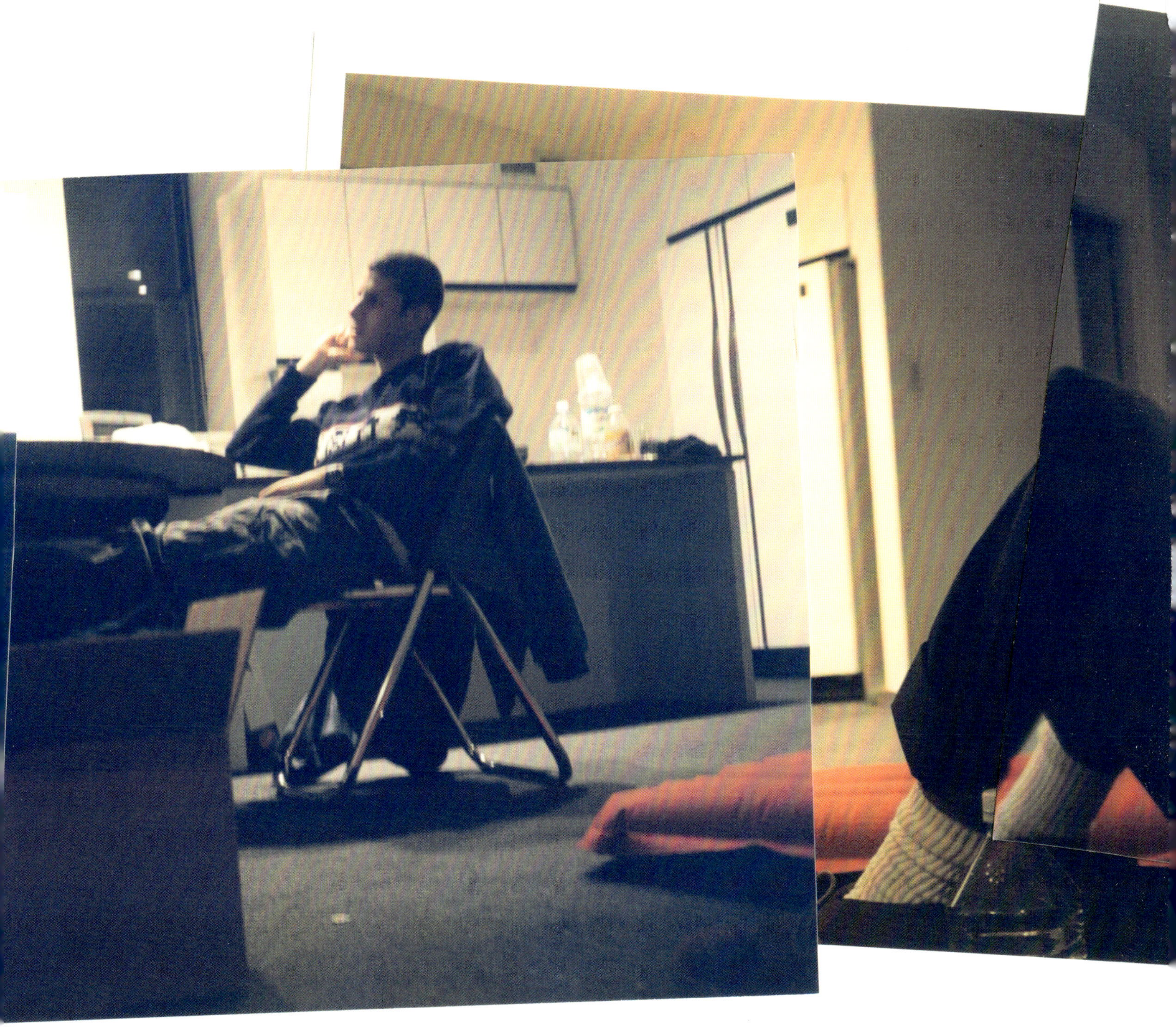

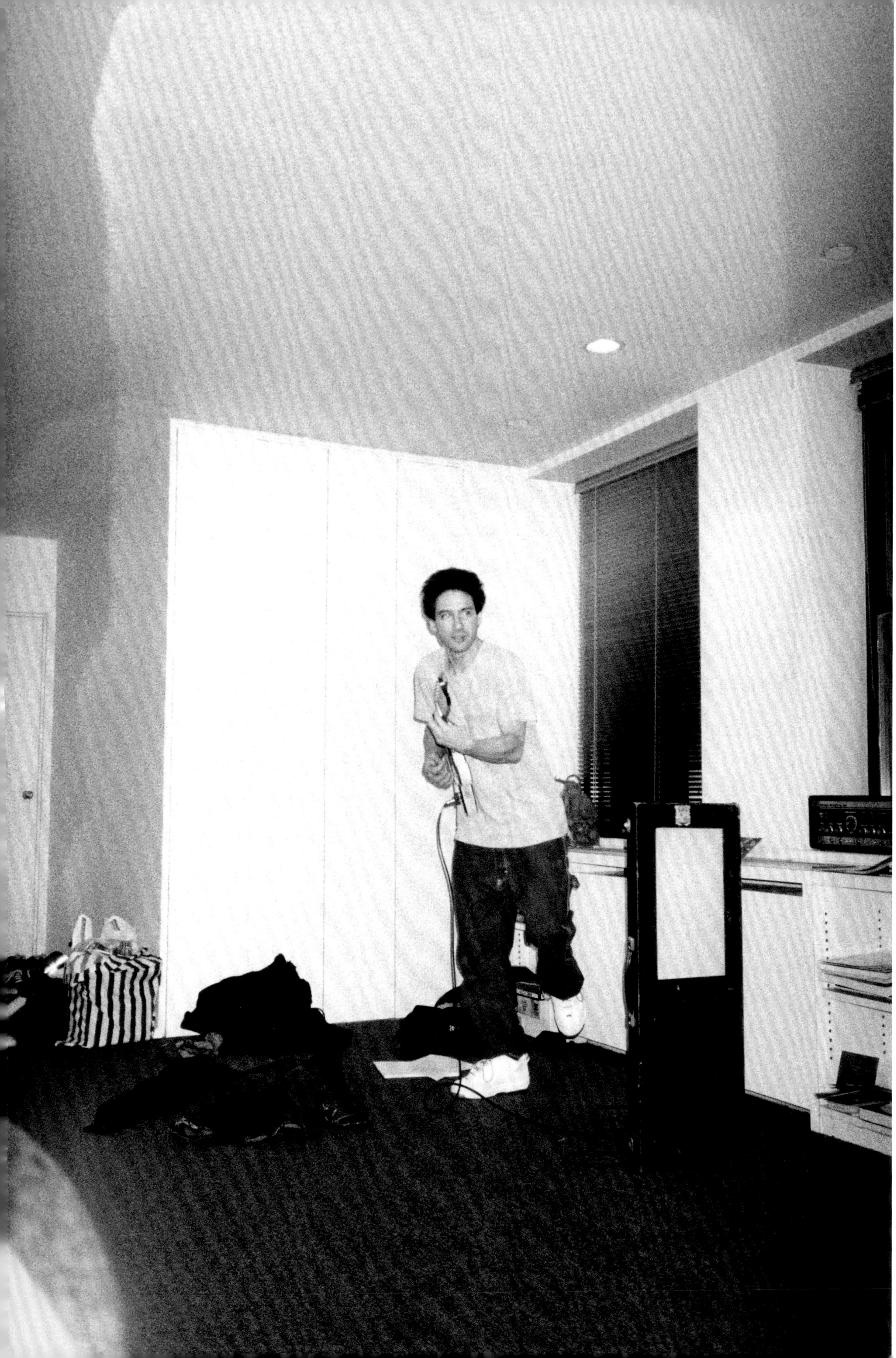

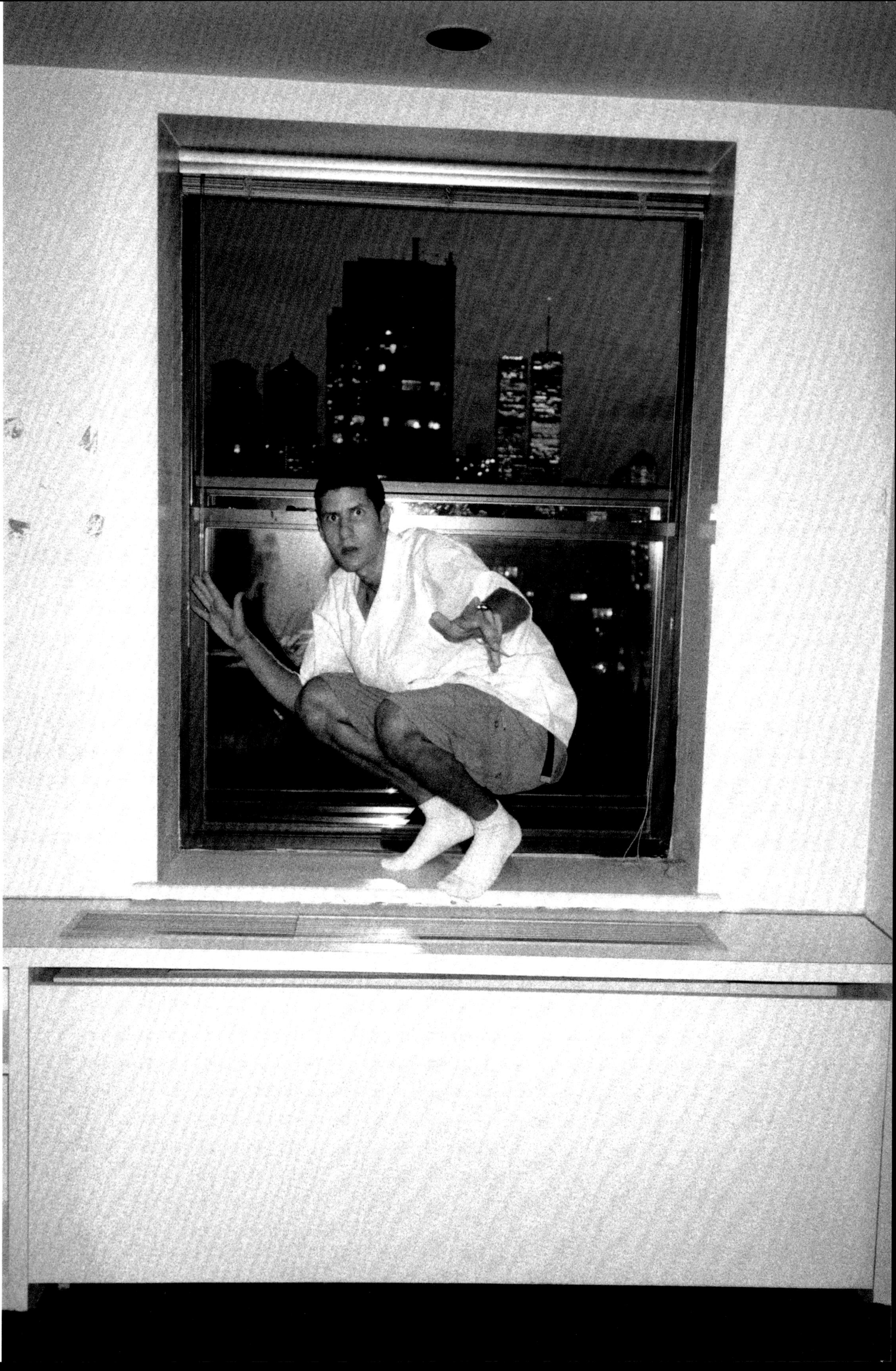

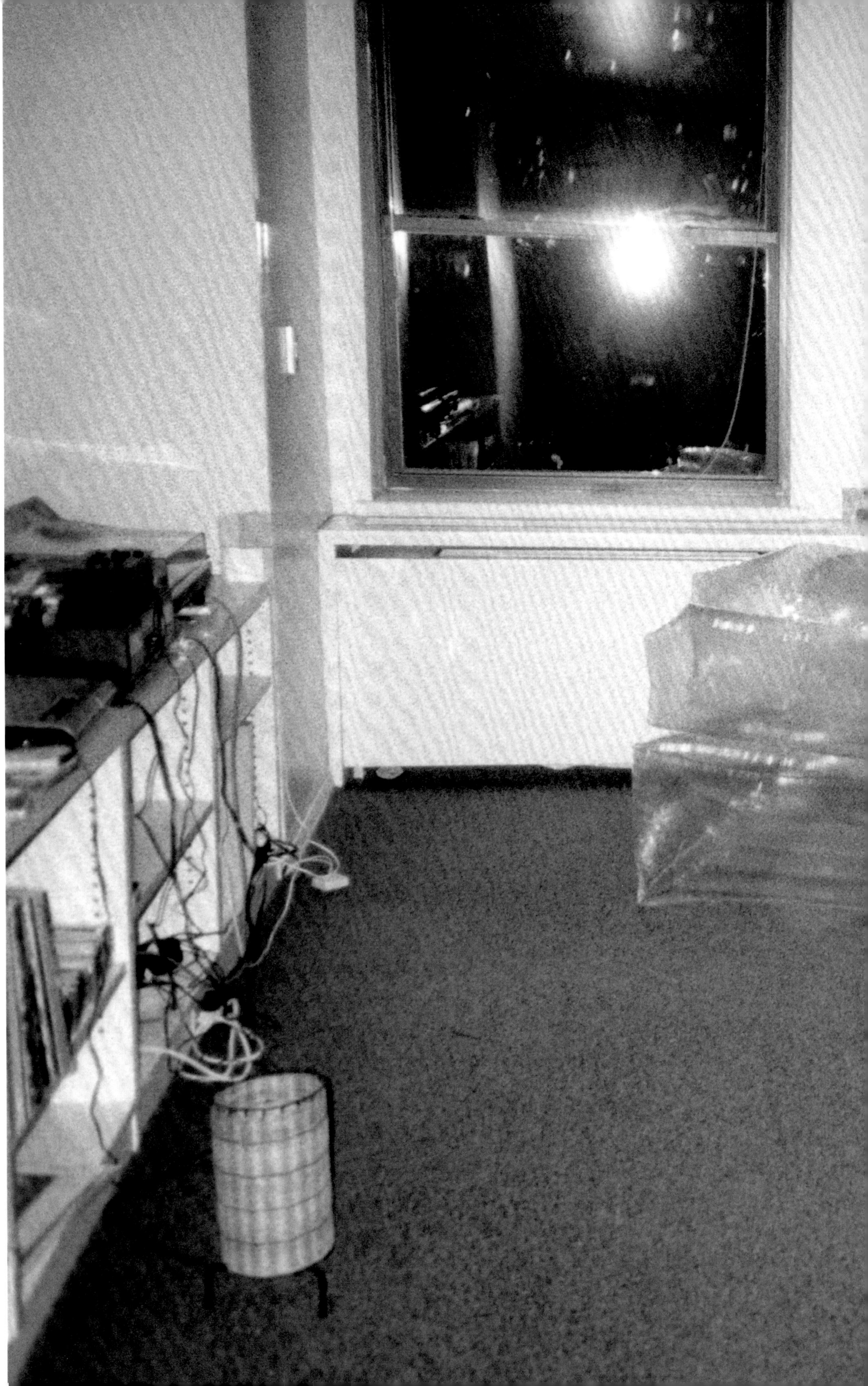

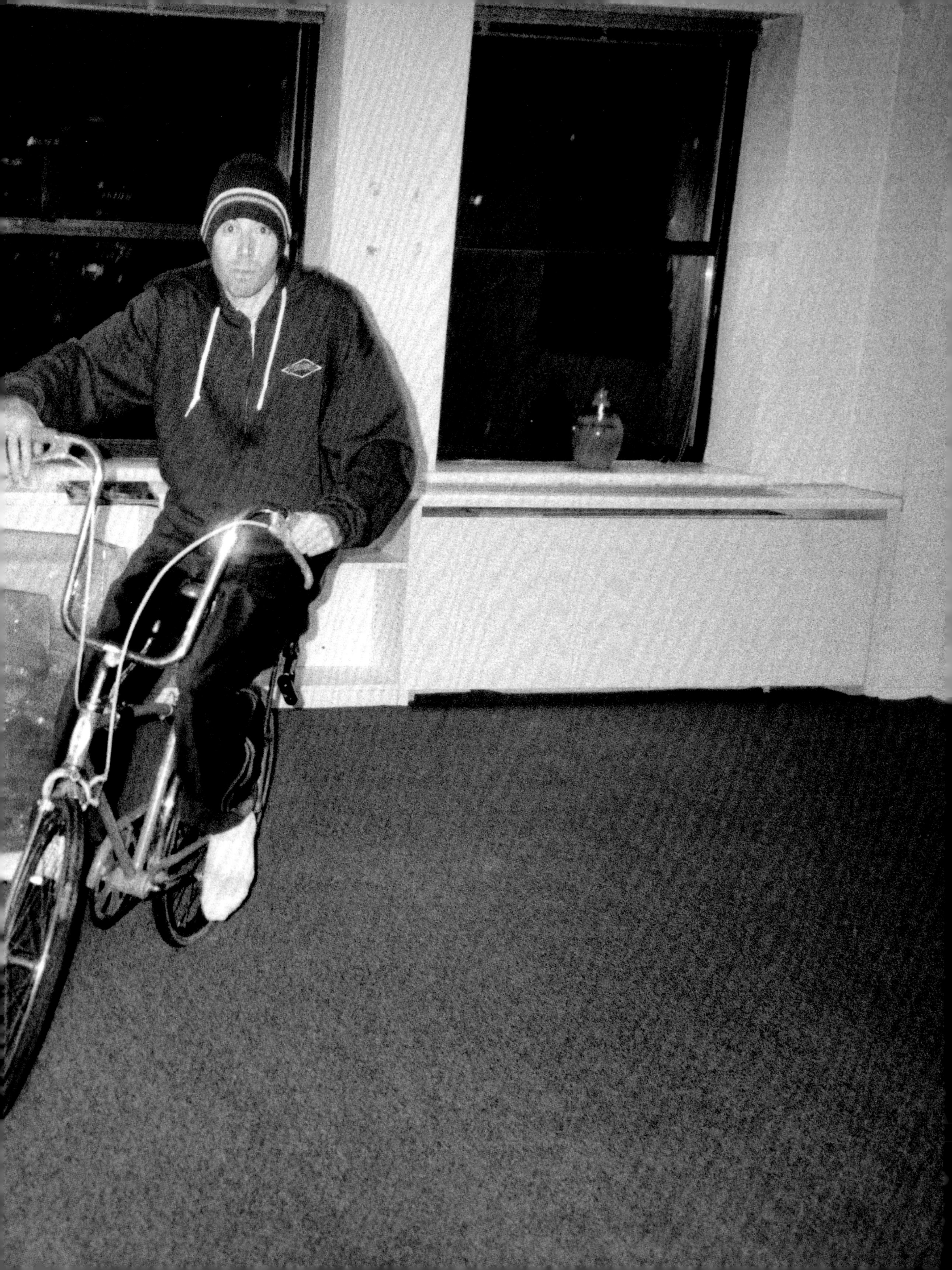

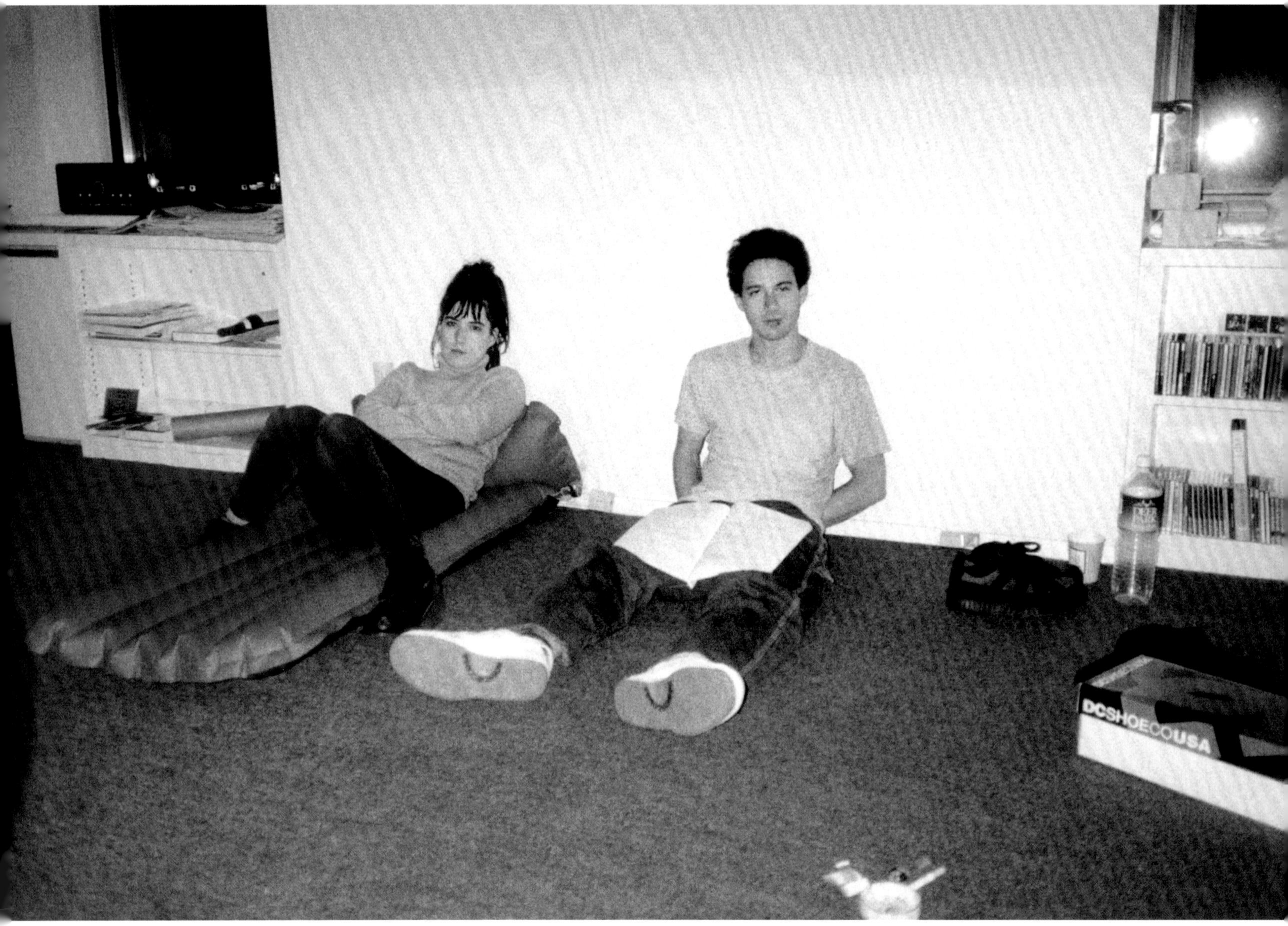
DCSHOECOUSA

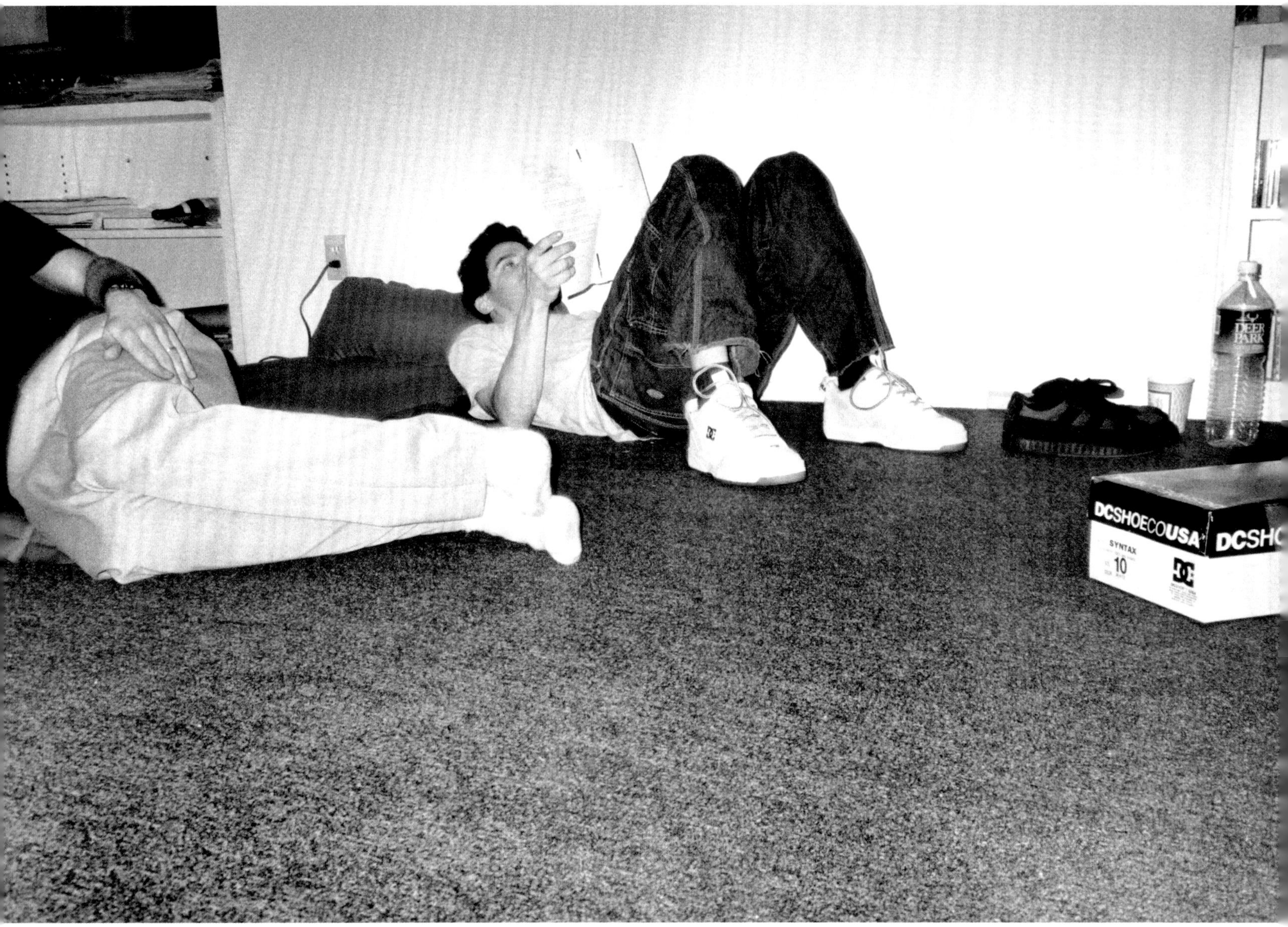
DEER PARK
DCSHOECOUSA
SYNTAX
10
DCSHO

Yauch wastrying to explain this to Bob Mack yesterday. He was saying, "Bob, you just say what you want to say, the way you want to say it and even if it's not decipherable to anyone, you've said what you wanted to say. The people who know what's up will know what's up. And the other people..."

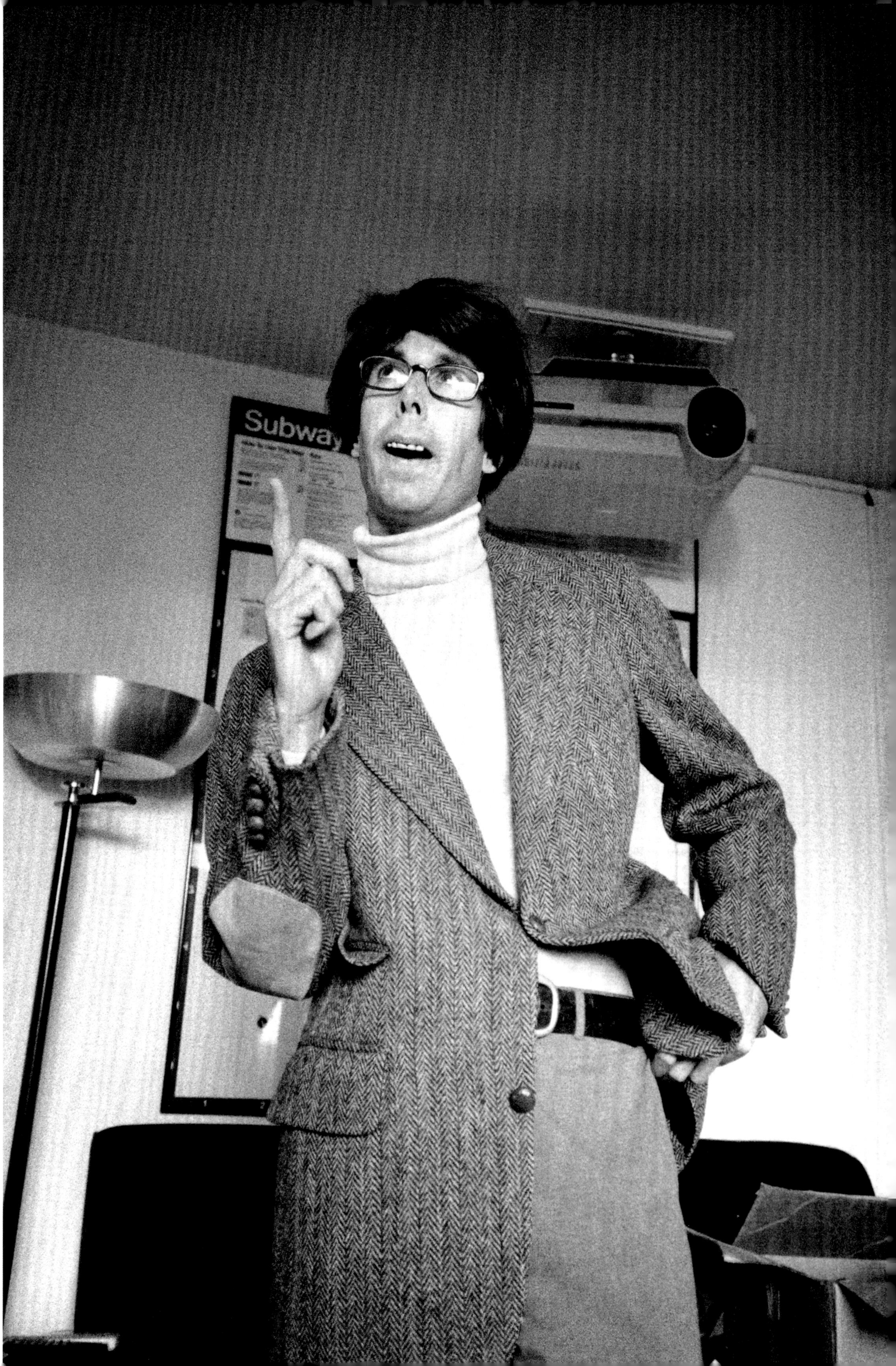
Subway

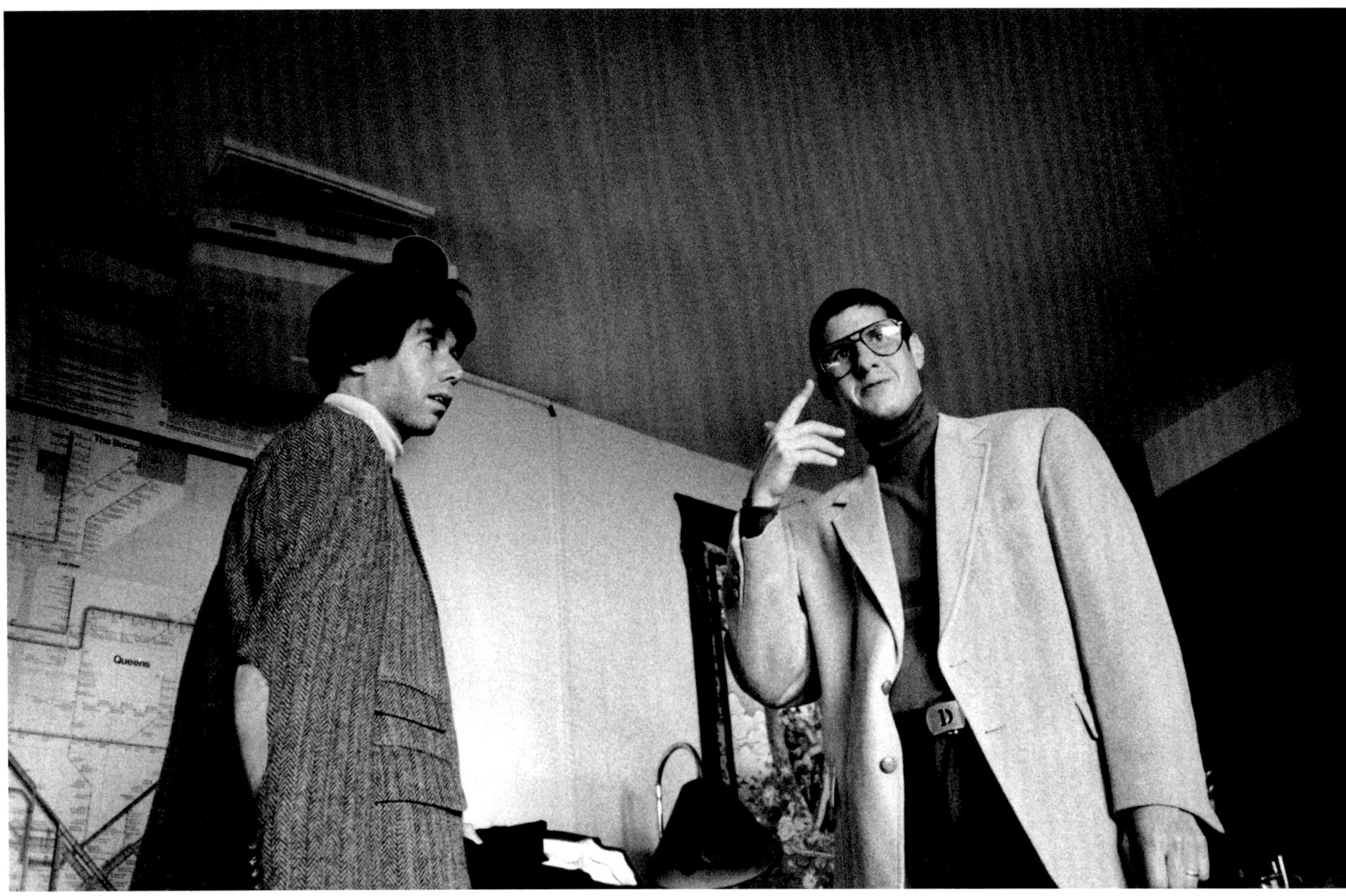
Queens

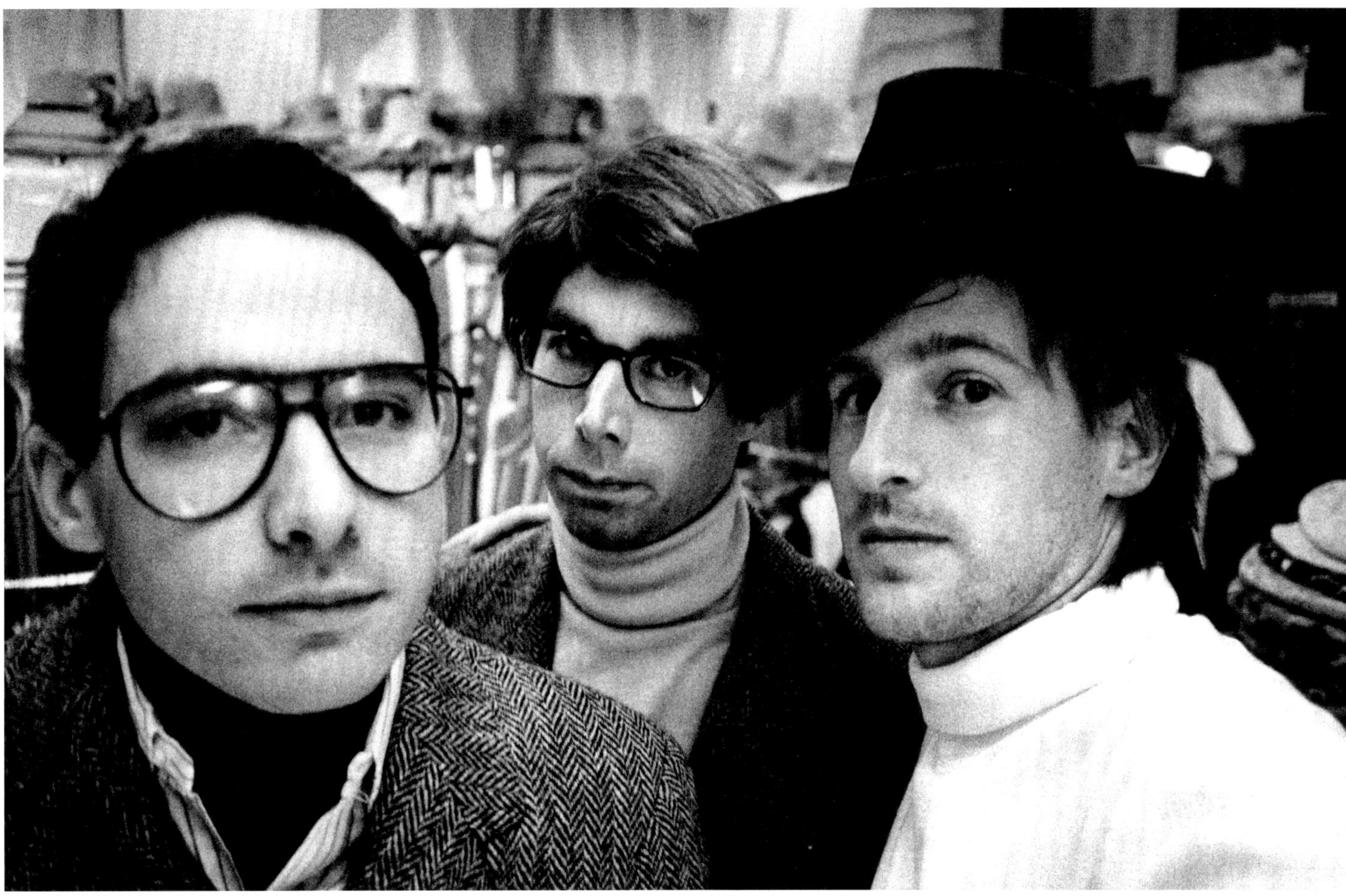

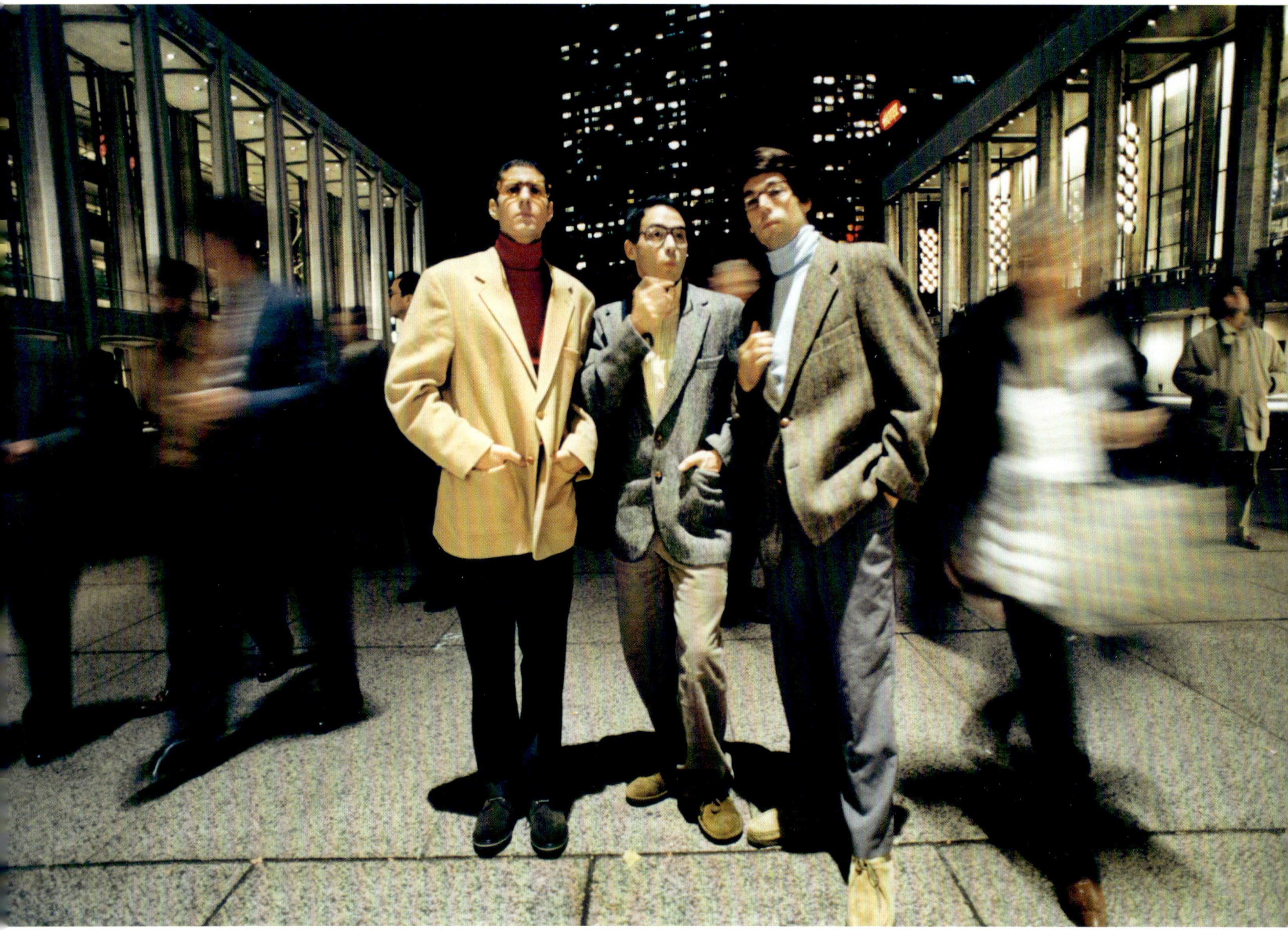

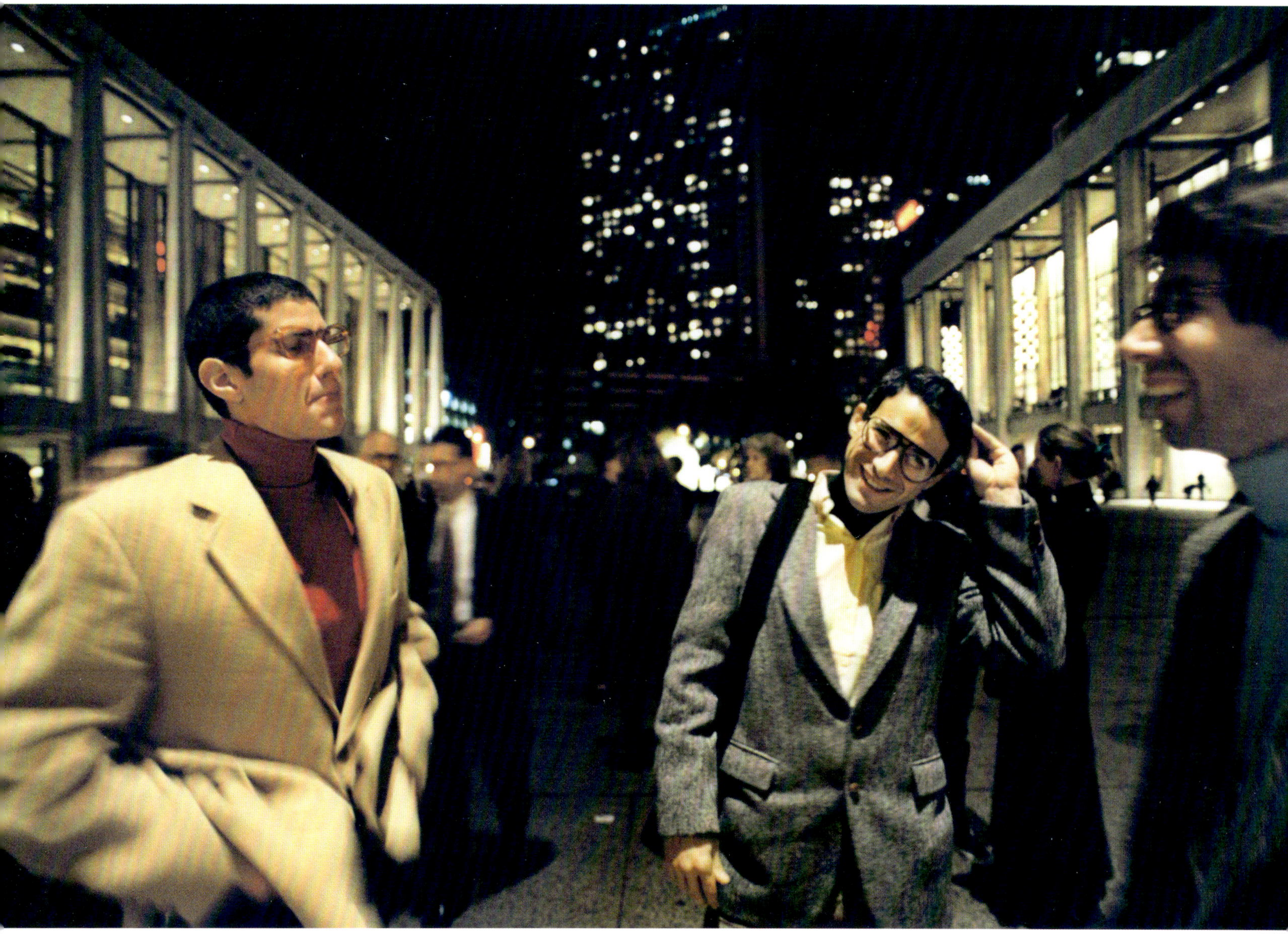

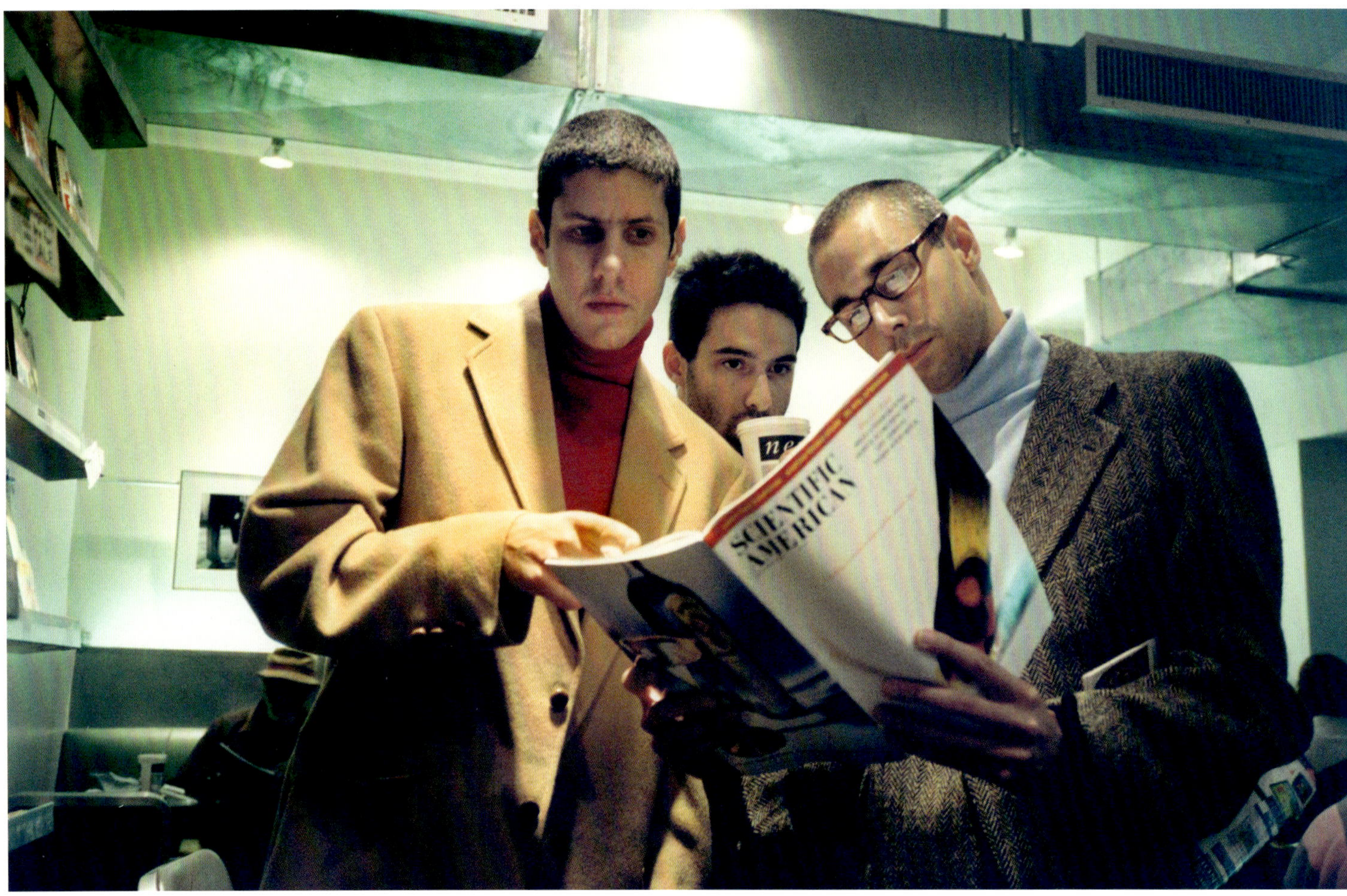
SCIENTIFIC
AMERICAN

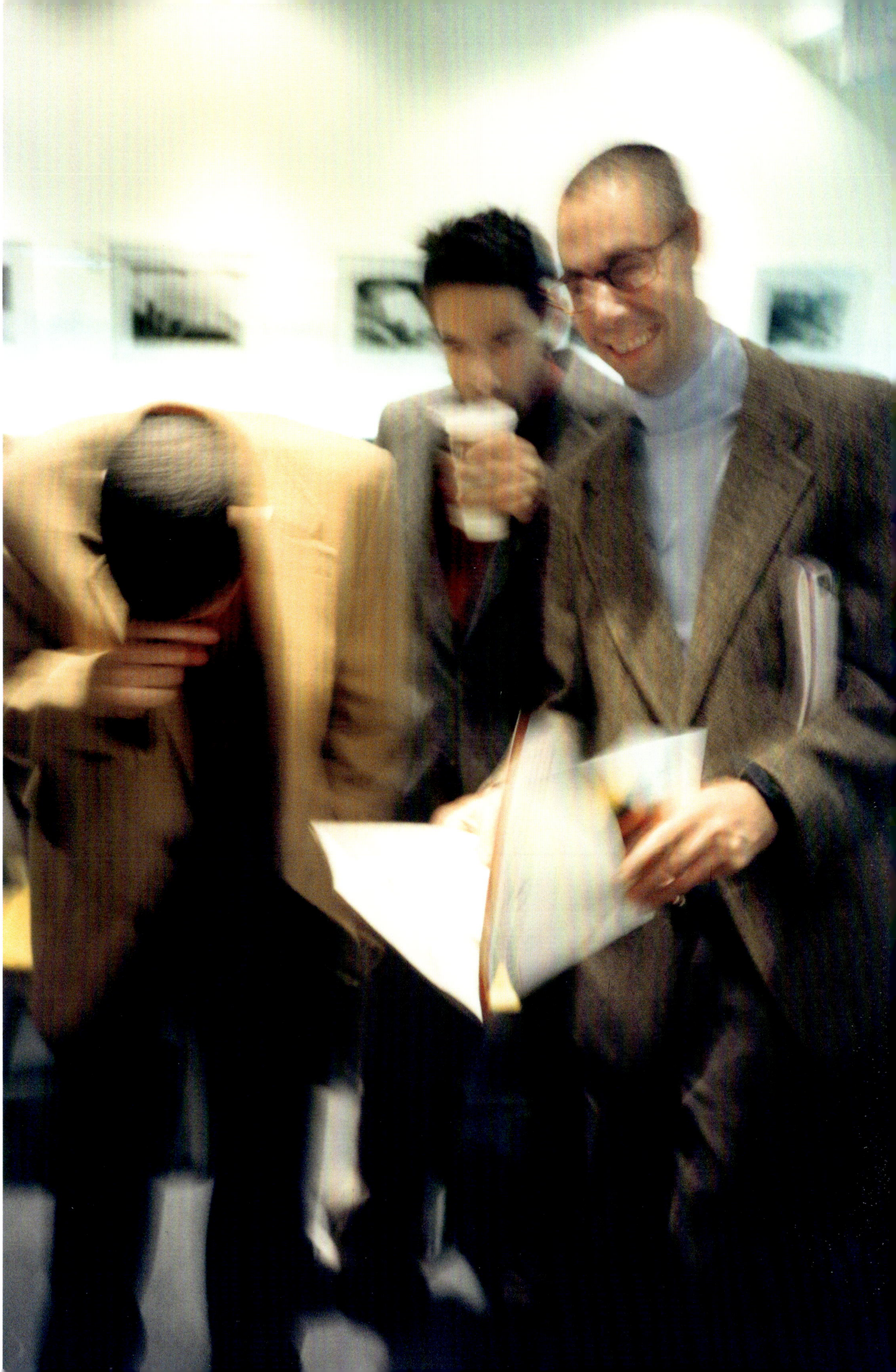

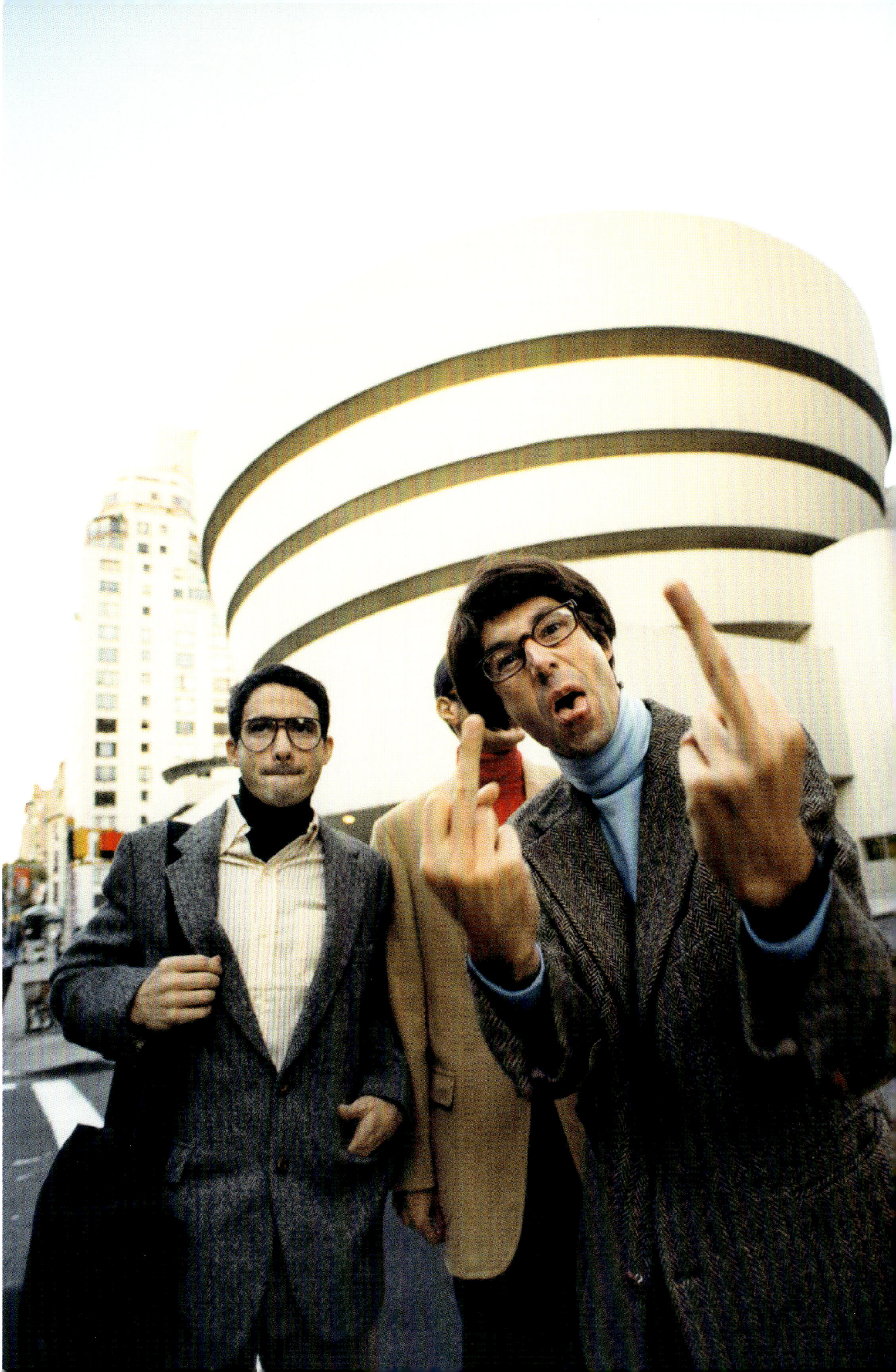

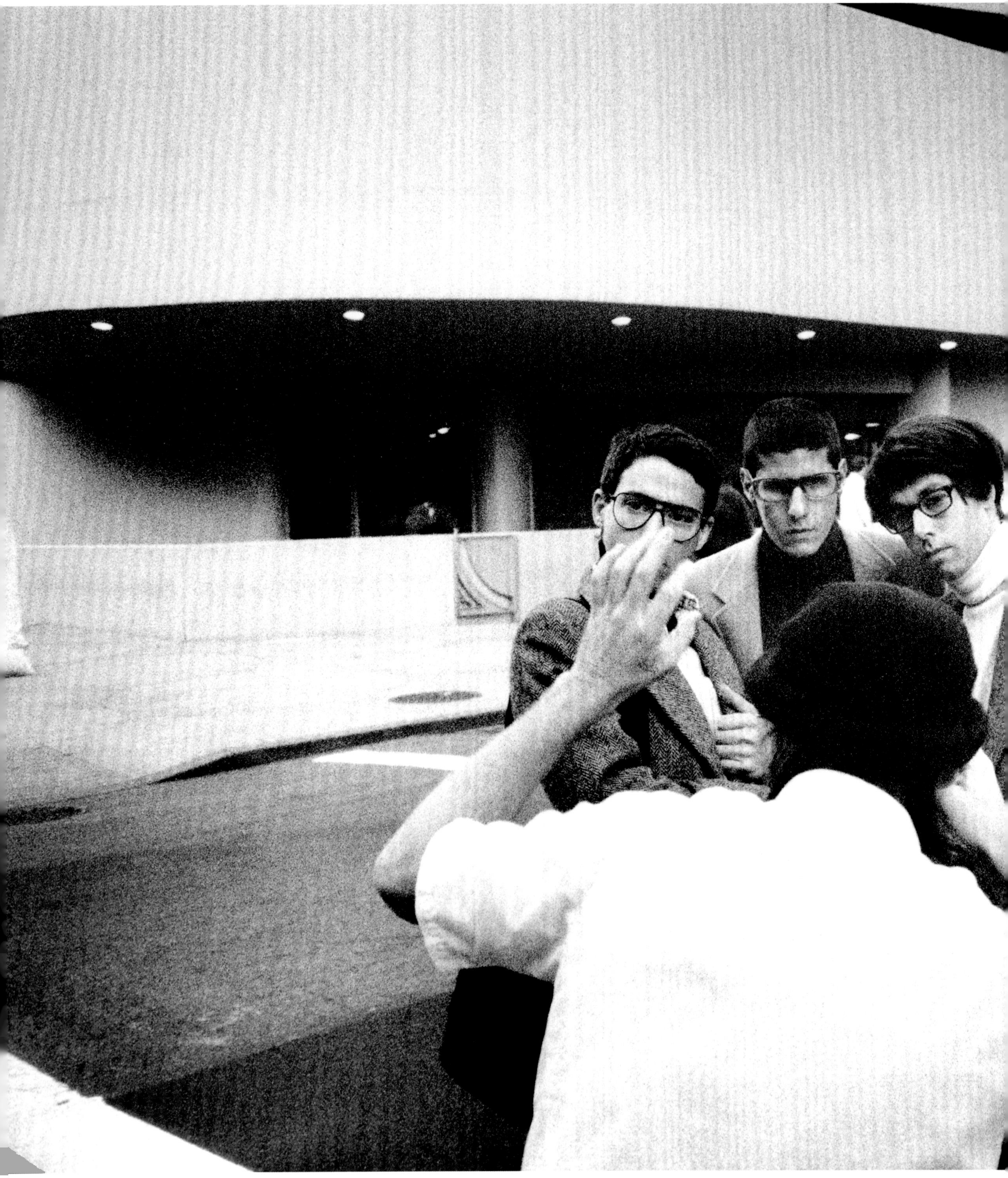

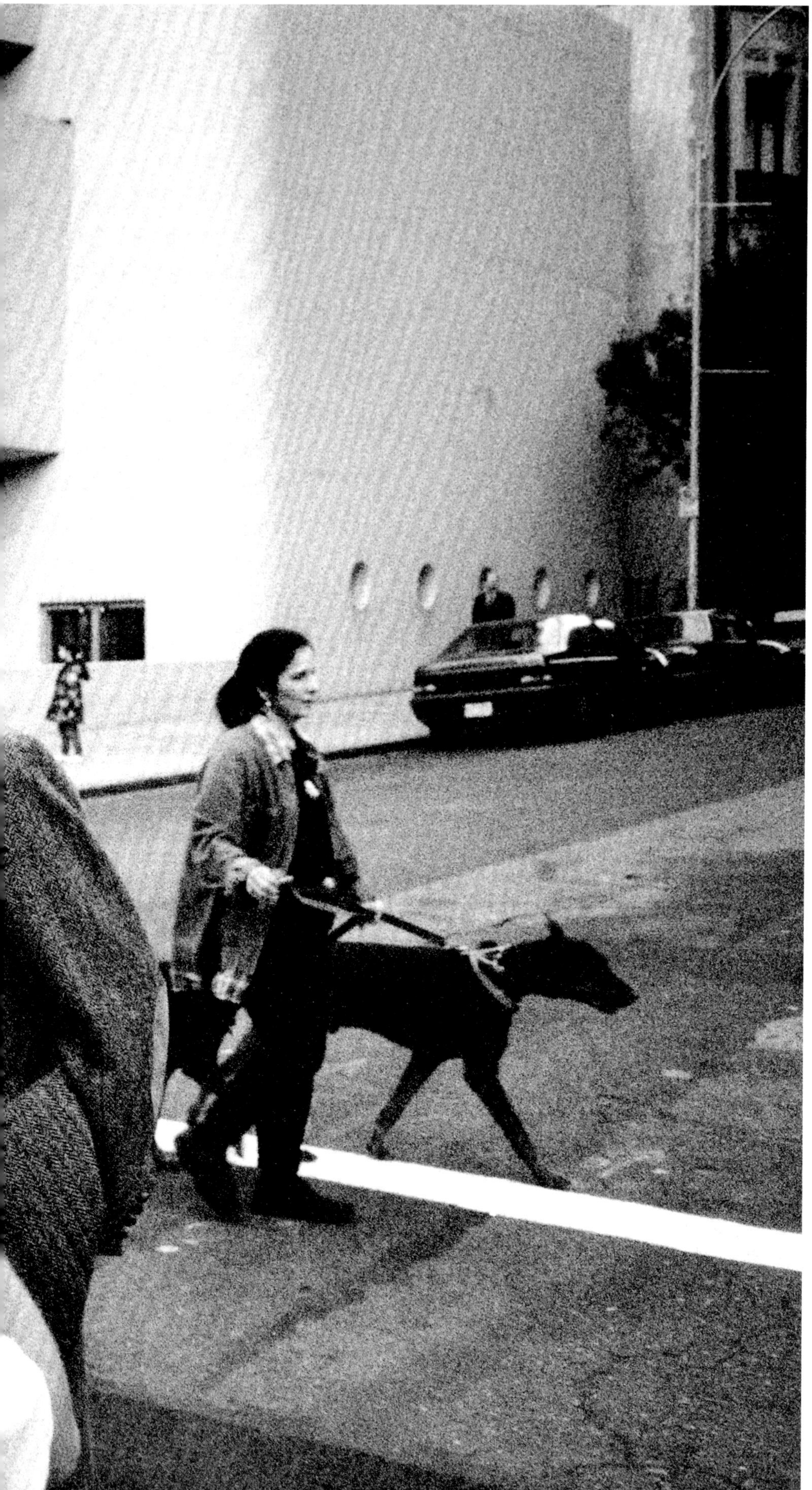

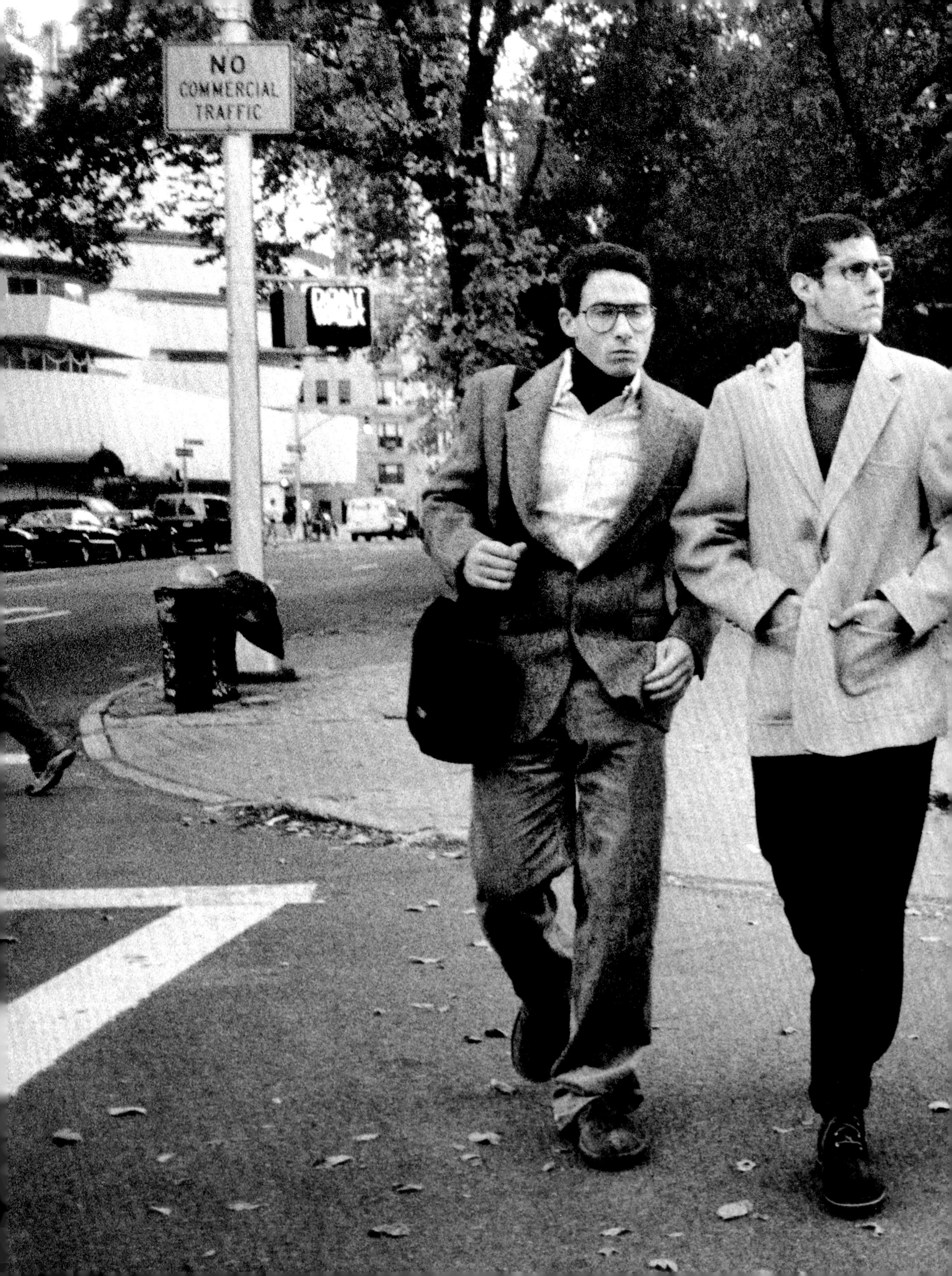
NO
COMMERCIAL
TRAFFIC
DON'T
WALK

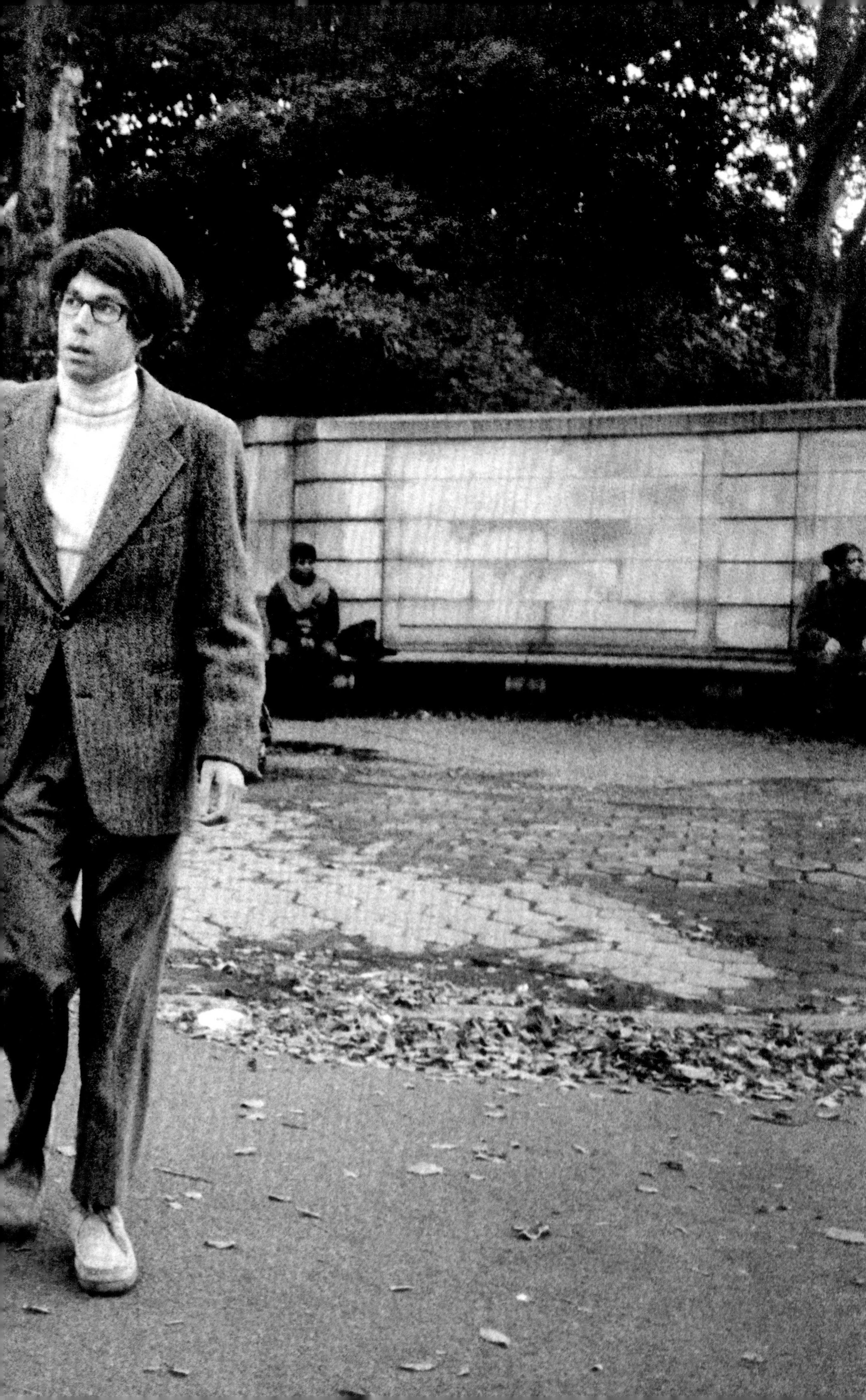

T-SHIRTS BY THE AIRPORT BY SPIKE JONZE

In 2009 I was in London trying to finish a movie we made, *Where the Wild Things Are,* that I'd been working on for 5 years, which felt like twice as long because of how difficult it had proved to be in so many ways. Not the least of which were epic battles and battles with the movie studio because basically, they didn't like the movie, it freaked them out. We had finally made it past all of that by sheer endurance and relentlessness (and a lot of help from our friends) and now we were in the last home stretch of it, everything was finished except the visual effects.

We were in the final 10 months where we had over 1,000 visual effect shots to complete, all of which required very detailed facial animation to add the final piece to the performances of the Wild Things themselves. We had had almost a year to do it, but when we got down to the last three months of it, we only had a few shots actually completed. So we'd moved to London, where the visual effects house was, to basically live at the place and mind-meld with these very talented animators to try to grind the shots out.

Our editor Eric Zumbrunnen and our producer Vince Landay, who were both old friends, had come to London, too, and we are spending 12 hours a day in dark rooms in Soho tweaking and re-tweaking the eyes and the brows and the curl of the lips on the big beastly furry faces to get it just right, the slightest wrong tweak and the eyes would look crossed or a sweet smile would look sociopathic. Needless to say, as much as I loved the movie, the process and labor of trying to finish it felt like my face was being ground into very very slow-moving asphalt.

Just when the grind was about to make my face pop off, I came into work one day and Eric (who, as a side note, had edited a Beasties video for 'Sure Shot' with us 15 years earlier, which isn't so much of a coincidence really because he had always edited most everything I made since I started directing) says, "I ran into Mike D walking to work. He is staying at the Soho Hotel and said to give him a call."

That little tremendous weirdo Mike D is in London? I was very happy to have something to be excited about and called him immediately. Not only was he here but he was with Yauch and Adam on a press tour and they would be in town for a few days. He said to come over to their hotel after work and we could eat and drink and he would make everything better.

I had been swimming so hard and so long on the movie that I hadn't really lifted my head too much to look around. So as I walked over to see Mike and the guys after work that evening, I felt like my head was back above water and I was looking around remembering my life beyond eyebrows, Wild Things, and battles with the movie studio. And suddenly I had the spark to go back and remember all the memories I had around these three humans and how much I loved them.

I was one of those lucky few, too, who had grown up loving them as a band and eventually got to become friends with them and eventually even got to make things with them. When I was 16, *Licensed to Ill* had been on repeat in my friend's station wagon. We would be driving to skate a ramp in a neighboring town in Maryland and have every word memorized and be laughing and rapping along feeling like we were the band or the band was us. And we were, in a way; me and my friends thought us and the things we thought were cool were the only things of any importance in the world and that most people were clueless. We went to a high school that was probably like most high schools in the suburbs in the eighties, with a lot of preppy entitled jocks who did cocaine at their parties on the weekends. Needless to say, we weren't that popular. But the Beastie Boys were kind of the absurd superhero cartoon version of what we were all into. Somehow they were both larger than life and making fun of it too, like we wanted to be.

Jump forward a couple years to when I was 19. I had moved to Torrance, CA, to write and shoot photos for a BMX magazine. I worked with two of the coolest people I knew, my friends Lewman and Andy Jenkins, who were, when I think about it, my first truly unbound creative friends. We lived together, skated together, and all we wanted to do was make stuff together: photos, painting, music, zines... it didn't really matter, we were just exploring it all. So when *Paul's Boutique* comes out, again I felt like the Beastie Boys were right with us, or we were right with them. They had tumbled out of adolescence into beginning to discover all the other ways of looking at the world, and we were, too. *Paul's Boutique* was cracking us up and tripping us out in a way that felt like we were on the inside of it, like we were the only ones who really got it.

And *Check Your Head* was just an extension of that. I had met the Beastie Boys before that record but only briefly, when Andy, Lew and I photographed them and interviewed them for a new magazine we were starting called *Dirt.* The magazine wasn't just about BMX or skating, it was also about all the other things we were into and learning about, like music, books, movies, all kinds of stuff you discover as the world gets bigger and bigger when you're 21. We were writing about, and even getting to interview, some of the people who we were inspired by and fascinated by: novelists, songwriters, and filmmakers. I was starting to sort of understand what those things really were and how they were made by people, in the same way we made stuff, as opposed to before, when I imagined some mythical fantasy version of how things I loved were made.

And when *Check Your Head* came out, it only felt more like they were us and were into what we were into. But obviously, they were way way cooler and more talented, and still seemed very mysterious.

And it was right around that record when I really got to know them. Becoming friends with them was both quite surprising and also seemed exactly simple and right. Through a crazy set of events involving the magic of Mark Gonzales, the curiosity and fairy godmotherhood of Kim Gordon, and the generosity and impromptu music video teachings from Tamra Davis I ended up rolling around with Mike, Adam, Yauch and this huge barrel of creative people my age making things on the Eastside of Los Angeles in the then-quiet neighborhoods of Silverlake, Echo Park, and Atwater Village.

They had built a homemade studio/office space/skate ramp/basketball court in a dusty old Elks Lodge in Atwater, and that became a meet-up place and creative hub. It would seem like a band that big wouldn't just have an open door for all their friends to roll through at any time, but they did, and it was wide open to maximize spontaneity, discoveries and stumbling on other creative weirdos. I don't think it was even intentional or thought out in that way, it was just who they were, but I clocked it for sure.

And even though it was exciting to suddenly be hanging out with this band I grew up loving, it also seemed like it couldn't have been more natural, and they made it feel that way, too, that we were all just making things together. So we all fell right in with them... Andy and Lew and I helped them start a magazine, I got to tag along with Yauch as he helped his uncle Hornblower direct their videos, and I shot photos and helped make videos for them and the other artists on the label they were starting (like Luscious Jackson, Hurricane, and Sean Lennon, among lots of others coming through Grand Royal at the time).

And I got to have such different relationships with each of them. Adam Horovitz was always still the most mysterious and cool, but he was also really fun to seek out at some weird party we would end up at with our girlfriends. I would find him and hang out in the corner and find things to obsess on and laugh about. I also always admired the way he would weave fantasy in with real life. I remember inviting him to something I had to go to for work or something and he said, "Oh man I would love to, I just can't, I gotta go pick up some t-shirts down by the airport. Wish I could." It was constant with him, all mixed up like pasta primavera, it was all true and all completely wise-guy too. And I still use that excuse to this day if there's something I don't want to go to.

Mike and I probably were the closest in that we were both probably the sensitive-feelings guys. Adam still makes fun of us to this day about us and our "emotions."[1] Mike was always so open with me about what he was doing, what he wanted to do with the label or the magazine and really why he wanted to do it all. If our relationship was one thing, it was driving around L.A. in his Volvo wagon talking about what we were into or what we were thinking about. I could sleep on his floor and I loved his dog like he was mine and I was just part of the family and part of his house.

One of the things that doesn't always happen is when someone who's inspired you and influenced you growing up ends up inspiring and influencing you even more if you meet them. I've always wrestled with the saying, "Don't ever meet your heroes." While I understand it and have a few times been disappointed, almost always it's the opposite. Maybe the saying should be: "Try to meet your heroes but just be very careful when you choose them." Yeah, I like that better. And it's definitely true with Mike, Adam and Yauch. It wasn't just their humor and creativity that inspired me, but it was also their true belief that you are just making things you and your friends would be into or think was funny. Nothing else matters. And set up your life and business like that, too.

I think Yauch maybe influenced me the most in how I worked in that I related to him and his desire to question everything. Not just to be contrarian (although that's fun, too) but to truly understand everything so you can decide if you agree. A lot of people you meet tell you this is how it is, this is how it works. "Are you sure, though? Really? This is the only way a music video or a movie can be made? Why?" Yauch was someone who never took things as they were told to him and never took no for an answer. No just meant to ask more questions, maybe you weren't asking the right ones. He was so strong in what he was into and what he believed in, it was like trying to bend a flagpole. But that being said, he was also a true listener and constantly wanting to learn new ways of thinking. I saw Yauch operating with so much independence and defiance and when I was young, to see him be that way up

[1] But, quick note: don't be fooled by Adam's ever-present smart-aleck smirk, he's got as big a heart as anyone I know. Like city-bus size. He'll pretend he doesn't, so don't tell him I told you.

against all these people who are supposed to "know everything" like labels, production companies, movie studios, really inspired me to double down on myself like they did.

When I started figuring out how to make music videos that were "mine," that felt like me, I was a little self-conscious because I thought my ideas were too goofy, like the idea that cracks you and your friends up but it can't be a real thing. But getting to see and be part of their band who did exactly that gave me permission to do what me and my friends had always done in skateboarding or the magazines or skate videos, but to just do it in these other forms and be given much bigger budgets. By still just taking whatever absurd idea you're into, making it with total commitment and treating it like it's a real thing... then it becomes a real thing to you and everyone around you.

And as Yauch and I got more into directing and films, we could talk endlessly about movies we wanted to make and how we wanted to do it. Yauch was going to be radically independent and not just make films on his own, but would start a distribution company to actually release them himself. And once he created a system to release his first film, he wanted to help other filmmakers release theirs with the same independence. With Yauch's strength of will alone, he created one of the few independently owned film distribution companies, Oscilliscope Laboratories. And they distributed legit films. Films with real actors and directors. Films in the Cannes Film Festival–type legit.

Ok, so needless to say, I was inspired by all of them in many different ways. As artists, definitely, but maybe even more so as friends, as the kind of people who treat each other and everyone in their life with respect and honesty. As we got older and went through real life shit together too, we really became close. We had the kind of relationships that you can only have when you get in fights with people you love and not only survive them together but get closer and understand each other more. I remember sitting in a shitty sake bar in the East Village in the mid-nineties with Mike, and he felt so badly that he had inadvertently been part of something that hurt me, that he started crying. That was the kind of friend he was to me and the kind of friend I hoped to be to him.

Wait, I think I got carried away... Back to London, 2009, 18 years after I first met them to shoot their photo with my friends. A few lifetimes later now and we were inescapably part of each other's lives, both through our friendships and what we all made together.

It was a perfect summer evening and I was running through Soho, escaping the grind of the asphalt to the face to go find my old friends who were in town. I had seen Mike and Adam and Yauch separately plenty, but I couldn't remember the last time I got to hang out with all of them together? It may have been 5 or 6 years earlier? Before I'd started on the movie I was now finishing.

So when I got to the hotel and saw all three of them, I was so happy. And even though I just went over to catch up with them that night for a drink, it tumbled into a much bigger adventure as it does with them and their contagiousness to all who's around. It became almost a week of hanging out, being stupid and laughing at complete nonsense that was maybe only funny to us and the people in our pile at the moment. The three of them were on a press tour for their new record and after Eric, Vince and I got to have a few ridiculous and fun nights with them in London, they were going to do more press in Paris and they persuaded me (did they really even have to persuade me though?) to come with them for a few more days of fun.

That week with them all was a real gift to me. Right in the middle of this visual effects asphalt grinder, I was dropped into this stew of very familiar and family-style fun. Even though I hadn't been with all three of them together in many years, it felt like it always had, just like kids playing and being stupid. But we were just staying at nicer hotels and now Mike was very into fancy French white wines, which he could describe in that very specific Mike-absurdist detail that fluctuated between highly knowledgeable savant-like genius and completely indecipherable thoughts that meant something very vivid to him but just sounded like funny words coming out of Mike's crooked grin. And as always, this entertained us all to no end. His new wine habit not only brought us to eat at really delicious fancy French white wine type restaurants, but also gave Horovitz endless fodder to make fun of and roll his eyes at Mike, which only made Mike laugh and get even more goofy and ridiculous, which gave Adam more to make fun of and so on... they had perfected this chemistry to a refined 30-year joy that was hilarious just to watch and soak in.

At the end of the week, they went on to finish their press tour and start to play shows to get ready to launch their new record, and I went back to London to finish my movie with a drop of magic in my beard.

It was a month or so after I saw them in Europe that I heard what was going on with Yauch. When he had gotten home from that trip, he felt a lump in his neck and went and got it checked out and found out he had cancer.

I don't know who I had heard it from, but when I talked to Yauch, he sounded just like Yauch... open, thoughtful, and here's another new thing to get to learn about and dive into. Another new experience to have, and as he did with everything, he did it fully. For the next few years he focused all his powerful intention on learning about his sickness and fighting it. And all the while, he never stopped being curious about what was going on in my life or stopped making and distributing great films, and never stopped being creative and playful.

He was the same funny dude who would laugh excitedly as he told me a new ridiculous idea he had for a video where Will Ferrell and John C. Reilly and all these epic actors play both the young and old versions of the Beastie Boys and they cross paths through a time machine, *Back to the Future* DeLorean–style, and have an epic battle over who are the real Beastie Boys. By the time he was telling me his ideas for the end of the video that climaxes in a giant pissing contest where they are all peeing on each other, Yauch and I are both laughing till we were crying. And the only thing more absurd than the fact that Yauch had these ideas was the fact that he went and made them. Just willed them to be. If you haven't seen his magnum opus 30-minute music video pee-soaked epic, please go watch it now. It's called 'Fight for Your Right Revisited.' Make sure to watch the long one. There is no one I'll ever know like Yauch. Who else could both teach me about the fundamental beliefs of empathy and compassion in Buddhism and in the same conversation tell you about his idea for Elijah Wood to be pissing on Jack Black?

So that week with them in Europe became even a bigger gift to me as time went on. It was this magical innocent moment stolen in time. On one of those nights in Paris, we all wanted to go to some famous ice cream place we heard about on the other side of town. And Yauch as always wanted to make an adventure out of it, so he and I rented bikes and rode around town, sort of sight-seeing and sort of just wandering around meeting people and goofing. At one point, we were riding through the plaza where those glass pyramids of the Louvre are and Yauch with his mischievous gravelly voice casually said, "I bet you could do a wall ride on that." Now we have no business in any way wall-riding on the Louvre in the first place, and also it had been probably 10 years since I'd done a wall ride on a bike, and this rental bike is like 50 pounds and I can barely bunny hop it... But I did it, of course, and the only reason I did was because Yauch had seen my nervousness and upped it with that grin of his that tells you there are no rules.

Since that week, we still had and have many laughs together. Through the last few years of Yauch's life, it never stopped. And to this day, when I see Mike and Adam, it's instant laughter, it's hard not to have fun when you're around them. Hanging out, laughing, creating things... it's all the same to them, one doesn't go without the other. I still try to live that to this day, no matter what I'm making. That has to be what it's all about.

And that's the way they've always been since I met them. So it turns out, they were very wise men for being 23 years old. They always knew that's what it was about: laughing with your friends and making things together. What else is there?

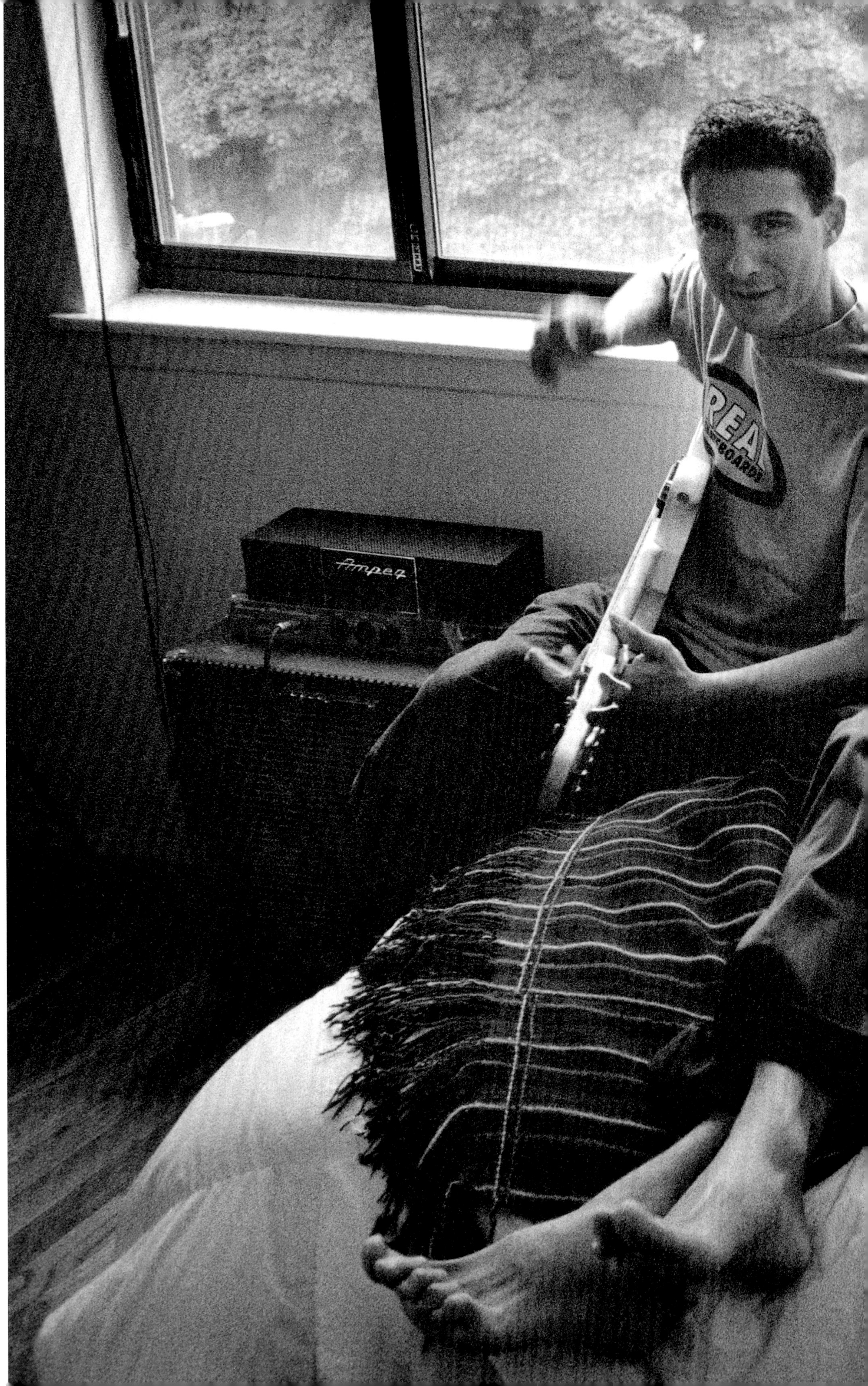
Ampeg

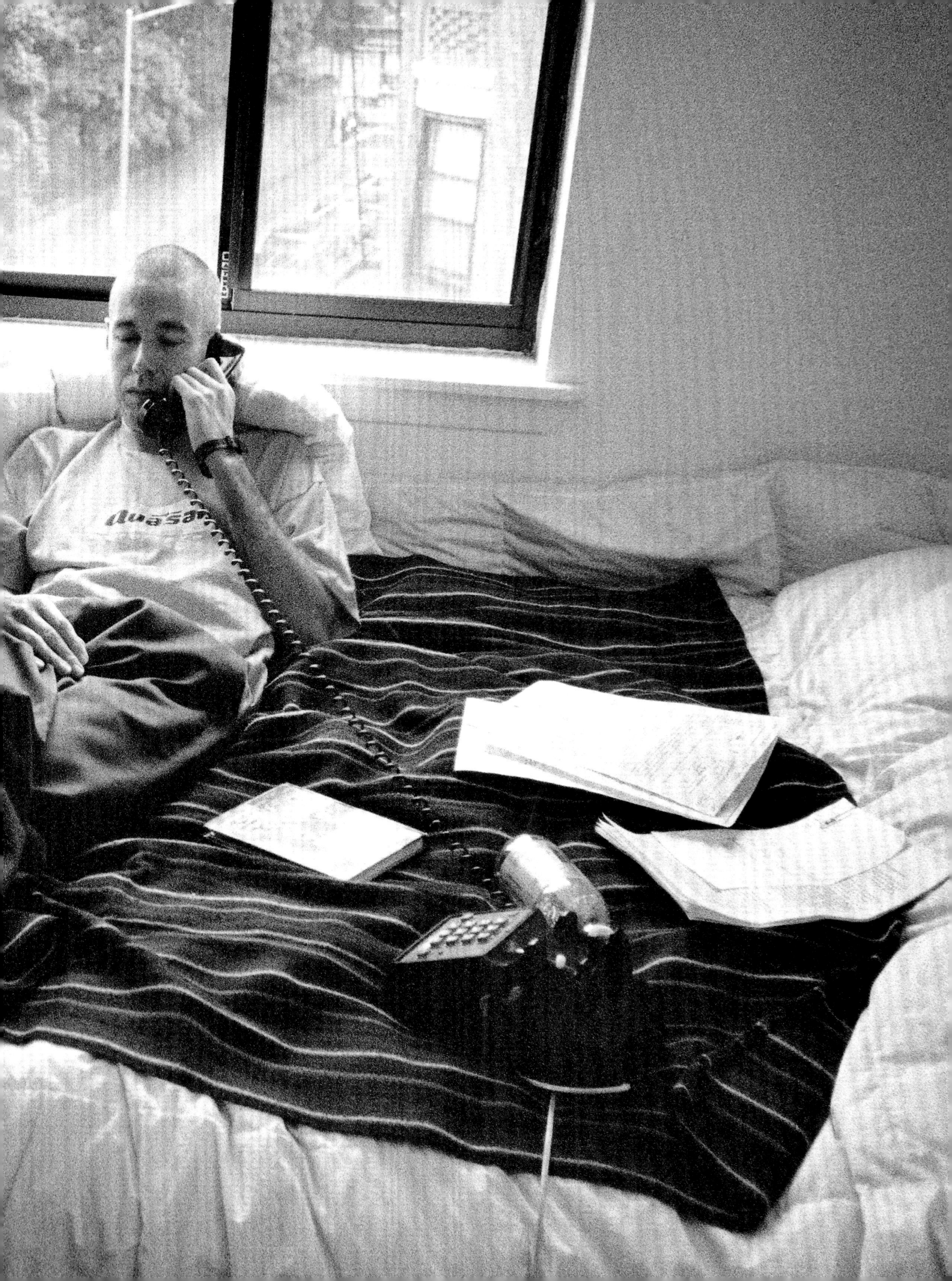

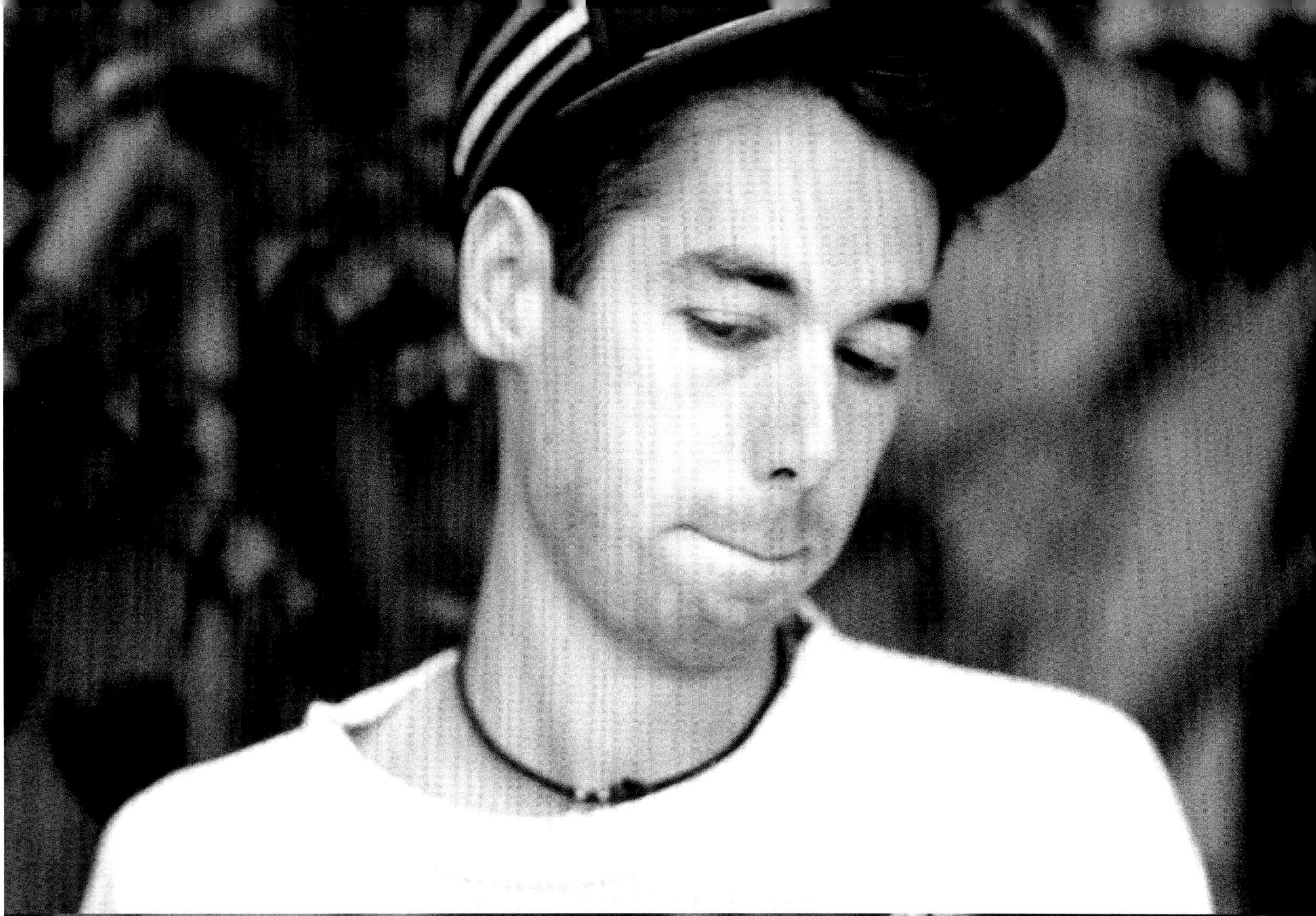
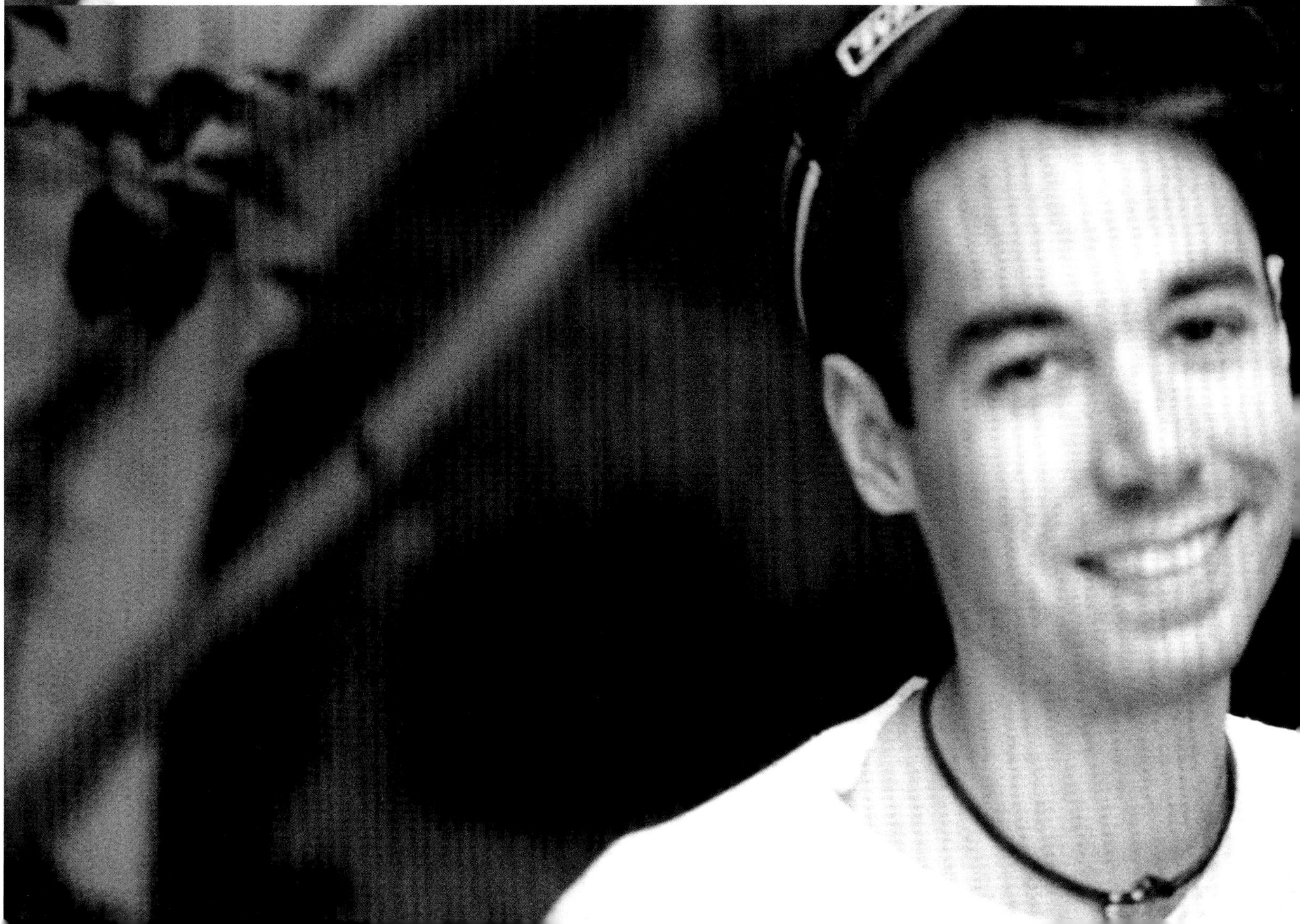

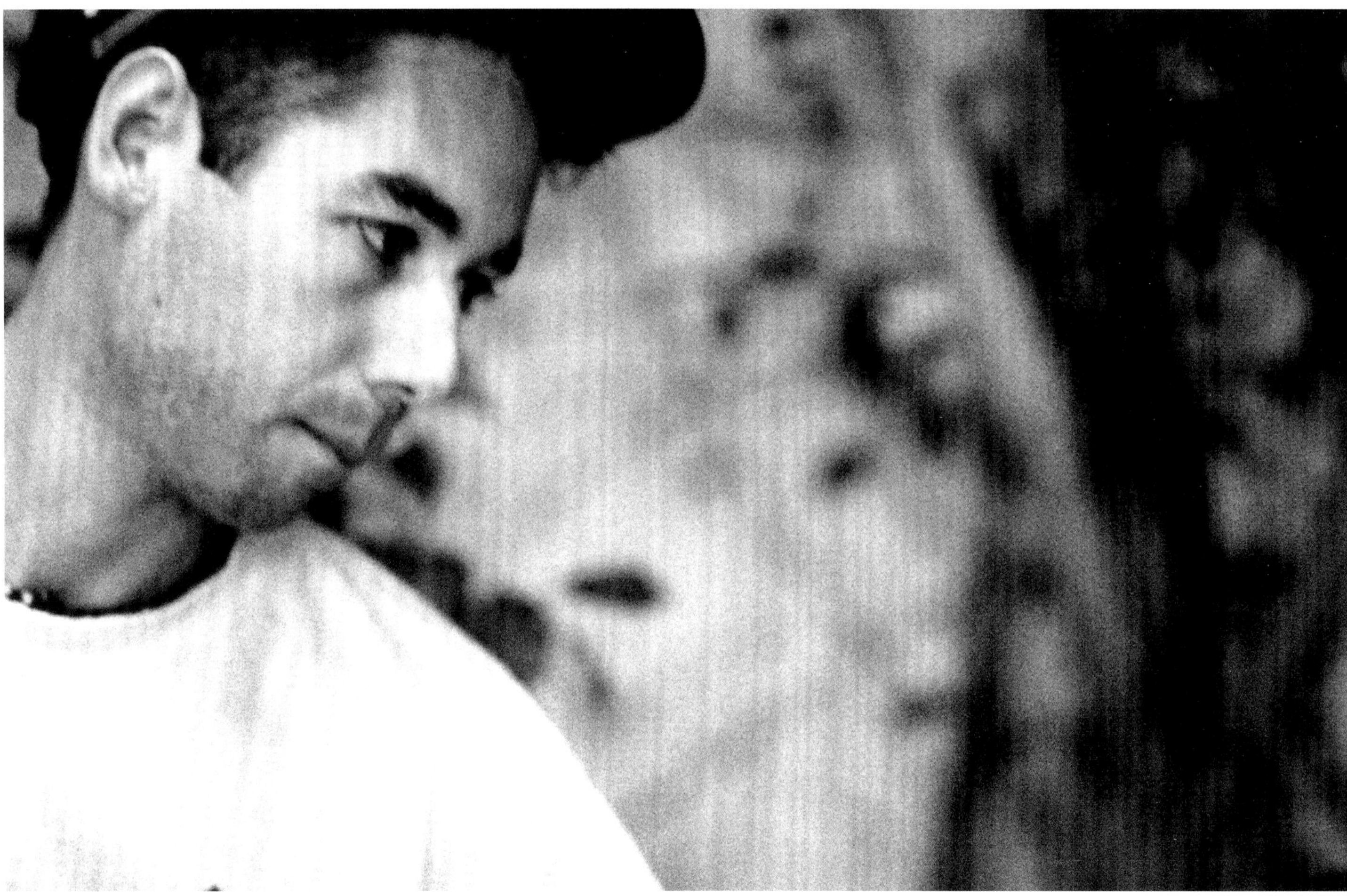

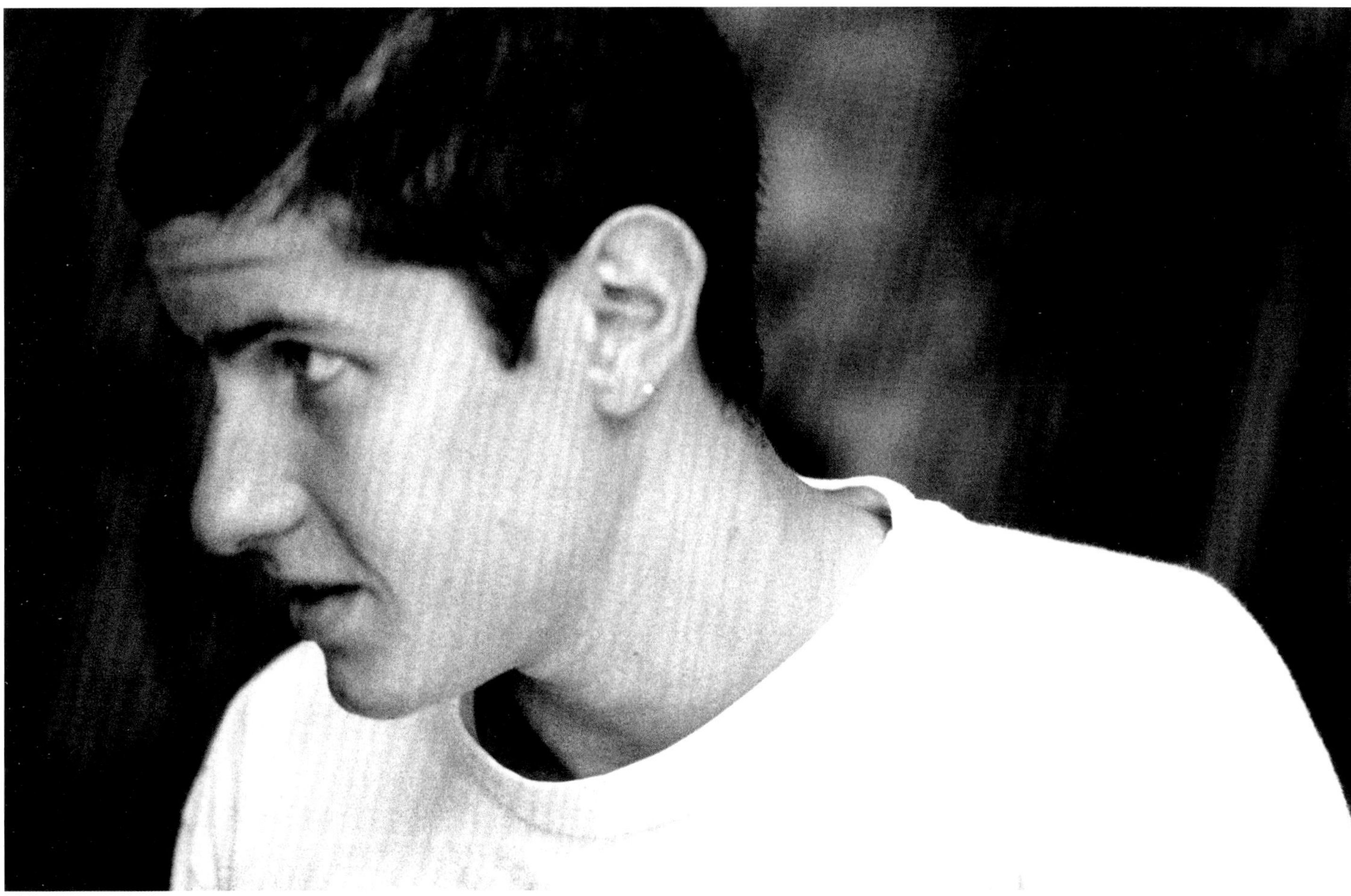

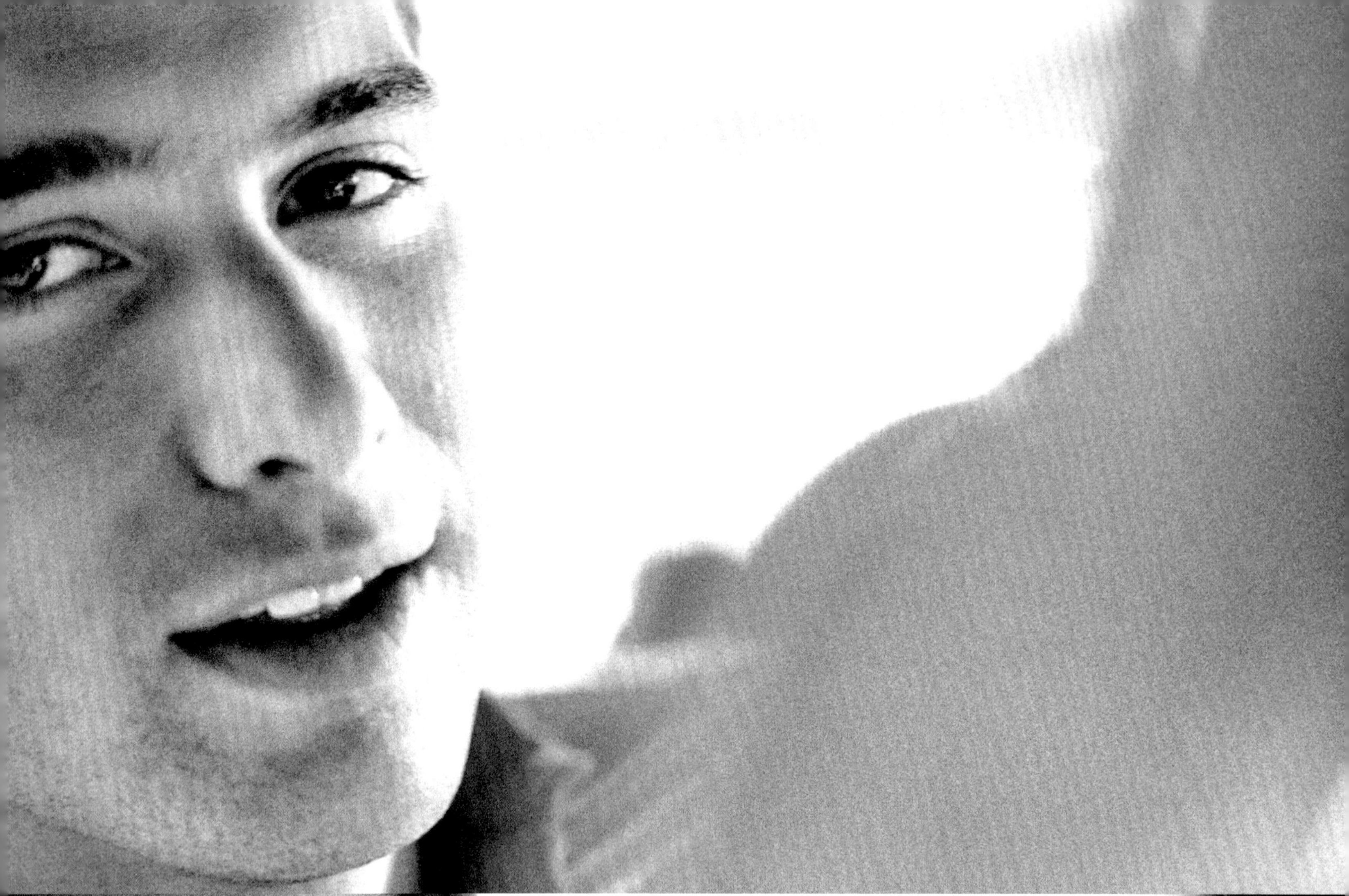
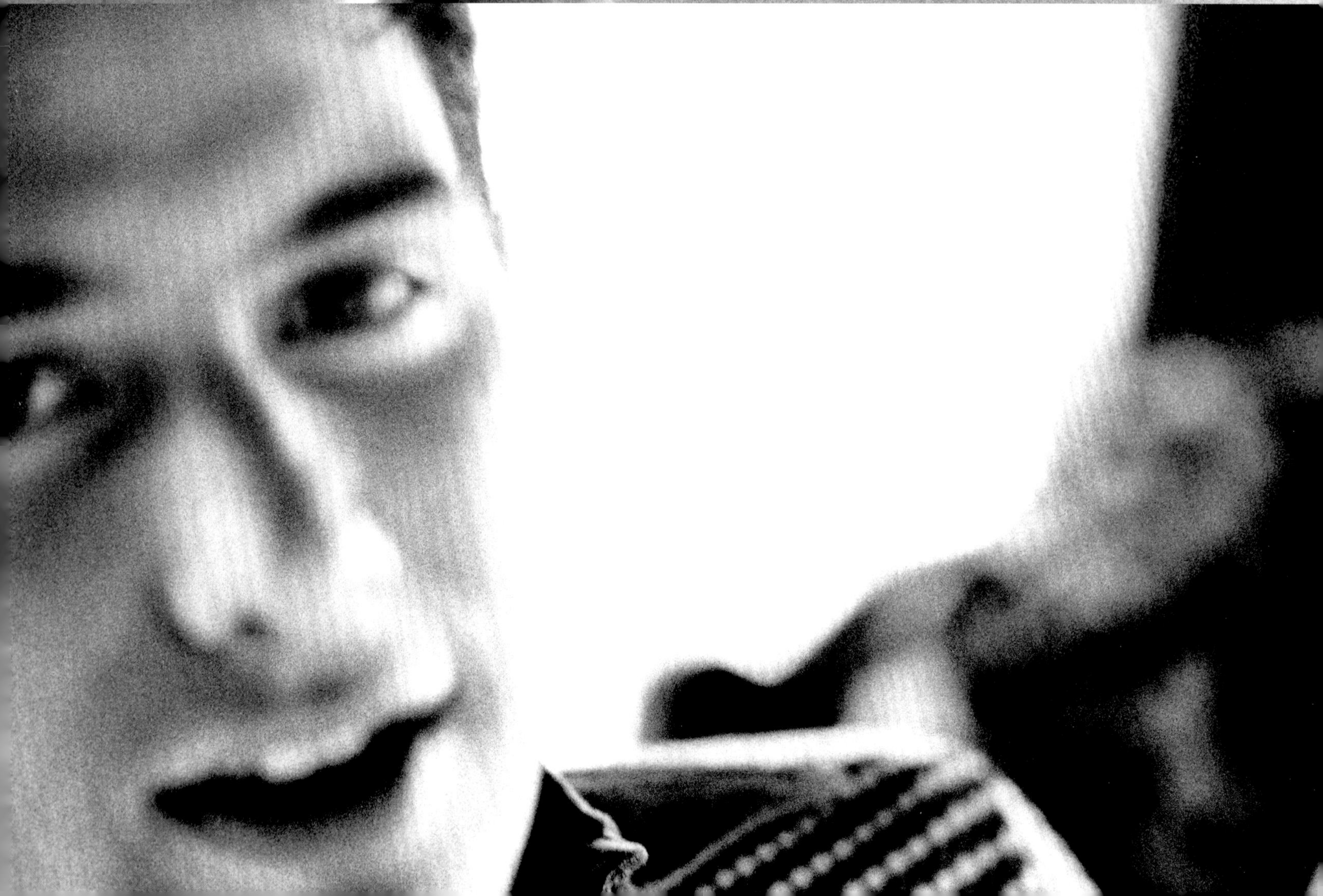

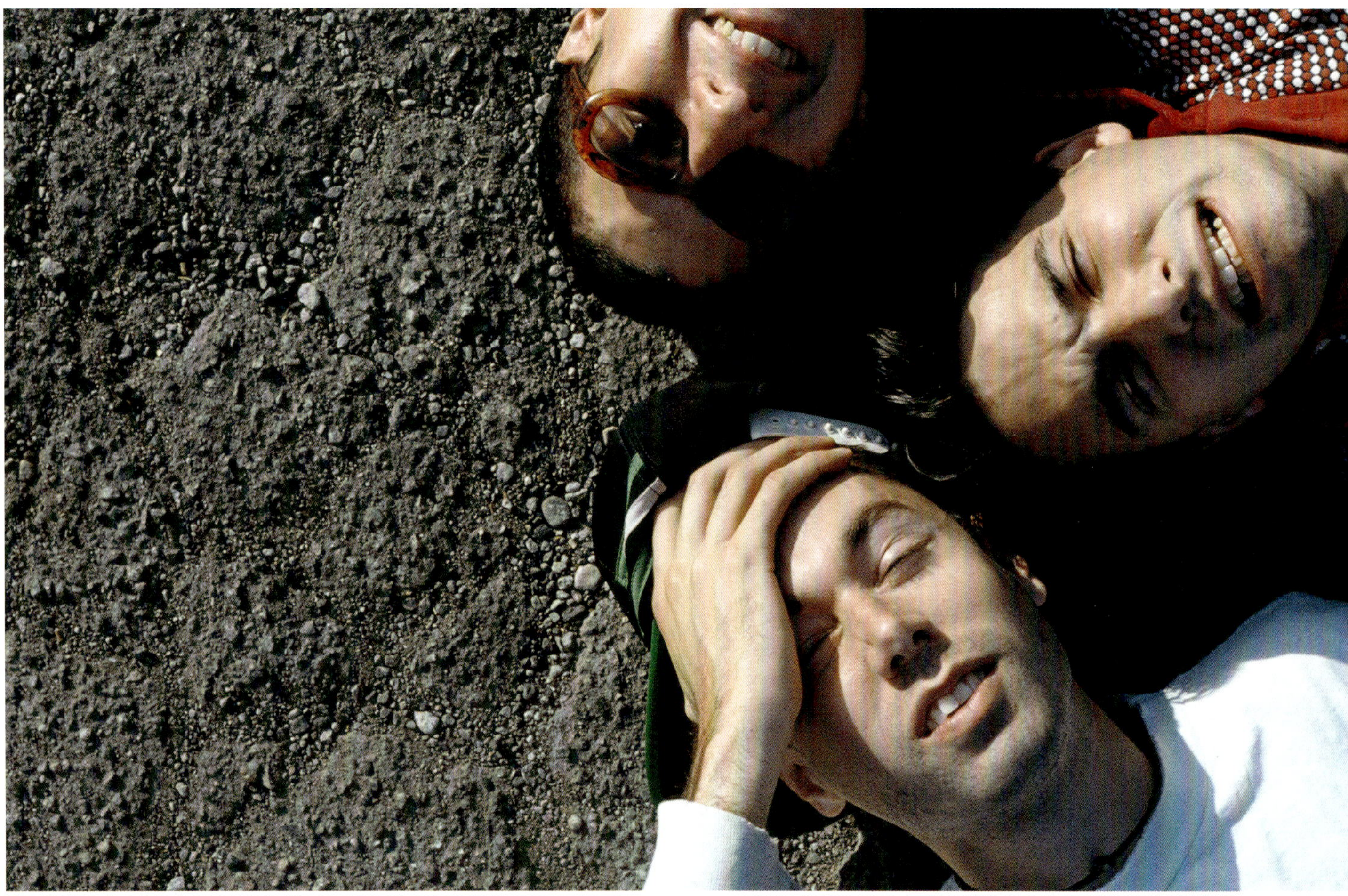

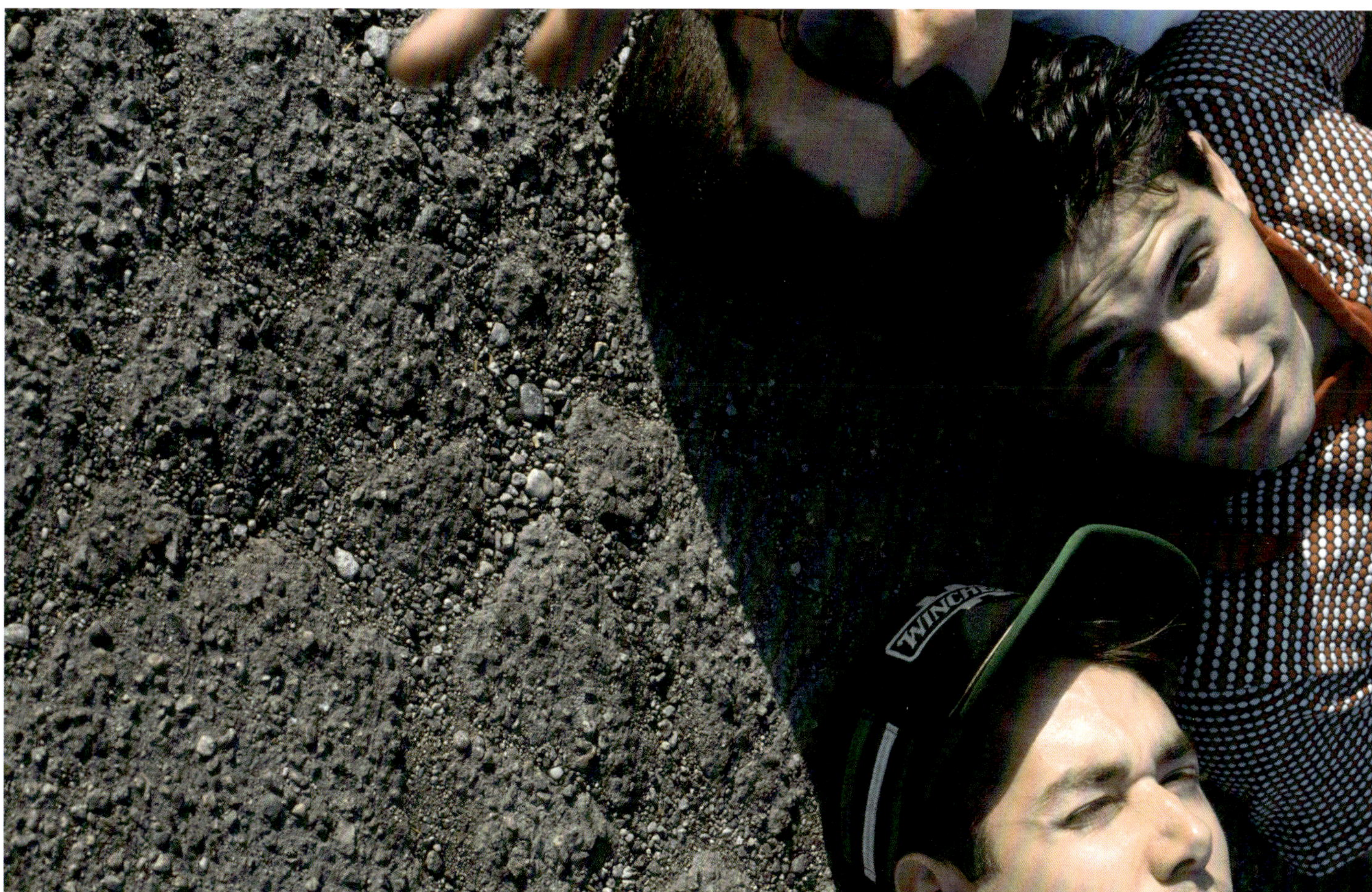

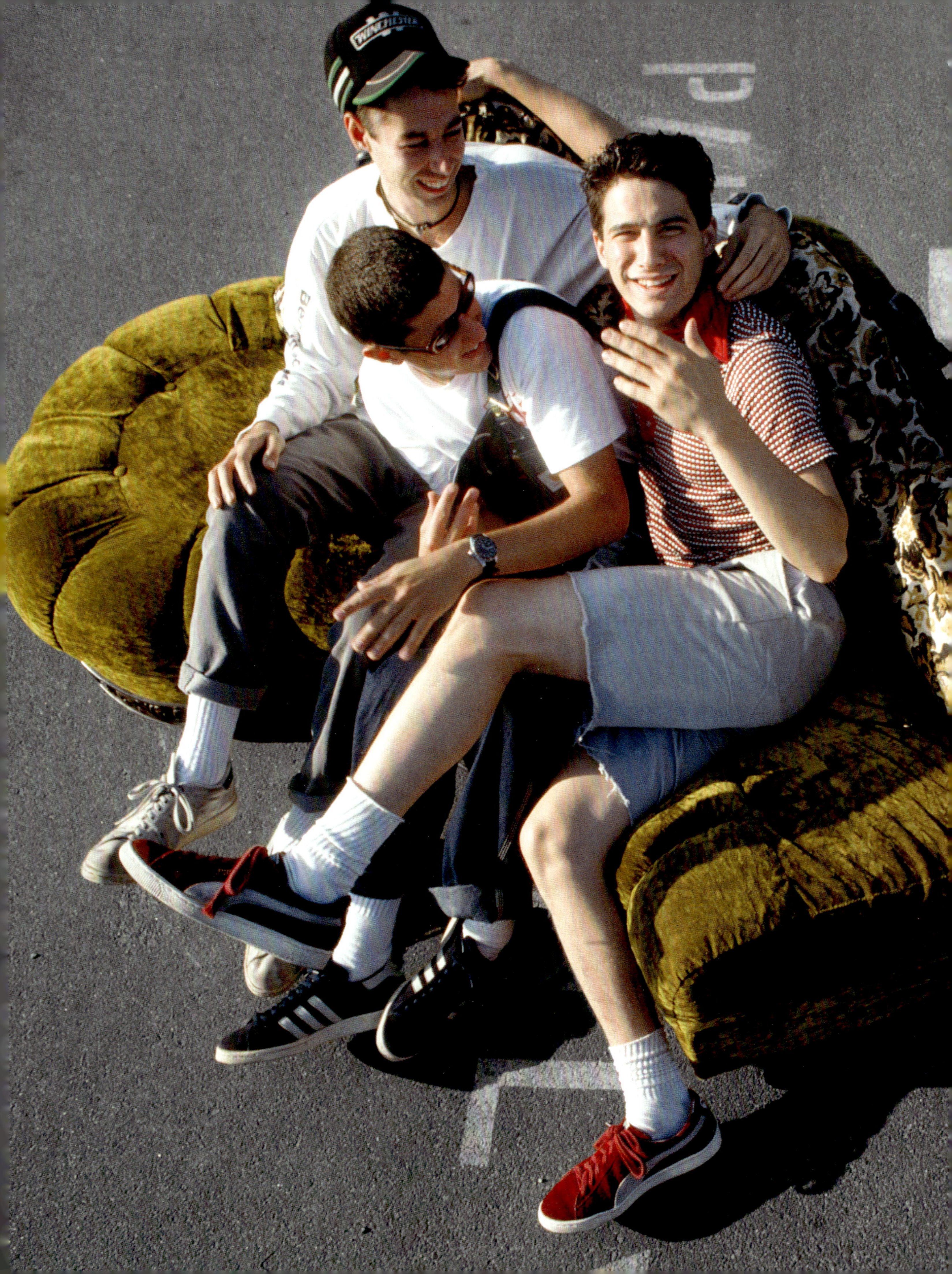